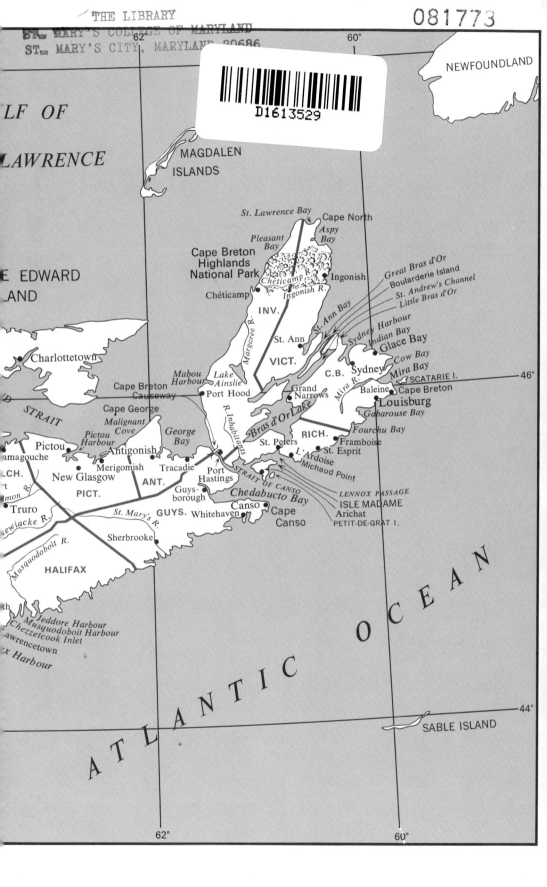

NEWFOUNDLAND

LF OF
LAWRENCE

MAGDALEN
ISLANDS

E EDWARD
LAND

St. Lawrence Bay
Cape North
Pleasant Bay
Aspy Bay
Cape Breton Highlands National Park
Chéticamp R.
Ingonish
Great Bras d'Or
Boularderie Island
St. Andrew's Channel
Little Bras d'Or
Chéticamp
Ingonish R.
INV.
Margaree R.
St. Ann Bay
St. Ann Bay
Sydney Harbour
Indian Bay
Glace Bay
St. Ann
VICT.
C.B. Sydney
Cow Bay
Mira Bay
SCATARIE I.
Charlottetown
Mabou Harbour
Lake Ainslie
Cape Breton Causeway
Port Hood
Grand Narrows
Mira R.
Baleine
Cape Breton
46°
STRAIT
Cape George
Malignant Cove
Bras d'Or Lake
Louisburg
Gabarouse Bay
Pictou Harbour
George Bay
R. Inhabitants
Fourchu Bay
Pictou
Antigonish
RICH.
Framboise
LCH.
Merigomish
Tracadie
St. Peters
St. Esprit
mon R.
New Glasgow
ANT.
Port Hastings
L'Ardoise
Michaud Point
amagouche
PICT.
Guys-borough
STRAIT OF CANSO
LENNOX PASSAGE
Truro
St. Mary's R.
GUYS.
Whitehaven
Chedabucto Bay
ISLE MADAME
Arichat
PETIT-DE-GRAT I.
ewiacke R.
Canso
Cape Canso
Sherbrooke
Musquodoboit R.
HALIFAX

A T L A N T I C   O C E A N

44°

Jeddore Harbour
Musquodoboit Harbour
Chezzetcook Inlet
awrencetown
x Harbour

SABLE ISLAND

62°   60°

ACADIA

ACADIA

The Geography
of Early Nova Scotia
to 1760

Andrew Hill Clark

THE UNIVERSITY OF WISCONSIN PRESS
MADISON, MILWAUKEE, AND LONDON
1968

Published by
The University of Wisconsin Press
Box 1379, Madison, Wisconsin 53701

The University of Wisconsin Press, Ltd.
27–29 Whitfield Street, London, W.1

Printed in the United States of America by
Kingsport Press, Inc., Kingsport, Tennessee

Standard Book Number 299–05080–7
Library of Congress Catalog Card Number 68–9829

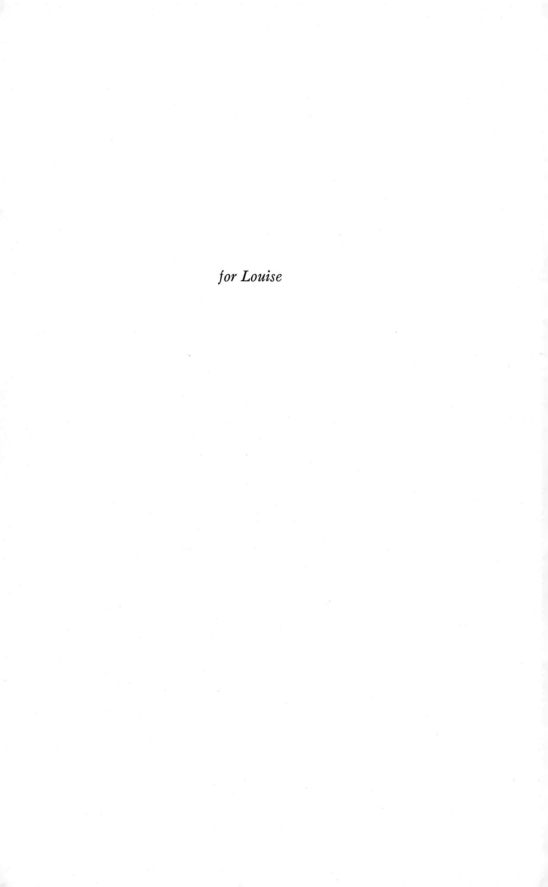

for Louise

Preface

THIS VOLUME is the first of two which will be devoted to an exposition of geographical change in the lands of Nova Scotia before that province, rather painfully evolved out of Acadia and Isle Royale in the eighteenth century, joined most of the other units of British North America in the later nineteenth to form the Dominion of Canada. The present book concerns itself with the period before 1760 and thus is sharply concentrated on Acadia and the pre-dispersion Acadians as those dedicated, stubborn, resilient, pettifogging, inventive, exasperating, peace-loving, and, in many ways, altogether magnificent people created a geographical entity which was absorbed in or replaced with, but never quite obliterated by, the Nova Scotia which succeeded it. Indeed the names "Acadia" and "Nova Scotia" may be said to have run concurrently from the 1620's, when Sir William Alexander's abortive colonization efforts introduced the latter term, through the period of the early eighteenth century when it became the official territorial designation for the present peninsula of that province (and in British eyes of much of present New Brunswick as well) and until "British" Nova Scotia became a demographic reality with the establishment of Halifax, the wholesale deportation of the Acadians, and the beginning of immigration from New England.

The Acadians of the late twentieth century are, very largely, descended from the protagonists of this report and are most easily identified in the same lands that once comprised the Greater Acadia or Greater Nova Scotia of the seventeenth and eighteenth centuries. Most of the inhabitants of the present provinces of Prince Edward Island and Nova Scotia who claim French origin have clearly identifiable Acadian surnames. In 1881 the Canadian census recorded 10,751 in

vii

the former and 41,219 in the latter; these had increased to 17,418 and 87,833 in 1961. They are now roughly one-sixth of the people in the smaller province and one-eighth in the larger. The population of French origin in New Brunswick increased in the same period from 58,635 to 232,127, or from 16 per cent to 41 per cent of the provincial population. Not all of the French Canadians in New Brunswick are of Acadian origin, but assuming that at least four-fifths of them are we may suppose that Acadians in the three Maritime Provinces now number from 250,000 to 300,000, or from one-sixth to one-fifth of the total population, and that roughly two-thirds of them live in New Brunswick. They are widely distributed within that province but the major concentration is in the southeast, and Moncton, on the Petitcodiac River, is considered to be the Acadian "capital." The principal Acadian newspaper, *L'Evangeline,* is published there and L'Université de Moncton is considered to be "the" Acadian University. Thus, the center of Acadian culture still lies on the margin of the Bay of Fundy tidal lands as it has since the seventeenth century.

The dispersion of the Acadians in the decade following 1755 scattered them widely. Many returned to the Maritimes later in the century but the only other area in which they were able to maintain a cultural identity was in Louisiana where so many of them finally gathered and where, in the 1780's, there may have been the largest single bloc of Acadians. Indeed, that concentration has been able to maintain its numbers better than the group in the Maritimes; the latter has experienced mass emigration, within the past century especially, to New England and other parts of the United States. Rather fulsome estimates have suggested that there may be a million or more in the Republic with Acadian names. But most of the Acadians in the United States are strongly anglicised, however strongly they cherish their traditions. Even Louisiana's "Cajun" country is fighting a losing battle against acculturation. Only in the rural Acadian areas of the Maritimes where they form relatively compact groups, and share in the traditions of a bi-cultural, bi-lingual nation, do we find a vigorous, self-conscious *acadien* culture comparable to the flourishing *canadien* culture of Quebec. And, although the Acadians of New Brunswick far outnumber those of Nova Scotia, the territory where most of them live was widely claimed as both Acadian and Nova Scotian before 1784. Despite the mid-eighteenth century break, and its convenience for dividing the historical geography of the European settlement of Maritime Canada into two chronological sectors, that geography was a continuum through time and the past, at any time, was ever prologue to what followed. What Nova Scotia is today derives in no small part from what it had become in the century and a half before *le grand dérangement* and its sequels, which signaled the end of the first Acadia.

The evolving economic and cultural geographies of Isle St-Jean (present Prince Edward Island) and Cape Breton Island in the early eighteenth century were very closely intertwined with that of the Acadian homelands to the south and west and by the middle of the eighteenth century the people of St-Jean were largely Acadian emigrants. I have already published a description of the changing geography of Isle St-Jean in *Three Centuries and the Island: A Historical Geography of Settlement and Agriculture in Prince Edward Island, Canada* (Toronto, 1959), and have also given some attention to Cape Breton in my article "New England's Role in the Underdevelopment of Cape Breton Island during the French Regime" (*Canadian Geographer, 9,* 1965, 1–12), but a much fuller treatment of the latter seemed necessary to the balance of this study and hence is included in a separate chapter. Some seven years ago, at an early stage in the collecting of materials for this book, I attempted to distill some of the essence of the story, for the seventeenth century only, in a brief essay, "Acadia and the Acadians: The Creation of a Geographical Entity," published in John Andrews, ed., *Frontiers and Men,* a volume in memory of Griffith Taylor (Melbourne, 1966). Unfortunately the publication of that volume was delayed for many years and many of its conclusions have changed with a fuller examination of the evidence.

The historiography of the Acadians in general has tended to have a genealogical flavor and emotional overtones especially when written by Acadians themselves. In many ways the most useful study for my purposes was the two-volume work of François-Edmé Rameau de St-Père, *Une Colonie Feódale en Amérique: l'Acadie (1604–1881)* (Paris, 1889), although an earlier three-volume English-language study by Beamish Murdoch, *A History of Nova Scotia or Acadie* (Halifax, 1865–67), was also helpful. Each made rather full if somewhat erratic use of the various documentary sources. Much the best modern study is that of the late J. B. Brebner, *New England's Outpost: Acadia Before the Conquest of Canada* (New York, 1927), which covers exactly the same period as does this volume. Indeed it was Professor Brebner who really introduced me to the Acadians and, along with Daniel Cobb

Harvey, then the Provincial Archivist of Nova Scotia, and Harold A. Innis, historian of the cod fishery, urged the study upon which this volume and its successor are based. Especially did these scholars go out of their way to direct the writer to a critical appraisal of the documentary sources upon which, finally, any such study must depend heavily. The primary sources and other published materials are discussed briefly in an appended bibliographical note.

But to a geographer, the documents, however central, can only be a part of the evidence. The historical human geography of any territory or people is the closely interwoven story of man and land; the rocks, the rain, the rivers, the winds, the tides, the trees, the fish—all the aspects of nature which become integral parts of that story—are of the utmost importance as well as the people and their culture, and it is the pleasure and duty of the student of changing regional character to attend closely to their significance in place and time. Chapter 2, which follows a brief introductory chapter establishing the initial coordinates of time and place, describes in some detail the endowment of nature in a series of partial geographies of Acadia's physical and biotic characteristics. Then the Micmac, pre-European Nova Scotians, are introduced. Thereafter the exposition carries on with description and explanation of the changing human geography of a century and a half. A combined chronological and chorological treatment is essential. The concern of the geographer for the locational attributes of the Acadian settlement and economy is reflected in many cross-sectional surveys but it is hoped that the point is made that any and all of these represent relatively instantaneous glimpses of an uninterrupted continuum of change and, throughout, the processes involved in the course of geographical change are of major concern.

The orthographic license, if not anarchy, of both English and French officials, cartographers, and casual observers of the Acadian scene in the seventeenth and early eighteenth centuries has made decisions on the spelling of personal and place names difficult. Gratitude is expressed to the staff of the *Dictionary of Canadian Biography* who, through the offices of the University of Toronto Press, provided their standards for names of seventeenth-century figures and these have been used throughout the text. For the names of places, particularly as these changed through time, and from one language to another, there is no satisfactory established standard despite the valiant efforts of the Canadian Board on Geographic Names. For late twentieth-century spelling and identification major reliance has been on the published maps of the federal Canadian Department of Mines, Energy, and Resources. But, understandably, there are many instances where maps of the same area, drawn at different scales, or for different purposes at different times, have different names, or different forms of the same name, for individual features. Many times the decisions were made on the basis of local usage. For maps and text describing the seventeenth and early eighteenth centuries one simply has to make individual choices; sometimes the form used may not be the one that was in widest contemporary use but it is intended that it should represent something of a "central tendency" within the orthographic range. In many places alternative names, often in the other language, or present-day names believed to apply to the same location or feature, are inserted parenthetically. It was not found possible to observe the unity of time in all cases; for clarity, later well-known names are cited, on occasion, for dates before they ever had been employed. Nor was it always possible to be consistent in the method of using names from one or another language. Sometimes a different form of the same name is used for the eighteenth century than that assigned for the seventeenth, but again, no rigid formula has been followed. There has been much greater freedom in using later, or English, forms where the cognate is obvious, as in Louisburg for "Louisbourg." The decision in each case was made in my judgment of what would aid most in communicating with the reader at any point in the text.

Literally scores of people have contributed invaluable aid to my understanding of Acadia and the Acadians, to helping me find the evidence and put it together, and to the preparation and drafting of the maps. Only a few of them will find mention here but to them all a most heartfelt expression of thanks is due. Perhaps first mention should be made of the many historians of Canada and its parts, besides Brebner, Harvey, and Innis, whose scholarship and interpretations I have drawn on so freely. Their numbers, swelled by the ranks of economists, sociologists, anthropologists, geologists, geographers, and many others, are beyond remembering let alone listing, but most of them whose work was consulted helped at least a little and some a great deal. The librarians and archivists of a great many libraries have created unpayable debts. The directors and staffs of the Public Archives of Canada and Nova Scotia, of the Reading Room of the British Museum, of the British Public Records Office, and of the Wisconsin State

Historical Society, however, must have special mention, and perhaps the unmentioned dozens will be forgiving if special thanks are tendered here to Dr. C. Bruce Fergusson of Halifax and Miss Ruth Davis of Madison. Quite a few research assistants did yeoman service over a period of twenty years but, again, most recently or most directly, gratitude must be expressed for work on this book to Cole Harris, Brian Reynolds, Arthur Ray, Leonard Brinkman, Grant Head, and Tom McIlwraith—good soldiers all and both severe and imaginative critics.

The debts to those who have provided funds for research and writing over a long period of time are also substantial. To the John Simon Guggenheim Memorial Foundation, the Social Science Research Council, the Fulbright organization, the Research Committees of Rutgers University and the University of Wisconsin (especially), and to whoever else has helped, these debts are gratefully acknowledged. Indeed, in one way or another (and in dozens of them), perhaps the greatest thanks should go to the University of Wisconsin and, particularly, to the faculty and secretarial staff of its Department of Geography. Finally, deep thanks are tendered to Randall Sale, Director of the University of Wisconsin Cartographic Laboratory, and to Cherie Edwards and Judy Olson who, under his supervision, prepared all the maps. To the single person who helped the most, in myriad ways, this book is dedicated.

A. H. C.

"The Island"
Rough Rock Lake
Minaki, Ontario
June, 1968

ABBREVIATIONS USED IN FOOTNOTES

AC   Public Archives of Canada

AC, NSA   A series of Nova Scotia materials in the Public Archives of Canada copied from Colonial Office records held by the Public Record Office

AC, NSB   As above, specifically "Minutes of Nova Scotia's Executive Council"

AdC   Archives des Colonies, Archives Nationales, Paris

MG   Manuscript Group in the holdings of the Public Archives of Canada

PANS   Public Archives of Nova Scotia

PRO, CO   Public Record Office, Colonial Office Papers, London

Contents

Illustrations and Tables

FIGURES

PLATES

TABLES

ACADIA

1

Introduction

🖋

THE ENSUING account of Acadia and the Acadians,[1] over a period of a century and a half, is a case study with potentially wide implications for the understanding of the ways in which individual immigrant groups of men have coped with the opportunities and limitations of newly occupied parts of the earth's surface. Sometimes such groups made substantial changes on the face of the earth; sometimes they appeared to make little impression on the natural milieu but were themselves profoundly affected in culture as they adapted, and often radically changed, their society and economy by developing new technologies, habits, and attitudes adequate to assure the viability of their occupancy. But whatever happened, whatever the setting, the kinds of people who invaded it, or the course of events of their history in it, the persistence of an exotic people and culture in a new home led inevitably to a new combination of nature and culture in the area and, thus, to the appearance of a new geographical entity.

The great migrations of the seventeenth, eighteenth, and nineteenth centuries from western Europe to the middle-latitude lands overseas settled therefrom, provide many examples in which such entities, created in a relatively few decades, existed long enough to leave an

1. Some sections of this chapter are borrowed from my article, "Acadia and the Acadians: The Creation of a Geographical Entity," pp. 90–119, in John Andrews, ed., *Frontiers and Men* (1966) either *verbatim* or with greater or lesser changes in wording.

3

indelible stamp on the regions in which they appeared, however heavily it may have been overlaid by succeeding patterns. The peopling of New England in the first half of the seventeenth century is a particularly good example of the creation of such an entity. Left much alone by their mother country, the settlers increased their numbers rapidly, and within the seventeenth century had become a new people in a new land—no longer transplanted Englishmen but North Americans of a very individualistic kind. It is true that it took most of another century for either themselves or contemporary Englishmen even to recognize the fact, let alone understand its implications. But long before the American Revolution, the name "New England" was little more appropriate to its people and the regional character they had helped to create than that of New Jersey or New York and arguably much less so than that of New France in the St. Lawrence Valley, where patterns unmistakably Norman, Breton, Parisian or whatever (but clearly French), had left deep impressions well before the British conquest of the Seven Years War. A new *canadien* people did also develop a new entity, Canada, there, but its major influx of population came decades later than the waves of non-conformists and separatists which reached the shores of New England in the 1620's and 1630's, and the sharply contrasting institutional structure of the French settlement made the process of cultural adaptation and evolution slower there.

It is the fate of small bands of people in small areas to be overlooked and even forgotten as, in our predilection for historical and geographical generalization, we attach them for convenience to larger groups or regions. This book is concerned with such a group, *les acadiens,* whose identity has been obscured by sweepingly inclusive descriptions of New France and its people in the sesquicentury from the beginning of the seventeenth century to the middle of the eighteenth. Their principal ancestors crossed the Atlantic in the same decade as did most of those of the colonial New Englanders, established themselves a few hundred miles to the northeast along the same coast, and rapidly assumed their new identity. They were far more isolated from the world and far fewer in number than their Puritan contemporaries who raided them persistently (in part because they could not get at their real enemies, or fur trading rivals, *les canadiens*), traded with them eagerly between raids, and probably knew them, in many ways, quite as well as did the rest of the people of New or old France. And even more precipitately than the New Englanders, these emigré Frenchmen were forced into a revolutionary adaptation of attitudes and ways of life in a new environment.

The human geography of Acadia begins, so far as solid evidence now available to us indicates, with the Paleo-Indians who hunted and fished and gathered food on the shores of the northeasternmost inlet of the Bay of Fundy more than ten thousand years ago, when that region cannot long have been freed of the stagnant ice remaining from the last advance of the many continental ice sheets of the Pleistocene period. Thus there were people in the area coping with its climatic and biotic hazards and exploiting its resources well before the plant and animal husbandmen of the Near or Far East of the Old World, or the lower-latitude piedmont dwellers of the New, created conditions of settled agricultural village life which were to blossom into the great nurseries of civilization. It is interesting that our first eyewitness accounts of the area (perhaps in the Norse sagas and certainly by the time of the reports of European visitors from the first Cabot onward) describe a human occupation that was still based essentially on the same economic pattern of ten millennia before. Some improvement in the making of tools, the diffusion into the area of a rather inferior kind of potting, the possible attempts to grow maize or tobacco, or increased knowledge of wild plants and animal life and ways of using them, may have added less than was lost with the disappearance of large game animals known to have roamed those periglacial lands. There may have been few inhabited parts of the world (Australia is the only one that comes to mind) where there had been as little change for as long a period before they first appeared on the world stage or in written history.

This record reflects very clearly the peripheral location of the shores of northeastern North America with respect to the major centers of cultural innovation and diffusion, whether of Meso-America, the Middle East, or East Asia. Far more than the arctic lands, where the movements and inventiveness of the Eskimo and their predecessors brought such a rapid change in a relatively short period, was this an Ultima Thule, an end of the world. Even when the first of the great geographical extensions of European culture reached through Iceland to Greenland, Labrador, and Newfoundland at the turn of the eleventh century of our era it either missed or ignored this land just beyond its reach. From the opposite direction that superb dietary trio of crop plants, maize, squash and beans, which had altered so much the life and economy of Indians as near as the St. Lawrence Valley, and had

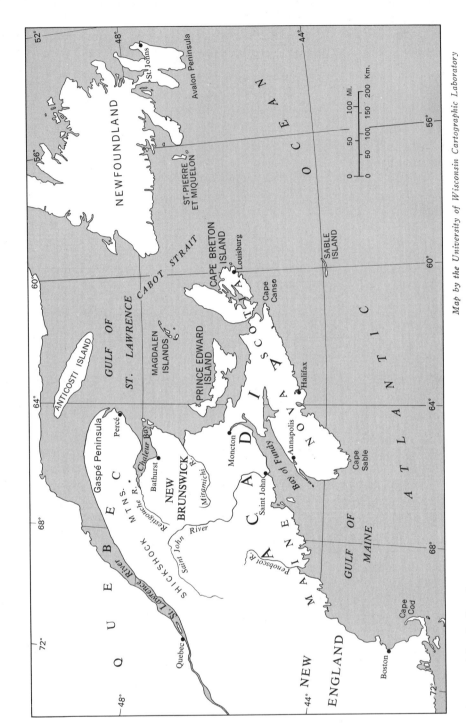

Fig. 1.1 Atlantic Canada.

Map by the University of Wisconsin Cartographic Laboratory

even begun to affect those of peoples living on the very fringe of the Acadian lands, still had not established itself in present Nova Scotia or the shores of the Gulf of St. Lawrence when the coasting voyages of the early explorers and the visits of many hundreds of European fishermen in the sixteenth century suddenly brought the region into the forefront of consciousness of the literate western world.

The reasons for the relative lack of interest of northwestern Europe in the area after the first contacts, about 1,000 A.D., have been discussed elsewhere.[2] Fundamentally they involved the fact that the Greenlanders and Icelanders could not have mustered the numbers of settlers necessary to defend themselves against Indian (or Eskimo) attacks, that the climate provided progressively colder winters as they moved farther and farther west, and that the plants, land animals, and sea-life involved nothing with which they were unfamiliar. The contrasts of conditions on opposite sides of the North Atlantic at the same latitudes (Baffin Island and Norway, Labrador and the British Isles, Nova Scotia and the Biscayan coasts of France) were all most unfavorable to North America and most of what was discovered was not particularly wanted. The one great resource of the region, and one almost unparalleled in the world, was the demersal fish off the shores and over the banks of the continental shelf. Why, or whether, these resources, apparently recognized in the oral traditions of the Vikings and later written down in their sagas, were not utilized sooner by Europeans is a mystery. Well before Cabot and Columbus, fishermen from the shores of the North Sea were making good use of the cod-rich Icelandic waters. At any rate, it was the lure of codfish which, within a decade of the Cabot reports, had initiated what was to be a great annual fleet of fishing ships repairing to these waters, Spanish, Portuguese, French (Basque, if we may consider them separately) and later, English. But Spanish overseas interest was concentrated in lower New World latitudes; Portugal's was distributed over many parts of the world, and England's, while focusing fitfully on Newfoundland's southeastern coast in the sixteenth century, tended to bifurcate north to the search for a northwest passage to Asia or south to more benign mainland climates and more fertile soils. Only the French, partly in reaction to other pressures, notably English, in the Newfoundland-Grand Bank fishery, and partly in the hope of discovering new Mexicos and Perus,

2. A. H. Clark and D. Q. Innis, "The Roots of Canada's Geography," a chapter in *Canada: A Geographical Interpretation* (1968), pp. 28–29.

pushed inland to the region where, in the seventeenth and eighteenth
centuries, New France was to blossom. With the forays of Jacques
Cartier into the Gulf and River of St. Lawrence in the 1530's, France
staked out her claim to this hitherto neglected eddy in the great stream
of world cultural diffusion and technological advance. Two-thirds of a
century more were to elapse before that claim was exploited—France
had many troubles at home in the 1500's—but it was not disputed
effectively by others and, meanwhile, a rational economic motive and a
cogent religious one led her, in the first decade of the seventeenth
century, to develop the first settlements that were more than wintering
camps.

The economic motive was that of a trade in furs. Furs had appeared
spasmodically, and rather incidentally, among the goods and trophies,
other than fish, which had trickled back to western Europe in the early
sixteenth century. Even before the visits of Cartier (among those
which were reported), Parmentier had taken skins to France and
Gomez to Portugal. Fur bales appeared more frequently in the latter
part of the century as the European market proved receptive. Most of
these clearly were incidental by-products of contacts by fishermen who
anchored in coves to cure their codfish or to procure wood and water
but, increasingly, the profitability of fur, easily obtained for baubles,
brandy, bits of clothing, or old pots and tools, drew the interest of
merchants who financed the fishing voyages. More effort was devoted
to the development and maintenance of Indian contacts, and to the
provision of trade goods more attractive to them; perhaps most often
the initiative lay with the Indians themselves, for iron pots were as
vastly superior in cookery to stone boiling or the use of fragile clay
vessels, as iron knives were to flint. Iron axes, large or small (and,
ultimately, firearms), gave any tribe a marked edge in weaponry until
its rivals were similarly provided. News of the ways of obtaining such
technologically advanced equipment diffused rapidly through the lands
of the Naskapi, the Montagnais, the Micmac, the Malecite and the
Iroquois. It became apparent that, properly organized and supplied, a
fur trade offered even greater opportunities for profit to the Europeans
than did the cod fishery. From the 1550's onward, either as an adjunct
of codfishing, walrus-hunting, or whaling in the waters of the Gulf of
St. Lawrence, or for itself alone, at a series of locations around the St.
Lawrence shores and as far up the estuary of the great river as Tadoussac, the trade slowly grew in volume. One voyage of 1583, to the

southern shores of the Gulf, is said to have realized a 1,000 per cent profit. In 1600 a fur depot was made for wintering over at Tadoussac, although scurvy and the severity of the winter almost wiped it out. The ill-fated colonization effort of the Marquis de La Roche on Sable Island at the turn of the century may not have advanced the fur trade but it drew further attention to its possibilities.

The religious fervor that made France a leader in the Counter Reformation was already evident in suggestions for missionary activity in the North American lands where the French had made contacts well back into the sixteenth century. Thus, with the beginning of the seventeenth, the opportunity to convert uncounted thousands of savage souls to the true faith seized the imagination of Churchmen. In the van were such holy orders as the Recollets and Jesuits, the latter in particular with strong supporting voices and hands in high places. So, with the desire for betterment in this world through the profits of the fur trade went that of preferment in the next through possibly massive additions to the ranks of the faithful.

Whether as a matter of policy, or incidentally, the missionary activity greatly aided the fur trade by attaching many of the Indians to a French cultural institution and, by extension, to the commercial representatives of France. Whether the new technologies in hunting, trapping, cooking, and clothing and the new deep commitment to production for an exchange economy, together with whatever different values or standards of belief and behavior they accepted from *les robes noires*, compensated the Indians for measles, smallpox, and new venereal diseases, for the demoralizing effect of brandy, for the vastly increased destruction of life in native warfare because of firearms, and for the general breakdown of social patterns, must remain a value judgment. For good or ill, the future economy and society of the Indians was set on a course of steady and irreversible change.

Finally, it was clear that both the French Crown, with its combined hope for royalties and ecclesiastical blessing, and the (often Protestant) merchants of the Channel and Biscayan ports, eager for trading profits, were alive to the necessity, or desirability, of planting the fleur-de-lis firmly in some substantial part of the New World, in rivalry with Iberia and the British Islands for the inevitably intertwined motives of grand strategy and commerce. No one really knew what lay behind the coast, and, even if the findings of the great sixteenth-century explorers who had penetrated the interior—Coronado, De Soto, and Cartier—had proved disappointing, some bonanza or other still might be hoped for. Only a substantial investment of the land by Frenchman could assure these opportunities for France as against its rivals.

Thus for the lands that are now Canada's provinces of Ontario, Quebec, New Brunswick, Prince Edward Island, and Nova Scotia, and on the fringes of present New England and New York, the first footholds of New France were established early in the seventeenth century in the Port Royal (Annapolis) basin of present Nova Scotia and at the site of present Quebec City, commanding the junction of the St. Lawrence River channel with its great estuary. The fur-trading interests, a westward extension of fishing, and sea-mammal hunting led the parade, but religion and international politics joined to sustain and accelerate the effort.

A geographical entity in which any group of people lives for any considerable period of time is a blend of qualities of the mutual reactions and adaptations of nature and culture. That Acadia was settled by seventeenth-century Frenchmen contributed one major group of ingredients to its character, but that it was situated where it was, with a particular congeries of physical and biotic characteristics and that, when the French arrived, it was occupied by a long resident group of North American Indians who continued to share the area with the Acadians, all contributed important additional elements. To a consideration of the geographies of nature and of the Micmac Indians, thus, the next two chapters are devoted.

2

The Endowment of Nature

THE ACADIANS lived in a very intimate relationship with nature. Their decisions as to where they would live and how they would sustain themselves were deeply influenced by the forms of the land, the climate, the vegetation, the soils, and the characteristics of the never distant sea. An attempt to understand the spatial components of their occupation of Acadia thus demands a clear, if summary, view of the intraregional geography of nature.

THE FORMS OF THE LAND

Appropriately enough, geomorphologists have classified the area of the three traditional maritime provinces of Canada, east of the New Brunswick highlands and Gaspé's rugged Shickshock mountains, as the "Acadian" landform region.[1] Along with coastal Maine these were the lands that, historically, comprised "Acadia" in its broadest territorial

1. That is, the area east of a line drawn from Chaleur Bay to Milltown on the St. Croix River where the Maine–New Brunswick border meets tidewater. The "Maritime Provinces," traditionally, include New Brunswick, Nova Scotia, and Prince Edward Island; the addition of Newfoundland in 1949 has created a new four-province group which is now being termed "Atlantic Canada" by way of distinction.

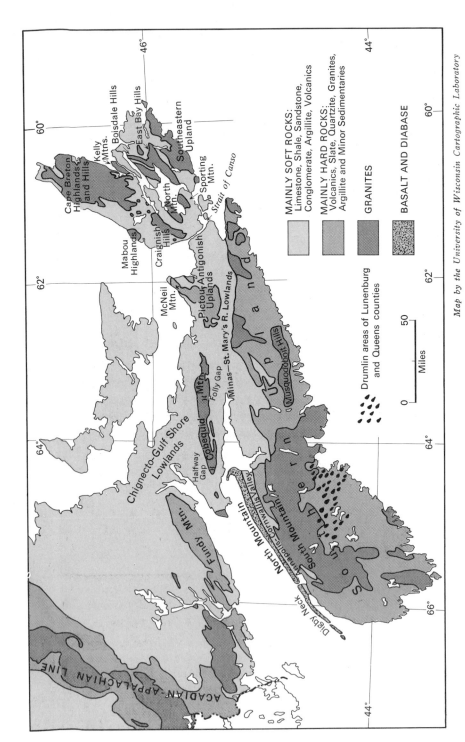

Fig. 2.1 The Acadian Lands: Hard and Soft Rock Areas.

MAINLY SOFT ROCKS:
Limestone, Shale, Sandstone,
Conglomerate, Argillite, Volcanics

MAINLY HARD ROCKS:
Volcanics, Slate, Quartzite, Granites,
Argillite and Minor Sedimentaries

GRANITES

BASALT AND DIABASE

Drumlin areas of Lunenburg
and Queens counties

Miles

0   50

Cape Breton
Highlands
and Hills

Kelly
Mtns.

Boisdale Hills

East Bay Hills

Southeastern
Upland

Mabou
Highlands

Craignish
Hills

North
Mtn.

Sporting
Mtn.

Strait of Canso

McNeil
Mtn.

Pictou-Antigonish
Uplands

Minas–St. Mary's R. Lowlands

Upland

Musquodoboit Hills

Chignecto-Gulf Shore
Lowlands

Folly Gap

Cobequid Mtn.

Halfway
Gap

Fundy Mtn.

North Mountain

Annapolis-Cornwallis Valley

South Mountain

Southern

Upland

Digby Neck

ACADIAN-APPALACHIAN LINE

Map by the University of Wisconsin Cartographic Laboratory

The Uplands

The greatest single upland block, named by J. W. Goldthwait the "Southern Upland,"[5] stretches for 275 miles from Cape Canso to Cape Sable and covers much of Guysborough County, most of Halifax, half of Hants, and virtually all the land to the west that lies southeast of the depression formed by St. Mary's Bay and the Annapolis-Cornwallis Valley (for place names see End papers). It has a land surface and pattern of drainage characteristic of much of the rock-scour area of the Canadian Shield. This dominant element of Nova Scotia's landscape is not really very high, reaching elevations of only 600 to 700 feet in the heart of the peninsula; it slopes generally from northwest to southeast. Two general kinds of terrain within it are attributed to bedrock differences. The surfaces of the granite areas (Figure 2.1) tend to be undulating, with gentle slopes and with a heavy sprinkling of granite boulders. The remaining hard-rock areas are rather mixed in bedrock types; ancient folded sedimentary rocks often metamorphosed into slates and quartzites, tend to be dominant. Where the latter two alternate we may have quartzite ridges alternating with shallow depressions based on the less resistant slate. Glaciation may have accentuated the inherent inferiority of the hard-rock areas for agricultural use, but within those areas the slate has provided the best opportunities in muddier soils and in the scattered, half-egg shaped drumlins scattered over Lunenburg and Queens counties (see End papers and Figure 2.1)[6] which offer the best of the limited farming opportunities on Nova Scotia's Atlantic coast.

Apart from North Mountain which forms the Bay of Fundy's southern margin the other major uplands of peninsular[7] Nova Scotia are Cobequid Mountain north of Minas Basin which was a very significant terrain feature to the Acadians, and the more compact hilly area straddling the border between Pictou and Antigonish counties. The former stretches from near Cape Chignecto almost to the western

5. J. W. Goldthwait, *Physiography of Nova Scotia* (1924), is the most important and nearly definitive work on the geomorphology of Nova Scotia.

6. There is an excellent map of the drumlin area in J. Tuzo Wilson, "Drumlins of Southwest Nova Scotia" (1938), with a base showing the distribution of quartzite and slate.

7. Despite the recently-constructed causeway across the Strait of Canso, Cape Breton Island is still recognized as insular.

sense. They have a rather irregular surface of hills and valleys; there are no true mountains and few of what would popularly be called plains, although there are extensive rolling surfaces of very moderate relief.[2]

There are two major types of terrain. The first is that underlain by crystalline rocks which have been comparatively resistant to erosion and usually have substantially greater elevations. The soil of these areas generally has not been useful for agriculture. The second has a surface eroded to lower levels in softer sandstones, shales, and limestones and characteristically covered by better soils on which most of the limited agricultural activity in the area has taken place during the last two centuries (see Figure 2.1). Yet there is no widespread, consistent contrast between the two types of terrain in local relief or intricacy of dissection. Differences in terrain quality often show their clearest expressions along some of the boundaries between the hard rock "upland" and the soft rock "lowland" rather than in broad contrasts between one or the other.[3]

Pleistocene continental glaciation was universal with almost all of its expected attendant phenomena.[4] Its major effect well may have been to exaggerate the differences between upland and lowland in terms of the soil-making potential of the regolith; the upland soils are characteristically thinner, there is much bare rock, and the incidence of stones and boulders is very much greater. Again, although disarrangement of drainage was also virtually ubiquitous, more regular patterns have been reestablished over most of the lowland.

2. In lieu of any recent general descriptive study of the geomorphology of whole, or any major parts, of the Acadian region, I have depended on my observations, air photos, and topographic sheets, as well as on a series of publ studies on special topics. See Bibliography.

3. Almost all the rocks are believed to be of pre-Cambrian or Paleozoi exceptions are the Triassic rocks of North Mountain, the Annapolis-Co Valley, and the shores of Minas Basin. The significant contrast in age "upland" and "lowland" is that the rocks of the former are mostly of pr iferous age (North Mountain excepted) whereas those of the latter, apar valley and the Minas Basin shores, are chiefly of Mississippian or Pe age.

4. Extensive evidence of terminal and recessional moraines is, hov on the present territory of Nova Scotia. Presumably, these were mo well out on the offshore banks and only Sable Island represents a p expression of one, by analogy with Long Island, the islands south o and Cape Cod.

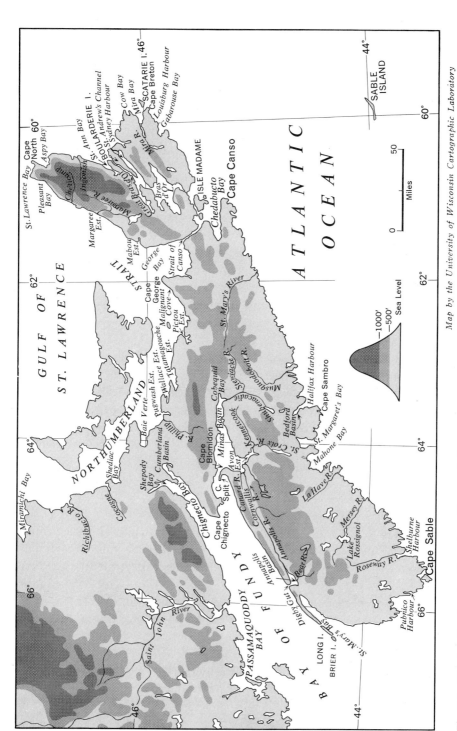

Fig. 2.2　The Acadian Lands: Elevations, Names of Capes, Bays, Islands, and Rivers.

Map by the University of Wisconsin Cartographic Laboratory

of the Bay of Fundy from Cape Split and Cape Blomidon in Minas
Basin to Brier Island, the westernmost extension of Digby Neck. In
only three places is it deeply broken, two of them giving access from
the Bay of Fundy to St. Mary's Bay and the third, Digby Gut,
providing the historic entrance to the Port Royal (Annapolis) Basin
into which Champlain and de Monts sailed to establish a settlement
several years before the first pioneers disembarked at Jamestown in
Virginia. There are, too, a number of wind gaps through North Mountain but none as prominent as those in Cobequid Mountain.

The cross-section of North Mountain is quite asymmetrical east of
Digby Gut. It has a fairly steep scarp slope to the southeast which
walls in the Annapolis-Cornwallis Valley. The change in slope is abrupt and the rise is on the order of four hundred feet. The greatest
heights in the ridge, of six to seven hundred feet, are immediately
above the escarpment, and the slope down to the Bay of Fundy is
generally fairly even at the rate of about 150 feet per mile. East of
Digby Gut the southern scarp is least sharply defined where the valley
behind it has its highest elevations, near the border of Kings and
Annapolis counties; on Digby Neck the height of the ridge is much
lower and the slopes toward the Bay of Fundy and St. Mary's Bay
much more even and symmetrical. It is not an imposing mountain in
any sense of the word but its abrupt scarp face, towering above the
dyked tidal meadows of the Acadians, made it a reassuring barrier for
them against the outside world.

The Lowlands

The lowlands have supported most of the agricultural settlement of
the area and the lines of land transportation have run across them,
wherever possible. The Annapolis-Cornwallis Valley, the first and historically most important of these, lay just south of North Mountain.
To traverse it is to have no doubt of its lowland character, and from it,
through much of its area, both North Mountain and South Mountain
are clearly in view. The latter, really the northern edge of the southern
upland, is as high as North Mountain and with slopes to the valley
only slightly less abrupt. Structurally the valley is a differentially
eroded lowland in comparatively soft, brick-red sandstones which
grade off to occasional pebble conglomerates or shales. The bedrock is
significant only in relation to the comparatively thin overburden of till

derived from it, but there is much glacio-fluvial sand in the valley and, at either end, tidal marshes and flats. The irregular deposition of till and sand has contributed to the unevenness of the floor of the narrow lowland which varies in height, longitudinally, from 150 feet above sea level to as much below in the flooded bays and basins. Indeed its surface is somewhat rougher than that of the granitic upland to the south. Transversely the elevations run from roughly twenty-five feet above mean sea level along the Annapolis and Cornwallis rivers to three hundred feet on the north side of the valley at the base of the North Mountain slope and to from two to five hundred feet on the south side. The boundary of the valley with the upland to the south is a bit indistinct in places with a sort of rolling "foothill"[13] transition.

The valley is narrowest, roughly two to three miles, just where the Acadian culture and economy was cradled, from the present town of Annapolis Royal to the village of Paradise, a distance of some twenty miles. To the east it retains its identity as a well-defined valley at least as far as Kentville, in places widening to as much as seven miles. Then at Wolfville, if not before, it merges with the Minas lowland. There it becomes three flattish peninsulas with elevations of 100 to 200 feet, their undulating surfaces sloping gently to the marshes. These peninsulas are separated by short water courses, around which were the extensive tidal flats where an early large Acadian expansion from the Annapolis Basin took place.

Adjacent to the valley, to the north and east, are the lowlands bordering Minas Basin. They are relatively narrow to the north, on the southern flank of Cobequid Mountain. Eastward they extend to the Pictou-Antigonish uplands;[14] southward they broaden to include much of Hants County, nearly all of southern Colchester, and even the bit of Halifax County in the upper Musquodoboit River valley. The border with the southern upland is sinuous as the softer rocks overlap the harder in a far from even line, and this border is one of the most difficult of the boundaries between harder and softer rocks to discern in the field.

The base rocks are most generally sandstones and shales, well represented in the ground moraine, but there are marls, limestone, and

13. The term is not very apt but so this area is known locally to its inhabitants and their near neighbors.
14. By a corridor north of St. Mary's River they continue to the "lowlands" of Guysborough, Antigonish, and Richmond.

gypsum (or "plaister");[15] the last makes its presence apparent at the surface in some expectable, and some highly individual, solution forms. The surface of the lowland is in places rougher than that of the upland to the south with a good deal of local relief and a rather disorderly arrangement of drainage. Either side of the border might be described as a "rough plain" or "subdued hill-land," the result of irregular ground moraine deposition. Yet some of the relief is clearly related to preglacial differential erosion and the "grain" of the country is related to underlying folds and faults more than to the direction of glacial movement. In nothing is this more clear than in a pseudo-"drumlin" field near Windsor on the upper and middle parts of the Avon estuary; the "drumlins," though close to real drumlins in shape, are in fact rock hills with a thin mantle of drift and their orientation is with the strike of the rock, not the movement of glacial ice.

North of Cobequid Mountain, in much of Cumberland and northwestern Pictou counties, lies a rolling plain, much of it less than two hundred feet in elevation although it may exceed three hundred feet near the foot of the mountain and there are residual hills rising as high as Springhill's 610 feet. Sometimes it is relatively flat, in other areas quite undulating, but the principal relief is seen along the valleys of the entrenched rivers. The till surface reflects the character of the sandstones and shales of most of the underlying bedrock.

East of the Pictou-Antigonish upland, in Antigonish and Guysborough counties, is another lowland area merging with that of Colchester County in a broad belt north of the west branch of the St. Mary's River. This is, indeed, of softer rocks but with elevations and surface forms barely, if at all, distinguishable from the uplands north and south of it except for fewer lakes, swamps, and muskegs, a reflection of the generally better organized drainage. There is a well-defined scarp south of the river, however, which marks the northern edge of the upland and justifies in part the designation of "Musquodoboit Hills." In relation to its later settlement history one must remember that this northeastern lowland of the peninsula is nowhere near a plain and that its surface is much dissected, with a considerable local relief. Eleva-

---

15. This out-of-date form of the now also generally obsolete "plaster," as a term for gypsum, was widely represented in Nova Scotia's place-names as seen on maps and in much contemporary description of the eighteenth and nineteenth centuries, indicating the fairly widespread occurrence of the gypsum beds and their economic importance at the time.

tions and roughness increase from George Bay south to the Guysborough County section.

As one moves across the Strait of Canso into the lowland strips of Cape Breton, which alternate with the hard-rock uplands in nearly parallel lines with a northeast-southwest strike, we are again, for the most part, dealing with very rolling or hilly surfaces in which interfluve elevations of up to five hundred feet may be reached in the west. As with the uplands, general elevations of the lowlands decrease from northwest to southeast. This considerable relief is carried over in the varying depths of the great "inland sea" of Bras d'Or Lake. Most of the bottom of the lake, indeed, is less than two hundred feet below the surface but in St. Andrew's Channel southeast of Boularderie Island, a depth of nearly 850 feet has been recorded.

A descriptive term for the lower valleys of the short rivers was "intervale" or "interval." Apparently imported from New England and applied widely through Nova Scotia in the late eighteenth century, it has no accepted scientific definition; its popular use has extended to almost any lowland, whether along a river or not. But generally it implies limited floodplain and terrace land into which the rivers were often incised and which, though perhaps flooded occasionally, was nevertheless much valued for meadow and plowland and often provided what little of the latter there was in the extensive hard-rock areas.

The Shoreline

Nova Scotia has a variety of shoreline types.[16] On the south and east from Yarmouth around Cape Sable and almost continuously therefrom to the province's easternmost tip at Scatarie Island, the hard-rock edge shows a consistent roughness and intricacy of outline with almost a skerry guard of islands or reefs in many places. Indeed, it shows most of the same features as the nearby coast of northern Maine. Sometimes the inlets are shallow bays or bights; sometimes they are deep, fjord-like estuaries leading miles inland from the open sea. Much of the irregularity of shore outline is unquestionably attributable to glacial deposition (drumlin and kame islands are very common) and there appears to be much less effect of glacial scour than one might expect, although ice-erosion has been called upon to explain many of the

16. For references on the shoreline, see Bibliography.

estuaries as excavated river valleys, and the mysterious existence of Bedford Basin behind Halifax Harbour.

The shores of the Strait of Northumberland are also uneven, but the outline fits a pattern in which lower valleys of rivers of dendritic form were flooded by a positive change in sea-level, presumably by postglacial sea rise; the estuaries at Pugwash, Wallace, Tatamagouche, and Pictou are almost classic examples. In contrast, the coast of Cape Breton on the Gulf of St. Lawrence is almost without indentation of any kind even in the soft-rock areas (the Mabou and Margaree estuaries are mild exceptions to the rule) although this coast does have a few offshore islands, free or bar-tied (as at Chéticamp and Port Hood), that have allowed port facilities of a limited kind to be developed.

The Fundy shores are different again. There are remarkably straight and unbroken coastlines in the harder rock areas and some deep estuaries in the soft-rock zones but nothing of the raggedness of the south coast is apparent. Sharp, if often low, cliffs are common. The famous tidal flats have contributed a special character to the shoreline which changes radically in appearance from hour to hour in a tidal cycle with ranges of such magnitude (see Figure 2.4 and Plates 1 and 2).

From the point of view of a settlement geographer the character of such an area's shoreline is of the utmost importance in the understanding of its exploration and early utilization, especially when it was approached, explored, and tried out by people with the freedom of movement made possible by the small shallow-draft transatlantic ships of the seventeenth century. Granted the enormous fishery resources off the coast and over the vast offshore banks, the myriad of rocky coves and natural harbors of the south coast provided ideal opportunities for landing and "making" (that is, salting and drying) codfish. The soft-rock, drowned, ria shoreline of the peninsula's western and northern shores provided a few, but enough, good small harbors for the needs of the agricultural activity in the lowland behind.[17]

The Offshore Banks

The continental shelf to the southeast of Newfoundland and Nova Scotia and east of New England is broad and contains rather extensive

17. This also provided for industrial activity, too, when the coal mines and the later iron and steel works of the New Glasgow area in Pictou County were developed.

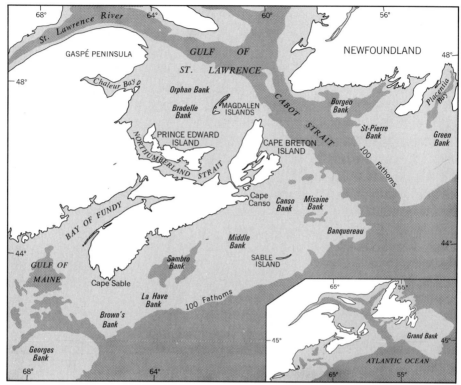

Map by the University of Wisconsin Cartographic Laboratory

Fig. 2.3 Atlantic Canada: Continental Shelf and Fishing Banks.

areas with depths of less than one hundred fathoms. On the largest single one of these offshore banks, Newfoundland's Grand Bank, with an area of 50,000 square miles, some shoals are virtually at the surface, and 170 miles east-southeast of Halifax lies Sable Island, the only surface indication of another of these shallow-depth submarine plateaus (see Figure 2.3). The shallower parts of the floor of the Gulf of St. Lawrence are so designated (Orphan Bank and the Magdalen Islands area). The significance of the banks is of course that above them were concentrated areas of plant and animal plankton, with successively larger forms of sea life feeding on the smaller, culminating in the world-famous richness of demersal fish, above all the cod.[18] The nearness of the banks to the Nova Scotia coastline, together with the

18. Included also were haddock, hake or whiting, ling, pollock, and perhaps rose fish.

suitability of the coves for shelter and of the sandy or rocky margins
for drying fish, provided a natural invitation for early European contacts. Much of the fishery, however, was always concentrated in the
immediate coastal waters, notably in the Canso region and along the
southeastern and eastern shores of Cape Breton Island.

The Tidal Marshlands

Around the Bay of Fundy and its various branches there are,
roughly, some 120 square miles of salt marsh and associated bogs.[19] Its
origin lies in the extraordinarily high tidal range of the Bay of Fundy
area (see Figure 2.4). The tidal range on the coast of the Strait of
Northumberland varies from more than two to less than five feet; at
Halifax it is about four feet, at Cape Sable six feet, and at Yarmouth
over twelve feet. But it is within the bay that spectacular ranges of
thirty to forty feet at normal tides, and fifty feet or more at spring
tides, occur. The ranges are still higher when gales are combined with
spring tides, and are somewhat greater in Minas Basin than in Chignecto Bay. Seasonally, the highest ranges occur in spring and fall and
there is special danger of floods between August and November when
the prevailing winds drive up the bay from the southwest sometimes
reinforced by the tail-end effect of hurricanes which, every few years,
can be felt even this far north along the coast.[20]

The tides of Fundy have been well studied and the details of the
oceanography need not be discussed here.[21] However, it is important to
remember that the tidal movements are not strictly surficial: speeds
down to depths of nearly 250 feet are close to those of the surface

19. W. F. Ganong, "The Vegetation of the Bay of Fundy Salt and Diked
Marshes: An Ecological Study" (1903), pp. 164–65, and D. W. Johnson, *The New
England–Acadian Shoreline* (1925), p. 567, estimated that there is ten times as
much dyked marsh around the Bay of Fundy as along the entire Atlantic coast of
the United States.

20. One in the late autumn of 1759 seriously damaged the dykes, neglected for
four years after the deportation of the Acadians, just before the New Englanders
moved in (see Chapter 8). In the Saxby Gale of October 5, 1869, the range exceeded seventy feet and reached a point 9.52 feet above the lowest high tides and
at least three and one-half feet above ordinary spring tides. In many places it
covered the dykes by a foot or more and lay ten to thirteen feet deep on the
dyked marshes, 16,000 acres of which were flooded. A gale in November 1901 had
almost as great an effect.

21. For references on oceanography, see Bibliography.

Nova Scotia Information Service

1   Low Tide in the Marshlands

Nova Scotia Information Service

2   High Tide in the Marshlands

which may be five to eight miles an hour. It has been estimated that with each tide some two cubic miles of water race in and out of Minas Basin through the channel between Cape Split and Cape Sharp which is less than five miles wide at high water. The tides carry along with them great quantities of sediment (fine sands, silts, and clays) as they erode, transport, and deposit. In the tidal creeks this sediment is commonly up to 2 per cent by volume. Unquestionably the high tides deposit the sediment across the flatter areas on their flood and they also take sediment out again into the deep parts of the bay on their ebb, but the very existence of the marshes supports the opinion that the tides deposit more than they erode: one tide can deposit up to two inches of sediment. Examination of the strata of the tidal marshes of the Fundy area indicate that, essentially, they have all been built up in this way. Borings have indicated that in depth they may reach thicknesses of at least eighty feet, and surveys of the marshes and associated fresh water bogs around the Bay of Fundy show that there are some 75,000 acres of them (Figure 2.4).

The largest part of this area (about 40,000 acres) lies around the shores of Cumberland Basin (about 15,000 acres in present Nova Scotia and about 25,000 acres in present New Brunswick). This is the only really large and continuous marsh area, although some of the smaller blocks (like that at Grand Pré in Minas Basin) may be more celebrated. Most of the rest of the marshland lies in bits and pieces along the coast or bordering the courses of the tidal rivers and streams. Even in the Cumberland Basin area the flat, treeless, marsh surface seems much like a sea around an irregular coastline as it surrounds "islands" and pushes into "bays" and "estuaries" of the solid land. As D. W. Johnson put it: "But the sea which spreads far up the submerged valleys is here a sea of green, and the wind sets in motion only waves in the grass, which leave no trace on the rocky shores."[22] The most devoted student of the marshlands, W. F. Ganong, thus described them at the end of the nineteenth century:

The country around Cumberland Basin is of ancient (Palaeozoic) formations, rounded into low smooth hills and ridges separated by radiating river valleys. Among the ridges lie the marshes, seemingly level as the sea; and, like it, they fill bays, surround islands and are pierced by points. Seen from the neighboring ridges, the marshes have an aspect characteristic and beautiful. They are treeless, but are clothed nearly everywhere with dense rich grasses in many shades of green and brown, varying with the season, with the light,

22. Johnson, *New England–Acadian Shoreline*, p. 566.

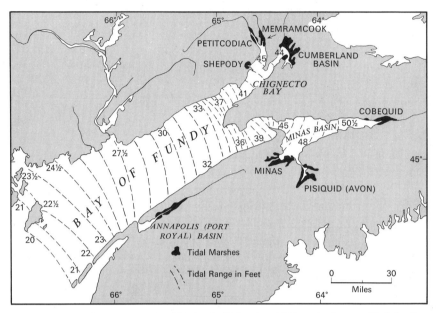

Map by the University of Wisconsin Cartographic Laboratory
Fig. 2.4   Bay of Fundy: Tidal Ranges and Tidal Marshes.

and even with the winds. For the most part the merging of colors is irregular; but in places, owing to the different treatment given by different owners to their land, or to the presence of fields of grain or pasture-lots, there is something of the checkered appearance usual in highly cultivated land. The frequent ditches marked by denser growths, the rare fences and the occasional roads or railways are other signs of the operations of man. Towards the sea are narrow fringes of unreclaimed marsh, poorer in vegetation and generally duller in color, while farther back the green of the marshes gives place to the brown and gray of the bogs, which are further distinguished by irregular shrubbery and trees, and many little lakes. Nobody lives upon the marshes, but scattered upon them are many great barns, all of one and the simplest pattern, unpainted and gray from the weather, standing at any and every angle. These barns are one of the distinguishing features of the marshes, and give to them a suggestion of plenty which is a true index of the economic condition of this region, for here are the most prosperous and progressive farmers, and the most thriving country towns in eastern Canada.[23]

This marshland, which largely supported the Acadian people for more than a century, and contributed so much to the economy of both Nova Scotia and New Brunswick for another century and a half after

23. Ganong, "Bay of Fundy Marshes," pp. 165–66.

the Acadian dispersion, in several important respects hardly deserves that name. The bottom, away from the fresh water peat bogs up the streams and toward the edges of the upland, is firm, composed of tightly-packed fine sand, silt, and clay. One walks on it, when the tide is out, as easily as on most upland soils after a heavy rain. Its texture is coarser near the seaward margins, finer inland. There is every evidence that the silt out of which it is built largely originated deep in the bay (although ultimately derived from the deposition of the rivers and the wearing away of the sea cliffs) and, immediately, comes only to a very small degree from the nearby lands and their rivers.

The sediments vary in composition, in part because they are directed by the meandering channels of the tidal "rivers." These channels move back and forth with time, as successive old river bank "running" dykes in roughly parallel lines near Aulac indicate, although with peculiarities resulting from the regularly reversing movement of the tidal currents (see Figure 2.4). In a quite specific way, the marshes are the flood plains of these tidal currents, showing both channel-meander features and channel-margin levees, with back swamps behind, below the level of the banks of the streams and the coastal margins. Because the tides are compressed in the channels they reach higher levels farther up the estuaries than they do at their mouths, and the bordering marshes themselves can thus be at somewhat higher elevations upstream than lower down; nevertheless the general level of the marshes decreases inward from the sea coast. Shallow pockets may develop in the higher lying back-swamp areas.[24] Unusually high floods or shifts in channels may later expose their vegetation to the killing effect of salt water and the deposition of bay silts. Several lenses of such fresh water peat bog material have been discovered by borings, or exposed by the shifting of channels in the present salt-marsh areas. Of more interest are the drowned or buried forests (including spruce, hemlock, birch, alder, ash, and elm stumps *in situ*) known on the "marsh" areas in several places where erosion has exposed them. Their existence, at up to thirty-five or forty feet below the present surface, has been used to suggest that there was a settling of the coastline, or a rise of sea level, in late post-Pleistocene time. We have a good deal of evidence to suggest, rather, that the "marshes" settled steadily by

24. Johnson, *New England–Acadian Shoreline*, p. 570, says that in 1883 Monro estimated that bogs covered 8,700 acres on the inner borders of the Cumberland Basin marshes.

compaction. Yet, the fact that forests of white pine, oak, and beech, that grew for up to two hundred years (by ring count), should have been established on soils of marsh origin, but yet at sufficient elevation, and with enough drainage, to have maintained themselves so long before being overwhelmed by salt water and silt, presents a tough problem of interpretation. It is not known if they are contemporaneous with the lenses of interbedded peat. But it is doubtful that when the necessary research to solve this problem is undertaken (and much research needs still to be done, as Schott remarked in 1955),[25] it will change our present conception of the essential nature of the marshland.

Another feature of the action and reaction of sea tides and currents with the marshland is the effect of sea-ice. It contributes to sea-margin beach ridges and to the transport of silt, frozen within or on top of cakes of ice which often become stranded high on the marshes by unusually high tides in late winter or early spring and, upon melting, leave heaps of material scattered over the marshes in a disorderly array.

Natural processes have been markedly affected by the dyking of the marshes to exclude salt water, the cutting of drainage channels on their surfaces, and the construction of sluice gates (*aboiteaux*), large and small, which allow the fresh water to drain out at low tide but exclude the salt water automatically when they close with the incoming tide. When the dykes were built high enough and maintained well enough to keep out the salt water and its silt over long periods, the natural settling, together with the compaction attributable to the working of the land, brought them to steadily lower elevations. The French rarely used deliberately the remedy that would have helped to maintain them best—that is, the compartmentalization of the marshes into polders with dividing dykes, and the periodic admission of silt-laden salt water to build up their level again. To be sure, however, nature did the job whenever unusually high tides, neglect of the dykes, or their destruction by marauders from New England, admitted the salt water. But clearly there was a good deal of interference with what could be called "natural" processes. Some interesting restoration work was done in the nineteenth century. Salt water loaded with silt was admitted into fresh water marshes and lakes far toward the inland edge of the marsh area in order to kill the vegetation and fill the depressions with soil-making silt. Several such lakes were thus filled in a short time.[26] The large

25. Carl Schott, *Die Kanadischen Marschen* (1955), p. 21.
26. Ganong, "Bay of Fundy Marshes," p. 179.

dykeland rehabilitation program, underway now for some years, probably will have the effect of steadily lowering the level of the lands behind the dykes. No natural rehabilitation seems to be planned.

CLIMATE

The climate of the Acadian lands had great significance for the kinds of vegetation and soil that clothed them and for the genre de vie of their settlers.[27] The following discussion will be concentrated upon a few indices of climatic character using recorded data from various Nova Scotia stations and will compare them, in part, with those of some others in central Canada, in the United Kingdom, and in France. The comparisons may help to elucidate those qualities of the Acadian climate that must have impressed the settlers from France and the British Isles as they tried to adapt techniques of the Old World, and a variety of immigrant plants and animals, to the conditions of their new homes. At the same time, it will make possible some useful comparisons with the St. Lawrence Valley and the Ontario peninsula where other French or British settlers, contemporaneous in time, had similar problems.[28]

Annual means for air temperatures in Nova Scotia are about the same as those for the Great Lakes–St. Lawrence area and 5° to 10° F. lower than those for the western European stations (see Table 2.1). January means are comparable with those in southern Ontario, substantially higher than those in Ottawa, Montreal, and Quebec, but 15° to 20° F. below those of London, Paris, Nantes, and Bordeaux. Summer temperatures, using July means for comparison, are roughly 5° F. below those of Toronto and Montreal, slightly above those of London, and somewhat below those of Paris, Nantes, and Bordeaux. The range of temperatures thus is less than that of central Canada but roughly

27. For references on climate, see Bibliography.
28. One caveat must be entered at once. Climates do fluctuate from year to year, decade to decade, and century to century. A study of M. K. Thomas, "Climatic Trends along the Atlantic Coast of Canada" (1955), using ten-year running means for the combined records of Yarmouth, Halifax, Sydney, and Sable Island from 1895 to 1950, showed that annual means had fluctuated within a range of nearly 3° F., summer means within a range of a degree and a half, and winter means within a range of some 4° F. But no clear trend for a period of a century is discernible and we have no firm evidence that the climate of the seventeenth, eighteenth, or nineteenth centuries was essentially different from that of the twentieth, nor, indeed, any good reason to think it might have been.

TABLE 2.1 *Air temperature (°F.) at selected stations in Canada and Europe*

Station	Mean annual	Jan.	Feb.	Mar.	Apr.	May	June	July	Aug.	Sept.	Oct.	Nov.	Dec.
Sydney	43	23	20	28	37	47	56	65	65	58	49	39	29
Halifax	45	24	23	31	40	50	58	65	65	59	50	40	29
Yarmouth	44	27	26	33	40	49	56	62	62	57	50	41	31
Moncton, N.B.	41	16	16	27	37	50	58	66	64	56	46	34	22
Quebec	41	12	13	25	38	52	62	68	65	57	45	32	18
Montreal	44	15	16	28	42	56	66	70	68	60	48	35	21
Ottawa	42	12	13	25	41	54	64	69	66	58	46	33	17
Toronto	47	25	24	32	44	55	65	71	69	62	50	39	28
London, Ont.	46	23	22	32	43	55	65	70	68	61	49	37	26
London, England	50	40	41	45	49	54	60	63	63	59	52	46	42
Edinburgh	48	38	39	42	45	50	56	59	58	55	48	43	40
Paris	52	36	39	46	53	58	64	68	66	61	52	44	38
Nantes	53	40	42	47	53	57	62	66	66	61	54	47	41
Bordeaux	54	41	43	48	53	58	64	68	67	62	55	48	43

Source: The records have been culled from a variety of official sources for Canada, the British Isles, and France. Certain minor adjustments have been made in the interests of greater comparability. As a result these figures should not be used as raw data for any other purpose but it is believed that they do represent the comparative situation fairly for the first half of the twentieth century —and probably, in comparative terms, for earlier centuries as well. Similarities with New England are so close (except for the latter's rather warmer summers) that climatic data for that area have not been included.

TABLE 2.2 *Precipitation (inches) at selected stations in Canada and Europe*

Station	Total annual	Jan.	Feb.	Mar.	Apr.	May	June	July	Aug.	Sept.	Oct.	Nov.	Dec.
Sydney	51	4.9	4.4	4.2	3.8	3.7	3.2	3.0	3.9	4.3	5.2	5.0	5.2
Halifax	54	5.2	4.0	4.3	4.5	4.4	4.3	3.6	4.1	4.6	5.1	5.0	5.2
Yarmouth	47	5.2	4.1	4.0	3.9	3.4	3.2	3.0	3.1	3.8	3.8	4.4	5.1
Moncton, N.B.	41	3.0	3.6	3.2	3.2	3.4	3.7	2.9	3.2	3.8	3.2	4.3	3.5
Quebec	45	3.6	2.8	3.0	3.3	3.6	4.5	4.4	4.4	4.2	3.7	4.0	3.3
Montreal	42	3.6	2.7	3.3	3.4	3.3	3.8	4.0	3.5	3.7	3.4	3.9	3.4
Ottawa	35	2.7	2.2	2.8	2.6	2.8	3.4	3.5	3.0	3.1	2.7	3.0	3.0
Toronto	31	2.7	2.3	2.6	2.6	2.7	2.7	3.2	2.4	2.7	2.3	2.6	2.3
London, Ont.	38	3.4	2.8	2.9	3.0	3.1	3.4	3.7	2.8	3.5	2.8	3.5	3.3
London, England	24	2.0	1.7	1.5	1.5	2.2	1.9	2.2	2.4	1.8	2.7	2.3	1.8
Edinburgh	27	2.5	1.6	1.7	1.7	2.2	2.0	3.0	2.7	2.4	2.8	2.2	1.9
Paris	25	2.1	1.8	1.8	1.6	2.5	2.0	2.0	3.3	2.0	1.7	2.3	2.1
Nantes	30	2.6	1.9	2.0	2.0	3.0	1.9	2.0	2.5	2.6	3.5	3.0	2.1
Bordeaux	30	2.1	2.3	2.3	2.4	2.4	1.8	2.0	2.4	2.8	3.4	2.9	3.2

Source: See Table 2.1.

half again as large as that of coastal northwestern Europe. Rarely do air temperatures rise above 90° F. or fall below 0° F.

The yearly regime of air temperature reflects the maritime situation of Nova Scotia better than does the annual range. As compared with Ontario and Quebec, spring is cold and late, autumn, warm and protracted; the parallel is rather with coastal northwestern Europe. June in Nova Scotia is generally cooler than September, and even May than October; February may be colder than January and August compares with July in warmth. A lasting snow cover and persistent freezing temperatures, well established in most of settled Ontario and Quebec in November, do not fasten themselves on most of Nova Scotia until well on in December. A "green" or "English" Christmas is often experienced even if closely followed by a "white" and very "Canadian" New Year. Most of the agricultural areas of the province have four to five months of frost-free weather; only in the interior uplands (especially the southern upland and the Cape Breton highlands) does the period between the average dates of the latest killing frost in spring and the earliest in autumn fall below one hundred days, although it is less than four months in the Chignecto isthmus. The forward displacement of the frost-free period, and the peak of the temperature curves, by the lag of the seasons, however, means that the growing season may average less sunlight. The annual total of hours of bright sunshine compares with that of the St. Lawrence Valley but is less than that of Ontario.

Precipitation of forty to sixty inches a year, fifteen to twenty-five or thirty inches of it coming between May and October, usually has been considered adequate for agricultural needs. Although fairly evenly distributed (for example, Liverpool on the southeast Atlantic coast, on a twenty-six-year average, showed no month with less than four inches or more than six inches and, for the same period, Nappan had no month below two inches or above four inches), the August–October period usually has one-tenth to one-fourth more rain than the May–July period (see Table 2.2). Taken in concert with relatively cool summers this is much more like the regime of northwestern Europe than that of Ontario, for example, and is a much better distribution for grass than for grain-growing, a fact Nova Scotia's farmers have taken a full three centuries to appreciate.

Snow, five to eight feet of it falling and between one and two feet of it covering most of the land (except some of the immediate Atlantic shores) from late December to mid-April, affords one of the sharpest

TABLE 2.3   *Other climatic data for selected stations, Nova Scotia, New Brunswick, Quebec, and Ontario*

Station	Snow (inches)	Wind (av. speed in m.p.h.)	Hours of sunshine	Days with thunder	Days with freezing temp.	Frost-free days
Sydney	97	13	1745	7	162	137
Halifax	64	10	1876	8	134	152
Yarmouth	83	12	?	7	127	160
Moncton	108	13	1877	12	194	105
Quebec	124	9	1714	16	162	147
Montreal	101	11	1811	20	143	172
Ottawa	81	10	2010	21	165	141
Toronto	55	12	2047	22	123	165
London, Ont.	77	10	1922	26	156	137

Source: See Table 2.1.

contrasts to western Europe and one of the closest parallels with central Canada (see Table 2.3). There are also many more days with freezing weather than in western Europe, and somewhat higher winds, more fog, and generally higher humidity than in Ontario or Quebec.

By adding shorter-term records for Nappan (Chignecto area), Annapolis (in the valley), Liverpool, Springfield (in the western interior), Windsor, Truro, and Pictou we can get some notion of variations within the province. For example, the northern and western parts are more "continental," with colder winters, longer summers, warmer springs, and cooler autumns; they also have lower total precipitation but more of that in winter comes as snow so that more snow may actually accumulate and lie deeper on the ground. Locally the same contrasts are seen as between the coastal and more inland areas.

Nova Scotia is an upper-middle-latitude east coast maritime region strongly affected by air masses moving from the west where they have been continentally conditioned. It is situated in the heart of the area of favored storm-track exit from the continent and, in consequence, has rapid, day-to-day changes in temperature, humidity, and cloudiness and more than usual windiness. The concentration of the inhabitants along the sea coast and their long and intimate relationship with the sea for fishing and transport make conditions along the coasts of unusual importance. Indeed, no place in Nova Scotia, or in the southeastern parts of New Brunswick settled by Acadians, is more than thirty-five miles from tidewater, and 95 per cent of the population and of productive agriculture is within ten or fifteen miles of the coast. The unusual fogginess of the south coast, and the frequent gales and the cooling effects of the sea in summer, combine with the deficiencies of terrain to create serious problems for farming from Cape North to Cape Sable.[29] The Annapolis-Cornwallis Valley, however, is protected somewhat from the Fundy fogs by North Mountain. That barrier also gives the valley some shelter from bitter northwest winds in winter and Cobequid Mountain gives similar protection to much of Minas Basin.

VEGETATION

There is perhaps no single feature of the Acadian region that had more importance for the Indians and the Europeans who attempted to exploit it or to make their homes in it than the varied mantle of vegetation which covered it, particularly the forests and the herbaceous vegetation of the tidal marshlands. Both were unquestionably subject to change before the seventeenth century. The latter certainly, and the former probably, were altered in varying degrees in the seventeenth and eighteenth centuries. In the past two hundred years the alteration in the forest cover has been widespread and spectacular, although, since our major detailed evidence about the forest comes from surveys conducted in this century, we often are forced to extrapolate backwards to reconstruct its character in the seventeenth and eighteenth centuries, and our hypotheses cannot always be subjected to rigorous checks. Figure 2.5 and Table 2.4, based on information from the mid-twentieth century,[30] indicate that most of the land of Nova Scotia is still forest-covered. We assume that almost all of the agricultural land also was forested three to four centuries ago, and that some of the non-forest, non-agricultural land, especially areas of serious and repeated burnings where the soil cover was thin, was then predominantly clothed with trees. The unforested land of those centuries was of wide variety: brushland, rock barren, tidal mud flats, marsh and muskeg[31] for the most part. In all probability, as today, it was most

29. Each year, Halifax has thirty-five to forty days with gales and up to forty summer days with fog.

30. L. S. Hawboldt and R. M. Bulmer, *The Forest Resources of Nova Scotia* (1958), p. 74.

31. I.e. shallow bogs filling in (or filled in) with vegetation, and sometimes containing stunted trees, especially black spruce.

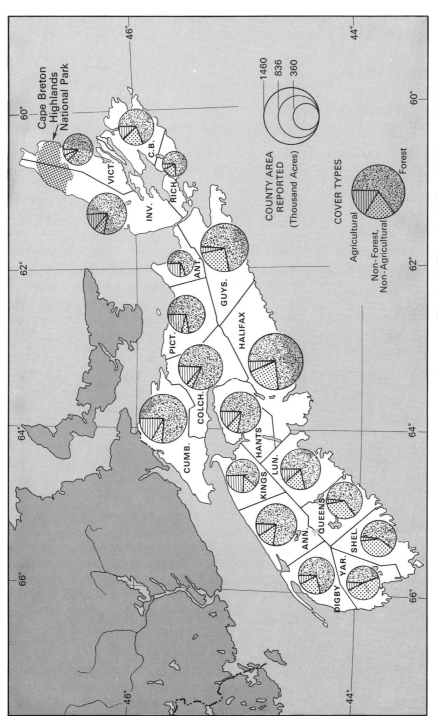

Fig. 2.5 Nova Scotia: Land Cover by Counties, 1950's.

Map by the University of Wisconsin Cartographic Laboratory

TABLE 2.4 *Land area of Nova Scotia classified by cover, 1950's*

Land area	Acres	Per cent of total area
Productive forest		
Softwood	5,159,172	38.7
Mixedwood	3,652,407	27.4
Hardwood	566,939	4.2
Total productive forest	9,378,518	70.3
Depleted forest	272,460	2.0
Non-forest land and non-productive forest (brushland, rock barren, and old burn not restocking)	1,037,744	7.8
Waste land (tidal mud flats, marsh, muskeg with stunted trees, sand and gravel pits, cape and quarry)	544,643	4.1
Agricultural and other improved land	1,453,378	10.9
Water (lakes, rivers, and estuaries)	655,367	4.9
Total (exclusive of Highlands National Park and area north of Park)	13,342,110	100.0
Highlands National Park	249,600	
Area north of Highlands National Park	120,080	
GRAND TOTAL of land and fresh water areas	13,711,790	
Bras d'Or lakes (salt water)	267,086	

Source: L. S. Hawboldt and R. M. Bulmer, *The Forest Resources of Nova Scotia* (1958), p. 74.

extensive on the Atlantic slopes of the interior upland, and especially in present Queens, Shelburne, and Yarmouth counties. But, in all, forest must have covered 85 per cent to 90 per cent of the land of Nova Scotia and perhaps 95 per cent or more of present New Brunswick and Prince Edward Island.

The Forest

Today most of Nova Scotia is forested; three and a half centuries ago almost all of it was. The proportions of the different species have changed—in some instances rather radically—under centuries of attack by axe and fire, and with the increased effect of insects, bacteria, and viruses encouraged by the alteration of ecological conditions. But the major forest trees are, as well as one can judge, given the uncertainties of terminology, the same trees reported by visitors since the early sixteenth century. A forest flora is much more than trees of course, but whatever use was made of the shrubs, ferns, mosses, grasses, and herbaceous plants in the forest,[32] it was the trees that characterized it and, to a very large degree, established the essential qualities of the land itself in the eyes of the explorers and settlers.

For so extensive a forested area, sharing the trees of at least three of the major continental vegetation regions,[33] the number of tree species is surprisingly small. Only thirty of the thirty-five species have been recognized as natives, and only two dozen or fewer have had any real importance. It is interesting that Titus Smith, in the first decade of the nineteenth century, had identified all of these but the wire, or grey, birch and the heart-leaf birch as separate species.[34] The total thus included a fir, a hemlock, a larch, a cedar, three spruces, three pines, an oak, a beech, an elm, an ironwood, two maples, two ashes, three or four

32. See A. E. Roland, "Flora of Nova Scotia" (1945). G. C. Cunningham, *Forest Flora of Canada* (1958), has photographs and descriptions of most of these plants.

33. The poverty of species is somewhat surprising in that Maritime Canada, including Nova Scotia, is a zone of mixing and competition between three major forest associations: the Northern or Boreal forest (the "taiga," mainly coniferous), the Northern Mixed forest (mainly deciduous broadleaf), and the Appalachian or Southeastern forest (predominantly broadleaf). It does have more variety than the taiga, but much less than the fully representative forests of its other two contributory associations. The fact that the Southeastern broadleaf forest is so poorly represented in Nova Scotia, as compared with Ontario, for example, where such trees as the tulip (*Liriodendron tulipifera*) and sour gum (*Nyssa sylvatica*) were abundant, is attributed to climate and especially to the effect of the cooling Labrador current in reducing summer temperatures. This may also account for the limited distribution of Northern white cedar, or arbor vitae (*Thuja occidentalis*) which, although a common species in New Brunswick, was until quite recently known in only a few localities in Nova Scotia, namely in the interior of Digby and Yarmouth counties and in the Annapolis Valley. A. J. Drummond, "How Plant Life is Distributed in Canada and Why" (1910), p. 25, pointed out that, in Ontario, 76 species of native trees had then been recognized as compared with 33 species in Nova Scotia.

34. For an account of the work of Titus Smith, a report on his famous traverses and diary, and an attempted reconstruction of his route in detail see A. H. Clark, "Titus Smith, Junior, and the Geography of Nova Scotia in 1801 and 1802" (1954). For an account of his more professional botanical and ecological work see Eville Gorham, "Titus Smith, a Pioneer of Plant Ecology in North America" (1955). One assumes that Smith meant red pine by "yellow pine" and jack pine by "mountain pine." He actually multiplied species of conifers by listing, as separate species, variant forms of these two pines. Professor Loucks has pointed out that with Smith's sensitivity to species it is amazing, and probably significant, that he does not list wire birch. From its rapid spread toward the eastern part of the peninsula in the last forty years we might hypothesize that it had invaded the western region since Smith's time. If, indeed, it was there, it must have been rare.

TABLE 2.5 *The more important Nova Scotian trees since 1600 (common names and botanical names)*

Needle-leafed trees
  Balsam fir: *Abies balsamea* (L.) Mill
  Red spruce: *Picea rubens* Sarg.
  White spruce: *Picea glauca* (Moench) Voss
  Black spruce: *Picea mariana* (Mill.) B.S.P.
  Eastern hemlock: *Tsuga canadensis* (L.) Carr.
  White pine: *Pinus strobus* L.
  Red pine: *Pinus resinosa* Ait.
  Jack pine: *Pinus banksiana* Lamb.
  Tamarack (larch or hackmatack): *Larix laricina* (Du Roi) K. Koch
  Eastern white cedar: *Thuja occidentalis* L.

Broadleaf trees
  Yellow birch: *Betula lutea* Michx. f.
  White birch: *Betula papyrifera* Marsh.
  Grey (wire) birch: *Betula populifolia* Marsh.
  Heart-leaf birch: *Betula cordifolia*
  Sugar (hard) maple: *Acer saccharum* Marsh.
  Red (soft) maple: *Acer rubrum* L.
  Beech: *Fagus grandifolia* Ehrh.
  Red oak: *Quercus rubra* L.
  Large-tooth aspen: *Populus grandidentata* Michx.
  Trembling aspen: *Populus tremuloides* Michx.
  Balsam poplar: *Populus balsamifera* L.
  American (white) elm: *Ulmus americana* L.
  Ironwood (hop hornbeam): *Ostrya virginiana* (Mill.) K. Koch
  White ash: *Fraxinus americana* (K. Koch)
  Black ash: *Fraxinus nigra* Marsh.
  Mountain ash: *Sorbus americana* Marsh. (S. decora?)

birches, and three poplars (see Table 2.5). Some of the shrubs, such as mountain ash (*Sorbus* spp.), occasionally assumed tree form.

At the present time conifers predominate everywhere both in areal extent and in volume of wood. In more than half of the forest area they are unmixed with broadleafs and they compose a substantial part of the mixed forests that occupy so much of the rest of the country (Figure 2.6 and Table 2.6). However, the scattered evidence of the seventeenth and eighteenth centuries, reinforced by Titus Smith's surveys of the early nineteenth century, suggest that in Acadian times (and probably well into the nineteenth century) the "hardwood" deciduous broadleafs were much more important. Indeed, the general forest cover of the north and east in the fifteenth to seventeenth centuries is reconstructed as one in which there were widespread sub-

TABLE 2.6　*Species composition of Nova Scotia's forests, 1950's*

Species	Volume in cubic feet	Per cent of group	Per cent of total
SOFTWOOD			
Balsam fir	2,987,303,445	38.33	25.35
White spruce	1,010,432,396	12.96	8.57
Red spruce	2,131,903,732	27.35	18.09
Black spruce	547,677,974	7.03	4.65
Eastern hemlock	469,647,316	6.03	3.98
White pine	506,748,450	6.50	4.30
Red pine	42,553,847	0.55	0.36
Jack pine	4,273,906	0.05	0.04
Tamarack	92,238,155	1.18	0.78
Eastern white cedar	1,775,231	0.02	0.02
Total	7,794,554,452	100.00	66.14
HARDWOOD			
Yellow birch	949,985,583	23.80	8.06
White birch	327,687,316	8.21	2.78
Sugar (hard) maple	645,266,248	16.17	5.48
Red maple	1,299,025,717	32.55	11.02
Beech	352,178,408	8.82	2.99
Balsam poplar	17,021,761	0.43	0.14
Ironwood	3,413,741	0.09	0.03
Red oak	124,346,117	3.12	1.06
White elm	2,100,043	0.05	0.02
White ash	141,499,554	3.55	1.20
Black ash	5,347,853	0.13	0.04
Trembling aspen	40,507,184	1.01	0.34
Large-tooth aspen	67,107,491	1.68	0.57
Grey birch	8,765,768	0.22	0.07
Others	6,868,934	0.17	0.06
Total	3,991,121,718	100.00	33.86

Source: L. S. Hawboldt and R. M. Bulmer, *The Forest Resources of Nova Scotia* (1958), p. 77.

stantial areas of almost purely broadleaf stands forming islands in a mixed forest often dominated by broadleafs,[35] and the present strong

35. See, especially, P. A. Bentley and E. C. Smith, "The Forests of Cape Breton in the Seventeenth and Eighteenth Centuries" (1956). M. H. Drinkwater, *The Tolerant Hardwood Forests of Northern Nova Scotia* (1957) and G. E. Nichols, "The Vegetation of Northern Cape Breton Island, Nova Scotia" (1918) are also relevant here. Limited as hardwoods are in Cape Breton today the accounts of Nicolas Denys in the seventeenth century and such observers as the Sieur de la

position of red maple west of Halifax and Minas Basin is one of several
kinds of evidence suggesting more extensive "hardwood" cover in the
west as well.[36]

Figure 2.6 is an attempt to show the relative distribution, by volume
of wood, of ten of the leading species which account for roughly nine-
tenths of the wood in the forests at the present time, arranged in seven
groups. The column on the left, for each county diagram, shows the
proportion of provincial wood-volume of each group; the right-hand
column shows the proportions of the same groups for each county.
The effect of clearing in the east is particularly evident. Balsam fir
and white spruce are heavily dominant (together comprising more
than half of the total volume of wood) in Cape Breton today, and
as farms have been abandoned in steady and accelerating procession,
particularly in the past fifty years, the colonization of old fields, by
white spruce in particular, has been spectacularly evident. Since the
maples, beech, and yellow birch, in particular, were considered very
generally to be indicators of potentially better agricultural land at the
time of initial clearing, the inferred changes as a result of cultural
process are clear. Yet similar changes appear to have occurred on land
never cleared; perhaps this is to be attributed in part to widespread
forest grazing and browsing. The long-term effects of repeated fires in
selective changes in this regard are not clear. But, for whatever rea-

---

Roque, Thomas Pichon, Thomas Jefferys, and Samuel Holland of the eighteenth
century make it clear that broadleafs were widespread, and dominant over large
sections of the island until the immigrants from Europe began moving inland and
agricultural settlement began. See "Tour of Inspection made by the Sieur de la
Roque," AC *Report for 1905* (1906); Thomas Pichon, *Genuine Letters and
Memoirs, Relating to the Natural, Civil, and Commercial History of the Islands
of Cape Breton and Saint John* (1760); Thomas Jefferys, *The Natural and Civil
History of the French Dominions in North and South America* (1760), p. 119;
and *Holland's Description of Cape Breton Island*, comp. and ed. D. C. Harvey
(1935). Relevant comments throughout the nineteenth century literature are
frequent and indicate the rapidly changing nature of the forest cover. That of
R. J. Uniacke in the 1860's is worth quoting for he was a good observer who had
traveled widely in the island: "A great variety of wood grows in Cape Breton,
amongst which the spruce, the pine and the fir most abound. . . . But fine hardwood trees (as they are called here) also clothe the rich and mineral soil of this
island, such as oak, ash, birch, beech and a great variety of maple. *Uniacke's
Sketches of Cape Breton*, ed. C. Bruce Fergusson (1958), p. 101.

36. See O. L. Loucks, "A Forest Classification for the Maritime Provinces"
(1962), p. 127, for a contrary view.

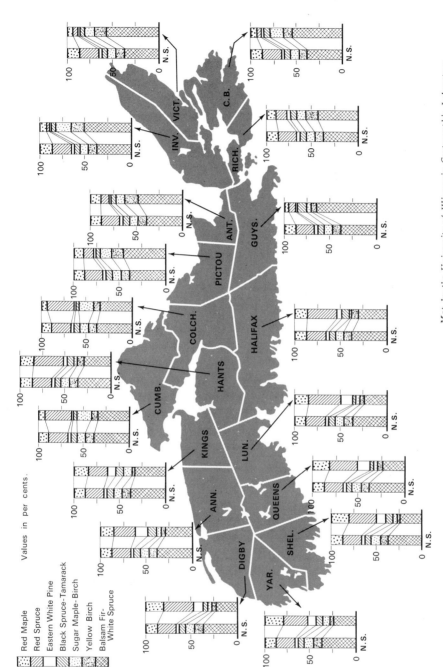

Red Maple
Red Spruce
Eastern White Pine
Black Spruce-Tamarack
Sugar Maple-Birch
Yellow Birch
Balsam Fir-
White Spruce

Values in per cents.

Fig. 2.6 Nova Scotia: Forest Species Groups, 1950's.

sons, the trend toward replacement of broadleafs by conifers has continued without abatement over most of the province for the past century and a half at least, most notably in the east but, I judge, also in the west and in the Fundy borderlands where the chief Acadian settlement took place.[37]

It is difficult to divide the Maritimes' area into distinct sections by forest types. Whatever the pattern may have been four centuries ago it is a disorderly mosaic today. Loucks[38] has provided an interesting attempt, from the point of view of a forest ecologist writing for those interested in silviculture (see Figure 2.7).

In a sense, each of his categories is a mixed forest association in which both conifers and broadleafs are found, but the proportions of each vary quite widely, as Figure 2.6 suggests. The Acadian areas were associated principally with what he calls the Fundy Bay ecoregion of the spruce-fir zone and the red spruce-hemlock-pine zone with a dividing line roughly along the road between Halifax, Windsor, and the Annapolis-Cornwallis Valley. The characteristic trees of the former are red spruce, balsam fir, and red maple, with scattered white spruce, white birch, and yellow birch; of these the wood of the spruces and the yellow birch was most widely used by the Acadians, although the bark of the white birch was always important for containers, canoes, and house insulation. The red spruce and hemlock are most characteristic of the lands further inland (especially in the Minas Basin areas). White pine and red maple are very common west of Halifax; east of it there may be rather more black spruce in wetter areas and jack pine on sandy soils. In the Annapolis-Cornwallis Valley, white and red pines and red oaks were common on the sandier soils of the central valley bottom; on the slopes some sugar maple and beech are found now; they, along with the red oak and the white pine, may have been much more widespread in the seventeenth century.

37. To enable us to have more confidence in this interpretation of trends, reference may be made to B. E. Fernow, C. D. Howe, and J. H. White, *Forest Conditions of Nova Scotia* (1912). The survey involved a good deal of field work extending over at least two seasons, and although it had nothing like the systematic care that went into Hawboldt and Bulmer's *Forest Resources of Nova Scotia*, and was intended only as a reconnaissance, it offers the only general account of forest conditions between that of Titus Smith at the beginning of the nineteenth century and the recent study.

38. Loucks, "A Forest Classification," p. 127.

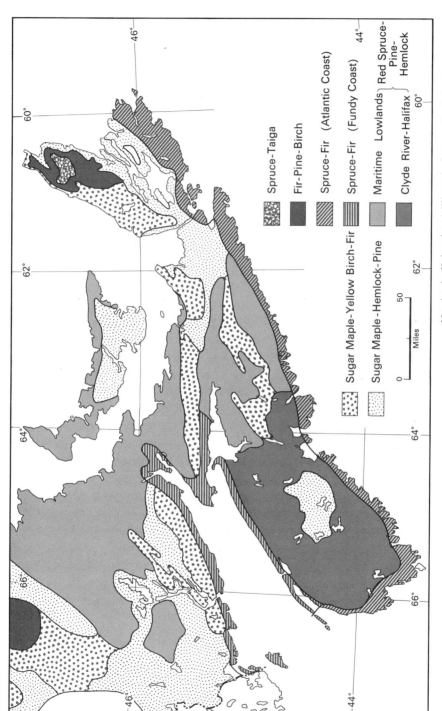

Legend:
- Spruce-Taiga
- Fir-Pine-Birch
- Spruce-Fir (Atlantic Coast)
- Spruce-Fir (Fundy Coast)
- Maritime Lowlands } Red Spruce-Pine-Hemlock
- Clyde River-Halifax
- Sugar Maple-Yellow Birch-Fir
- Sugar Maple-Hemlock-Pine

Map by the University of Wisconsin Cartographic Laboratory

Fig. 2.7 The Acadian Lands: Forest Zones and Regions.

The Plants of the Salt Marshes

The cover of the tidal flats and neighboring bays in the areas where settlement and farming took place the first century and a half around the shores of the Bay of Fundy was largely of grasses and associated herbaceous plants. Champlain, Lescarbot, Demeulle, Dièreville, and indeed all of the visitors of the seventeenth and early eighteenth centuries who commented upon them at all, support the position that the salt marshes were naturally treeless meadows. Carl Schott, in *Die Kanadischen Marschen*, has examined much of the literary evidence on these marshes in the past, has made detailed field studies of them, and strongly supports these views.[39] The significance of the buried forests (see the discussion of the marshlands above), is moot but it is certain that there can have been no arborescent species in this area sufficiently salt-tolerant to colonize land with the salt content of the present marshes. That in unusual circumstances, on reclaimed marshes near roads or hay barns, an occasional dwarf willow or birch may now appear, and that adjacent bogs or muskegs (see below) may support dwarf black spruce or tamarack, does not alter this conclusion.

The whole marshland area (see Figure 2.4) varies substantially within itself. Near the "inland" (really a better term here than "upland") border of the salt marshes there are often moderately extensive fresh water bogs of what Schott calls the *hackmoore* type. Interspersed (especially on the northern borders of the Cumberland Basin marshland area) are lakes of some considerable size on which floating bog a yard or more in thickness may be found. The same thing can sometimes be seen back of the natural levees of the tidal channels much nearer the sea. In all of these, peat mosses, cotton grasses (several species of *Eriophorum*, especially "rusty" cotton grass, *E. chamissonis*), sedges (*Carex*) in great variety, several horsetails (*Equisetum* spp.), rhodora (*Rhododendron canadense*), willow herbs (*Epilobium* spp.), sweet gale (*Myrica gale*), and the various kinds of cranberry and blueberry (*Vaccinium* spp.) may be found, and, as indicated, in bogs solidified to the status of muskeg, black spruce, tamarack, or even white birch.

All of this is beyond the innermost reach of the salt water. The next zone (not lower, for the "flats" may actually rise toward the sea and the

39. Schott, *Die Kanadischen Marschen,* p. 21.

tidal channels—see the discussion of the marshlands above) begins where the salt water of an occasional exceptionally high spring tide reaches; and the type changes as inundation becomes more frequent or prolonged or where, for reasons of upward movement of salt, the salt content of the soil increases.

Usually the first, sometimes the only, and always the most important colonizer of the outermost bare salt-mud flats, regularly flooded and exposed by the tides, is the cord grass (*Spartina alterniflora*).[40] It can establish itself even where the high tide may cover it with as much as ten feet of water. The plants tend to be low, only a few inches in height, and to spread largely by their tenacious rhizomes;[41] they increase in size and density as the duration and depth of flooding decreases progressively inland. Ordinarily the first other plant to appear in that direction is a chenopod, the glasswort or samphire (*Salicornis europaea*); it can tolerate as much salt but not so long a period of inundation as the *Spartina alterniflora*. It reaches about three inches in height and appears to have a reddish color. Other members of the *Chenopodiaceae* also appear on this inner tidal zone, notably the sea blite (*Suaeda maritima*) and *Atriplex* (esp. *A. patula*), and with them the spurreys (*Spergularia canadensis* and *S. marina*) of the *Amaranthaceae*. As annuals these plants can rapidly take over new alluvial deposits (as when individual dyked fields are flooded by dyke-breaks) but may be rapidly displaced on the deeper areas by *Spartina alterniflora* and, in the higher, by *Spartina patens*.[42] In the old marsh, the chenopods and the amaranths appear not as an association but as individual plants, and if the spartinas become depressed under grazing or cutting the glasswort can again become important. A leadwort (of the *Plumbaginaceae* or *Staticeae*,[43] *Limonium nashii*) and some salt-tol-

40. This has had many local names. "Sedge" (often pronounced "sage") was once common and locally it may be called "broadleaf" although this latter is a rather generic name for the spartinas and is also, and sometimes exclusively, used for *Spartina patens*.

41. It is wind pollinated and wind (or water) disseminated, but seeds and seedlings are rare.

42. Often confused with *Sp. alterniflora* by observers, and in terminology; both are called "broadleaf." One of the differentiations, as used by Ganong, "Bay of Fundy Marshes," was between "salt marsh-grass" for *alterniflora* and "salt meadow cord grass" for *patens*. See V. J. Chapman, "A Note on the Salt Marshes of Nova Scotia" (1937), for a slightly different interpretation of *patens*.

43. Schott, *Die Kanadischen Marschen*, p. 23, refers to these as *Staticeae* and mentions *Limonium carolianum*.

erant plantains (*Plantago juncoides* or *P. aliganthos*) may also appear.

As well as earlier descriptions can be interpreted, it was other spartinas, especially *S. patens*, that were dominant plants of the upper, drier phases of the flooded marshes at the time of the arrival of the Europeans. They dominated and suppressed the other species and often formed nearly pure stands. When not cut for hay they formed thick mats outside of the dykes, greatly aiding the building up of silt deposits there. With their cutting for hay, however, they tended to be replaced by *Spartina alterniflora* in the lower areas, and in the upper especially by *Puccinellia* (*glyceria*)[44] and leadwort. This association, because it yielded poor hay, was seldom cut. Also important on the inner border of the marsh was red fescue (*Festuca rubra*) and, widespread on the old dykes, couch grass (*Agropyron repens*).

In the salt-free dyked marshes the most important plants in the association that is most widely used for hay and grazing today are timothy (*Phleum pratense*), couch grass (*Agropyron repens*), and redtop (*Agrostis alba*). When the fertility runs down in an old marsh area, the last named tends to disappear. Red and white clovers and oxeye daisies (*Chrysanthemum leucanthemum*) are common too. Poor drainage will induce the spread of *Spartina cynosuroides* (*patens?*) and it may develop pure stands. There will also appear water hemlock (*Cicuta maculata*), sedges like *Carex maritima* or C. *paleacea, Calamagrostis canadensis,* and other wet land plants. If neglect leads to the development of swamps then the sedges may become dominant and be joined by bulrushes (*Scirpus paludosus*) and, maybe, *S. atrovirens,* meadow rue (*Thalictrum polygamum*), willow herbs (*Epilobium* spp.), loosestrife (*Lysimachia stricta*),[45] and blue flag (*Iris versicolor*).

The Acadians harvested for hay the grasses that naturally colonized the marsh areas. When they had dyked a section, with a sluice (*aboiteau*) to keep out the salt water and let the fresh water through, they

44. *Ibid.*, p. 24. Apparently, this is not Roland's "milkwort" (*Glaux maritima*); *Polygala sanguinea* is the only member of the milkwort family known in Nova Scotia. According to Schott this association also included a fescue (*Festuca avena*) and a rush, black grass (*Juncus gerardi*). Others noted by Schott include arrow grass (*Triglochin maritima*), foxtail barley (*Hordeum jubatum*), one of the wheatgrasses (*Agropyron vulgare*), silverweed (*Potentilla anserina*), a cinquefoil, seaside goldenrod (*Solidago sempervirens*), and seashore saltgrass (*Distichlis spicata*). In addition, Roland, "Flora of Nova Scotia," notes the bulrush (*Scirpus paludosus*) and the knotweeds (*Polygonum* spp.).

45. Roland, "Flora," does not list *L. stricta.* Either his "fringed loosestrife" (*L. ciliata*) or "water loosestrife" (*L. thyrsiflora*) may be meant. Schott's botanical nomenclature appears often to be *sui generis.*

sometimes grew crops of wheat, peas, and other grains, pulses, or vegetables, and sometimes simply let volunteer grass colonize the area for grazing. The silts were rich and, as the salt was slowly washed out and the water table lowered by ditching, the better grasses and clovers took over naturally. Whether as permanent pastures or as rotation leys with other crops, these improved grasslands were important in supporting the livestock for which the Acadians became locally noted.

There is a great deal more that might be added to a description of the vegetation of Nova Scotia, including a discussion of the ferns, mosses, flowers, grasses, and herbaceous growths of various kinds as the settlers first encountered them, used them, or contended with them. Notable, for example, were the fruits, especially the blueberries and cranberries (*Vaccinium* spp.). There also have been hundreds of immigrant plants introduced intentionally for husbandry or decoration, or adventitiously as weeds. In the sections that follow, they will be discussed as they are relevant to the unfolding story of the changing settlement geography.

SOILS

The general conditions of land form and surficial geology, climate, and vegetation under which soils developed in Nova Scotia have been described.[46] The vast preponderance of the surface was covered with glacial ground moraine and such material thus forms the regolith from which most of the soils evolved. There is a certain amount of partially water-sorted material of periglacial origin, as on the floor of the Annapolis Valley and in or near the gaps (Halfway and Folly) in Cobequid Mountain, and in a few kames, eskers, or valley-train deposits elsewhere. There is some limited alluvial material in the terraces and true flood plains of the lower valleys ("intervales") of the short, swift-flowing rivers. There are also extensive marine alluvial deposits, particularly in the estuaries of the Bay of Fundy where they are associated with the unusually high tides. Scattered over the surface of the southern upland in particular, but in all the other sections, too, are lakes, swamps, bogs, and swamp- or bog-forests (the last two categories often being subsumed under the title "muskeg"), that reflect the glacial legacy of disordered drainage. Where recognizable soils develop in these circumstances they are described as peats or mucks, or are so

46. For references on soils, see Bibliography.

heavily waterlogged that no profile of a normal, zonal kind can develop. Chiefly on the uplands, and especially on the vast surface of the Atlantic slope of the southern upland, there are large areas of bare rock or thin lithosols barely covering the base-rock skeleton of the peninsula.

As we have seen, except for the inland swamps and bogs, the bare rock, and the coastal salt water marshes, the seventeenth-century surface was covered with forest, here and there purely coniferous or broadleaf, but mostly a mixture of the two. Locally, the kind of forest cover both reflected the qualities of the soil and contributed directly to those qualities. The best of the hardwoods demanded better soil but also, in the annual accumulation of leaf litter from deciduous trees, helped to build up the organic content, to promote more vigorous bacterial action, and to reduce the acidity. The variation in the acidity of the soils, however, was all within a range that, in a comparative pedological view, could only be called high.

Where mature soils develop under such conditions they are called podzols. Beneath the forest litter the top layer has most of the clay washed out of it, and much of the iron and aluminum is leached out. These move into lower layers, sometimes consolidating into a hardpan. If the regolith, the soil-forming material above bedrock, is thick enough the whole soil-forming process may affect a depth of from twelve to thirty inches. The degree of podzolization in the soils of Nova Scotia is such that none of the mature soils is of high fertility for most crops and that only a small percentage of even those soils which are free enough of stone, gentle enough of slope, and with texture or structure satisfactory for plant nutriment, growth, and tillage, can in fact be used for agriculture with any hope of success. The margin between use or neglect depends on factors of individual entrepreneurial attributes, the purpose of farming, the state of the market, capital supply, technical knowledge, and so forth, and these all may change with time. But under no circumstances existing since Europeans first attempted to use them for agriculture have any of Nova Scotia's soils, apart from the dyked tidal marshland, been considered of high fertility, and at no time has more than a small proportion of the province's surface been improved for agricultural or pastoral use.

There are a few areas in which the proportions of more useful soils are very much above the low provincial average. These are mostly on the lowland areas of the classic geomorphological divisions, although there are exceptions, as in the drumlins of the slate-drift area of western Lunenburg (see Figure 2.1). The best agricultural soils are on the flanks of the Annapolis-Cornwallis Valley, the Cobequid Bay hinterland of Colchester and Hants counties, and the rolling plains between Cobequid Mountain and the Strait of Northumberland. Somewhat poorer are the discontinuous patches that have been found suitable for cultivation in the lowlands further east in Pictou, Antigonish, and Guysborough counties and in Cape Breton Island.

The Soils of the Acadian Settlements

Following are descriptions of soils in the four principal areas where the Acadians settled. Two of these areas were reasonably suitable for agriculture; two were much less satisfactory. The descriptions are based on detailed surveys, by the Nova Scotia Soil Survey, of the soils of all counties (with the exception of those parts of Annapolis and Kings counties outside the Annapolis-Cornwallis Valley) published with accompanying maps between 1943 and 1964.

THE ANNAPOLIS-CORNWALLIS VALLEY[47]— This lowland area (including for the purpose of the survey the left bank of the Avon River below Falmouth) covers 386 square miles, or 245,981 acres, between the edge of the crystalline upland to the south and the trap rock of North Mountain to the north. Only a small fraction of the total area of Kings and Annapolis counties, it includes almost all their agricultural land of any value, all the cities and towns of any size, and almost all of their rural population. Yet less than half of the lowland is, or ever has been, used for agriculture, and much that has been experimented with in the past has long since been surrendered once more to wild vegetation. Over a third of its extent, soil is developed on sandy, water-laid materials mostly along the floor of the valley. Indeed if one followed the center of the valley from Kentville to Annapolis, most of the trip would be on such soils and the impression one would have would be of a largely neglected or reverted wilderness of jack-pine, spruce, birch, aspen, and such low-growing bushes as blueberry, sweet fern, broom crowberry, Hudsonia, and leatherleaf.

The well-known orchards are rather on the glacial tills along the sides of the valley and the lower slopes of the flanking "mountains," or

47. L. C. Harlow and G. B. Whiteside, *Soil Survey of the Annapolis Valley Fruit Growing Area* (1943).

toward the sea at either end.[48] It is true that the even more famous dyked lands cover 14,035 acres or nearly 6 per cent of the area, but, however primary they were to the Acadians, they have been of only minor interest and importance to the people of the valley for most of the last two centuries. Even if they supported one person per acre, which they are far from doing, they would not contribute very greatly to the total agricultural base.

CUMBERLAND COUNTY[49] — In the county as a whole there are 1,683 square miles, or 1,077,120 acres. Three-fourths of this surface is still under "natural" vegetation; that is, no serious attempts to farm it have ever been made, although its sixteenth-century vegetation has been much altered by forest cutting, rough grazing, and burning. Less than 30 per cent is suitable for cultivation in its present state and enough of that is marginal, under current conditions of management, that the hopeful estimate that still another 25 per cent might be brought into agricultural use with various improvements in practice seems a rather distant dream. Nearly half, at the very least, is quite unsuitable for agriculture under any conceivable circumstances. Except for the salt-marsh land, whether dyked and reclaimed or yet undyked, and the limited alluvial soils along the river valleys, almost all the used, or potentially useful, agricultural land is on well-drained loams developed on glacial till on the plain adjacent to the Strait of Northumberland. With dyked and alluvial soils (less than 2 per cent of the total), these comprise only about 25 per cent of the county area. Roughness of surface, stoniness, porosity, thinness, poor drainage, etc., combined with the general limitations of even the best of the podzolized soil, mean that the most that can be hoped from the rest is a good forest crop.

LUNENBURG COUNTY[50] — Lunenburg lies within the hard-rock up-land area west of Halifax. It has a long, deeply embayed, Atlantic shoreline and a total area of some 1,200 square miles or 767,808 acres. In 1951 less than 400 square miles were in farms and only some 50

48. Orchards are no longer the agricultural mainstay of the area; the income they produce is long since exceeded by that yielded by both poultry and dairy products.

49. G. B. Whiteside, R. E. Wicklund, and G. R. Smith, *Soil Survey of Cumberland County, Nova Scotia* (1945).

50. D. B. Cann and J. D. Hilchey, *Soil Survey of Lunenburg County, Nova Scotia* (1958).

square miles (32,402 acres), or less than 5 per cent of the whole area, was improved. In fact only about 110,000 acres, roughly one-seventh of the whole, is really even potentially satisfactory agricultural soil. Most of this is on drumlins developed on slaty till in the southwestern half of the county, and their irregularity of outline, frequent inaccessibility, stoniness, and steep slopes put a great deal of the actual drumlin surface (probably more than half of it) beyond all practical use. Away from the drumlins, the usual problems of droughtiness, stoniness, surface roughness, thin soil, and poor drainage rule most of the rest of the land out of consideration for any kind of productive, progressive agriculture. For example, the most expansive single soil series is the Bridgewater sandy loam occupying over 190,000 acres. The till is generally extremely thin and bedrock is frequently exposed. It is very sandy and stony with rapid internal drainage. Fortunately it does support good stands of white pine and hemlock.

YARMOUTH COUNTY[51] — If there are any patches in Yarmouth's 518,733 land acres that would fall into the provincial Soil Survey's first or second classes of soil they are too small to be mapped. The best is class three which has "fairly good agricultural land but [with] moderately severe limitations in use," and soil of that class covers only 17 per cent, or about 90,000 acres, of the county. On this land were to be found most of the 70,000 acres in farm land in 1951, but of that total only 12,717 acres were improved, about half of them in hay and the rest in pasture. Dyked-land soils, only about 700 acres, are no significant addition although possibly a good deal more of the 8,416 acres of salt marsh might be dyked. Again, most of the county's area has soil too thin, sandy, stony, or wet to be used, and even the good soil is often so scattered in small and irregularly shaped pieces, here and there in the general wilderness, as to be of little value. Fortunately, however, most of the possible agricultural soil does lie in a belt ten to fifteen miles wide in the western third of the county, just north and east of Yarmouth and west of the main Tusket chain of lakes.

The Acadian Use of the Soil

From the middle of the seventeenth century to the deportations of the mid-eighteenth, most of the Acadians depended primarily on the

51. D. B. Cann, J. D. Hilchey, and J. I. MacDougall, *Soil Survey of Yarmouth County, Nova Scotia* (1960).

unusually deep and fertile soils of the tidally flooded salt marshes which had been dyked in from the sea. Here and there attempts were made to clear and farm non-marsh soils but with limited success. The strongly podzolized forest soils have their virgin fertility exhausted in a very short period of use. They can be made continuously productive for most purposes only with continual manuring, the application of lime to counteract their acidity, and much labor. In the last two centuries the level of husbandry for most of the farmed area above the salt marshes has been too low to yield anything but a meager living from farming alone. Market opportunities rarely justified more intensive efforts to maintain or improve its fertility. There are many reasons why pioneer farmers should, initially at least, support themselves with the fruits of many kinds of labor beyond farming. But that most of Nova Scotia's farmers, for most of its history, remained part-time farmers, with one hand ready to lay on the tiller of a fishing skiff, and the other on a woodsman's axe, is to a great degree the result of the fact that farming alone, on the generally indifferent soils and with the limitations imposed by climate, land forms, and drainage, yielded too scanty a living or asked too high a competitive price in labor and investment.

The expansion of Acadian agriculture was confined chiefly to the marshland areas. Repeatedly their governors urged them to clear and farm the wooded areas, but with little effect. The great fertility of their dyked fields gave Acadian soils a reputation for richness which they were far from deserving and which led to continual disappointment as the post-Acadian colonists cleared the forests and made their farms. Even had they made full use of the Acadian dyked lands, as they did not, those lands would have accommodated only a fraction of Nova Scotia's immigrants of the late eighteenth and nineteenth centuries.

CONCLUSION

Nova Scotia's terrain, soils, and climate may be said to have allowed, but not encouraged, most of the forms of plant and animal husbandry known in the British Isles and northwestern France. The greatest differences lay in colder winters with much more snow and a more limited proportion of land surface and soils suitable for arable agriculture. Conditions for road building were definitely poorer because of disorganized drainage and its concomitant lakes, swamps, and bogs, and because of colder, snowier winters. The difficulties of making roads, the small peripheral population, and the opportunities for coastal water transport combined to inhibit land transport.

The forest vegetation covering so much of the land area was of major importance, both as an inhibitor of agricultural development when dykable tidal marshes were available, as a source for construction and fuel, and as the habitat for animals providing food, skins, and furs. In the Acadian period there was far more hardwood than at present and the effects of axe, fire, and forest grazing and browsing of domesticated animals was little in evidence before the middle of the eighteenth century.

Features of the coast line were outstanding contributors to the nature of land use and occupation in the Acadian period. The intricate serration of the Atlantic coast provided superlative coves and harbors for the cod fishery, and the tidal flats around the Bay of Fundy offered both an opportunity to make farms with the spade rather than the axe and soils of a fertility greatly exceeding that of most of the dry land areas.

3

The Micmac Indians:
First Residents of Acadia

🌿

THE PEOPLE

There are gaps of some thousands of years in the archeological records of the Acadian lands, notably between those of the Paleo-Indians of the Debert site to shell heaps of the more recent past.[1] Many of the latter suggest a material culture like that of the Micmac Indians at the time of the first French contacts and imply some centuries of prior occupation. In the sixteenth and seventeenth centuries the inhabitants of the Maine-Gaspé-Maritimes peninsula of northeastern North America had some variety in language, or dialect, and in other characteristics of non-material culture, but the most important aspects of their economy and material culture were remarkably uniform. Our concern here is with those people who lived in the three traditional Maritime Provinces. East of the drainage basin of the Saint John River in present New Brunswick, on the Gaspé peninsula, and everywhere in present Nova Scotia and Prince Edward Island there was only one tribe or (if that word be meaningless in this context, as it may) only one language-group, one "people," the Micmac. The borders to the east were no doubt variable through time but the watershed between the Saint John River and the Gulf would appear to have been a

1. R. Stuckenrath, Jr., "The Debert Site: Early Man in the Northeast" (1964), and H. I. Smith and W. S. Wintemberg, *Some Shell-Heaps in Nova Scotia* (1929).

well-established boundary.[2] It was the Micmac with whom the Acadians had the most intimate contact in the seventeenth and eighteenth centuries. The Malecite[3] of the Saint John river valley, and the Passamaquoddy and other tribes to the west in Maine, as the Montagnais to the north and occasionally the Iroquois (especially the Mohawk) further to the west, were also peripheral ethnic groups making their contributions to the unfolding cultural and economic geography of the Acadian region, but the Micmac are of central importance.

Wallis and Wallis identify the Micmac Indians as representatives of the Eastern Woodland culture and, within it, group them with the Malecite, Passamaquoddy, Penobscot, Abenaki, and Womenack—all Wabanaki tribes of closely related Algonkian speech.[4] Frank Speck saw the relatively simple culture and economy of the Micmac, compared even with the other tribes of the Wabanaki group, as reflecting an early migration to the area and a geographical isolation from the diffusion of ideas and technology to the south and east from the Iroquois and other groups.[5] The distinction from their only immediate neighbors, the Malecite to the west, was chiefly one of language. That the latter had some minor concern with agriculture, whereas the Micmac probably had none in 1600, may be of less importance.[6]

2. R. G. Thwaites, in the introduction to *The Jesuit Relations and Allied Documents . . . 1610–1791* (1896–1901), *1*, 9, has summarized the problem of describing tribal boundaries as well as anyone: "The migrations of some of the Indian tribes were frequent, and they occupied overlapping territories, so that it is impossible to fix the tribal boundaries with any degree of exactness. Again, the tribes were so merged by intermarriage, by affiliation, by consolidation, by the fact that there were numerous polyglot villages of renegades, by similarities in manner, habits, and appearance, that it is difficult even to separate the savages into families. . . ." W. D. Wallis and R. S. Wallis, *The Malecite Indians of New Brunswick* (1957), discuss some of the problems of the Malecite-Micmac boundary from the seventeenth to the nineteenth centuries. W. D. Wallis, "Historical Background of the Micmac Indians of Canada" (1961), p. 54, has the Mohawk occupying Gaspé in 1638 and driving the Micmac south of "Nesisiquit" (Nipisiguit?). See also Frank G. Speck and W. S. Hadlock, "A Report on Tribal Boundaries and Hunting Areas of the Malecite Indians of New Brunswick" (1946).
3. Sometimes called Maliseet, these were the "Etchemins" of the early French. On the Malecite, see Wallis and Wallis, *The Malecite Indians*.
4. Wallis and Wallis have been the principal contemporary students of the Micmac Indians. See esp. their monograph, *The Micmac Indians of Eastern Canada* (1955). There are very brief accounts of the Micmac and the Malecite in Diamond Jenness, *The Indians of Canada* (1960), pp. 267–70.
5. Frank G. Speck, "Culture Problems in Northeastern North America" (1926).
6. The possibility of tobacco growing is still moot, but unlikely.

The origin of the name "Micmac" is obscure, but may be derived from "Miscou" and the fact that Chaleur Bay, the entrance to which is guarded by Miscou Island, was an early point of French contact with the tribe.[7] To the French of the early seventeenth century they were the Souriquois, under which sobriquet they are often, and fully, described in the early accounts. In an area of roughly 30,000 square miles there were, in Champlain's time, about 3,000 of them, a density of one person for each ten square miles of land and inland lake, stream and swamp.[8]

One of the first descriptions of the Micmac Indians tells us most graphically the view in which they were held by many of the French, a view not dissimilar to that held of many more southerly tribes by the English in the seventeenth century:

The nation is savage, wandering and full of bad habits; the people few and isolated. They are, I say, savage, haunting the woods, ignorant, lawless and rude: they are wanderers, with nothing to attach them to a place, neither homes nor relationship, neither possessions nor love of country; as a people they have bad habits, are extremely lazy, gluttonous, profane, treacherous, cruel in their revenge, and given up to all kinds of lewdness, men and women alike, the men having several wives abandoning them to others, and the women only serving them as slaves, whom they strike and beat unmercifully . . . . With all these vices, they are exceedingly vainglorious: they think they are better, more valiant and more ingenious than the French; and, what is difficult to believe, richer than we are.[9]

7. Wallis and Wallis, *The Micmac Indians,* p. 15. The first use of the name "Micmac" they have seen in the records is in a memoir of M. de La Chesnaye, in 1676. Popularly, Micmac often is taken to mean "allies"; see T. F. McIlwraith, "Micmac" (1966), p. 60, among many such ascriptions.

8. Father Pierre Biard, one of the first missionaries (1611–13), estimated numbers at something under 2,000 in 1612 (*Jesuit Relations, 2,* 73), but, in 1616, further familiarity led him to increase the figure to from 3,000 to 3,500. *Ibid., 3,* 111. One Colonel Frye, in a letter to the governor of Nova Scotia in March 1760, reprinted in Massachusetts Historical Society *Collections* (1809), also reported a French missionary's estimate of 3,000 as a good figure for a century and a half later, after the Acadian deportations. Other estimates in these two centuries are within the same range. The hazards of European contacts and acculturation (notably disease and dietary changes) would seem to have maintained a balance with tendencies toward natural increase. In the early twentieth century those who called themselves Micmac had increased to 4,000 or so (and since to more than 6,000), but these figures include many mixed-bloods and have no relevance to our period of interest.

9. *Jesuit Relations, 1,* 173. In fairness, it should be said that Father Biard, who wrote this in 1611, was anxious to impress his superiors with the difficulties of the missionary enterprise.

Lescarbot gives a more balanced view at many places in his writings[10] as does Chrestien Le Clercq in his *Gaspesia*,[11] but there is very little liking for the Micmac evident in the early French reports.

The periodic movement of the Micmac living quarters followed the seasons.[12] In the spring they left their summer camps, along inland lakes and streams in the forest, and made their way to the seashore to catch lobsters and a variety of fish, to gather clams, oysters, scallops, and other shellfish at low tide, or even to hunt sea mammals (seal, walrus, and porpoise) in offshore waters. In the autumn they returned to the forest. The most favored locations for inland and coastal camps are difficult to identify. Probably they were chosen in part because of relationship to transportation routes, which were by water as far as possible, but there are innumerable waterside locations scattered through the province and this must have left a wide choice. The Gaspé coast, Miramichi and Chaleur bays, the south shore of the Gulf of St. Lawrence as far east as present Pictou County in Nova Scotia, many places in Prince Edward Island, the shores of Bras d'Or Lake, the estuary of the La Have River, and Mahone Bay, all are known to have been the sites of summer camps. Inland the Micmac spread out more in winter; some favored sites were up the Restigouche, Nipisiguit, Miramichi, and Richibucto rivers toward their head waters, along the Shubenacadie River, and on the shores of Lake Rossignol. As we shall see, movement was relatively easy winter or summer.

The simple social structure involved quite small settlements usually of closely related families under a chief who probably allotted hunting grounds to his own members. Although there appears to have been no discernible hierarchy of such chiefs in the seventeenth century and most observers saw them as equals in rank, chiefs of larger groups probably had comparably larger influence and distributed their people over rather larger areas. In the later seventeenth and eighteenth centuries a hierarchy of chiefs did develop, perhaps through the exigencies

10. See esp., *The History of New France by Marc Lescarbot*, trans. and ed. W. L. Grant (1907–14), *3*, 211*n*. Wallis, "Historical Background of the Micmac," also quotes many examples of a more favorable view by different writers.

11. Chrestien Le Clercq, *New Relation of Gaspesia, with the Customs and Religion of the Gaspesian Indians*, ed. W. F. Ganong (1910). This edition gives the original 1691 text and a carefully and fully edited translation. Le Clercq was a Recollet missionary who worked among the Micmac for most of the years from 1675 to 1686.

12. A. H. Clark, *Three Centuries and the Island* (1959), pp. 22–24.

of conflict and negotiation with Europeans, and at any one time there appear to have been quite well defined districts with one local chief exercising some sort of loose hegemony over substantial areas, probably in the assignment of specific territory to specific groups if in nothing else. Just how decisions of this kind were made in the seventeenth century is not certain, but the assignment of territory to assure a reasonably even distribution of people in relation to the availability of game for winter sustenance must have been achieved by some kind of intergroup agreement or arbitration if not by force.

THE ECONOMY

The best early account of the yearly round of economic activity comes from Father Biard. He reported seal hunting in January on some of the nearby islands where the pregnant females repaired to calve (a bit in conflict with the accepted evidence that the Micmac generally were deep in the woods in winter quarters by that time). They ate seal flesh but particularly valued the oil which was collected in large moose bladders and used as a sort of sauce, or condiment, throughout the year. February to mid-March was the time for emphasis on the hunt for beaver, otter, bear, moose, and caribou—the great danger then being rain and thaw. In March they focused on streams or rivers that were already open and, continuing into April, made a good thing out of the runs of spawning fish—smelt, herring, shad, sturgeon, and salmon in particular (Biard does not mention the shad). Also, in spring the northward migration of ducks and geese to nesting grounds in the area began and both birds and eggs were readily taken. "From the month of May up to the middle of September, they are free from all anxiety about their food; for the cod are upon the coast, and all kinds of fish and shellfish . . . ."[13] The summers also yielded pigeons, partridges, hares, and rabbits.

Now our savages in the middle of September withdraw from the sea, beyond the reach of the tide, to the little rivers, where the eels spawn, of which they lay in a supply; they are good and fat. In October and November comes the second hunt for elks [i.e. moose] and beavers; and then in December (wonderful providence of God) comes a fish called by them *ponamo* [tom cod?] which spawns under the ice. Also then the turtles bear little ones . . . .[14]

13. Biard, in *Jesuit Relations, 3,* 81.   14. *Ibid.,* p. 83.

. . . the people are nomads . . . never stopping longer than five or six weeks in a place . . . . These Savages get their living in this manner during three seasons of the year. For, when Spring comes, they divide into bands upon the shores of the sea, until Winter; and then as the fish withdraw to the bottom of the great salt waters, they seek the lakes and the shades of the forests, where they catch Beavers, upon which they live, and other game, as Elk [moose], Caribou, Deer, and still smaller animals. And yet, sometimes even in Summer, they do not give up hunting: besides, there are an infinite number of birds on certain islands in the months of May, June, July and August.[15]

Shellfish were dug out principally at low tide. Line fishing was done with a bone gorge, but nets and rather elaborate weirs also were made, the latter especially for trout, bass, and salmon.[16] Fishing in the inland streams and rivers was also of some importance. Probably spears were used more for fishing than for hunting on land. Whether sea hunting for seals, walrus, and porpoise (apart from taking seals on offshore rocks) was undertaken in pre-European times, or even during the seventeenth century, is not clear.

The bow-and-arrow was the Indians' chief hunting weapon but they also used a wide variety of traps and snares. Many observers mention the use of dogs.[17] Beaver were prime objects of the hunt from the earliest times of French contact, although whether they had occupied so prominent a place before the advent of the fur trade is uncertain. Beaver provided both food and fur, as did bear, which were hunted with both spears and bow-and-arrow, and also taken in traps or snares. Moose was probably the most desired game, in autumn or early winter especially. Denys describes moose calls used to attract the animals in the rutting season.[18] Deer and a wide variety of smaller animals as well as moose were taken with both bow-and-arrow and snares. They also killed quantities of ducks and geese by a variety of methods.

Vegetable foods were abundant in season and may have played a larger role in nutriment than the records indicate. As early as the first decade of the seventeenth century, Lescarbot may refer to the use of

15. Marc Lescarbot, "The Conversion of the Savages . . . ," in *Jesuit Relations, 1,* 83–85.

16. Lescarbot, *History of New France, 3,* 236, mentions sturgeon and salmon being taken in weirs on the Dauphin (Annapolis) River.

17. See, for example, Lescarbot, *History of New France, 3,* 221. Nicolas Denys describes the use of dogs to locate beaver and hunt moose in *The Description and Natural History of the Coasts of North America (Acadia)* (1672), trans. and ed. W. F. Ganong (1908), pp. 429–32. Le Clercq, *Gaspesia,* p. 226, implies their use for hunting as well.

18. Denys, *Description,* pp. 427–28.

maple sap: "S'ilz sont pressez de soif ils ont l'industrie de succer certains arbres, d'où distille une douce & fort agreable liqueur, comme ie l'ay experimenté quelquefois."[19] There is evidence for the use of beechnuts, possibly of acorns. Apparently various roots were eaten, most likely as "starvation foods" in times of shortage.[20] Blueberries, cranberries, huckleberries, and shadberries (or wild pear),[21] all were gathered, no doubt often eaten fresh, but also dried after cooking, and preserved in cakes. Despite Lescarbot's "noz Sauvages font aussi grand labourage de Petun, chose tres-precieuse entr'eux, & parmi tous ces peuples universelement . . . ,"[22] there is a reluctance by scholars to accept the fact that the Micmac had even this touch of plant husbandry in their economy.

An essentially nomadic life, in a culture without domestic animals (except the dog) or wheeled vehicles, and in a countryside where forest, lakes, streams, and swamps made land travel difficult, led to

19. *History of New France*, *3*, 409. Denys, *Description*, p. 380 (French text, pp. 316–17), also refers to the use of sap, although not to boiling it down. In *Jesuit Relations* there are several early seventeenth-century descriptions of the St. Lawrence valley in which maple sap is mentioned. It may well be that boiling down was hardly possible before, and not discovered until, metal kettles were introduced. Micmac pottery was of indifferent quality.

20. Wallis and Wallis, *The Micmac Indians*, p. 66, imply the use of *Ligusticum scothicum*, the "wild potato" or "wild carrot." There appear to have been others as well. Le Clercq, *Gaspesia*, p. 298, states: "They have, moreover, a quantity of roots and herbs which are unknown to us in Europe, but whose virtues and properties the Indians know wonderfully well, so that they can make use of them in time of need." Neither of the Helianthes (sunflower or Jerusalem artichoke), which are commonly seen in the Nova Scotia countryside today, seem to have been present in the seventeenth century. See A. E. Roland, "The Flora of Nova Scotia" (1946), p. 505.

21. *Amelanchier weigandii*. Roland, "Flora of Nova Scotia," p. 295, thinks reports of *A. Canadensis* in Nova Scotia are incorrect. The shadbush or shadberry was so-called because it bloomed when the shad were running, hence also "Juneberry." Other *Amelanchier* species are widely known in North America as, for example, the "Saskatoon" of the Canadian Prairie Provinces; it will be known to many as the serviceberry and is sometimes confused with *Sorbus* spp., although *Sorbus domesticus* is not known in Nova Scotia.

22. *History of New France*, *3*, 439. His further description leaves little doubt that he refers to *Nicotiana rustica* which was grown by many "non-agricultural" tribes beyond the limits of agricultural food crops. "Noz Sauvages" might refer to any of the Wabanaki tribes. In 1691, Father Le Clercq averred that "the Gaspesians, all of them together, men, women, girls, and boys, use tobacco." *Gaspesia*, p. 298.

heavy concentration on the use of waterways for transportation. The principal means of travel was by birch-bark canoe in summer and by snowshoe and toboggan in winter. The winter snows alleviated some of the problems of land travel but favored routes followed the waterways to avoid the forests in all seasons. Freeze-up and break-up periods, although usually a matter of only a week of two, were thus times of limited movement.

Most of the longer-distance canoe travel was accomplished from spring until late autumn. The birch-bark vessels were relatively easy to construct, very light in weight, and extremely shallow in draft, yet an ordinary canoe, perhaps up to sixteen feet in length was ". . . so capacious that a single one of them will hold an entire household of five or six persons, with all their dogs, sacks, skins, kettles, and other heavy baggage."[23] They were thus peculiarly suitable for use on inland routes where water was often very shallow and where portages from a few yards to a mile or more in length were common. Six portages, for example, were involved in crossing from the Miramichi River to the Saint John, around rapids, from stream to stream, or from stream to lake. "The Savages of Port Royal can go to Kebec in ten or twelve days by means of the rivers, which they navigate almost up to their sources; and thence, carrying their little bark canoes for some distance through the woods, they reach another stream which flows into the river of Canada, and thus greatly expedite their long voyages."[24] Biard thought that they could make thirty to forty leagues a day in good weather.[25] Canoes were used along all the coasts in summer and even,

23. Biard, in *Jesuit Relations, 3,* 83. The canoe had few distinctive features other than an inverted, double-cusp, undulating profile of the gunwale which suggests diffusion to or from Newfoundland where a similar peculiarity was noted in Beothuk canoes. Essentially it was the same vessel made and used almost everywhere in North America that *Betulus papyrifera* could be found in abundance. Locally, slats were made of white fir, the ribs, of cedar; spruce roots were used to sew the bark, and spruce gum (or often an adhesive made by boiling the gum with animal or fish fat) to seal the stitches or tears that might appear. A canoe might take a week or two to build and with reasonable care might last twenty years (spruce and birch for repair work were ubiquitous in seventeenth-century Acadia). Accounts of construction of canoes in that century can be found in Denys, *Description,* pp. 420–22, and, more briefly, in Lescarbot, *History of New France, 3,* 192.

24. Lescarbot, "Conversion of the Savages," p. 101.

25. In *Jesuit Relations, 3,* 85. (This is some paddling! Probably it would need good help from wind or current.)

on occasion, in winter. Apparently the Indians crossed in them to the islands of Cape Breton and Prince Edward and perhaps they even paddled across the Gulf of St. Lawrence to Newfoundland and Labrador.[26]

For short journeys, if there were no canoes available, various other kinds of craft were improvised. Doubtless timber rafts of a crude kind were made, although we have no sure record of them. Other expedients well may have been like those described by the Wallises for later periods: ribless sheets of spruce bark, shaped more or less like canoes, and canoe-shaped coracles made of moose hide.[27] Dugouts, in rare later use, probably were not made as early as the seventeenth century.

Winter travel involved principally two kinds of aids: snowshoes for rapid travel, in hunting in the woods especially, and toboggans for transporting heavy loads. The French were particularly taken with the former, likening them to the *racquettes* used in court tennis in France, only "trois fois aussi grandes que les notres."

Of rather special interest to a geographer is the ease with which the Micmac got around the country. The writer's personal experience with many Indian guides or companions bears out the logical presumption that they had no mysterious inner "sense of direction" and were quite as likely as anyone to get lost in unfamiliar territory, however easily they moved through country they had previously traversed, carefully observed, and tenaciously remembered. The manner of transfer of knowledge of terrain from one individual to another apparently involved the occasional use of crude maps. "They have much ingenuity in drawing upon bark a kind of map which marks exactly all the rivers and streams of a country of which they wish to make a representation. They mark all the places thereon exactly and so well that they make use of them successfully, and an Indian who possesses one makes long voyages without going astray."[28]

26. "It is wonderful how these Savage mariners navigate so far in little shallops, crossing vast seas without compass, and often without sight of the Sun . . . ." Anon., "Letters sent from New France . . . ," in *Jesuit Relations*, 45, 65. These may not always have been birch-bark canoes, however. Father André Richard, quoted in the "Relation" of 1661/62, describes the Indian purchase of shallops in Gaspé which ". . . they buy of the French who frequent their shores for the sake of fishing, and they handle them as skillfully as our most courageous and active Sailors of France." *Ibid.*, 47, 223. Such may have been the means of much Micmac migration to Newfoundland.

27. Wallis and Wallis, *The Micmac Indians*, p. 50.
28. Le Clercq, *Gaspesia*, p. 136.

OTHER   ELEMENTS   OF   MATERIAL   CULTURE

A conical or "domed" wigwam, widely used in the continental north-east, was the form of housing most commonly in use among the Micmac for their winter quarters and for temporary camps. Its array of supporting poles was covered with the best available material, usually with overlapping strips of birch bark. Sometimes mats woven of swamp grass might be used instead of bark, or under it, to insulate against wind, wet, and cold. Animal skins, almost universally used for door flaps, might on occasion cover the whole wigwam. Biard has given us the earliest full description:

Arrived at a certain place, the first thing they do is to build a fire and arrange their camp, which they have finished in an hour or two; often in half an hour. The women go to the woods and bring back some poles which are stuck into the ground in a circle around the fire, and at the top are interlaced, in the form of a pyramid, so that they come together directly over the fire, for there is the chimney. Upon the poles they throw some skins, matting or bark. At the foot of the poles, under the skins, they put their baggage. All the space around the fire is strewn with leaves of the fir tree, so they will not feel the dampness of the ground; over these leaves are often thrown some mats, or sealskins as soft as velvet. . . . they are very warm in there around that little fire, even in the greatest rigors of the Winter.[29]

Warm the wigwams may have been, but smoky, filthy, and stench-filled they were too, to the great discomfort of the eyes, noses, and sensibilities of Frenchmen who occasionally lodged in them. We are also reminded of "the constant danger of burning alive from too large a fire on a winter night, or a worse death from burns and slow gangrene."[30]

The only early description of a non-conical dwelling is from Biard: "In Summer the shape of their houses is changed; for then they are broad and long, that they may have more air; then they nearly always cover them with bark, or mats made of tender reeds . . . ."[31] Dixon

29. Biard, in *Jesuit Relations*, 3, 77. This has been widely quoted. Other useful early descriptions are found in Le Clercq, *Gaspesia*, pp. 100 ff., and in *Relation of the Voyage to Port Royal in Acadia or New France, by the Sieur de Dièreville*, trans. Alice Webster, ed. J. C. Webster (1933), p. 177. Le Clercq wrote of the wigwams and, in contrast to Biard, said they were "of a coldness which cannot be described."

30. Wallis and Wallis, *The Micmac Indians*, p. 60.

31. Biard, in *Jesuit Relations*, 3, 77.

implies more widespread use of the long house among the Micmac, but gives no details.[32] It did appear sporadically among the Algonkian neighbors of the Iroquoian peoples, perhaps by diffusion from the latter. Joseph Jouvency, writing about Canada in 1710, describes what must have been such a hut: "They construct their huts by fixing poles in the ground; they cover the sides with bark, the roofs with hides, moss and branches. In the middle of the hut is the hearth, from which the smoke escapes through an opening at the peak of the roof."[33]

No other buildings are recorded for the Micmac in the seventeenth century. Even food storage seems to have been rather haphazard. Thus Biard, writing of Port Royal in 1616: ". . . they will sometimes make some storehouses for the Winter, where they will keep smoked meat, roots, shelled acorns, peas, beans, or prunes bought from us, etc. The storehouses are like this;—They put these provisions in sacks, which they tie up in big pieces of bark; these they suspend from the interlacing branches of two or three trees so that neither rats nor other animals, nor the dampness of the ground, can injure them."[34] The mention of smoked meats suggests smokehouses but although these are well known for later periods,[35] no evidence of them for the seventeenth century has appeared. Smoked meat and fish continued to be noted by observers through the seventeenth and eighteenth centuries.[36]

Much household equipment such as cups, dippers, boxes, and other containers was also made from birch bark. "Pots" of bark for stone-boiling were known, but more usually they were made by hacking or burning out a block of wood, or an old stump. Pottery making, if indeed it was practiced in the seventeenth century (it has been found in shell heaps in the area from several centuries earlier) was not well established among the Micmac at the time of the French arrival and the introduction of kettles acquired in trade appears to have spelled its end.[37]

32. R. B. Dixon, "The Early Migrations of the Indians of New England and the Maritime Provinces" (1914), p. 73.

33. In *Jesuit Relations, 1, 257.*   34. Biard, in *ibid., 3,* 107 and 109.

35. Wallis and Wallis, *The Micmac Indians,* p. 61.

36. For example, see Gamaliel Smethurst, *A Narrative of an Extraordinary Escape* (1774), in New Brunswick Historical Society *Collections* (1905). Passage is from p. 372.

37. For the wooden kettles see Denys, *Description,* pp. 401–2. Lescarbot, in the same passage in which he attributes agriculture to "Our Souriquois" in former times (but lost before the seventeenth century), says that they had also made

There are few early references to basketry or weaving but Lescarbot's detailed description leaves little room for doubt of its importance at the time of the very earliest contacts. The women made ". . . mats of rushes, wherewith they garnish their cabins, with others to sit upon. . . . they scrub and make supple the skins of beavers, moose, and others. . . . If these are small they sew a number together, and make cloaks, sleeves, stockings, and shoes. . . . They also make baskets of rushes and roots, to hold their provisions. . . . They also make purses of leather . . . [and] . . . dishes of bark to drink out of, and to put their meats in."[38] Stone tools included knives, tomahawks, adzes, scrapers, and the like, but these were among the first of the native artifacts to be replaced by trade goods. Many bone and horn tools, and the more durable shellfish shells, appear to have been employed widely.

The skin-and-fur clothing which the Micmac wore seems to have been typical of that used throughout the northeastern continental area. There were some small differences between the sexes, especially in how robes were worn. Subsequent to the earliest contacts the Micmac showed a great desire for European blankets, hats, caps, shoes, shirts, and many other items and more often than not their dress was a motley of Indian and European bits and pieces. Rain capes of birch bark or skin were used while canoeing.[39]

CONCLUSION

The Micmac Indians were a small group thinly scattered over a large area when the seventeenth century opened. Contacts throughout the previous century, chiefly through fishermen, had prepared them for trading relationships with the French, but they were little acculturated when Champlain, Lescarbot, and Biard first reported on them. However, it is worth noting the kinds of acculturation to French goods which developed as early as the second decade of the seventeenth

earthen pots. *History of New France*, 3, 194–95. Wallis and Wallis, *The Micmac Indians*, p. 63n, imply that stone boiling disappeared rapidly, presumably with the introduction of metal kettles.

38. Lescarbot, *History of New France*, 3, 201.

39. There is a plethora of seventeenth-century descriptions of clothing. See, for example, Lescarbot, *History of New France*, 3, 132; Denys, *Description*, pp. 411–13; Biard, in *Jesuit Relations*, 3, 73–77; and Le Clercq, *Gaspesia*, p. 94. See also Wallis and Wallis, *The Micmac Indians*, pp. 78–83, 87, for a useful summary.

century (presumably for the Souriquois, i.e. Micmac, as well as for the others). "[The tribes] assemble in the Summer to trade with us, principally at the great river. . . . They barter their skins of beaver, otter, deer, marten, seal, etc., for bread, peas, beans, prunes, tobacco, etc.; kettles, hatchets, iron arrow-points, awls, puncheons,[40] cloaks, blankets, and all other such commodities as the French bring them."[41]

The smallness of their numbers and the lack of effective political organization between the scattered units ("settlements" seems an inappropriate word) meant that they offered no serious, concerted threat to French occupation. Gradually they came to a position of mutual interdependence with the French and in places, as at La Have (La Hève), interbred with them to produce small *métis* populations. However, although some Micmac contributions to the subsequent Acadian gene-pool must thus have taken place, the mixed-blood offspring generally were raised as Micmac by their (almost exclusively) Indian mothers and the physical results of miscegenation were seen much more among the Indians than the French.

Although their economy changed with new implements, weapons, clothing, and food as a result of their relationships with the French during the "Acadian century" from the mid-seventeenth to the mid-eighteenth century, and the interrelationship between the two peoples has been described, rather loosely, as "symbiotic," the Micmac remained chiefly migratory hunters, fishers, and gatherers, living still, in the late eighteenth century, much as they had in the early seventeenth. Almost no adoption of farming took place and they proved to be of little use for labor in agriculture, forest clearing, or as hands on vessels. Since the Acadian occupation was peripheral, and was concentrated largely in the tidally flooded lands that could be dyked, the interiors of the present territories of Nova Scotia and eastern New Brunswick remained largely undisturbed for the Micmac to practice much of their traditional economy.

The chief services of the Micmac to the French, consistent with the maintenance of their own basic culture patterns, were as guides, paddlers, hunters, and procurers of the furs and feathers for which a market existed in Europe, the St. Lawrence settlements, or the English colonies to the south. From time to time they were organized by the

40. An obvious mistranslation of *poinçons*, which could have meant bodkins, stilletos, or (like *aleines*, the previous word in the original) awls.
41. Biard, in *Jesuit Relations, 3*, 69.

French into effective guerilla units for attacks on the English—either in New England, with other members of the Wabanaki tribes, or in the precarious English footholds in the Acadian region in the early eighteenth century.

The slow, but ultimately almost universal, attachment of the Micmac to the Roman Catholic faith reinforced their ties to the French. These ties were maintained assiduously by missionaries largely based on Quebec[42] and, as we shall see, the Micmac were more actively hostile to their nominal British masters after 1710 than were the Acadians themselves. Their close and amicable association with the Acadians meant that, despite the inoffensive and largely neutral role that the latter played under British occupation, the frequent forays, large or small, planned or spontaneous, conducted against the British by the Micmac were often charged to the Acadians' account. And should the Acadians have decided to sacrifice their friendship for the Indians to their fear of British accusations they ran, themselves, the risk of becoming victims of the "hit and run" raids which the Micmac, despite their limited population, could manage so successfully, easily foiling retributive pursuit by dispersing in the forested, lake-strewn, interior wilderness. Thus were the Acadians forced into a situation which must have weighed heavily in the decision for their forcible, wholesale deportation in the mid-eighteenth century (see Chapter 8).

The Indian contributions to the Acadian culture and economy were many and important. The use of birch bark for canoes, containers, and the insulation of building walls and roofs was of major importance. So too were the valuable lore of fishing and hunting, the knowledge of local nuts, roots, and berries, the making of clothing and footwear from

42. The list of missionaries active among the Micmac even in the seventeenth century is a long one. Beginning with the secular priest Jesse Fléché, who came to Acadia with the Sieur de Poutrincourt in 1610 (see below, Chapter 4), they included Biard and Énemond Massé, the first Jesuits, from 1611 to 1613, several Recollets from Tadoussac to the Gaspé area in the 1619–24 period, five Jesuits who joined the Recollets in 1625 (including Charles Lalemant, Massé, and Jean de Brébeuf), and one Perreault, who founded a Jesuit mission on Cape Breton in 1634. An enduring mission in the Gaspé region was established by Fathers André Richard, Martin de Lyonne, and Jacques Fremin; until 1657, the Jesuits were dominant. In addition to Le Clercq, there were several others in the later seventeenth century, perhaps the most interesting being Father Thierry who had a mission at Miramichi from 1684 to 1686 and who, in 1699 at Chebucto (Halifax) harbor, announced a "plan" for resettling all the Micmac between that harbor and the Shubenacadie River (actually a major route from the Atlantic coast to the Bay of Fundy).

skins and furs, of fibers from roots and animal sinews, and of dyes from a wide variety of vegetable sources. As in other parts of eastern North America, however, the local tobacco (if any!) was not taken over by the French; rather the Micmac became acculturated to the use of imported tobacco which became a trade good of major importance.

There is little doubt that a fishery would have been established along most of the Acadian coasts washed by the Gulf and the Atlantic Ocean whether the hinterland had been inhabited or not. But the lodgement of French on the Saint John River, at Port Royal, and at Chignecto, on which the Acadian settlement was to be based, was directly related to the existence of a native hunting people who could supply furs, the most desired trading goods from the land, in some quantity. Although a small agricultural population was introduced in the 1630's, it was intended only to provide a supply base for the fur trade or the fishery. So far from being designed to replace the Micmac its purpose was to strengthen an economic activity based upon Indian hunting and trapping. The scanty legacy of evidence from the French occupation of Cape Breton Island for nearly fifty years in the eighteenth century,[43] based as it was chiefly on the fishery and the maintenance of a strategic fortress, suggests that the fur-trading activities of Canada and Acadia were the important attractive forces for ultimate settlement and fuller exploitation of the land. Had there been no Micmac[44] in the Acadian area, its settlement almost certainly would have been later and, perhaps, of an altogether different order of significance to the development of the subsequent economic and settlement geography of the area.

43. See a discussion of this in A. H. Clark, "New England's Role in the Underdevelopment of Cape Breton Island during the French Regime, 1713–1758" (1965).
44. Perhaps we should include the Malecite and others of the Wabanaki tribes as well.

4

Acadia to 1670

🖋

Since the beginning of the seventeenth century the boundaries of Acadia[1] have been perceived quite differently by a variety of observers,

1. The two leading theories of the origin of the name Acadie (or Acadia) are: (1) that it derives from the appearances of the name "Arcadia" or "Larcadia" on various sixteenth-century maps (perhaps in turn from reports of the Verazzano expedition of 1524), or (2) that it derives from a Micmac word (Quoddy or Cady), generally rendered in French as "cadie," meaning a piece of land (generally with a favorable connotation). Of the substantial literature on the question one of the more interesting notes, supporting the first theory, is that of Henri Froidevaux, "Origine du mot 'Acadie'" (1920). This theory is also supported, in scholarly depth, by E. H. Wilkins, "Arcadia in America" (1957), who in turn acknowledges his indebtedness to W. F. Ganong, *Crucial Maps in the Early Cartography and Place-Nomenclature of the Atlantic Coast of Canada* (1929–37), ed. with introduction and notes by T. E. Layng (1964); see pp. 110–11, 125, 132–33. See also, W. F. Ganong, "The Origin of the Place-Names, Acadia and Norumbega" (1917). A recent contribution is P. C. Cormier, *L'Origine et l'histoire du nom Acadie, avec un discours sur d'autres noms de lieu Acadiens* (1966). The second, and less romantic, theory, which many scholars find inherently more likely, is supported by the fact that, with the notable exception of Champlain's use of "arcadie" in *Des Sauvages* (1603), reprinted and translated in *The Works of Samuel de Champlain,* ed. H. P. Biggar, *1* (1922), 83–192, virtually all the French references, after significant contact with the Micmac inhabitants, use the form without the "r." Perhaps the most sensible conclusion is that the cartographic ancestry of "Arcadie" for various parts of the coast of eastern and northeastern North America prepared the way for the acceptance of "Cadie," "La Cadie," "L'Acadie," and so "Acadie" from its Indian source. In any event a deep interest in the question requires an antiquarian taste for disputation in the resolution of a dilemma that is of no importance to the subsequent historical geography of the area.

including those who have lived in or near it and those who have written about it from afar. In this book the geographical title, Acadia, will be seen to have had two distinct, basic meanings.

The first was that of an area which, roughly, comprised the territory of the present three Maritime Provinces of Canada. In realistic terms the northern coast of Maine, the southern coast of the Gaspé peninsula, and the Magdalen Islands were included at one time or another, but Newfoundland and its fringing islands and the rest of the territories of present Quebec and northern New England were not (see Figure 1.1). This was, in effect, the Acadia of the French before the Treaty of Utrecht in 1713 and the Nova Scotia of the British after 1763. But, to the former, Acadia continued to exist as an entity after 1713, if, for convenience, under other names and in spite of being partly in enemy hands; and the British view of the proper territory of Nova Scotia (and thus, Acadia) was essentially unchanged from the third decade of the seventeenth century onward.

Of course there was a good deal of diplomatic double-talk on both sides about the boundaries. Temporary concessions were made in the occasional intervals of peace or armed truce. A spate of literature, based largely on the conflicting claims of the British and French commissioners who were appointed to confront the problem, has been devoted to analysis of the rather obvious special pleading indulged in by both sides.[2] But, to sum it up I think it is fair to say that, to Paris and Quebec on the one hand, or to London and Boston on the other, "Acadia" and "Nova Scotia" remained comprehensive concepts, embracing essentially the same area, and viewed as rightfully belonging, intact, to one crown or the other, for well over a century regardless of the temporary concessions in treaties or of *de facto* occupation or control.

A great deal of confusion has arisen, not only from the casuistry of political argument following the Treaty of Utrecht, but also from the

2. On the disputed limits after Utrecht, see Thomas Jefferys, *The Conduct of the French in relation to Nova Scotia from its First Settlement to the Present Time* (1754); *Mémoires des Commissaires du roi et de ceux de Sa Majesté britannique sur les possessions et les droits respectifs des deux couronnes en Amérique* (1755–57); *The Memorials of the English and French Commissaries Concerning the Limits of Nova Scotia or Acadia* (1755); M. F. Pidanzat de Mairobert, *Discussion Sommaire sur les anciennes limites de l'Acadie et sur les stipulations du Traité d'Utrecht* (1755).

vagueness in many minds as to the territorial extent of "New France," the particulars of the dismemberment of greater Nova Scotia in the later eighteenth century, and the special status of Isle Royale (Cape Breton) and Isle St-Jean (Prince Edward Island) from 1713 to 1763. The heart of New France was always "Canada," the lands along the St. Lawrence, but it included the distinctly separate "Acadia" as well. It served the French interest, in 1713 and afterward, to consider the two islands (Isle Royale and Isle St-Jean) as a still different and distinct unit of New France under the government of Louisburg, to claim those territories of ancient Acadia which now lie in New Brunswick and Maine as part of Canada, and officially to claim that the "Acadia" surrendered at Utrecht consisted only of present peninsular Nova Scotia. But always they hoped, and strove, to reestablish their seventeenth-century hegemony, while the British in the same spirit, never gave up their official claim to any of the mainland portions of the ancient Acadia or Nova Scotia. Moreover, despite the concessions of 1713 and 1749, the latter were unremitting in their efforts to recover the two islands, as they ultimately did, for good, in 1758.

The second basic territorial meaning of Acadia is that of the land occupied by the Acadians. In this sense Acadia not only was much more limited at any one time but was a constantly changing area, and generally an expanding one, throughout the period with which we are concerned. By the 1650's solidly established at Port Royal, where they learned to exploit the tidal flats by dyking to make their arable fields, most Acadians remained very close to similar locations around the shores of the Bay of Fundy until the cataclysmic denouement of the 1750's. Some usually were scattered along the western and southern coasts of present peninsular Nova Scotia and there was some movement to the tidal marshlands of the Chignecto Bay estuaries which lie in present New Brunswick. Many Acadians migrated to Isle St-Jean; only a few moved to Cape Breton Island, but there was a brisk, if illegal, trade between the main body of the Acadians and the people engaged in the activities associated with the fortress and fishery there. There were small settlements of Acadians, or of others in close contact with them, here and there on the coast of the Gulf of St. Lawrence from Chaleur Bay to the Strait of Canso. Finally, Acadians continued some interest in the fur trade up the rivers of the north shore of the Bay of Fundy and the Gulf of Maine from the Saint John to the Penobscot.

Thus, most of the Acadians lived in a small part of the present province of Nova Scotia but their interests and activities extended broadly in the lands of Acadia, *sensu latiore*.

Because most of the Acadians did continue to live in the peninsula of present Nova Scotia, and because their ecclesiastical and trading connections (and, in an even more clandestine and largely involuntary sense, political and military contacts as well) with Cape Breton Island were so strong, this book is, properly, most largely concerned with Nova Scotian territory as it is delimited today. Even while the lands of Acadian occupation expanded steadily as the major feature of their changing human geography, settled Acadia bore only the same fractional relationship to the broader Acadia, or Nova Scotia, that the lands occupied by Canadians do to the vast empty reaches of the present Kingdom of Canada. Peripheral Acadia will not be ignored but our attention will be focused sharply on the heartlands where most of the Acadians lived. However, in the period before 1632 our view of Acadia must have its first, and broader, connotation, for there were few "Acadians," by any definition, until that year.

BEGINNINGS TO 1632

The First Contacts

The possibility of Viking visits to the area, at least to the rocky coasts of Cape Breton Island, from their probable base in northern Newfoundland, and the likelihood of its "descry," if not "discovery," by generations of pre-Columbian European fishermen and traders plying the waters of the North Atlantic, are now well-known hypotheses in the historiography of the exploration of the shores of the northwestern Atlantic. Even better publicized have been the recorded post-Columbian landings of Cabot on Cape Breton and Cartier on Prince Edward Island, and the "coastings" of the Corte-Reals and Verrazano.[3] But for significance to the history of Acadia in the seven-

3. There are, as well, a great many others of lesser renown as, for example, Fagundes, Hore, Strong, and Leigh. See esp. T. J. Oleson, *Early Voyages and Northern Approaches, 1000–1632* (1963); James A. Williamson, *The Cabot Voyages and Bristol Discovery under Henry VII* (1962); and H. P. Biggar, *The Precursors of Jacques Cartier, 1497–1534* (1911).

teenth century, none of these may compare with the annual visits of small fishing vessels throughout the sixteenth century. First in dozens, then in scores, and finally in hundreds, they came to the coasts of Newfoundland and gradually to the offshore banks and the coasts of Greater Acadia in search of codfish.[4] Norman and Breton, West-country English and Basque, Spanish and Portuguese, they gradually added to the technique of packing the cod down in heavy salt on their vessels (the "green" or "wet" fishery) the practice of curing their catch on shore, in the open air soon after catching, with much less salt. This (the "dry" fishery) made a much more valuable product and required landing on, and learning the nature of, the rocky Atlantic shoreline. Disembarking only briefly in the summers at first, they began to find the shore phase of their work important enough to require leaving men to winter in the new land in order to protect structures and to prepare for the following season. Much has been made of formal "settlement" by fur traders and missionaries but quite probably they were greatly outnumbered by the fishermen—and certainly by the seasonal ones— until far into the eighteenth century. We have records of many who virtually lived their lives in such a fishery and whose knowledge of the coasts of today's Atlantic Canada must often have been profound. Lescarbot described a meeting at Canso, in 1607, with a French fisherman who was on his forty-second annual voyage to the area.[5]

We must suppose that throughout the last half of the sixteenth century these fishermen in their increasing numbers had made contact with the Micmac Indians of Nova Scotia, and that much, if desultory, trading for a variety of goods on both sides had occurred. The importance of the opening decade of the seventeenth century for this area is, thus, not that it introduced the first Europeans to the land, nor established the first lasting contacts with the Indians, nor initiated the fur trade—for all of these had had a respectable local history in the previous century. What is significant is that the incidental fur trade of the fishermen and the sporadic and abortive beginnings of Cartier,

4. See Biggar, *Precursors;* Harold A. Innis, *The Cod Fisheries: The History of an International Economy* (1954), chs. 2 and 3; and Charles de La Morandière, *Histoire de la pêche française de la morue dans l'Amérique septentrionale* (1962), *1,* 215–70. Innis concludes that the early fishery was confined to the coasts and that the names of Gaspé and Cape Breton Island may have been used before the banks were exploited or, perhaps, even known. P. 25.

5. *The History of New France by Marc Lescarbot,* trans. and ed. W. L. Grant (1907–14), *2,* 362. See also Biggar, *Champlain's Works,* esp. *1,* 467n.

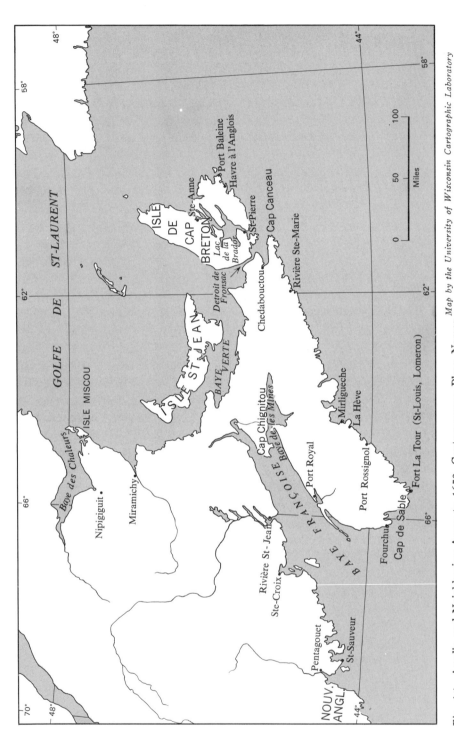

Fig. 4.1 Acadia and Neighboring Areas to 1670, Contemporary Place Names. *Map by the University of Wisconsin Cartographic Laboratory*

Roberval, and their successors were followed by trading schemes involving actual settlement, undertaken with a view toward the posts' being self-sufficient in agricultural and pastoral products, with minor or negligible interest in the fishery, and which, with some few short breaks, led directly (in the 1630's) to the first Acadian agricultural settlement which did not have a broken subsequent history. These posts were designed primarily as bases for the exploitative staple trades, and were not intended for colonization in the usual sense, but they were soon associated with missionary activity and they were settlements in which men committed themselves (with whatever subsequent or rapid changes of mind) to make their homes in the New World.

North of the northernmost Spanish outposts on the Carolina coastal islands the first such settlements were French. In the Bay of Fundy first, and soon thereafter in the St. Lawrence valley, the seeds of New France were planted. Although Acadia was of less economic and political significance than Canada to the Old World, it had wealth in both fish and furs and, located on the exposed flanks of both Canada and Newfoundland in the all but perpetual British-French struggles of the seventeenth and eighteenth centuries, it proved to be of major, and occasionally vital, strategic importance. Until the days of the great naval fortresses of Louisburg and Halifax in the eighteenth century and the climax of the struggle to control the St. Lawrence lifeline of New France, the chief military importance of Acadia was as a base for supplying and inciting Indian forays into New England and for sheltering the predatory shipmasters whose alternating roles as pirates or privateers were determined less by them than by distant decisions on war and peace, of which they often knew little and cared less. But these matters of attack and defense, in a sparring rivalry with New England for control of Indians and the fur trade, were not of little moment for either Acadia itself or the broad arc of North Atlantic shorelines, stretching from Florida through Greenland and Iceland to the British Isles, of which it found itself to be the keystone.

The Earliest Lodgements

If we may pass quickly over the sorry tale of the convict settlers of the Marquis de La Roche on Sable Island in 1598 (something of a parallel to Raleigh's "Lost Colony" at Roanoke), the first attempt at

settlement proper was that of Pierre Du Gua de Monts, who was
granted extensive rights to settlement, trade, and fishery in the area.[6]
Backed by an association of merchants, de Monts crossed to Acadia in
1604 with seventy-nine men.[7] A brief survey of the coasts of southwestern Nova Scotia, including the Annapolis Basin, led de Monts to cross
the Bay of Fundy and settle on an island at the mouth of the St. Croix
River. François Gravé Du Pont and Jean de Biencourt de Poutrincourt (two of his associates) returned to France the same year, leaving
de Monts to pass a disastrous winter during which thirty-five of his
men died and, according to the account of another, and soon-to-be-fa-
mous, associate of de Monts, Samuel de Champlain, "plus de 20. qui en
furet bien prés."[8]

In mid-June of 1605 Gravé Du Pont arrived back at St. Croix with
two ships, supplies, and a substantial reinforcement of men. A period
of six weeks was spent exploring the coast to the south as far as Cape
Cod in search of a better spot to settle, and then the decision was made
to shift south across the Bay of Fundy to the present Annapolis Basin.

6. The large number of known, and much larger number of supposed, contacts
with the land that is now Nova Scotia, for the refreshment of fishing vessels, the
beginning of the dry fishery, and fur trading, suggest the probability of many earlier
over-winter lodgements. Before Cartier, furs were being acquired and shipped back
to France and after the Roberval-Cartier enterprises in the lower St. Lawrence
River ended there was much activity if we can judge from the actual record. After
1550 the St. Lawrence estuary shores as far as Tadoussac were visited regularly,
with frequent penetrations as far as the Montreal area.

French attempts at lodgement were being made at the same time along the
Atlantic coast of Florida and the Carolinas, but were universally frustrated by the
power of Spain. All of this sets the background for the activities of Troilus de La
Roche de Mesgouez, whose record of continuous failure, unrivaled in the history of
the northeastern shores of North America, began with a first abortive voyage in
1578. Twenty years later he set out, armed with rather comprehensive letters patent
as lieutenant-general of the whole northeastern region, with some two-score "crimi-
nals" (or vagabonds) from the Rouen area and a few soldiers, and made an
establishment on Sable Island, a crescentic sandbank in the ocean at latitude 44° N.,
longitude 60° W., which even then was a well-known mariner's hazard. It is said
that he maintained this colony for five years, or at least that some eleven survivors
were still alive in 1603, when they were rescued or removed. See Gustave Lanctot,
"L'Établissement du Marquis de La Roche à l'île de Sable" (1933).

7. See the account in Lescarbot, *History of New France*, 2, bk. 4.

8. Biggar, *Champlain's Works*, 1, 304. Father Pierre Biard, reporting eleven years
later, said that of the seventy-nine, only eleven remained well. *The Jesuit Relations
and Allied Documents . . . 1610–1791*, ed. R. G. Thwaites (1896–1901), 3, 52.
Scurvy was a problem in all subsequent settlements dependent on ship's food to see
them through the winter.

There they established Port Royal, as it was to be known until 1710, erecting buildings and fortifications on the north side of the basin, opposite Goat Island[9] (see Figures 4.1 and 4.2). Gravé Du Pont and Champlain remained for the winter of 1605/6 with some forty-five men; de Monts and Poutrincourt returned to France.

When Poutrincourt sailed back to Port Royal with supplies and new personnel[10] in July of 1606, he found that all but two members of the establishment had left for Canso, the best known fishing harbor of Nova Scotia's coast and certain to have had dozens of ships visiting it. The men were recalled and immediate attempts were made to sow vegetables and field crops. A lime kiln was built, a forge set up and charcoal made for it, and paths were cut from the settlement to the fields and the valley. Tradesmen of many kinds spent a brief part of the day at their trades, the rest of it fishing, hunting, and gathering shellfish. They had a good winter, and toward the end of March started sowing seeds and building a water-powered gristmill to take care of the anticipated harvest. Then, in the summer of 1607, the news came that the de Monts grants, patents, and monopoly were withdrawn.[11] After various tidying-up operations, including a visit to St. Croix and the "copper mines"[12] up the bay—party conceived to delay their departure until samples of ripe grain were available for exhibits at home—the longest and most elaborate post-Viking settlement of Europeans on the North American continent north of Florida was abandoned—in the same year that Jamestown was established.

For three years, as Champlain turned to the founding of Quebec, the vestiges of settlement at Port Royal remained for the edification of the Micmac only. Then, in 1610, Poutrincourt, who had received a concession of the Port Royal Basin area (with loose and ill-defined limits) in 1604 from de Monts, succeeded in getting permission, financial aid,

9. This was done partly by "cannibalization" of the buildings of the St. Croix settlement. The Port Royal establishment has recently been reconstructed on its original site, on the north side of the Annapolis Basin, as nearly as possible to the original plans following the descriptions of Lescarbot and Champlain, and forms one of the more interesting tourist attractions in Canada.

10. These included his son Biencourt, the lawyer Marc Lescarbot, to whose descriptions we owe so much, a cousin Louis Hébert, who was both an apothecary and an enthusiastic horticulturist, and some fifty men.

11. Involved were rivals' resentment of the monopoly and de Monts' position on that year's wrong side of civil-war politics in France.

12. This is the origin of "Mines" or "Minas" Basin as a name; the deposits were in the Cape Chignecto region; no "mines" for copper ever developed.

Fig. 4.2 Port Royal Basin and Valley in the Seventeenth Century.

Map by the University of Wisconsin Cartographic Laboratory

BAYE FRANÇOISE

(BAY OF FUNDY)

N

65°30'W

44°45'N

44°45'N

(DIGBY GUT)

(Granville
Peninsula)

*PORT ROYAL
(ANNAPOLIS)
BASSIN*

ISLE AUX
CHÈVRES
(GOAT ISLAND)

(N   O   R   T   H   M   O   U   N   T   A   I   N)

(De Monts-Champlain Habitation
and later Scotch Fort)

Rivière Port Royal (Dauphin)

(Annapolis River)

300'

300'

600'

600'

(Bridgetown)

chapel ✝

Pré Ronde
(marsh)

Belle Isle
Marsh

moulin

Port Royal
(After 1632)

moulin

R. Lequille
(Mill or Allain R.)

R. Orignal

(Moose R.)

(S   O   U   T   H   M   O   U   N   T   A   I   N)

600'

300'

R. Imbert
(Bear R.)

300'

Paradis
terrestre

44°45'N

65°30'W

0   5

Miles

manpower, and a ship, and returned for another try at settlement.[13] After hurriedly sowing crops on his arrival, he remained for the autumn and winter with more than forty men; his son, Charles de Biencourt, returned to France with the ship and a cargo of furs. The next year, under court pressure, along with his mother and some additional men, he brought out with him two Jesuits, fathers Pierre Biard and Énemond Massé.[14] For the winter of 1611/12, while his father returned to France, Biencourt remained with the missionaries and a score of men and faced the trading rivalry of Gravé's son who had set up on the Saint John River across the Bay of Fundy. Conflict of interests with the Jesuits was immediate because, as Parkman put it, "He wished to make a trading post; the Jesuits wished to make a mission."[15]

In 1613 a contingent was sent out by Jesuit-inspired interests of the Marquise de Guercheville and others to take over the whole of the area (presumably all of "Acadia") outside of Poutrincourt's seigneurie.[16] They were to pick up priests at Port Royal and found a colony elsewhere; this they proceeded to do at St-Sauveur on Mount Desert Island, off the present Maine coast, with thirty settlers and some goats and horses. Meanwhile, the little colony at Port Royal had increased its agricultural activity and now extended up the river as far as Pré Ronde (see Figure 4.2). Very late in the year Poutrincourt sailed with relief ships from La Rochelle, but before he arrived, Samuel Argall, a trader-freebooter out of Jamestown, authorized by Governor Dale to dispossess any French south of latitude 45° N., had sacked the infant settlement at St-Sauveur and, in November, looted and burned the Port Royal settlement, dispersed its people, and destroyed its livestock.[17]

13. His companions included the young Biencourt, his son, a priest, and a number of men to serve as aides, soldiers, and artisans. Several head of cattle are believed to have come with this group.

14. After the assassination of Henry IV, Marie de Medici was in effective control in Paris. The assignment of the Jesuits led to the withdrawal of the support of the Dieppe merchants, du Jardin and du Quesne, but this support was matched or "bought out" by the Jesuits or their supporters. See *Jesuit Relations, 1, 6,* and various references by Biard in subsequent "Relations."

15. Francis Parkman, *Pioneers of France in the New World* (1910), *2, 122.*

16. The Marquise de Guercheville and her friends had obtained a grant of all the area outside of Poutrincourt's royally confirmed, but still roughly bounded, seigneurie. Indeed the wording for the larger grant could have included the whole Atlantic coast north of Florida.

17. François-Edmé Rameau de Saint-Père, *Une Colonie Féodale en Amérique: l'Acadie (1604–1881)* (1889), *1,* 59–60, well describes the expedition as "demi-marchande, demi-flibustière."

When Poutrincourt arrived early in 1614, after a hard winter voyage, he found the remains of his group barely ekeing out an existence; many had died. However, when Poutrincourt decided to give up and return to France, his son Biencourt, with one Claude de Saint-Étienne de La Tour, the latter's son Charles, and a few others determined to continue to find furs for the La Rochelle merchants. The next year, 1615, Poutrincourt *père* was killed in France and his son assumed his title and his rights or claims in Acadia and with his companions settled in at Port Royal.

For nearly a decade thereafter, Biencourt and his associates carried on a combined subsistence and trading economy. It has been speculated that they may have built cabins and storehouses and have cultivated fields up the river out of sight of ships entering the basin, and that they used the gristmill (which on this theory had escaped destruction by Argall, or had been rebuilt) to grind their grain.[18] Yet it seems improbable that an enterprise so heavily focused on the fur trade, and with the opportunities to buy food, or to leave, presented by the frequent and easy contacts with fishermen, could have held any large body of men at the monotonous and back-breaking labor that hand cultivation entailed. It may be more sensible to assume that the lands at Port Royal were largely abandoned and that they learned to live on fish, game, and wild berries as did the Indians with whom they were in constant association in their fur-gathering enterprise. We know that several fur-collecting posts were established, as at Fort Lomeron[19] (near Cape Sable), possibly at Pentagouet (Penobscot), and on the Saint John River (see Figure 4.1); a record 25,000 pelts from all of Acadia was reported for 1616. There is no conclusive evidence as to numbers of Frenchmen present in any given year and no doubt they fluctuated widely; there was constant contact with France through the fishery, especially at Canso, and that fishery must have both siphoned off the discontented and provided new recruits. In 1623 Jean de Biencourt died and Charles de Saint-Étienne de La Tour[20] took the leader-

18. *Ibid.*, p. 67. He was in fact speaking of the period after the Argall raid when he suggested the matter of concealment.

19. Named after David Lomeron. A partner in the firm that supported Poutrincourt and the La Tours after the Argall raid, he was the principal Poutrincourt agent in France.

20. The "St-Étienne," like the "de La Tour," may have been added by father and son to lay claim to a gentle family background. Their detractors and apologists have argued the point.

ship of the group together with the claims of the Poutrincourt family to
the Port Royal "seigneurie," although the headquarters was moved,
probably sometime in 1623, to the Cape Sable area.[21]

Meanwhile Sir William Alexander, one of the Scots who had moved
into court circles in London with the accession of James I, spent several
years promoting a variety of often fantastic schemes to colonize and
develop Acadia as a Scottish (under the joint crown perhaps we may
say, in anticipation, a British) possession.[22] He had received a charter
for roughly the territory of Acadia, *sensu latiore* (possibly including
Gaspé), in 1621, as "Nova Scotia."[23] His first expedition, of early
1622, did not make it to Nova Scotia and wintered in Newfoundland.
The second, in 1623, found that the "colonists" of the previous year
had hired out to the fishery so, after a bit of scouting along the south
shore of Nova Scotia, it picked up a cargo of cod and returned.

For a brief period, between 1628 and 1632, the English and the Scots
were the dominant power in Acadia and Canada. The Kirkes forced
Champlain to surrender Quebec in 1629, and Alexander, who had
joined his interests with theirs, established a settlement at Port Royal
in either 1628 or 1629.[24] Another Scottish settlement was founded at

21. In the period 1619–24 four different Recollet missionaries spent some time in
the area.

22. See Sir William Alexander (later Earl of Stirling), *An Encouragement to
Colonies* (1624), which reveals a good deal about the man and his interests (see
also map reproduced in text). The text of the original *Encouragement* is reproduced
in E. F. Slafter, *Sir William Alexander and American Colonization* (1873). For
further secondary discussion, the following are useful: T. H. McGrail, *Sir William
Alexander, First Earl of Stirling: A Biography* (1940); D. C. Harvey, "Sir William
Alexander and Nova Scotia" (1954); H. P. Biggar, *The Early Trading Companies
of New France* (1921), pp. 133–66 (fuzzy in some details, but very complete);
George Patterson, "Sir William Alexander and the Scottish Attempt to Colonize
Acadia" (1892); and G. P. Insh, "Sir William Alexander's Colony at Port Royal"
(1929–30).

Cape Breton Island and Prince Edward Island were detached from the grant and,
shortly after, given to Robert Gordon of Lochinvar. See *Royal Letters, Charters,
and Tracts Relating to the Colonization of New Scotland,* ed. David Laing (1867),
section on "Charters," beginning on p. 1.

23. This was the first use of the name, although "New Scotland" was more
widely used at the time.

24. Harvey, "Sir William Alexander," pp. 1–2, discusses the problem of the date
of the first occupation of Port Royal by the Alexander colonists and settles on 1628
for an Alexander settlement at Gaspé with "70 men and tua weemen" (p. 20) and
1629 for the establishment of Port Royal, after moving the 1628 group. The
problem exists because the documentation is largely associated with conflicting
English and French claims at the time of the peace settlement that "restored" Port

Port Baleine on Cape Breton in 1629, by James Stewart, Lord Ochiltree, who was landed there with fifty colonists by Alexander's son on
his way to Port Royal with a fleet. The Baleine settlement was captured and sacked by a Frenchman, Captain Charles Daniel, three
months later, and the Scottish settlers were deported.

When Alexander's son arrived at Port Royal he found that thirty of
the Scottish colonists had died. The colony carried on, however, visited
each year by representatives of the joint English-Scottish company
while negotiations for a peace treaty to settle the fate of Quebec and
Acadia dragged on. The brief period of British control in Acadia came
to an end in 1632 with the Treaty of St. Germain-en-Laye when the
British holdings in Acadia and New France were surrendered to the
French. It is believed that many of the Scottish settlers at Port Royal
left in 1629 and 1630, either for New England or the south shore
fisheries. However, at least forty-six of them are said to have been
disembarked in England in early 1633 suggesting that there had been a
substantial number in the settlement until the end.[25]

The Changing Geography of Settlement and Resource Use

At the beginning and end of the period the principal actors on the
scene were the same: scores of fishermen visiting the Atlantic coves

Royal to France. The years 1627, 1628, and 1629 have been cited by various
scholars: Gustave Lanctot, *A History of Canada, 1* (to 1663), trans. Josephine
Hambleton (1963), p. 141, chooses 1627; Biggar, *Trading Companies,* pp. 141–42,
implies both 1627 and 1628; and Patterson, "Alexander," p. 92, favors 1628. The
year 1629 is chosen by Ganong in his introduction to Nicolas Denys, *The Description and Natural History of the Coasts of North America (Acadia)* trans. and
ed. W. F. Ganong (1908), p. 3; by Azarie Couillard-Després, "Les Gouverneurs
de l'Acadie sous le régime français, 1600–1710" (1939), p. 229; and by Rameau,
Une Colonie Féodale, 1, 72. Émile Lauvrière, *La Tragédie d'un peuple* (1922), *1,* 43,
has the vessels involved (*Morning Star* and *Eagle*) arriving in 1628 (although he
has the fort built in the wrong place). Women may have been part of the 1629
reinforcement if the first group came in 1628. At any rate there is abundant
evidence of the *presence* of the Scots from 1629 to 1632 even though we know so
little about how they lived, or precisely when they arrived.

The "Kirkes" involved were a father and three sons, reported as having been long
residents of Dieppe, but then in London, whose operations—rather of a privateering
sort at first—received full official support when Quebec fell to them in 1629.

25. *La Gazette de Renaudot,* February 11, 1633, reported that Razilly's ships had
returned to France "après avoir deschargé aux dunes de la coste d'Angleterre les
quarante-six Ecossais qui estoient au Port Royal." Quoted in Genevieve Massignon,
Les Parlers Français d'Acadie (1962), *1,* 18.

each year (with wintering-over undoubtedly on the increase) and the Indians, living much as before, but with increasing interest in the trade goods on which they were learning to depend, and thus gathering furs more systematically and spreading more widely to acquire them. By 1632, however, there were beginnings of actual French settlement of promising permanence. If the various attempts to colonize Port Royal had proved abortive, by 1630 there were posts in the Cape Sable area, at Pentagouet, and on the Saint John River,[26] and also at Miscou (Gaspé), and probably for a time at present St. Ann in Cape Breton, established by the French captain, Daniel, after the eviction of Ochiltree (see Figure 4.1). In none of these was agriculture of any importance. Yet agriculture had been practiced in the period, first most tentatively at St. Croix, and then more extensively and intensely at Port Royal, with enough success to suggest that permanent colonies could be assured of self-support in food.

In the autumn of 1605 Champlain and Poutrincourt visited the previous winter's settlement at St. Croix and reported on the results from the grain (in fact, rye) they had sown there, "lequel estoit beau, gros, pesant & bien nourri" (translated variously as "healthy, fat, full and well grown" and "fair, big, and weighty").[27] On virgin soil this might well have been expected, and a handful of mature ears proved little; but that little included the fact that the climate would allow bread grains to mature.

Most of what we know of that first settlement on the shores of the Annapolis Basin comes from the 1606/7 observations of Lescarbot who had a deep interest in farming and plant husbandry. He speaks of ". . . the pleasure which I took in digging and tilling my gardens, fencing them in against the gluttony of the swine, making terraces, preparing straight alleys, building store-houses, sowing wheat, rye,

26. Fort Lomeron, in the Cape Sable area, was subsequently called Fort St-Louis, and still later usually known as Port La Tour. A fort was apparently established at Pentagouet by La Tour in 1623 and the group doubtless maintained posts west of the Saint John River, if not at this spot, in the succeeding decade. Although Ganong, in his introduction to Denys, *Description*, p. 5, suggests that the La Tours established their post on the Saint John only in 1635, Couillard-Després, "Les Gouverneurs," p. 229, and Lauvrière, *La Tragédie, 1,* 52, both have satisfied themselves of the 1630 date.

27. The original as well as the first translation can be found in Lescarbot, *History of New France, 2,* 319, 553–54. The more familiar translation, by Pierre Erondelle in 1609, is *Nova Francia, A Description of Acadia, 1606,* available in Broadway Travellers Edition (1928), where the second translation is given on p. 26.

barley, oats, beans, peas, garden plants, and watering them, so great a desire had I to know the soil by personal experience."[28]

The experience with grain at Port Royal was, by Lescarbot's continued testimony, even more satisfactory than at St. Croix:

. . . the rye was as tall as the tallest man . . . and we feared that this height would hinder it from bringing forth seed [a eulogy of the results follows]. . . . I sowed wheat without allowing my land to remain fallow, and without dunging it at all; and nevertheless it grew up in as fair perfection as the fairest wheat in France, although the corn and all that we sowed was over a year old. . . . in the month of April in the year 1607, having sown too thick and too near one another some grains of rye that was gathered at St. Croix, ... they multiplied so abundantly that they choked one another, and did not come to perfection.[29]

Seeds were sown in April or even March, a bit early for most crops but these were times of experiment. In addition to the principal food crops of northwestern Europe, both swine and sheep were brought out in 1605.

. . . French domestic animals prosper very well in those parts. We had hogs which multiplied abundantly; and although they had a stye, they lay abroad, even in the snow and during the frost. We had but one sheep, which enjoyed the best possible health, although he was not shut up at night, but was in the midst of our yard in winter time. M. de Poutrincourt had him twice shorn, and the wool of the second year was reckoned in France two sous a pound better than that of the first. We had no other domestic animals save hens and pigeons, which failed not to yield the accustomed tribute, and to multiply abundantly.[30]

Nor did the first visitors fail to bring with them the ubiquitous pest of sailing ships, the grey rat: ". . . we had ample provision of them, and made unceasing warfare on them. The savages had no knowledge of these animals before our coming; but in our time they have been beset by them."[31]

The water-powered gristmill that was built to grind the grain suggests that a fair amount was grown (or anticipated) but exactly how or where we are uncertain. In all likelihood the fields were near the "habitation," i.e., the fort, on the north shore of the basin, and the tillage was an axe, spade, and hoe operation in land cleared from the forest; there is no suggestion of the use of a plow. We should like to

28. Lescarbot, *History of New France*, 2, 266.   29. *Ibid.*, 3, 247.
30. *Ibid.*, p. 226.   31. *Ibid.*, p. 227.

know how many arpents[32] were cleared and the proportions of different crops grown, but we do not. Nor are we much better informed as to the agricultural activities in the period between 1610 and the Argall raid in 1613, or for the decade and a half from 1613 until the arrival of the Scottish expeditions. Some kind of farming may have continued along the shores of the northern end of the basin and along the lower course of the Port Royal or Dauphin (Annapolis) River. If so it probably involved cattle and swine and we should assume that the salt-marsh grass and even fresh-water marsh grass, so invitingly present, would have been cut for hay. There is no evidence whatsoever of the dyking of the salt marshes, the successful establishment of fruit trees or, indeed, of any lasting improvements that could be part of the capital equipment of subsequent settlers.

The Scots' settlement, again, is an enigma in terms of land use and settlement. What crops they may have grown, or where they may have grown them, what livestock or implements they may have had, how many, and what kind of buildings they built—all these are unknown to us. All the probabilities point to a very limited and sketchy agricultural activity while, as the Alexander group barely survived in Annapolis Basin, La Tour and his followers roamed the interior and made rendez-vous with their Indian friends at their various permanent or temporary posts. Rameau has given a vivid reconstruction of the life of the latter (even if based more on probability than evidence):

Meanwhile young La Tour carried on, both in the interior and at posts along the shore, with his program of trading with the Indians for furs. For fully fifteen years he and his associates maintained this exotic way of life among the Micmac. In a letter he reported that they depended on the friendship of the natives, living and dressing as they did. The winter passed in traveling through the woods, in hunting, and in trading their beads and trinkets for the peltry of the Indians. They lived in snow houses [highly unlikely!] and subsisted on roots, game, and smoked fish. From time to time they made their way to the coast with the packs of furs they had collected. In the springtime and summer they kept to the coast, living by hunting and fishing, and watched for the ships that came there in search of cod. These they signaled to come in to the little

32. The arpent was a basic French unit of land measurement, both linear and areal, but its size at the time is uncertain. In length, 200 feet may be a rough equivalent for an arpent in the seventeenth and eighteenth centuries; it was later standardized at 192 feet. An areal arpent may have been something less than an acre (the usual equivalent was .845 acres) although it has been given the equivalent of as much as an acre and a half in some twentieth-century definitions.

palisaded forts or warehouses where the skins were stored, and in return for the skins they obtained arms, ammunition, and general supplies.[33]

Retrospect from 1632

In conclusion there are a few points to be underlined. In numbers of men involved, the value produced, the areal distribution of activity, and the interest in Europe, it is clear that the agricultural experiments and even the fur trade remained of very minor importance in comparison with the cod fishery. The events on which the majority of the historians of the area have focused most of their attention were economically and demographically rather incidental. The overwhelming significance of the apparently inexhaustible codfish near the shores and on the offshore banks, and of the hundreds of miles of deeply broken Atlantic coastline offering innumerable coves for shelter, refreshment, and the erection of drying flakes, cannot be overlooked in any geographical assessment of the area. Indeed, the fur-trading and settlement activities, such as they were, were heavily dependent on the ease with which small vessels could move along the coast, from Havre à l'Anglois (Louisburg) to Cape Fourchu (Yarmouth), or even around the shores of the Bay of Fundy, "hopping" from one of the closely spaced harbors to another.

There are perhaps enough reasons for the scantiness of agricultural settlement without attempting to single out any one for emphasis. The experiments suffered grievously from political troubles in Europe, more from internal strife and factionalism in France than from British-French differences, although later overseas settlements often had similarly unpropitious auguries on the home front. The Indians were generally friendly and cooperative as they continued to be to the trading entrepreneurs and settlers for the following century and a half. The distraction of the interest of potential farmers to sea and forest (in this case fishery and fur trade) was a theme that, established in the early seventeenth century, was to outlast the Acadian period and be of central importance through the two succeeding centuries; it was a major factor at the time but perhaps hardly more so than later. But it may be that one notable lack in the "equipment" of the settlements was primarily responsible for their failure. In the history of the

33. Rameau, *Une Colonie Féodale, 1,* 73. My translation.

transference of people, plants, and animals overseas from northwestern Europe to the mid-latitude lands overseas colonized by them, it has been abundantly demonstrated that an agricultural colony needs its own women and the stability of family life. Poutrincourt brought his wife briefly, and two women may have accompanied the Alexander settlers of 1628 or 1629, but if there were any more we have no record of them.

Resort to Indian women must have been common enough among the fur traders but it never became an accepted or established practice in the organized settlements, in good part because of the influence of the priests. In any event, dalliance with the Indian maids was more likely to lead the men to the forest than the women to the cornfields. There is no doubt that the blending of French and Micmac genes did get underway in the period and that this process continued, clandestinely at least, through the remaining Acadian residence, somewhat diluting the "genetic purity" of both Acadian and Indian groups (principally the latter). But it was the absence of wives and settled families that may well have been the greatest handicap agriculture faced. It was demonstrated that the desired immigrant plants and animals would thrive in the soil and climate, and the need for the products of husbandry was great and continuous. But of women of their own kind to cook and sew, harvest and hoe, and provide the solace and affections of home, there were none, and to their absence, as much as to any other problem or difficulty, the lack of success may be attributed. The attempts at agricultural settlement in Acadia prior to 1632 were largely abortive but, in proving that agriculture of the west-European mixed-farming character (which could be largely self-sustaining) was feasible, they proved that permanent colonization was possible as well.

In several important ways these first three decades established the pattern of life for the Acadian century that followed. Argall's raid was to be repeated ten times in well under a hundred years. The support and friendliness of the Indians, doubly reinforced by interbreeding and a widespread if often superficial conversion to the French Catholic faith, was established and endured through the entire period of Acadian occupation, a fact of particular importance during the years of English rule. All three occupations of the subsequent regional economy —fishing, fur-trading, and agriculture—were in operation concurrently for the first time. The three were to shift in relative importance in the succeeding 120-odd years but each was always an integral element of the Acadian scene.

FRENCH SETTLEMENT AND NOMINAL FRENCH CONTROL, 1632–1654

For twenty-two years after the Treaty of St. Germain-en-Laye in 1632, the Acadian lands were in French hands and there became established by 1654 a resident population, more or less sedentary and agricultural, from which a large proportion of the later Acadians were descended. Indeed this is the real beginning of French settlement in Acadia. An enduring lodgement of agricultural settlers, with a social structure adequate to their needs, was made at Port Royal in the Annapolis Basin and several new posts were established around the coasts. Husbandry and population expanded to the point that the intrusion of France into these maritime lands assumed an air of permanence. As was to be characteristic of Acadia, these events took place almost in spite of, rather than in conscious and studied direction from, the leaders in the New World or the authorities in the Old.

The history of these twenty-two years has often been written as a sort of *opéra bouffe* libretto based on the vendetta between Charles de La Tour and Charles de Menou d'Aulnay for control of the fur trade. It is true enough that the energies of the settlers were greatly occupied by that minuscule civil war between rival fur-trading seigneurs. The struggle originated and persisted for many reasons: because of the inconsistency and inaccuracy in the statement of terms of the grants, or the failure to annul earlier rights in granting new ones; because the responsible people in Paris knew little of Acadia and cared even less; because Acadia was too far away for adequate enforcement of authority from France or Quebec; and because in Acadia there was no single authority. Of importance to us is that this armed feud diverted so much attention from the actual settlement and its agricultural activities that the few settlers brought out, when they were not drafted for service on attack or forced to be active in their own defense, were often left to fend for themselves.

The charter of the Company of New France stressed settlement as its outstanding responsibility and with each concession there was stipulated the number of colonists to be brought out within a given time limit.[34] As was the rule with the dozens of French and English charters granted in the seventeenth and eighteenth centuries in eastern North America, these quotas were never met. As we shall see, only d'Aulnay and Isaac de Razilly brought out immigrants specifically as agricultural settlers. There was no immediate or significant profit to be earned from colonization; on the other hand the fur trade and fishery could be highly rewarding. Between 1632 and 1635 some 3,700,000 arpents of land in Acadia were granted to the Company, but for all of their interest in land as such it might as well have been 3,700 arpents, or very little more.

The Narrative

The Company of New France had been established in 1627 to bring order to, and increased (or assured) crown revenues from, the North American fur trade.[35] Although temporarily frustrated by the activities of the brothers Kirke in the Gulf of St. Lawrence, and by the Alexander enterprises in Cape Breton Island and at Port Royal, its directors were able to organize an expedition immediately after the conclusion of the peace treaty and to reestablish French control of the fishery and fur trade in Acadia as well as on the St. Lawrence. Razilly, one of its leaders,[36] sailed from France on July 4, 1632 in *L'Espérance à Dieu,* shepherding two transports, and disembarked some three hundred people (mostly men) and a variety of livestock, seeds, tools, implements, arms, munitions, and other supplies at La Have (La Hève, at the mouth of La Have River in present Lunenburg County) on September 8. Shortly thereafter the Scottish settlement at Port Royal was taken over, and all but the possible one or two families who elected to remain departed; the new settlement on the south coast was undisturbed for the moment.

Meanwhile, La Tour was confirmed in his possession of his forts near

34. The Company of New France—i.e., the Company of One Hundred Associates —is fully described in Biggar, *Trading Companies,* pp. 133–65.

35. The problems of the early years of the fur trade are treated in great detail in Harold A. Innis, *The Fur Trade in Canada: An Introduction to Canadian Economic History* (1956).

36. Razilly was a cousin of Richelieu and a royal councillor. He was designated lieutenant-general of all the parts of New France called "Canada" and governor of "Acadia."

Cape Sable,[37] at Pentagouet, and on the Saint John River. Most of his men, by now thoroughly at home in the restless, dangerous, but profitable life of the fur trade, stayed with him. In 1635 he shifted his headquarters from the Cape Sable area to the Saint John. The move may have been related to the death of Razilly at La Have in that year which left both La Have and Port Royal under the control of his lieutenant, d'Aulnay. Whether by Razilly's testamentary direction or not the French court appears, at this time, to have awarded control of much of the northern shore of the Gulf of Maine and the Bay of Fundy to d'Aulnay and of the Fundy and Atlantic coasts of the present Nova Scotia peninsula to La Tour.[38] Thus La Tour had moved to a spot from which he could prosecute the fur trade vigorously in "d'Aulnay territory" whereas d'Aulnay's posts at La Have and Port Royal were in "La Tour country." Perhaps fortunately for the ultimate agricultural interests of the colony, but apparently not for that reason, he decided to shift the settlement at La Have around to the Annapolis Basin. He had become a keen and bitter rival of La Tour for the fur trade, and the contemporaneous moves of the two rival headquarters may be seen as an element of the steadily changing geography of the continental fur trade as fur seekers pushed west after their retreating resources. There followed fifteen years of most active feuding between the two adversaries, involving all but incredible behind-the-scenes maneuvering in

37. Fort St-Louis, later Fort La Tour. Neither archeological nor documentary evidence has resolved the problems of nomenclature, chronology, or locations of the several forts or fur-depots (*magasins*) which were built and used in the Cape Sable area at different times in the seventeenth century, chiefly by the La Tours and their descendants (Forts Lomeron, St-Louis, La Tour, etc.). Henri Leander d'Entremont, *The Forts of Cape Sable in the Seventeenth Century* (1938), has argued passionately for one of the more westerly locations.

38. Razilly's intention with regard to division of authority between himself (and d'Aulnay), La Tour, and Nicolas Denys has been argued but not resolved. See the suggestion of Ganong in his introduction to Denys, *Description*, p. 11. In 1633 the Company had given La Tour extensive privileges which were to last for six years. See Azarie Couillard-Després, *Charles de Saint-Étienne de La Tour . . . et son temps, 1593–1666* (1930), pp. 205–8. There appears to be no definitive documentation but it is argued by the La Tour apologists that before his death, Razilly had set up three lieutenancies: the coast of present Maine west of the St. Croix River for d'Aulnay; from St. Croix to Canso for La Tour; and Canso to Gaspé for Denys. Denys became something of an apologist for La Tour. Robert Le Blant, "Les Études Historiques sur la colonie française d'Acadie 1603–1713" (1948), has a summary of Denys' career.

France, England, and New England as well as skirmishes, blockades, fort-storming, and the capture and recapture of posts.[39]

By 1647, d'Aulnay had destroyed La Tour's fort on the Saint John River and had been confirmed as governor of all of Acadia. La Tour was forced into exile. The tide was reversed suddenly in 1650 when d'Aulnay died at Port Royal and La Tour, having procured a new commission for himself, returned to Acadia.[40] His own wife having died after attempting to defend the fort on the Saint John, he now arranged a *mariage de convenance* with d'Aulnay's widow and stood off Emmanuel Le Borgne, d'Aulnay's chief creditor, who had arrived from France and established himself at Port Royal.

The other leading member of the Acadian cast of characters in this period was Nicolas Denys, the most attractive but in many ways the least fortunate.[41] In 1632, under Razilly's patronage, he had posts for a fishery, and perhaps for cutting timber, at Port Rossignol, the site of present Liverpool at the mouth of the Mersey River, and at La Have, but after Razilly's death in 1635 he was ousted by d'Aulnay. For the next three decades he was very active both as an agent for others in France, and on his own in Acadia, in promoting Acadian enterprises. In the 1640's he established a post at Miscou, at the entrance to Chaleur Bay, which was soon seized by d'Aulnay and later, in 1650

39. Feelings among historians partial to one side or the other still run as high as those of the early seventeenth-century antagonists themselves. A bibliography of the literary feud would be long. We may call to attention as pro-La Tour, Couillard-Després, "Les Gouverneurs," and *idem, La Tour;* and, as pro-d'Aulnay, Lauvrière, *La Tragédie.* The latest published study, Gustave Lanctot, *L'Histoire du Canada, 1,* (1960), esp. chs. 21 and 22, manages to be anti-La Tour without being notably pro-d'Aulnay. Ganong, in his introduction to Denys' *Description,* pp. 5–7, gives a more objective assessment.

40. La Tour had been "resting" in Quebec after his ouster in 1647. When he returned as governor of Acadia he brought with him one Lieut. Philippe Mius d'Entremont whose descendants played a large role in Acadia in the next century. Le Borgne was d'Aulnay's *procureur-générale* at La Rochelle and advanced large sums both for supplies and for sending out engagés. D'Aulnay had gambled heavily in his investments in men and supplies in the struggle with La Tour and his death came just at the time when he might have been expected to start cashing in on them.

41. Much is known about Denys and about Acadia in the period, from his viewpoint, because of his magnificent *Description.* Ganong's introduction to the book includes an extensive assessment of the man, the period, and its principal figures. Le Blant, "Études Historiques," is more critical.

and 1651, indefatigable, he built posts at St. Peters and St. Ann[42] on Cape Breton Island, only to be again dispossessed, this time by the agents of the widow d'Aulnay, now Madame La Tour. Trying again both at St. Peters and at Nipisiguit on Chaleur Bay, he was ousted by Le Borgne and carried off to Port Royal as a prisoner. There, in 1654, he was released through the English capture of Port Royal by Robert Sedgwick. This expedition, diverted from an attack on New Netherland by the inconvenient arrival of news of peace with the Dutch, sailed instead to the northeast and seized the French establishments on the Saint John River, at Port Royal, and at La Have. They were to remain under English control until 1670. Meanwhile Denys returned to France in 1654 and received authority, sufficiently impressive to be recognized by his rivals (who were greatly inhibited by the English presence in any event), for control of the territory of Cape Breton, the Gulf shore westward to Gaspé, and, probably, of Isle St-Jean as well. He held firm in St. Peters and Nipisiguit until the winter of 1668/69.[43]

THE SETTLEMENTS

The Outports and Outposts

Except for Port Royal, the evidence for agricultural settlement in Acadia in this period can be summed up in a few words. We know that Razilly's original passenger list for La Have in 1632 included some three hundred, mostly men, many of whom may have left after the first buildings were erected and the first fields cleared. Denys reported some forty *habitants* there in 1635.[44] Apparently there were but a dozen

42. Ganong, in Denys, *Description,* pp. 183–84n2, attributes the fort at St. Ann to Denys' brother.

·43. In 1668 Denys ran afoul of the pretensions of the Sieur de La Giraudière at Chedabucto. During that winter he was burned out at St. Peters and retired to Nipisiguit in 1669. Shortly thereafter he returned to France, wrote and published his book (partly a defense of his own pretensions), and probably remained in France until he died in 1688.

44. Denys, *Description,* p. 482. Massignon, *Les Parlers Français, 1,* 35–36, reports a *mémoire* of date 1644 concerning those who accompanied d'Aulnay which reported that the Razilly group had comprised two hundred men "tant soldats, laboureurs, qu'autres artisans, sans compter les femmes, les enfants ni les Capucins." Also there were twenty French households "qui sont passés avec leur familles." B. N. Nouv. acq. fr. MS. 9281, fol. 104.

or fifteen women in the original group. Assuming that most of these survived, and that they had a reasonable number of children, we may estimate roughly a hundred people in all living at La Have in 1635.

Between 1635 and 1640 most of this group moved to Port Royal. It seems likely that those who had taken Indian wives were not encouraged to move and that La Have, thus, became a settlement for métis families.[45] How many there were we do not know, for population figures given in the mid-forties and in 1650 combine Port Royal and La Have.

While it is traditional to refer to the farmland in the La Have area as poor, in fact the drumlins (see Chapter 2) provided soil as good or better than other upland soils used in the seventeenth century and quite adequate to the needs and techniques of the time. Razilly had apparently organized a fairly elaborate seigneurial machinery for the forty allotments; Rameau interprets it as very like that of the later seigneuries of New France.[46] If so it was perhaps the only example of a serious attempt to establish such an apparatus in the present territory of Nova Scotia. Before Razilly's death, cabins (type unknown) had been built on most of the allotments, the seeds, tools, and animals brought from France had been employed effectively, and, according to Denys, at least one wheat harvest had been garnered. Some settlement apparently continued with the métis group here, although Le Borgne appears to have captured and burned the fort at La Have in 1653.

As for the other coastal settlements, there are suggestions in the mid-1640's of a hundred or more residents at the mouth of the Saint John River, near the fort or forts at Cape Sable, and at Pentagouet and other posts on the Maine coast. Some of these would have been from the group of *colons* which La Tour brought with him in 1633, almost certainly as hands for his fishing or trading enterprise.[47] Undoubtedly these posts were still almost purely for trade. There may have been some gardening in the Cape Sable area, and a report that

45. Lauvrière, *La Tragédie, 1,* 81, refers to some "anciennes familles métissées" being left as caretakers of the establishment by d'Aulnay. The degree of Acadian intermixture with the Micmac, and the degree and significance of an Indian strain in the Acadian people, has not been studied adequately.

46. Rameau, *Une Colonie Féodale, 1,* 81.

47. The distinction between *colons* and *engagés* was, simply, that the latter were indentured and the former were not. The terminology has been used very loosely by later writers and is not even consistent in documents of the period.

Charles de La Tour destroyed a farm of d'Aulnay's near Pentagouet in
1644 suggests some attempt at agriculture there.[48]

Champlain's map of 1632 indicates some kind of settlement at Fourchu though it may have been a brief one, perhaps a wintering spot for
fishermen (see Plate 3). Denys places Fort Lomeron at Fourchu instead of in the Cape Sable area but this was probably in error.[49] Port
Rossignol was such a strategic situation for both a fishery haven and
for open or clandestine trade in furs and skins to the interior that there
may well have been more settlement at this period than Denys' short-
lived one from 1632 to 1635.

Eastward of La Have, the trading post established by the Sieur de La
Giraudière on the St. Mary's River, some distance above its mouth and
near present Sherbrooke, may possibly date from 1654.[50] Chedabucto (Canso and Chedabucto Bay), while of increasing importance as
a port for fishing vessels, offers no evidence of a permanent post or of
attempts at agriculture before the 1660's. The Port Baleine settlement
of Lord Ochiltree[51] did not survive the attack by Captain Daniel and
there is no record of further settlement or wintering there before
1654.[52] Finally, before 1654, we have Denys' short-lived posts on Cape
Breton Island and those along the shores of the Gulf of St. Lawrence,
one on Miscou Island from 1645 to 1647 where he had some gardens,
possibly one at Miramichi, and, after 1652, one at Nipisiguit.[53]

Port Royal and Its District

Perhaps there were members of the Poutrincourt-La Tour group at
Port Royal each year from 1613 to 1628, and of the Razilly-d'Aulnay
group from 1632 to 1635, but continuous agricultural settlement in this

48. Denys, *Description*, p. 98n1. A farm "house" some miles from the fort was
attacked and some cattle killed. Two studies by G. A. Wheeler describing this area
at the time are *History of Castine, Penobscot, and Brooksville, Maine* (1875), and
"Fort Pentagoët and the French Occupation of Castine" (1893).

49. Denys, *Description*, p. 128. Perhaps the most convenient source for the
Champlain map is Biggar, *Champlain's Works*, in a special portfolio of plates and
maps, which accompanies the series.

50. Denys, *Description*, p. 158.

51. Figure 4.1 indicates Port Baleine (or des Baleines) as it was specified on later
maps, and represented by the hamlet of Baleine today; it is not known whether this
was the same site in the early seventeenth century.

52. Biggar, *Trading Companies*, p. 147.

53. Denys, *Description*, pp. 11 and 177.

PLATE X.

Samuel de Champlain, Oeuvres

3   Champlain's Map of Atlantic Canada, 1632

seedbed of the Acadian people dates from the firm establishment there of d'Aulnay's "habitans" from La Have in the late 1630's. This decision to move from La Have was to be of critical importance for the changing geography of the Acadians for more than a century afterward and it deserves some attention. As was pointed out above, the motive of finding a more satisfactory spot for agriculture may have to be discounted. As far as we know there had been no use of the Bay of Fundy's tidal salt marshes for agriculture before 1635 and the upland soils previously used in the Port Royal area were not significantly better (and may have been worse) than those around the La Have estuary. It is true that the shelter of North Mountain from the prevailing northwest winds of winter has been advanced as an attraction, yet Annapolis, in fact, has lower temperatures in January and February than has the Lunenburg coast.

But such records as we have suggest that agriculture was of secondary interest to the leaders of the French settlements. The fishing and the fur trade supplied commodities marketable in Europe. Nicolas Denys, it is true, was always more interested in the fishery, with agricultural settlement coming ahead of the fur trade (or so he protested, after having been rather brutally handled by his fur-trading rivals):

Although it has been believed that my principal object in all my enterprises in these parts has always been the trading in furs with the Indians, I have never considered that as anything other than an accessory which could serve in some measure to make capital for that which might be done in the country, which is the settlement fishery [pesche sédentaire] and the cultivation of the land, presuming the establishment of one or several colonies in all those places of the coast where one or the other can be advantageously carried on.[54]

Razilly, too, seemed to have had a balanced program of resource exploitation in mind in which agriculture, the fishery, and even lumbering each had an important place. But d'Aulnay, as his original assignment to the Maine coast suggests,[55] was primarily interested in quick profits from the fur trade, and he wanted to move nearer to the chief source of furs which was on the continent, not on the peninsula. His chief rival, La Tour, had an advantage with his post north of the Bay

54. *Ibid.,* p. 146. "Pesche sédentaire" is perhaps more acceptably translated as the "dry," or at least "sedentary," fishery.
55. Ganong, in his introduction to Denys' *Description,* p. 11. See also note 38 above.

of Fundy, and Port Royal was a much more satisfactory base for competitive activity than La Have.

The greater attraction of Port Royal (Annapolis) Basin as a harbor, and its superior defensibility, as compared with La Have, should not be given too much weight. La Have was quite adequate for the needs of the time, and though batteries or lookouts on either side of Digby Gut, and a series of message relay-stations for warnings to the fort, might have given Port Royal a great defensive advantage, none of these (probably too elaborate and expensive) preparations was made. Indeed there are few harbors outside of the Mediterranean Sea that have had as sorry a history of vulnerability to sea attack as did Port Royal. In all, there seems little doubt that the fur trade, and the rivalry with La Tour for it, were of overwhelming importance in the decision for this site. However, there is a danger in overemphasizing the actual fighting between the rival factions as a deterrent to the progress of settlement and agriculture. In fact the "war" lasted little more than a decade and the personnel of both sides must have spent most of their time in the actual trade.

Of much more importance to the development or neglect of Acadia were the events of the main stream of western European history on both sides of the Atlantic. Cardinal Richelieu's partly successful attempts to bring some international diplomatic order out of the near chaos of the early century, to France's benefit, were not matched by comparable progress within the country, and his successor, Cardinal Mazarin, was preoccupied with domestic problems during Louis XIV's minority in the 1640's and 1650's. Further international gains were made in the famous "charter of Europe"—the Treaties of Westphalia —in 1648; but La Fronde, the French civil war of the mid-century years, left little money or interest available for the struggling commercial enterprises across the Atlantic. England had its own civil war and that, and its aftermath, similarly left the New World plantations largely to fend for themselves.

POPULATION GROWTH — In the uneasy fifteen years after Argall's raid (1613) and before Alexander's Scottish settlers arrived at Port Royal there may have been a score or two of the residue of Poutrincourt's settlement—with many additions and subtractions—wintering each year in the Fundy hinterlands. As indicated above, there is confusion as to how many the Alexanders may have temporarily added to the population of Acadia. Perhaps as many as seventy wintered in one year, but the numbers are believed to have fluctuated widely and, generally, to have dwindled progressively during the four years.

Even before the move to Port Royal by the group at La Have, which perhaps was underway before 1635 and largely concluded by 1640, there may have been some new immigration. There are records of *contrats d'engagement* for Acadia in large numbers, by the notaries of La Rochelle, for the period between 1630 and 1654. It is true that few of their names, as far as we know them, are found in the first Acadian census of 1671, but, while serving their contracts of from one to three years, they must have swelled the population not only at Port Royal but at the outlying posts as well. Among those recruited for Port Royal by Emmanuel Le Borgne were five sawyers in 1645 and a gunsmith in 1646. Even more numerous were those sent out to Charles de La Tour by his intendant, Guillaume Desjardins. For example, in 1640 his *engagés* included a gunsmith and a joiner and, in 1641, a nailmaker-blacksmith, a sawyer, a mason, and a baker; in 1642 these were joined by twenty-two men who were hired as laborers and soldiers for the fort on the Saint John. In addition we know that some twenty-five men and five women were signed up for Acadia in 1640, but we know neither their names nor their destinations.[56] Couillard-Després quotes at length from a contemporary source a list of sixty-three men sent out on the vessel *Saint-Clement* in 1642 to reinforce La Tour.[57] Rameau concludes that d'Aulnay also imported some families in 1640,[58] and Lauvrière estimates that, at one time or another before his death, d'Aulnay may have added a score of married couples or families to the original La Have nucleus.[59]

For 1650 an estimate of forty-five to fifty European households at Port Royal and La Have has been made,[60] with some sixty single men—possibly 300 or 350 people in all. Denys estimated perhaps 270, perhaps considerably more, when the English captured Port Royal in 1654, including Le Borgne and ". . . six vingts hommes des siens avec

56. These records are cited and discussed by Massignon, *Les Parlers Français, 1*, 38–39.

57. Couillard-Després, "Les Gouverneurs," pp. 242–44.

58. *Une Colonie Féodale, 1*, 93. He does not cite his evidence.

59. Lauvrière, *La Tragédie, 1*, 80–81. By the time of the estimate they had all removed to Port Royal.

60. Rameau, *Une Colonie Féodale, 1*, 110, cites a memoir of Father Ignace de Senlis to this effect.

les habitans qui, faisoient [sic] bien cent cinquante . . . ."[61] We can be satisfied that at least two to three hundred folk, half of them in settled families, lived in the Port Royal area at the time of its capture in 1654 (see Figure 4.3).

ORIGINS OF THE SETTLERS — The "Frenchness" of Port Royal is widely believed to have been diluted by some carryover of Scots. Acadian names claimed to be so derived include Peselet or Pesely (from Paisley), Pitre (from Peter or Peters), Caissy or Caisse (from Kessey or Casey), Colleson or Coleson, and Melanson.[62] The doubts that have been raised on this question are of little importance here for there is no evidence of any significant cultural inheritance. Presumably the core of the settlement in Port Royal in the 1650's was composed of those who had come out with Razilly in 1632 and who have long been believed to have been drawn largely from Touraine and Britanny.[63]

In speculation on the localities of origin of the Acadians in France there has been little advance beyond Sulte's conclusion of 1905 that ". . . their dialect would indicate their place of origin to be in the neighborhood of the Bay of Biscay and the mouth of the River Loire,"[64] except for the recent research of Geneviève Massignon[65] which implies that the 1632 settlers and perhaps others introduced by d'Aulnay before mid-century, may have come chiefly from the Loudunais area in northeastern Poitou (the northern part of the present Département of Vienne). The discussion of origins is amplified in the Appendix, but the significance of Massignon's conclusions, if we accept them, is that few of the earliest settlers would have come from the vicinities where dyking of tidal marshes, recently introduced from the Netherlands, was in progress at the time they left France. Yet we may also suppose that the men even of inland Poitou, perhaps occasionally following river tributaries flowing into the Loire and so to Nantes and the sea, may well have known of such activity along the coasts and estuaries

61. Denys, *Description*, p. 466.
62. This list is given by Lauvrière, *La Tragédie, 1,* 63. Couillard-Després, "Les Gouverneurs," p. 234*n*, argues against the probability that most are, in fact, Scottish names. His arguments against Colleson are convincing and he insists that Pitre and Caisse are "noms bien français." Moreover Melanson may have arrived with the Sedgwick expedition of 1654. Currently, scholars are inclined to accept the possibility only of Caisse (Kessey or Casey), presumably ultimately of Irish origin.
63. Lauvrière, *La Tragédie, 1,* 63.
64. Benjamin Sulte, "Origin of the French Canadians" (1906), p. 99.
65. Massignon, *Les Parlers Français, 1.*

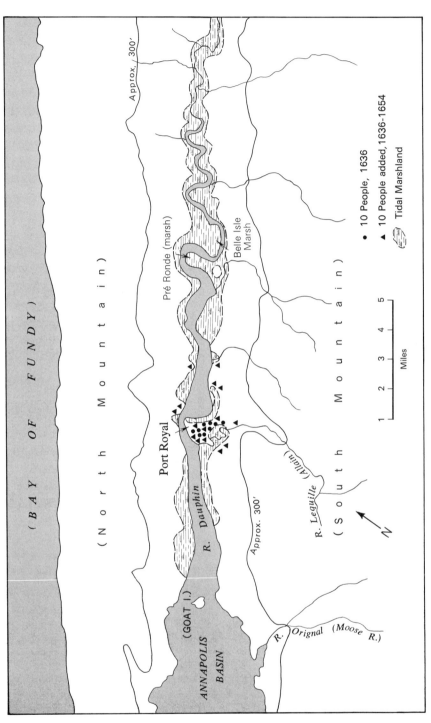

Fig. 4.3 Port Royal Basin and Valley: Population, 1636–1654.

Legend:

• 10 People, 1636
▲ 10 People added, 1636–1654
Tidal Marshland

Map by the University of Wisconsin Cartographic Laboratory

from the Loire to the Gironde.[66] Certainly dyking got under way in the basin near the mouth of the Dauphin (Annapolis) River within the first decade or two after d'Aulnay's move to Port Royal.

AGRICULTURE AND HOUSING — D'Aulnay began at Port Royal with advantages for the success of settlement not heretofore present. Farming activity of one kind or another had been under way in the area for nearly three decades and his own people had had at least three years of acclimatization to Nova Scotia in their prior stay at La Have. D'Aulnay not only settled his people on individual allotments on which they could contemplate some security of future, but developed two large farms for his own use worked by his own engagés. He may have restored Poutrincourt's old mill which was on the Rivière Allain, near present Lequille and near his new headquarters on the present site of Annapolis (see Plate 4).[67]

Denys, who had visited (indeed, been a prisoner in) Port Royal in 1653, wrote, in the next decade, of his memories of the settlement:

There are numbers of meadows on both shores, and two islands which possess meadows, [and] which are three or four leagues from the fort in ascending. There is a great extent of meadows which the sea used to cover, and which the Sieur d'Aunay had drained. It bears now fine and good wheat, and since the English have been masters of the country [the English took over Port Royal in August 1654], the residents who were lodged near the fort have for the most part abandoned their houses and have gone to settle on the upper part of the river. They have made their clearings below and above this great meadow, which belongs at present to Madame de La Tour. There they have again drained other lands which bear wheat in much greater abundance than those which they cultivated round the fort, good though those were. All the in-

66. In the reign of Louis XIII (1610–1643) extensive reclamation of tidal marshlands by dyking had taken place near La Rochelle and in Saintonge and Poitou, under the supervision of Dutch engineers. Many of the Razilly group (or others) might have been familiar with the techniques. See Carl Schott, *Die Kanadischen Marschen* (1955), p. 28.

67. This site was on the south side of the Annapolis River, on a peninsula formed by the last bend of its channel before it reaches the open basin. (The de Monts establishment of 1605 had been on the north shore of the basin, opposite Goat Island, some six or seven miles to the west. See Lescarbot, *History of New France*, pp. 280–81. The Scottish settlement appears to have been adjacent to it.) The new location was bounded on the south by the marshy flood plain of the meandering Allain River, with a "neck" less than a mile wide which rises to an elevation allowing extensive prospects both down the basin and up the river. It was an ideal headquarters site and it was here that d'Aulnay's and subsequent forts were built and the first nucleated settlement slowly developed. See Plate 4.

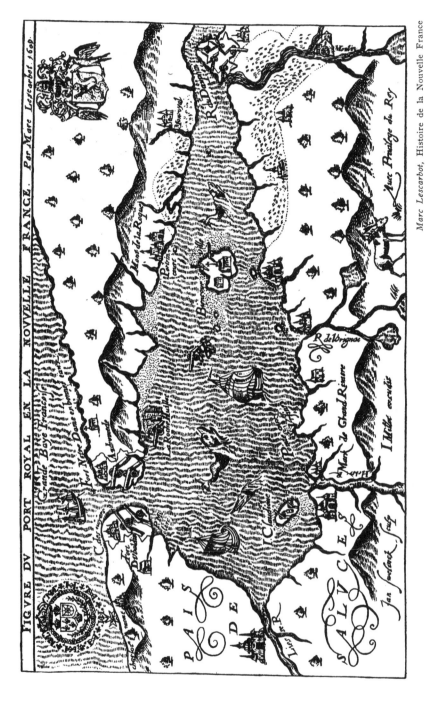

Marc Lescarbot, Histoire de la Nouvelle France

4 Lescarbot's Map of Port Royal, 1609

habitants there are the ones whom Monsieur le Commandeur de Razilly had brought from France to La Haive; since that time they have multiplied much at Port Royal, where they have a great number of cattle and swine.[68]

We are poorly informed on the kind and conditions of buildings, furnishings, agricultural implements, crops, dykes, etc., for this period. Rameau describes the houses, but his prefatory phrase, "sans doute," and his obvious dependence on later observers (as Saccardy, Dièreville, and others) make one wonder if, indeed, he had the evidence he does not cite. Nevertheless, he says:

The houses were doubtless very rough: many were built of tree trunks piled one on another without even being squared; some were based on heavy piles, driven in the ground, which were interlaced with branches and then plastered with mud. The better built ones, and the manor house [of d'Aulnay] itself, were made of great roughhewn beams laid, one on the other, in tiers [assemblées par les extrémites]. This construction is still called *pièces sur pièces*.[69]

He may well have been intending to describe the horizontal log cabin which many have assumed had not even reached New England, from its alleged introduction to the New World along the Delaware River, until long after this. He could have been wrong about the full log-cabin technique with interlocking corners, but there is no doubt of the *pièces sur pièces* (usually "pièce-sur-pièce") construction, and the question remains whether, unlike seventeenth-century New Englanders, the Acadians employed it widely.[70] Perhaps usually in Acadia, as in Canada, the horizontal logs of the walls abutted on vertical corner posts.

68. Denys, *Description*, pp. 123–24.

69. Rameau, *Une Colonie Féodale, 1*, 95. My translation.

70. Rameau may have been a victim of one aspect of the "log cabin myth" widely accepted in American historiography. H. R. Shurtleff, discussing the myth, hypothesized that this form of building originated with Swedo-Finns on the Delaware River before the middle of the seventeenth century, diffusing thence, like ripples on a pond, but not reaching Maritime Canada until the late eighteenth century. *The Log Cabin Myth* (1939). Shurtleff, however, did not face the problem of the many evidences of *pièce-sur-pièce* construction; Champlain, for example, had used the technique in the "habitation" at Port Royal and in Quebec before the Swedes had even heard of the Delaware. Although there has been no adequate discussion, or indeed investigation, of the construction of Acadian houses in the 17th and early 18th centuries, and we are yet without satisfactory evidence either documentary or archeological, Marius Barbeau's study, "Types des maisons canadiennes" (1941), is most suggestive by analogy. He accepts the Shurtleff hypothesis that the round-log cabin with interlocking ends ("battisses avec encoigners en queue-d'aronde [dovetailed] ou en têtes de chien") remained unknown among *canadien* colonists, even in Louisiana or Missouri, until well into the 18th century. He demonstrates quite effectively that the standard *canadien* style consisted of

Summary

The Razilly settlement is interesting as something of an anomaly in that it actually did plant a lasting agricultural population, if only by accident. The conditions of grants of territories and trading or fishing privileges usually involved commitments to bring out settlers in specified numbers, within specified periods. But these were blandly and, for the most part, completely ignored in Acadia. The clauses in the charters represented lip service to colonizing theory, but government officials, like the grantees themselves, were interested in exploitative profits, missionary enterprises, or tactical and strategic military considerations, and the colonization motif tended to be conveniently overlooked. Something has been made of the "feudal" nature of the seigneurial grant to Razilly, and its inheritance by d'Aulnay, as the transference of an Old World system to Port Royal.[71] But it has been argued that this is a misinterpretation even for New France: "A society in which everyone enjoys equal protection from the state, and in which everyone is on the same footing with regard to public duties is not feudal."[72]

In any event, after 1654 Acadia never had even whatever degree of institutionalization was known in New France; the relation between seigneur and habitant was loose and fluid and one would have been hard put to it to have recognized anything like our traditional conception of seigneurial forms and practices in any of the later Acadian settlements. It may be that the form had some substance at La Have and in Chapters 5 and 6 we shall see that there was a slight carry-over

---

squared logs or beams or thick planks (*le colombage*) set one on another (clearly. *pièce-sur-pièce*), horizontally between posts which were sunk in the ground or erected on a foundation of logs or stone. The interstices were stuffed with moss, grass, or clay or with lime mortar perhaps mixed with oat straw or hair. The inside might be boarded or plastered; the outside covered with shingles, boards, or bark. Whether the standard *canadien* plan, of a house with two rooms, each with a fireplace on the end walls, with doors front and rear centered on the long walls and a hall running between, separating the rooms was also used in Acadia is likewise uncertain. The few maps indicating farm buildings (as in large scale plans of the Port Royal area in the early eighteenth century), suggest many small outbuildings (in the same style?) rather than single large barns of the American type.

71. See esp. Rameau, *Une Colonie Féodale*, and Lauvrière, *La Tragédie*.

72. Marcel Trudel, *The Seigneurial Regime* (1956), p. 14. This theme has been elaborated in R. C. Harris, *The Seigneurial System in Early Canada* (1966).

to the later Acadian settlements, but we have very little evidence on which to go.

After the takeover of 1654 the English effectively controlled the ports and posts on the Maine coast and the Fundy shores (and their immediate hinterlands) until 1670. The sovereignty of France in the area, indeed, was recognized by 1667 in the Treaty of Breda, but Sir Thomas Temple, who had taken over the governorship by Commonwealth authority in 1657 (a position renewed or confirmed after the Restoration in 1662),[73] managed to delay the effective transfer of control until the end of the decade. Temple also made some attempt to extend his authority to the Atlantic coast. In 1658 he dispossessed a group of Le Borgne's men at La Have; in 1664 he forced out some French fishermen at Port Rossignol and established himself there and at Mirligueche (Lunenburg).

Meanwhile Emmanuel Le Borgne, who laid claim to all the inherited d'Aulnay rights and disputed the claims of both La Tour and Denys, was engaged in a desperate struggle to hold out and hang on. In 1654 he had to face the fact of Denys' unquestionable royal grant to the Gulf of St. Lawrence area and turned over the posts at St. Peters and Nipisiguit to him. In 1667, with the return of French sovereignty, his son and heir, Alexandre Le Borgne de Belle-Isle was named by the home authorities as governor from Canso or Baie Verte to New England, assuming all of La Tour's rights, but he had rather poor luck in the face of English aggressiveness. However there is some indication that he had continued to collect and ship large quantities of furs from the peninsula even during the interregnum.[74]

Denys, so unfortunate in his earlier ventures, was left relatively undisturbed in the Gulf by the English, and engaged variously in a

73. Temple had a Cromwellian grant of "Acadia" shared by La Tour and William Crowne; the patent is printed in Beamish Murdoch, *A History of Nova-Scotia, or Acadie* (1865–67), *1*, 138. The restoration confirmation is discussed in *ibid.*, p. 134 and in Couillard-Després, "Les Gouverneurs," p. 256.

74. W. A. Calnek *History of the County of Annapolis* (1897), p. 31, gives a figure of 387.000 livres worth of furs shipped by Belle-Isle in 1660. No evidence in support is presented. although he refers to a letter of La Verdure to the daughter of d'Aulnay in that year which I have not been able to locate.

little fishing, a little farming, a little trading with the Indians, and even the making of some timber. About 1660 he established a post at what is now Guysborough town at the head of Chedabucto Bay. In 1664, part of his "dominions" (Prince Edward Island and the Magdalen Islands of today) were granted to one Sieur Doublet but neither he nor Denys exploited them. In 1667 Denys was dispossessed at Chedabucto by another trader, the Sieur de La Giraudière, who earlier had established himself on the St. Mary's River near Sherbrooke. Later, Denys was burned out at his St. Peters establishment and the double loss forced him into virtual retirement at Nipisiguit. He appears to have been in France when the heart of Acadia, in the Bay of Fundy, was restored to French control.

We know that in 1670, when Hector d'Andigné de Grandfontaine accepted the surrender of the English forts at Jemseg, on the Saint John River, and at Port Royal, and somewhat later in the Cape Sable area, there was a substantially larger number of settlers up the Port Royal River above the fort than there had been sixteen years earlier; in Acadian terms almost a generation had grown up. Although we may accept Denys' belief that they gave up their homes near the fort to move away from immediate English surveillance, the direction of the move was a natural one if they were seeking new marshlands and there is no evidence that the English paid much attention to them. Certainly their new masters, whether from New or old England, had not the slightest interest in settling or actively developing the part of Acadia they controlled; their interest was solely in furs and in the control of Indian attacks on New England, and the Acadians at least were protected from attacks from that area. Documentation on the conditions of settlement and agriculture is almost completely lacking. It has been inferred that after 1654 many of the French settlers moved on to Quebec or returned to France. For those who remained (and they were, we think, the majority), we have to assume the gradual but inexorable increase of numbers and expansion of agriculture, the planting and reaping of grain, peas, flax, and vegetable crops, and the tending of sheep, swine and cattle. If the period is largely a *tabula rasa* in the historical record, it was nevertheless one of consolidation and expansion of this nucleus of the Acadian population.

5

The Acadian Expansion, 1670-1710

🌿

By 1670 a settled and thoroughly acclimated people had become firmly established at Port Royal. Most of them had been born in the country; almost all of the men and women had had a generation of experience with farming it and with the special problems of dyking and using the tidal marshlands. In the succeeding four decades offshoot colonies took root in the two other major Acadian settlement areas to the north and east, each destined to surpass the hearth area in population and importance by the middle of the eighteenth century.

The Minas settlement expanded from its initial foothold between the mouths of the Rivière St-Antoine (i.e., Rivière des Habitants or present Cornwallis River) and the Gaspereau River, where the buildings of those farming the Grand Pré marsh were to assume an almost village-like density, north across the broad mouth of the great valley with its three other streams (the Canard, Petit Habitant, and Pereau) to the foot of North Mountain (see Figure 5.9). To the south and east it pushed far up the Pisiquid (Avon) estuary and deep into Cobequid Bay.

In Chignecto Bay, settlement began at Beaubassin, just north of Cumberland Basin along the lower Missaguash. Thence there were many later extensions: up the Missaguash itself, the La Planche, the Hébert and Maccan rivers and on the edges of the "champs élysées,"

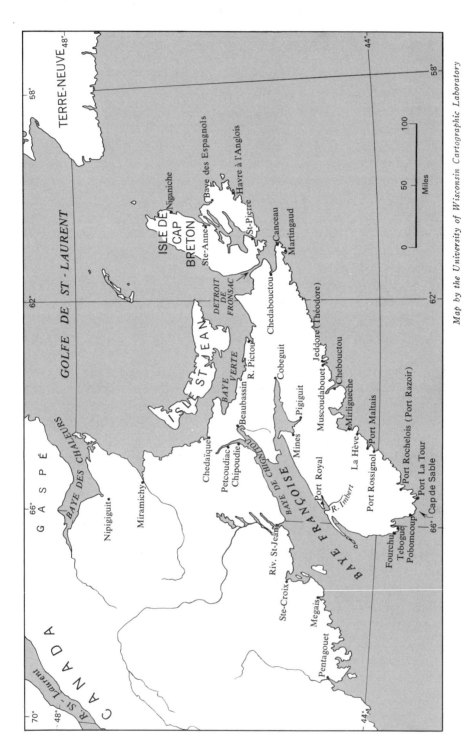

Fig. 5.1 Acadia: 1670–1710, Contemporary Place Names.

Map by the *University of Wisconsin Cartographic Laboratory*

the great marsh of the Minudie peninsula; up the Aulac and Tantramar through the largest marsh of all and on its western margins; and
even out of Cumberland Basin around Cape Maringouin into Chignecto's other head, Shepody, Bay, where Acadians were to exploit the tidal
marshes of the Shepody, Petitcodiac, and Memramcook rivers.

This steady progress of settlement was achieved despite the fact that
fighting between the representatives of the French (largely organized
and directed from Quebec) and of the English (chiefly based on Boston) was almost continuous. The French held the advantage on land on
the northern frontiers of New England with the effective work of
Canadian *capitaines des sauvages* and their Indian allies; the English
more often than not controlled the seaways, and attacked the coastal
establishments and settlements almost at will. Apart from references to
the fur trade, this activity dominates the documentary record, and
would suggest that the peaceful occupations of agriculture, fishing,
lumbering, and trade were of relatively minor importance. Yet, in these
years, hundreds of people lived in Acadia, steadily expanded their
numbers, raised their crops and animals, sold their surpluses (usually
to New England) in return for much needed hardware and other
sundries, and, in fact, became the only significant, largely self-reliant,
settlement east of New Hampshire and Canada in North America in
the later seventeenth century.

A CROWN COLONY: THE ACADIAN SECTOR OF NEW FRANCE

With the recognition of French sovereignty in 1667 in the Treaty of
Breda, the English agreed to leave, although Temple managed to delay
the formal takeover until 1670.[1] Then Hector d'Andigné de Grandfontaine assumed the governorship for France, establishing his headquarters at Pentagouet on the Penobscot rather than at Port Royal. In the
subsequent forty years there were at least seven other fully authorized

1. Sir Thomas Temple was the heir to the claims of the Alexanders. With
William Crowne and Charles de La Tour (who had turned his coat for the
purpose), the Commonwealth granted him the government and monopoly of trade
in the area after Robert Sedgwick's expedition had captured the forts on both
shores of the Bay of Fundy. La Tour then made an arrangement to occupy and
exploit the Cape Sable area. The rest was under strictly English control, more or
less *de jure* until 1667 and *de facto* until 1770.

governors and several deputy charges d'affaires who filled in at intervals: these were Hector d'Andigné de Grandfontaine (1670–73);
Jacques de Chambly (1673–78), captured by Dutch pirates in 1674;
Pierre de Joybert de Soulanges et de Marson (1677–78), to resume
control; Michel Leneuf de La Vallière (1678–84); François-Marie
Perrot (1684–87); Louis-Alexandre des Friches de Meneval
(1687–90); Joseph Robinau de Villebon (1691–1700); Sébastien de
Villieu (1700–1701), administrator; Jacques-François de Brouillan
(1701–1704); Simon-Pierre Denys de Bonaventure (1704–1706); and
Daniel d'Auger de Subercase (1706–1710), who made the final surrender to the English in 1710.[2] More often than not their headquarters
were elsewhere than at Port Royal: on the Penobscot or the Saint John
or, in the case of La Vallière, at Beaubassin.

Conflict with the English

There were repeated raids on the Acadian settlements throughout
this period by ships from New England, stimulated by or serving as
stimuli for the almost continuous French and Indian raids, by land, on
the outlying New England settlements. Dutch attackers on the continental shores in the 1670's carried off Chambly. Although the Treaty
of Whitehall of 1686 solemnly declared that even if England and
France were at war in Europe "their colonies in America shall continue
in peace and neutrality," this declaration was ignored, if, indeed, it was
widely known of across the Atlantic.

Sir William Phips forced the surrender of Port Royal in 1690 and
did much damage to the settlement; "pirates" did an even more thorough job a few months later, virtually wiping out the village; and
Benjamin Church wreaked heavy damage in Chignecto in 1696 and
both there and at Minas in 1704.[3] However, these forays did not lead to

2. Azarie Couillard-Després, "Les Gouverneurs de l'Acadie sous le régime français, 1600–1710" (1939).

3. Beamish Murdoch, *A History of Nova-Scotia, or Acadie,* (1865–67), *1,* 195,
paraphrases P.-F.-X. de Charlevoix, *Histoire et description générale de la Nouvelle
France* (1744), *3,* 101–8, in reporting the 1690 incident. Murdoch refers to a
mémoire of February 5, 1691, in which it is said that twenty-eight houses were
burnt with the church, but that the mills and farms further up the river were
spared. Later in the same year two English pirates burned some more houses and
killed some residents as well as cattle.
Some accounts of the Church expeditions are given in [Benjamin] Church, *The
History of the Great Indian War* . . . (1716 and many later editions). The details

English occupation and there were two more abortive attacks on Port Royal by the English after 1700. Port Royal finally fell to Nicholson's forces in 1710, after which it was never again under French control.

After 1690, when Phips carried off Meneval as a prisoner, the English claimed sovereignty of the area, although they left no garrison at Port Royal, and the government of Acadia, under Villebon, kept its headquarters on the Saint John River. Only in 1700 was Port Royal reestablished as the *de facto* capital of Acadia. During this last decade of the century, as between 1654 and 1670 and at many other times, the settlers at Port Royal were without any effective local government.[4] Except during La Vallière's regime, when the operative headquarters of the colony was at Beaubassin, the outlying settlements there and at Minas had even less contact with government.

Seigneuries in Acadia

Many of the interpreters of Acadia and the Acadians have seen the period from 1670 to 1710 as one marking the firm establishment of French institutions among the Fundy settlements. Often it has been assumed that this was in a strongly feudal or, at least, seigneurial framework. That assumption deserves some attention here.

Every Frenchman of the seventeenth century, at least every French-

---

may be unreliable. Of the 1696 expedition it was recorded that the people of Beaubassin "were troubled to see their cattle, sheep, hogs and dogs lying dead about their houses, chopped and hacked with hatchets." Rev. ed. (1845), p. 232. Of the 1704 attack on Minas, "the Colonel [Benjamin Church] gave orders to his men, to dig down the dams, and let the tide in, to destroy all their corn . . . ." *Ibid.*, p. 275. At Chignecto, again, in the same year, he "did them what spoil he could." *Ibid.*, p. 282. Benjamin Church is supposed to have dictated or supplied the basis of this from memory.

4. Exception has been taken to this viewpoint. It is true that under Grandfontaine, Alexandre Le Borgne de Belle-Isle (son of d'Aulnay's creditor Emmanuel and inheritor of the latter's rights, claims, and pretensions) was appointed deputy governor of Port Royal. Earlier, in 1654 or shortly thereafter, a sort of council of the inhabitants, with one Guillaume Trahan as leader, had been set up by the English. No doubt the priests performed a major role. In the period before 1710, forty to fifty different priests and missionaries had been present in Acadia at one time or another and there were regular parish priests in Port Royal from 1676, in Grand Pré from 1687, and at Beaubassin from 1686. While French authorities effectively controlled Port Royal there were, of course, many *notaires, greffiers,* or *procureurs du roi* who filled out the thin cadres of government, and men with such experience helped the priests and the few with seigneurial pretensions to solve problems when formal governmental machinery was absent.

man north of the Roman Law area, must have believed that the only way to hold land was, as always, from a lord, a seigneur, who held it in turn from the king. There is no reason to suppose that this was not true of the Acadian emigrés from France. With whatever freedom they took land in the Port Royal area, or moved to the new lands to the north, on which they settled and farmed, they must still have assumed always that their use of it was, somehow, by way of concession from some individual or institution who, or which, in turn, held it from the crown.

J. B. Brebner has observed that "the Canadian seigneuries had a way of being magnificent on paper and somewhat unimposing in fact. The Acadian seigneuries were equally vast and infinitely less practical."[5] Seigneurial grants in the "greater Acadian" area may have been intended to be of the same general kind as those in Canada but the majority of the grants made remained paper entities and, of those which had more or less reality, we are poorly informed about their actual operation, the payment of dues of various kinds, the geographical limits of the individual *rotures* or seigneurial "domains," and the processes of granting, inheriting, or transferring the rights to either. Indeed there are serious doubts as to whether understanding of them is advanced by thinking of them as seigneuries of the Canadian type.[6]

Grants that would appear to have had essentially a "seigneurial" character, but perhaps not held fully *en seigneurie* in the technical sense that these words were to have in later years, included those to de Monts, Poutrincourt, the Marquise de Guercheville, Denys, and Razilly, which have been described in Chapter 4. Some of the commissions to La Tour also would seem to have given him similar rights at one place or another. From these grants stemmed the major conflicts in claims to territory later in the century between the heirs, associates, and creditors of one or another of these people. Grants were poorly described and often overlapped, and prior grants were rarely extin-

5. J. B. Brebner, *New England's Outpost: Acadia before the Conquest of Canada* (1927), p. 43.

6. Despite a substantial literature on the seigneuries of Canada, it is doubtful if we have understood them very well in economic and demographic terms. The most complete recent discussion of them, clarifying many of these problems from the point of view of an historical geographer, is in R. C. Harris, *The Seigneurial System in Early Canada: A Geographical Study* (1966). On the seigneuries and seigneurial grants see W. F. Ganong, "A Monograph of the Origins of Settlements in the Province of New Brunswick" (1904), pp. 32–33; Brebner, *New England's Outpost*, p. 40*n*; and "Les Seigneuries de l'ancienne Acadie," ed. Placide Gaudet (1927), p. 343. Ten of the seigneurial grants from 1632 to 1693 are copied in AC, M-*371*.

guished before new ones involving the same territory were made. Much of the confusion must have been based on ignorance of the fundamental place geography of the area as, for example, when d'Aulnay was given the north, or fur-trading, coast of the Bay of Fundy but not the mouth of its principal river, the Saint John, which was granted to La Tour, while at the same time, La Tour was granted most of the coasts of peninsular Nova Scotia but not its principal settlement, Port Royal, which was d'Aulnay's headquarters. As has been noted above, Razilly's settlement at La Have was perhaps the first of the Acadian lodgements to be organized along seigneurial lines and, albeit in a very faint and approximate fashion, this pattern was continued in the Port Royal area and extended to Minas and Pisiquid. In a very loose and skeletal way, such forms were also in existence at later periods at Cobequid and in the dyked marshlands tributary to Chignecto Bay.

The Acadians appear to have treated the system, and the obligations it imposed on the individual land holder or farmer, in a very cavalier fashion. Few would have challenged the right of someone to ask for those dues and duties traditional in the *coûtume de Paris* (codification of customary law) or one of the other *coûtumes* of northern France. But the amount of the dues, the ways of performing the duties, and the identity of the seigneur were often so vaguely established or understood, and the *acadiens* shared so fully the litigiousness of the *canadiens* and the latter's unwillingness to pay anyone anything but token amounts except under heavy pressure, that the burdens of the system did not rest heavily upon them and the nominal or claimant seigneurs usually derived very little from the agricultural use of the land. For almost all practical purposes the *censitaires* of the Acadian seigneurs might as well have been freeholders with nominal quitrents or land taxes.

The precise number of seigneurial grants made in greater Acadia is uncertain and likely to remain so. J.-E. Roy attempted a map of them in 1894[7] in which he located some fifty-five between Gaspé and the Penobscot River in Maine, including all of present New Brunswick and peninsular Nova Scotia and even one grant in Isle St-Jean. Figure

7. "Carte de l'Acadie et d'une partie de la Nouvelle France, sur laquelle sont marquée les anciens noms des lieux et les divisions en seigneuries . . . jusqu'en 1703 pour accompagner une étude lué dévant la Société Royale du Canada, Mai, 1894." Apparently a map showing the boundaries of the Acadian seigneuries in 1700 was prepared in Acadia and sent to Versailles but no trace of it has turned up. See *Bulletin des Recherches Historiques, 33* (1927), 345–46.

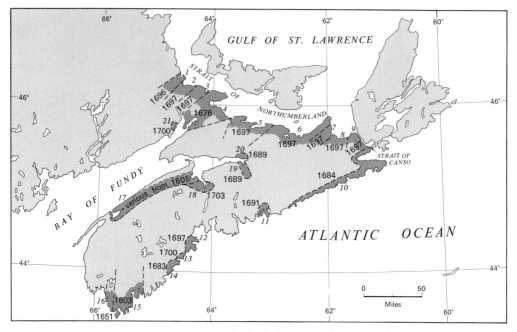

Fig. 5.2   The Acadian Lands: Seigneurial and Territorial Grants in the Chignecto Region and Peninsular Nova Scotia. 1. Cocagne River area to Sieur Duplessis. 2. Linoville to Mathieu Martin de Lino. 3. St-Paul (or Dupuy) to Sieur Paul Dupuy. 4. Chignecto (or Beaubassin) to Michel Leneuf, Sieur de La Vallière. 5. Tilly (or Tatamagouche) to Sieur Le Gardeur. 6. Boisselery (or Cap St-Louis) to Sieur de La Boissellery Noël (there may have been an earlier grant in 1690). 7. Articogneth (or Antigonish?) to Charles Denys de Vitre. 8. D'Outlas (or Antigonish) to Sieur d'Outlas. 9. De Cottentré to Marc-Antoine, Sieur de Cottentré. 10. [Grant, seigneurie?] to Bergier, Gauthier, et al. 11. Mouscoudabouet to Mathieu Des Goutins. 12. Mirligueche (or Minitiguich or De Randin?) to Hugues Randin (the date may be 1697). 13. Port Maltais (or Baronnie de Beauville) to Baron de Beauville. (Regranted in 1707 to M. de Beauharnois.) 14. Port Rossignol [grant, seigneurie?] to Aubert de La Chesnaye. (This may be a confusion with another seigneurie in present New Brunswick.) 15. Cape Sable [grant, seigneurie?] claimed by La Tour heirs from several grants beginning with first grants to De Monts and Poutrincourt. 16. Pobomcoup (Baronnie de P.) to Mius d'Entremont, a subgrant from Charles La Tour. The precise date is uncertain, but it may have been in the early 1650's. 17. Port Royal and Minas. The various claims of heirs of the La Tours, Mme. D'Aulnay-Charnisay, and Emmanuel Le Borgne were not consolidated until after 1713. There were a number of smaller subgrants or conflicting grants (e.g. Granville Peninsula, see Fig. 4.2, to M. Des Goutins in 1695. 18. Pigiguit (or Pisiquid) to heirs of Charles La Tour. The boundaries would seem to have excluded lands east of the Pisiquid (present Avon) River, but dues were claimed on the Quennetcou (Kennetcook) and Ste-Croix rivers. 19. Chicabenacady (or St-Joseph) to Demoiselle Marie-Joseph Leneuf (daughter of the Sieur de La Vallière of Beaubassin). The date is uncertain. 20. Ouëcobeguy (or St-Mathieu) to Mathieu Martin of Port Royal. 21. Chipoudy to Sieur de Villieu (son-in-law of the Sieur de La Vallière).

5.2 is an attempt to show locations, dates of concession, and approximate boundaries as largely as possible from the original wording of the grants in the area of the major Acadian settlements and throughout the peninsula of Nova Scotia.[8]

The first six on Roy's map were in present Gaspé Peninsula, north of Chaleur Bay. From that bay (or rather from the Restigouche River at its head) the shore of the Gulf was granted in almost continuous series (one gap) to the Strait of Canso. Thence along the south shore of the peninsula and around the Bay of Fundy the grants are territorially discontinuous. Not shown are a large number of similar grants along both sides of the Saint John River from its mouth to latitude 47° N. and along the New Brunswick and Maine coasts as far to the west as the Penobscot. Figure 5.2 has made some changes in Roy's map based on other evidence or a reinterpretation of the documents he used.

It will be noted that, with one exception, the grants along the Strait of Northumberland were made in 1696 and 1697, apparently as part of a vigorous royal policy of the time to achieve more rapid progress in economic development. Indeed, if we set aside the one at the mouth of the Cocagne River (the first estuary north of Shediac) all but that of Chignecto, or Beaubassin, were made in 1697, but there is no evidence that any of the 1697 grants developed beyond the paper stage. There were Acadian settlers in the first half of the eighteenth century at Tatamagouche (and possibly briefly at present Pugwash and Wallace as well), and there is some evidence of contemporaneous settlement in the four grants to the east: in Boisselery, or Cap St-Louis (around Pictou), Articogneth, d'Outlas, and de Cottentré (in order, from west to east, in the area of present Antigonish County) (Figure 5.2, numbers 6, 7, 8, and 9). But these settlements were late, associated with illegal trade with Cape Breton or Isle St-Jean, or with refugees from Chignecto or the Minas Basin, and apparently the settlers were ignorant of the seigneurial grants even if the new British government would have recognized them. Except for La Vallière's establishment at Beaubassin the grants along the Strait of Northumberland were of no significance to the changing settlement geography.

8. The identification of individual grants and the basis for locating them are to be found chiefly in Pierre-Georges Roy, *Inventaire des concessions en fief et seigneurie, fois et hommages, et aveux et dénombrements, conservés aux archives de la province de Québec* (1927–29), *1–6*, although in Figure 5.2 some other sources, including the notes on the 1894 map of J.-Edmond Roy, have been used.

Ignoring the Bergier-Gauthier group (Figure 5.2, number 10) for the moment, there were three other grants on the south coast for which I can find documentary evidence: Mouscoudabouet (Musquodoboit) to Mathieu Des Goutins in 1691, Minitiguich (probably Mirligueche) to Hugues Randin in 1697, and Port Maltais (Port Medway) to Baron de Beauville in 1700 (and to M. de Beauharnois in 1707?). The 1894 Roy map indicates one at Port Rossignol (Liverpool), granted to Aubert de La Chesnaye in 1683, but this probably is a misinterpretation. The seigneurial status of the La Have area at this time is obscure.

The La Tour claims around the Cape Sable area, including their sub-grant to the d'Entremonts at Pobomcoup (Pubnico), do not appear to have been challenged despite the dubious or contested status of the other lands claimed by the family heirs. Passing over the lands of Port Royal and Minas proper (the Cornwallis end of the present Annapolis-Cornwallis Valley) three grants apparently were made elsewhere in Minas Basin. The first, on the west shore of the Avon River and abutting Minas proper on the south, is given on Roy's map as "to the La Tour heirs in 1703." Along the Shubenacadie River, Marie Leneuf (of the Leneuf de La Vallière family) had been given a grant in 1689, in the same year in which Mathieu Martin received his at the head of Cobequid Bay, in the present Truro area and northwest (Figure 5.2, numbers 18, 19, and 20).

Nothing apparently remained in our area of interest of the rights granted to Nicolas Denys along the shores of the Gulf in earlier decades. Even the French sovereignty over Cape Breton Island was dubious and when the French established themselves there in the eighteenth century the official policy was against seigneurial grants (although essentially similar concessions were made, as in the case of Isle Madame and the island between the Great and Little Bras d'Or channels to the Sieur de La Boularderie). The concessions to the Bergier-Gauthier group, west from Chedabucto and Canso, do not appear to have been in the usual seigneurial form. The western boundary of the grant in the "Bay of Islands" region was vague; it could have been anywhere between Ship Harbour and Sheet Harbour.

The degrees of reality in the seigneurial forms and procedures, such as they were, were largely restricted to the settled areas of Port Royal and its river, Minas, Beaubassin, and, to some degree perhaps, in the Pisiquid, Cobequid, and Pubnico areas. These were, of course, the only agricultural settlements. It is probable that the other seigneurs had been more interested in fish or fur than in agricultural lands in any event. In the central areas the La Tour-d'Aulnay-Belle-Isle heirs contested with each other for *cens et rentes*[9] and continued to make some small collections well into the eighteenth century under British rule. The whole system officially came to an end, in British eyes, when one of the heirs, Agathe de La Tour (who had married one Campbell, an officer of the Annapolis Royal garrison and had carried on a long and unremitting campaign for her "rights"), was, in 1733, granted a substantial "composition" of £2,000 by the British government.[10] Since Charles de La Tour had married Mme. d'Aulnay and had a second family by her, and one of his daughters had married Alexandre Le Borgne de Belle-Isle (son of Emmanuel Le Borgne the original d'Aulnay creditor who had come out in the 1650's, and who surrendered Port Royal to the English in 1654), and there was much subsequent intermarriage, the seigneurial inheritance was rather complicated. Two of the young d'Entremonts also married La Tour girls. Probably much of the Port Royal settlement and Minas proper was tacitly recognized as "belonging to" Belle-Isle, although Pisiquid was not, and Belle-Isle was popularly known as the "Seigneur of Port Royal."[11]

There are many references in the documents to confirm this position or role of Belle-Isle. An Act of Concession by him to one Pierre Martin in 1679 of land bounded "à l'est, par la grande prairie, à l'ouest, par le ruisseau Domanchin [i.e., probably, du Moulin], au midi, par la rivière Dauphin, et au nord, par la montagne" asked, for *cens et rentes, a* penny, a capon, and one bushel of oats per year.[12] A letter of Meneval of November 7, 1689, makes clear that Belle-Isle was recognized officially as having seigneurial title to most, but not all, of the Port

9. A *cens* was a token payment always levied on *rotures* (the ultimate divisions of land granted by a seigneur or sub-seigneur) and paid by the *censitaire* as a legal or traditional recognition of the relationship. In a sense it was rather like a fee for a license or document of possession. A *rente* carried the English connotation of rent, could be much more onerous, and provided the chief source of a seigneur's revenue if he could collect it.

10. For further discussion of the sources on this case see Chapter 6, p. 197, note 22.

11. There is a tendency to confuse the Le Borgnes, *fils et père*. "Belle-Isle" should be used only for the son, who adopted the title.

12. This document is printed in François-Edmé Rameau de Saint-Père, *Une Colonie Féodale en Amérique: l'Acadie (1604–1881), 2,* (1889), 318.

Royal lands.[13] There are many similar references to La Vallière at Beaubassin as he conceded lands and collected, or tried to collect, his dues, and attempted to evict squatters whom he did not want, or who would not acknowledge his seigneurial rights.

The situation of seigneurial grants in Acadia at the end of the seventeenth century may be summed up best in the instructions given to the Sieur de Fontenu, Commissaire Ordinaire de la Marine, on his departure for Acadia in 1699. It was pointed out to him that Acadia had been divided in the past into a great many grants to individuals, some of whom were still resident and some of whom had left. (It might well have been added that some had never arrived.) Many disputes had arisen over the concessions which had hindered the development of the colony, and many were currently continuing in conflict with the king's desire to see Acadia firmly established. Even some with claims to the oldest titles to the lands were trading with the English or giving the latter permission to come to Acadia to trade themselves. Consequently the king had prepared a new ordinance (arrêt), which was attached. The ordinance was quite explicit that each grantee or title-holder, whether by inheritance, purchase, gift, sub-grant, or whatever, was directed to present his title, or authorized copies of his documents, on pain of revocation of the grants and redistribution of the lands. The date for compliance was later moved forward, and various other references to this flurry of interest appear in the documents for these years, but nothing constructive seems to have been accomplished.[14]

One may conclude that the Acadian seigneurs, such as they were, performed few if any of the traditional seigneurial functions, even in the emasculated form in which these were represented along the St. Lawrence. There is no record that they built mills, or bake-ovens, for example, or, indeed, did anything but act as landlords whose only role was that of rent-collector. On the other hand they do appear to have confined their demands largely to cens et rentes, with perhaps occasional lods et ventes (the seigneur's commission on the sale of a roture, in effect, a fine of alienation). We do not hear of corvée, of charges for fishing, for timber cutting, or for the use of a common.

One hesitates to be too certain about many of these things because we are so grievously lacking in evidence. Much of what paper record

13. *Ibid.*, pp. 326–31.
14. AC, B-*20*(2), 93, 95, 114; B-*22*(1), 144–45; B-*22*(2), 38, 84. These have been printed in Gaudet, "Seigneuries," pp. 343–47.

may have existed from the activities of the notaries at Port Royal, Beaubassin, and Minas has not been found and very likely has been destroyed. But we do suspect that official correspondence would have contained more hints if the "system" had been more elaborate or had had deeper impact on the people. Yet, flimsy and fragmentary as the institution undoubtedly was, it provided the only framework in which the Acadians could identify the land they held for right of occupation, for devisement to their heirs, or for sale and exchange, and, as such, it may have performed a vital service for the settlers.

POPULATION GROWTH AND LOCATION

Grandfontaine initiated the first census of the colony, which was completed in 1671.[15] In all, nearly 400 heads were counted of whom some 375 were in the territory that is now Nova Scotia. The census was most nearly complete in the Port Royal area; it clearly was both incomplete and ambiguous in the outlying settlements. Assuming an additional twenty to thirty settlers with year-round homes in various harbors on the southwestern and southern coasts (and even ignoring completely the large seasonal influx or fishermen and traders), there cannot have been many fewer than 500, of whom roughly 450 must have been on the present Nova Scotia peninsula.

The census disclosed that Port Royal's population had risen to 340 or 350 individuals in perhaps sixty-seven families, including roughly 65 men, 67 wives or widows, 125 sons, and 91 daughters. Their distribution is suggested in Figure 5.3. Perhaps 400 arpents were cultivated;

15. AC, G1-*466*, 2–13. Most of the censuses cited in this chapter are in AC, G1-*466:* for 1671, pp. 2–13; for 1686, pp. 14–57; for 1689, pp. 58–59; for 1693, pp. 60–102; for 1698, pp. 107–45; for 1701, p. 169; and for 1707, pp. 215–31. One for 1687/88, prepared by M. de Gargas, is published in *Acadiensia Nova, 1578–1779,* ed. W. I. Morse (1935), *1*, 144–55. Many of the others have been included, in full or partially, in published works; these sources are recorded in subsequent notes in this chapter.

The 1671 census is reproduced in detail in François-Edmé Rameau de Saint-Père, *La France aux colonies: études sur le developpement de la race française hors de l'Europe* (1859), pp. 124–27, with deviations. Unhappily, the nominal census has a number of duplications: married daughters and sons are counted in two households (their own and their parents'), or married daughters (whose husbands may be living elsewhere) are counted in both places. What appear to be precise numbers, therefore, are actually estimates in this and later censuses.

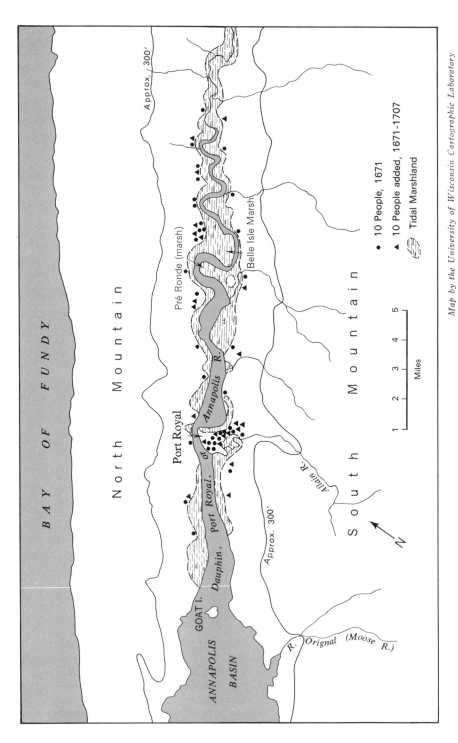

BAY OF FUNDY

North Mountain

Approx. 300'

Pré Ronde (marsh)

Belle Isle Marsh

Port Royal

Annapolis R.

of Port Royal,

Dauphin,

GOAT I.

ANNAPOLIS BASIN

R. Orignal (Moose R.)

Allain R.

South Mountain

Approx. 300'

N

Miles
1 2 3 4 5

• 10 People, 1671
▲ 10 People added, 1671–1707
⌂ Tidal Marshland

Map by the University of Wisconsin Cartographic Laboratory

Fig. 5.3 Port Royal Basin and Valley: Population, 1671–1710.

there were some 650 cattle and about 430 sheep. The rough count of outlying areas listed fourteen people at Pubnico including the families of the Sieur d'Entremont (his wife and five children) and two others. A family of four was counted at "Cap Neigre" (Port La Tour?) and one of three at Port Rochelois (near present Birchtown, on the northwest arm of Port Razoir).[16] There were rather vague numbers listed at

TABLE 5.1 *Census of 1686*

Location	Persons	Families	Remarks
Port Royal	583	96*	Plus thirty soldiers
Cape Sable area	15	4	One single European (Charles de La Tour) and one single Negro man
La Have and Mirligueche	13	14	Only three children and one "servant"; several Indians and métis
Chedabucto	20*	5*	Sieur de Laboulais and a rather indefinite number of domestics and laborers, plus many Indians and four "habitants"
Minas	57	10	
Beaubassin	127	17	
Saint John River	8	3	
St. Croix or Passamaquoddy (Pesmonquady)	4	–	Plus "domestiques" (Indians?)
Machias (Megais, Megays)	2	–	Plus "domestiques" (Indians?)
Pentagouet	1	–	Old Sieur de Castine (Baron de Saint-Castin) surrounded by his Indian family and retainers
Nipisiguit (Nipissigny or Népisiguy)	1*	–	One Enaud and Indian wife plus other Indians
Isle Percé	26	5	
Miramichy	1*	–	Richard Denys de Fronsac ("Denis de Fronsac") plus many Indians; Denys was the son and heir of Nicolas Denys

* Not certain. Since the scattered records of this census are conflicting the figures given represent a choice of interpretations. The discrepancies are not large. The totals may lie between 850 and 900.

Sources: AC, G1-*466*, 14–57. See also note 19 of this chapter.

16. Port Razoir (later called Port Roseway) was the name by which the entire Shelburne Harbour was then known. There was also a settlement called Port Razoir, in the northeast arm, at the present site of Shelburne. The present place-name "Roseway," southwest of Shelburne Harbour, is of post-Acadian origin, but it and Roseway River clearly derive their origin from "Razoir."

Pentagouet and Muskadaboucs (Musquodoboit?), and a family of six or seven at St. Peters on Cape Breton Island (see Figure 5.1).

There are reports of 515 in 1679 or 1680[17] and of 800 in 1683[18] and a complete census was taken again and submitted by Perrot in 1686 (see Table 5.1).[19] By then, the total had risen to roughly 875, some 800 of whom were living somewhere on the peninsula or just beyond it in Chignecto; of these 583 were at Port Royal, including 192 men and women, 205 boys, and 177 girls, and 9 children of unrecorded sex—in all more than 90 families and 30 soldiers. Among the places missed where some settlers may have been living were Pubnico, Shelburne Harbour, Musquodoboit, and Canso so that the true total may have exceeded 900.

We have additional evidence for this decade from the very detailed census taken over the winter of 1687/88 by a man named Gargas (first name not known) who was *écrivain principal*—sort of colonial secretary and record-keeper—in Acadia during that winter.[20] It differs slightly from the 1686 census but we must expect discrepancies under the probabilities of error that existed for both censuses and Gargas was under the handicap of the opposition of the new governor, Meneval himself. Port Royal came out at 450, a good many fewer (and more than 100 fewer even if we ignore the thirty soldiers of 1686), but Meneval's attitude may have created the greatest problem just there. There were 122, slightly fewer, at Beaubassin too, but the population of Minas had roughly doubled; perhaps some of the Minas folk were counted at Port Royal in 1686. The Cape Sable area had 24; Port Rochelois (present Shelburne Harbour), omitted in 1686, is included with 20; and La Have and Mirligueche had three more. On the Saint John River and along the Maine coast to the west 86 are listed, including 24 women and girls. This large increase over 1686 suggests omissions in the earlier census, or the inclusion of more métis and Indians living like, or with, Europeans. East of Mirligueche (present

17. AC, C11D-*1*(2), 328–39.

18. O. A. Lemieux, "The Development of Agriculture in Canada during the 16th and 17th Centuries" (1940), p. 404.

19. The census was assembled by Jacques Demeulle, Intendant of New France, during a visit to Acadia in 1685–86. It was a nominal census of which more than one manuscript version exists. That in AC, G1-*466*, 14–57, totals only 879 persons, omitting the six at "Miramichy." It has been printed twice in full nominal form: first, in Rameau *Une Colonie Féodale*, 2, 394–402, and later as "Un Recensement de l'Acadie en 1686" in *Bulletin des Recherches Historiques* (1932). There are discrepancies between the two. It is summarized in *Census of Canada, 1870–71* (1876), *4*, 20.   20. *Acadiensia Nova*, *1*, 144–55.

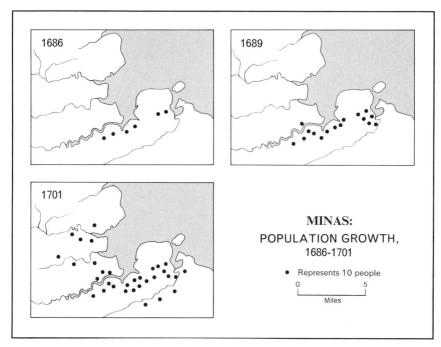

Map by the University of Wisconsin Cartographic Laboratory

Fig. 5.4   Minas: Population, 1686–1701.

Lunenburg) there were three now at Chebucto (Halifax Harbour), fifty-one at Chedabucto (Guysborough Harbour, where he may have included Canso seasonal fishermen), and six for all of Cape Breton. The locational detail is the best to that date and mapped distributions have been tried for the head of the Bay of Fundy as well as for Port Royal (see Figures 5.3 through 5.7).

In 1689 the final count of this census-rich decade was taken.[21] A total of more than 800 included 461 people and 80 heads of families at Port Royal, 164 at Minas, and 83 at Beaubassin, together with two priests at Port Royal and one each at the other two settlements. Other places listed included Cap de Sable, 24, La Have, 20, Chebucto, 3, Passamaquoddy on the St. Croix, 21, the Saint John River, 17, Megais (Machias?), 2, Pentagouet, 4, Lincour, 5, Petit Plaisance, 3, Larigimagnan, 2—these last three presumably also on the Maine coast. These hundred people were rather evenly divided between the New Brunswick–Maine coast and the south shore of the peninsula. This census

21. AC, G1-*466*, 58–59. It has been published in Rameau, *Une Colonie Féodale,* 2, 403, with slightly different totals.

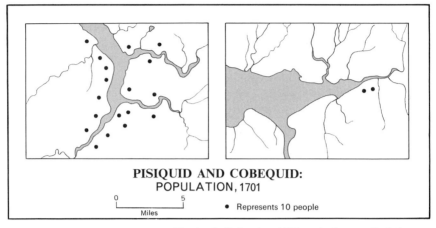

Fig. 5.5 Pisiquid and Cobequid: Population, 1701.

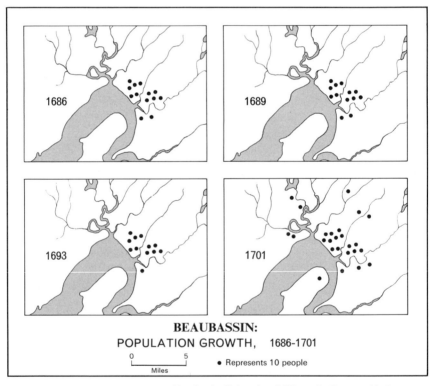

Fig. 5.6 Beaubassin: Population, 1686–1701.

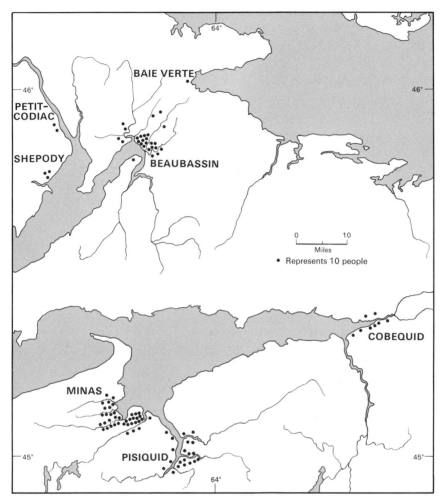

Map by the University of Wisconsin Cartographic Laboratory
Fig. 5.7   Northern and Eastern Acadian Settlements: Population, 1707.

is clearly incomplete, missing Isle Percé, Miramichi, Nipisiguit, Cape Breton, Chedabucto and Canso, Port Razoir (Shelburne Harbour), and Pubnico, at least. A separate count of the same year credited 103 to "Nipissigny,"[22] which might have included all the population on the Gulf of St. Lawrence coasts from Cape Breton Island to Isle Percé off Gaspé, and even Chedabucto and Canso.

22. Although this would seem to be Nipisiguit, place names like "Nipissigny" have been found in lists along with Nipisiguit.

Five more censuses, of varying detail and completeness, have been reported for the French regime. In 1693[23] Port Royal still had roughly 80 families and the total population was 499: some 55 families and 305 people were counted at Minas, 20 families and 119 people at Beaubassin, 6 and 32 at Cap de Sable, 2 and 12 at Port Razoir (probably a continuation of the earlier "Rochelois" group), and 4 families (but only 6 people!) at La Have. There is no separate count for Pubnico (probably included with Cape Sable) and none east of La Have on the south coast. Allowing for omissions it seems probable that the overall total was approaching 1,200, almost all on the present Nova Scotia peninsula.

The incomplete census of 1698 lists only three localities: Port Royal, Beaubassin, and the Saint John River.[24] The 575 people for the first and the 174 for the second are consistent with the earlier accounts, allowing for normal growth. A census believed to be of 1700 gives the same figures for these two places.[25] Another limited count in 1701[26] listed Port Royal as 456, Minas as 299, Pisiquid, 188, and Beaubassin, 188, giving a total of over 1,200 on Beaubassin and the peninsula. This has been interpreted by Rameau to represent, in fact, more than 1,400, distributed as shown in Table 5.2. The 182 must have included the other population on the south coast, which may have been a score or more. The rest of this group would have been scattered along the Gulf and Fundy coasts of present New Brunswick and Maine, north or west of the Chignecto isthmus.

It has been observed before that the absorption of Micmac by the Acadian community has not been well studied. There was a rather conspicuous métis settlement in the La Have-Mirligueche region which, Rameau estimated, numbered seventy-five or more at the turn of the century. This settlement had a continuous history from the arrival of Razilly's settlers in 1632. It has been assumed that those who did not move to Port Royal later in the decade included many who had made alliances with Indian women; further recruitment may have involved daughters of the Port Royal settlement (especially those with Indian blood) or Indian girls from the interior. It is likely that, in any event,

23. AC. G1-*466*, 66–102.
24. *Ibid.*, pp. 107–45. Two separate totals are given for Port Royal: 505 (p. 106) and 575 (p. 133). Lemieux, "Agriculture," quotes 583 for Port Royal and *Census of Canada, 1870–71, 4,* 44, quotes 573. The Beaubassin figures are, from the same sources respectively. 178. 183, and 175.   25. AC, G1-*466*, 146–68.
26. *Ibid.,* p. 169. See also Rameau, *Une Colonie Féodale, 1,* 205–6.

this group became highly inbred, but that was a situation characteristic of the small Acadian groups everywhere.[27]

A partial census of 1703 is generally in accord with that of two years earlier but is of interest in recording "Cobequit" separately from the rest of Minas.[28] (Three families, but no details of population, had been listed as there in 1701.) The totals given for the different settlements

TABLE 5.2 *Distribution of population in the peninsula in 1701*

Port Royal, Beaubassin, and Minas	1,153
La Have (including métis living like Europeans)	75
Pubnico and Cape Sable area	40
"Divers lieux sur la côte et dans l'intérieur"	182
Total	1,450

Source: François-Edmé Rameau de Saint-Père, *Une Colonie Féodale en Amérique: l'Acadie (1604–1881)* (1889), 2, 205–6.

are: Port Royal, 504; Beaubassin, 246; Minas and Pisiquid, 440; and Cobequid, 87—a total of 1,277 for the three main settlement areas. An estimate of 1,400 to 1,450 for the isthmus and the peninsula would seem reasonable for the turn of the century.

The last known proper census of the French regime in what is now peninsular Nova Scotia was taken in 1707 and shows a continued advance in numbers.[29] Port Royal advanced again to 570, Beaubassin (east of Shepody) was up to 271, and Minas (including Pisiquid) was up to 585, although Cobequid had dropped by 5 to 82. Presumably

27. There is an interesting discussion of these points in Rameau, *Une Colonie Féodale*, 2, 348–49. In *Origine des Acadiens* (1874), Pascal Poirier, an Acadian, attacks Moreau and Rameau for even suggesting Acadian-Indian intermarriage.

28. AC, G1-*466*, 207–14, gives the totals as Minas, 498, Beaubassin, 189, and Port Royal, 466. For the same year Rameau, *Une Colonie Féodale*, 2, 129, has copied respectively 427 (plus 187 at Cobequid), 245, and 485. *Census of Canada, 1870–71*, 4, 45, has used the same figures as Rameau.

29. AC, G1-*466*, 215–31. Using what is probably the same census, but ascribed by him to 1706, Rameau, *Une Colonie Féodale*, 1, 275, gives slightly different totals: for Port Royal, 554, for Minas, 659, with no separation of Cobequid, and Beaubassin 270. He also includes "Chipody," separately from Beaubassin, giving it 55 and "fiefs épars," 300, the last presumably an estimate. For this census, Lemieux, "Agriculture," quotes 566 for Port Royal, apparently using the same documentary source.

there was confusion of location within the Minas area. The indicated total for all of Chignecto and the peninsula would be between 1,700 and 1,800.[30] In 1708,[31] a census added 53 for the Cape Sable area, 15 for Shelburne Harbour, and 42 for the La Have-Mirligueche region. Whatever differences there may be in the interpretation of these data we are safe in assuming at least 1,500 and perhaps as many as 2,000 Acadians, distributed roughly as indicated in Figures 5.3 and 5.7 when the British assumed permanent control of the peninsula in 1710. And these, now almost all second-to-fourth generation settlers, were thoroughly "Acadian" in feeling, habits, and ecoromy.

It is significant that while the total Acadian population tripled or quadrupled in number in these four decades, the population of Port Royal had increased by only half in the same period. The push to the north and east was such that before the end of the century the Minas settlers outnumbered those at Port Royal and by 1710 the population of the Chignecto marshes was half that of the mother settlement. Most of the effective emigration from Port Royal appears to have taken place in the 1680's and 1690's. By the beginning of the new century, population growth at Port Royal had resumed its normal course. If young people continued to migrate they must have been balanced by new arrivals.

Most of the total increase was natural, but there was a larger influx of outsiders than we have been led to suppose. Grandfontaine sent a score or more of soldiers to Acadia in 1670 (he actually dispatched a company of fifty men but twenty-six of them were lost in a shipwreck). These probably were mostly used in the posts along the northern shores of Fundy and the Gulf of Maine from the Saint John to the Penobscot. When Grandfontaine arrived at Port Royal in 1671 an accompanying vessel brought sixty passengers including four girls and one woman. There is also a record of provision for passage money and feeding of thirty boys and thirty girls, but the records are so incomplete we are not certain of their destination.[32] There are scattered

30. Lemieux, "Agriculture," p. 326, however, estimates 1,600 persons for 1710.

31. AC, G1-466(2), 224.

32. For the 60 passengers known to have come to Port Royal, see a letter of Grandfontaine accompanying the dispatch to France of the record of the census of 1671. It is reprinted in Rameau, *Une Colonie Féodale, 2,* 316, from the original in the Archives de la Marine. The records of the soldiers and the mysterious sixty children are cited by Geneviève Massignon, *Les Parlers Français d'Acadie* (1962), *1,* 39–40.

records thereafter of soldiers and artisans brought out for the garrison or to work on the fortifications and on a church building. How many found wives in competition with the Acadian youths themselves and settled down is unknown. The problem of assimilating this group is referred to in a dispatch of 1671 from Talon, who reported that Grandfontaine had written to him that ". . . nearly all the soldiers wished to settle, and even get married, if girls are sent out from France, and already twenty-two (fourteen soldiers and eight engagés) have settled at one league from the fort."[33] The 1686 census has the names of many who came to Chignecto from Canada with La Vallière, a native of Three Rivers. The marriage register of the church at Port Royal lists forty soldiers or other male immigrants from France who were married there in the period from 1702 to 1715, and there also were five women immigrants whose marriages were recorded in 1704, 1710 (three), and 1712.[34] We have similar records from 1707 at Grand Pré and from 1712 at Beaubassin (although immigrants were very few during the English regime). A check of the nominal census reveals that, even allowing for the inevitable orthographical fancies of census-takers among a largely unlettered people, by 1693 some fifty new male names and at least fifteen new female ones had been added, roughly doubling the numbers of each present in 1671.[35]

It is clear that a relatively significant infusion of new blood had been made, but the family names in the nominal census of 1693 were still predominantly those recorded in Port Royal in 1671. Indeed, Geneviève Massignon appears to support Rameau's conclusion that at least two-thirds of the Acadians of the mid-eighteenth century were descended from people recorded in that first, 1671, count. It may be worth noting here that the identification of Acadians in the twentieth century, whether in Maritime Canada or elsewhere in the country, in Europe or in the United States is very largely by name. Massignon estimates that seventy-six Acadian names borne by at least one hun-

33. "Lettre de Talon au ministre Colbert," November 1671, reprinted in *Rapport de l'archiviste de la province de Quebec pour 1930–31* (1931), p. 163. My translation. A dispatch of Talon to Colbert, November 1670, expressed similar sentiments. *Ibid.*, p. 131.

34. Documents published in Rameau, *Une Colonie Féodale, 2*, 350–51. The Port Royal registers are in PANS.

35. Massignon, *Les Parlers Français, 1*, 42. Among new Acadian names appearing in Beaubassin between 1676 and 1678 as engagés of La Vallière were: Chiasson, Cottard, Haché (*dit* Gallant), Labarre, Lagacé, Leger, Mercier, Aubin, Mignault, Mirande, Perthuis.

dred families each in the mid-twentieth century, covered fully 86 per cent of present Acadians.[36]

THE SETTLEMENTS

Port Royal

Cadillac's description of 1692 gives us the setting of Port Royal: "Ce lieu est environé de montaignes tout à pic, au bas desquelles il y a un petit vallon d'une lieue de largeur et de sept lieues de longeur, ou il n'y a que de prairies de chaque costé de la rivière, qui sont inondées par les marées, les habitants ont fait des levées, des digues et chaussées, affin que l'eau sallé ni puisse entrer."[37]

The scattering of settlers with their homes just above the pre-dyking high-tide land is reconstructed for 1671 in Figure 5.3.[38] The seigneurie of Port Royal was still the chief claimant of lands in the area and these claims had been strongly pressed by Emmanuel Le Borgne and his son. At some time in the period it is reported to have been divided into seven sections and to have extended twelve and a half miles upriver and five miles on either side.[39] Perrot, on taking up the government, wrote in 1686 that the people had scattered themselves in such a way that they were very far removed from one another; he complained that

36. *Ibid.*

37. AC, C11D-*10*, 17–52: "Mémoire de l'Acadie, Nouvelle Angleterre, Nouvelle Hollande, et Virginie," 1692, p. 22. Cadillac's full name was Antoine Laumet de Lamothe de Cadillac and he was known, while he lived in Acadia in the 1680's, as "Laumet." Several versions of this report are known, including one in AC, C11D-*2(2)*, 432–71, and that given above, which includes a somewhat longer version in English. The original is in the Archives de la Marine, Paris, designated "Description de l'Acadie par M. de Cadillac," 1692, No. 74. W. F. Ganong has translated what he considered to be the best French version and published it as "The Cadillac Memoir of 1692" (1930).

38. There are several rather detailed plans of the farms and buildings of the settlers along both the basin and river of Port Royal, copies of which are held by the PANS or AC, which attest to this.

39. This was presumably from Goat Island up the river to present Bridgetown, and possibly, but not likely, to Paradise. The description of the Port Royal seigneurie, as understood by the British in 1730, had it commencing 2,000 feet up river from the fort and continuing five leagues farther up and two leagues in depth on either side. AC, NSA-*19*, 60–61.

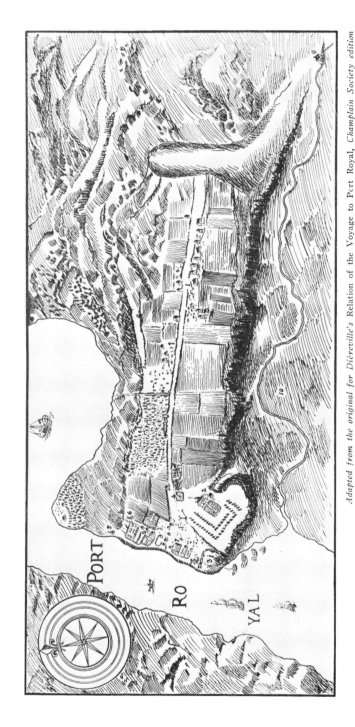

Adapted from the original for Diéreville's Relation of the Voyage to Pcrt Royal, Champlain Society edition

5 Demeulle's Plan of Port Royal, 1686. The legend is as follows: 1. House at Gros Cap. 2. Parish church. 3. Ruined fort. 4. Cemetery. 5. Storehouse of an Englishman. 6. Storehouse of an Englishman. 7. Governor's residence. 8. House of Sieur Le Borgne. 9. Water mill. 10. Marshland

some of the grants had sixty leagues of frontage.[40] He was presumably referring to Belle-Isle, who "controlled" nearly all the grants, or to other "shadow" seigneurs. The latter, in turn, had granted the same concessions to different people, which led to much litigation.[41]

Meneval, in 1688, describes the settlers as ". . . dispersé esloignés les uns des autres dans l'espace de six ou sept lieues, au dessus et au dessous le long des bords de la rivière du Port Royal . . . ."[42] Saccardy said there were no settlers below Goat Island and twenty-nine along the shores of the basin above it in 1689.[43] It is probable that prior to 1710 the settlement remained largely confined to the shores of the basin above Goat Island and to the banks of the Dauphin (Annapolis) River as far as present Bridgetown. De Labat, an engineer living at Port Royal during the administration of Governor Jacques-François de Brouillan (1701–1704), wrote "In going up the said river one finds no habitations except between L'Isle-aux-chèvres and about five leagues above the fort. These represent 54 or 55 families . . . ."[44]

Lacking true cadastral maps or precise information one must estimate the size of individual holdings; the evidence is consistent with average frontages of one-half to two miles per settler along the basin or river and no great depth behind. However, there clearly was a marked clustering near the largest areas of dykable marsh; there the length of an individual frontage may well have dropped to a few hundred feet or less in places. But these would be balanced by substantial stretches with no salt-marsh border. Perhaps one or two hundred acres is a reasonable size to postulate for the individual *granges* (farms), al-

40. AC, C11D-*2*(1), 24. The statement of sixty leagues is patently absurd unless all the windings of all the rivers and streams of Port Royal, Minas, and perhaps even Pisiquid, were included in the total claims of the Le Borgne and La Tour families.   41. AC, C11D-*2*(1), 27.

42. AC, C11D-*2*(1), 179–221: "Mémoire du Sieur de Meneval, Gouverneur de la Cadie, touchant les affaires de cette province pour l'année 1688," p. 186.

43. AC, C11D-*2*(1), 302–33: January 10, 1690, p. 310. Vincent de Saccardy, an engineer, was sent to Port Royal in 1689 and spent a month there in the autumn drawing up plans for restoring and improving the fortifications. He returned briefly in 1690 to find that the settlement had been ravaged once more by the English. Another version, dated January 12, has been printed in translation in *Acadiensia Nova, 1,* 207–22.

44. De Labat (also Delabat, De la Bat, etc.) wrote a description of Port Royal in 1703 where he served briefly as an engineer on the fortifications. It is printed in translation in *Acadiensia Nova, 2,* 7–12. Quotation is from p. 9. Incidentally, referring to "l'isle-aux-chèvres," he says there were none.

though in fact their homesteads on the edge of the marsh and the few acres of dyked marshland that each cultivated occupied only a small fraction of this. There are, indeed, suggestions of the pattern of long rectangles extending back from the river, which was found throughout the French settlements on the St. Lawrence River and in the interior of North America, and which was repeated later in Clare Township in Digby County (see Chapter 8). But there is little to support these suggestions; just the existence of fifty to one hundred holdings, spread along perhaps as many miles of river bank and basin shore, hardly sustains them, and if such rectangles did exist the interior parts of them were used at best for wood lots and rough pasture for animals.

The stringing out of population along lines of communication was characteristic of a great deal of North American settlement, both French and English. And in the Acadian areas it had a powerful incentive beyond the concentration of attention on the marshlands. The roads or tracks along the river were slow to be made suitable for vehicles; the river itself was the major avenue of communication in all seasons—by canoe for most of the year, and by snowshoe when it was frozen over and snow-covered—and this perpetuated the stringing out. The dependence of the Acadians on canoes and the skill of men, women, and children in using them was cause of frequent comment by observers. Cadillac remarked: "The *creolles* [i.e., the Acadians] . . . travel most of the time by bark canoes. Their wives do the same, and are very bold on the water."[45] Meneval described the use by Acadians of ". . . canots d'escorce comme les sauvages, ou d'autres petits canots qu'ils font eux mesme d'une troue d'arbre creusé."[46] Longer and stronger boats of the fishing-skiff type were also used, especially for moving heavier goods.

The number of people living in the Port Royal settlement grew very slowly from the 348 of 1671 to some 456 in 1701, but then advanced rapidly to 570 in 1707 and doubtless to roughly 600 by the time of the British takeover. There is considerable doubt as to the number actually inhabiting the roughly triangular "peninsula" on which the fort was situated. Plate 5 and Figure 5.8 are taken from two cartographic interpretations of the inhabited area: the former is Demeulle's plan of

45. "The Cadillac Memoir," p. 81.
46. .AC, C11D-2(1), 206: 1688. It is uncertain whether these were dugouts or whether he was really referring to a canoe made of one large piece of bark.

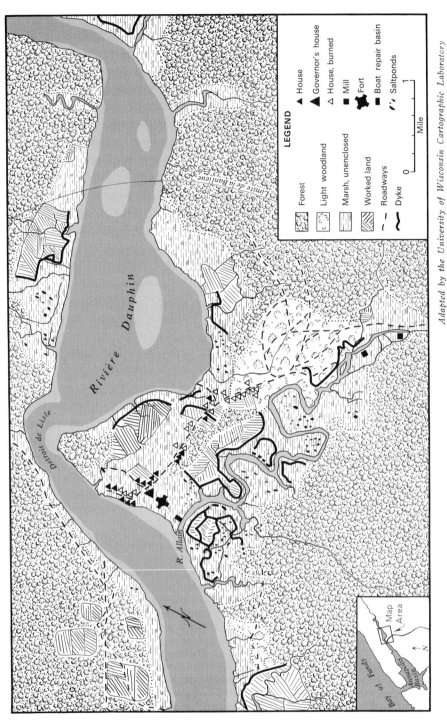

LEGEND

Forest	▲ House
Light woodland	▲ Governor's house
Marsh, unenclosed	△ House, burned
Worked land	■ Mill
Roadways	✪ Fort
Dyke	■ Boat repair basin
	⸌⸍ Saltponds

0   Mile   1

Riviere Dauphin

Detroit de L'Isle

Limite de la Banlieue

R. Allain

Bay of Fundy

Annapolis Basin

Map Area

N

Adapted by the University of Wisconsin Cartographic Laboratory

Fig. 5.8 Port Royal Area, 1709. After a Carte Marine in The Newberry Library, Chicago.

1685 or 1686,[47] and the latter is one of the beautifully-drafted series known as the Cartes de la Marine and dated 1709.[48]

Dièreville described the "town" in 1699–1700 as spread over an area a league and a half in length and almost as wide,[49] which suggests that what was called the "town" of Port Royal differed with different observers. The major node was probably near the fort in most of this period. Settlement extended northeastward from the fort and to the southeast along the sandy ridge where a settlement called the "upper town" slowly developed.[50] In 1686 there appear to have been one hundred to one hundred twenty people in the area, some of whom in all probability were the thirty soldiers known to have been in Port Royal in that year.[51] The Gargas count of 1687/88 listed only thirty at "Port Royal" and fifty at "Le Cap." Although he locates the latter at about two musket shots away and says it consisted of eight to ten families (his count listed seven men and thirteen women) he may have confused some of these with those on the ridge to the east.[52]

The vulnerability of Port Royal to attack and the long succession of incidents of pillage and burning had left their mark on the town and the fort, which was continually in disrepair. Gargas reported that the houses were low, built of logs (pièces) laid one on top of another, and roofed with thatch; only the one in which the governor lived was covered with planks.[53] Meneval, in 1688, described Port Royal as

47. Demeulle, at the time Intendant of New France, made his inspection tour of Acadia in 1685. See *Acadiensia Nova, 1*, 15–29, and Rameau, *Une Colonie Féodale, 1*, 164–65. His "Account of the Voyage of Monsieur de Meulles to Acadie, 1685–1686" is published in full, with a map identifying his route, in *Acadiensia Nova, 1*, 91–124.

48. The *Cartes Marines* are a collection of more than one hundred maps and views relating to French voyages of exploration, trading posts, and colonial expansion (1640–1726). This example is in the Edward E. Ayer Collection of the Newberry Library, Chicago. The date of this map, done in water colors on heavy paper, is somewhat uncertain, but must be at least as late as 1708, from a date on the map, and before the British capture of 1710.

49. *Relation of the Voyage to Port Royal in Acadia or New France by the Sieur de Dièreville*, trans. Alice Webster, ed. J. C. Webster (1933), p. 86. This volume includes the full French text as well as the translation.

50. The local topographical terminology is very confusing. Both "Le Cap" and "Gros Cap" may refer to the "upper town" southeastern settlement near the neck of the peninsula. But "Le Cap" may sometimes refer to the northwest point, the whole Port Royal peninsula, or even to the Granville peninsula, extending to Digby Gut, the entrance to the Basin.   51. AC, C11D-*2*(1), 54.

52. *Acadiensia Nova, 1*, 144, 146, 181. For problems of location see note 50.

53. *Ibid.*, p. 179.

consisting of but twenty wretched dwellings of mud and wood, and only six inhabitants (presumably six families). He must have referred only to the area immediately around the fort.[54] Saccardy disagrees with Gargas for he reported the houses as covered with shingles or boards. In his inspection of Port Royal he found the old fort ". . . not even large enough to be a simple Acadian dwelling. It was more than a quarter undermined by the sea and was crumbling everywhere."[55] A decade later, Dièreville found the houses built rather far apart and nothing more than cottages, very badly constructed, and with chimneys of clay; he had not been able to identify the church which he thought looked more like a barn.[56] Baron Lahontan, a visitor of the same decade, said it ". . . n'est au bout de compte, qu'un tres-petite Bicoque. . . . n'est donc qu'un petit nombre de Maisons à deux étages & où peu de gens de distinction habitent."[57] These remarks have been translated as "no more than a little paultry Town" with "only a handful of Houses two Story high."[58]

Rameau describes housing in the colony in general at the turn of the century; how much he depends on documentary sources not available to the writer and how much on his imagination or inference is uncertain. Many houses, he says, were built by driving large piles (presumably side by side) in the earth and filling in the cracks with moss and clay. The chimneys were built with posts and pounded clay and the roof covered with reeds, bark, or on occasion even with sod. The better ones were built *en pièce-sur-pièce,* that is to say with stout logs, squared off, piled one on the other and interlocked (*s'enchêvetrant*) at each corner. These were easily built from the abundant wood and at the first alarm they could be abandoned without worry and lost without excessive regret, a matter of some importance in a place so frequently attacked.[59] We have nothing to go on for the houses of the farming community away from the town but presumably they were at least as roughly if perhaps more solidly built.

54. AC, C11D-*2(*1), 186.   55. *Acadiensia Nova,* 1, 216–17.

56. Dièreville, *Relation,* pp. 82–83.

57. Louis-Armand de Lom d'Arce, Baron de Lahontan, *Mémoires de l'Amérique septentrionale, on la Suite des voyages de Mr le Baron de Lahontan* (1703), pp. 29–30 (bound with his *Nouveaux Voyages* . . . , as the second volume).

58. Translation to English is from the London edition of the same year (*New Voyages to North-America*), 1, 224–25. Also printed in *idem, New Voyages to North America,* ed. R. G. Thwaites (1905), *1,* 330–32.

59. Rameau, *Une Colonie Féodale, 1,* 150.

The Expansion Settlements up the Bay

Perhaps the most important development of this forty-year period was the establishment and rapid expansion of new settlements in the two branches of the head of the Bay of Fundy: Chignecto Bay and Minas Basin (see Figure 5.9). There were other minor sources for their peopling but most of the settlers were sons and daughters from the Port Royal settlement. The first movement was, apparently, coincident with the return of the French government to Port Royal in 1670, for it was in 1671 that the first settlers established themselves on the shores of Cumberland Basin, the eastern head of Chignecto Bay, in 1671. A decade later there was a settlement on the Minas shore of the great valley at the other end of which nestled the mother settlement of Port Royal. By the turn of the century several other settlements had been begun as expansions of these two.

It is easily assumed that this migration reflected the filling up of the Port Royal marshlands and the natural inclination of the habitant, whose agriculture was centered around the tidal flats, to seek out similar lands where he could build his dykes and continue the same sort of agriculture. But in 1671 there were just under 350 people at Port Royal and some fifty or sixty farms; this small farming population had not nearly exhausted the lands that could be dyked around Port Royal or farther up the Dauphin (Annapolis) River, as subsequent expansion was to show. Perhaps they were avoiding the claims of the seigneurial heirs (and there were many complaints that usable land was tied up and kept out of production) but, as we have seen, the seigneurial dues were never very burdensome. It seems more likely that a desire to escape from a place that was a focus for English attacks and where, due to official surveillance, it was more difficult to conduct the indispensable trade with the New Englanders in the more peaceful interludes, weighed more heavily than any form of seigneurial harassment, land hunger, or resource depletion. Above all, the Acadians sought to live their own lives in their own way and outward expansion had in it much of the same search for freedom and escape from restraint that sparked so much of the westward movement by other European settlers to the west and south in the seventeenth, eighteenth, and nineteenth centuries.

Certainly, although perhaps unintentionally, Perrot painted a pic-

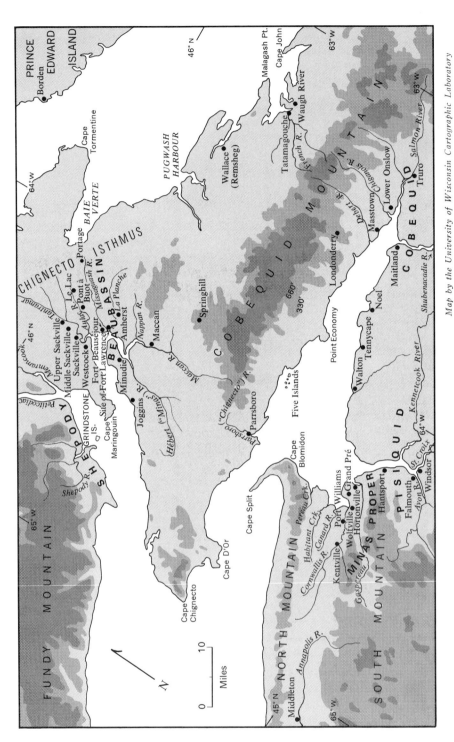

Fig. 5.9 Northern and Eastern Acadian Settlements as of the Early Eighteenth Century, Modern Place Names.

Map by the University of Wisconsin Cartographic Laboratory

ture of a contented, if sparse and simple, pastoral existence among the Port Royal folk in the 1680's. He reported that they lived better than the Canadians, and never were without meat and bread, although they were less industrious and never thought of saving against bad harvests or other disasters. He attempted to gauge the meagerness of their life by an accounting of their dowries: seldom, he indicated, did a dowry amount to more than twenty or twenty-five francs in goods, a cow in calf, a ewe, a sow, and, in the case of the better-off families, perhaps a feather bed.[60] In the Acadian context this sounds quite satisfactory.

There are, of course, indications to the contrary. Meneval, writing in 1688,[61] noted the shortage of labor and manure for developing the uplands, and implies a shortage not of dykable land but of tidelands that could be dyked with an absolute minimum of effort. It was to this cause that he attributed the movement to Minas to which place twenty-five or thirty persons, mainly of the younger age groups, had migrated in the previous six years.

BEAUBASSIN — Not long after 1671 Jacques Bourgeois, the former surgeon of d'Aulnay and a well-to-do farmer of Port Royal,[62] decided to move to Beaubassin. He had known the area in younger days in the course of extensive fur-trading activities and his move was undoubtedly aimed at the freer activity of Indian trading as well as of farming. But he persuaded five other families to go with him and the prospects of farming were certainly bright enough with a situation on the edge of the largest continuous expanse of dykable marshland in eastern North America. Even without dyking, the resources of salt-marsh hay, and of grazing, must have seemed limitless. Within five years the group was well established, other settlers followed, more and more land was reclaimed, and the flocks and herds increased.

The success of this "établissement demi-commercial et demi-agricole"[63] did not go unnoticed by others. Michel Leneuf de La Vallière, a son-in-law of Nicolas Denys, had seen the Bourgeois establishment in its first year and, in the autumn of 1678, was granted a seigneurie in the Chignecto area ten leagues square (about 1,000 square miles) by

60. AC, C11D-*2*(1), 40–41: 1686.   61. AC, C11D-*2*(1), 206–7.
62. Rameau, *Une Colonie Féodale, 1,* 168, describes him as a man fifty years old, with ten children, thirty-three cattle, a small flock of sheep, and five arpents of wheat land.
63. *Ibid.* Rameau describes it at some length, with adequate documentation.

Frontenac. It included much of Chignecto Bay, Cape Tormentine, and Baie Verte. His grant specified that he leave undisturbed any settlers there, together with the lands they used or had planned to use for themselves; the Bourgeois group was thus protected. La Vallière established himself on an "island" of higher ground in the marshes between the Fort Lawrence and Fort Beauséjour ridges (known as Tonge's Island today). He enclosed his buildings with a stockade, cleared some upland, and dyked some marshland. The buildings were mostly of logs, like those of the Bourgeois settlers, although some of the out-buildings (stables and barns) may have been made of planks.[64] A subpoena to his censitaires of Beaubassin in 1682 (for having refused to accept the contracts of concessions) lists eleven men (presumably heads of families) who may well have represented the families of the whole settlement in that year. Two of them were named Bourgeois; either they had taken new lands outside of the Bourgeois "reserve" or La Vallière was asserting at least nominal control over the whole area.[65]

After 1686 there seems to have been little migration from Port Royal to the Chignecto area and it probably grew largely by natural increase, although some accretions from the fishing fleet, from France, or even from New France are assumed. Rameau says that La Vallière had several engagés, whom he names, and who are clearly not from Port Royal. At least one of them married an Acadian.[66] The census evidence of total population is sketchy and, for some years, obviously incomplete (see Table 5.3), but the growth would appear to have been steady after 1690 at least.

We have a detailed description of the area from the 1680's,[67] usually ascribed to Demeulle. The vast extent of meadows, thought capable of

64. A great deal of detail has been dug up and presented in Rameau, *Une Colonie Féodale, 1*, ch. 5, and Will R. Bird, *A Century at Chignecto: The Key to Old Acadia* (1928), pp. 7 ff.

65. AC, FM-*9:* 1682. Names of the eleven men were: Pierre Morin, Guyou Chiasson, Michel Poirier, Roger Kessy, Claude Du Gast, Germaine and Guillaume Bourgeois, Germaine Giroir, Jean Aubin Mignaux, Jacques Belou, and Thomas Cormier.

66. Rameau, *Une Colonie Féodale, 1*, 171, in part based on registers of the church at Beaubassin.

67. It is pp. 110–16 of "Mémoires généraux," AC C11D-*2*(1), 93–134: 1686. The fullest use of this document, ascribed variously to Demeulle and Francquillier, has been made by Rameau, *Une Colonie Féodale, 1*, 172–74, and Bird, *Century at Chignecto*, pp. 19 ff. Demeulle's diary account of his trip to Acadia (on which this must be based) is printed in *Acadiensia Nova, 1*, 91–124. Regarding his five months enforced stay at La Vallière's home he says he was "bored to death."

supporting a hundred thousand cattle, and the upland borders with their virgin forests, are fully described. More than a score of dwellings had been built on the borders of the marsh or on the "islands" above the tide. Each farmstead had many outbuildings and had perhaps a dozen to twenty cattle, a dozen pigs, and as many sheep. The livestock were stabled only for two or three months in the winter or for fattening before butchering; Demeulle thought this resulted in undue loss from wolves. The dependence on livestock had meant a neglect of field crops

TABLE 5.3   *Population of Beaubassin in various years, 1686–1707*

Year	Pop.	Year	Pop.
1686	127	1698	174
1687/8	101	1701	188
1689	84	1703	246
1693	119	1707	271

Sources: The following censuses are in the AC, G1-*466* series: 1686 census, pp. 14–57; 1689 census, pp. 58–59; 1693 census, pp. 60–102; 1698 census, pp. 107–45; 1701 census, p. 169; 1703 census, pp. 207–14; 1707 census, pp. 215–31. The census for 1687/88, prepared by Gargas, is published in *Acadiensia Nova, 1578–1779*, ed. W. I. Morse (1935), *1*, 144–55. See also note 15 of this chapter.

but he thought they had cultivated enough land to raise the hope that they might soon be independent in bread grains. The women made both linen and woolen cloth for clothing and, for shoes, both sexes wore Indian moccasins that they made themselves.

Demeulle's report made a good deal of the short portage route across the isthmus to Baie Verte and he may well have been the first to suggest a canal to shorten the trip from Quebec to Port Royal by over five hundred miles. The purpose of such a canal would have been to strengthen commercial as well as administrative and ecclesiastical connections with Canada. The New Englanders were now the suppliers of Acadian needs, taking furs in exchange and thus depriving France of both furs and markets for manufactured goods. The New England connection also led to Acadians' seeking work with the English, especially in the fishery, to pay off debts, or simply to earn the money that was so often in short supply.

Despite the large number of cattle, and the ideal situation for them, they were, in Demeulle's opinion, "d'une méschante espèce qu'il faudroit changer"[68] (unfortunately this advice was not taken) and he makes the comment that is also made by other visitors that the cows could be milked only while the calves were active sucklings, and, as a result of the shortage of milk, little butter was made.

By the later 1680's both La Vallière and Bourgeois had built gristmills at Beaubassin and the latter appears to have had a sawmill as well. Grain was being produced in some quantity. Gradually the settlement adopted all of the field crops and animals known at Port Royal, and fruit trees (plums, pears, and apples) were well established by the turn of the century, perhaps introduced by Roger Quessy (Kessey, Casey?), one of the early settlers. Apparently the more severe winter of Beaubassin kept out cherries.

Beaubassin failed to achieve the rate of growth of the Minas Basin settlements. The departure of La Vallière and his family for Canada and the actions of his son-in-law and agent, Sébastien de Villieu, probably were factors, but the raids from New England under Benjamin Church in 1696 and 1704, with their destruction of buildings and cattle, were reason enough for discouragement. Nonetheless, Table 5.4, which gives agricultural statistics over a twenty-year period, shows a substantial, steady advance.

It is interesting that the gypsum and coal, commented on by Cadillac in a *mémoire* of 1692,[69] and probably used locally, should have drawn so little attention. Nor is there good evidence that Grindstone Island was yet yielding its later widely famed product. The Chignecto isthmus was, still, rather a crossroads for Indians moving from the Bay to the Gulf or from the mainland out to the peninsula and their frequent presence may have deterred some more timid souls. Perhaps the progress may be considered surprisingly good in the face of the difficulties.

La Vallière himself may have got on well with his own servants or engagés but his son-in-law, de Villieu, made himself unpopular by, among other acts, getting eviction orders for settlers who had squatted in Shepody Bay and dispossessing them. No doubt this was within the rights of a rather expansive seigneurial grant but it did not encourage settlement, for others could not be induced to replace them.

68. Rameau, *Une Colonie Féodale, 1,* 174, with slightly modernized spelling.
69. "The Cadillac Memoir," pp. 89, 91.

THE SHEPODY ESTUARIES — The story of the beginnings at Shepody and along the Petitcodiac River which, with the valley of the Memramcook River, represented the chief marsh areas on the western arm of Chignecto Bay (see Figure 5.9), has a slim documentary base, but appears to have paralleled that at Beaubassin, with a lag in time of a quarter-century.[70] In 1698 Pierre Thibaudeau, a resident of Port

TABLE 5.4 *Agriculture at Beaubassin*

	1686	1698	1707
Arpents "cultivated"	426*	298	286
Farms in cultivation	20†	25	40
1–4 arpents cultivated	(3)	(4)	(14)
5–10 " "	(6)	(9)	(20)
11–50 " "	(11)	(12)	(6)
Cattle	236	352	510
Farms with cattle	19	28‡	42§
1–4 head	(3)	(4)	(2)
5–10 "	(6)	(9)	(17)
11–24 "	(9)	(13)	(23)
over 25 "	(1)	(2)	(0)
Sheep	116	178	476
Swine	189	160	334

* Clearly not all cultivated.
† Three of the twenty farmers were actually resident at Port Royal and were simply running livestock.
‡ There were 28 families with livestock, 3 without land.
§ There were 42 families with livestock, 2 without land.
Sources: See Table 5.3.

Royal, began his settlement at Shepody much as Bourgeois had done at Beaubassin. A miller of Pré Ronde, up the river from Port Royal (Figure 5.3), he and his sons explored the Shepody area in the first year, and encouraged friends (the Blanchards) to make a companion effort on the Petitcodiac. The first wintering by three of Thibaudeau's sons was in 1699/1700, when they did very well trading furs with the Indians. De Villieu heard of the activity and immediately protested that they were on his father-in-law's seigneurie without permission, although the precise boundaries of La Vallière's grant are almost im-

70. Rameau, *Une Colonie Féodale, 1*, ch. 7, deals with the founding of Shepody, with some documentary support in *ibid., 2*, 333–36. The topic is also dealt with in Esther Clark Wright, *The Petitcodiac* (1945), ch. 2, apparently with heavy dependence upon Rameau.

Nova Scotia Information Service

6   A View over the Cornwallis River Valley

possible to determine from the wording of the concession.[71] Thibaudeau had dreamed of a seigneurie of his own, like that of his old friend Mathieu Martin at Cobequid (see below) but showed a willingness to compromise which de Villieu declined. When in 1702 de Villieu himself was willing to compromise, the Thibaudeau group, believing that a petition of their own to Paris would succeed, in turn refused.[72] Indeed they were confident enough of success to invest a great deal of effort in dyking, building sluices (aboiteaux), and even erecting a grist-and-saw mill with machinery from New England. In 1703 they had their lands confirmed but "without prejudice" to the rights of La Vallière. The old man died thinking himself a true seigneur but, in an arrêt of June 2, 1705, the Thibaudeaus' right to the land was expressly granted as a concession from La Vallière's seigneurie. Officially, the Thibaudeaus could not extend their lands, nor could others settle without assuming the legal position and charges consequent to being censitaires of the seigneur of Beaubassin.

In 1702 there appear to have been seven households at Shepody (roughly thirty-three people) and five households (thirteen people) on the Petitcodiac, most likely near present Hillsborough. By 1707 fourteen families and seven engagés (fifty-five people in all) were estimated, with twelve horses, seventy cattle, and fifty sheep. The families settled there doubtless increased, but the outbreak of war with England and the unwillingness of potential settlers to subject themselves to de Villieu apparently stopped expansion. Shepody never actually was raided but English ships effectively cut it off from Port Royal and Quebec. Rameau estimated fifty to seventy-five people for 1715, four-fifths of them of European blood. It became a favorite summer camp-

71. Roy, *Inventaire*, *3*, 160, gives it as: ". . . avec l'étendue de cinq lieues de France de tous côtés du lieu et manoir seigneurial du d. Beaubassin en tirant de l'est nord-est à l'ouest sud-ouest et du nord nord-ouest au sud sud-est qui feront dix lieues en carré . . . ." In a map presented in *Acadia at the End of the Seventeenth Century* (1934), facing p. 228, J. C. Webster boldly shows the limits and also those of the Shepody seigneurie as granted to de Villieu in 1700.

72. One member of the Thibaudeau group, a son-in-law, was Mathieu Des Goutins (whose name has a dozen different orthographic variants in the documents). He was the second and last chief civil officer, or king's clerk, in Acadia. In 1793 he became *procureur-général*, performing functions somewhat parallel, although at a much lower level, to those of the intendants at Quebec. He succeeded Gargas and served from 1688 until the final surrender of Port Royal in 1710. He was constantly embroiled with the governors and became more and more identified with the local resident community, into which he had married. See Webster, *Acadia*, pp. 174–76.

ing spot for Indians, both Micmac and Malecite, and at least one engagé started a métis family with an Indian bride. As we shall see (Chapter 6) settlement on the combined Shepody-Petitcodiac-Memramcook tidal lands increased to some sixty-five families in 1734 and by an estimated further hundred families by 1750, shortly before the debacle that led to the deportation or dispersion of the Acadians and the destruction of their homes and livestock.

MINAS BASIN — This area, which was to assume demographic and economic leadership among the three Acadian farming regions in the eighteenth century, was the last of the three major Acadian centers to get started. But its fine marshlands, the weakness of its nominal seigneurial control, and, perhaps above all, its relative freedom from the attention of both New England raiders and French officials, allowed it to expand rapidly. From only 57 people in the Grand Pré area in 1686 the population soared to more than 580 in 1707.

The settlement appears to have begun in 1682 with the movement thither of two of the most prosperous of the Port Royal settlers. Pierre Melanson, ("*dit* La Verdure," son of the tutor of the d'Aulnay children and married to Marie-Marguerite Mius d'Entremont) settled with only one neighbor (perhaps a hired hand) at Grand Pré and that much-storied settlement's history began. Pierre Terriau settled on the Rivière St-Antoine (Cornwallis River) and four other settlers joined him at once, including a Le Blanc and a Landry. Four years later there was another family at Grand Pré and seven families in all on the St-Antoine, giving the total of fifty-seven people. The census lists only five farms but on four of them there was a total of eighty-three arpents "under cultivation" (perhaps simply enclosed by dykes). Two of these were apparently of some size since one of the four had less than four arpents improved and another only between five and ten. Altogether it was a remarkable start in four years. Rapidly the word spread and settlers came in from Beaubassin as well as Port Royal. In the winter of 1687/88 Gargas guessed "about thirty families" there "where all the young people from Port Royal [are] settled."[73]

All observers stressed the comparative isolation (and thus freedom from interference) of the settlers. The Grand Pré neighborhood at least, and probably also the mouths of the creeks to the north and of the Pisiquid to the east, apparently were recognized as belonging, along

73. *Acadiensia Nova, 1*, 181.

with all the Port Royal area not specifically alienated, to the seigneurie claimed by the heirs of Le Borgne. But their hold was light, their claims small (appearing content "de concéder les terres à rente censive à ceux qui les demandaient"[74]), and they did nothing to assist the settlers or, apparently, even to guide them. The latter may simply have squatted, but perhaps Melanson, who acted as their seigneurial agent or *procureur fiscal* (and was the "captain of militia" in the area and the recognized leader or local authority), guided them in their location. Gargas said ". . . the settlement is too remote for commerce: only small vessels can risk going there."[75] This in fact expresses correctly the degree of isolation but it is not correct in terms of commerce, for these people, like those at Port Royal and Beaubassin, depended on New England goods, and the small vessels out of Boston made the journey through the tidal race north of Cape Split, allowing themselves to be stranded far "inland" at low tide for friendly trade as the privateers could hardly risk doing.

By 1701 there were 33 families and 188 persons at Pisiquid, and even three families at Cobequid where, in 1689, Mathieu Martin (who had been trading there for furs) was granted a seigneurie with the nominal dignity of the "Sieur Mathieu de Saint-Martin."[76] By 1707 there were 17 families and 82 people at Cobequid. The Pisiquid settlement also appears to have grown, but at a slightly more moderate rate.[77] All the Minas Basin settlements enjoyed the fruits of their own abundant natural population increase greatly aided by the continued migration of young couples from Port Royal with the wives at the peak of their child-bearing capacity.

There is no doubt that agriculture flourished in Minas beyond any experience at Port Royal or Beaubassin. It was better balanced than the latter; not neglecting livestock, in which Beaubassin rather specialized, it developed the best and most extensive arable farming in Acadia.[78] Table 5.5 indicates the trend.

Brouillan first saw Minas in 1701 when he left his command at

74. Rameau, *Une Colonie Féodale, 1,* 188.   75. *Acadiensia Nova, 1,* 181.

76. Rameau, *Une Colonie Féodale, 1,* 189–93. Martin believed himself to be born in Acadia of the d'Aulnay group. The act of concession is printed in Roy, *Inventaire, 4,* 38–39.

77. In 1707, the figures for Minas and Pisiquid were entered as one, the combined population having grown from 487 to 585.

78. According to an anonymous chronicler of 1710, Minas grew more grain "than all the rest of the country." *Acadiensia Nova, 1,* 45.

Plaisance (Placentia) in Newfoundland and went to assume the government of Acadia. Landing at Chebucto (Halifax Harbour), he proceeded by way of the Shubenacadie River to Cobequid and thence via the basin to the Minas settlement, before going on to Port Royal. He reported that cattle were abundant and that they could easily export

TABLE 5.5　*Agriculture in the Minas Basin*

	1686	1693	1701		1707	
	Minas and Pisiquid		Minas	Pisiquid	Minas and Pisiquid	Cobequid
Population	57	305	299	188	585	92
Farmers with land	5	47	39	28	73	17
Farmers with livestock	8	50*	43	29	81†	17
Arpents cultivated	83	360	329	199	315	101
Farms with:						
up to 4 arpents	1	8	10	7	48	2
5–10　　"	2	31	20	19	21	15
11–20　"	1	7	9	2	4	0
over 20　"	1	1	0	0	0	0
Cattle	90	458	547	283	766	180
Farms with:						
up to 4 head	2	6	7	5	16	2
5–10　　"	2	23	10	11	30	7
11–25　"	3	18	25	13	28	8
over 25　"	1	0	0	0	3	0
Sheep	21	320	518	188	718	124
Swine	67	315	385	125	639	114

* 47 with cattle.
† 78 with cattle.
Sources: See Table 5.3.

700 to 800 hogsheads of wheat but that the inhabitants were half-republican, of very independent character, and accustomed to deciding things for themselves![79]

The fullest account of Minas in the period is that of Villebon of October 1699.[80] He remarked on the lack of cod fishing but on the presence of shad and gaspereau (alewives) in the tidal streams.[81] He

79. As quoted by Rameau, *Une Colonie Féodale, 1,* 220.
80. Webster, *Acadia,* pp. 132–33, prints it in full in translation.
81. Gargas had reported in 1687/88 that the Minas rivers contained shad, trout, gaspereau, and shellfish. The second major river, bordering the Grand Pré settlement to the south, was named the Gaspereau.

thought the ground excellent for the main crops of wheat, rye, peas, and oats and all sorts of vegetables which were found in abundance. Curiously, he makes no mention of apple trees at Minas nor do the other chroniclers, but from the descriptions of later visitors they appear to have been planted before the end of the first decade of settlement, and they were widespread in both Minas and Beaubassin in 1698. Like most new observers of the Acadians he complains of their laziness—they worked only to maintain themselves and showed little ambition to "get ahead." He does mention the industry of the women in spinning and weaving wool and linen. He noted one sawmill in existence with another planned, a windmill, and some seven or eight water gristmills. There is no clue, however, as to whether any of these really were "tidal mills" for which such unusually good conditions existed.[82]

The Outlying Settlements

The outlying settlements were largely fishing and trading stations. After Gargas' description of them on his tour of 1687/88 he reflected the usual official judgment: that they were most precariously situated, depending for food on fishing, hunting, or what they could obtain from trading vessels, and that the settlers should be obliged to cultivate the soil and establish deeper roots.[83]

Moving counterclockwise around the peninsular coast from Port Royal the first settlement was that at Fourchu (present Yarmouth, see Figure 5.1). Although recorded in none of the censuses, Villebon's report of a visit in 1699 implied successful farming. There was a good harbor and the cod fishery was aided by the early appearance of the cod (at the end of March). He thought gardens were possible, that there was a good supply of hay for livestock, and that enough grain could be grown to load more than one hundred shallops.[84]

Exactly what the situation was in the Cape Sable area is uncertain. Cape Sable, Pubnico, Barrington (Bacareau) Passage and Bay, Port

82. Webster, *Acadia*, p. 133n1, believes that there were many such mills used by both the French and the New England settlers who replaced them.
83. *Acadiensia Nova, 1,* 190–91.
84. AC, C11D-*3*(2), pp. 437–53: "Mémoire sur les establissements et havres que sont depuis les Mines dans le fond de la Bay française, jusques à l'Isle de Cap Breton," October 1699, p. 443. This has been translated in Webster, *Acadia*, pp. 132–37. Ref. is to p. 134.

La Tour (or the general area of Cape Negro) are all referred to and evidently confused. In 1671 there seem to have been some dozen or so people in the area, perhaps half at Pubnico and half further east. There was a substantial number of sheep and goats.[85] In 1684, we are told that at Port La Tour there were two buildings of the "Sieurs" La Tour and Mius (d'Entremont) and six or seven people, all very poor.[86]

The Sieur Bauregard was as vague as most of the reporters but writing in 1686 he spoke of ". . . Pouboncour autrement Latour [the usual confusion] 6 lieux du capes sables ou il y a cinq familles composée de 18 personnes."[87] Actually the census counted four families with more than one person and fifteen in all. Other censuses do not list Pubnico separately but Gargas in 1687/88 was careful to point out that there were two occupied places in the Cape Sable area ("Cap de Sable and Poubouncou").[88] The totals for the whole district in successive censuses are shown in Table 5.6. They indicate a steady and healthy growth, possibly mostly in the d'Entremont seigneurie at Pubnico.

The count of 1671 gave eight arpents cultivated, twenty-six cattle, twenty-nine sheep, forty-nine pigs, and thirty-two horses;[89] that of 1686 listed seven arpents cultivated and seventeen cattle; and the Gargas census four and a half arpents cultivated, thirty-two cattle, and seven sheep.[90] No reliance can be placed on these figures for the whole area nor can we attach them to a particular location, but there were farming people and livestock, and some attempts at cultivation were

85. The summary in the *Census of Canada, 1870–71, 4*, 10, and the analysis of the nominal census by Rameau, *La France aux colonies*, pt. 1, pp. 126–27, disagree:

	Census of Canada	Rameau
People	14 (and 14 at Cap Neigre)	7 (and 7 at Cap Neigre)
Cattle	12 (possibly horses)	26
Sheep	8	25
Goats	12	—

86. AC, C11D-*1*(2), 398.

87. AC, C11D-*2*(1), 2–3: "Déscription abrégée des lieux habités de la Coste d'Accadie." Ref. is to p. 3. Some of this is printed in Harold A. Innis, ed., *Select Documents in Canadian Economic History, 1497–1783* (1929), pp. 62–63, with slightly different spelling.   88. *Acadiensia Nova, 1,* 189.

89. Of these, 7 people, 6 arpents, all the cattle and sheep, 20 pigs, and 12 horses were given for "Pobombon."

90. The 1689 census listed 40 cattle, 13 sheep, and 21 swine; that of 1693, 54 cattle and 42 swine; in 1689 there were 6 houses and two farms, but only 3 arpents listed as cultivated. See above, note 15, for sources.

being made. Apparently the d'Entremont family represented the chief settlers in Pubnico and the nominal census of 1686 makes it clear that other descendants of La Tour were living in the area, although probably not at the old fort site. Villebon was quite specific about two of the sites in 1699.[91] At Pubnico he reported a son of d'Entremont living with

TABLE 5.6   *Population of the Cape Sable area for various years, 1671–1708*

Year	Pop.	Year	Pop.
1671	14	1693	32
1686	15	1701	40
1687/88	22	1708	53
1689	24		

Sources: 1671 census, AC, G1-*466*, 2–13; 1708 census, AC, G1-*466*(2), 224. For sources of other censuses, see Table 5.3.

his wife and eight children. The soil was fertile, they raised peas and wheat, and they had thirty head of cattle, three sheep, eighteen pigs, and a water mill. There was good offshore fishing within sight of land. Sailing around Cape Sable proper he commented on the seals, and in Barrington Passage he reported a settler with a wife and seven children; they had six cattle and raised enough grain for themselves.

The present Shelburne Harbour area had two settlement sites at its head, Port Rochelois and Port Razoir; again the visitors and census-takers confused, combined, or sometimes ignored them. In actual numbers of people, three were counted in 1671, twenty in 1687/88, twelve in 1693, and fifteen in 1708; these figures indicate only that there was some settlement, but probably not very much. Gargas thought the area as a whole could support thirty or forty people. Villebon, in 1699, mentions no settlers at Rochelois, but at Port Razoir he found another of d'Entremont's sons with his wife and four children, ten or twelve horned cattle, and some sheep. Another settler with a wife and two children was not so prosperous but was a capable fisherman.[92]

Port Rossignol (present Liverpool) apparently had no settlement and we know of nothing there from Denys' time until 1686 when a small warehouse belonging to some New Englanders was reported.[93]

91. AC, C11D-*3*(2), 444–45.   92. *Ibid.*, p. 446.
93. AC, C11D-*2*(1), 123. Printed in Innis, *Select Documents*, p. 55.

Descriptions and statistics of La Have and Mirligueche are confused but continuous settlement through the four decades is likely. In 1684 four or five inhabitants who fished or traded with the Indians were reported; they had little gardens.[94] The later recorded census counts (for one or another, or both of the locations) are shown in Table 5.7. Farming is reported only for 1686 and 1689: two "farms" in each case, with three arpents cultivated and one pig in the former year, and

TABLE 5.7 *Population of La Have and Mirligueche for various years, 1686–1708*

Year	Pop.	Year	Pop.
1686	13	1693	6
1687/88	22	1701	75 *
1689	20	1708	42

* This figure includes métis and perhaps Indians.
Sources: 1708 census, AC, G1-*466*(2), 224.
For sources of other censuses, see Table 5.3.

four arpents cultivated, seven horses, and five swine in the latter.

The evidences of the agricultural settlement of the 1630's were still present; the fields were largely overgrown but as late as 1701 the apple trees planted by Razilly's group still flourished: "La plus grande partie des pomiers qui ont esté plantes du temp de Monsieur le commandeur de Rasily y sont encore et aporte du fruit tous les ans, j'en ay bien de sidre cette annee . . . ."[95] Demeulle mentions settlers in both locations in 1686. He points out that La Have was regularly visited by a dozen or fifteen large English vessels for drying cod. He thought the three or four French residents had begun "des habitations assez raisonables."[96] He took four sailors from here to visit the rest of the coast. He noted that the few settlers on the Little La Have River (Petite Rivière, behind La Have Island) lived well enough not by cultivation but by trading furs with the Indians and later the English, on whom they depended for supplies. As he correctly pointed out, the fur trade did

94. AC, C11D-*1*(2), 398.
95. AC, C11D-*4*(2), 209. Printed in Innis, *Select Documents*, p. 60.
96. AC, C11D-*2*(1), 124. Printed in Innis, *Select Documents*, p. 60. See also *Acadiensia Nova*, *1*, 116.

not result in people's striking their roots in the country, as they would if they became farmers. Although they liked to fish, they had been pillaged so many times they had pretty well given it up.[97]

Gargas, two years later, thought that more than a hundred settlers could be accomodated at La Have and twelve or thirteen at Mirligueche.[98] Villebon was very enthusiastic about the area. La Have had, he thought,

> . . . the best harbor and the most magnificent situation on the east coast. Like the others it is surrounded by hills but has much more land suitable for cultivation. It is true there is not much beach available for a large fishing industry, but it could be extended; moreover, flakes could be used, and they without question produce the finest quality of fish. The old fort is at the mouth of the very beautiful river, and vessels of 50 guns can enter and anchor under its cannon. Lumber mills could be built, for pine and spruce fir [?] are plentiful. Two families are at present living there. There is plenty of hunting, and many good things to eat, such as herring and mackerel in season, eels at all times, as well as plaice, lobsters, oysters and other shell-fish.[99]

His only comment on Mirligueche was that the soil was fair and that there was a large number of red oaks.

Chebucto is given very little attention by the reporters. Demeulle found it occupied by three or four settlers in 1686, ". . . qui prétendent y faire de fort bonnes habitations; ce lieu est considérable par la pesche de la morue seiche, parcequ'il s'y trouve des isles, couvertes de caillous plats que les pescheurs apellent galet, où ils font seicher la morue."[100] Gargas noted one house, three French settlers, and thirty-three Indians in 1687/88 (the three are confirmed in the count of 1689), and Cadillac thought it the most beautiful and best harbor on the coast,[101] but Villebon only notes it in passing. Similarly Musquodoboit was largely ignored; the thirteen people recorded there in 1671 are the only notice of settlers we have and Villebon in 1699 thought little of its harbor.[102] There may well have been intermittent settlement here as well as at Jeddore, the St. Mary's River estuary and, indeed, at dozens of other places along the haven-rich coast. But there is no record until we reach Martingaud (Whitehaven), just west of Canso.

97. *Acadiensia Nova, 1,* 116. 98. *Ibid.,* p. 189.

99. Webster, *Acadia,* p. 135. In a footnote Webster points out that this is the farthest southwest along this coast that oysters have been reported.

100. AC, C11D-2(1), 126. Printed in Innis, *Select Documents,* p. 55.

101. "The Cadillac Memoir," p. 84. 102. Webster. *Acadia,* p. 136.

where Cadillac noted a sedentary fishery about 1690 ("but the war has ruined their project and their means").[103]

One of the great mysteries of the French accounts of Acadia in the period is the relatively little attention paid to the great fishery depot of Canso. No census indicated permanent settlement by recording numbers, but every visitor speaks of the number of fishermen seen, and the various fishing stations. Gargas' report (1687/88) is typical: "Canceau is one of the best places for codfishing. There are several fine beaches to dry the fish on and several small islands where ships can be sheltered. In this place the gentlemen of the Company [des Pêches sédentaires de l'Acadie] have established their fishing station."[104]

Chedabucto Bay between Canso and the Strait of Canso was too open and deficient in coves to provide shelter except at its head where, in the estuary now known as Milford Haven, behind a treacherously shallow bar, there was a natural harbor (near present Guysborough town) and soil more suitable for cultivation than at any place on the south coast east of Mirligueche. There Bergier, a La Rochelle merchant, and his associates in the Company of Acadia had obtained a grant in 1682, and built Fort St. Louis with a storehouse and a barracks for the men.

Bergier, who was made king's lieutenant in Acadia, under Perrot, declared, in a dispatch shortly after that event, that he had sowed wheat, rye, and barley on May 28, reaped it on September 16, and taken it to France for exhibition. He claimed that he had taken out vines and all sorts of fruit trees from France and that flax, hemp, peas, beans, and all manner of vegetables did well. He thought it incomparably superior to Quebec.[105]

This bit of propaganda received damaging blows from succeeding visitors. In 1684, 130 persons are reported (outside of women, if any, and sailors employed by the Company). Besides a dry fishery they had a seal fishery and a tryworks for rendering seal oil, they cut wood to make fishing shallops, and had opened a coal mine.[106] In 1686 fifteen or twenty "domestics" and four families were recorded as working the land. Demeulle was not negative about it, just noncommittal. He described the buildings as several roughly built huts. The farm was three

103. "The Cadillac Memoir," p. 82.   104. *Acadiensia Nova, 1,* 188.
105. AC, C11D-*1*(2), 361–62, 373: 1682.
106. AC, C11D-*2*(1), 397. It is hard to know just where the coal mine might have been. Conceivably they were taking sea-cliff coal from Cape Breton's coast.

leagues away from the fort (at the head of Milford Haven?). There, three acres had been cleared and the ground manured, and he had "no doubt that grain will flourish there." Demeulle is quite specific on one point: "Ils font toute leur pesche entre les Isles de Canseaux à une ou deux lieues au large."[107]

There are reports of 150 residents, including 80 fishermen, based on Chedabucto in 1687 (this may include any population for Canso and explain the absence of records for that area) and two large buildings, a barque of thirty tons, and a number of shallops.[108] More than a year later Gargas was openly depreciatory; he thought the soil not very good and said very little land had been cleared. He did think the fishing fairly good; he reported an iron mine and thought "a few settlers could support themselves."[109] In 1690 Saccardy, the engineer, was even more discouraging about the actual headquarters area: "There is no natural wood or wood for carpentering; nor are there three acres of meadow in ten leagues of the countryside. It is scarcely possible to make a garden, for the sand is too dry and too light, and water is too scarce and too distant to be used. The house [block house, or fort] is built of stone and mud, and is about to fall down."[110] In all there were then seven settlers and twelve soldiers, who depended entirely on imported food and other supplies. The "fort" was sacked by New Englanders in 1688 and 1690 and appears to have been out of business thereafter. By 1710 the Company of Acadia was moribund.

Cape Breton Island remained essentially empty (see Chapter 7). No attempt will be made to discuss here the settlements on the Saint John River or the coast to the west or those on what is now the Gulf shore of New Brunswick. They became, increasingly, simply fur-trading posts and bases for raids on New England. The Acadians in the settlements appear to have had almost nothing to do with them, and they were little more relevant to their farming community than the more distant Canadian people along the St. Lawrence. The north shore of the Bay of Fundy and east to the Penobscot River appears to have had fewer than one hundred settlers in any of the seventeenth-century accounts. Rameau estimated a total of ninety-six for 1701, on the Saint John River and westward.[111]

---

107. AC, C11D-*2*(1), 135. Printed in part in Innis, *Select Documents*, pp. 55–57, 60.
108. Webster, *Acadia*, p. 207.   109. *Acadiensia Nova, 1*, 188.
110. *Ibid.*, p. 210.   111. Rameau, *Une Colonie Féodale, 1*, 205–6.

THE ECONOMY

Agriculture[112]

The economy of the Acadians in the major settlements did include fishing, hunting, lumbering, the building of boats and small vessels, a great many household industries, blacksmithing, trading locally with the Indians for furs, and trading their surplus livestock and grain to the New Englanders or to vessels from France for a wide variety of goods which they could not produce themselves. But, for the vast majority, for most of each year, the occupation was farming and, so far as cropping was concerned, almost exclusively the cultivation of the tidal marshlands after these had been dyked in from the sea. Indeed this had been so since soon after the reestablishment of settlement in the Port Royal area in the late 1630's. As Demeulle reported in 1686: "Il y a quelques habitans dans ce lieu [near the town]; mais la plus grande partie est sur une rivière qui aproche de la baye des Mines; cette rivière est continué a ce bassin du Port Royal et fort utilé par la quantité de bonnes terres qui s'y trouvent dont les habitants ont defrichez une bonne partie pour leur subsistance."[113]

UPLANDS AND TIDAL MARSHLANDS — The persistent neglect of the "uplands" (i.e., any land but the dyked marshlands) for agriculture was the subject of repeated comment in criticism of the Acadians by visitors and newly arrived officials from France. Governor Perrot, writing in 1686, thought it was the "fear of work" that kept men from clearing and cultivating the forested uplands.[114] By avoiding them they had saved themselves the work of cutting wood, gathering it in piles, burning it, and hoeing by hand (since they could not plow among the stumps) or removing the stumps. Moreover, upland would require manuring. In contrast the marshes, once dyked, enclosed, and drained, and then left idle while the rain washed out the salt, were easily plowed

112. Some statistical and other descriptive information on agriculture at Chignecto and Minas has been given above. This section focuses strongly, although not exclusively, on the Port Royal district for which we have a continuous record throughout the period.

113. AC, C11D-*2*(1), 119: "Mémoires Généraux," 1686.

114. Perrot's "Relation de la Province d'Accadie," from which these references come, is in AC, C11D-*2*(1), 38–60. Refs. are to pp. 41–42, quotation from p. 41.

and very fertile for grain. The difficulty with the concentration on the marshlands, as Perrot saw it, was that their cultivation made unavailable the natural pasture and hay land, a fact which may help to account for the reduction (or slow growth) in cattle numbers suggested by the successive censuses. Perrot thought that the upland provided only sufficient forage for sheep—"du pâturage court propre aux moutons . . . ."[115]

Meneval, in a dispatch to Colbert in 1688, reported on the same problem: "Je n'en ay encore pu rien descouvrir les habitans ne trouvant point d'endroits où les terres hautes y soient propres."[116] He thought they might be forced to the uplands ultimately by a shortage of land but felt that the prospect of the heavy work discouraged them and added that they were short of labor and animals to make the manure, "qui y est absolument necessaire."[117] They undertook the heavy task of dyking and draining more willingly because the fertility of the marshlands guaranteed nearly perpetual annual harvests if unusually high tides did not break down the dykes.[118] Meneval ascribed the scattering of settlement to the irregular and discontinuous location of bits of suitable marsh, and he saw the exhaustion of the supply of such marshland as the chief reason for the emigration to Minas which had started in that decade.

Saccardy summarizes his condemnation of the "meadow cultivation," which maintained the "beaded" settlement pattern, under three heads. First, once cultivated these, the only meadows they have, no longer supply hay and pasturage for cattle. Second, the system promotes laziness; it is not necessary to manure the "meadows" and the children are brought up in idleness, and cultivation of the higher ground would remedy this trouble. Third, living this sort of life cramps their outlook and results in their children leaving home for other low-lying lands, such as those at Grand Pré.[119] At the end of the century the same sort of critical observations continued. Governor Villebon supported the conclusion that disinterest in the hard work of clearing the upland was

115. *Ibid.*, p. 41.   116. AC, C11D-2(1), 206–7.

117. *Ibid.* Meneval points out that the Acadians would have had to clear a substantial area around their houses and fields to keep the wild predators (bears and wolves?) away from themselves and their livestock if they moved further inland (i.e., away from the streams).

118. Meneval noted that there had been three or four unusually high tides that March that had flooded most of the land already seeded to wheat. *Ibid.*

119. AC, C11D-2(1), 310: 1690, and *Acadiensia Nova*, 1, 203–8.

a major cause of the migration to Minas, and he insisted that the Acadians were in error in their judgment. The upland, he felt, was much more reliable in view of the danger of dyke failure and the need for a two-year lapse in use after dyke repair to wash out the salt.[120]

However, the Sieur de Dièreville, a man of some little scientific and literary education, visited Port Royal in the same year, 1699, and provides us with a different point of view on the marsh versus upland problem. "It costs a great deal to prepare the lands which they wish to cultivate; those called Uplands, which must be cleared in the Forest, are not good, & the seed does not come up well in them; it makes no difference how much trouble is taken to bring them into condition with Manure, which is very scarce; there is almost no harvest, & sometimes they have to be abandoned."[121]

Brouillan picked up the theme again in a dispatch of 1701.[122] He thought that the lands could be more productive, but for the indolence of the inhabitants. The failure to attack the uplands he attributed to laziness; and he thought this a major reason why the settlers were limited to such small pieces of cultivated land on the marshes, although their concessions were very large. He suggested a redivision of the lands on the basis of what could or could not be worked, and hoped that this would encourage the young men to work the uplands. More-over, he felt that a sorting out of individual holdings, with a redrawing of boundaries, might correct the fact that some of the original allot-ments were too small. He also alluded to another abuse, the concession of lands that had been reserved for common pasturage so that holders of small allotments near the post had nowhere to take their cattle. The same complaint is echoed by Des Goutins, writing in 1703, who charged that Meneval had been guilty of such practices in 1688.[123] Finally the engineer, De Labat, living at Port Royal during the admin-istration of Governor Brouillan, complained that land was being held

120. AC, C11D-3(2), 441: October 1699. Most of the Villebon material is in AC, C11D-2 and C11D-3; much of it has been translated and published in Webster, Acadia, where ref. is to p. 133.   121. Dièreville, Relation, p. 94.

122. AC, C11D-4(1), 114–77: "Mémoire de ce qui regarde les interests du Roy touchant l'establissement que Sa Majesté a dessein de faire dans la Province de la Cadie," attached to a letter of October 1701. There is an extract of this printed in Rameau, Une Colonie Féodale, 2, 337–38.

123. AC, C11D-4. A short extract from this dispatch is printed in Rameau, Une Colonie Féodale, 2, 336. Although Rameau ascribes it to 1703 its date was November 29, 1702.

out of use, and that if it were all used the Acadians would be in good shape.[124]

There is an air of unreality about all the complaints regarding failure to use the uplands; the observers were making comparisons with France and with much better soils than the Nova Scotia uplands provided. In the conditions of the time and place the Acadians followed what was, for them, the most sensible policy. As long as there was productive marshland to be dyked they preferred to move to where it was easily available, and as we have seen they did move—to Minas and Chignecto—long before even all the dykable marsh in the Port Royal area was employed. They were not afraid of axe-work as they amply demonstrated.[125] They simply observed the comparatively poor yields and short life of unfertilized upland soils and made, for their situation, a good judgment.

FARMS, CROPLAND, AND CROPS — The first reasonably full account of marshland agriculture was given by Dièreville:

To grow Wheat, the Marshes which are inundated by the Sea at high Tide, must be drained; these are called Lowlands, & they are quite good, but what labour is needed to make them fit for cultivation! The ebb & flow of the Sea cannot easily be stopped, but the Acadians succeed in doing so by means of great Dykes, called Aboteaux [he was confused as to terminology], & it is done in this way; five or six rows of large logs are driven whole into the ground at the points where the tide enters the Marsh, & between each row, other logs are laid, one on top of the other, & all the spaces between them are so carefully filled with well-pounded clay, that the water can no longer get throug̑h. In the centre of this construction, a Sluice is contrived in such a manner that the water on the Marshes flows out of its own accord, while that of the Sea is prevented from coming in. An undertaking of this natʹure, which can only be carried on at certain Seasons when the Tides do not rise so high, costs a great deal, & takes many days, but the abundant crop that is harvested in the second year, after the soil has been washed by Rain water compensates, for all the expense. As these Lands are owned by several Men, the work upon

124. *Acadiensia Nova*, 2, 6.

125. The Gargas census report (1687/88) shows 44½ arpents of upland and 254 arpents of marshland cultivated in 1687 (clearly an incomplete figure, see Table 5.4), a higher proportion of upland than the reports of the period imply. *Acadiensia Nova*, 1, 154. Moreover, the 1689 census has counts for Port Royal of 136 arpents of upland and an additional 45 cleared but abandoned, as compared with 342 arpents of marsh, which is an even more striking proportion. AC. G1–466, 58–59. It probably should be added that Acadians always seemed to prefer to use dyked land if it was available, even if it required a great deal of work.

them is done in common; if they belonged to an Individual, he would have to pay the others, or give to the Men who had worked for him an equal number of days devoted to some other employment; that is the manner in which it is customary for them to adjust such matters among themselves.[126]

The description is generally good. The word *aboiteau* is a curious one, used not for the dyke itself but for the clapper valves (wooden gates on horizontal hinges) which opened seaward to let out the fresh water from the streams and drains behind the dykes at low tide, and were forced closed by the incoming tide to keep out the salt water.[127] Dièreville was overly optimistic about the period necessary to "wash out" the salt; two full years was a minimum and perhaps more usually three years was involved. Cadillac was one of many, however, to mention the two-year period: "Ils les laissent dessécher pendant deux ans, au but de ce tems là, ils rompent et labourent ces terres ou marois, dans lesquels tout ce qu'on y sème y vient merveilleusement bien, sans qu'il soit besoin d'y mettre jamais du fumier."[128]

The marshland agriculture, however productive, had not only its hard work but its hazards. In a report of 1706 Des Goutins described the great flood of November 5, 1705, that had overflowed "tous ceux du pays sans exception."[129] While the extent of the damage may have been exaggerated (he was arguing for the turning of attention to the uplands), there is no question that the land flooded would regain its previous level of production only after a desalinization period following rebuilding of the dykes. There is a good deal of disagreement on the length of such a period after chance inundation, doubtless depending upon how long the land had remained under salt water. A *mémoire* of 1701 states that four years were necessary,[130] but during that time drains could be dug and increasing use made of the marshes for hay and pasture, as the vegetation association changed rather rapidly.[131]

126. Dièreville, *Relation*, pp. 94–95.
127. J. C. Webster, *The Forts of Chignecto* (1930), p. 33.
128. AC, C11D-*10*, 22. The following is the translation in "The Cadillac Memoir," p. 86: "They allow them to dry during two years. At the end of this time they plow and till these lands or marshes, in which everything that is sown produces marvellously without need for ever adding manure."
129. AC, C11D-*5*, 280: December 1706. A small part of this has been reprinted in Rameau, *Une Colonie Féodale*, 2, 340–41. Rameau is inconsistent in his quoting; he may quote exactly for several lines, and then put the sense of what follows in his own words. He also leaves portions out and makes insertions.
130. AC, C11D-*4*(1), 179–80: "Mémoire de Port Royal et des Costes d'Acadie." Some of it has been printed in Innis, *Select Documents*, p. 66.
131. See discussion of marsh vegetation in Chapter 2.

Unfortunately, the actual cropping activity is not well reported in the various censuses. In 1671 about 380 arpents were cultivated and the harvest consisted of over 500 *barriques* of grain. Without knowing how much of the land was in grain, or the precise volume of a barrique, the yields cannot be calculated but the fact that little more than one arpent (about an acre) per person was cultivated suggests a heavy dependence on foods other than the grain, pulse, and vegetables that were raised on these marshland acres.[132] If both the 1671 and 1686 figures are accurate, there was little extension of cultivation in the Port Royal area in those fifteen years, for the latter estimate of arpents cultivated was still under four hundred.

There were perhaps sixty to seventy "farms" recorded by the 1686 census, for a total population of fewer than six hundred persons.[133] There were one hundred and two heads of family, ninety-five households of more than one person, seventy-five households with land or livestock, and fifty-nine credited with some land in cultivation. Even if roughly one hundred persons were living in a more or less nucleated group of hamlets on the Port Royal peninsula, this suggests at least eight people per farmstead—and of the fifty-nine holdings of land only nine had ten or more arpents in cultivation, twenty-two had from five to nine, and twenty-eight had fewer than five; sixteen families who held animals had no improved land.[134] The 1689 count listed about five hundred arpents of farmland but fewer *granges* (farms) than in 1686 (fifty-seven as against sixty-one). Its total of seventy-eight houses may indicate some twenty-one homes, presumably largely on the peninsula, not directly connected with farming (of course more than one "house" may have been associated with any one farm).[135]

The Gargas census of 1687/88 and that for 1689 are the only ones which distinguish between upland and marshland and, as remarked upon above, Gargas showed that a much larger proportion of the

132. AC, G1-*466*, 2–13, give values of 379½ arpents and 525 *barriques*, 57 *mines*, 25 *boisseaux* of grain in 1671. The capacity of the hogshead indicated by *barrique* is uncertain; the *mine* also had a fluctuating value, but is usually quoted at 78 litres or two *minots*. A "bushel" fluctuated at around 32 litres so that 25 bushels should have been more than one *mine*, and 57 *mines* probably more than one *barrique*. Possibly there were 5 *boisseaux* per *mine* (or 2½ of our present standard bushels) and 5 *mines* per *barrique*, making a *barrique* about 100 gallons. At this approximate calculation, the yield comes to about 15 bushels per cultivated acre, which is reasonable since only part of the tilled land was in grain.

133. AC, G1-*466*, 14–57. What constituted a farm is not clear in this or other censuses; here it is taken as a household holding either land or animals.

134. *Ibid.*   135. AC, G1-*466*, 58–59.

upland areas had been cleared than the comments about neglect of those areas would lead one to imagine. Perhaps most of the upland simply had trees cut down to make rough pasture, although at least one farm, consisting entirely of land away from the marshes, is evident in Figure 5.8.

In 1693 the total amount of cultivated land reported took a big jump to some 1,300 arpents,[136] and remained at figures around 1,200 arpents in the varying totals given for 1698.[137] The count for 1701 is given as both 462 arpents (consistent with the figures for 1689 and earlier) and 1,361 (consistent with those for the 1690's).[138] It may be that the larger figures represent a more accurate count or that the smaller refer only to dyked marshlands and that there was no sudden acreage increase in the 1690's. If, however, the 1,300-acre figure for 1693 is correct, it indicates an average of nearly twenty arpents per farm, placing the role of arable land in a somewhat more prominent light, if, indeed, clearing (*défrichement*) implies arable.

Some of the farms were becoming quite large establishments. Of the seventy-one holdings of "land worked" (*terres labourées*) in Port Royal in 1698, three holdings had forty or more arpents worked, eleven from thirty-one to thirty-nine, eleven from twenty-one to thirty, twenty-six from eleven to twenty, thirteen from five to ten, and only seven with four arpents or fewer.[139] Also, as time went on, there were increasing numbers of non-farming families at Port Royal, although there were few at the other settlements that held neither land nor animals.

The major crops throughout the period, from the evidence available, were wheat and peas, the standard Acadian combination of the seventeenth, eighteenth, and even early nineteenth centuries. Sometimes they were forced to other expedients; thus Grandfontaine appears to have reported that, in 1670, they were sowing maize (*bled d'Inde*) because they had no seed wheat[140] but Indian corn was, almost certainly, a rarity. There are also several references to other crops, hemp (*chanvre*) being mentioned as early as 1670,[141] and there is frequent

---

136. AC, G1-*466*, 60–102.

137. The 1698 counts yield figures of 1,140, 1,257 and 1,275 arpents, as variously totaled by the census reporter (AC, G1-*466*, 106–7) and the author (whose addition made 1,275, from *idem*, pp. 107–33).

138. AC, G1-*466*, 169, and Rameau, *Une Colonie Féodale, 1*, 223 (quoting from some unspecified source), respectively.   139. AC, G1-*466*, 107–45.

140. "Lettre de Talon au ministre Colbert," p. 163.   141. *Ibid.*, p. 164.

reference to the weaving of linen from locally-grown flax as well as to the spinning and weaving of wool from local sheep. Perrot's comments of the 1680's were that the Port Royal area harvested a surplus of wheat and that a fair quantity of peas, apples, and cherries was available.[142] Oats, barley, and rye also were widely used and cabbages and a great variety of garden stuff were indispensable to the settlers' diet. The harvests were very reliable on the dyked lands and only occasionally did failures occur. One such instance, in 1698, is described in a joint report of Des Goutins and Villebon: the people were "sans bled ny farine à cause de la mauvaise récolte des bleds et pois de l'année dernière."[143]

For the early 1690's the report of Cadillac fills in the production picture: "This district . . . produces wheat, rye, Indian corn, every kind of legumes [vegetables?] and pot herbs, especially headed cabbages. . . . Fruit trees also thrive there very well, among others apple trees and pear trees. Grain is sown about 15 of April, and is reaped towards the end of August."[144] For the last year of the century there is the useful descriptive *mémoire* from Villebon. He mentions many vegetables, including "choux, betteraves, oignons, carottes, cives, eschalottes, navets, panets, et touttes sortes de salades,"[145] and seems to suggest that d'Aulnay started the practice of sowing wheat and peas together. He gives special attention to the apples: "Port Royal is a little Normandy for apples. They might have a great many more, and could easily make cider; but apart from the fact that they are not very industrious and most of them work only enough for a bare living, they neglect the propagation of fruit trees for use as the country opens up."[146] Among the kinds of apples were Calvilles, Rambours (or Rambures), Reinettes,[147] and three or four other varieties. There were *poires des rousselet* (and other pears) and trees yielding both the regular cherries (*cerisiers*) and red-and-white ones (*bigarotier*, i.e., *bigarreautier*). In 1698, the census reported a total of 1,766 fruit trees scattered over fifty-four of the seventy-three farms so that fruit grow-

142. AC, C11D-2(1), 39: 1686.   143. AC, C11D-3(2), 504.
144. Ganong, "The Cadillac Memoir," p. 80.
145. That is, cabbages, beets, onions, carrots, chives, shallots, turnips, parsnips, and a variety of salad greens. AC, C11D-3(2), 436–67. Quote is from p. 455.
146. Webster, *Acadia*, p. 128.
147. The Calville was a Norman apple (same root as Calvados); the Rambour (Rambure, Rambutan) a large green or yellow apple; and the Reinettes were. apparently, highly variable in size and color. Webster, *Acadia*, p. 128n.

ing, with an average of some 35 trees per farm, represented a rather important part of their husbandry by the turn of the century. There were three orchards with more than 150 trees each, although more than half of the orchards had 30 trees or fewer.

Writing in the same year, Dièreville describes the several varieties of apples "which they keep carefully in their cellars to eat during the Winter"[148] as excellent but *sauvages* (i.e., uncultivated, neglected, or gone wild).[149] However, he does mention (on the shores of the basin below Port Royal) a few yards "as well planted with Apple trees as they would have been in Normandy," but with the difference that the trees were not grafted.[150] He says first that, although himself a Norman, he was unable to recognize any of them, but almost immediately retracts and says that he recognized Calvilles. He mentions cider but makes rather more of the brewing of spruce beer (new tips fermented with yeast and molasses), a well-known anti-scorbutic of the seventeenth century that had apparently caught on in Acadia.[151]

Dièreville places *Brassicas* (the cabbage family) in a more prominent position in farming and in the diet than do most other writers. There was a heavy dependence on cabbages and turnips, and a soup made from a combination of the two with slices of pork was popular in the winter. Interestingly, the turnips were stored in cellars (possibly usually under the houses) whereas the cabbages were left in the fields after being pulled and covered with snow.

LIVESTOCK — Livestock of all the major kinds, but especially cattle, were of great importance and it may be that they figured as largely as the grains, fruits, and vegetables together in food supply. Livestock numbers were reported for Port Royal in various censuses from 1671 to 1707 (see Table 5.8). One of the major deficiencies of the censuses of livestock is the sketchy and obviously very incomplete record of horses: nine and seven in the censuses of 1687/88 and 1689 for Port Royal, and six for Beaubassin in the former count. None was reported for Minas. Yet as early as 1671 there were thirty-two listed for the Cape Sable settlements (presumably between Pubnico and Shelburne), and there are frequent references to horses in the documentary

148. Dièreville, *Relation*, p. 116.   149. *Ibid.*, p. 83.   150. *Ibid.*, p. 85.
151. *Ibid.*, p. 91. His words are "On n'y fait que de la Biere avec des sommitez de Sapin." *Ibid.*, p. 256. "Sapin" could be either fir or spruce but clearly means spruce here, although Webster translates it as fir.

record, by both Cadillac and Dièreville, among others. It is possible that the infrequent use of plows (see discussion in Chapter 6) and the very poor roads meant that horses were not nearly as important as we believe them to have become to the Acadians in the eighteenth century.

The smaller numbers of cattle and sheep in 1689 and 1701, as compared with totals of three years before, in each case do not seem to have any connection with known effects of raids during these troubled years and may reflect only less careful counts; it is questionable if any substantial part of the swine population ever was counted. Again, the

TABLE 5.8 *Numbers of livestock reported for Port Royal in various censuses, 1671–1707*

Livestock	1671	1686	1689	1693	1698	1701	1707
Cattle	652	647	573	955	982	715	952
Sheep	430	617	617	1,279	1,136	768	1,237
Pigs	—	348	619	733	568	462	855
Horses	—	—	7	—	—	—	—

Source: AC, C11D-2(1), 124. Printed in *Select Documents in Canadian Economic History, 1497–1783*, ed. Harold A. Innis (1929), p. 55.

time of year of the counts was important; with winter fodder always in short supply and the autumn slaughter usually heavy, December counts may have been 30 per cent to 40 per cent less than those of the previous June in some years. Perhaps the most notable impression one gets is that of relative stability of cattle numbers but of general increase in sheep and swine. It is difficult to gauge the importance of deliberate slaughter during attacks, or in anticipation of them, to prevent animals falling into the hands of the New Englanders. In a dispatch of December 25, 1707, Subercase reported: "Il [Subercase] a esté obligé dans la première attaque des Anglais de faire tuer une grande quantité de boeufs et de vaches appartenant aux habitans de peur que les ennemis n'en profitassent."[152]

The kind and quality of the animals is hard to identify with confidence. Cadillac throws some doubt on the usefulness and reliability of his other observations by his rhapsodies on the livestock: "The sheep are . . . as fat and big as in the Pyrenees, and their wool is as fine. . . . The ewes bear young twice a year and have two young each time."[153]

152. AC, C11D-6, 14.   153. "The Cadillac Memoir," p. 80.

He described the horses as ". . . de belle taille, bien traversés, forts, la jambe bonne, l'ongle dur, la teste un peu grosse, mais on ne prend point de soin pour en élever, à cause qu'on n'en trouve point le débit."[154] If indeed the case, no other observers have joined with him in praise of these animals. Finally, Cadillac observed that "there is also much poultry," including geese and pigeons as well as barnyard fowl (coqs d'Inde).[155] Villebon had a less happy picture of the livestock which were showing the deleterious effects of long and unselective inbreeding: "Another thing which appears indispensable is our need to obtain from them [the New Englanders] mares and stallions for breeding purposes and for trade in the Islands, and cattle, so that the stock may be changed entirely. The Acadian cows do not yield a third of the amount of milk which the cows of Boston give, and even that with difficulty."[156]

The comparative value of livestock is indicated in a price list recorded by Villebon in 1699 (Table 5.9).[157] For comparison with field products, wheat and peas sold for one sou (sol) per livre weight.

Dièreville, at about the same time as Villebon, has a number of remarks regarding the animals. He echoes Villebon's comment upon the impressive size of the sheep (up to 100 pounds weight, as big as those of Beauvais) and adds that, being kept for wool, they were rarely slaughtered. He comments on the difficulty of keeping stock through the winter (the perpetual problem for settlers in northeastern North America) and on the problem of keeping meat after the fall slaughtering (one could not freeze it and depend on its staying frozen in Acadia,

154. Rameau, Une Colonie Féodale, 1, 230. Ganong, "The Cadillac Memoir," p. 80 translates it: "The horses there are of fine build, broad-shouldered, well legged, with lasting hoofs, the head a little large, but no care is taken in raising them." There is not the added phrase: "because there is no market for them."

155. Again Rameau, Une Colonie Féodale, pp. 230–31, has a fuller version than Ganong. One must assume a variety of poultry from the 1630's onward.

156. Webster, Acadia, p. 139. The "Islands" are the French West Indies.

157. Ibid., p. 128. The list gives prices and weights in livres. A livre (weight) was about 17 ounces, roughly a pound. A livre (monetary) was a franc, but actually worth much less than a gold franc or crown or an ecu sol. By 1689 the value of an ecu sol was roughly 61.t. 5s. (6 livres tournois, 5 sous). The livre, like the monetary pound, was divided into 20 units (sous or sols) and each sou into 12 units (deniers, from Latin denarius; compare the British "d." for a penny). But the livres were not coins, simply monnaie de compte or French money of account, and one must equate them neither to gold nor to the apparent English or British equivalents. See, especially, Harold A. Innis, The Cod Fisheries: The History of an International Economy (1954), pp. 28–29, and Webster, Acadia, p. 128. These equivalents tell us more about the local value of a livre than of the value of the items, except to give us a comparative scale.

as in Quebec) which meant a great activity in preserving meat in the fall and a consequent greater demand for salt. Dièreville does mention the pigs being wintered on scraps of turnip and cabbage and on the offal of slaughtering: "The Acadians are great lovers of fat bacon . . . which they prefer before partridges and rabits [sic]. . . . They never

TABLE 5.9 *Comparative values of livestock and livestock products in 1699*

Stock and game		
Cattle	40 to 50	livres per head* (monetary)
Sheep	7 to 7½ livres	"
Suckling pigs	15 to 18 sous	"
Fowl (all kinds)	4 to 10 "	"
Partridge and hare	4 to 5 "	"
Animal products		
mutton	3	sous per livre (weight)
bacon	2 to 3	" " "
beef	2	" " "
butter	8	" " "
eggs	5	" per dozen

* For an explanation of the livre as monetary unit and weight unit, see footnote 157 this chapter.

Source: Acadia at the End of the Seventeenth Century, ed. J. C. Webster (1934), p. 128.

eat veal, nor lamb, but let them all grow up, and throw the sheeps heads, trotters and pluck to their swine . . . ."[158]

Although butter was made in the country it was not considered good; the settlers made and kept only a small supply, preferring to use the milk. Of the latter Dièreville thought they were too fond: ". . . on y aime trop le lait . . . ."[159] This desire for milk he saw as a major reason that calves were rarely killed for veal, for ". . . it is the peculiarity of the Cows in that Country, that if a Calf is taken from its Mother, her udder yields nothing more."[160] He also comments on the plenitude of poultry but felt that, in a country of such abundant game, it did not serve much purpose.

The major role of cattle in supplying much needed surplus agricul-

158. *Acadiensia Nova, 1*, 44–45. It is described as being from the account of "a French gentleman, who visited Port Royal in 1699" and must come from one of the Dièreville editions. The parallel passage, with some additions and omissions is given in Dièreville, *Relation*, p. 107 and (in French) p. 265.

159. Dièreville, *Relation*, p. 266.   160. *Ibid.*, p. 110.

tural commodities for sale is stressed again and again. At the beginning of the period Grandfontaine had reported that the supply of cattle was such that they could send 6,000 pounds (livres) of salted beef to Quebec in exchange for cloth and other goods.[161] Moreover, in the frequent official complaints made of the settlers' trading with the New Englanders, cattle figure largely.

Because there is so little information on the sale of farm products (in part because so much of it was illegal) and because we have much more quantitative data about livestock than about crops, livestock holdings offer our best clues to comparative degrees of commercial emphasis on the part of Acadian farm families. The standard of comparison used is the ratio of livestock units per capita, one unit being composed of one head of cattle, or five sheep, or five swine. We begin with the assumption that a farm family required at least one livestock unit for each of its members to satisfy its own needs. For example, a family group of two grandparents, two parents, and four children is considered to have been no more than self-sufficient in animals if it owned two oxen, four cows, five sheep, and five pigs, and unlikely to have had any surplus for sale. On the other hand, such a family with as many as three livestock units per capita (say, four oxen, ten cows, four other cattle, twenty sheep, and ten pigs) almost certainly would have had a surplus, and the possibility of sale (of live animals, salt meat, wool, and hides) provides the only rational explanation for the maintenance of such numbers.

The precise ratio for a clear subsistence/commercial division probably varied from family to family, or even among the different settlements, within the range of one to three livestock units per capita; a ratio of two may perhaps serve as a rough gauge of the threshold of commercialism in livestock holdings. Using this measure, Table 5.10 and Figure 5.10 indicate the relative positions of the different settlements in the various census years and, within each settlement, the relative proportion of clearly subsistence farming and of various degrees of commercial interest in farming operations. Since livestock in general, and swine in particular, are likely to have been underrepresented in the censuses, it is judged that the relative degree of commercial emphasis is, if anything, suggested less strongly than it should be. Table 5.11 suggests two general trends in time and space. Port Royal

161. "Lettre de Talon au ministre Colbert," p. 163.

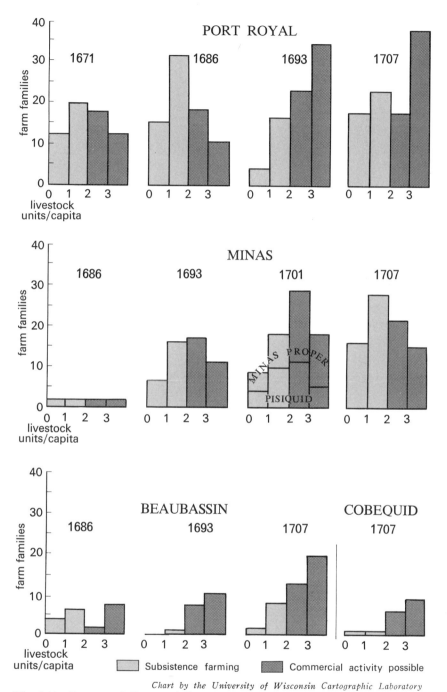

Fig. 5.10 Degrees of Commercialism as Measured by Holdings of Livestock Per Capita among Farm Families.

TABLE 5.10 *Degrees of commercialism in the Bay settlements as revealed in various censuses 1671–1707*

Year and location of census	Number of farm families* with:				Total number of:	
	less than 1 livestock unit† per capita	1 to 2 livestock units per capita	2 to 3 livestock units per capita	more than 3 livestock units per capita	farm families	non-farm families
1671 Port Royal	12	20	18	12	62	5
1686 Port Royal	15	31	18	10	74	27
" Minas	2	2	2	2	8	2
" Beaubassin	4	6	2	8	20	0
1693 Port Royal	4	16	23	35	78	2
" Minas	7	16	17	11	51	4
" Beaubassin	0	2	7	10	19	1
1701 Minas proper	4	9	17	13	43	1
" Pisiquid	5	10	12	5	32	1
1707 Port Royal	18	23	18	38	97	7
" Minas	16	28	22	15	81	7
" Cobequid	1	1	6	9	17	0
" Beaubassin	2	8	13	20	43	2

* A farm family is one having either land or livestock.
† One livestock unit = 1 head cattle = 5 sheep = 5 swine.
Sources: 1671 census, AC, G1-*466*, 2–13, and see Table 5.3.

became more commercial in interest (or at least in opportunity) between 1686 and 1693, and between 1701 and 1707. In terms of livestock, Beaubassin tended to be rather more commercially oriented than Port Royal, and Minas less so. It is true that of the three main districts, Minas emphasized grain production and the Chignecto area, livestock. The caveat thus should be made that a measurement of commercial emphasis only by livestock per capita ratios is far from

TABLE 5.11   *Livestock units per capita in the Bay settlements as shown in various censuses, 1671–1707*

Location	1671	1686	1689	1693	1701	1707
Port Royal	2.1	1.4	1.8	2.7	2.1	2.4
Beaubassin	–	2.3	2.8	3.3	2.5	2.5*
Minas	–	1.9	1.1	1.9	2.4	1.8
Pisiquid†	–	–	–	–	1.8	–
Cobequid†	–	–	–	–	1.6	2.8

* Including the population at Shepody, this figure drops to 2.3.
† Figures for Pisiquid and Cobequid may have been included with Minas figures.
Source: See Tables 5.3 and 5.10.

giving the full picture. Minas clearly had surplus grain for the other two settlements and Beaubassin, surplus livestock. The balance could have been one of a large degree of subsistence for the overall Acadian community. In fact, however, there was a substantial surplus of livestock for the colony as a whole throughout the period and there is much evidence that advantage was taken of this situation. Moreover, the Minas "bread basket" may have supplied visiting traders with grain even when the other settlements were short and, in Cobequid, Minas had its own livestock surplus area.

In all the settlements, cattle represented the major focus of livestock interest throughout the period; the strength of this emphasis is shown in Table 5.12. In general sheep and swine are seen to have advanced in proportion slightly through the period. Of the two, through time, swine declined and sheep increased in relative importance. At any time swine were somewhat more prominent in the newer settlements than in Port Royal, sheep increasing in significance only as fields were abandoned to pasture from cultivation, perhaps, or as more forest land was opened, offering both more grazing and less danger of predators. This

TABLE 5.12 *Percentages of cattle, sheep, and swine in the total livestock in the Bay settlements in various years, 1686–1707*

Location		Cattle	Sheep	Swine
	1686			
Total Bay of Fundy area		78	12	10
Port Royal		77	15	8
Minas*		84	4	12
Pisiquid†		–	–	–
Cobequid†		–	–	–
Beaubassin		79	8	13
	1689			
Total Bay of Fundy area		74	13	13
Port Royal		70	15	15
Minas*		81	12	7
Pisiquid†		–	–	–
Cobequid†		–	–	–
Beaubassin		80	13	7
	1693			
Total Bay of Fundy area		74	16	10
Port Royal		70	19	11
Minas*		78	11	11
Pisiquid†		–	–	–
Cobequid†		–	–	–
Beaubassin		79	14	7
	1698			
Total Bay of Fundy area		78‡	13‡	9‡
Port Royal		74	17	9
Minas§		–	–	–
Pisiquid§		–	–	–
Cobequid§		–	–	–
Beaubassin		84	8	8
	1701			
Total Bay of Fundy area		77	14	9
Port Royal		74	16	10
Minas		75	14	11
Pisiquid		82	11	7
Cobequid		81‡	13‡	6‡
Beaubassin		80	13	7

Table 5.12 (*continued*)

Location	Cattle	Sheep	Swine
1707			
Total Bay of Fundy area	73	15	12
Port Royal	70	18	12
Minas‖	74	14	12
Pisiquid†	–	–	–
Cobequid	79	11	10
Beaubassin	76	14	10

* May include Pisiquid and Cobequid.
† Unsettled or included with Minas.
‡ Estimated.
§ No data.
‖ May include Pisiquid.
Sources: See Table 5.3.

characteristic was to be noticeable in Nova Scotia during the next two centuries. But the nominal censuses made clear that in any setttlement at any time, there was a good deal of variation as between different farming families in the proportions of different livestock held.

There was not much raising of cattle in a large way at Port Royal during the period: there was simply no space nor adequate supply of wintering fodder to support a cattle-focused economy such as that which developed at Chignecto. All but six of the seventy-five farms of Port Royal in 1686, it is true, had cattle, but of them, eleven had fewer than 5 head, forty from 5 to 10 head, fifteen from 11 to 20 head, and only three had more than 20 head apiece.[162] Perrot pointed out in 1684 that by the use of their marshlands for agriculture rather than for grazing or hay they could not support as large a number of animals as they had done in the past, and the cattle they had were "fort méchante" and "de peu d'utilité."[163] Cattle of this kind and in these numbers were clearly adequate not only for their needs for meat, traction, leather, and milk, but, when the trade with New Englanders (usually clandestine, always officially interdicted, but sometimes of substantial dimensions) was at its freest, there was opportunity to market substantial surpluses. However, because it was more nearly and more regularly under an official eye, Port Royal never could enjoy the

162. AC, G1-*466*, 14–57.   163. AC, C11D-*2*(1), 42.

benefits of this trade as freely as could the outlying settlements up the bay.

Secondary Economic Activities

CRAFTS AND MILLING — The discussion of trade, below, will make it clear that the Acadians, even in their closely knit group of communities, were by no means self-sufficient. They imported a good deal in the way of tools, implements, and other hardware, particularly from New England. Their shortages of such goods are suggested by Talon's request, in 1670, that they be sent one hundred hoes and two hundred axes[164] to supply two of the three or four most urgently needed implements for farming. A third necessity was the spade; it was vital for dyking and making drains, but it also, with the hoe, was a major tillage implement; as we shall see in Chapter 6, there appear to have been few, if any, plows in use in Acadia in the seventeenth century. No doubt they also had to import sickles.

Apart from specifically agricultural needs there also must have been a strong demand for carpenters' tools, blacksmithing equipment, and bar iron with which some of the needed tools could be made. Similarly the import of much of the necessary hardware, sails, and rigging for small vessels made their modest but vital building of boats and small vessels possible.

The romantic picture of the self-sufficient Acadian household, which Longfellow's *Evangeline* has imprinted so firmly, needs a good deal of modification. We know that there was much specialized activity and exchange of labor throughout the settlements and particularly in the village of Port Royal and the quasi-villages of Grand Pré and Beaubassin. Even the agricultural activities required a good deal of artisan skill at times, notably in the planning and building of dykes and sluicegates. It is quite possible, indeed probable, that many of the tradesmen were also farmers and that farming may have absorbed most of their time in summer. But in the winter season, when the varied household industries were unusually active, the specialists could make wider use of their particular skills.

Among the occupations listed for heads of family in the 1671 census were: surgeon, weaver, cooper, farrier, gunsmith, joiner, mason, carpenter, tailor, and maker of edge tools. The absence of a specialist

164. "Lettre de Talon au ministre Colbert," p. 164.

cobbler is interesting; we know that to some degree the Acadians followed the Indian practice of using the skins of wild animals for moccasins. Dièreville, for example, mentions shoes made of elk (i.e. moose) hide and sealskin. In 1686 Perrot described the Acadians as "tissarons, massons, charpentiers, menuisiers, taillandiers" and builders of small vessels to sail along the coasts.[165] Clearly, however, the needed skills were not always in good supply. In 1688 Meneval gave his list of artisans needed by the colony: "charpentiers, charon [a wheelwright], menuisier [a joiner], sieurs [sciers, i.e., sawyers] de long pour faire des planches, gens a faire du bardaux [shingles] à couvrir les maisons, forgerons [blacksmiths], serrurier [a locksmith], cloutier [a nail-maker], masson, faiseur de briques, boulanger, gens qui sachent travailler au gazon [a fortification specialist], d'autres pour faire les estofes [textile workers], cordoniers [shoemakers], faiseurs de bas [stockings].[166]

There is no need to elaborate on the household carpentry, metalwork, spinning, weaving, tanning, cobbling, and salting and smoking of food, nor the endless household chores that were part of the way of life for men and women in a largely subsistent frontier economy. The role of hunting and gathering in providing food (meat and berries), and articles for trade (feathers, hides, and furs) may have been very large. Yet references by observers to such dependence on the wilds is rather infrequent and generally unfavorable when it appears. This was "la vie sauvage," too much like that of the Indians and too distracting from a settled agricultural life to appeal to governor, trader, priest, or casual observer from France.

Mills were established much earlier in the century at Port Royal and (although there may have been others) we do know that two grist mills (one water and one wind) and a second water mill, doubling for grinding grain and sawing wood, were in operation in the late 1680's.[167] The wind mill was a sound idea, for an occasional summer drought (as that of 1707) stopped the water mills.[168] Cadillac, who reported the mills in 1692, stated that the saw mill was neglected because of a lack of market. The Acadians could make planks of pine of any desired length, width, or thickness because of the height and diameter of the trees. They used cherry wood, the best wood they had and better than anything in France; it was a bit heavy but very durable. Oak was rare but there was ample material for ship-building, including trunks (of

---

165. AC, C11D-2(1), 44.   166. AC, C11D-2(1), 187.
167. AC, C11D-10, 23: Cadillac, 1692.   168. AC, C11D-6, 75.

pine?) for masts from a foot to two or two and a half feet in thickness.[169]

Dièreville also reported three mills, describing one as for grinding corn and two as for the sawing of timber, and locates them on the stream south of the settlement (Allain River).[170] Villebon mentioned boards from Port Royal, and says they had two saw mills and four water mills for grinding grain.[171] Certainly there were mills up the river; Pierre Thibaudeau, who established the first settlements at Shepody, had been a miller at Pré Ronde. Moreover these mills were turning out a good deal of flour to supply the garrison and visiting ships, and even for trade.

FISHING — Fishing had two connotations for Port Royal: that tied to the interest of the French commercial and official sponsors and (in theory at least) protectors of the colony, and that done by the Acadians themselves for their own food needs. The major resource of the commercial fishery was never, of course, in the Fundy area, but always along the southern and eastern coasts from Cape Sable to Canso, both for a shore-based boat fishery and for drying grounds for fish caught on the offshore banks. Fishing rights figured in many of the grants and disputes over grants but these were not significant in the immediate coastal regions of the actual Acadian settlements. Sometimes the Acadians did go out to the open Atlantic to participate in the increasingly international fishery there. Encouraged by Bergier, of the Company of Acadia, who was established at Chedabucto, the inhabitants of Port Royal once fitted out six small craft for the fishery, but these were taken by New England buccaneers[172] and although Acadians continued to have some interest in the Atlantic fisheries, it was a relatively haphazard one.

Although the documentary record is very weak on any Acadian fishery within the Port Royal Basin, or indeed in the Fundy area

169. AC, C11D-*10*, 23: Cadillac, 1692. According to Rameau, *Une Colonie Féodale, 1*, 125, masts, shingles, and staves or clapboards were also made and shipped.

170. Dièreville, *Relation*, p. 85. The 1688 plan of Port Royal is reproduced as one of three maps in *ibid.*, following p. 324; it shows a windmill near the fort.

171. Webster, *Acadia*, p. 116 *passim*, and p. 134. In *ibid.*, p. 106, there is a reference to 18 barrels of flour being shipped from Port Royal to Fort Nashwaak on the Saint John River in 1697.

172. Murdoch, *Nova-Scotia, 1*, 160, and Couillard-Després, "Les Gouverneurs," p. 264.

generally, the references existing leave no doubt as to its importance. Thus, Villebon remarked in 1699: "The settlers catch codfish for food, and there are small rivers opening into the Basin which yield many fish such as bass, shad, sardines, gaspereau and plaice. Large numbers are taken in weirs built across the rivers so that the fish are caught when the tide goes out."[173] Although food shortages were rare in the settlements at Minas and Chignecto they did occur periodically at Port Royal where the garrison, officials, and merchants put an extra strain on the food supply. No doubt when storms and unusually high tides flooded the dyked marshlands, or when English raiders disrupted the economy by cutting dykes and burning haystacks and harvests stored in barns, interest in fishing, as in hunting, took an upswing. Indeed, at such times local supplies of fish were of the utmost importance; once, of a population of 753 at Port Royal, one-third were said to be living on shellfish.[174] Cadillac noted that cod were taken at the mouth of the Rivière Imbert (Bear River) and that, also in the basin, they caught sardines (i.e., herring), shad, and bass.[175]

There is much discussion in the dispatches and *mémoires* of New England's actual or potential interest in the fishery off the Acadian shores and its effect on the Acadians. Brouillan suggested that it may have involved movements of families to Canso and other south coast points:

It is necessary to establish [a fishing settlement—and fortified post—at] La Hève, and one cannot begin too soon because of the large number of young [Acadian] residents who are now in that area without land or any other occupation than that of consuming the small amount of grain and vegetables available in the colony after two years of poor harvests, and inevitably many families are going over to the English as four or five small families did last year. I have taken the liberty of warning you that this could not help but happen, as much because of the liking they have for the English as because they find nothing to do here.[176]

TRADE AND TRANSPORTATION — Between 1670 and 1710 the interest of the administrative officers of either old or New France in Acadia was chiefly peripheral: in the Maine-New Brunswick borderlands or

173. Webster, *Acadia,* p. 133. The "sardines" were probably herring; the "plaice" possibly halibut.   174. Couillard-Després, "Les Gouverneurs," p. 279.
175. "The Cadillac Memoir," p. 87.
176. AC, C11D-4(2), 468–69: November 1703. Quoted in part in Rameau, *Une Colonie Féodale, 2,* 340, my translation. See also a report of February 1703 from Brouillan in *ibid.,* p. 343.

in the fishery on the Atlantic and Gulf coasts. In so far as they gave any attention to the agricultural settlements at Port Royal, in Minas Basin, and at the heads of Chignecto Bay, they were concerned chiefly with trade. They wished to encourage Acadian commerce with France and Canada and to prohibit or greatly diminish that with New England. The fur trade from the peninsula declined steadily but continued to yield cargoes for France up until the time of the British takeover. On the Saint John and the other rivers leading from the Gulf of Maine into the interior the French interest in furs was more active. The fur supply was diminishing there, too, but the strategic problems of attack and defense *vis-à-vis* the New Englanders were inextricably tied up with their relations with the Indians who, in turn, remained closely associated with the trade.

But of greater importance to the Acadians was the trade with New England, always of considerable importance and always technically illegal during periods of French sovereignty, although engaged in or conveniently overlooked (for considerations) by the French officials themselves on occasion. Talon commented on it in 1671, pointing out the importance of reserving it for France: "We must put a stop (without violence) to the commerce which the English carry on with Port Royal, from whom they take every year a quantity of meat in exchange for a few druggets and other cloths; it would suffice to send out from France, or from here [Quebec] to Port Royal, cloth and other things for their most pressing needs, and even a few looms which the colonists asked me for so that they could work their own wools and hemps [linens?]."[177] In 1686 Meneval pointed out that the English at Boston continued to be regarded as the masters of all the commerce on the Acadian coasts.[178] He reported that he had seen English trading at Minas, the Saint John River, and Port Royal, which was particularly galling since French merchants were not allowed to trade at Boston. But Meneval excused the Acadians; they received no help from France and they were completely dependent on the New Englanders for imported goods. Each spring three or four English vessels came loaded with goods the Acadians needed and traded them for furs and other produce.[179] Meneval, indeed, apparently conducted a flourishing trade

177. "Lettre de Talon au ministre Colbert," p. 164.
178. Émile Lauvrière, *La Tragédie d'un peuple* (1923), *1*, 135.
179. There are many documented references to this trade in *ibid*. Apparently wood was an item in the trade along with grain and cattle, according to a rather ambiguous, undocumented note in Rameau, *Une Colonie Féodale*, *1*, 225.

with Boston on his own[180] although this may have been largely from the northern shores of the Bay of Fundy and the Gulf of Maine. Des Goutins, king's clerk in Acadia, insisted that Meneval was deeply involved in the trade (including grain, cattle, and timber) and specified particular instances.[181] Meneval, in turn, wrote at length of the clandestine trade in eau de vie carried on with the Indians by Des Goutins and others.[182] The war of letters and *mémoires* between Meneval and Des Goutins makes the facts doubtful, but the charges are suggestive.

In any event it was a very difficult matter to control. The New Englanders conducted here the same irregular, hawking trade that they carried on along all the coasts from Newfoundland to the West Indies.[183] They picked up what they could find and dispose of—furs, feathers, fish, grain, livestock, meat, or even wood products. They gave in exchange iron products (utensils, implements, tools, firearms, mill machinery, etc.), textiles, sugar, spices, and other luxury food and drink, and a wide variety of oddments to satisfy the demands for which they were the only dependable outside providers. The French at Port Royal or on the Saint John River, with tiny garrisons and no permanently stationed war vessels, had no way of halting these peripatetic merchants and every spring they sailed into La Baye Française (the Bay of Fundy) as if it were an English gulf.

One of the curious and ironic results was the partial realization, through the New Englanders, of a trade between Acadia and the French West Indies, illegal if not exactly clandestine at both ends. Such trade had long been advocated by Acadian officials. There can be little doubt that some of the Acadian wheat, lumber, cattle, and fish found their way thus to the French Antilles and that some of the sugar, molasses, and rum they bought had non-British origins,[184] for the extent

180. Murdoch, *Nova-Scotia, 1,* 178, and Couillard-Després, "Les Gouverneurs," pp. 269 ff.

181. See a memoir of Des Goutins for 1690 in AC, C11D-2(2), 357–75, printed in Rameau, *Une Colonie Féodale, 2,* 324–25. Three different dates—September 2, October 2, and October 8 (perhaps the usual practice of sending several copies by different vessels)—are assigned to it.

182. See AC, C11D-2(1), 245–57, 275–300, one part of which is printed in Rameau, *Une Colonie Féodale,* pp. 326–31.

183. See R. G. Lounsbury, "Yankee Trade at Newfoundland" (1930), pp. 607–26.

184. But much of it was from the British West Indies also. See M. Tibierge, "Memoir on the Present State of the Province of Acadia," from Fort Nashwaak, June 1697, as printed in translation in Webster, *Acadia,* pp. 152–55. Reference is to p. 155.

of the trade of the New Englanders with the French islands, despite official English mercantilist prohibitions, was notorious.

During Villebon's governorship (1691–1700) there are numerous references to a continuation of this trade between New England and Port Royal, involving Acadians as well as New Englanders. Apparently the priests encouraged it, or at least pointed out that the French trading company charged extortionate prices. Moreover, they were often more fearful of English reprisal than of French authority. Villebon reported in 1695 that the Port Royal settlers were afraid to trade with the French on the Saint John River lest the English burn them out, and, like Meneval, he may well have had to supplement his own supplies by clandestine trade to the south.[185] One M. Tibierge, an agent of the Company of Acadia, writing June 30, 1697, from Fort Nashwaak on the Saint John, reported of Beaubassin, Minas, and Port Royal:

Every year the English bring to these places trade-goods, brandy, sugar cane from Barbadoes, molasses and the utensils which are needed, taking in exchange pelts and grain, which has been a great boon during the recent years of famine in Boston. M. Dubreuil, Boudrot and le Marquis, of Port Royal, took shipments to them, for they have passports from both M. de Villebon and the English. M. Dubreuil made four or five voyages laden with wheat. . . .

Those who live at Minas, Beaubassin and Port Royal buy very little here [i.e., on the Saint John River] because it is difficult to reach the fort, which is 25 leagues from the mouth of the river, and because they fear to be caught by the English . . . although they admit that it [our merchandise] is better and cheaper than that of the English.[186]

Unquestionably, however, the trade and possibilities for it fluctuated greatly. At the turn of the century Dièreville observed: "In such a vast Country, where Trade should be open to all in order that it might be established, no one dares to do any business; if a Settler attempts anything of the sort even in the Neighborhood, from one House to another, trouble is made for him on some fine but specious pretext, suggested by base interests; his buildings are taken from him, & in this

185. Webster, *Acadia*, pp. 5–6, 84, 141, and an undocumented reference in W. A. Calnek, *History of the County of Annapolis* (1897), p. 40, referring to supplies of Indian corn and meal obtained from Boston by Villebon.

186. Tibierge, "Memoir," pp. 154–55. It is highly doubtful that regulations were ever enforced to this point.

way districts which might have become productive, are rendered forever barren."[187]

Without the New England trade, life in Acadia would have lacked many of the simplest necessities as well as the luxuries. That Port Royal was poor in even minor elegancies is evident from an inventory of the choice pillage of the Phips' expedition which captured and sacked the settlement in May, 1690: "twenty-four girdles; two caps; one hood; twenty-four canonical gowns; four more gowns with silver clasps and laced; beds and bedding; one white coat; two pairs of shoes; one red waistcoat; fourteen old kettles, pots and stew-pans."[188] But it was not only little luxuries or iron pots, spades, and axes that were needed—when a sawmill or gristmill was built or needed repair, New England was the most accessible, the cheapest, and often the only source of supply for the iron-work. This was doubtless true of rope, sails, and metal fittings for their small craft as well.

Probably much of the trade was by barter, for a severe and perennial problem was the shortage of currency. However, this is not meant to imply a moneyless economy. Provisions were bought for the garrison from time to time and when the troops were paid, as on occasion they were, some of their pay undoubtedly made its way into general circulation. New England may have supplied some of it, but also may have been the chief ultimate recipient of it. The frequent mention of money prices for produce, and the raising of 800 livres from the inhabitants of Port Royal toward a church,[189] both suggest the existence of adequate currency. In discussing trade in his report of 1692, Cadillac speaks of "le vin, l'eau de vie, les étoffes, les toilles, les armes, la poudre, le plomb, s'y debitent le fort bien, les habitans payent en argent, en castor, pelleteries ou poisson sec."[190] Just at the end of this period, in the first decade of the eighteenth century, governors Brouillan and Subercase both issued card money, since they received no money from France to pay the garrison or the workmen on fortifications, or for supplies. This was quickly disapproved and ordered withdrawn. In a letter from Versailles to Subercase in August 1710, the official observes: "Therefore, as you inform me that there is plenty of money in

187. Dièreville, *Relation,* p. 100.
188. From the State Archives of Massachusetts, as quoted in Gerald S. Graham, *Empire of the North Atlantic* (1950), p. 70.
189. AC, C11D-*4*, 473: Brouillan to the Minister, November 1703. Summarized in Murdoch, *Nova-Scotia, 1,* 266–67.   190. AC, C11D-*10*, 24–25.

Acadia, but that the inhabitants do not put it in circulation, it is your business to discover the means of getting it into circulation. . . . it is the King's determination that you should not have any card money issued, no matter in what position you might find yourself . . . ."[191]

The officials believed the Acadians were hoarding metal currency (for trade with New England, among other reasons) and they were probably right. A dispatch of Des Goutins to Paris in 1707 said that the issue of paper money was unavoidable, though Subercase was trying to call it in. The report continued that forty-three families were destitute owing to depredations of the English. They were without such vital necessities as iron pots, scythes, sickles, knives, other iron goods, salt, and blankets. They had no hatchets or kettles for the Indians. They would be lucky if the enemy would sell them goods again for their beaver, but Subercase was opposed to such trade and the dispatch adds that the people would not deal with the enemy (a rather doubtful judgment).[192]

Transportation by land was of minor importance. Almost certainly there were trails across the peninsula used by the Indians to communicate with La Have and Mirligueche and other places on the southern coast but most of the land trails were short portages around rapids, and between headwaters of opposite-flowing streams. At the turn of the century, when the settlement at Minas was beginning to rival Port Royal in importance, there was still no cart road between them; only a foot-and-bridle track was serviceable. On the connections with Minas, Villebon stated in 1699:

[The route to Minas] is by boat up to the head of the tide of the Port Royal River, a distance of six leagues from the old fort; thence over land thirteen leagues [forty miles?] on a good level road to the outlying homesteads of Minas; the whole journey can be made in a day. There are five leagues of sandy soil without trees, and eight of wooded country on the portage, and a road for carts could easily be made; whatever was needed could be trans-

191. Adam Shortt, V. K. Johnston, and Gustave Lanctot, *Documents relating to Currency, Exchange and Finance in Nova Scotia . . . 1675–1758* (1933), p. 16. Other relevant documents for this period will be found, in translation, in *ibid.*, pp. 13–16.

192. AC, C11D-*6*, 64–88. Excerpts have been printed in Rameau, *Une Colonie Féodale, 2,* 341–43, and a rather full summary in translation appears in Murdoch, *Nova-Scotia, 1,* 295–96.

ported from Minas quickly and without any risk. The settlers now bring their [large] animals, sheep, and even pigs, from one place to the other with great ease.[193]

An "inland" route of communication between Minas and Beaubassin went from the site of present Parrsboro up the Parrsboro River, over a short portage to the River Hébert, and down the latter to Cumberland Basin. Interestingly the Parrsboro thus came to be known as the Chignecto River and the Hébert as the Minas River. The Port Royal people used canoes or small wooden vessels, built by themselves, on the river, in the basin and even for journeys to the River Saint John, but they had some sizeable ones for voyaging on the Bay of Fundy. In Chapter 6 there is a fuller discussion of their vessels.

193. Webster, *Acadia*, p. 129.

6

Acadian Nova Scotia, 1710-1748

🖋

SOVEREIGNTY, GOVERNMENT, AND THE COURSE OF EVENTS

The period of permanent British control of present peninsular Nova Scotia, including most of Acadia and the Acadians but not Cape Breton Island, began with the capture of Port Royal in 1710, and French recognition of British sovereignty over that area was confirmed in the Treaty of Utrecht in 1713. Even then the British and French were to contest for the area now included in New Brunswick and Maine for most of the following half century, debating whether or not it had been included in the cession of "Acadia." In fact, the lands north of the Bay of Fundy remained largely under French control until the military collapse of French power in North America during the 1750's.

The control of a province, the small population of which was closely attached to Britain's perennial enemy by language, faith, and total culture, presented a nearly insoluble problem. It arose when, in 1714, the British decided against a policy of deportation of the Acadians. Indeed, it is uncertain whether any who really wished to go were prevented from leaving but certainly they were not encouraged to leave. The reasons advanced for leaving the Acadians on their lands, despite the potential military danger they represented, included the advantage of having a settled farming population to supply the garrison at Port Royal (immediately renamed Annapolis Royal), the obvious difficulties of getting other colonists to move into the area, the sheer lack of shipping to effect the removal, and the danger of having such an accession of strength to Cape Breton.[1]

On the whole the Acadians remained as much for lack of any positive policy as because of one. If the authorities in Isle Royale (as Cape Breton Island was renamed) wished them to remove thither, those in Quebec clearly could see advantages in their remaining in a territory they one day hoped to see restored to New France. Some Acadians did move to Isle Royale but most of those who left the Fundy settlements to look over the prospects there returned. In a letter to the governor of Isle Royale in September 1713, the resident Recollet missionary, Father Félix Pain, summarized the general attitude of the people toward moving to Cape Breton.

"It would be to expose us manifestly (they say) to die of hunger, burthened as we are with large families, to quit the dwelling places and clearances from which we derive our usual subsistence, without any other resource, to take rough, new lands, from which the standing wood must be removed. . . . One-fourth of our population consists of aged persons, unfit for the labor of breaking up new lands, and who, with great exertion, are able to cultivate the cleared ground which supplies subsistence for them and their families."[2]

The Acadians continued to live on their ancestral lands for the next four decades without any resolution of the vexing questions of their right to the lands they farmed or their duties to their new sovereign and his representatives. There was no lack of pronouncements, ordinances, warnings, and exhortations, but until mid-century either the will or the means (or both) were of insufficient strength to enforce the political anglicization of the population. For most of four decades, and even amid military activity after 1744, the Acadians continued to occupy, multiply, expand, and colonize new areas as they had done since 1670.

The earliest scandal-ridden administrations of Samuel Vetch and Francis Nicholson (the latter largely in absentia and through his officer, Thomas Caulfeild) gave way in 1717 to that of Colonel Richard Philipps who retained the government of Nova Scotia, nominally at least, until he was superseded by Colonel, The Honorable Edward

1. PRO, CO 217-*1*, 97–99. It was observed that Acadians, if only for their knowledge of snowshoes and canoes, were worth five times the number of new men.

2. As quoted in a presumably literal translation in Beamish Murdoch, *A History of Nova-Scotia, or Acadie* (1865–67), *1*, 336.

Cornwallis in May of 1749 when Halifax was established. Philipps spent little time in Nova Scotia; he was "in residence" at Canso or Annapolis Royal for less than five years in two separate periods, 1720–23 and 1729–31. As a result the local administration was in the hands of lieutenant-governors, sometimes without the title and usually without the emoluments of office, sometimes two at once (at Canso and Annapolis Royal), sometimes overlapping in terms of appointment, and sometimes without command of the troops with whose presence, weak although they invariably were in numbers and morale, the actual power lay. The principal subordinates to Philipps, with whom the Acadians had to deal directly, were Captain John Doucett (1717–26), Major Lawrence Armstrong (1725–39), and Major Paul Mascarene (1740–49).

As Brebner pointed out long ago[3] "government by analogy [with Virginia] and rule of thumb" presented most unusual problems in the absence of British settlement beyond the garrison and a few New England merchants at Annapolis Royal. A council was created for which the governor when in residence, the lieutenant-governor, or the senior councillor present (in the absence of either of the above) served as president. This body, as well as it could, exercised not only the executive but the judicial and (in the absence of an assembly and when without specific instructions from the Board of Trade) the *de facto* legislative powers of the province. Their religion debarred the inhabitants from assuming any of the duties upon which the design of government, to be modeled after Virginia, was based. The Test and Corporation Acts forbade their taking oaths allowing them to vote for, or serve in, the required elective assembly. The actions of council established thus a *modus operandi* of "case law" unless, rarely, they were annulled by the home authorities.

Excepting Celtic Britain and, possibly, the beginnings of New York and Jamaica overseas, this was the first attempt of a British government to rule a large number of alien people. As late as 1740, Mascarene pointed out that there were still only two or three English families besides the garrison, and that a largely military council had to meet on call in a civil judiciary capacity to decide matters of *meum* and *tuum* among the Acadian habitants, usually brought to them by deputies who were elected, or otherwise chosen, to represent each district. By that

3. J. B. Brebner, *New England's Outpost: Acadia before the Conquest of Canada* (1927), ch. 6, deals in superb fashion with the problems of government involved.

time, in theory at least, there was also in each district a messenger called a constable and a notary, who acted as a recorder of legal documents and receiver of quitrents. At Canso, justices of the peace were appointed from the garrison officers or the three or four settlers wintering there.[4]

It is interesting that this quasi-representative system of deputies probably was established by Mascarene himself as early as 1714, when he was at Minas on a tribute-collecting mission: ". . . [the inhabitants] desir'd of me to have the Liberty to choose some particular number of men amongst them who should represent the whole, by reason of the most of the people living scattered far off & not able to attend a Considerable time, I easily consented to it and they chose Mr. Peter Melancon & ye four formerly Capts of their Militia with another man for Manis [Minas], one for Chicconecto & one for Cobequid."[5]

By 1748 the system had become formalized and elaborated: according to Mascarene, eight deputies were chosen from eight districts on the Annapolis River and Basin and sixteen others from the outlying districts around Minas and Chignecto.[6] Charles Morris' extensive survey of the same year has many details, no doubt colored by his own bias as a New Englander, after insisting that the real government of the people was in the hands of their priests:

Indeed they have some officers of Publick capacity call'd Deputys, but they have no Power Committed to them being only servants to the People, they are annually chosen by the several Districts. . . . The use of these Deputys is to call the District together, to Publish Proclamations and orders to receive the minds of the People and to transmitt their results to the Govr and Councill. . . . Besides the Deputy they have a Register or Clark in each District . . . to record orders of Government, Deeds and Conveyances and to keep the Publick papers, besides these I know of no other Civil Officer among them . . . .[7]

4. AC, NSA-*25*, 3–8: Mascarene to Lords of Trade, August 1740 (duplicate of letter of March 1740).

5. AC, NSA-*4*, 170. "Manis" was the English reading of the French pronunciation of "Mines."   6. Murdoch, *Nova-Scotia*, *1*, 371–72.

7. [Charles Morris], "A Breif Survey of Nova Scotia" (MS. in Library of the Royal Artillery Regiment, Woolwich, n. d.), cap. 5, pp. 3–4. J. B. Brebner identified the author by comparing statements on pp. 54–59 of this manuscript with pp. 115–17 of the British Museum Add. MSS. 19071, known to be by Morris. The writer has made a verbatim transcription of the original; AC has a photostat catalogued as MG18, F10. In 1748 Captain Charles Morris was instructed by Governor William Shirley of Massachusetts to survey land in the Bay of Fundy area for English settlement.

Clearly the deputies were rarely happy with their lot. To the council at Annapolis Royal they were symbols of Acadian independence if not intransigence; as appointed rather than elected officials (at first) the inhabitants saw them as arms of the government. This was why Armstrong, in 1730, had insisted on their election by the people themselves.

Morris believed that there was a much more effective *de facto* local government and system of justice administered by the priests and headed by the Bishop of Quebec. He thought the priest's judgment ("Sentence") ". . . generally Definitive, for if the offending Party comply's not he excommunicates them which to a People so Superstitious is very terrible . . . ."[8] The role of the French priests in Acadia in providing a sort of clandestine local government in the different settlements, especially outside of the Annapolis Royal area, has yet to be clarified.[9] Perhaps no one has carried its study much further than Abbé H.-R. Casgrain did some eighty years ago.[10] Understandably his writing reflects a strong sympathy for the Acadians, their missionary priests, and the French colonial governments in Quebec and Louisburg. In a good tempered and scholarly indictment of the British government from Annapolis he has a number of rather important points to make.

There were many attempts by that government to enforce an order that all missionaries in Acadia (whose presence was guaranteed, inferentially at least, to the settlers by the provisions of the Treaty of Utrecht about religion) should be approved by it and that their location and movements should be closely regulated by British orders. At the same time, as Casgrain conceded, the missionaries were appointed by, directed by, and responsible to, Quebec and Louisburg and the lieutenant-governors of Annapolis were confident, with reason, that the missionaries were not always careful to distinguish between inculcating loyalty to the Roman Catholic faith and to His Most Christian Majesty in France. Many times orders were given for individual missionaries to leave the country; on more than one occasion, for example, Armstrong tried to get rid of Father Félix Pain. Often the orders were ignored or protested; usually the worst penalty was for the priests to appear before the council for reprimand or, rarely, to remain briefly in custody

8. Morris, "A Breif Survey," cap 5, p. 3. Shades of the Salem witch trials!

9. Hopefully this may be done in an exhaustive study of the ecclesiastical records of the Acadian missionaries now being done by Father Jules Leger, Assistant Professor of History at the University of Moncton, who is doing a doctoral dissertation under Professor Marcel Trudel of the University of Ottawa.

10. Abbé Henri-Raymond Casgrain, "Coup d'oeil sur l'Acadie" (1888).

at the fort. More commonly the priests continued about their business, there was so little the authority at Annapolis or Canso could do. Perhaps the greatest pressure came from refusal to allow new churches to be built or old ones to be repaired. Yet somehow the churches got built and the government did not risk having them torn down.

The chief civil function performed by the priests, and one which profoundly irritated the governors, was the settlement of a host of minor civil differences between their parishioners. Presumably their ukase was usually accepted gracefully; when it was not and the priests resorted to ecclesiastical penalties the reaction sometimes reached Annapolis. Certainly the Acadians who felt put upon were not above appealing to Annapolis from the discipline of the church. Governor Mascarene wrote menacing letters to Abbé Desenclaves, one of the missionaries, because he refused absolution to some individuals who did not wish to make some retributions he had ordered them to do. But since there was almost no workable alternative to the clergy acting as substitute minor civil magistrates, it is clear that they continued to do so. The criteria they applied in their judgments came from the only bodies of law they knew, those of the church and the ancient *coûtumes* of France, which often differed sharply from the precedents of English common law.

British subjects, and especially colonials from Massachusetts, were familiar with the major role religious rules and precepts could play in the minute regulation of their own civil affairs. But to have, in effect, a "shadow government" of representatives of a hated faith, operating in British territory, appointed by and responsible to Great Britain's chronic enemy, usurping much of the governing function for which they were responsible, was galling and quite unacceptable to Nova Scotia's governors. Indeed, the situation added much fervor to the attempts to get the Acadians to take the hated unequivocal oaths and to the inevitably abortive but repeated proposals from London, Boston, and Annapolis to attempt to convert the Acadians to Protestantism, to bring in substantial numbers of Protestants to be settled among them to dilute their faith and allegiance and, for nearly half a century, to round them up and deport them as the only ultimate and effective solution.

"Exposed" Canso and "protected" Annapolis Royal as well as the "out" settlements of Minas and Chignecto and, to a lesser degree, the "cove" settlements along the coast, were subject to the harassments of the undeclared war that continued in America between the French and British during the "Great Peace" of 1713–44 and the very active hostilities of the war of 1744–48 which saw the fantastic capture of Louisburg by one of the world's most motley assemblages of land and sea forces and its even more incredible return to France as a pawn of the peacemaker's game in the ensuing formal settlement. The Indian War of 1722–26 was assisted by the French at least covertly and there were many attacks on settlements, individuals, and trading and fishing vessels. After 1739 the commencement of the war with Spain made New England even more conscious than before that Nova Scotia was her outpost against French power and that its defense likely would rest largely in her hands. During the uneasy five years that followed, however, neither old nor New England had the desire, or found the means, to treat Nova Scotia with any more attention than it had enjoyed in the years since 1710. When open war broke out in 1744, the French in Cape Breton learned of it first and easily captured the small fort at Canso. In the ensuing year Mascarene held out at Annapolis with a decaying fort and a dispirited garrison "only through a combination of personal courage, New England aid, poor French leadership, and the honest neutrality of the great majority of the Acadians."[11] This period included a land siege of Annapolis, first by a band of Indians led by the French and then by a rather odd force under François Dupont Du Vivier, from Louisburg, each of which had its almost comic aspects. A small French naval force arrived only after Du Vivier had withdrawn.

Early in 1745 (May), a force of five to six hundred Canadians and Indians came to Annapolis by way of Minas but retired after capturing two Boston schooners in the basin. After the siege and capture of Louisburg and Isle Royale in 1745 there followed, in a curious reversal of land and sea roles, the deployment, in the North American theatre, of a vast naval force by France and of great land armies by Britain— and quite abortively in both cases. The Duc d'Anville's fleet with a substantial part of the total French naval power of the time, set out for North America and its storm-tossed, disease-ridden remnants finally reached Chebucto (French "Chebouctou," soon to be Halifax) harbor. The death of its leader and a further disrupting storm ended its threat, but intelligence of the French plans gave the garrison at Annapolis a very uneasy time, especially as they faced a besieging land force under

11. Brebner, *New England's Outpost,* p. 111.

the Canadian Ramezay in the late autumn which was to be coordinated with D'Anville's attack by sea. On the other hand, the imposing British colonial land forces, organized for the attack on Quebec, never got under way and a later New England attempt to impress the Acadians and defend Annapolis by quartering several hundred troops on the inhabitants of Minas in the winter of 1746/47 backfired when that garrison, dispersed in individual Acadian homes over a stretch of two and a half miles, was surprised by a Canadian force based on the Beaubassin settlement at Chignecto, partially destroyed, and forced out of the area.

This was also an important period in the ultimate fate of Acadia in that it saw the debut of the controversial priest, Abbé Jean-Louis Le Loutre. In Acadia as a missionary priest to the Indians since 1738, he had, by 1744, a devoted following among the Micmac and some small influence with the Acadians themselves, both directly and through the implied retaliatory powers of his Indian brigades. Few men involved in Acadian history, even including the La Tours, have aroused more acrimonious debate among later historians. The stealth and savagery of the Indian attacks he directed or inspired, and his position as a religious leader of a proscribed and hated faith, led to his vilification by British, and especially New England, authorities of the 1740's and 1750's and a scarcely better reputation with later British scholars. Yet his obvious concern with ultimately religious purposes (whatever the means), in his effort to extirpate heretical and anglicizing influences on the Acadian life and mind, and his considerable local successes in a warfare that the French ultimately lost, and that led directly to the deportation of the Acadians in 1755, have resulted in a kind of apotheosis of his person by many chroniclers of Acadian origin or sympathies.[12]

The outstanding, and rather astonishing, fact is that most of the Acadians, despite suffering from the pressure of repeated raids and the coming and going of larger or smaller contingents of regular or irregu-

12. J. C. Webster, *The Career of Abbé Le Loutre in Nova Scotia* (1933). Although showing much of the traditional English viewpoint, this is factually the best account of his activities. The fact that the French noun "loutre" (otter) is feminine has led some scholars to use the form "La Loutre" but, following the documents, Webster and W. F. Ganong have preferred "Le Loutre," from his own signature. There is a substantial Le Loutre bibliography. One might note in addition, at least "Une autobiographie de l'abbé Le Loutre (1709–1772)," ed. Albert David (1931), and Casgrain's "Coup d'oeil sur l'Acadie."

lar forces of both sides, remained throughout the whole period, and
especially in the most troubled years of declared war from 1744 to
1748, almost completely neutral. That there was widespread sympathy
and even passive support for the French among many of the Acadians
is unquestioned; understandably this was greater in Minas than Annapolis, stronger in Pisiquid and Cobequid than at Grand Pré, and
most evident in the Chignecto settlements. Indeed the principal support for the authorities in Canada and Cape Breton (and through them
for France) lay in the Chignecto region—the Acadian fringe and the
doorway to Quebec and Cape Breton Island. This unfriendly attitude
of the settlers on the isthmus was suggested much earlier by Mascarene. In June of 1741 he observed: "The inhabitants of Chignecto
appear in all things of a refractory spirit; their paying the king's dues
unwillingly and in bad species [sic], doth not show well in their
favour . . . ."[13]

Mascarene was, in general, one of the most vocal and effective
apologists the Acadians had. After the attack of Du Vivier in 1744, he
laid the preservation of the garrison to a number of causes (as well he
might), but not least to "our French inhabitants refusing to take up
arms against us."[14] However in 1744, in dispatches to the Secretary of
State, he recognized that the Acadians could be, even involuntarily, of
great aid to the enemy. The second force attacking Annapolis had
conscripted guides, cattle, and nearly two hundred draft horses from
them.[15] He followed this with a suggestion that if the Acadians could be
removed and Protestant subjects established in their place, the interests of Britain and New England would be well served.

The greater partisanship of the Acadians at Chignecto after 1750
was aided by the presence of forts Beauséjour and Lawrence, established on opposite sides of the Missaguash River at mid-century (see
Figure 8.3). From the former to the west, supported from Quebec and
Isle Royale via Baie Verte, the Abbé Le Loutre set out once again in
1749 to restore the Indian threat and to convert the local Acadians
from their stubborn neutralism. The chief result was the establishment
of Fort Lawrence; he had a very limited success in attracting Acadians
to open partisanship.

On the whole, and with the notable exception of Le Loutre, the
priests who ministered to the Acadians were on the side of neutrality

13. Quoted in Murdoch, *Nova-Scotia*, 2, 14.   14. *Ibid.*, 38.
15. AC, NSA-*27*, 211–22.

despite the fact that they were appointed by and largely supported from Quebec (the Acadians were scarcely more willing to pay tithes than quitrents) and that they were often harried by the British authorities.[16] Yet the British attributed the refusal of the Acadians to take an unqualified oath largely to the influence of the priests and held them responsible for the sporadic killing, scalping, and burning by the Indians nominally under their care.

THE TENURE OF THE LAND

There is no more vexing question in Acadian historiography than that relating to the circumstances and characteristics of land tenure after 1710. Cloudy as the situation was before (see Chapter 5), especially on the fringes of Minas, and in Shepody, Pisiquid, and Cobequid, it became deeply confused by the ambiguity of the terms of the Treaty of Utrecht and of their interpretation by the Board of Trade or by the governor or his representative on the spot. The original supposition that the Acadians would leave and would be replaced by New Englanders or other Protestants having proved false, the Acadians simply stayed on. Those in Annapolis, Minas proper, and Beaubassin, who held land by some inherited or negotiated seigneurial arrangement continued to pay the trivial amounts demanded to attest to their "rights": those who had squatted usually paid nothing.

Quite substantial purchases, some of large areas, were made by the members and associates of the conquering "wave" of 1710. On the one hand the sales may have been made under duress with low prices and deferred or dubious payment; on the other hand, the right of the Acadians to "sell" was often questionable and the purchasers of houses or lots other than those near the fort realized little from them, for the expected purchasers did not arrive, and perhaps most such transactions were unrecorded and forgotten. However, many relatively small grants, usually near the fort, were made later to members of the garrison, to resident New England merchants, and to other British subjects.[17]

16. Most notable for a peaceful, accommodating approach was Abbé de Miniac, grand archidiacre (archdeacon) and pastor of the parish of St. Joseph of the Canard River. For some time he was vicar-general of Acadia for the Bishop of Quebec.

17. *Nova Scotia Archives. III* (1908), 228 *passim*. Note entries for June 19, 20, and 28, 1732, and for June 6, 1733. See also references to large grants in the late

Lord Dartmouth, Lord Keeper of the Privy Seal, had put the interest of the Acadians clearly in instructions to Nicholson in 1713: ". . . you permit and allow such of them as have any Lands or Tenements in the Places under Your Government . . . & are Willing to Continue our Subjects to retain and Enjoy their said Lands and Tenements without any Lett or Molestation . . . or to Sell the same if they shall rather Chuse to remove elsewhere . . . ."[18] No term was placed on how long they might have to remove, although one year was elsewhere specified. Of 169 heads of family at Annapolis Royal, 146 agreed to go to Cape Breton after two officers (Louis Denys de La Ronde, and Jacques d'Espiet de Pensens), sent by the governor at Louisburg, Brouillan de St-Ovide, had been allowed to talk with them in 1714.[19] Later, 139 heads at Minas and 17 at Cobequid yielded to La Ronde's persuasiveness and signed. But they were canny enough to send a few of their number to Cape Breton to look things over. This group was not impressed; the main body did not move and then it was ruled that the time for allowing them to do what probably very few of them wanted to do had elapsed.

Tenure of land, then, became, in British eyes, inextricably associated with the Acadian's willingness to "continue our subjects," which involved an unqualified oath of allegiance. For more than forty years the government tried to get them to take an unqualified version of such an oath (which would have involved their bearing arms against the Micmac and French forces if necessary) and they consistently refused in the face of the only kinds of pressure that could be applied, admoni-

1730's, as two 50,000-acre grants to Philipps, his officers, and various prominent Englishmen, in Chignecto and Minas, (later escheated, in 1760), and to various small grants (essentially village lots) to officers and other residents at Annapolis in 1737 and 1738. See especially Murdoch, *Nova-Scotia*, 1, 519–20, 526, 531.

18. PRO, CO 217-1, 95, 95ᵛ. See also PRO, CO 217-1, 105–6: "The Case of Coll. Vetch," about 1714. Vetch complained not only that the Acadians were confirmed in their lands when these had been promised to the New Englanders of the 1710 expedition to encourage them to enlist, but that the missionaries had been telling the people about these generous terms some several months before he, Vetch, was notified of them. In a letter to the Lords of Trade late in 1714 he repeats the same complaint about a breach of promise to the captors, if the Acadians were allowed to sell their lands. PRO, CO 217-1, 97–99.

19. AC, NSA-5, 80: August 1714. Of the 146 heads of families signing, 89 used marks in place of signatures. Brouillan de St-Ovide was governor of Isle Royale at the time and should not be confused with Jacques-François de Brouillan, governor in Acadia, 1701–1704. De Pensens and de La Ronde Denys (as he is often referred to) were French officers at Louisburg.

tions, harangues, and abortive threats.[20] The British continued to dodge the ultimate alternative of deportation until 1755.

For many decades before the British takeover, but perhaps more regularly in the eighteenth century than in the seventeenth, most of the Acadians at Port Royal, and some at Minas and Chignecto, continued to pay their token seigneurial dues and rents to the various La Vallière, La Tour, d'Aulnay, and Le Borgne heirs who had successfully established claims with French authorities. After the takeover of 1710 British governors had been insisting on such payments being made to the Crown, but with little success. In 1730 Philipps reported that "three or four insignificant families . . . pretend to Right of Seigneury that extend over all the Inhabited part of the Province . . ." and that ". . . the chief of these [claimants] is a woman who has been wife to two subaltern officers of this Regiment, she has by cunning address got the others to make over their Pretensions and is going over [to England] to Solicit . . . ."[21] The lady, Agatha La Tour Campbell, finally succeeded, in 1733, in winning an award of £2000 to buy out her (i.e., presumably *all*) seigneurial rights or pretensions in the Annapolis and Minas areas.[22] She was to continue to collect her own rents.

Thereafter the collection of old seigneurial dues and some rents now clearly owed to the crown involved much discussion, accounting, and correspondence but never much cash or kind. Various detailed accounts of *cens et rentes* and fines of alienation are scattered through the documents. In 1734 rents due for the two previous years for the Annapolis district were thus recorded: for *cens*, 20 *deniers parisis*, 72 *deniers tournois*, and 6 *oboles parisis;* for *rentes*, a beaver tail, 4 partridges, 2 pullets, roughly 150 capons, 200 bushels of wheat, and a few small payments of cash. Commuting to cash values in New England currency the amount due was only about £68 (including some £8

20. Brebner, *New England's Outpost,* pp. 93–99, discusses in detail the circumstances of the "unqualified" oaths taken in 1729 and 1730 and concludes that they were extracted by Philipps on his verbal promise that the Acadians would not have to bear arms. This question is still open, however, and may never be resolved.

21. AC, NSA-*19,* 52–59.

22. There is very full documentation of the progress of her suit, especially in PRO, Board of Trade, Nova Scotia, *33,* mostly copied in AC, NSA-*22* and NSA-*23.* Much of this has been printed in Adam Shortt, V. K. Johnston, and Gustave Lanctot, *Documents relating to Currency, Exchange and Finance in Nova Scotia, 1675–1758* (1933), esp. pp. 190 ff. For the concern of the council at Annapolis Royal with her, see *Nova Scotia Archives. III,* 290–362, which is a printing of the AC, NSB series as far as the meeting of August 17, 1736.

or more in fines of alienation) and of this some £48 was collected. On this amount a little more than £7 was paid in commission, and the net yield of nearly £41, when converted to sterling at 260 per cent discount, amounted to only slightly more than £11 for the two years.[23] In 1745 Mascarene observed that the settlers paid no taxes but ". . . only a small Quit-Rent for their Lands in Fowles and Wheat amounting in the whole to about £15 Sterling excepting what they voluntarily allow to their Priests . . . ."[24] Rents, seigneurial dues, and fines of alienation on land were no burden on the Acadians.

Beyond the cores of the older settlements most often not even these nominal tributes were paid. Morris described Acadian squatting in 1748: "Their Title of Lands arises from Old French Grants, but these extend only to their Old Settlements; But since the Rendition of that Country [i.e., in 1713] many are settled contrary to the order of Government and have no other Title than the Law of Possession."[25] In 1738 Armstrong was complaining in a letter to Alexander Bourg (Bourq or Burke, one of the deputies) that several people who had merely got leave to visit and mark out lands "laying about Chepody, Memramcoup and Petitcoutiak and report on them [with a view to application for grants] have taken possession of and improved large portions of the crown lands, disobeyed repeated orders and defied the government."[26] Two years later Mascarene was echoing him. The Acadians had presumed to mark out crown lands in the Shepody area and had gone ahead to settle there and improve the lands with no permission.[27] However they were by temperament and tradition a litigious people[28] and perhaps most of them sought, by the payment of

23. The details of this "rent roll" can be found in AC, NSA-23, 7–19. The conversion factors (in New England currency) were: for wheat, 50d. per bushel (about 18 pence sterling); for capons, 18d. each; for partridge and pullets, 5d. to 9d. each; and for the beaver tail, 5 shillings. The total cens for two years amounted to little more than one New England pound.

24. AC, NSA-27, 211–22. Printed in Shortt, Currency, Exchange and Finance, p. 237.   25. Morris, "A Breif Survey," cap. 5, p. 4.

26. Nova Scotia Archives. II (1900), 221. For locations from Minas around to Shepody mentioned in this chapter, see Figure 5.9.   27. Ibid., p. 236.

28. Armstrong, in a dispatch to Lords of Trade, noted that ". . . they are a Litigious Sort of people and so ill natur'd to one another as Daily to Encroach upon their Neighbours propertys . . . ." AC, NSA-20, 112: 1731. Armstrong was exasperated but he describes a situation quite to be expected among agricultural people in a poorly surveyed area. Good fences have always been important to good neighborliness. As a result a committee or commission of the council existed to adjudicate claims and it had lots of business. "The owners of such unruly cattle as break

trivial *cens et rentes,* to assert "legal" claims to land for themselves or their children.

The matter of title also was muddied by general lack of survey or of precise designation of parcels when the British took over. The first major official effort to correct the situation was associated with abortive plans of the 1720's and 1730's to settle Irish and Palatine Protestants in Nova Scotia.[29] Armstrong pursued the matter in 1731: "There is not an inhabitant who pays a farthing Rent towards the defraying of Such necessary charges that attends all governments . . . ," and he went on to insist on ". . . the necessity of having the french Inhabitants Estates survey'd and Measur'd . . . to lay before Your Lordships any just plan of this Country, for it is said that some, if not all, of them possess and claim Greater Tracts than they are anyways Intitled to. . . ."[30] The next year Armstrong was empowered to grant land,[31] and, in 1733, one George Mitchell was instructed to survey the woods and lands on both sides of the Annapolis River from Digby Gut upward; the inhabitants were ordered to plant poles on their boundaries. In November 1733, Armstrong sent the Board of Trade "an exact plan" of the Annapolis River with a survey of property boundaries.[32] In December of that year he commissioned one Prudent Robichaud, Sr. to collect on the river all quitrents, fines of alienation, etc. In a letter to Father Maufils, the resident priest at Pisiquid, Armstrong indicated

---

through or jump over the fences declared good by the commission, must dispose of them; or be under the same penalties as those who do not keep their dykes in repair." *Nova Scotia Archives. II,* 206: 1735.

29. AC, NSA-*18,* 134–36: 1729.   30. AC, NSA-*20,* 98–110.

31. AC, NSA-*21,* 73–77. Also in 1732, the Lords of Trade informed Armstrong that while it might be reasonable that the immediate possessors of lands should enjoy what they actually cultivated, claims of large areas should be suspect. *Nova Scotia Archives. II,* 194.

32. In April of 1734, Mitchell was ordered to do the same for Minas, Pisiquid, Cobequid, Cap D'Or, Chignecto, and Shepody, as well as to map extensive stretches of coastline as far west as Passamaquoddy. See AC, NSA-*21* to NSA-*23.* The "Plan of the River of Annapolis Royal" bound on to the back of vol. 1 (1914) of *An Historical Journal of the Campaigns in North America from the Years 1757, 1758, 1759 and 1760 by Captain John Knox,* ed., Arthur G. Doughty (1914–16), together with accompanying notes (both prepared by Placide Gaudet) may be based on this survey, no other results of which I have yet seen. They should be in PRO, if in mapped form. PRO has several maps based on the Mitchell survey of Annapolis Royal and the river and basin settlements (copies of all of which are in PANS and AC) but so far as the Minas Basin settlements are concerned the writer could find no further documentary or cartographic evidence that this herculean task was ever carried out.

that the Minas residents had brought in records of their lands (to be registered, presumably) and that he wanted those of Pisiquid to do the same. By 1738 Acadian agents were being sent by the council as far away as Shepody for the same purpose.[33]

The efforts of the council to control settlement are indicated in a number of entries in the council minutes and the official correspondence. The minutes for July and August 1740 are concerned with a petition of eight settlers who wished to go to Tibogue (i.e., Chebogue, near present Yarmouth) for the winter only. They went before permission was granted, were called back, and finally allowed to go for the one season provided they engaged only in fowling and fishing and dyked no land.[34]

We may conclude that the Acadians themselves had always had a rather specific conception of their own plots of land, that they were ready to argue with anyone about their limits, that they paid the token fees involved in seigneurial dues without too ill a grace, and that most Acadians, in 1710, had some sort of tradition of individual tenure of the lands they occupied and worked. As the British intentionally or unwittingly destroyed or undercut the old system, the Acadians became increasingly uncooperative. They appeared to associate the payment of quitrents to the British government with the hated oaths which they were being pestered to take. The hope of restoration of French sovereignty remained strong and was fanned by officials of the nearby French areas of Cape Breton, Isle St-Jean, and Quebec, and by the French missionaries. As with most conquered people they tended to act as independently as circumstances allowed and they very quickly discovered that British power as represented by the governor and council at Annapolis had little bite to it.

THE GROWTH AND DISTRIBUTION
OF POPULATION

With the end of official French government we also come to the end of those frequent, detailed annual censuses which have provided so much information about Acadia's changing human geography. In their place we have estimates, often simply of numbers of families, and such

33. Council actions as summarized in Murdoch, *Nova-Scotia, 1*, 524.
34. AC, NSB-*2*, 188, 189–92, 213, 217–22. *Novia Scotia Archives. II*, 244–45.

counts as of those rounded up and deported in 1755 and succeeding years. Perhaps the most useful and reliable count remaining to us for this period is one made by the missionary, Father Félix Pain, at the request of the government of Isle Royale in 1714.[35] More than 2,300 were named and a population of at least 2,500 is assumed, including the extension of the Chignecto area to the estuaries of Shepody Bay.

The less satisfactory later estimates suggest five thousand in the early thirties and more than ten thousand by the fifties—a doubling of the population in, roughly, each twenty years. This is a remarkable rate of growth for its time in that it seems to have involved little or no immigration. That rate of growth, as far as we can tell, was remarkably constant from 1671 to 1748 if our estimates are reliable. From 1671 to 1714 numbers roughly quintupled, from 500 to 2,500 and by mid-century, in approximately the same period of time, it may have again increased five times to between ten and fifteen thousand.

We have no evidence on which to base birth and death rates. We conclude that there was no substantial loss of life in military action during the period nor have we any record of epidemic disease or of serious shortages of food. Most young people married at least by their early twenties and set up for themselves as soon as they could. There were few spinsters over thirty and widows were quick to remarry. However, the nominal censuses of the previous half century often included many young men and women in their twenties as children in families and so unmarried and the parish registers show very few marrying before eighteen. Indeed, most Acadian girls were in their twenties when they wed. Anything approaching child marriage was unknown.[36]

Family size ranged from no children in the case of newly married

35. This is summarized in AC, G1-*466*, 232 ff. *and* AC, NSA-*5*, 74–80, and the complete nominal census has been printed in François-Edmé Rameau de Saint-Père, *Une Colonie Féodale en Amérique: l'Acadie (1604–1881)* (1889), 2, 403–11. There are minor discrepancies between the two and the regrouping by Rameau is used here.

36. An examination of the parish records of St. Jean Baptiste of Annapolis Royal from 1727 to 1742 and of St. Charles of Grand Pré from 1730 to 1748 revealed that of 224 marriages for which the age of both partners was given, only sixteen of the brides were younger than 18 and only one, at 15, younger than 16. The median age of girls at marriage was 21, the modal age 20. Thirty-four were 25 or older at first marriage. In twenty-five cases, slightly more than 10 per cent, the woman was older than the man. In the cases (189) where the man was a year or more older, the median difference in the ages of the partners was four years; the modal differences were two and four years.

couples or older people with all their offspring married, up to a dozen or more, but the average and modal sizes of family "in residence" imply three to four children. In the principal division of the parish of Port Royal (in Pain's count of 1714) of 83 families which included 300 children, only 14 contained more than six children, while 13 had none, and 13 had only one child. In the Grand Pré section of Minas, 48 families had 192 children, or an average of exactly four per family although only one family had the average number (see Table 6.1).

TABLE 6.1   *Number of children per family in two districts of Annapolis Royal in 1714*

Location	Number of children												
	0	1	2	3	4	5	6	7	8	9	10	11	12
Annapolis (upriver)	13	13	6	12	9	8	8	7	2	1	3	1	–
Grand Pré	6	7	6	4	1	7	7	5	3	1	–	–	1

Source: Father Félix Pain's census of 1714. Summarized in François-Edmé Rameau de Saint-Père, *Une Colonie Féodale en Amérique: l'Acadie (1604–1881)* (1889), *2*, 403–11.

However the number of families was no indicator of the number of households. Although young married couples clearly made efforts to become established on their own and unquestionably so contributed to the rapidity of spread of settlement, there are many indications of multi-family households with three or four generations under one roof. Both Otis Little[37] and the anonymous author of *A Geographical History of Nova Scotia*[38] thought that up to three or four generations, and perhaps that many related families, normally lived in one dwelling, suggesting a dozen to a score of people under one roof. If this were the case a general underestimation of population is possible, but neither of these sources is considered to be a highly reliable one. The consideration of average family size becomes important when, for estimates of population, we are given simply the number of families or heads of households. The evidence for 1714 suggests that a factor of six would

37. *The State of Trade in the Northern Colonies Considered with an Account of their Produce and a Particular Description of Nova Scotia* (1748), p. 35. Little was a colonial and pamphleteer.

38. Pp. 20–21. This was published in London in 1749. There was a German edition of the book in 1750 and a French one in 1755. This volume also has been attributed to Otis Little.

provide the most reliable multiplier for conversions; it is probably a bit closer than five and a half.

Changes in the distribution of people during the period were associated with a faster growth in the Minas and Chignecto areas than at Annapolis and their spreading out in a way not possible in the home area, although in fact no entirely new districts were colonized.[39] There were no substantial areas of tidally flooded land that had not been tried before 1710, but there was plenty of opportunity for expansion in most of them. Spotty although the settlement of the outlying areas was in 1710, by mid-century almost every area where marsh could be easily dyked, and many that involved much labor and ingenuity to enclose, had some settlers.

The parish registers of baptisms, deaths, and marriages, incomplete as they are, provide some interesting indications of the circulation and geographical mobility of the population.[40] Recently, geographers and sociologists have given some attention to the location of marriage partners as a measure of such circulation and the registers were checked for this purpose. Of some 117 marriages of which we have record at Annapolis Royal (the parish of St. Jean Baptiste) between 1727 and 1755, for which we are reasonably confident that we know the residence of both partners, only thirty-two had one, usually the man, from outside of the parish. The true proportion is certainly much lower than these figures suggest for it is necessary to assume that most of the marriages for which no location of partners is given were between two members of the local parish. Indeed a number of those involved can be identified as locals from comparison with earlier nominal censuses.

However, at Minas, extra-parochial marriage partners were much more common. Of some 272 marriages, on the registers of the parish of St. Charles at Grand Pré which have survived, we have adequate residence information for some 164. Most, of course, were of pairs from within the two adjoining parishes of Grand Pré and Canard (St.

39. Movement from the Cumberland Basin or Shepody Bay into the tidal estuaries of the Petitcodiac and Memramcook rivers may have been the major expansion. New settlements along the south shore of the Strait of Northumberland, as at Tatamagouche and Remsheg (Wallace Bay), were associated with emigration to Isle St-Jean and trade with Cape Breton. There was little settlement at Baie Verte before the establishment of Fort Gaspereau.

40. The surviving parts of the registers for St. Jean Baptiste of Port Royal and St. Charles of Grand Pré are catalogued in AC as MG9, B-*8*, lots 12(3) and 24(2).

Joseph). Some twenty-nine were between Minas and one of the two Pisiquid parishes (of the Assumption of the Holy Virgin and of the Holy Family), four had both partners from Pisiquid, one had both from Cobequid, and one was a Pisiquid-Cobequid combination. Forty-eight were clearly extra-regional matches of a Minas man or woman (usually the latter). The distribution of outsiders showed sixteen from France, fourteen from Annapolis, eight from Canada, four from the Chignecto estuaries, three from Cape Breton Island, two from the Saint John River, and one from the Penobscot (Pentagouet). In addition, at Grand Pré there were thirteen marriages in which two outsiders were involved: Pisiquid-Annapolis eight, Annapolis-Canada two, Pisi-quid-Canada one, Mirligueche-France one, and Chignecto-France one. Thus, in 61 out of 272 marriages the partners were from different areas and, if we add the twenty-nine Minas-Pisiquid combinations, ninety, or almost exactly one-third, involved partners from different areas. This indicates a high rate of circulation by Minas people and a great many visitors to Minas from the outside. Indeed the eighteen marriages which had one partner from France, the eleven with one from Canada, and the three with one from Cape Breton (more than 10 per cent of all marriages) suggests a rather remarkably cosmopolitan touch. Even the Annapolis records suggest a good deal of contact outside of that settlement; the records of Grand Pré show the precise opposite of bucolic isolation.

One other kind of information about the degree of circulation in the population that is given in the marriage records, comes from the dispensations for consanguinity. The Acadian population has been supposed to have been rather highly inbred genetically and the records, especially those at Annapolis, tend to bear this out. Of some 297 marriages in the St. Jean Baptiste parish records between 1727 and 1755, for which there is enough information to allow us to make a judgment, at least 131, or 44 per cent, had to have such dispensations (usually between second-cousins). Pre-marital pregnancy, a standard reason for such dispensations and less than a major sin if followed by marriage, may have been the usual reason for the dispensation—the officiating priest or missionary often adds that it was for good reasons known to him. But there are many arguments against such an interpretation; one of the best being that, on the average, the brides were in their twenties. Another is the undoubtedly deserved reputation of the Acadians for the avoidance of extra-marital liaisons, which may have carried over to pre-marital experience between young lovers (although the latter is common enough in farming communities and generally condoned if followed by marriage). What is reflected, unquestionably, is simply the degree of isolation, whether the marriages were forced or not, and the sheer difficulty of finding someone to marry who was not a second cousin.

Pain's account listed more than nine hundred people in the Annapolis area (not including twenty-two entered as "absent" and eleven who were away fishing[41]). Above the fort, along the river, were the largest number, 449. A total of 239 is listed as "basse ville" and "proche de la Fort," 209 come under the heading "Cappe" or "le Cap," and 28 as in the "Banlieue." It is possible to interpret all of these titles as being on, or near, the peninsula on which the fort was situated but it is nearly impossible that all the people listed were settled there and it is known that there was settlement on both sides of the basin below the fort. The assumption has been made that "Cappe" or "le Cap" refers to the higher ground leading to the neck of the fort peninsula in the bend of the river (as it had in seventeenth-century censuses and maps) and not to the Granville Peninsula between the Bay of Fundy and the Annapolis Basin. Perhaps "proche de la Fort" could mean all the area as one approaches the fort after entering the basin through Digby Gut— which would include much of the same area. Not a great deal of preference can be given to one or the other interpretation but the latter is preferable to the assumption that 466 people lived in quite close proximity to the fort peninsula. There was not nearly enough marshland to support them there. Although the suggestion that "proche de la Fort" refers chiefly to population west of the fort is an hypothesis, it cannot be a bad distortion of reality. We have to assume a reasonable number of families below the fort. Mascarene had observed in 1720 that "from Goat Island to five leagues above the ffort, on both sides of the Brittish [Annapolis] River are a great many fine farms Inhabited by about two hundred familyes."[42] Although assuming six per family his round figure of two hundred may well have been too large.

The sources for population figures in the 1730's are a bit skimpy.

41. The twenty-two may well have included the eleven. The total may have been 917 or 920.

42. PRO, CO 217-*3*, 184–93[v]: "Description of Nova Scotia," p. 188[v]. This document has been copied in AC, NSA-*12*, 124–38, and an edited version has been printed in *Nova Scotia Archives. I* (1869), 39–49, where Mascarene is described as an "engineer."

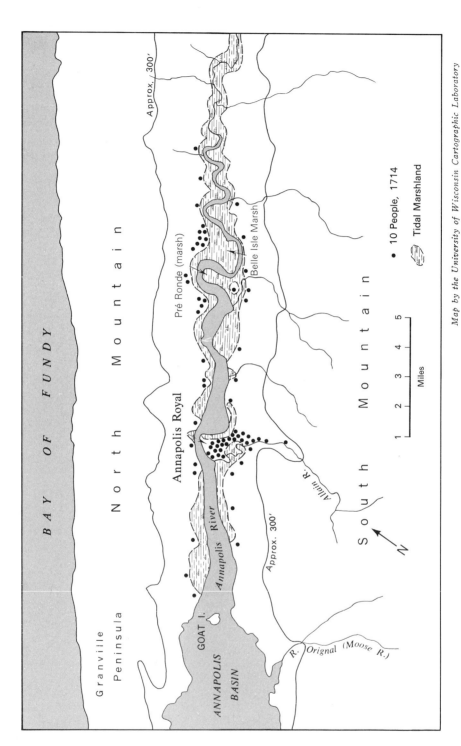

Fig. 6.1 Annapolis Basin and Valley: Population, 1714.

For Annapolis Royal there are estimates of 900 people in 1730, of 160 families in 1731, and of 180 families in 1732, which tend to support each other unless they are derived from the same source.[43] In 1737 our single source gives a grand total for Acadia of 7,598 from subtotals that add up to 640 less (see Table 6.2).[44] Rameau, perhaps on the

TABLE 6.2   *Population of the four Bay settlements in 1737*

Annapolis Royal	1,406
Pisiquid	1,623
Minas	2,113
Beaubassin (all of Chignecto)	1,816
Total	6,958

Source: AC, G1-*466*, 262.

assumption that he had found one source of the error, transposes the Annapolis figure to 1,046 but that reduces the total to 6,598, or 1,000 less.[45] About all we can conclude is that the Annapolis population was somewhere between one thousand and fourteen hundred.

There is little to go on except Le Loutre's estimates of numbers of Annapolis communicants for that year as two thousand.[46] Rameau believed that the only way to reconcile that figure was to assume that it was meant to be one thousand, although the two thousand figure is repeated in another estimate for 1753. He then converts the communicant numbers to a population of fifteen hundred for Annapolis.[47] Charles Morris, who had ample opportunity to know the region, estimated only two hundred families there in 1748–49.[48] This figure,

43. The figure for 1730 appears in Rameau, *Une Colonie Féodale*, 2, 16–17; that for 1731 in *idem.*, *La France aux Colonies* (1859), p. 36, and in *Census of Canada for 1870–71* (1871), 4, 56; and that for 1732 in AC, G1-*466*, 290: a dispatch of Brouillan de St-Ovide at Louisburg to the Minister of Marine.

44. AC, G1-*466*, 262.   45. Rameau, *La France aux Colonies*, p. 36.

46. Abbé Jean Louis Le Loutre, "Description de l'Acadie," in *Collection de documents inédits; Documents sur le Canada et l'Amérique*, comp. Abbé Henri-Raymond Casgrain, *1* (1888), 42.

47. Rameau, *La France aux Colonies*, pp. 133–34; *idem.*, *Une Colonie Féodale*, 2, 146.

48. Morris, "A Breif Survey," cap. 5, p. 8, and *idem.*, "Judge Morris' Remarks Concerning the Removal of the Acadians," Nova Scotia Historical Society *Collections* (1881), 158. This report has also been printed in Casgrain, *Collection de documents inédits*, *1*, 130–37. The factor for multiplying the number of communicants to get population is uncertain, but probably is from 1.33 to 1.5.

roughly consistent with Rameau's estimate of fifteen hundred people, suggests very little growth in the forties and the writer would advance it to no more than 1,750 (plus or minus 500) for mid-century. Substantial emigration from Port Royal throughout the period is indicated, especially of young couples in their most fertile years.

By mid-century the inhabitants appear to have used all the available marshland on the north shore of the basin, although it was not all dyked, and on the map accompanying the second of the Morris reports[49] no settlement is shown below Goat Island on either side. Between that island and the fort, then, there were twenty settlers on the north side and eight on the south. It is possible to assume a much heavier settlement than this on the northwestern shore below present Granville Ferry and some even below Goat Island, in all perhaps 150 to 200. If we assume some 250 in the neighborhood of the fort peninsula, that would leave 1,150 to 1,200 strung out above the town along the river "for nearly thirty miles"—certainly at least to *paradis terrestre* (present Paradise). Beyond the farthest conceivable settlement (present Lawrencetown or Middleton) there was a stretch of at least fifty miles of empty country in "The Valley"—which was "for the most part barren, [and] has no inhabitants"[50]—until the first of the Minas settlements.

On the basis of any reasonable assumption or evidence, the population grew more rapidly in the Minas district than in those of either Annapolis or Chignecto. The Pain account listed 540 for the Minas settlements west of Pisiquid, 336 on that river, and 155 in Cobequid. Rameau's figure for all of Minas in 1731 was 386 families; the 1732 estimate of "habitans" (presumably heads of family) was 217 west of Pisiquid, 110 in Pisiquid, and 92 at Cobequid. At a conversion factor of six, these would be, respectively, 1,302, 660, and 552, or a total of nearly 2,500.[51]

For 1737 Minas was given a total of 2,113 and Pisiquid and Cobequid combined some 1,623.[52] These figures again call into doubt Le Loutre's estimates of 3,400 communicants for Minas proper and Pisiquid, for the year 1748, a total which seems too high regardless of the

49. PRO, A & WI-*63*, 106: "Report by Captain [Charles] Morris to Governor Shirley upon his survey of lands in Nova Scotia available for Protestant Settlers, 1749." Printed in AC *Report for 1912* (1913).

50. "Report by Captain Morris," p. 80.

51. For sources see above, notes 35 and 43.

52. AC, G1-*466*, 262.

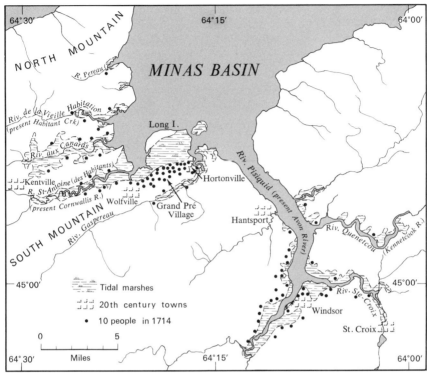

Map by the University of Wisconsin Cartographic Laboratory

Fig. 6.2   Minas and Pisiquid: Population, 1714.

conversion factor used. To support his own position Le Loutre had every reason to be generous in his estimates.

We have separate estimates for Cobequid (apparently all the shores from the mouth of the Pisiquid, i.e., Avon River to the head of the Bay and back along the entire north side of Minas Basin and Channel) of 136 in 1714, 442 in 1730, and 92 "habitans" ($\times$ 6 = 552 persons?) in 1732. For 1737 it is quite unclear what share of the regional total to assign to Cobequid; for 1748 Le Loutre's claim of 800 communicants (1,200 persons?) may be too large as usual.[53] Estimates for all of Minas Basin in the mid-century period vary from perhaps 3,500 to as many as 6,500.[54]

53. For sources see above, notes 35, 43, and Le Loutre, "Description."

54. Rameau, *Une Colonie Féodale, 2,* 148, estimated some 6,000, a good round figure to compare with Le Loutre's implied 6,300. Morris, "Remarks Concerning the Removal," pp. 158–59, estimated only some 650 families: 150 at Canard, 200 at Minas proper, 150 at Pisiquid, and 150 at Cobequid.

In Morris' "Remarks Concerning the Removal of the Acadians," he suggests 180 families for the Grand Pré area, 30 for the "Gaspero," and 16 for the "River Habitants" (Cornwallis River), 150 for Canard and 150 for Pisiquid, or, at best, fewer than 4,000 people for 1748.[55] J. S. Martell, who was thoroughly familiar with the sources, came out flatly for 4,800 at Minas and Pisiquid in 1755,[56] while Winslow's journal recorded 2,242 and 1,100, respectively, as having been embarked by his forces during the 1755 deportations.[57] The writer's choice in round figures for mid-century is 2,500 for Minas, 1,500 for Pisiquid, and 1,000 for Cobequid (the first, if anything, a bit low and the last possibly a bit high). Perhaps the most striking thing about the estimates is the important place held by the Avon River area by the 1750's. Le Loutre rated Pisiquid as more populous than Minas proper, but the other evidence doesn't support him.

The Chignecto area presents the most acute regional problem in estimating population for the first half of the eighteenth century. The Pain count of 352 families for 1714 makes no distinction between Beaubassin (Cumberland Basin) and the areas further north and west. For 1730 Rameau assigned 840 to Beaubassin and 170 to Shepody; in 1732, 140 and 65 "habitans" (840 and 390 people?) were reported. The total had soared to 1,816 by 1737, perhaps indicating a more complete count. By 1748, however, the picture is very clouded. People were moving into Beaubassin from the other settlements and out of it, especially to Isle St-Jean. Rameau accepts Le Loutre's estimate of 2,500 communicants (and 3,750 people) which seems high to the writer, who prefers a figure under 3,000—say 2,800. In 1748 Morris estimated 200 families in the Cumberland Basin, four at Baie Verte, and 140 in the Shepody Basin (perhaps 2,000 people in all),[58] which seems a bit low.

In 1756, Judge Morris (as he had then become) made the estimates shown in Table 6.3 for the period before deportation, but they are too

55. Pp. 158–60.
56. J. S. Martell "Pre-Loyalist Settlements around Minas Basin" (1933), pp. 19–20.
57. "Journal of Colonel John Winslow, of the Provincial Troops, while Engaged in Removing the Acadian French Inhabitants from Grand Pré, and the Neighbouring Settlements, in the Autumn of the Year 1755." Printed in Nova Scotia Historical Society *Collections*, *3* (1883), *4* (1885). Ref. is to *4*, 114–22.
58. Morris, "A Breif Survey," cap. 5, pp. 14–16.

TABLE 6.3   *Judge Charles Morris' estimate of the number of French families in the Bay settlements in 1756*

River of Annapolis Royal	200
River Canar & its dependencys	150
Grand Pré, Gasparo & its dependencys	200
River Pisgate, St. Croix, &c.	150
River Cobequet Cheganois Shubnacadie & round Cobequet Bason	120
Shepody	40
Patcoutycak	45
Marooncook	50
Chiegnecto & its dependencys	150
	1,105

"And several other scatering Familys . . . ."

Source: Collection de documents inédits . . . sur le Canada et l'Amérique, comp. Henri-Raymond Casgrain, *2* (1889), 86.

close to those of "A Breif Survey" for us to feel much confidence that they were based on new evidence or reasonable allowances for natural increase less emigration.

If we use a factor of six we should have 6,630 folk, or too few. A factor of nine to allow for extended families would give a reasonable total of nearly 10,000, but it may be more reasonable to assume that the number of families is underestimated.

Allowing a very generous figure of five hundred to account for all the possible people in outlying settlements (but not including Isle St-Jean or the Acadians on Cape Breton Island) the writer suggests that there were approximately 10,000 Acadians in the settlements of present peninsular Nova Scotia and New Brunswick about mid-century, distributed thus: Annapolis Royal district, 1,750; Minas north and west of Pisiquid, 2,500; Pisiquid, 1,500; Cobequid and the Gulf Shore, 1,000; Chignecto, 1,600; Memramcook, Petitcodiac, and Shepody (together), 1,200; and outlying settlements, 500 or fewer. If the Acadians on Isle St-Jean and Cape Breton Island were added the total might reach 12,500.[59] He finds it difficult to accept figures for the mainland as low as the 7,500 implied by Morris for 1748 or as high as the 12,000 used by Rameau for the same year. Yet both may come just

59. See A. H. Clark, *Three Centuries and the Island* (1959), p. 33. Also, see below, Chapter 8.

within the dimension of possibility. As we shall see in Chapter 7, Abbé
l'Isle-Dieu in his "Tableau des Missionaires . . . à l'Acadie française
et anglais" estimates, on the basis of the reports of Le Loutre, some
18,000 on the peninsula at the time of the deportation.[60]

THE INDIVIDUAL SETTLEMENTS

Annapolis Royal

The old "home" settlement of the Acadians differed from the others
in several ways. In the first place the fort with its hundred or more
soldiers and the small official community, usually with at least two or
three resident New England traders, formed a nucleus and a special
sort of area that consumed and did not produce. It provided a market
for agricultural products, although the residents of the basin below the
fort, and of the valley above it, felt that it was a forced market with
prices kept at as artificially low a level as the garrison dared try to
enforce.

The principal church of the region was twelve miles from the fort,
upriver on the north side, and formed the Acadian social nucleus of the
Annapolis area, although there were "chappells of ease" elsewhere. The
garrison and the few New England families lived a life apart from the
general Acadian community although a few Acadian families, generally
those living near the fort, effected a partial integration by marriage of
their daughters to soldiers of the garrison. The habitant society largely
must have ignored the small British group and have lived in the same
bucolic fashion as their cousins in Grand Pré and Beaubassin. Such
hints of elegance, or of exotic sophistication as there were in housing,
clothing, and furniture, were confined closely to the *banlieu* of the fort.

The age structure of the population was somewhat different from
that of the other major settlements. Newly married couples tended to
move out as they had from the 1680's onward, although this difference
probably diminished steadily after 1710. There were, of course, many
reasons for emigration besides overcrowding in the Annapolis Basin
and River valley. The greater freedom from official surveillance (in-

60. Quoted by Casgrain in "Coup d'oeil sur l'Acadie," p. 117.

cluding often a much wider choice of markets for surplus grain or livestock, and greater ease of dealing in furs and feathers with the Indians) may have been particularly compelling. An older population may have emphasized the imbalance between production and consumption. But the greatest distinction between the residents of Annapolis and the other areas probably lay in their more limited contacts with Isle Royale, Isle St-Jean, and Quebec (areas of French sovereignty), with the Indians and, indeed, with the illegal New England traders who escaped surveillance from Annapolis and visited Minas, in particular, with some regularity.

The fort was still where it had been established by d'Aulnay in the 1630's, on a peninsula formed by a meander of the river just where a small tributary entered from the south (see Plate 4). The lower town was along the main river adjacent to the fort. The upper town stretched south from the fort along a ridge parallel to the tributary Rivière Allain, or Allen's River.

Farms, singly or in groups, "where the Soil is good and where they have marshes to raise their bread corn on,"[61] were dotted along the shores of the basin and river from Goat Island to as far as five leagues above the fort as early as 1720.[62] Following the marshes on both sides, which were intermittent, settlement tended to be in nodes, almost hamlets, commonly of five to ten families. The largest group was around the great Belle Isle marsh, six to eight miles above the fort, and included thirty families, or 150 to 200 people, within a space of two miles.

The fullest reports that we have for the end of the period come from Morris.[63] We learn something of problems of navigation that must always have been present but which were becoming more acute with the steadily increasing size of transatlantic naval and merchant vessels. The channel south of Goat Island was shallow and rocky and could not be used; that to the north was both wide and deep enough but the ebb and flow of the great tides was so strong that vessels might get out of control without a strong leading wind. From Goat Island to the fort the five-mile stretch formed a most commodious harbor with six fathoms even at extreme low tide. The river was navigable for small vessels about eighteen miles above the fort (present Bridgetown) and large boats could go nine miles further to "the falls" on the tide if they were

61. Morris, "A Breif Survey," cap. 5, p. 9.   62. PRO, CO 217-*3*, 188ᵛ.
63. "A Breif Survey," and "Report by Captain Morris."

able to be beached at low tide but, Morris observed, "the bottom at Low Water is intollerably Rocky and foul."

The inhabitants were mostly farmers, using any spare time they had for hunting, fowling, trapping, or fishing. A certain amount of lumbering was essential for their needs. Most of these were off-season activities but occasionally younger men, able to leave their home because of a surplus of family labor, hired out to the cod fishery for the summer season. Apparently the Acadians still were content with modest houses. A report of 1745 speaks of them as ". . . wretched wooden boxes, without conveniences, and without ornaments, and scarcely containing the most necessary furniture . . . ."[64] and in the following decade a visitor observed that "the houses of the village [Annapolis Royal] . . . are mean, and in general built of wood."[65] The use of "wood" or "wooden" as a derogatory epithet, however, is surprising. Quebec, Boston, and even Montreal had many substantial stone buildings, but to have supposed that farmers in a wooded country, especially where suitable building stone and masonry skills would have been hard to come by, should have built of any other material is absurd. However, more use of stones and baked clay bricks for foundations, fireplaces, and chimneys might well have been expected.

Minas Basin

MINAS PROPER — The title "Minas" was applied in three progressively narrowing territorial contexts: to all of the settlements inside Cape D'Or and Cape Split (i.e., all of the shores of the Minas Basin); to all of the settlements in the area between Cape Blomidon and the mouth of the Avon (i.e. excluding Cobequid and Pisiquid); or, finally, just to the heart of the Acadian settlements, the Grand Pré nucleus and the banks of the present Cornwallis River (see Figure 5.9). The eastern end of the Annapolis-Cornwallis River valley is drained by four tidal streams or creeks that enter the basin in roughly parallel courses between North Mountain and South Mountain: Pereau Creek nearest to the former, Habitant Creek (which had many other names

64. This is from a letter from the Marquis de La Boische de Beauharnois, Governor of Canada, and the Intendant, Gilles Hocquart, to the Comte de Maurepas, printed in full in *Documents relative to the Colonial History of the State of New York*, ed. E. B. O'Callaghan. *10* (1858). 3–19.
65. Knox. *An Historical Journal, 1*, 97.

and is not to be confused with Rivière des Habitants), Canard River, and Cornwallis River (Rivière St-Antoine of the seventeenth century, but known in the eighteenth as Rivière des Habitants).[66] Still further south, and parallel to the last, draining the granite upland (the northern edge of which forms South Mountain) in a 500-foot gorge until within five miles of its mouth, was a fifth river, the Gaspereau. There were settlements along all of these by 1714 according to the Pain census presented in Table 6.4.

TABLE 6.4 *Population of Minas District in 1714*

Gaspereau River	37
Grand Pré	287
Cornwallis River	94
Canard River	76
Habitant Creek (and/or Pereau Creek)	36
Total	530

Source: See Table 6.1.

In 1715 Caulfeild called Minas "by much the best improvement in This Collony."[67] Referring to Grand Pré, Mascarene, in his description of 1720, described it as ". . . a platt of Meadow, which stretches along for near four leagues, part of which is damn'd in from the tide, and produces very good wheat and pease." As for the settlement, "the houses which compose a kind of scattering Town, lyes on a riseing ground along two Creeks which runns betwixt it, and the meadow, and makes of this last a kind of Peninsula."[68] This was where the center of Minas lay until the time of the dispersion.

The perhaps two hundred houses of Grand Pré were spread out over two or three miles along the northern slope of the ridge that descended gently from the height of land near the Gaspereau valley to the edge of the great thousand-acre marsh. There were houses roughly from pres-

66. Perhaps to add to the confusion both Pereau Creek and Habitant Creek are sometimes referred to, collectively or individually, as "Rivière des Vieilles Habitants."

67. PRO, CO 217-2, 49–53ᵛ: Caulfeild to Lords of Trade, November 1715, p. 50. This letter has been copied in AC, NSA-7, 164–74.

68. PRO, CO 217-3, 190–90ᵛ.

ent Hortonville to present Wolfville. The houses along the lower Gaspereau (at two settlements called, then, Gasparaux and Melanson) usually were lumped with Grand Pré. As in the case of Pré Ronde in the Annapolis Valley, the settlement took its name from the marsh but the houses and other buildings were well above it on permanently dry land. The area from present Wolfville and Port Williams to present Kentville along the Cornwallis River was a relatively minor section of Minas; the area second to Grand Pré in importance was Canard, which

TABLE 6.5   *Estimated population of Minas District in 1750*

Pereau Creek		50
Habitant Creek (Rivière de la Vieille		
Habitation, or des Vieux Habitants)		75
Canard		750
Upriver, around Dyke Village	350	
Downriver, along both banks	150	
Canard-Cornwallis interfluve	250	
Cornwallis River (Rivière des Habitants)		100
Grand Pré		1,350
Gaspereau		125
Total		2,450

Source: Author's estimate based on [Charles Morris], "A Breif Survey of Nova Scotia" (n.d.), cap 5, p. 10.

had a comparable stretch of marshland in its broad lower valley. Assuming that the population had increased some five times between 1714 and mid-century when we have reports from Morris, the writer suggests a distribution of 2,500 people at mid-century as given in Table 6.5.[69]

Morris reported a parish church (of St. Joseph) at Canard and indicated a larger use of upland there for agriculture than in most of the other settlements: ". . . for the production of Grain [it] well answer'd their Labour; but not like their Marshes, but much more uplands are here improved then [sic] in any other District."[70]

The anonymous author of *A Geographical History of Nova Scotia* estimated four hundred houses within a radius of 8 or 10 miles and assuming three or four families under each roof, came up with fifteen

69. Morris' 1755 figures included the two more northern settlements; he listed only 180 families for Grand Pré, which seems too few.

70. Morris, "A Breif Survey," cap. 5, p. 10.

people "per roof," or a total of some six thousand.[71] The date is clearly in the late forties but even for "greater Minas" seems a bit too high. His radius of 8 to 10 miles presumably from the center of Grand Pré seems to have excluded Pisiquid.

From the detailed accounts of the near destruction of the British forces at Minas in January of 1747 we have a description of the Grand Pré buildings as ". . . low Houses fram'd of timber and their Chimney fram'd with the Building of wood & lined with Clay except the fireplace below . . . ." There were a few stone houses in the "center of town." So scattered were the individual houses that ". . . our Quarters must have been extended above a mile [even] had we taken up the nearest houses in the thickest part of it . . . ."[72] Apart from homes, barns, and stables, the only buildings were the churches and mills.

PISIQUID — Pisiquid, which lay along the present Avon River and its branches, was the next largest settlement in the Minas Basin. It seems to have grown very rapidly from 56 families (and 351 people) in 1714, to 1,400 or 1,500 people by mid-century.[73] Evidence for the distribution of people is difficult to interpret. The writer's estimate for a population of roughly 1,400 (say as of about 1750) is shown in Table 6.6. The primary center, including one of the churches with its presby-

TABLE 6.6   *Estimated population of Pisiquid in 1750*

Left bank (present Hantsport-Falmouth area)	800
St. Croix River (and present Windsor area)	500
Kennetcook River and right bank generally	100
Total	1,400

Source: Author's estimate based on Charles Morris, "Judge Morris' Remarks Concerning the Removal of the Acadians," Nova Scotia Historical Society *Collections* (1881), p. 159.

tery, appears to have been near present Falmouth. There were two parishes: that of the Assumption of the Holy Virgin on the right bank and that of the Holy Family on the left.[74]

71. P. 21.   72. Morris, "A Breif Survey," cap. 2, pp. 25–26.
73. Morris, "Remarks Concerning the Removal," p. 159, estimates only "upwards of 150 families" but clearly he knew far less about this area than the other settlements.
74. The other Acadian parishes included that of St. Charles at Grand Pré, St. Joseph at Canard, St. Jean Baptiste at Annapolis, and St. Louis at Beaubassin.

By the time of the deportations a large number of the Pisiquid settlers had already left. Pisiquid was the Acadian settlement closest to Halifax and to attack it Indians had to come from the general direction of the Avon River or Cobequid-Shubenacadie settlements. As a result the Halifax garrison tended to hold the Pisiquid and Cobequid inhabitants responsible for Indian depredations; moreover, fairly or not, both settlements had been accused of open and substantial aid to both Indians and Canadians in the 1744–48 period. They also were the groups most conveniently accessible for the demands of Cornwallis and his successors for labor on the roads, especially the main one from Halifax to Minas. For all of these reasons the settlers were attracted to the Chignecto isthmus region, to the shores of the Strait of Northumberland (as at Tatamagouche), or to Cape Breton.

The great tidal range created problems for water communication. Large vessels usually had to lie well out and even then were usually aground at lowest tide, but small vessels could come up to all the settlements if they could withstand beaching. Anchorage was also a problem so rapidly did the tidal race enter and leave the channel.

COBEQUID — East of Pisiquid, on Cobequid Bay, the settlers were much more scattered in pockets over more than a hundred miles of shoreline and had much less social cohesiveness than those already described. They reached at least from Tennycape (east of Walton on the south shore of Cobequid Bay) and along the whole north shore of Minas Basin from the head of Cobequid (present Truro), to Grosse Isle (present Parrsboro) or beyond. The densest settlement was, naturally enough, close to the most extensive marshes, from the mouth of the Shubenacadie River on the south to the present Masstown on the north. There were churches near present Truro and Masstown (Cove d'Église) and an Indian chapel some twenty miles up the Shubenacadie River (near present Stewiacke). F. H. Patterson has done some revision of an estimate of numbers made by Morris in 1755 (but as of 1748)[75] and the writer, using these sources as well as "A Breif Survey . . ." suggests in Table 6.7 the distribution for a population of 900 (roughly 150 families) which is probably a minimum figure. Patterson also followed Morris in his estimate of some twelve families at Tatamagouche and of six at Remsheg.

75. Morris, "Remarks Concerning the Removal," and F. H. Patterson, "Old Cobequid and its Destruction" (1936).

TABLE 6.7 *Estimated population of the Cobequid area in 1748*

Tennycape (Petite Rivière?)	25
Noel (Ville Noël or "Nela" Noël)	50
Maitland (Ville Robert?)	25
Elsewhere west of Shubenacadie	25
Shubenacadie up to Stewiacke	100
South side, Shubenacadie to present Truro (Villes Percé, Burke [Bourcq], Michael Oguin, Jean Doucet, etc.)	180
North side, east of Chiganois River (North River, Onslow, etc.)	120
Chiganois River and Lower Onslow (Isgonish)	100
Masstown (Cove or Cape d'Eglise)	100
Debert (Ville Burke) to Point Economy	75
Point Economy	30
Five Islands	30
Five Islands to Cape D'Or	40
Total	900

Source: Author's estimate based on F. H. Patterson, "Old Cobequid and its Destruction" (1939), and Charles Morris, "Judge Morris' Remarks Concerning the Removal of the Acadians," *Nova Scotia Historical Society Collections* (1881), p. 159.

Presumably the two churches and perhaps five mills were the closest things to foci of community interests, although the movement of cattle to Tatamagouche (en route to Cape Breton) by way of the Chiganois River valley must have led to some concentration there. Even within the nuclei of these settlements, so widely scattered over present Hants, Colchester, and Cumberland counties, the houses must have been widely separated (as they were even at Grand Pré). The area east of the longitude of the mouth of the Shubenacadie had been granted as a seigneurie to Mathieu Martin in 1689 and his rights had been assumed by the Crown on his death in 1724, but as far as we know the area never had been properly surveyed or assessed and the hand of government from Annapolis, tentative enough in its reach at Minas and Pisiquid, scarcely ever poked its fingers into Cobequid's affairs.

As at Canard, but here because of more limited tidal marsh, relatively more upland was cultivated than was normal for the Acadians. This was particularly true on the Gulf shore around Tatamagouche Bay from Cape John to Malagash Point and in Remsheg (Wallace Bay) west on the way to Baie Verte. The dozen families of the former area at mid-century must have been spread through an extent of one hundred square miles along the present French and Waugh rivers. It may be that the breadwinners often were more active in ferry services to Isle St-Jean and Cape Breton than in agriculture. Tatamagouche was second only to Baie Verte as a depot of illegal export and emigration, and the connection with Cobequid by land may have allowed greater secrecy for such movements than that from and via the Chignecto isthmus. The Chiganois route, involving movement over a height of land of about 1,000 feet, was apparently in use in 1744 when two droves of cattle and sheep went through,[76] and is commented upon as early as 1720 when Mascarene observed that the inhabitants had communication ". . . by a road across the woods at the distance of about twenty leagues . . . [to] . . . the Bay of Verte, in the Gulph of St Lawrence by which they drive a Trade to Cape Breton."[77] The long established Indian route by the Shubenacadie to Chebucto (Halifax Harbour) also was commented upon frequently.

Chignecto

As with "Minas," "Chignecto" was a somewhat elastic regional designation. It might include everything from the rivers Maccan, Nappan, and Hébert to the east of Cumberland Basin, to the Memramcook, Petitcodiac, and even to the Shepody marshes off Shepody Bay (see Figure 5.9). Sometimes it excluded these latter and sometimes it referred narrowly to the original Beaubassin settlement along the Missaguash. The panorama of the ridges rising like islands or peninsulas in a sea of marshy grassland was ". . . one of the most Beautifull prospects the Bason of Chignecto affords in Summer for which Cause it is called by the French Beau Basin here may be seen a Number of Villages built on gentle rising Hills interspers'd with Gardens and Woods the Villages divided from each other with long intervalls of marshes and they at a great distance bounded by Hills covered with Trees the Natural growth of the Country here may be seen Rivers turning and winding among the Marshes then Cloath'd with all the Variety of Grain."[78] The main marsh areas, north of Cumberland Basin, were drained by the La Planche and the Missaguash to the east and, through the Tantramar (the greatest of the North American

76. *Nova Scotia Archives. I,* 151–52.   77. PRO, CO 217-3, 191ᵛ.
78. Morris, "A Breif Survey," cap. 5, p. 15.

Atlantic tidal marshes), by the Aulac and Tantramar rivers. There was a low ridge between the Missaguash and the La Planche and a much higher one between the La Planche and the Aulac. On these were to be built, respectively, Fort Lawrence and Fort Beauséjour in the 1750's and here the British and French forces confronted each other, making of the Missaguash a *de facto* boundary which was later chosen to be that between Nova Scotia and New Brunswick. But no such division existed in the seventeenth century or the first half of the eighteenth.

As had been the case during the French regime the Chignecto settlements were among the least well known to the government and population estimates are likely to be very rough approximations. Those available suggest some 350 in 1714 (Pain), 450 in 1720 (Mascarene's seventy to eighty families), 800 to 1,200 in the early 1730's, 1,800 for the late 1730's, and 3,000 to 4,000 for 1748. In the late forties the situation became confused with the coming and going of armed bands and activity in trade and emigration by way of Baie Verte to Isle St-Jean and Cape Breton. It was further complicated by Le Loutre's policy of attempting to get all the Acadians in the area east and south of the Missaguash to move to *de facto* French territory.

Certainly in the mid-forties we can assume that at least several families each were settled in the following locations: Westcock (Weskak, Wehehauk, Oneskak, Peshkak, etc.); Sackville (Pré des Bourcqs, Burkes, Bourgs); Middle Sackville (Pré des Richards); Upper Sackville (Tintamare, Tantramar); La Butte, Le Coupe, and Le Lac (on the Jolicoeur ridge); Portage (at the head of the Missaguash); Minudie (Menoudie, the Elysian Fields); Maccan (Makan) and, perhaps separately, Nappan (Nepane); Hébert River; and along the old central Beaubassin lands along the Missaguash and the La Planche, and they filled in and extended these where they could until active hostilities started. Unquestionably greater activity in dyking and damming (as with the great aboiteau sponsored by the Abbé Le Loutre—see Chapter 8) would have supported many times this population. In the estuaries of Shepody Bay there was still a good deal of marshland available for use, even with the simplest of dyking and draining techniques.

The observers from Annapolis were uniformly impressed with the potential of the area and recognized its strategic location for trade with the Indians and for commercial, military, or ecclesiastical intercourse with Quebec, Isle St-Jean, and Cape Breton. Caulfeild, Mascarene, and

Morris all refer to Joggins coal; its veins could be seen in sailing by but the lack of a harbor and the range and rapidity of the tide made it difficult to exploit. Both Mascarene and Morris mentioned the resources of Grindstone Island. The white pine Caulfeild thought useful but inferior to that of the Maine coast. Before Le Loutre's scorched earth policy (to force migration of those who would not move voluntar-

TABLE 6.8 *Estimated population of the Chignecto area in 1750*

Cumberland Basin east of the Missaguash		850
Minudie peninsula	175	
Hébert River	125	
Maccan River	75	
Nappan River	150	
La Planche River (east)	50	
Beaubassin (Missaguash to La Planche)	275	
Cumberland Basin west of the Missaguash		650
Beaubassin (Fort Beauséjour Ridge)	225	
Aulac and La Coupe	150	
Tantramar	150	
Pré des Bourgs	25	
Pré des Richards	75	
Baie Verte	25	
Cumberland Basin, scattered		100
Total		1,600
Shepody Basin		1,200
Memramcook	300	
Petitcodiac	400	
Shepody	500	

Source: To a considerable extent these figures are based on various estimates of the source of refugees or numbers of old residents in the 1750–55 period. See AC, G1-*466*, 267–91, especially, and below, Chapter 8.

ily) the old Beaubassin nucleus was described by Morris as having fifty houses, centered on the Missaguash about half a mile from the sea. He noted possible sites for a fort, the portage route to Baie Verte, the roads or tracks (or lack of them), and the existence of "several villages." At Baie Verte there were four families who cut hay for their cattle in their 1,000-acre "midden" but who "subsist wholly on their trade to and with Louisburg and Canada."[79]

79. Morris, "A Breif Survey," cap. 5 *passim* (last quotes from p. 14).

Before the forts were built and the ensuing dislocations of the populace occurred, the numbers of people are uncertain, but if they are taken as some 3,000[80] in the whole Chignecto region then a reasonable guess as to population distribution excluding two or three hundred scattered, might be as shown in Table 6.8.

The Shores from Digby to Lunenburg

It is ironic that we have no record of any pre-dispersion occupation or exploitation of St. Mary's Bay or the Digby Shore where the greatest post-dispersion concentration of Acadians in Nova Scotia was to take place (see End papers). A settlement of eight families at Chebogue (Tibogue, Tebak, Thebok) in 1740 was forbidden to raise dykes or farm, but presumably they followed the good Acadian custom of ignoring the council's more absurd, or least enforceable, orders for it was reported in 1748 that Chebogue Point had 12 families and ". . . la terre y est bonne et fertile Le bled et les fourages y sont abondans."[81] For 1746 and 1748 respectively Le Loutre listed ten and twenty-five people at "Tebak."[82] There is no record of settlement at Fourchu (present Yarmouth) in this period and it is possible that there never was any settlement there earlier; it was but a few miles from Chebogue and locations are rather hazy in references to the south and east coast.

We assume continuity of settlement in the Pubnico area throughout the period, although growth was rather slow. The references are sometimes to Cape Sable, however, and may include settlers in the Barrington Passage-Port La Tour-Cape Negro area as well.[83] In Pubnico as such there were fifteen to twenty families by the end of the period, and usually some Indian families.[84]

80. This is a compromise between Morris' implied 2,000 and Rameau's 3,750. See "Report by Captain Morris to Governor Shirley" and Rameau, *Une Colonie Féodale*, 2, 148. See also Morris, "A Breif Survey," cap. 5, p. 8, and *idem*, "Remarks concerning the Removal," p. 158.

81. AC, C11D-*10*, 144. Reprinted in part in Harold A. Innis, ed., *Select Documents in Canadian Economic History, 1497–1783* (1929), p. 239, with slightly modernized spelling.

82. Le Loutre, "Description," pp. 43–44. This detail is presumably based on word of mouth, and baptismal and marriage records, but perhaps also on hearsay.

83. In a deposition given to the council at Annapolis by Denis and Bernard Godet ("inhabitants at the top of the River of Annapolis Royal") in September 1714, they mention three inhabitants at the Passage de Baccareau (Barrington Passage) one of whom had gone to Cape Breton. PRO, CO 217-*2*, 10.

84. See AC, C11D-*10*, 143–54, Anon., *A Geographical History*, p. 26, and Le Loutre, "Description," p. 43.

Further east, there are scattered references to locations at the head of Shelburne Harbour (Port Razoir settlement in the northeast corner, and what was later to become Birchtown in the northwest). It is probable that of the ten families assigned to Ministiguesch ("autrement dit la passage") between Port La Tour and Pubnico in 1748,[85] some may have belonged to Shelburne Harbour. The lack of reference to even tentative settlement at places like Port Mouton or Port Rossignol (Liverpool) in the eighteenth century is puzzling for their attraction as fishing depots would seem to have been at least as great as that of Shelburne Harbour.

There are references to settlement in the neighborhoods of present Petite Rivière, the La Have River estuary, and Mirligueche (present Lunenburg) at both the beginning and end of the period. There were fifteen to twenty families in the area in the late 1740's according to one report. ". . . Mirligueche . . . est un port pour des marchands. . . . Il est habité par 12 ou 15 familles françoises. . . . Ensuite est le Port de la haive. . . . Les habitans françois que consistent en 4 ou 5 familles ont leur maisons à la petite Rivière."[86] In their dispatch of September 12, 1745 Beauharnois and Hocquart had listed eight settlers at Mirligueche and two at Petite Rivière.[87] Le Loutre has a dozen French families at "Misliguesch" and eight at "La Haive" "et 2 à 300 cents sauvages [sic., i.e., two to three hundred Indians] qui s'y assemblent."[88] When Governor Cornwallis visited "Merliguiche" in 1749 he observed: "There are but a few families with tolerable wooden houses covered with bark—a good many cattle and cleared ground more than serves themselves. . . . [They] say they . . . have their grants from Colonel Mascarene, the governor of Annapolis . . . ."[89] There are no references to Mahone Bay, the Chester area, or St. Margaret's Bay.

The Shores from St. Margaret's Bay to Canso

There are two general localities in the western part of this stretch of shore mentioned in what accounts we have: Chebucto (Halifax Harbour and Bedford Basin) and Chezzetcook (in various spellings), which presumably included the Jeddore and Musquodoboit areas (see

85. AC, C11D-*10*, 143–54. Ministiguesch was presumably on Barrington Passage.
86. *Ibid.*, p. 145. Reprinted in Innis, *Select Documents*, p. 239.
87. *New York Colonial Documents, 10*, 10.   88. "Description," p. 43.
89. Murdoch, *Nova Scotia, 2*, 137–38.

Figure 6.3). The former, one of the finest harbors in North America, was widely known and praised. It was the Atlantic end of a much used portage-and-stream route from Cobequid via the Shubenacadie River, and a less used one from Pisiquid. A common resort of Indian tribes, it was the rendezvous for the Duc d'Anville's fleet in 1746, and the burial ground for scores of his forces. Yet it seems never to have had any continuous French settlement in the period. Beauharnois and Hocquart, in a long dispatch from Quebec in 1745 after the fall of Louisburg, reported a man and his three children "three leagues east of the entrance of Chibouctou" which might have been at Chezzetcook.[90] In 1748, seven or eight families are reported for "Chegekkouk."[91] Cornwallis, in 1749 mentions " a few French families on each side of the bay, about three leagues off."[92] These suggest not only some at Chezzetcook but also some to the west at Sambro, Prospect, or even St. Margaret's Bay. There is no listing of Musquodoboit by Caulfeild, Mascarene, Le Loutre, or Beauharnois and Hocquart, in successive lists of south coast locations from 1715 to 1748, but another report of the latter year avers: "Il y avoit autrefois des habitans a Mouschkodabouet; pour la traite des Sauvages mais il n'y en a plus depuis longtems."[93]

Looking eastward in the first half of the eighteenth century, the most obvious peninsular focus of economic activity was the fishery centered on Canso and the fort and garrison established to protect it (see Figure 6.3). The Treaty of Utrecht may have left the area around Chedabucto Bay, as that around Chignecto, in some doubt as to sovereignty in French official minds, but the effect of the fort at Canso appears to have been to eliminate settlement at the head of the bay. The only evidence of settlement there we have for the period is a dubious reference in *A Geographical History of Nova Scotia* to a "town [which] consists of a good Number of Inhabitants" on the west bank of the Guysborough River and near enough the fort to be commanded by it.[94] This well may have been an extension of the Canso settlement which is described as of ". . . a few Inhabitants who are wholly employ'd in the Fishery . . . ."[95]

Indeed we have in the documents a great deal of information about the English fishery at Canso, the garrison that was established there to

90. *New York Colonial Documents*, 10, 10.   91. AC, C11D-*10*, 145.
92. Quoted in Murdoch, *Nova-Scotia*, 2, 138.   93. AC, C11D-*10*, 144.
94. P. 31.   95. *Ibid.*

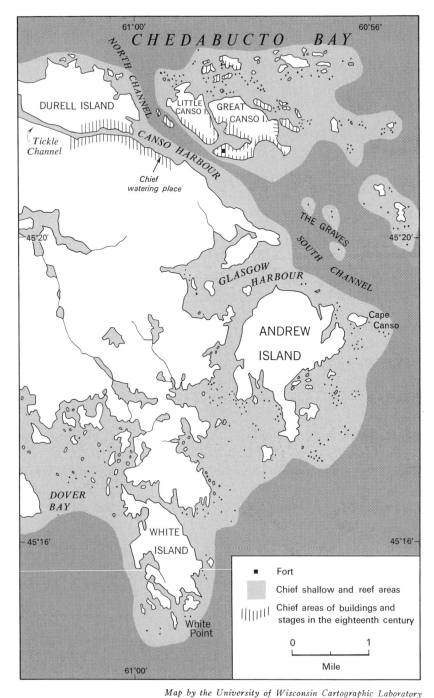

Map by the University of Wisconsin Cartographic Laboratory

Fig. 6.3 Canso: Peninsula and Islands.

protect it, and the wide network of trade involving England, New England, the Mediterranean, and the West Indies of which it became an important center.[96] Yet it never had more than a handful of settlers besides the garrison. New Englanders began to fish from the area from about 1715 and repeated difficulties with French and Indians in the next few years led to the fishermen themselves building a small fort and the detachment of a few of the Annapolis garrison to occupy it in 1720.

The fishery in the Canso area was simply an extension of the New England schooner fishery on the various offshore banks (from Georges to Grand, see Figure 2.3) which had developed so strongly in the previous two or three decades. No residents or byeboatmen were involved; there was virtually no shore-based boat fishery there in this period nor did fishing ships come from England.[97] The schooners came from New England in spring, from late March to early May, and returned home in late September or early October. The voyages to the banks, fifty to one hundred miles away, lasted from ten days to a month, depending on the fishing and the weather, during which time they caught, split (headed and cleaned), and temporarily put down in salt 150 to 250 quintals (hundredweight) of cod. This took a hogshead of salt for each ten or twelve quintals of fish. Upon arriving at Canso the fish were washed out in the sea and then laid out on clean gravel beaches, or roughly constructed tables, or "flakes," to dry. A rather elaborate process of repiling and respreading went on until the fish were completely hardened and cured. Many entrepreneurs (usually with one schooner, but some operators had four or five) had some shore hands in the season but most of the work on land and sea was done by the five hands (rarely fewer or more) who, including the master, manned each vessel. The schooner crews generally worked on a

96. These documents are in the PRO, CO 217 series, and most are transcribed in the AC, NSA series (esp. from NSA-*18* to NSA-*24*). Some have been printed in Innis, *Select Documents*, pp. 153–62, and in Shortt, *Currency, Exchange and Finance*, pp. 133, 156, 160, 165, 174–80, 190–91, 194–95, 205–7, 218.

97. Between 1720 and 1760, only one English ship (in 1732) has been noted by the writer. AC, NSA-*21*, 80. The only reference to a possibility of others was in an answer to an inquiry on the Canso fishery for 1734 which stated: "The Fishery is chiefly Carried on by His Majesty's Subjects from New England, Some from New York also, and from Annapolis Royal, the Metropolis [!] of Nova Scotia, with some few from the West of England," but this may well refer to the sack ships and supply ships and perhaps some hands from Annapolis. PRO, CO 217-*7*, 107.

share basis. From three to five trips to the banks and back from Canso might be ventured each season.

Each year a number of sack ships[98] came from Britain bringing supplies to sell to the fishermen and taking away the cured fish. The schooners also brought supplies with them from New England, some of which may have come from Europe originally. Some of the fish also was taken back to New England with the schooners when they went home, or by ships from Boston or other colonial ports. Markets of particular importance included the Mediterranean countries of Europe and, for the poorest grades, the West Indies and the southern colonies where they were used as food for slaves. The best fish went east across the Atlantic and there were complaints that it didn't always arrive in good condition. In part this was an unavoidable handicap of the schooner fishery in which the fish had to remain piled and heavily salted on board the vessels for days (or even weeks), whereas a boat fishery allowed lighter salting and immediate start on the air-and-sun curing process. But the official reporters also suggested that the masters of the sack ships, anxious to be off in the race for European markets, often loaded fish before the curing process was complete. There was a wide fluctuation in the numbers of New England schooners. The reports included numbers of 197 in 1725 ("vessels" but probably at least 175 schooners), 223 schooners in 1729, 80 in 1732, and 46 in 1736. The numbers of men involved must have varied from five hundred or fewer to fifteen hundred or more. From four to a dozen sack ships came from England each year and as many as eight (perhaps also partly to fish) from the American colonies.

The structural accommodation of this activity, which involved many buildings to store gear, supplies, and fish and to shelter the shoremen during the season, dozens of stages for loading or unloading vessels, and acres of flakes for drying them, was spread over many miles of beach of both mainland and adjacent islands and must have been an impressive sight in mid-season (see Figure 6.3). The small garrison and half dozen or fewer permanent residents lived somewhat apart and would have been relatively inconspicuous in the mid-summer activity;

98. "Sack" ships sailed to North America not to fish but to bring supplies, notably salt, and to take back cargoes of cured fish. Many of them were routed directly to major markets in the Iberian peninsula. One derivation suggested for the name is that they were so called from the cargoes of sack wines (Canary, Malaga, Sherry, etc.,) which they took back to the British Isles.

in the winters, however, they were all the population Canso boasted except for the English garrison and a handful of servants (inferentially southern Irish, and probably from Newfoundland) who watched over and repaired flakes, stages, and buildings belonging to the New Englanders. There were rarely more than ten or a dozen taverns licensed (mostly to members of the garrison and presumably for its convenience) but there was a great deal of illegal grog-selling from the temporary storehouses. Indications of "settlement" in the ordinary sense were few. A comment of 1749 was that, although the handful of settlers had been there thirty years, they ". . . have little more Improvements to shew than a few Patches to supply them with Kitchen Ware."[99]

Other forms of illegal activity caused perennial official concern: a French boat fishery based on Isle Madame (by French ships and local residents) ten miles to the north, which fished in Canso waters and was virtually impossible to control, an illegal trade in fish and French West Indian goods with such boats or to the nearby harbors of Cape Breton as far as Louisburg itself; and the spiriting away to New England of seamen and artificers who came to Canso with naval vessels, with the official garrison supply ship, or with the several sack ships. Very few outright passengers came to Canso from England. But the greatest difficulties lay in the harassment of the fishermen by Indians and French, especially after the opening of the war with Spain in 1739. The boom conditions of the late twenties and early thirties declined in the later 1730's and Canso became something of a ghost town during many years of the open English-French hostilities of the forties and fifties, although some New England schooners continued to come each year.

The Gulf Shore

There was some exploitation of the forests in the present Pictou area by the French from Cape Breton; whatever the English claims to the peninsula, the Gulf of St. Lawrence was a French sea and protests from Annapolis Royal or Canso were ineffective. Settlements of a minor sort at Baie Verte, Remsheg, Tatamagouche, and Cape John associated with the traffic (illegal from the English viewpoint) to Isle St-Jean and Cape Breton have been noted above. In the 1750's small settlements were to appear to the east (the evidence is sketchy but persuasive) on Caribou Island, Pictou townsite, Little Harbour, French River,

99. Anon., *A Geographical History,* p. 30.

and Merigomish and probably in the inlets of George Bay in Antigonish County as well.[100]

Agriculture

DEVELOPMENTS — The basis of farming remained the exploitation of the dyked marshlands: the crops and animals were largely unchanged. There was experiment with a few specialty crops like tobacco (the potato had still not arrived) and probably a substantial increase in the number of horses. Port Royal may have expanded its own agricultural lands only modestly, for there was not full use of them by 1710, but there was an extension in this period to nearly all reaches of Minas Basin and Chignecto Bay. Moreover, as in the islands of St-Jean and Cape Breton,[101] there was more serious and widespread development of forest clearing beyond the reaches of the Fundy tides—as at Chebogue, Pubnico, and the Atlantic coves and along the intervale lands in the Gulf coast settlements.

Perhaps the greatest change that occurred was the appearance of receptive markets in Cape Breton Island and the more frequent appearance of New England trading schooners, an increase in commercialization reflected in so many of the rather pathetic reports of the struggling and neglected little British garrison at Annapolis, which found itself in active competition for supplies with these financially more rewarding outlets. Such trading, especially to Cape Breton, is often referred to as clandestine although it was so widely known and so openly practiced that the adjective loses much of its meaning. What is meant is that the trade to Louisburg was completely, and that with the New England vessels, intermittently, illegal and contrary to the frequent proclamations of a governor and council powerless to stop it.[102]

Sometimes the trade may have been in the traditional "wild" com-

100. George Patterson, *A History of the County of Pictou, Nova Scotia* (1877), F. H. Patterson, *Acadian Tatamagouche and Fort Franklin* (1947), and J. C. Webster, *The Forts of Chignecto* (1930) have discussed much of the evidence.

101. See A. H. Clark, *Three Centuries and the Island,* and below, Chapter 7.

102. See AC, NSA-*11*, 186–94; NSA-*17*, 32–35; NSA-*20*, 165–69; NSA-*22*, 173–74; NSA-*26*, 29–33, 50–54; NSA-*32*, 74–76; Murdoch, *Nova-Scotia, 1,* 377–78, 380, 470–71, 480–81; British Museum Add. MSS. (NSM 651a, pp. 129–32) 141–44; BM Add. MSS. 19070, fol. 55 (also AC, MG-*21*).

modities of furs and feathers (taken by the Acadians themselves, or acquired by them in trade from the Indians) but New England schooners, and French vessels calling at Baie Verte, as well as small vessels of the Acadians themselves carried off substantial quantities of grain and livestock in return for textiles, metal goods, brandy, rum, tobacco, and, above all, for specie (especially from Cape Breton) for which the Acadians developed a peasant passion that observers described as miserly. At any rate it would be grossly inaccurate to describe their agricultural economy as self-contained and, although it was largely subsistent, it was far from being completely so.

Even if we include the labor involved in building and repairing dykes, drains, and aboiteaux, farming was as easy for the Acadians as it ever was to be for Nova Scotians until the technological revolution of the late nineteenth century made its tardy way into the province. The easy going attitude of the Acadians mystified and irritated the observers from both New and old England. Mascarene, writing in 1720, found them ". . . for the generallity very little industrious, their land not improved as might be expected, they liveing in a manner from hand to mouth, and provided they have a good feild of Cabages and bread anough for their familyes, with what fodder is sufficient for their Cattle they seldome look for much further improvement."[103] He went on to point out that they spent their spare time in hunting and trapping and that many of the young men, underemployed in farming, went off to the Atlantic fishery in the summer.

Governor Philipps, who had far less knowledge of the Acadians than Mascarene (who, a Huguenot, spoke French and had known them intimately for decades), was even more caustic. Writing in 1734, he found them ". . . rather a pest & Incumbrance, than of an advantage to the Country being a proud, Lazy, obstinate and untractable people, unskillfull in the methods of Agriculture. . . . they have not in almost a Century clear'd the Quantity of 300 Acres of Wood Land. From their Corn and Cattle they have plenty of Dung for manure which they make no use of but when it increases to become troublesome then instead of laying it on their Lands they get rid of it by moving their barnes to another Spot . . . ."[104] Finally, that most thorough observer and reporter from New England, Charles Morris, described them at mid-century as ". . . but indifferent Husbandmen in General, and do

103. PRO, CO 217-*3*, 186ᵛ.   104. AC, NSA-*23*, 50.

no more labour than what necessity urges them to, and their Land being so easily Cultivated, it does not take up one third of their time. . . . they cheifly aim at raising stocks of Neat Cattle and sheep, for which they had heretofore a ready Markett at Louisburg. Their surplusage of Grain the [New] England Traders generally purchase . . . ."[105]

Tools and Implements—Acadian farming did not change very much in the eighteenth century. Its tools were still of the simplest: pickaxes, spades, axes, hoes, sickles, scythes, flails, and wooden forks and rakes for the most part."[106] Seguin makes the point that even the somewhat better equipped and more sophisticated *canadiens* had virtually the same kinds of implements as western European peasants and rural English American colonials to the south. Since the Acadians were in almost constant communication with both *les canadiens* and *les bastonnais* (from the latter of whom they probably obtained most of the little farm equipment they did not fashion themselves) they undoubtedly had as many of the same tools and implements as they could afford. Possibly their shortage of metal was matched by shortages in certain skills like that of the blacksmith or wheelwright, but they seem to have been rather competent carpenters and joiners. At any rate it is clear that their desire to trade with the Yankees was based on real needs.

It is worth noting that the spade, pickaxe, and hoe were the major implements. In an agriculture based on dyked lands rather than forest clearing the axe must have assumed a much less prominent place than in Canada or New England, although the Acadian too had need of much fuel and structural wood, and the aboiteaux, or sluice gates, in the dykes took large amounts of timber.

That there is neither documentation nor artifactual evidence for the plow or harrow in the seventeenth century is bothersome for while it is just conceivable that neither was used before 1700 it is highly unlikely. Plows were introduced into Canada early in the seventeenth century

105. "A Breif Survey," cap. 5, p. 7.
106. Respectively, *pioches, bêches, hâches, houes, faucilles, faux, fleaus, fourches,* and *rateaus.* For comparison with the contemporary *canadiens* see R. L. Sequin, *Équipement de la ferme Canadienne aux xvii⁰ et xviii⁰ siècles* (1959). Perhaps, following Seguin, one might add the *serpe* or *crocheton,* a bill-hook for harvesting peas, or the *van* (a fan for cleaning the flailed grain), although the writer has seen no evidence for their use in Acadia.

(1628) although it was not until after mid-century, and perhaps after the assumption of royal control, that one can assume that each farmer had his own.[107] If it took two generations or more to establish plowing generally in Canada, where a rather more extensive agriculture was practiced, one might as well expect to find a further delay in the case of the few acres of marshland which sufficed for the cropping needs of most Acadian farmers. As in Canada the early use of cattle may have been chiefly for beef, leather, and dairy needs. Although rarely listed in inventories we are inclined to feel that horses were relatively widely held and the carts that were in general use in the eighteenth century may have been largely horse-drawn. In the Canada of the time the horse was widely used as a draft animal. When plows were used more extensively in Acadia (as they were by the middle of the eighteenth century) the interesting question remains whether it was the wheelless plow, as used in New England, or *la charrue à rouelles ou avant train*, like that exported from France to Canada, may have been employed. The impression one gains from the slight evidence is that hardware of all kinds, and especially common tools and implements employing iron, may have derived more largely from New England, and Judge Isaac Deschamps' description of Acadian plowing (written after 1760) as never exceeding three inches in depth, certainly suggests a light, wheelless, skim plow.[108] However, Morris' description of deep plowing for drainage—". . . it is Plowed up in Ridges about five feet Wide for the sake of Draining of the Water into Trenches . . ."[109]—with two yoke of oxen might suggest the heavier implement.

THE EXPANSION OF FARMING—After 1707, when the erstwhile frequent French censuses ceased, we have very little guide to numbers of animals and extent of cultivated land. The ecclesiastical head counts of communicants and the various estimates on which we must depend for this period did not include agricultural data. Table 6.9 is an

107. *Ibid.,* p. 21. Seguin gives three reasons for slowness of adoption: the necessity for specialized blacksmithing, the fact that each *censitaire* might not earlier have had the requisite ox-power, and that until the stumps and roots were removed or rotted away the use of a plow might have been difficult. In Acadia the first reason was probably most important early on; cattled increased rapidly and the dyked lands presented no stump problem.

108. Isaac Deschamps, undated MS. (but probably written soon after 1760, from internal evidence), in the Public Archives of Nova Scotia, uncatalogued. Deschamps lived at Pisiquid before the Acadians were removed.

109. Morris, "A Breif Survey," cap. 5, p. 6.

(almost certainly incomplete) census inventory, taken just before the period began. Table 6.10 combines Father Pain's nominal census of 1714 with no figures on livestock and some estimates of population and livestock in 1715 by the Lieutenant Governor Caulfeild.

TABLE 6.9 *Acadian census of people, land, and livestock, 1707*

	Port Royal	Beaubassin	Minas	Cobequid
Total population	570	271	585	82
Number of heads of family	104	45	88	17
Families with two or more people	96	45	86	15
Heads of family with cultivated land (number of farms?)	83	41	73	17
Arpents of cultivated land (all dyked?)	398	286	315	101
Arpents of cultivated land per capita*	0.70	1.06	0.54	1.23
Arpents of cultivated land per (head of) family*	3.83	6.36	3.58	5.94
Number of cattle	952	510	777	180
Cattle per capita*	1.67	1.88	1.33	2.20
Cattle per arpent of cultivated land*	2.39	1.78	2.47	1.78
Number of sheep	1,237	476	732	124
Sheep per capita*	2.17	1.76	1.25	1.51
Number of swine	855	334	643	114
Swine per capita*	1.50	1.23	1.10	1.39
Livestock units† per capita*	2.41	2.48	1.80	2.78
Cattle/sheep ratio*	0.77	1.07	1.06	1.45
Cattle/swine ratio*	1.11	1.53	1.21	1.58
Sheep/swine ratio*	1.45	1.43	1.14	1.09

* Calculated from census data.
† One livestock unit = 1 head cattle = 5 sheep = 5 swine.
Source: PAC, G1-466, 215–31.

Clearly the two accounts do not agree very well in numbers or proportions of the different animals and we do not have any more counts or estimates of livestock. Above we have estimated a population of some 2,500 for 1714 and it was almost certainly over 2,000 when the British took over in 1710. Perhaps we may hazard the following guesses for numbers of livestock at that time: cattle, 4,000, sheep, 4,000, and swine, 3,000, and assume that Caulfeild was over rather than under in his estimates. Perhaps we may also assume some 2,000 arpents in cultivation, of which more than three-fourths would have

TABLE 6.10 *Population, livestock, and grain production figures for the Bay area, 1714 and 1715*

Location	1714 Population	1715 Population	Cattle	Sheep	Swine	Bushels of grain
Port Royal	917	———	2,000	2,000	1,000	10,000
Minas (the whole Basin?)	666	540(90 × 6)*	3,000	4,000	2,000	20,000
Beaubassin (all of Chignecto?)	345	300(50 × 6)*	1,000	1,000	1,000	6,000

* Caulfeild's figure for number of families in 1715 multiplied by estimated number of persons per family.

Sources: 1714 census, PAC, G1-*466*, 232, and François Edmé Rameau de Saint-Père, *Une Colonie Féodale en Amerique: l'Acadie (1604–1881)*, (1889), *2*, 403–11. 1715 census, PRO, CO 217-*2*, 49–53ᵛ: Caulfeild's letter to Lords of Trade, November 1715. This letter has been copied in AC, NSA-*7*, 164–74.

been dyked marshland. There were also numerous poultry of various kinds, many fruit trees, and probably some scores of horses, although there seems to be almost a conspiracy to hide the presence of horses from us. By mid-century the population had increased to, very roughly, some ten thousand,[110] just under half of whom lived around Minas Basin and, of the rest, more lived on the Chignecto shores than in the Annapolis Basin and River valley. Just under one-third of the whole lived at the eastern end of the valley, between North Mountain and the mouth of the Pisiquid (Avon) estuary which we have called Minas proper. The contrasts we have noted above are that Annapolis grew more slowly and Minas more rapidly than the Acadian average.

Precisely how many farms, of what size or area (or even how we might define a farm), and with how much land in crops, no one really knew at mid-century and our estimates have to be in very round figures indeed. Some guidelines on dyked land are provided by Eaton's estimates of 4,100 acres dyked in Minas and up to 1,000 acres for Cobequid in 1755.[111] Similarly we have some guide lines for livestock numbers in the totals rounded up at Minas in 1755: with the 2,743 people there were counted 5,007 cattle, 8,690 sheep, 4,197 hogs, and 493

110. Perhaps 12,500 if those on Isle St-Jean and Cape Breton were included.
111. A. W. H. Eaton, manuscript notes on Colchester County, quoted in Martell, "Pre-Loyalist Settlements," p. 20.

horses.[112] Assuming that the round-up was most nearly complete there (considering the difficulty of driving livestock away) these numbers may give us a reasonable census of animals present at mid-century. Allowing for the different nature of the other settlements, Table 6.11 shows the estimates for 1748–50.

TABLE 6.11 *Estimated number of livestock and acres of dyked land in the Bay area, 1748–50*

Location	Cattle	Sheep	Swine	Horses	Acres of dyked land
Annapolis	3,000	6,000	3,000	350	3,000
Minas proper	5,000	9,000	4,000	500	4,000
Pisiquid and Cobequid	2,500	3,500	1,500	200	2,500
Chignecto	7,000	8,000	4,000	500	3,000
Outlying settlements	250	150	250	50	100
Totals	17,750	26,650	12,750	1,600	12,600

Source: Author's estimate based on "Journal of Colonel John Winslow, of the Provincial Troops, while Engaged in Removing the Acadian French Inhabitants from Grand Pré . . . 1755," Nova Scotia Historical Society *Collections* (1885), p. 122.

The estimates of the amount of land worked per capita, or per farm, have presented a great deal of difficulty. Since the middle of the seventeenth century—and until the removal in 1755—the agricultural base remained the always limited area of dyked marshland. With very minor exceptions on the Gulf and Atlantic coasts, settlement expanded only where land available for the same kind of exploitation could be found. Every farm that amounted to anything had its small parcel of marsh above an aboiteau. In 1701 the average worked (*défrichée*) was one acre per capita (five to ten acres per farm family), and in 1707 it was no greater (Table 6.9). It is clear that the dyked land was a small part of each farm. For the late 1680's Rameau inferred "holdings" of fifty to one hundred hectares.[113] Allowing that arpents was meant, and that he exaggerated, even fifty acres was a lot of land in comparison with the normal share of plowed dyked land. Armstrong categorically asserted in 1734 that they had many times this amount (most of them, he reported, had a mile in frontage and a league in depth—i.e., roughly

112. Winslow, *Journal*, p. 122.   113. *Une Colonie Féodale, 1*, 163.

two thousand acres) without any condition of enclosing and fencing.[114] We need not speculate on the credibility of such a claim for, in fact, little upland was used; claims to larger areas of upland were not likely to cause dispute since they served largely as rough pasture and wood lots. The small holdings of precious dyked marshland might be sections of narrow strips along the shore of a bay or tidal stream or a variably-shaped sector of a larger marshland area.

FARMS AND THE FARMING ROUTINE   From Armstrong's observation it has been inferred that the individual holdings were of severely oblong rectangularity like the *rotures* of Canada, the nineteenth century farms of Clare Township leading back from St. Mary's Bay, or the farms of Chéticamp on Cape Breton. There may have been some such rule but there is no evidence of it, nor would it have made much sense with the uneven distribution of marshlands. The shape and spacing of "total farmland," whatever that may have been for an individual *grange,* was of little moment compared with the location and amount of marshland. The conditions that created and maintained parallel strips with dimensions of ten or twenty to one elsewhere simply did not exist in Acadia.

That the marshlands were of high and lasting fertility is attested abundantly: "They are Naturally of a Fertile Soil and produce (communibus annis) about twenty Bushells of Wheat from an Acre English Measure and they are of so strong and Lasting a Nature that their Crops are not Diminished in ten or twenty Years Constant Tillage."[115] A little later we have the following estimate: "In the year 1754 upwards of 6000 Bushels of Wheat, were Shipped from the different Settlements, now known by [the names] Horton Cornwallis Falmouth & Newport [i.e., Minas and Pisiquid], besides that the Acadian Inhabitants . . . were amply Subsisted & great part of their food was Bread."[116] The surprisingly small amounts of "arable," or even "improved," lands on which upland (i.e. non-marshland) settlers of the nineteenth century depended make the estimates of five to ten acres per family of dyked and tilled farmland per Acadian farm family seem quite reasonable, with the size of the rest of the "farm" of little importance. It is evident that little upland was cleared by 1750, proba-

114. AC, NSA-*22*, 209–10.   115. Morris, "A Breif Survey," cap. 5. p. 6.
116. Deschamps, MS.

bly less than 500 acres as against a putative 13,000 acres of dyked marshland.

It must be borne in mind that much more marshland was dyked at any one time than was actually in use.[117] The breaking of dykes, overflowing at excessively high tides, concentrating of salt in old fields, and the constant bringing of new lands into production, with a desalinization period under ordinary rainfall of two or three years, lead us to conclude that in any given year a substantial area cannot have been in crop. Moreover some of it was used for pasture. Perhaps as little as two-thirds of the dykeland was cropped in a given season. If it is cropped land that was reported in the censuses the estimate of total dyked land could be raised to 20,000 or 25,000 acres (but the writer feels that figure to be rather high). One must also remember that much of the undyked marshland provided salt hay, cut at low tide and dried and cured on dry land, so that the use of dyked lands for grazing may not have been very extensive.

The Acadians evidently had a very keen property sense from the number of boundary disputes that are reported. If a more readily available legal apparatus had existed they might well have proved as litigious as their Canadian neighbors. Thus they were careful to mark divisions between individual holdings on the upland with barriers or fences of wood—or at least piles of brush and trunks of trees. The marshland drainage ditches, shared with a neighbor, seem to have served such purposes admirably.

THE DYKING PROCESS — The methods of dyking, the building of aboiteaux (the clappervalve gates) to drain the fresh water and exclude the salt, and the digging of intra-marsh ditches apparently changed very little from the mid-seventeenth century to the mid-eighteenth. Given either a marginal strip of marsh on a coast or river bank, or large blocks as at Grand Pré at Minas, Pré Ronde on the Annapolis River, or any of several areas in the Cumberland Basin-Tantramar Marsh region (where single units of up to one thousand acres of marshland existed), the first problem was to get the dyke built in the face of the rapidly moving tides. This was done by cutting deep sods (held together by the matted roots of salt-marsh grasses) in rectangular or trapezoidal shapes (rather like peat-turf) and erecting a barrier

117. Although it is not clear whether the land listed in any given census represented the total dyked, or the total in use.

7   A Typical Dyke in the Marshlands

perhaps five feet high and with a base twice or more the width. Three
observations of the mid-eighteenth century probably apply to earlier
operations as well: "The dykes are in General on the Main Rivers 11
and 12 feet thick at bottom and gradually slope till they become a foot
& half thick at top, and are five feet in height."[118] ". . . their Dykes
are made of large Sods of Marsh cut up in square Pieces, and raised
about five Feet higher than the common Surface, of a competent
Thickness to withstand the Force of the Tides, and soon grow very
firm and durable, being overspread with Grass, and have commonly
Foot-paths on their Summit . . . ."[119] "These Dykes being made with
dry Sods, intermixed with Marsh, grow very compact in a little Time,
the Marsh serving the use of Mortar to the Sods; they are soon
covered with Grass, and furnish the Farmer with Footways to his
Lands."[120]

The earliest seventeenth-century dykes had been "running dykes"
protecting small areas of river margin, closed off by local high spots or
by turning the dykes inland and thinning them out up-slope. But no
considerable area could be so enclosed without some exit lest it become
water-logged and swampy: it had to be drained. Many of the marshes
had natural creeks that drained not only the uplands behind but the
marshes themselves at low-tide. The aboiteau was placed as near the
sea on the creek as possible to provide the largest possible area of
marsh behind and to minimize the amount of "running dyke" required.
The more seaward it was placed the higher the bounding dyke had to
be and the stronger the aboiteau itself to withstand the tide. "Across
the large Creeks are considerable dams composed of spruce Brush and
sods from the salt marshes with large Sluices in which are two or three
gates or valves for stopping the sea water and drawing off the fresh
water, and the dimentions of the trunk is according to the size of the
creek, or sluice. From these dams the dikes run along the sides of the
main Rivers."[121] There clearly was a limit beyond which the technical
resources of the Acadians could not reach and the largest Acadian
venture, on the Rivière Aulac in the Tantramar marshes, begun by

118. Deschamps, MS.   119. Little, *The State of Trade*, p. 70.
120. Anon., *A Geographical History*, p. 22. This may be derived from Little, or
vice-versa, if Little did not write both.
121. Deschamps MS. The ultimate in aboiteaux are huge engineering structures
built in the twentieth century in the Minas and Chignecto areas. They resemble
hydro-electric power dams in size and strength.

the Abbé Le Loutre in the early 1750's but never completed, was the most elaborate project undertaken.[122]

During the two or three years of waiting for rain to "wash out" the salt after dyking, the land was used for hay and pasture. Progressive desalinization led to the replacement of the coarse "broadleaf" and other marsh grasses by more useful volunteers (see Chapter 2). Two descriptions of the working of the land are informative:

They ploughd the land Intended to be sown with wheat, between the month of august or middle of September, and the month of Decr. and if the whole intended to be sown was not plough'd by that time and that they found the Ground (which in some seasons was the Case) clear of snow in february, they ploughd more, and as soon as possible in the month of april they sewed wheat, & they laid it down as a rule, never to sowe Wheat, after the month of april. . . . There is a particular nicety required in ploughing them, & ploughs are constructed on purpose; about an inch and half is the depth of the first ploughing, and must never Exceed three inches, the Crop of Grass will yield two tons of hay to an acre.[123]

Their Tillage is performed with much ease being Intirely free from Stones; that two Yoke of Cattle is Sufficient to Plow up their Stubble which is usually done in the Fall of the Year, it is Plowed up in Ridges about five feet Wide for the sake of Draining of the Water into Trenches which are cutt in the Meddow and inclose about four or five Acres. These Trenches drain of the Water into Channells which were formerly Creeks in the Meddow, and thus in the Ebb of the Tide all the Fresh Water is drain'd into the Sea which without these Trenches and this manner of Plowing would rest upon the Land and render it unfitt for Tillage. The Land thus Plow'd up Lays open to the Winter Frosts and by that means the Gleb is so dissolved and Montored that in the Spring in the Beginning of April they have no further trouble but to sow their seed and harrow it in and from thence good crops are produced from Year to Year. That part of the Marsh which is expos'd To the Inundation of the Tides produces their Hay which support their Cattle in the Winter Season. This salt Grass is the first and natural produce of all their Marshes, and by means of them, they have been enabled to extend their Settlements over the Bay of Fundy. The upland is made use of for the Production of all sorts of Roots and Garden stuffs but very little is used by them either for Grass or Grain, some particular Rich spotts do Produce good Wheat

---

122. The money for this ambitious project (50,000 livres) was given to Le Loutre in 1752 and it appears to have been begun but abandoned during the siege of Fort Beauséjour, never to be completed. Webster, *Forts of Chignecto*, p. 33, says that portions of the associated dyke still may be identified. See also *idem, Le Loutre.*   123. Deschamps, MS.

and other Grain, but that is not general, the Lands are well adapted for English Grass, but as they have fodder enough from the Marshes without any other Labour then that of Mowing and Making it they have hitherto much neglected the Improvements of their uplands, which require a good deal of Labour to Clear & which afterwards must be fenced in, to prevent their Cattle destroying it who are turn'd loose into the Woods all the Summer Season.[124]

Many observers commented upon the obvious difficulties that ensued if the dykes were broken through neglect, unusually high tides, severe storms, or the action of New England raiders: ". . . the Damage is severely felt, since besides all other Losses, nothing will grow upon the Land for two or three Years after."[125] Nevertheless, the disaster was mitigated by the rest given the soil and the addition of new silts brought in by the tides: ". . . but afterwards, by Means of the new Recruit of Salts, which are incorporated with the Mold, the Soil is renewed, and produces [after three years] as fine Crops as ever . . . ."[126]

CROPS — All of the major western European "white crops" were grown but wheat probably exceeded in acreage oats, rye, and barley combined and field peas were little, if any, less important than the coarse grains. Some flax and hemp were grown throughout the period but apparently less than enough for domestic needs. Cabbages were grown so extensively as often to be considered a field crop but the residents also depended upon beans and a wide variety of other garden truck. Many of the truck gardens and the surprisingly extensive orchards (plums appear in this period to join the pears, apples, and cherries) were on the borders of the marshland or on the slopes above, near the homesteads and barns, and thus, technically, upland. As in the seventeenth century, comments upon the orchards are frequent. Knox, in 1757, refers to extensive groves of apple and pear trees, the boughs bending under the weight of their fruit: ". . . finer-flavoured apples, and greater variety, cannot in any other country be produced; there is also great plenty of cherry and plumb trees; but the fruit were either gathered, or had rotted and fallen off."[127] We are virtually without clues as to varieties of grains, fruits, or vegetables used. Their flour,

124. Morris, "A Breif Survey," cap. 5, pp. 6–7.
125. Anon., *A Geographical History*, p. 23.
126. Little, *The State of Trade*, p. 70.
127. Knox, *An Historical Journal*, p. 105. See also pp. 86, 97, and 103.

whether because of the kinds of grain used or the milling process employed, did not find favor at Louisburg[128] but surpluses of grain and flour (mostly the former) were picked up regularly by New England traders to make ship's biscuit. It is likely that Acadian flour, as with other produce of less than the best standards collected at Boston (as, for example, "refuse codfish," cited earlier in this chapter), went to tropical plantation areas as slave food.

LIVESTOCK — The Acadian cattle, which seem to have increased in number very rapidly in the period, were the chief draft animals besides supplying milk, meat, and leather as required. Regarding processed dairy products, Morris described "a little bad Butter but no Cheese"[129] at mid-century and this would seem to be a fair report. Indeed they had abundant protein and fat not only from their poultry and livestock but from fish and game. The cattle were not prepossessing to the English observers; scrawny and poor would sum up the many comments. In describing the rations of the soldiers at Grand Pré just before the surprise attack in early 1747, Morris asserted: ". . . our Provision was the Flesh of Lean cattle, that a whole Ox did not afford a Pound of Tallow, & sometimes it looked like Carrion that the Soldiers choose rather to go without their allowance then to Eat it."[130] Of course the good habitants of Grand Pré may have been culling their herds for the forced provisionment. But as early as November 24, 1726, Armstrong had written that to provision the garrison he had killed about sixty cattle "who weighs very small."[131]

If these comments do not reflect simply the anti-French bias of the English garrison they describe a situation not unusual for colonial cattle during a winter season when, as wintering feed grew short, the least promising animals were butchered. All reports tend to emphasize that adequate amounts of wild marsh hay were made but it was not a very nutritious feed. However, there are other suggestions that the best animals were killed in the autumn to be salted away for sale or use, or were driven and shipped at that season to Cape Breton or sold to the New England trading ketches.

Sheep and hogs received virtually no notice from eighteenth-century observers, except as reported in cargoes shipped to Louisburg for meat. The function of sheep in Acadia was chiefly to provide wool, especially

128. Morris reported flour of "a moist Quality." "A Breif Survey," cap. 5, p. 7.
129. *Ibid.*   130. *Ibid.*, cap. 2, p. 27.   131. AC, NSA-*17*, 65–68.

for caps, stockings, and other knitwear. How heavily they depended on homespun woven cloth we don't know. In their increasingly active trade the Acadians imported much cloth, including woolens and linens. Sheep must have had some care to have allowed steady increases in numbers in the face of active predators such as wolves, bears, and wild dogs. Swine, like sheep, were ubiquitous and apparently present in comparable numbers. Pork was an important element of the diet; indeed with wheaten bread, peas, and cabbages it was one of the four mainstays of the daily fare. The pigs appear to have had little attention and may have subsisted largely on offal, garbage, deadfalls, and other waste, together with mast and roots in the forest. Little use was made of any animal manure, although the winter was a light labor season that would have allowed time for spreading it.

Subsidiary Economic Activities

FISHING AND VESSELS—The confinement of the main Acadian settlements to the Fundy shores severely limited their fishing opportunities. Yet their precise relationship to that economic enterprise off the coasts of northeastern North America which was of keenest interest to the rest of the world is not easy to establish. The great codfishery had its impact on them in a dozen indirect ways. It profoundly affected them in terms of British-French rivalry, of the demands for supplies by the fishery and its protecting garrisons, and in the large number of New England schooners that came their way each year. The Acadians were intricately involved with the activity of the fishery and the fishermen, but they were not *of* them to any significant degree:

. . . they had some shallops, in which they employ'd themselves in the catching of Fish just upon their Harbours, being out but a few days at a Time; This was rather for their Home Consumption then foreign Market the Surplusage being no great Quantity was generally sent to Boston for a Market in the New England Traders. The present Inhabitants being settled Chiefly in the Bay of Fundy, are not conveniently situated for the Fishery. It is only in the Summer Season that the Fish strike into the Bay they are then to be taken in the greatest plenty on two small Banks, one a league north of Grand Passage the other about three Leagues West of Long Island [Digby peninsula]. The Borders of the Shores afford fishing but they are not in so great plenty as to make any considerable Tairs.[132]

132. Morris, "A Breif Survey," cap. 5, p. 4.

Nova Scotia Information Service

8   Drying Cod on Flakes, Nova Scotia

The number of New Englanders making fish along Nova Scotia's Atlantic coast in any summer season of the 1720's and 1730's, at least, was far greater than the total number of Acadian settlers there. Although they were concentrated at Canso, they frequented many other coves as far as Cape Sable, despite the ever-present threat of Indian attack. Although a scattering of Acadians lived in these same coves, their participation was relatively insignificant.

One should interpolate here that the Acadians were, nevertheless, seasonally engaged in a home fishery for their own food needs. They were particularly interested in salmon, shad, gaspereau, and the like, during their spring runs up the rivers and creeks, and the freshwater fish in the plentiful lakes and streams of the interior wilderness. Writing in the twenties, Mascarene observed of the Minas area that "in the road they ketch white Porpasses, a kind of fish, the plubber of which, turn'd into Oyl, yeilds a good proffit."[133] Whether these were in fact porpoises, which were well known in the Gulf and St. Lawrence estuary at this time, is unclear. It has been suggested that Mascarene meant halibut, in which the Fundy waters are rich, but it is hard to imagine him calling halibut flesh "blubber."

There is some evidence which has been interpreted to indicate a more active interest in the cod fishery by the Acadians themselves. Rameau thought the Acadians did a lot of fishing at the turn of the eighteenth century, "bienque Dièreville semble insinuer le contraire" and he had made a good deal of the coopers present at Port Royal in 1671 as evidence of greater fishing than agricultural interest. But in an economy in which "barrels" of all sizes from tiny kegs to tuns formed the principal packaging for most fluids and for grain, flour, meat, furs, refuse fish, indeed almost anything not shipped in bulk, one can hardly argue firmly from such indications.[134] Rameau was more specific in a

133. PRO, CO 217-3, 190ᵛ.
134. See Rameau, *La France aux Colonies*, p. 28. The terminology of the barrel family was international but it is doubtful that the capacities were at all uniform. Perhaps "keg" could be restricted to very small containers of two gallons or less. A rather widely used capacity series (in English wine gallons), known as the "London Assize," was:

1 barrel = 31½ gal.	1 puncheon = 84 gal.
1 tierce = 42 "	1 pipe = 126 "
1 hogshead = 63 "	1 tun = 252 "

This puts 8 bbl. = 6 tierces = 4 hhd. = 3 puncheons = 2 pipes = 1 tun. See AC, NSB-7, 423–28: 1754. Various other capacities, up to 20 per cent different, have been attached to each of these names, and sometimes, apparently, "hogshead" was

later volume when he describes Pierre Landry of Port Royal as "à la tête d'une véritable entreprise pour la pêche maritime," surely, however, an exaggeration.[135]

More to the point, Caulfeild in his report of 1715 observed of Minas that "they have between Thirty and fourty Sale of vessells which are employed in fishing, Built by Themselves,"[136] but none of the later reporters supports this view. Needless to say they had an abundance of canoes, boats, and small vessels throughout their history. They depended heavily upon them for transport and, because of their attachment to the tidal marshes, all lived close to the water. Thus the number of vessels listed by Caulfeild at a time when the number of families at Port Royal exceeded 100, does not seem out of line. Vetch had estimated in 1720 that "their Shipping Consists only in sloops, ketches, shalops and small Boats from fifty tunns, and under and of those [few] above 25 or 30."[137] Of their vessels in 1748–49 Morris observed that ". . . they are small Vessalls not exceeding fifteen to Twenty Ton and therefore they have not been Capable of being employ'd by them [the Canadians] to infest the Navigation to and from Annapolis with New England."[138] But Morris also noted that they had two or three vessels "before the War that used the West India Trade."[139] These may have belonged to Nicholas Gauthier of the Belle Isle community up river from Annapolis Royal.[140] In 1741 Mascarene, referring to vessels said to be being built in Minas, reminded the local deputy that all vessels of five tons or more had to have an official license from Annapolis before engaging in trade.[141]

The principal direct connection of the Acadians with the cod fishery probably lay rather in their contribution of extra hands to the French and New England fishing vessels. It was a practice generally frowned

---

used to mean a puncheon or pipe. The most uncertain term, however, was "barrel" itself.

135. *Une Colonie Féodale, 1*, 224.   136. PRO, CO 217-2, 50.

137. PRO, CO 217-3, 111–14. The quote is from p. 111. Vetch was answering one of the several questionnaires directed to him as a result of his early experiences with Nicholson and later as governor at Annapolis.

138. "A Breif Survey," cap. 5, p. 5.   139. *Ibid.*, cap. 5, p. 4.

140. Rameau, *Une Colonie Féodale, 2*, 79–81. Gauthier was an example of the more ambitious or more fortunate Acadian who built up a large estate. He controlled much land up the river, owned two lots near the Fort, and operated two gristmills and a sawmill. His total wealth may have exceeded 80,000 livres; in Acadian terms, at least, he was a veritable tycoon.

141. *Nova Scotia Archives. II*, 157.

upon and we hear of it only faintly and occasionally through complaints; it may have been exaggerated in the special pleading typical of
such dispatches or it may have been poorly reported because of its
clandestine nature. At any rate we are safe in assuming a good deal of
it. In February, 1717/18, several merchants at Annapolis petitioned to
be allowed to continue to trade with the Acadians following ". . . our,
former priviledge of employing the french Inhabitants in our Sloops
and other fishing vessels."[142] Mascarene in his 1720 report speaks of
"their young men who have not much work at farming begett themselves to fishing in the summer."[143]

A final observation on the cod fishery is that in the eyes of officials in
London and Paris it was of such critical national importance as to make
all the enterprises and activities of all the Acadians fade into relative
insignificance. Canso meant far more to London and Boston than
Annapolis, Minas, and Chignecto combined. As has been observed,
there were many more men engaged in the fishery operating from Nova
Scotia's Atlantic coves in any normal year than farmed Fundy's tidal
marshlands. Furthermore between the activities of the Acadians and
the New Englanders the cod fishery made the whole coastline of Acadia
known in much detail, even if it was not always adequately charted.

LUMBERING AND FOREST PRODUCTS — All rural settlements of the
seventeenth and eighteenth centuries in eastern North America were
heavily dependent on a plentiful supply of wood, and that of the
Acadians more than most. From the forests came their fuel, their
building material for houses and barns, furniture, sluice gates, fences
(where they existed), and bridges, and most of the material for the
construction of implements, tools, household utensils, carts, and sleds.
To the degree that they built their own boats and vessels the forest
supplied most of the raw material. Thus, although the Acadians cleared
relatively little land for agriculture, they must have been felling timber
constantly, and without its bountiful supply the relatively comfortable
life they led would have been impossible. Yet they made very little use
of it as a raw material for export, a matter of some surprise since they
had many sawmills scattered through the settlements and since their
economy was, indeed, commercial to a degree. A major reason may be
that timber for masts, chiefly white pine, was not plentiful near the

142. AC, NSA-9, 11–14.   143. PRO, CO 217-3, 189.

Acadian settlements and it was masts, above all, which interested the French before 1710 and the British afterward. Caulfeild, in his survey of the province in 1715, was cautiously optimistic about masts from Chignecto but pointed out that it was the north shore of the Bay of Fundy and the Gulf of Maine (present New Brunswick and Maine) which had the important resources. As for Port Royal he could observe only that "masting is to be had with difficulty."[144] The urgency of the needs at Louisburg in 1743 led the French there to cut timber on the Gulf coast near present Pictou: ". . . the French . . . Winter there and build Vessels and cut Oak Timber & a large Quantity of fine large Masts and carry them off before the Man of Warr arrives here [Canso] in the Spring without which Timber they could not well build nor go on with their Fortifications and Fishery as they do . . . ."[145] Charles Morris observed in his lengthy account:

I shall just mention their materials for ship Building. It has been said by some that this country abounds with Oak this is a mistake I have traveled through all the Countrys bordring on the Bay of Fundy and through the Isthmus to Bay Vert and dont remember to have seen one Oak in my Travels a Compass of more than 100 Leagues, and the Inhabitants inform me that Oak trees are seldom found in their Woods on that side the Country and therefore they build their Vessalls of Ash, Beech and Mapple, which is the strongest wood they have but it decays so soon that their Vessall's Last not above four or five Years after which they are unfitt for any sea Voyage[.] But they inform'd me that some good Oak Timber was to be found in the Island of Poietu [Pictou?], where the French are now Cutting for repairs for Louisburg and on some of the Coasts Opposite to Cape Breton. And in a few places on Cape Sable shore but in no great Plenty there is all so but few Large Pines fit for masting but smaller ones in abundance.[146]

The problem that might have arisen had the lands occupied by the Acadians contained valuable timber is illustrated by the reaction of the council at Annapolis to what they considered exorbitant prices asked by the residents for firewood: ". . . his Majesty hath an undoubted right to the woods & they only to the Herbage & Vesturage of the Lands And Entitled only to the benefit of Such Woods as they may have immediate Occasion for their own proper use of buildings."[147] Firewood, indeed, figured largely in the concerns of the council. In the thirties it imposed a stumpage duty on cordwood cut on ungranted

144. PRO, CO 217-2, 49ᵛ.   145. AC, NSA-*26*, 35–36.
146. "A Breif Survey," cap. 5, pp. 5–6.
147. *Nova Scotia Archives. III*, 312: 1734/35.

lands[148] and it concerned itself with the detail of honest measure in a cord of wood: ". . . Eight foot long, four feet high and four foot over from one half Scarp to one half Scarp, Closely Piled . . . ,"[149] and with the prices charged, six shillings and eight pence a cord being judged fair in February 1734/35.[150]

TRANSPORT AND COMMUNICATIONS—The accompanying map (Figure 6.4) shows the major avenues of land communication on the peninsula in the first half of the eighteenth century, before the founding of Halifax. Only one route would appear to have been suitable for, and used by, wheeled vehicles: the main "artery" of communication by land from Annapolis through the valley to Grand Pré and so on to the Pisiquid settlement (to the present site of Falmouth, at least). Surprisingly the much-used portage route from Beaubassin (Cumberland Basin) to Baie Verte does not seem to have involved carts:

Cheignicto is Distant from the Bay of Vert which lies to the North East of it eighteen Miles as the Road is now travell'd but transportation by Land is no more than 4 miles. North of old Cheignicto Settlement is a Marsh which extends within Land almost to the Bay Vert in this Marsh the river is said to be Navigable within 4 miles of the said Bay but the Tide flows up but three Miles and a half and there I crosst it over a Bridge; above the Bridge a Brook of Fresh Water empty's its self into this River which would be otherwise dry at two Hours Ebb. This Brook is dry at some Seasons it was wholly dry in September Last when I crost it and at other times to prevent its failure a Dam is Built just above the Bridge which Stops the Fresh Water And the Marsh being on a Level fills the Channells of the Brook and thereby they are able to transport their merchandize. This Transportation is performed in Canoes made of Pine Loggs and the People walking on the Banks draw the Canoes after them Spring and Fall their Channell is full, it was about twenty feet wide where I crost it, The Canadians and Inhabitants have taken great pains to Build Bridges over the Morasses of the four mile Land Carriage, but the road is exceeding bad the upland being of a Clay Soil and intermixt with Low wet grounds thro out the Road make it almost impossible in the Spring. They use no wheel carriages on this Road but drag their Merchandise with Cattle in short Canoes made for that purpose.[151]

The development and maintenance of roads and bridges became one of the chronic concerns of the governor and council at Annapolis. Their attitude changed from initial discouragement, for fear of greater mobil-

148. Murdoch, Nova-Scotia, 1, 516.
149. Nova Scotia Archives. II, 189: order by Armstrong, 1732.
150. Ibid., III, 313.   151. Morris, "A Brief Survey," cap. 5, pp. 14–15.

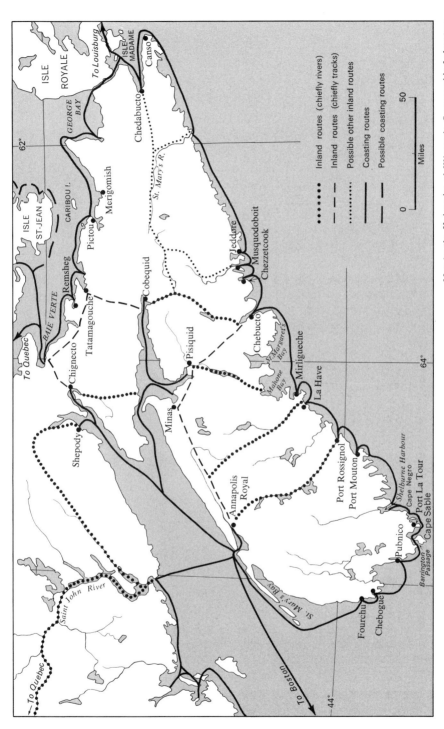

The following labels appear on the map:

ISLE ROYALE
To Louisburg
ISLE O MADAME
Canso
Chedabucto
GEORGE BAY
62°
St. Mary's R.
CARIBOU I.
Merigomish
ISLE ST-JEAN
Pictou
Remsheg
Jeddore
BAIE VERTE
Tatamagouche
Cobequid
Musquodoboit
Chezzetcook
To Quebec
Chignecto
Chebucto
St. Margaret's Bay
Pisiquid
Mahone Bay
Mirligueche
Shepody
Minas
La Have
Annapolis Royal
Port Rossignol
Port Mouton
Saint John River
Shelburne Harbour
Cape Negro
Port La Tour
Cape Sable
Pubnico
64°
Barrington Passage
To Quebec
Fourchu
Chebogue
St. Mary's Bay
To Boston
44°

Inland routes (chiefly rivers)
Inland routes (chiefly tracks)
Possible other inland routes
Coasting routes
Possible coasting routes

0   50
Miles

Map by the University of Wisconsin Cartographic Laboratory

Fig. 6.4 The Acadian Lands: Routes of Communication, 1710–1748.

ity of the settlers and greater exposure to Canadian and Indian attack, to one of encouragement, for the convenience of the Acadians, for routes of supply for the garrison and village, and for their very own tactical and strategic needs. Critical was the valley road joining Annapolis and Minas proper, that is, the Canard and Grand Pré settlements. In 1719 Philipps ordered the Minas people to desist from building a road toward Annapolis[152] and in 1720 warned the Annapolis folk not to assist them.[153] Yet in 1731 Armstrong was ordering them to complete this road[154] and in 1734 he pointed out that inhabitants were obstructing an order of Philipps of 1730 for the construction of the road because it went through their properties and was forcing traffic "through long round about unknown & almost impracticable paths." They were ordered to complete the said road under the direction of deputy surveyor Mitchell and an officer of the garrison, from the ". . . nethermost to the uppermost Houses on both sides of this River of Annapolis Royall; & to make and draw it through any up Land or low ground in as direct and streight a line as the nature & Situation of the ground will admit of."[155] The reference in Philipp's order of 1730 to "un chemin de Charete" suggests a cart road as the object if not the result.[156]

The work on this road, as on others, was done by the local people as something like corvée. There are several entries in the council minutes about deputies being directed to order the inhabitants to get on with the work. Road making, like the construction and maintenance of dykes, drainage ditches, and aboiteaux, was one of the communal duties that often needed government pressure to effect progress.[157] An order of 1735 pointed out that the Minas–Pisiquid road was in bad shape and it was decreed that the repair should be done half by Minas residents and half by Pisiquid men.[158] In 1736 there was a similar order about the road from Annapolis to the Cape (from the context, one assumes along the Granville Peninsula).[159] In 1740 an order to relocate the road from Annapolis village to Belle Isle was recorded.[160]

There were roads or trails along which cattle were driven from Cobequid Bay to Tatamagouche, to the north, and southerly by way of the Shubenacadie River to Chebucto. Whether cattle also went over

152. *Nova Scotia Archives. II*, 58; *III*, 9.   153. *Nova Scotia Archives. II*, 167.
154. *Ibid.*, p. 80.   155. *Ibid.*, p. 202: 1734.   156. *Ibid.*, p. 180.
157. *Ibid.*, pp. 205–6: order for repairing dykes at Pisiquid, 1735.
158. *Ibid.*   159. *Ibid.*, p. 211.   160. *Ibid.*, pp. 235–36.

the much-used foot-trail from Pisiquid to Chebucto (i.e., from present Windsor to the head of Bedford Basin) is uncertain. There was an "interior" line of communication from Chignecto to Minas Basin: "When they come from Cheignecto to Minas they pass up Minas [Hébert] River and thence on Cheignecto [Parrsboro] River into the Basan of Minas [the sources] of these two Rivers are within a mile of each other this was a safe Passage to them clear of all English Cruisers."[161] The distance along this route was estimated at ten leagues, that from Minas to Chignecto "47 miles as the Roads are commonly travell'd thro' the Country"[162] (although the route for this distance is obscure). The Minas–Chignecto route may have been used for cattle-droving but more likely any cattle from Minas or Pisiquid were taken to the mouth of the Chiganois River in Cobequid Bay, thence by trail to Tatamagouche and, if still by land, by a shore trail west by way of Remsheg to Baie Verte.

There are indications that land routes opened in the seventeenth century from Annapolis to La Have and from La Have to Pisiquid and Minas were still used but these may have been simply the normal canoe routes of the Indians. One inland route of importance was that from the Shepody to the Saint John River and thence up that river towards Quebec; this artery was much used by the Canadians, especially in winter. Another route used by the Indians, whose major interior rendezvous was on the Shubenacadie, was by the Stewiacke River and the west branch of the St. Mary's River to Chedabucto Bay and Canso. The vast interior "moose farm" remained the largely undisputed domain of the Indians until the late 1750's.

There were distinct seasonal differences in routes and methods of transport. In summer, canoes offered rapid transport and the Acadians presumably retained the skills in their use for which they had been extolled in the seventeenth century. But canoes were chiefly valuable for personal travel or for commodities of high value per unit weight, such as fur, spirits, or money itself. For the transport of heavier goods the winter had notable advantages; the interior water surfaces offered open, ice-supported, snow-covered highways for sledges if the snow was not too deep (and for snowshoe travel at all times), and the snow and frost made good thoroughfares of roads which were poor to impassable in the summer. Any long-distance land movement of grain,

161. Morris, "A Breif Survey," cap. 5, p. 11.   162. *Ibid.*

hay, or firewood was confined largely to the period from January through March. The comparative advantages of straighter and easier routes for livestock-droving in winter may have been pretty well balanced by occasional deep snows and by the problems of protection from exposure and the lack of graze and browse along the way.

Finally, all the Acadians lived close to tidewater and they had a more than adequate supply of canoes, boats, and small vessels. If their transport problems did not involve secrecy or the dangers of apprehension by an official British vessel, they moved themselves, their animals, and their goods largely by sea. The problems of the great tidal range, as a result of which vessels might have to be anchored far off-shore or be able to withstand "beaching" at low tides, had been familiar to them for generations and they coped with them successfully.

TRADE — Morris wrote, of the trade of the Acadians:

They have but Little Trade at present not one that uses any foreign Market. . . . The Inhabitants all this War have carried on a Trade with the Indians, whom they have supply'd with Blanketts, Provision, and Other Necessarys. The Furrs they Exchange with the English Traders for European Goods such as strouds, Blanketting, Cloth, Calam, Tammy, nails &c. When Louisbourg was in the Hands of the French the greatest Trade was carried on with them, whom they furnish'd with Cattle and other Live Stock and took in Exchange: Rum sugar Cotton Molasses Wine and Brandy and that Garrisons Demands for Live stock was so great as made the Trade much in favour of the Inhabitants that they furnisht themselves with a Silver Currency from it . . . .[163]

There is a danger in seeing too vivid a contrast in the first half of the eighteenth century between the Atlantic coast of Nova Scotia, its activity focused on Canso, as a region whose interests were, in the cod fishery and its international markets, almost wholly commercial, and the Acadian settlements of the Fundy hinterlands as being nearly completely self-sufficient. It has been pointed out that the New England trading connection was important throughout the seventeenth century and there is much evidence that it continued and increased in this period. But of even more importance was the ready market provided by the fishery and garrisons on Cape Breton and Isle St-Jean. Despite official prohibition, this trade flourished in the twenties, thirties, and early forties. It was conducted in the Acadians' own vessels, in French

163. Morris, "A Breif Survey," cap. 5, pp. 4–5.

vessels from Louisburg, and even by the New Englanders themselves, for the latter were engaged in a flourishing clandestine trade with Louisburg for a wide variety of products from both the Old and New worlds, and trading regularly with the Acadians they could and did take such cargoes covertly to Cape Breton. But most of the trade between the Acadians and the garrisons and settlers of the northern islands was by way of Baie Verte or Tatamagouche on Northumberland Strait; livestock could be driven overland to either although grain and flour, to the lesser extent that they were involved, went by the short isthmus portage route from Cumberland Basin to Baie Verte.

In Chapter 5 the number of livestock per farm or farm family was argued to be a reasonably good measure of the degree of commercial interest. On the basis of the numbers of livestock assumed for 1715 and mid-century (see Tables 6.10 and 6.11) all the settlements had substantial commercial surpluses of livestock at both times and these surpluses increased throughout the period.[164] Indeed, if the numbers of horses were anything like our inference, the cattle surplus would be even more impressive (fewer being needed for traction).

The formerly quite limited trade out of the Bay of Fundy to New England attained some variety in the early decades of the eighteenth century. A petition of fourteen merchants at Annapolis Royal in February, 1717/18, asking for greater supervision of the trade, said it consisted chiefly of "furrs, fish and grain" and that most of it was "carried on by some . . . from New England, Cape Bretton and Canada."[165] But writing in January of 1719/20, Vetch observed that ". . . the trade of that place . . . is as yet not at all Considerable and Consists cheifly in furrs, and peltry of all sorts; Cod fishing, some small matter of Naval stores as pitch, tarr, masts, Lumber of all sorts as pipe hhd and Barrell staves, shingles Boards poles and hoop poles."[166] In the same year, Governor Philipps made an estimate of the annual value of the New England-Acadian trade as £10,000 (probably in New England currency, but still a substantial amount) and said that it was carried on by four or five sloops from Boston, bringing English woolens, West Indies goods, and New England provisions to the Acadians for fur and feathers, and that he estimated they were making a

---

164. Thus at Minas, in 1755, if the numbers of people and livestock rounded up were reasonably complete and in proportion (see Tables 6.5 and 6.11, and below, Chapter 8), the ratio of livestock units per capita was 2 : 8, not counting horses.

165. AC, NSA-*9*, 11–14.   166. PRO, CO 217-*3*, 111.

profit of 400 per cent to 500 per cent and paid no duty.[167] Vetch thought most of the fur trade went to Canada and that the Acadians derived substantial imports therefrom,[168] but there is no evidence to support this view. It is clear that British manufactures such as "Course woolings, as strouds, and Duffles . . . Cutlery ware Nails Cordage Iron, Copper, and peuter tools, and vessels [iron and earthenware?], of all sorts"[169] came in from New England. If Vetch meant by "vessels," shipping, it might help to explain the poverty of reference to ship and boat building in the Acadian settlements. At the beginning of the fourth decade the New England trade may have subsided a bit: ". . . as to the Trade in this part of the Province, But very little, the same Being Carried on by only four or five Coasting Vessells from Boston hither, which supply the ffrench Inhabitants with European and West India Goods, who make two or three trips annually, and Carry from hence some time, Grain, a few fish, but cheifly ffurs."[170] However, a proclamation in March of 1730/31, by Philipps, to regulate currency and exports testified both to the vigor of the trade and the disinclination of the Acadians to accept the paper money of the garrison when he spoke of ". . . the great exportation of late years, of corn, cattle, sheep and hogs as well alive as slaughtered beyond what the yearly produce of the stock of this province can afford . . . ."[171]

We have noted above, in connection with fishing, that the Acadians had increasing numbers of vessels of their own and it appears that, as time went on, they used these more and more in trade on their own.[172] Probably, however, they were involved less in direct trade with New England than in trade with Cape Breton and in the later years more of them may have confined their activities to the Gulf of St. Lawrence.

A major concern of the governor or his representative at Annapolis was the effect on supplies to the garrison of the removal of surpluses by this trade. The Acadians were loath to sell to the impoverished garrison, for promises or debased paper currency, what they could dispose of so profitably to the Yankees or the French at Louisburg. Caulfeild's plea of 1715 that methods of supplying would have to be changed "if this garrison is to live through the coming winter"[173] was echoed repeatedly during the next thirty-five years.[174] A proclamation of Phi-

---

167. *Nova Scotia Archives. II*, 62–63, 69.   168. PRO, CO 217-3, 111.
169. *Ibid.*, p. 112.   170. AC, NSA-20, 165–69: 1732.
171. *Nova Scotia Archives. II*, 181–82.   172. *Ibid.*, p. 135: 1740.
173. *Ibid.*, p. 12.   174. See *ibid.*, esp. pp. 145 ff.

lipps in 1731, for example, forbade merchant vessels to sail with more than two month's provisions, forbade the Acadians to export at Chebucto, Chignecto, or "Tapenagoock" under penalty of a fine of fifty pistoles (pounds) of New England, to be levied on the delinquent's effects, half to go to the accuser.[175] Unable to stop the trade by cajolery, threats, or unenforceable embargoes, they sometimes tried to regulate the New England sector of it and even used approval as a kind of bribe to induce Acadians to take an oath.[176] Every effort was made to get Acadians to take out papers for their vessels at Annapolis before they did *any* trading[177] but with little success.

The Cape Breton trade became active as soon as Louisburg was established. Doucett reported in 1715 that:

Vessells from Cape Britton Spring and Fall come to Minis . . . bring Wine Brandy & Linnings which they can afford Four pence and Sixpence in a Yard cheaper then our Traders can Possibly doe, And Take from thence nothing but Wheat & Cattle which they Kill there & Salt up and from Chignecto . . . They Drive Cattle over to Bay Vert and from thence Transport them which is not only a great Detriment to Our Traders who Cant sell their Goods but will raise the Price of Provisions & impoverish the Collony. . . . The French Inhabitants . . . haveing the sole Trade with the Indians & what our Traders gett is intirely from the French.[178]

In a report of customs' collectors Newton and Bradstreet, of New England vessels trading to Louisburg in 1725 (roughly a dozen), there was appended a note of three schooners from Nova Scotia with cattle and sheep—two from Baie Verte and one from Chebucto.[179] This indicates that a track to Chebucto for driving livestock existed in the twenties. But most of the Cape Breton trade was by way of Baie Verte or Tatamagouche. Bradstreet reported that the next year: "The latter [the people of Cape Breton] as often as they want fresh Provisions or anything else [of] the Produce of Nova Scotia. They send their Vessells to two or three convenient Places in the Bay of Verd . . . and go by Land to Our Plantations, where they buy up most of our Cattle, Flower and Furrs. . . . Then they Drive them [the cattle] through the Woods to their Vessells. . . . The Inhabitants of Nova Scotia likewise have sent about Twelve Vessels of their own with which they follow the same Trade . . . and laugh't att all Orders to the Contrary."[180] The

175. *Ibid.*, pp. 181–82.   176. *Ibid.*, p. 51: 1717.
177. *Ibid.*, pp. 146, 156–57: 1741.   178. AC, NSA-*9*, 142–45.
179. Quoted in Murdoch, *Nova-Scotia*, 1, 430.
180. AC, NSA-*17*, 33: March 1725/26.

same story is repeated again and again in the documents. Its dimensions in 1743 were reported by Newton:

They [the Acadians] in a Clandestine manner supply the French at Lewisburg and St. Johns [Isle St-Jean] with 6 or 700 Head of Cattle and about 2000 sheep in a year, in short Lewisburg in my Opinion would starve if it was not for them, tho' at the same time they do this Our Garrison at Annapolis Royal and Canso, which is in their Neighbourhood are in great want, and can gett neither Beef nor Mutton, but at great Expences from New England, the Accadians before mentioned have their Woollen & Linnens and most of the Necessarys they want from Lewisburg, and are in a manner dependent on the French tho' they live in Nova Scotia.[181]

Later in the same year it was reported:

". . . they [the Cape Breton French] Supply the Nova Scotians from Lewisburg with Spanish Iron, French Linnens, Sail Cloth, Woollen cloths, & almost all sorts of Goods with Rum, Molasses, Wine & Brandy & this in considerable Quantitys. . . . Besides this there is so great an illicit Trade carried on by the People of Massachusetts Bay & New Hampshire."[182]

Table 6.12 is a record of supplies entering Louisburg from Acadia in 1740. Interestingly Annapolis Royal was said to have supplied more than half of the moose skins, all of the marten skins, some of the lynx skins, all of the beaver fur, most of the flour, the bulk of the oats, and all of the salt pork and beef. The mystery of how these exports could have escaped the notice of the officials there is not cleared up; perhaps they were officially cleared for New England. Presumably almost all the rest, including the livestock which was almost exactly half of the total value, went from Baie Verte or Tatamagouche. But the writer has found no other direct evidence of shipments to Cape Breton from Annapolis and, in view of the perennial shortages there for both the garrison and various "poor families," with repeated requests for flour (especially) from up the Bay, this must have been a rare exception.

With the coming and going of "armies" of Canadians and Indians in the several abortive attacks on Annapolis Royal in the 1740's these shortages for that town became acute and intra-Acadian trading (or need for it) became more urgent. In 1746 one enterprising Minas resident rounded up eighty cattle and five hundred sheep in Minas and drove them up the valley toward Annapolis hoping to sell them at a

181. AC, NSA-*26*, 29–33. This report has been reprinted in Shortt, *Currency, Exchange and Finance*, pp. 223–24.
182. AC, NSA-*26*, 51. Reprinted in Shortt, p. 225.

TABLE 6.12 *Supplies from Acadia entering Louisburg in 1740*

Item	Number	Price (in livres)	Total value (in livres)
Livestock			
Oxen	155	75	11,625
Cows	20	50	1,000
Calves	5	25	125
Pigs	10	20	200
Sheep	60	10	600
Poultry	246	1	246
Hides and skins			
Martens	20	2.10	50
Moose	322	15	4,830
Lynx	37	10	370
Bear	6	6	36
Otter	3	3	9
"chapts cerviers"*	6	8	48
Pounds of			
Beaver fur	20	4	80
Hundredweight of:			
Flour	95.50	12	1,146
Bread	5	10	50
Eels	6	15	90
Fish oil	2	30	60
Salt pork	10.80	35	378
Salt beef	6	30	180
Dried codfish	21	12	252
Sweetmeats	8	20†	169.12
Feathers	5.50	80	440
Casks of:			
Oats	349	12	4,188
Peas	18	20	360
Wheat	5	30	150
Dozens of:			
Bundles of spars	29	3	87
Plates	5	12	60
Cubic ft. of			
Hardwood	80	1	80
Numbers of			
Axes	6	5	30
Total			26,939.12

* Document unclear.
† Probably 20.015.
Source: AC, F2B, p. 12.

good profit, because of the shortages at the western end of the valley, to the Duc d'Anville's "invincible" fleet which was expected to take Annapolis easily. In the end he lost more than two thousand livres when he had to flee and the Indians killed or dispersed his animals.[183] Surely only in a commercial economy, with ample ready cash, could such a venture have been undertaken.

The larger surpluses, representing greater production and freedom from levies or forced sales to the garrison, was clearly one of the reasons Acadians preferred to live in the Minas and Chignecto settlements. There is no doubt that the "out-settlements" were prospering while Annapolis stagnated. And it was in those settlements especially that metal currency was sought and accumulated, for the inhabitants could count on being able to hang onto it. Many observers commented on this deep interest in coin among the Acadians: ". . . they are extremely covetous of specie. Since the settlement of Ile Royale they have drawn from Louisbourg, by means of their trade in cattle, and all the other provisions, almost all the specie the King annually sent out; it never makes its appearance again, they are particularly careful to conceal it. What object can they have, except to secure for themselves a resource for an evil day?"[184] The romantic picture of the simple frugal Acadian habitant, waiting with a sack of gold buried beneath his hearth against the dread day of his oft-threatened expulsion, has been painted by many writers. But his demand for hard cash is more likely to have been a desire to command a means to buy from the Yankee traders[185] and because he could absorb only a limited quantity of the West Indian and European products available at Louisburg in exchange for his produce. The balance of trade was in his favor and that balance he took in specie. Very little of these supposed hoards appear to have gone away with the exiles in 1755 or to have been discovered later by treasure seekers who dug among the abandoned house sites.

The activity of the Acadians in trade sheds much light on the Acadian character. Observed by the British most closely at Annapolis Royal, they have been pictured as dull, unenterprising peasants whose chief noticeable activity apart from farming was squabbles with neighbors over land boundaries and who were content to eke out a subsistence with a minimum of labor, having no interest in the Yankee

183. Deposition of Joseph Leblanc, an Acadian, in 1750, quoted in Rameau, *Une Colonie Féodale*, 2, 376–77.   184. *New York Colonial Documents, 10,* 5: 1745. 185. Murdoch, *Nova-Scotia, 1,* 470.

summum bonum of "getting ahead." But, by this evidence, at least in the settlements up the Bay from Annapolis where the vast majority of Acadians lived, the picture by mid-century is quite a different one. We have a great deal of energy and initiative going into the raising of surpluses and shrewd trading operations not only with the French at Louisburg but with the sharpest dealers of their time—the Yankee sea peddlers. When opportunity presented itself the Acadians were quick to grasp it. It is perhaps remarkable that they achieved as high a commercial level in their economy as they did in view of the obstacles placed in their path at every turn.

7

Cape Breton Island to 1758

🍃

FROM 1763 until 1784, and since 1820, the territory of the colony and province of Nova Scotia has included not only the peninsula but Cape Breton Island as well. Although it has been argued above that the island was a part of Acadia in its broadest sense, that is not the basis for its treatment here. There were few Acadians living in what the French chose to call Isle Royale at any time from 1713 to 1759. But there are compelling reasons why no treatment of Acadia in the early eighteenth century should fail to give a solid account of that island. Very soon it became one of the two major markets for the surplus farm production of the Acadians and their major source of hard money, matters of outstanding importance to their commercial aspirations and their economic well-being. It represented a French presence on the Acadian doorstep which did much to hold the Acadians to a strong, sentimental, if generally passive, allegiance to France, especially through their ecclesiastical ties and the effective control of the Indians who lived among them by the government at Louisburg. Finally, strategically as a strong military and naval base and economically as a major entrepôt of trade and the major base of the French North American fishery, it represented a continuous, substantial, nagging challenge to the English of both Old World and New, to the government they strove to maintain at Annapolis, and to the fishery to which they were so deeply committed at Canso.

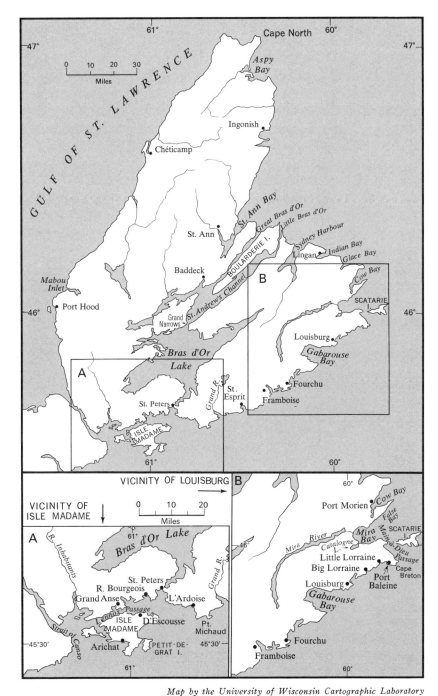

Fig. 7.1 Cape Breton Island to 1758, Modern Place Names.

THE COURSE OF EVENTS

Nicolas Denys made the first serious and successful attempts at European settlement on the island of Cape Breton in the two decades following 1650.[1] His earliest attempts were harassed and temporarily checked by rival claimants in 1651[2] but he got a "good title" in 1653 and settled down at St. Peters, on the narrow peninsula that separates the island's great internal salt water bay, Bras d'Or Lake (Figure 7.1) from the southern coast. In his remarkably informative (and, where he had no axe to grind, probably reliable) book he has left us the first geographical survey of the island extant, and one not to be rivaled for a century. He wrote that he had cleared nearly one hundred acres near his fortified post at St. Peters and had built a "road" on which to drag small vessels across the isthmian portage. It was a strategic location for trade with the Indians, for this portage was used by most of the peripatetic groups of Micmac who came and went between the Acadian mainland and the interior of the island. Denys accurately observed that the interior lake was surrounded by mountains (some of them, he noted, contained gypsum), clothed with "pins & sapins meslez de boulleaux & haistres,"[3] suggesting the mixed forest of spruce, fir, hemlock, pine, and larch with birch, maple, and beech which, in somewhat changing specific proportions, has dominated the island ever since.[4] His

1. Denys' observations are to be found in *The Description and Natural History of the Coasts of North America (Acadia)*, trans. and ed. W. F. Ganong (1908), pp. 175–87.

2. These were the relatives of Madame d'Aulnay (see Chapter 4). The Acadian-Gulf area was bedeviled throughout the century by the practice of the French court of issuing new grants and monopolies that overlapped in area, or otherwise encroached upon, previous grants. In part this was the result of geographical ignorance, in part of bureaucratic inefficiency, and in part of the constantly shifting power structure in the court so that the interests of the protegés of yesterday's favorites were subordinated to those of the men who had connections with the newest figures of influence. Even when rights and privileges were well defined geographically, the news of royal action was often slow in reaching the parties concerned in the New World.   3. *Description*, p. 492.

4. O. L. Loucks, "A Forest Classification for the Maritime Provinces" (1962), pp. 108–9, points out, of the land bordering Bras d'Or Lake, that although much of it which was once cleared for sheep pasture (actually for grain, hay, or root crops which later reverted to sheep pasture) has largely reverted to white spruce and balsam fir, scattered stands of tolerant hardwoods remain and hemlock and white pine are found locally. See also Chapter 2.

description of the outer coast follows a counterclockwise circuit from St. Peters. Of Havre à l'Anglois[5] (which became Louisburg) he noted that the fishermen of La Rochelle had come in old times to winter, in order to be fishing as early in the spring as possible—for it was France's early market that paid most handsomely. Of Spanish Bay (Sydney Harbour) he mentions a hill of coal ("une montagne de très-bon charbon de terre") and, among the trees, maple, ash, and oaks ("quelques peu"). There is a good account of the harbor of St. Ann with its all-but-enclosing bar and the cliff of gypsum at its foot, and brief mention of Niganiche (Ingonish), Cape North, Le Chadye (Chéticamp), and so around the shores (eighty leagues of circumference, he guessed) and through the Strait of Canso to St. Peters once more.

The whole tenor of his description is of a place long and well known to those who used its shores for a fishery and to whom its resources of timber, coal, and gypsum were familiar. Indeed, Cape Breton may have been known to post-Columbian Europeans as long as any other part of the continent. By Denys' time it had doubtless been seen, if not visited, by literally thousands of individuals and certainly many hundreds must have trodden its beaches and rocky harbor strands. Although the connection of Cape Breton with Norse exploration may always be debatable, and even the celebrated Cabot landfall of 1497 remains open to some doubt, known contacts become more frequent with the successive decades of the sixteenth century. The coastings of Verrazano and Gomez are well known; Fagundes may have wintered there with some Portuguese in 1520; Richard Hore of London paid a putative visit in 1536, and so the record continues.[6] The name of the little cape, northeast of Louisburg, that was to be attached to the whole island, probably goes back in cartographic record even beyond the certainty of the Maggiolo map of 1527[7] and before 1600 its use to mean all of the island, and the recognition of Cape Breton's insularity, was common.

To its shores came many ships from the great annual codfishing

5. A reference of 1597 to this harbor as "the English port" is found in the report of a voyage in Richard Hakluyt, *The Principal Navigations, Voyages, Traffiques & Discoveries of the English Nation* (1904), *8*, 174. This name, as that of Spanish Bay for present Sydney Harbour, must go well back into the sixteenth century.

6. A concise summary of the island's earliest history can be found in the introduction to C. Bruce Fergusson, ed., *Uniacke's Sketches of Cape Breton* (1958).

7. Ganong, in Denys, *Description*, p. 182n.

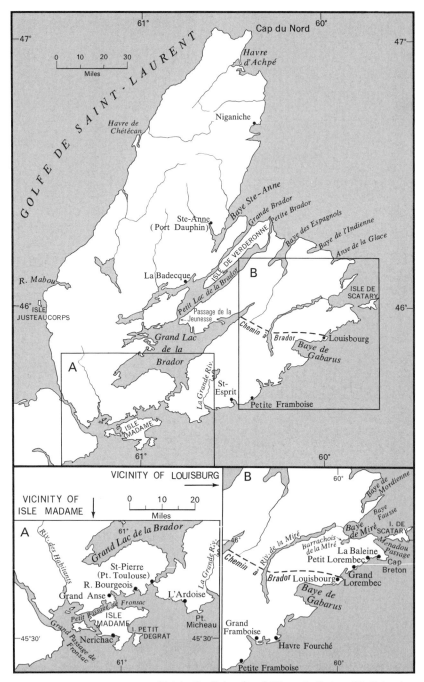

Map by the University of Wisconsin Cartographic Laboratory

Fig. 7.2 Cape Breton to 1758, Early Eighteenth-Century Place Names.

fleets crossing the ocean from England, France, Spain, and Portugal: ". . . de tems immémorial, les vaisseaux ont fait la pesche sur lles costes du Cap Breton, le Forillon, l'Isle Plate [these last two off Gaspé] L'Indiane Niganiche, Achpé, le Chadie, Canceaux, le Havre à l'Anglois, et la Balaine qui en dépendent ne sont jamais sans vaisseaux en temps de Paix. . . ."[8] As early as the middle of the sixteenth century the "dry" fishery (chiefly shore-based with the fish cured under the sun, with less salt, on beaches and platforms) was of major importance, and the beaches and coves of Newfoundland, the Gulf, and Cape Breton were in great demand for preparing the higher quality product.

Before the time of Denys' small but successful settlement, thus, many Europeans must have known the island and many wintered there through necessity, or to protect shore establishments from the destructive curiosity or animosity of the Indians. The coal, of which Denys wrote, so readily accessible in exposed cliffs at tidewater from Sydney Harbour to Port Morien (Cow Bay), became widely known and ships with excess hold capacity often called in to dig and carry off a few hundredweight, or tons, for New France, New England, the West Indies, or even Europe. The only significant attempt at settlement prior to Denys was associated with the Alexander scheme, of the 1620's, to turn Acadia into a New Scotland. In 1629, when Sir William Alexander (the younger) was taking settlers and supplies to the ephemeral Scottish settlement at Port Royal, he left his associate, Sir James Stewart, to set up a fort and settlement at Port Baleine, northeast of present Louisburg. Soon afterward this was attacked and destroyed by Captain Daniel of Dieppe who deported its residents and then made a temporary settlement himself at St. Ann.

After Denys was burnt out at St. Peters in the winter of 1668/69 and retired to Nipisiguit, we infer, rather than know of, only wintering fishermen temporarily in one or another harbor. The Indians, constantly on the move, fluctuated widely in numbers and generally camped on the shores of Bras d'Or Lake when they did winter there. Gargas' census of 1687/88[9] mentions one man and five engagés as the

8. AC, C11C-*8*, 39: "Mémoire . . . sur l'établissement d'une colonie dans l'isle du Cap Breton," November 1706. Most of this has been reprinted with some different wording in J. S. McLennan, *Louisbourg, from its Foundation to its Fall, 1713–1758* (1918), pp. 22–31.

9. Recorded in *Acadiensia Nova, 1578–1779,* ed. W. I. Morse (1935), *1*, 144–55.

European population, along with some Indians. An additional ninety Indians were listed for "Canceau" and "Isles St-Pierre," the latter possibly the Isle Madame area southwest of St. Peters.

Until the eighteenth century the claims of sovereignty over the island or its parts, formal or informal, were of little significance or effect; no country appeared to want to make permanent establishments there and the vessels of all the western European nations, and of their North American colonies, visited it freely. Indeed, one is reminded of the "hands off" attitude of European powers, especially Great Britain and France, toward New Zealand a century later."[10] It was an international haven for drying fish, for a shore-based boat fishery, and for obtaining supplies of wood, coal, or water. In the seventeenth century the French and British must have predominated and various grants (as that to Denys, made by France[11]) do not seem to have been seriously challenged.

Queen Anne's War (or The War of the Spanish Succession, 1702–13) pointed up some critical problems for the French who had failed to develop as successful an Atlantic empire as that of England in the later seventeenth century. As early as 1706 Jacques Raudot, the intendant at Quebec, had urged a French establishment on Cape Breton to serve three main purposes: (1) as an entrepôt between France, Canada, Plaisance (Placentia, in Newfoundland), and Acadia where cargoes could be transshipped; (2) as a location that would allow a winter fishery (*pêche d'automne*) as well as a summer one and a base for sealing and whaling; and (3) as a haven for French merchant and naval vessels and a base from which to annoy the English.[12] When, in 1713, by the Treaty of Utrecht, France lost not only mainland Acadia but its only settlement base for the fishery at Placentia, the preeminent needs of that fishery dictated the settlement, development, and military protection of the islands of St-Jean and Cape Breton which she obtained or retained in that agreement. The plans[13] included agricultural

10. See A. H. Clark, *The Invasion of New Zealand by People, Plants and Animals* (1949).

11. One of the fullest secondary accounts of the confusion of overlapping grants, rights, and sovereignties is contained in Gustave Lanctot, *A History of Canada, 1* (to 1663), trans. Josephine Hambleton (1963), esp. chs. 8, 12, 21, 22, and 23. For documentation of the Denys grants, see Robert Le Blant, "Les Études Historiques sur la colonie française d'Acadie, 1603–1713" (1948).

12. AC, C11G-*6*, *passim*. See also note 8 for a similar memoir.

13. See, among others, AC, F3-*50* (Collection Moreau St-Méry).

development of Isle St-Jean[14] and, if possible, of Cape Breton, importation of settlers from Placentia, Acadia, or New and old France, development of Cape Breton's resources of timber and minerals (especially coal), fortification of one or more harbors, establishment of a naval base and an entrepôt for commerce, and, above all, provision of an adequate accomodation for the all-important cod fishery, both for the sedentary or dry fishery and as a year-round haven for vessels coming from France to the Grand and other neighboring banks.[15]

By October of 1714 all of the settlers at Placentia (except the handful who chose to take the oath of loyalty to Queen Anne and remain) had been transferred and some 180 people were established around Louisburg, or nearby in Baleine or Scatarie Island (see Figure 7.1). It proved difficult to attract and hold year-round settlers for any purposes other than the resident fishery. As we have seen in Chapter 6, with only negligible exceptions the Acadians, for a variety of reasons, did not leave their dyked-land Fundy farms until the pressure of events in the 1750's brought a few score to Cape Breton—and most of these remained but a short time.

It was some years before a final decision on a site for the official headquarters, capital, and fortress was made. The choice of Louisburg was made early but it was not until 1718 that final orders came to establish the official headquarters there permanently,[16] and it was not until 1720 that the first major element (the King's Bastion) of the great fortress, the "American Dunkirk," was begun.

The long-drawn-out debate which led to the decision on this site is described in great detail in official correspondence and memoirs, with extensive arguments for the various alternative possibilities.[17] In addition to Louisburg serious consideration was given to present St. Ann (renamed Port Dauphin), St. Peters (Denys' old stand, renamed Port Toulouse), and the best known and most commodious harbor of all, Spanish Bay (present Sydney Harbour, see Figure 7.1). Their compar-

---

14. See A. H. Clark, *Three Centuries and the Island* (1959), on the agricultural development of Isle St-Jean in the early seventeenth century.

15. See AC, C11B-*1* (1), *passim* (note esp. pp. 13–21, 22–27): 1713, and AC, C11B-*1* (2), 373–79: 1715.

16. See AC, C11B-*1* (2), 651: "Mémoire sur l'Isle Royale," 1718. Also, AdC, B40, fol. 519, quoted in Charles de La Morandière, *Histoire de la pêche française de la morue dans l'Amérique septentrionale* (1962), 2, 660.

17. See, among others, AC, C11B-*1* (1), 13–21, 68–71: 1713–14; AC, C11B-*1* (2), 427–97: 1716; 650–70: 1718.

ative advantages and disadvantages were assessed with care. The case for "La Baye des Espagnols" was set forth eloquently in the anonymous *mémoire* of 1706, cited above (see note 8). Its spacious harbor was protected by a largely submerged sandbar which blocked much of the entrance; it had excellent, sandy beaches and holding bottoms; there was adequate space and depth of water for any size of fleet; the land around it seemed more attractive (or less unattractive) for agriculture than that near Louisburg; there were both good timber and open-face coal mines nearby; and, of great importance, it was fairly close to the fishery. Finally, by way of a short portage to Bras d'Or Lake, it had easy access to the interior and by way of St. Peters a protected avenue of connection with the Canso region and the Acadian (Nova Scotian) mainland.[18]

St. Peters had relatively good agricultural possibilities nearby and was quite well situated to protect the fishery of the Canso-Isle Madame region; there were hardwood forests in the vicinity and it had a spacious harbor, but a narrow entrance and a bar excluded ships of over 150 tons. Much more serious attention was given to St. Ann and indeed Philippe de Pastour de Costebelle, the first governor (1714–17), made his headquarters there and, with support from home,[19] clearly intended to make it, rather than Louisburg, the major center. The local soil and vegetation were good, it had a commodious harbor with a bar leaving a narrow channel which, adequate for peaceful entry, promised facilities for defense. But the Acadians who could have developed the area agriculturally did not come, the fishermen who had to provide the economic base found it too far from the fishing grounds for the use of shallops, and its encircling hills cut off the breezes essential for the "making" of the dried codfish. As had been pointed out in 1714: "Ce n'est pas un establissement pour la culture des terres que l'on cherche à l'Isle Royale, mais un endroit pour y faire la pesche en seureté . . . et pour les vaisseaux que iront de France."[20]

But Louisburg was the closest port to Europe and one of the longest and best known to French sailors in North America. As a major haven for the fishery and port-of-call for the transatlantic traffic, with a harbor that could handle a hundred ships, year-round access to the open sea, and capability for defense from naval attack,[21] it served well,

18. AC, C11C-*8*, 39: 1706.   19. AC B37, *passim*.   20. AC, F3-*50*, 11.
21. Its ability to resist military attack from the land was obviously not well considered.

although as a site for a naval fortress it faced the handicaps of a lack of building stone and lime, the agricultural unattractiveness of its hinterland, and the fogginess of the coast. In any event it was chosen.

The decision meant for Louisburg, as it doubtless would have for any other choice, a heavy concentration of administrative, military, and construction personnel which, with a continuation of a substantial resident and seasonal fishery, and the shipping and commerce that such a concentration implied, gave it more than half the total population of the island throughout the period from 1720 to 1758 (see Figures 7.3–7.6). For the sustenance of its people there were added to its large expenditures of public money, the yield of the fishery and the income of a major trading depot. French fishing and sack ships (which supplied the fishery and carried away its produce) had unused hold capacity on the outward voyage. Sugar ships from the West Indies found it a convenient station on the homeward voyage. Further, as we shall see, despite elaborate mercantilist trade regulations of both France and Britain and the hazards of piracy, privateering, or naval attack in open and undeclared war, the Acadian residents of British Nova Scotia and, especially, the shipmasters of New England, made it a focus of their own trading activities.

With the official French occupation of the island the record of fishing activity along all of the Atlantic coast becomes much fuller and it is apparent that Louisburg had stiff competition in the fishery from Ingonish and the Canso-Isle Madame areas (see Figure 7.1). In the latter there were associated activities of woodcutting, quarrying, brick-making, and some little agriculture; something of a bi-polarity of population centering on it and the Louisburg-Scatarie Island area became noticeable (see Figures 7.3–7.6).

The military and diplomatic history of Louisburg and Cape Breton Island (even the French sometimes forgot to use its impressive new title of Isle Royale) as a whole, in the French-British struggles of the eighteenth century, has been told many times.[22] The motives that induced New Englanders to yield to Massachusetts' Governor Shirley's cajoling and driving to mount an attack, which led to Louisburg's capture in 1745, have been the subject of much speculation. Louisburg represented no threat to open attack on New England although, after its capture, it is true that the Duc d'Anville's fleet, had it negotiated its

22. Notably in McLennan, *Louisbourg;* W. C. H. Wood, *The Great Fortress* (1915); and Gerald S. Graham, *Empire of the North Atlantic* (1950).

Atlantic crossing in better shape,[23] might well have retaken Louisburg, captured all of Nova Scotia, and engaged in some hit-and-run raiding on New England ports. Yet New England, which was profiting greatly from trade at Louisburg, saw the possibility of even handsomer profits from such trade if the port were in British hands (which seems somewhat dubious) and similarly greater advantages from New England's engrossing the Cape Breton fishery and destroying a base from which French privateers preyed on New England's fishermen and traders. Graham concludes that "The decisive elements in the Massachusetts resolve to take Louisburg were anger and greed."[24] At any rate the fortress fell, miraculously it seemed to many, after forty-seven days. The victory of 1745 was, perhaps, a tribute more to British command of the seas than to colonial military effectiveness, although the achievement of Pepperell and his "rustics and fishermen" foreshadowed later colonial successes in the American War of Independence. With the victory most of the resident French population, along with the garrison, was deported.

The return of Louisburg (and all of Cape Breton and Isle St-Jean) to France by the treaty of Aix-la-Chapelle in 1748 has been looked upon as a rather minor concession by the British who have been thought to have done rather better at the peace table than in the field. Certainly things were not quite in *status quo ante* when the French resumed control in 1749. Halifax was established simultaneously as a counterpoise, and the fortress was in drastic need of rehabilitation in view of its demonstrated weaknesses. A much more vigorous, more fully manned, and better financed administrative cadre and garrison were sent out from France and many residents, fishermen, and traders returned from France and Canada. Of the three governors in the brief interlude of peace,[25] Jean-Louis, Comte de Raymond, governor from

23. On June 22, 1746, a French expeditionary force consisting of ten ships of the line, three frigates, three bomb vessels, and sixty transports carrying 3,500 troops, escaped from the British blockade at Rochefort. It was under the command of de Roye de La Rochefoucauld, Duc d'Anville. A very bad passage reduced the fleet by twenty vessels before it reached Chebucto harbor in Nova Scotia. There scurvy, typhus, and smallpox combined to decimate his forces, d'Anville died, and a subsequent attempt to attack Annapolis with the remnant of the forces was frustrated by a gale. Upon arriving back in France the expedition counted 8,000 men dead and the only accomplishment a thorough scare of the British in Louisburg, Annapolis, and Boston. See Graham, *Empire*, ch. 7.   24. *Ibid.*, p. 120.

25. The list of French governors and commissaires-ordonnateur (in effect, intendants) of Cape Breton included: Philippe de Pastour de Costebelle, 1712–17 (gov.);

1751 to 1753, was especially active in trying to develop new settlements and a broader economic base, particularly in agriculture. The records of his administration are enlivened by lengthy and critical comments on his correspondence by the able Surlaville, the military commander whose sojourn in the colony paralleled that of Raymond and who received rather full accounts of later events there from correspondents.[26]

The needs of the enlarged garrison and army of artisans working on the fortifications alone would have made Louisburg an active port for supply ships but its oceanwide trading function greatly enhanced this role. At least seventy-five "legal" French-flag vessels entered the port in 1752, for example, and the visits of New England vessels greatly swelled this total. The trade is considered in more detail below but, with great public expenditures and the active fishery, it supported a busy, and at times rather cosmopolitan, garrison town with many parallels to Halifax in the same period.

These relatively happy conditions lasted only through 1754, however, when the undeclared war in North America picked up tempo. In 1755 came the French loss to the British of the area of present New Brunswick with the fall of Fort Beauséjour on the Chignecto isthmus, the abandonment of the mouth of the Saint John River, and the deportation of the Acadians. Louisburg was blockaded and although occasional supplies got through the garrison felt the pinch increasingly.[27] In 1757 the French navy temporarily achieved local supremacy

Pierre-Auguste de Soubras, 1714–18 (comm.); Joseph de Brouillan de St-Ovide, 1715–17 (acting-gov.), 1717–38 (gov.); Jacques-Ange Le Normant de Mézy, 1718–28 (comm.); Sebastien-François-Ange Le Normant de Mézy, 1729–35 (acting comm.), 1735–39 (comm.); François Bigot, 1739–46 (comm.); Isaac-Louis de Forant, 1739–40 (gov.); Jean-Baptiste-Louis Le Prévost du Quesnel, 1740–44 (gov.); Louis Dupont du Chambon, 1744–45 (acting gov.); Charles des Herbiers, 1749–51 (gov.); Jacques Prévost, 1749–56 (comm.); Jean-Louis, Comte de Raymond, 1751–53 (gov.); Charles-Joseph d'Ailleboust, 1753–54 (gov.); and Augustin, Chevalier de Drucourt, 1754–58 (gov.). During the British interregnum, 1745–49, the sequence was: Admiral Peter Warren and General William Pepperrell (joint), Commodore Charles Knowles, and Colonel Peregrine Hopson.

26. *Les Derniers Jours de l'Acadie (1748–1758). Correspondances et mémoires. Extraits du portefeuille de M. Le Courteois de Surlaville. Lieutenant-Général des Armées du Roi [et] Ancien Major des troupes de l'Ile Royale,* ed. and ann. Gaston du Boscq de Beaumont (1899).

27. The virtual impossibility of maintaining a complete blockade, with frequent fogs and winds onshore to a reefbound coast, had been strong recommendation for the site.

and opened the port with de la Motte's fleet, the presence of which deterred a projected British attack, but it was only a short postponement of the final blow which fell in 1758. Assembling an overwhelmingly superior force of some 27,000 men and thirty-five to forty warships (as compared with perhaps 7,500 men and fewer than ten warships in Louisburg harbor and fortress) the British made a landing in Gabarouse Bay (as had the New Englanders of 1745) on June 8, and won capitulation on July 26.

In 1759 Louisburg then served as the new advanced base for the expedition against Quebec. With Halifax well established and the memory of the return of Louisburg to France in the last peace treaty clearly in mind, it was decided that, the expedition to Canada launched, ". . . the said Fortress, together with all the works, and Defences of the Harbour, be most effectually and most entirely demolished."[28] Although neither time nor personnel allowed this order to be executed fully, the razing was generally effective.[29] In the peace treaty which followed, however, the island did not revert to France but, with most of the French empire in North America, became legally British in 1763.

POPULATION AND SETTLEMENT

Numbers and Changing Locational Patterns

With the exception of rare, small-scale ventures such as those of Denys, Stewart, and Daniel, there were only occasional groups of fishermen wintering on the island before 1713. Yet, as we have seen, its eastern and southern shores had been known to hundreds of visiting ships, chiefly engaged in the fishery before that year, and thereafter large numbers came annually, in times of peace, to its splendid array of harbors and coves. These included especially Aspy, Ingonish, St. Ann, Little Bras d'Or, Sydney Harbour (Spanish Bay), Lingan (Indian Bay), Glace Bay, Port Morien (Cow Bay), Mira Bay, Main-à-Dieu Passage, Scatarie Island, Louisburg and its satellites of Baleine and the Lorraines, Gabarouse, Fourchu, Framboise, St. Esprit, Point Michaud,

28. Pitt to Amherst, February 1760, quoted in McLennan, *Louisbourg*, p. 290.
29. Within the past decade a serious rebuilding program has been undertaken by the Canadian government, as a centennial project, to restore some of the more impressive buildings and sections of the fortifications.

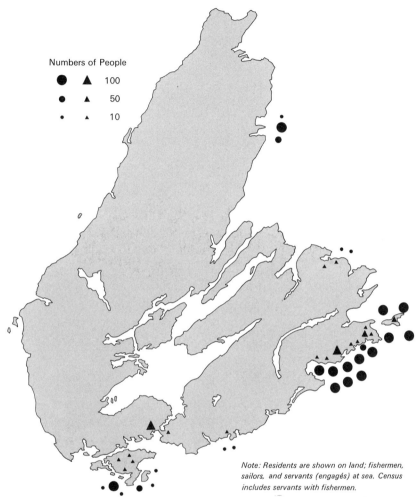

Numbers of People

● ▲ 100
● ▲ 50
• ▲ 10

Note: Residents are shown on land; fishermen, sailors, and servants (engagés) at sea. Census includes servants with fishermen.

Map by the University of Wisconsin Cartographic Laboratory

Fig. 7.3 Cape Breton: Population, 1716.

L'Ardoise, St. Peters, Isle Madame with its havens of Petit-de-Grat and Arichat, the havens along Lennox Passage, and River Inhabitants[30] (see Figure 7.1).

30. The contemporary names of some of these places (where different from the present) were: Achpé (Aspy), Niganiche (Ingonish); Port Dauphin (St. Ann), Baye des Espagnols (Sydney Harbour), L'Indienne (Lingan), Mordienne (Port Morien), Menadou (Main-à-Dieu), Lorembec (Lorraine), Gabarus (Gabarouse), Fourché (Fourchu, and not to be confused with Yarmouth), Pointe or Isles

TABLE 7.1   *Population of Cape Breton Island, 1716 to 1752*

	Louisburg			Outports			
Year	Inhabi-tants and families	Servants and domes-tics	Fisher-men	Inhabi-tants and families	Servants and domes-tics	Fisher-men	Total
1716	172	338	127	326	636	1,020	2,619
1720	188	261	?	433	858	?	1,740
1723	278	515	?	497	1,380	?	2,670
1724	431	77	377	609	70	679	2,243
1726	544	94	314	805	139	1,257	3,153
1734	673	157	296	751	163	1,349	3,389
1737	984	229	250	797	115	1,663	4,038
1752	1,349	437	674	1,662*	?	?	4,122

* May well include servants, domestics, and fishermen.

Sources: AC, G1-*406*, G1-*407*, G1-*409*(3), G1-*411*, G1-*467*; J. S. McLennan, *Louisbourg, from its Foundation to its Fall, 1713–1758* (1918), appendix 1; for the 1752 census, the De la Roque census, see Joseph, Sieur de la Roque, "Tour of Inspection made by the Sieur de la Roque," in AC *Report for 1905* (1906), pp. 1–172. These sources are discussed in footnote 31.

There are counts of population with some breakdowns by districts or centers for 1716, 1717, 1718, 1723, 1724, 1726, 1734, 1737, 1750, 1752, and 1753.[31] Attempts have been made in Figures 7.3–7.6 to show distributions of population in 1716 (controlled or modified by the counts of the next two years), 1724, 1737, and a combined map for 1752 and 1753. These are summarized in Table 7.1 to which the years 1720,

---

Micheau(x) (Point Michaud), Nerichac or Nerichat (Arichat), Petit Passage de Fronsac (Lennox Passage), and Rivière des Habitants (River Inhabitants). The failure to retain the older and simpler French spelling of "Gabarus" is particularly mysterious, as also is the change from Menadou to Main-à-Dieu.

31. Most of the known censuses of Cape Breton have been collected in AC, G1-*406*, G1-*407*, G1-*409*(3), G1-*411*, and G1-*467*. Some of these have been re-printed in McLennan, *Louisbourg*, appendix 1, and an elaborate nominal census of 1752 by Joseph, Sieur de la Roque, "Tour of Inspection made by the Sieur de la Roque," called De la Roque census, has been published in full in AC *Report for 1905* (1906). The census, listed as for 1718 in AC, C11B-*1*(2), pp. 650–70, is given in McLennan as for 1720, presumably an error in copying or printing. There also are occasional estimates of totals for Louisbourg itself, for certain specific areas of the island, or for the island as a whole. Most of the censuses omit certain places and all population estimates or counts are clouded by the ephemeral or seasonal nature of the fishing population, with its large numbers of seasonal engagés and servants and/or fishermen from France, which are often omitted for individual locations.

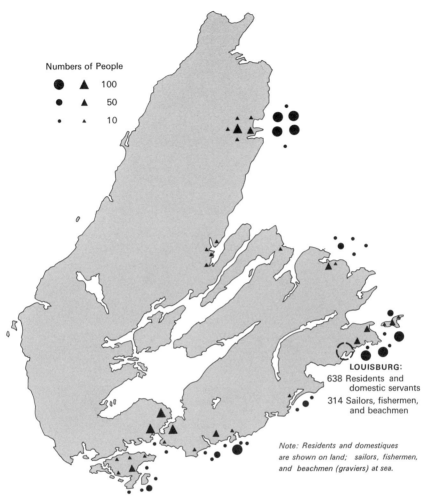

Numbers of People

● ▲ 100

● ▲ 50

● ▲ 10

LOUISBURG:
638 Residents and
domestic servants
314 Sailors, fishermen,
and beachmen

*Note: Residents and domestiques
are shown on land;   sailors, fishermen,
and beachmen (graviers) at sea.*

Map by the University of Wisconsin Cartographic Laboratory

Fig. 7.4   Cape Breton: Population, 1726.

1723, 1726, and 1734 have been added. No summary is given for 1753 which did not include Louisburg or the outports south and east of St. Esprit. The totals for 1716 seem reasonable, with the fishermen definitely listed by the census as ship's crews. Neither Ingonish nor Arichat showed any residents, which is possible. There were 510 at Louisburg, including 172 "habitans" (presumably residents) and families, whereas the actual headquarters of the time, St. Ann, held only forty-

eight. Since the category of "servants and domestics" includes fishermen serving as engagés to the residents, one can only guess how many
of this group were relatively permanent. None of the later censuses
lists ship's crews separately and there is an indeterminate line between
the "servants and domestics" and "fishermen." In 1720 it is probable
that ship's crews were not counted in the single category of "servants"
separate from "habitans" and families but they may well be included
in the single separate heading of "hommes" in 1723. In 1724 the
"fisherman" category is explicit but does not necessarily include ship's
crews. In 1726, the category of "sailors, fishermen and beachmen"
(*graviers*) probably does include them and the big increase in numbers
in two years supports this view. The numbers of "habitans" and families do not agree with those previously published because many
women in the different censuses were counted twice (as widows and
"habitans" or as both "femmes" and "filles").

In 1734, again, sailors are specifically included as they appear to
have been in 1737 under the title of fishermen. There is a report of six
thousand for that year[32] but it seems doubtful that the garrison *and*
any uncounted sailors could have added two thousand to the census
total. In 1744 we have an estimate of four thousand besides the
garrison, which is of the right order.[33] The large increase in numbers in
1752 (after the recovery following the deportation of most of the
population in 1745) is not only the result of steady growth but includes
the sudden influx of some 400 to 500 Acadians within the previous year
or two. By the evidence of the partial 1753 census they were shifting
around rapidly and, as will be seen, most of them returned to Acadia or
moved to Isle St-Jean before 1755. It should also be noted that the
Louisburg count of 1752 excluded thirty in the governor's household,
two hundred newly-arrived habitants (Acadians?), and a garrison of
fifteen hundred, which, allowing for the suspicious nature of the
round-figure estimates, gives some 4,200 for Louisburg and just under
six thousand for the island as a whole. The figures for the outports
probably included all fishermen but not ship's crews as such. Some
allowance must be made for the omission of Ingonish in both censuses
of the 1750's. If, as suggested below, the total for Louisburg is reduced
by between five hundred and one thousand, the overall figures are
likewise diminished.

If the totals are inexact, as they must be, the slow but steady growth

32. AC, C11B-*19*, 6, in a letter from St-Ovide.   33. AC, C11B-*38*, 39.

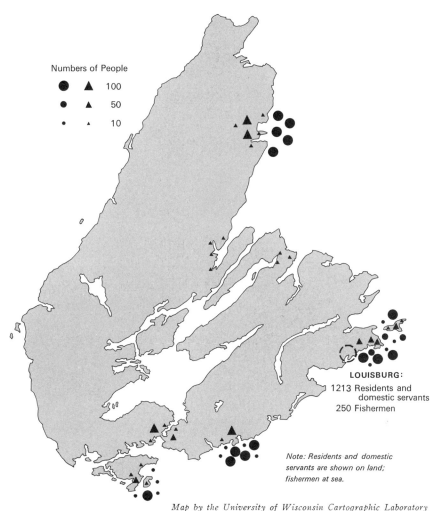

Numbers of People

Map by the University of Wisconsin Cartographic Laboratory

Fig. 7.5 Cape Breton: Population, 1737.

is clear and the distribution as shown on the maps must be close to the
fact. The main concentration was always in the Louisburg area, the
second in the St. Peters-Isle Madame area and the third around Ingonish. Except for the 1750's there was no interior population and even
then it was composed chiefly of refugee Acadians, most of whom left
before 1755, and the settlements along the Mira River of discharged
soldiers and a few dissident refugees from the "Foreign Protestants" at
Halifax.

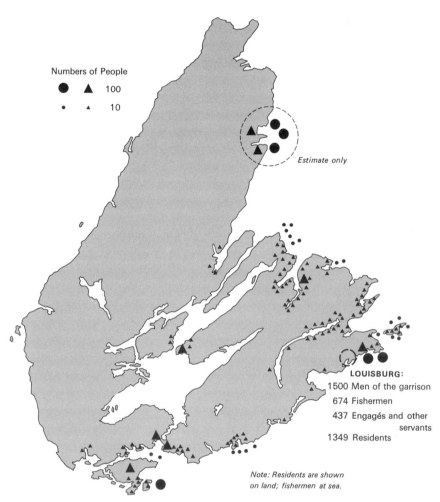

Map by the University of Wisconsin Cartographic Laboratory

Fig. 7.6 Cape Breton: Population, 1752/53.

The Individual Settlements

A reconnaissance geography of the general outlines of settlement at the mid-century point between the periods of open warfare can be reconstructed from the surveys of De la Roque in 1752, a description by Thomas Pichon who accompanied him on part of his journey, and from the survey of Captain Samuel Holland of 1765–67. Despite being written eight years after the British capture of the island and the deportation of its inhabitants, Holland's survey provides evidence of prior occupation and housing.[34] There are also other descriptive bits scattered through the official correspondence including some of the earlier censuses. In the following descriptions emphasis will be upon the changing character of the settlements throughout the French regime but must dwell most largely on the times for which the best information is available.

THE EMPTY WEST COAST — A review of the coastal settlements might well proceed in a clockwise fashion from the present Strait or Gut of Canso (Grand Passage de Fronsac). In the Strait itself at Plaster Cove (near the island end of the present causeway at Port Hastings) there had been substantial quarrying of gypsum, chiefly for Louisburg's needs for mortar and plaster, and hence some intermittent temporary occupation. Again, the known quarrying of building stone and the construction of some vessels at Justeaucorps (present Port Hood) necessarily meant at least temporary workmen's camps. There are few other references to the west coast that allow us to be more specific and as one proceeds north these become still fewer; a salmon fishery at Mabou inlet might be inferred, and Chéticamp may have seen some boat building as well as serving as a refuge for small fishing craft, but there are not even hints of the use of Judique (near Port Hood) or the barred estuary of the Margaree River.

CAPE NORTH TO PORT MORIEN — Most of the population and economic activity was on the eastern and southern coasts between Cape North and the Isle Madame-Canso area. There are frequent references to the fishery at Aspy, but if there was any permanent population there it must have been recorded with that of Ingonish. In the report of his survey of 1765–67, Holland estimated that some 45 boats had fished there in the middle fifties as compared with 160 at Ingonish. Although

34. For De la Roque, see above note 31. For Holland's survey see *Holland's Description of Cape Breton Island,* comp. and ed. D. C. Harvey (1935). For a note on Holland see W. Chipman, "The Life and Times of Major Samuel Holland, Surveyor-General, 1764–1801" (1924). Thomas Pichon published *Genuine Letters and Memoirs, Relating to the Natural, Civil, and Commercial History of the Islands of Cape Breton and Saint John,* anonymously (i.e., "by an impartial Frenchman") in London in 1760. Secretary to Governor le Comte de Raymond, Pichon later served in Fort Beauséjour where he was a spy for the British; still later he lived in England under the name of Tyrrell. Some of his papers are preserved in the library of Vire, France, and others, as the Tyrrell Papers, in the Public Archives of Nova Scotia.

Ingonish was a busy fishing area throughout the period, with 600 to 800 residents and families and ship's fishermen counted in censuses of the twenties and thirties, there probably were never as many as 200 permanent residents.[35] Pichon implies few settlers in the fifties and suggests that both seasonal and resident fishermen had to remove to St. Ann at the season of easterly gales when the open roadstead offered no protection. Although it never rivaled Louisburg in trading activity, it may have had more than any other outport; more ships visited it to pick up fish or sell supplies, and its residents usually had some sloops or schooners in the coastal trade (*cabotage*). In 1739, when Louisburg had twenty-nine vessels so employed, Ingonish had eight and St. Peters ten, with only seven others scattered through the rest of the coves and harbors.[36]

In 1720, St. Ann, under its new name of Port Dauphin, briefly described above, had seventy-nine "permanent" residents and its largest population record (133, and most of those, seasonal fishermen), but with the decision to build the fortress in Louisburg it rapidly declined and generally thereafter held fewer than ten or a dozen families. Too far away from fishing grounds (twenty to twenty-five miles), its later population cut timber and building stone for Louisburg but did little to develop the agricultural possibilities. In 1752 De la Roque counted only sixteen residents (the census of 1753 did count thirty-two, possibly a refugee augmentation) and only two or three dwellings, seven arpents of meadow, a small garden and orchard, and but two head of cattle. Pichon's statement that it "furnishes . . . [Louisburg] . . . with great part of its provisions, and a thousand cords of wood annually for firing"[37] must be largely, or entirely, nonsense.

The next inlet east of St. Ann is a strait a mile or two in width, generally known as the Great Bras d'Or; it is the principal entrance to the great interior salt water "lake" of the same name (often Grand Lac de la Brador, or simply "Labrador," in the documents). The shores of the strait had no known settlers during the French regime. Between it

35. The highest number recorded was of 186 (residents and families) with 55 servants or engagés, many of whom were seasonal. In 1737 Ingonish was described as one of the best fishing ports on the island, with more shallops (over 100) than any other harbor. AC, C11B-*20*, 45, 243. A large church is reported to have been erected there in 1729. Richard Brown, *A History of the Island of Cape Breton . . . with Some Account of the Discovery and Settlement of Canada, Nova Scotia, and Newfoundland* (1869), p. 173*n*.

36. AC, C11B-*21*, 151.   37. Pichon, *Genuine Letters*, pp. 60–61.

and the only other entrance to Bras d'Or Lake (a narrow, winding, creeklike strait known as Little Bras d'Or) lay the rolling surface of present Boularderie Island. Although Cape Breton had neither the fully operating seigneuries of Canada nor the shadowy ones of Acadia there were a few substantial private grants of land on Cape Breton, of which that of Boularderie Island[38] to Antoine Le Poupet de La Boularderie was notable.[39] The failure to grant seigneuries thus did not preclude substantial grants (Boularderie's included not only the island but a strip of land along the Little Bras d'Or a league in depth) which in the former case was given "en franc alleu noble sans aucune redevance" but nevertheless "sans justice."[40] But the exceptions were few; generally the crown stayed with the policy reported in 1718: "Sa Majesté ne voulant point qu'il y ait d'autre seigneur qu'elle dans cette Isle. . . . Elle y donne seulement des habitations de deux, trois et quatre arpens de front sur quarante ou soixante arpens de profondeur . . . ."[41]

Boularderie had also been granted special concessions at Ingonish and although by 1726 he had done nothing with his island,[42] in the following year he was reported to have arrived with one hundred engagés and many fishermen, presumably going to Ingonish.[43] Thereafter the record is conflicting as to what he did accomplish. In 1730 a dispatch from Louisburg reported him very active in the fishery; he had sent four vessels there from France and three had returned with 1,000 quintals[44] of fish. In the winter of 1729/30 he had had twenty-five shallops engaged in the "winter" fishery from November to early January, twenty-eight shallops fishing in the summer, and four sloops (*batteaux*) on the banks. In the previous winter he had had twenty shallops and one schooner built at Little Bras d'Or and for 1730/31 he planned to build a two hundred-ton ship. Fifty workmen were settled at the latter place, the needed wood was cut, many buildings had been

---

38. Sometimes referred to in the documents as Isle de Verderonne, although this same name has also been interpreted to mean an island off Ingonish. Yet one reference to Isle de Niganiche probably meant Boularderie Island.

39. AC, C11B-*8*, 54–58: a dispatch of St-Ovide from Louisburg, November 1726.

40. AdC, B41, fols. 562, 563: 1719, quoted in La Morandière, *Histoire de la pêche*, 2, 671.

41. AC, C11B-*1*(2), 653–54, 670: "Mémoire sur l'Isle Royale," 1718.

42. AC, C11B-*8*, 54–58.   43. AC, C11B-*9*, 18–19.

44. A quintal was roughly the English hundredweight, the basic unit of measurement of the Atlantic cod fishery.

erected, and a road had been cut across the island to the Great Bras
d'Or. Some garden cultivation was being attempted.[45] But the censuses
of 1734 and 1737 reported populations of only twenty-one and thirty-
two and in 1742 the Commissaire, Bigot, indicated that the promising
beginnings had not flowered. Boularderie had a good house and the soil
was good but he simply was not a farmer and was making a bare
living.[46]

The enterprise seems to have failed totally by the time of the war of
1744–48 but Boularderie's son, who had succeeded him on his death in
1748, claimed in a deposition made at Louisburg in 1755, that he had
brought out some artisans and farm workers and "touttes les ustenciles
nécessaire pour la culture des terres." He said that for eight years he
had had twenty-five employees who had erected a fine manor house, a
barn, stable, dairy, oven, dovecote, windmill, and water mill, and
tended twenty-five cows, six oxen, six mares, a stallion, and fifty sheep;
he claimed further that he had established an orchard and grown good
crops of grain and vegetables.[47] Whatever the exaggeration of these
claims, De la Roque listed a total of sixty-four residents, probably
some forty at Little Bras d'Or in 1752 and, in 1753, fifty-three residents and seventy-eight seasonal hands engaged in the fishery were
counted,[48] but since there were no records for Ingonish in any of these
years it is quite possible that any or all of these totals may have
belonged to the latter place, which was much better placed for the
fishery. Nevertheless, De la Roque estimated from 100 to 150 arpents
of land cleared by Boularderie and this could only have been in the
lands bordering Little Bras d'Or.

Next again to the east was Spanish Bay which had been considered
as an alternative site to Louisburg for the fortress, and the neglect of

45. AC, C11B-13, 55–56: Le Normant de Mézy to the Minister, Louisburg,
November 1730. See also AdC, C11B-11, fols. 67, 68: 1730, quoted in La Morandière, Histoire de la pêche, 2, 671.

46. AdC, C11B-24, fol. 114: 1742, quoted in La Morandière, Histoire de la pêche,
2, 671.

47. The complete deposition is printed in Surlaville, Les Derniers Jours, pp.
286–92; quote is from p. 287. The reliability is placed in question by, among other
things, the claim of eight years. Between 1738 and 1745 it was just possible but is
refuted by Bigot's comments of 1742. From 1749 to 1755 the maximum time he
could have been operating was seven years.

48. A somewhat doubtful figure of 159 (127 residents) for 1750 has been
recorded too; as in other cases the published figures in McLennan, Louisbourg, are
occasionally slightly off.

which by the French (in the face of nearly two centuries of familiarity) has been something of a mystery. This neglect was suddenly reversed when, in the 1750's, it became the site of a major Acadian refugee settlement and, temporarily, held one of the largest populations outside of Louisburg. De la Roque counted 185 there in 1752 and, for 1753, under headings probably all referring to the area (Bras du Sud, Bras de l'Ouest, and Banc de la Berichon), there were listed, respectively, 191, 108, and 32—or 331 in all. In 1753, too, a contingent of twenty-five soldiers was placed there for the dual purpose of providing protection and of finding wives among the nearly sixty Acadian daughters of marriageable age.[49] The increase in 1753 may have represented a northward movement of those counted at Passage de la Jeunesse (Grand Narrows) in 1752.

These Acadians, out of sheer necessity to survive by supplementing the inadequate "vivres" supplied from Louisburg, had cleared something under forty arpents at the time of De la Roque's visit and had livestock, surviving from those they had brought from Baie Verte or Tatamagouche, amounting to some thirty cattle, twenty pigs, and a few sheep, goats, and fowl. No doubt they cleared more land the next year but their situation grew worse and, despite grain sent to relieve them in 1754, they returned to Acadia at the end of the year with harsh words for the land and the unfulfilled promises of the government.[50] Among their other difficulties was lack of experience or equipment for the fishery; they had but two boats in 1752.

Between Little Bras d'Or and Port Morien (Cow Bay), coal is exposed at the surface and on sea cliffs, evidence of what was the best resource of mineral fuel on the whole eastern seaboard òf North America. In addition there were accessible cliffs of limestone and there was some good timber nearby at Spanish Bay. Some coal had been dug there intermittently through the previous century and some limestone and timber cut for Louisburg, but none of this activity had led to permanent settlement. Lingan (Indian Bay), next east from Spanish Bay, was a minor fishery haven that had counted as many as two hundred (mostly ship fishermen) seasonally in the twenties but had never had a resident population of as many as a dozen families or more than fifty people in all. Pichon opined that "the few inhabitants hereabouts

49. Surlaville, *Les Derniers Jours,* pp. 103–4. The minimum "marriageable age" would have been no more than fifteen years, although Acadian girls often remained single into their twenties.   50. *Ibid.,* pp. 114, 122, 126.

neglect all sort of agriculture,"[51] but De la Roque noted ten arpents cleared in 1752. Holland's estimate of 120 acres of cleared land in the sixties "partly overgrown with Brush"[52] may well have been a misreading by his survey crew of natural brushland and old burnt-over land. The decline of its fishery interest was partly attributable to beach gravel too fine to allow good curing of cod.

On a headland between Lingan and Glace (lit., frozen) Bay, next to the east, open-face coal mining had long been undertaken and a British fort built there in 1746 was burned down in 1752; indeed, accidental or intentional firing of the open seams was always a problem in the coal region. Glace Bay itself, although it had a good drying beach, had no protected harbor and rarely, if ever, true settlers, but it and several small coves to the east were used in season by scores of shallops. Port Morien, well sheltered on three sides, was nevertheless open to easterly gales and this created repeated problems not only for the fishery but for loading from its sea-cliff coal mine, the one most used for the Louisburg garrison. Yet sixty-six people were counted in 1752 and twenty-three in 1753 along with twenty head of cattle and two horses. Perhaps the people were either, or both, refugees and mine workers.

THE ENVIRONS OF LOUISBURG: MIRA BAY TO GABAROUSE BAY — Larger Mira Bay was even more open to the east. It contained both the outlet of the broad, estuarine, lake-interrupted Mira River which formed a crescentic western boundary to the immediate Louisburg hinterland and, behind a coastal bar, one of the typical east coast lagoons (*barrachois*[53]), Catalogne (now usually spelled Catalone) Lake. Mira first appears separately in the statistical summaries in 1734, although earlier population there and in Main-à-Dieu Passage may have been included with Scatarie Island. In that year there was a resident population of twenty-six, with ten servants or domestics in addition. These may have been in part along the lower river as well as on the bay near the river mouth. (Sometimes the expression "Mira Bay" apparently refers to the Barrachois de Catalogne, i.e., the lagoon behind its bar.) Forty-three residents were attributable to False (Fausse) Bay on its northern shore in 1753, but there is no record of

51. Pichon, *Genuine Letters,* p. 59.
52. Harvey, *Holland's Description,* p. 75.
53. The derivation of the application of what probably designated the bar, for the lagoon behind the bar, is uncertain.

earlier settlement there and these may well have been refugees. Small vessels drawing seven to nine feet of water could go a fair distance up the Mira with the tide to serve the farms along its banks and to bring firewood or lumber to Louisburg.

Between Mira and Gabarouse bays lay the easternmost projection of Cape Breton including Scatarie Island, Main-à-Dieu Passage separating it from the mainland, Cape Breton (after which the whole island had been named), and a series of coves including Baleine and Little and Big Lorraine which, with Louisburg itself, were among the most popular fishing havens in the colony. Used by scores to hundreds of fishermen each year since the early sixteenth century, they maintained, collectively, a resident population (outside of Louisburg) that rose from some 125 in the 1720's to perhaps 150 in the 1750's. In 1720, a total of more than 1,200 persons, including ship's crews, had been counted in the area at the height of the fishing season. In many ways this region was "suburban" to Louisburg and part of its economic complex; indeed the long-standing preference of European fishermen for this area, and its role as the "front door" to continental North America, had weighed heavily in the choice of Louisburg as the capital and fortress site.

Gabarouse Bay, the northern shore of which was the landing site for the invading armies of both successful sieges of Louisburg, in 1745 and 1758, had held some scattered settlement before the first (New England) invasion but had suffered severely from the associated scorched-earth policy that was carried out so effectively along the coast between Scatarie Island and Isle Madame. Nevertheless, some twenty to twenty-five residents were reported in the fifties, its chief attraction other than the fishery being swampy meadows for cattle (although no cattle are reported as surviving there in the 1750's).

GABAROUSE BAY TO ST. PETERS—Here were several coves occupied by a few permanent settlers and seasonal fishermen through most of the French regime: Fourchu, Framboise, St. Esprit, Grand River, Point Michaud, and L'Ardoise. Ascription of population to one or another of these in various census counts was rather loose and the situation in the fifties represented only a temporary recovery from the destruction in the late 1740's by New Englanders.

Apparently the Fourchu-Framboise district had been burned out and still was not reoccupied when De la Roque visited it in 1752. He ascribed all the population between Gabarouse and St. Peters bays to St. Esprit, although this may have included some in the Grand River-Point Michaud area. The resident population of the district, which was under a dozen before 1720, reached a maximum of ninety-six in 1737, and in that year some 450 additional servants, engagés, and ship's crews were counted fishing off the coast. Such a seasonal population, hired by the residents or from visiting ships, and coming out from France just for the summer, generally outnumbered the year-round population by four or five to one. The 1752 total included fourteen families of perhaps seventy to seventy-five; with hired seasonal hands there were eighty-six people counted. Only three of the families had gardens (which was as close as they came to farming), only seven had cattle (thirteen head in all), two had horses and most had barnyard fowl, geese, or turkeys; oddly, few had pigs. Holland's reports, in the next decade, of extensive clearances (as at Fourchu: "40 Acres of Clear Land which produces good Hay"[54] and at St. Esprit 100 acres) probably were a misinterpretation of the natural marshy margins of the lagoons, used in part as natural meadows for pasture and hay. Yet, in 1752 the settlers at St. Esprit were so short of hay locally they had to get additional supplies at Canso.[55]

The region of St. Peters Bay, including the area from L'Ardoise on the east to River Bourgeois on the west, had most of its population at St. Peters itself, and there are no separate locational listings before 1752. On the narrow neck of land between the Bay and Bras d'Or Lake, a favorite portage route of the Indians and the Acadians, Nicolas Denys had established a settlement in the preceding century and had claimed to have had eighty arpents of land in cultivation (doubtless a gross exaggeration).[56] There was an abortive French settlement there in 1715,[57] and it counted more than 100 residents in each census from 1716 onward, with peaks of 261 in 1724 and 199 in 1734 (including eighteen servants, engagés, and fishermen), until a large influx of Acadians swelled the regional total to 298 in 1752. Of these latter, fifty-nine lived at L'Ardoise and about eight or ten on the Bras d'Or side. The slate quarry (which gave L'Ardoise its name) was important in supplying roofing material for Louisburg and the economic base of

---

54. Harvey, *Holland's Description*, p. 81.

55. An imprecise designation. Any of the small islands off the south coast of Isle Madame may have been included in "Les isles de Canceaux."

56. Denys, *Description*, p. 177.   57. AC, C11B-*1*(1), 315.

the settlement rested on that, on cutting wood for the fortress, on coastal shipping (often with small vessels or shallops), or on their own garden plots and livestock. Nine families held forty-three head of cattle, four horses, fourteen pigs, and many fowl; such proportions were typical of Acadia rather than of Cape Breton.

In 1724 the occupations of all but two of the forty-six heads of family were given. One, a woman, was listed as "gardener," probably meaning that she lived off her garden plot. No fewer than forty-one claimed to be pilots or seamen ("navigateurs"), although a dozen of these listed a joint occupation ("constructeur" or "charpentier"). Clearly St. Peters was a port of some importance. Only three actually listed fishing as an occupation and the later activity in brick-making and wood supply is foreshadowed by one "briquetier et scieur." Of perhaps more interest in our view of the Lennox Passage–St. Peters Bay area as being a major route of contact with Acadia is that thirty of the heads of family had been born in Acadia, two in Canada, and the rest in France. Bordeaux, Dinon, St. Malo, Poitiers, Orleans, St. Denis, Paris, Normandy, Orleron, Brussels, Provence, and Granville were all represented; including the hired hands one could add Fontainebleu, Champagne, Brest, and Angers. There seemed to be no Norman, Breton, or Basque dominance, although the northern and western provinces were far in the lead. Incidentally, the population figures for St. Peters did not include the detachments of troops stationed there at any time.

In 1752 the farming activity had expanded, no doubt stimulated by the influx of Acadians to the chief Acadian doorway to the island. Holland reported three hundred acres of cleared land which may have been only a slight exaggeration. There was little shallop fishing based on St. Peters itself and the population was employed largely, as it had been for thirty years, in the coastal trade (in schooners, sloops, and skiffs) and in supplying Louisburg with timber and firewood, and with bricks from the local kiln.

LENNOX PASSAGE AND ISLE MADAME — Difficult as it is to locate population with much certainty elsewhere on Cape Breton, the problem is perhaps most nearly insoluble in the environs of Lennox Passage which divides Isle Madame from the larger island, and on Isle Madame itself. Sites include River Bourgeois, Grande Anse, D'Escousse, Petit-de-Grat, and Arichat (see Figure 7.1). Isle Madame itself was a most unattractive site for agriculture in terms of soil and vegetation (as it still is) but was very well situated for the excellent boat and small-vessel cod fishery of the Canso-Chedabucto region. Resident settlers in this whole archipelagic region probably numbered from fifty to one hundred throughout most of the French regime, with two or three times as many seasonal fishermen present in the best years. One D'Auteuil had been granted the whole island some time before 1722, and had arrived in that year, but appears to have abandoned it in 1724.[58]

This area was the French base for the Canso fishery and was much exposed to activities ranging from piracy and privateering to open military operations by New Englanders. In 1752 De la Roque counted ten "old" families and a dozen refugee families on the northern coast of Isle Madame; he also noted seven families with houses and ten families of fishermen with no permanent houses (about 150 people), together with some hundred single fishermen or engagés at Petit-de-Grat. The count may or may not have included people at Arichat, which he does not mention. Pichon may have been more accurate than usual in his description: ". . . being greatly streightened by the barrenness of the soil, they subsist by means of a little commerce. Some maintain themselves by fishing and hunting; others by cruizing winter and summer, and cutting wood for firing, which they sell for five livres the cord along the coast. The few horned cattle they are able to maintain, are likewise a considerable relief to them: in short, their distress was so great as to excite our compassion."[59] The "few horned cattle" were forty-one head by De la Roque's count. There were, in addition, a horse, many swine, and fowl. Some hay was obtained at Isle Verte, an islet just off the southeastern corner of Isle Madame. A major problem for the resident fishermen was the assumption of ownership or control of the Petit-de-Grat harbor area by two Basque entrepreneurs, the Sieurs Jean Hiriart and Pierre d'Aroupet. They had thirty-seven fishermen and six engagés, almost all from St. Jean-de-Luz. A rival merchant, the Sieur Larcher, employed thirty-nine men, also all Basques, in the fishery.[60]

The last of the coastal settlements was at the mouth of the River Inhabitants where some five Acadian families (thirty settlers in all) maintained themselves in 1752 with a little garden agriculture, stock-

58. AC, C11B-*8*, 55.   59. Pichon, *Genuine Letters*, pp. 46–47.
60. De la Roque census, pp. 33–34.

raising, and lumbering. There was a sawmill on a small island in the bay at the mouth of the river although the other settlers lived on the west (right) bank of the river where they were subject to flooding. Pichon observed that "the land produceth no sort of grain, except buck-wheat, oats, and rie: so that their riches consist intirely in cattle."[61] Since there were some thirty-eight head of cattle and only thirty people these were, indeed, comparative "riches" on Cape Breton Island.

THE INTERIOR — There were but two areas of interior settlement, at Grand Narrows, on the strait between the inner and outer expanses of Bras d'Or Lake, and at several places along the banks of Mira's lacustrine river. Until 1751, as far as we know, Bras d'Or's shores had known only the wigwams of the migratory Micmac. In August of that year a large number of Acadians came from the increasingly disturbed conditions on the Chignecto isthmus where the confrontation of French and English forts across the Missaguash River had taken place the previous year. When De la Roque visited them he counted 137; they appear to have entered by the St. Peters isthmus. Upon their arrival at Grand Narrows they had 240 head of cattle, 181 pigs, 173 sheep, and 17 horses; to De la Roque they reported only 30 cattle, 29 pigs, and no sheep or horses. He inferred that the rest had perished from lack of shelter and winter feed but some considerable number must have been killed for food and there was a substantial export of horses to the West Indies from Louisburg in 1752. They were "unanimous in reporting the ground as unsuitable for cultivation"[62] and all of them wanted to leave which, apparently, they did within the next year or two. There were lands of moderately good agricultural potential around the shores of Bras d'Or Lake, but these Acadians from the easily worked, dyked tidelands of the Bay of Fundy apparently were averse to clearing forests.

The other, and much older, interior settlement was that along the Mira River. To this area roads had been cut from Louisburg, originally to obtain the timber unavailable in the great stretches of muskeg, bare rock, swamp, and heath lands that dominated the eastern coastal areas and the immediate hinterland of Louisburg in particular. One ran north-northwest to approximately the present Albert Bridge area on

61. Pichon, *Genuine Letters*, p. 54.   62. De la Roque census, p. 38.

the lower river and another ran more or less directly west to the present Mira Lake (Grand Miré) with a continuation from the west shore of that lake to East Bay of Bras d'Or Lake. We have only scattered and incomplete information on settlements there before 1745 but the journal of a New Englander, James Gibson, reported on the discoveries of a scouting expedition to the Mira during the 1745 siege:

Sunday, [May] 26. This day, a scout, consisting of 153 men besides myself, marched to the west-north-west part of this island, which is twenty-five miles' distance, or thereabouts, from the grand battery. We found two fine farms upon a neck of land that extended near seven miles in length. The first we came to was a very handsome house, and had two large barns, well finished, that lay contiguous to it. Here, likewise, were two very large gardens; as also, some fields of corn of a considerable height, and other good lands thereto belonging, besides plenty of beach wood and fresh water. . . . The other house was a fine stone edifice, consisting of six rooms on a floor, all well finished. There was a fine walk before it, and two fine barns contiguous to it, with fine gardens and other appurtenances, besides several fine fields of wheat. In one of the barns there were fifteen loads of hay, and room sufficient for three-score horses and other cattle.[63]

Gibson's description of the location defies all attempts to pinpoint it on contemporary maps; it might well have been on the Upper Mira near the northward narrowing of present Mira Lake. However, there is every likelihood that there were a dozen or two residences between Louisburg Harbour, Main-à-Dieu Passage, and the lower Mira River (the sacking and burning of several are described by Gibson and others) and there may have been some (including the two described above) further up the river.

It was in the 1749–58 period, however, that the greatest development of the Mira area took place. In 1752 De la Roque's probably incomplete census counted twenty to twenty-five households (presumably on the lower river or near Lake Catalogne) not, however, including those farming the holdings of the Fathers of Charity who ran the hospital in Louisburg, and several plowmen for the farm of M. de la

63. James Gibson's journal was first published in London in 1745 as *A Journal of the Late Siege . . . against the French at Cape Breton . . . .* The above quotation is from a reprinting of it "by one of his descendants," published in Boston in 1847 as part of a small pamphlet entitled *A Boston Merchant of 1745: or, Incidents in the Life of James Gibson, a Gentleman Volunteer at the Expedition to Louisburg,* pp. 56–58. Both Sir John G. Bourinot in his "Cape Breton and its Memorials of the French Regime" (1891), p. 195, and Brown in *A History of the Island,* p. 222, quote parts of the above account with substantially different wording.

Borde, treasurer of the Colony. The count of 1753 increased the one hundred recorded in 1752 by one half, but included two villages which may have been missed the year before. Rouillé, at the end of a road to the upper Mira (north of present Gillis Mountain, "seven leagues from Louisburg on the Great Mira Road") was established in 1752 as a settlement of ex-soldiers, but had achieved no great success before its settlers were called upon to help defend Louisburg. It included twenty-one households but only eighteen married couples (only six with children), for a total of fifty-one people in 1753.

Some Germans, defectors from the "Foreign Protestants" at Halifax, also were established on the Mira, probably in the same year.[64] The "village des Allemands" included eight single men and eight married couples, four of whom had five children in all. It was situated about a quarter of a mile from Rouillé along the same road. The names in the nominal census included: Haas (two), Schumann, Chenk, Kuely, Bückler, Schattler, Colls, Pfisterer, Dubois, Gueff, Meyoffer, Geyler, Huff, and Müller, as entered by the recorder. In 1754, in a comment critical of Governor Raymond who sponsored these settlements, Surlaville indicates there were only twenty-two people at Rouillé, a reduction of more than a half in two years. A few Catholic Irish, possibly strays from Halifax or Newfoundland, were also vaguely reported for the area, but these do not appear in the nominal census of 1753.

LOUISBURG — Louisburg was the best known harbor, the center of the island's official and commercial life and one of the busiest of its fishing ports. Its civilian population grew slowly from some 700 in 1715 (118 men, 80 women, 170 children, 39 servants, and 300 fishermen) to 1,463 in 1737 (163 men, 157 women, 664 children, 229 servants, and 250 fishermen). Surlaville estimated the numbers at some 4,000[65] (mostly fishermen), and presumably including troops, in the early 1750's. This was after the population of the town, garrison, and

---

64. This group wrote several letters, abstracts of which have been preserved. One, signed by six heads of families, written from Cape Breton in 1752 (and perhaps before they had left Louisburg for the country) reported that: ". . . each of us has fifty acres of Good cleared land three years' provisions Tools Cloths, a bed and everything else given him." From the translated abstract, AC, NSA-*48*, 69. They were doubtless disappointed in the amount of land cleared, unless unstumped cutover resulting from the lumbering for Louisburg was so described.

65. Surlaville, *Les Derniers Jours*, p. 14.

environs had been evacuated by the British in 1745, and in part had returned from France and Canada in 1749. Interestingly, the officers (often married and living in the town) usually were included in the civilian population, as the noncommissioned officers and private soldiers never were. Between the 1720's and the 1750's, the latter varied from six to twenty-four companies which themselves, at full complement (as they rarely were), ranged in size from fifty to sixty-five men. In all likelihood Louisburg's garrison generally numbered from 500 to 1,000 men. In a dispatch of June 28, 1752, Raymond estimated fewer than 1,000 men and Surlaville thought there were only some 700.[66] Perhaps a total of about 3,500 for Louisburg in 1752 would be nearer the mark than the figure given in Table 7.1. This was more than double the total of 1,500 to 1,600 (allowing for vagueness) reported by De la Roque for the rest of the island. Since we know that he missed some (on the Mira River) and we may suppose that he missed substantial numbers of others (as at Ingonish), the fortress harbor may not have held two-thirds of the island's population, but almost certainly it held more than half.

McLennan's fully documented history of Louisburg gives many interesting references to the changing character of the town. We learn less about urban life and character from official correspondence and other documents than one might suppose except for regulations published from time to time. The shortage of building stone, which was needed for the fortifications and major buildings when it could be secured, meant that most of the buildings were of wood (*en gros rondins*) and a distinct fire hazard; at one time bark siding for the houses was forbidden from this fear. A regulation that no building should be higher than two *toises*[67] at the corner posts was widely ignored and a few private two-story structures had stone to the height of the first story, with the superstructure of wood. The restrictions had been promulgated to allow free movement for air to aid in the drying of fish, always a major occupation of the inhabitants in season. That Louisburg was always a major fishing port, and that the fishery was a dirty, stinking, generally noisome industry, created obvious problems. Cattle, horses, sheep, and goats were herded outside the walls or folded or stabled within, but the

66. Surlaville, *Les Derniers Jours*, p. 47.
67. Literally, this is two fathoms or twelve to thirteen English feet (one toise = 6 pieds = 6.4 English feet), but both La Morandière, *Histoire de la pêche*, and McLennan, *Louisbourg*, interpret the arrêt to have meant six to seven feet.

swine tended to run at large. The pigs did provide an informal sanitary service but they were a danger to poultry, drying fish, and even to small children.

The site of the town was on a peninsula between the harbor to the north and the open sea to the south (see Figure 7.1) and formed a triangle roughly 1,300 yards along the harbor, 500 yards along the sea, and some half-mile along its base on the landward side. The entrance to the harbor lay between this peninsula and another to the north and was partially blocked by islands, one of which was fortified. The harbor itself, trending northeast-southwest, was roughly two miles in length by a half-mile in width and had enough expanse over eight fathoms deep to shelter as many as three hundred ships of the line. The townsite, roughly a hundred acres in 1734, was surrounded by walls on all three sides. Those on the land side to the west were most formidable with an elaborate glacis, drymoat, and bastions. Despite the triangular shape of the peninsula, and a large and oddly-shaped lagoon included within it, a formally rectangular block system with some deviations on the harbor side was laid out to give the basic cadastral pattern. In 1734 there were four east–west streets more or less paralleling the harbor front and lagoon, and some nine or ten shorter north–south streets; some changes were made in the rebuilding between 1750 and 1758.

In this latter period the housing needs of the military and civilian officials, and some relatively large residences of merchants, took up much of the space; the working population was largely crowded into meaner dwellings along the shore of the harbor. There were at least two rather imposing structures, L'Hôpital and the Bastion du Roy, which towered over most of the others. The general descriptions and sketches extant stress the fortifications and such buildings. McLennan turned up only two accounts of individual houses. One held, on the ground floor, a kitchen, scullery, servants' room, diningroom, bedroom, and two small closets; in the attic were a study and some small bedrooms. Another house, fifty by fifteen feet in plan, had two principal rooms running the width of the house, some smaller rooms, a loft and a lean-to; there was a garden behind it sixty feet square and, in front, a court sixty by thirty feet. These two buildings were of wood and, presumably, were representative of the homes of such mercantile and bureaucratic bourgeoisie as the town boasted. Some of the officials must have had more elaborate quarters in town as they certainly had country places either on the northern side of the harbor or off the road that ran north-northwest by Catalogne Lake to the lower Mira River. On the whole the residential and commercial areas were unpretentious, not only in comparison with contemporary Quebec or Boston but even with newly founded Halifax (a fairer criterion).

The lists of occupations in the different censuses reflect the changing life of the fortress city. Only some four men were listed as merchants in 1724 as compared with twelve innkeepers, eight carpenters, seven masons, and a wide variety of other trades including pilots, surgeons, shoemakers, barbers, tailors, launderers, joiners, glaziers, coopers, and blacksmiths. Another census of 1734 showed that the number of inn-keepers had grown to approximately nineteen, while "marchands," "ne-gociants," and resident fishermen had increased to practically equal numbers. The most detailed inventory of occupations ever listed was that for the winter of 1749/50. Interestingly a sort of upper-class, or middle-class, group was listed first. Of some eighty-eight such families, seventy had servants. (There were 337 in these families employing about 183 servants, making a total of 520 in all.) Approximately twenty were merchants and clearly many more were involved in trad-ing. Of the rest of the population there were roughly 250 households and from 1,350 to 1,400 people. There was a very wide range of occupations, with "pêcheurs" comprising the greatest number.

The 1724 census asked for birthplaces of the 108 heads of families and the replies give evidence of a remarkable diversity of origin. Placentia understandably led the list, with ten; Paris, with nine and Canada, with eight were close behind. Other places or provinces listed (some are indeterminate because of spelling or illegibility) included: Limoges, six; St. Malo, St. Jean-de-Luz, and Armagnac five each; Nantes, Saintonge, and Bayonne four each; Bordeaux, Picardy, and Rochefort three each; Granville, Brittany, La Rochelle, Poitou, Nor-mandy, Dendaye, and Perigord two each; and, among the remainder, Auvergne, Angers, Guiennes, Avranches, Marennes, Avignon, Angou-lême, Toulouse, Constance, Besançon, St. Brieux, and Lyons. The Channel and Biscayan coasts are prominent but it was a representative population from all over France and neighboring states. It is interest-ing that there were no Acadian single men or heads of family known to be living in Louisburg at this time whereas some thirty heads of family in St. Peters had been born in the mainland Acadian settlements. However, we know of at least one Acadian bride, from Minas, and probably there were others.

THE ISLAND'S ECONOMY

The economy of Cape Breton was concentrated so much on the fishery, and there was so little other economic development, that outside supplies of all kinds, and particularly food, were always needed in large amounts for the garrison and workmen employed on the fortifications at Louisburg as well as for the support of the resident and seasonal fishermen.[68] For very good reasons immigration to develop the resources of soil, timber, and minerals failed to come from France, Canada, or Acadia.[69] Fundamental to the whole situation was the failure of agricultural development.

The Problems of Agriculture

Cape Breton Island as a whole, compared with the St. Lawrence Valley, Isle St-Jean, the Fundy dyked marshlands, or the Connecticut, Hudson, or lower Delaware river valleys in the early seventeenth century, had a relatively low agricultural potential. Yet it had qualities of terrain, vegetation, and climate (in a somewhat variegated pattern it is true) as favorable as those of the bulk of Nova Scotia's peninsula away from the Fundy slope and the shores of Northumberland Strait and, indeed, as good opportunities for agriculture as much of the land in both Canada and New England that was being farmed at the time. The evidence of the successful farming of the Highland Scottish immigrants of the nineteenth century, with a technology little advanced over that available to the Cape Breton settlers of the early eighteenth, suggests that the island could have supported many thousands of farming families and have established an agricultural and pastoral enterprise to feed the fortress and the fishery.

Yet agricultural activity and production remained so small as to be considered negligible throughout the period. A major factor was that most of the residents, most of the time, lived close to the sea along the eastern and southern coasts which were in every way the least suitable

68. For further discussion see A. H. Clark, "New England's Role in the Underdevelopment of Cape Breton Island during the French Regime, 1713–1758" (1965).

69. Detailed in *ibid.*, pp. 3–4.

farming areas. The view that agriculture was difficult if not impossible
was derived from generalizations based on knowledge of these coastal
areas. As early as 1713 it was stated unequivocally that "la plupart des
terres sont peu propre à la culture."[70] The southeastern coastal land
was rocky and swampy, the soil thin, and the vegetation poor. In one of
the first appraisals which suggested that good land was to be found
elsewhere on the island the agriculturally negative qualities of the
south and east were emphasized:

". . . dans la partie au nord de la Grande Baye de Labrador tous les bois y
sont francs et de constructions et la terre est capables d'être ensemencées
qu'avec quelque travail du défrichement et que au contraire toutte la partie
de l'Isle au Sud de la même Brador ne contient que de mauvais bois de sapins
et terres remplies de pierres, il est vray que cette moytié du Cap Breton est
plus propre que l'autre pour la pesche des morues . . . ."[71]

The prevailing cool, foggy, maritime weather, also least favorable in
the east, was not particularly suitable for wheat and for every warm
summer that would allow wheat to ripen there were several too cool. A
comment of 1741 pointed out that the French could not hope to
increase agricultural production on Cape Breton ". . . non seulement à
cause de la mauvaise qualité des terres, si on peut en admettre, mais
encore par l'intempérie du climat qui est continuellement brumeu pour
l'ordinaire pendant l'été, ce qui empêche les grains de murir. . . ."[72]
The French dietary preference for wheat and peas, neither of which
ever were to be really successful under the local conditions of soil and
climate, was clearly a major problem. Yet later experience was to show
that oats, barley, hay, and potatoes did well enough that they could
easily have been produced in quantities far beyond the needs of the
largest population ever present. Moreover, cattle, sheep, and swine
could thrive with the pasture and fodder the soil and climate would
support.

In the Mira area, where the major experiments in agriculture were
undertaken, hemp and flax as well as wheat, peas, and oats were
grown; vines were planted, and also plum, apple, and pear trees.
Neither there nor anywhere else, from our records, does it appear that
potatoes were even tried; these were wheat-eating people and, as in

70. AC, C11B-1(1), 13–21: an unsigned description of the island.
71. AC, C11B-1(2), 382: Louisburg, January 1715.
72. AC, C11B-23, 23: from Du Quesnel and Bigot, Louisburg, October 1741.

New France, they tended to become discouraged with grain farming if wheat was unsuccessful: "On n'a point l'usage du seigle qui rendroit le pain meilleur et donneroit des pailles pour le long ébergement [penning up] des bestiaux pendant l'hiver, d'ailleurs ces pailles feroient des fumiers pour amender les terres . . . ."[73] In fact there appears to have been very little manuring of the few arpents that were cleared and lack of straw no doubt was a hindrance. In any event there were few stables in which the livestock could have been housed for the winter.

The discussion of population and settlement has made abundantly clear that most of the residents were fishermen. The timetables of agriculture and the fishery so overlapped that the most a fisherman could attempt was a garden patch, a little rough grazing for a cow and a few sheep, the care of a few swine or perhaps a horse, or the cutting of wild hay on the marshy margins of the coastal lagoons. Most of the necessary farming labor, moreover, was supplied by the women and children. When the weather was fit for agricultural operations of any kind it was generally also suitable for the fishery. Like the fur trade the fishery provided both a more exciting and varied life than farming and a salable staple in constant demand. Even the fluctuations in the price of codfish offered the excitement of a gamble; there was always the chance of a bonanza season and a subsequent winter of comparative ease and affluence. An observer in the beleaguered fortress in 1758 summed it up very well. The fishery, he observed, ". . . being the most profitable occupation and the gain less uncertain, very few employed themselves in the cultivation of the country; indeed husbandry seemed to want a requisite time for the products to attain to their proper maturity . . . ."[74]

The fishery, trade, some vessel construction, and the demands of the fortress capital for wage labor, timber, firewood, limestone, building-stone, and bricks absorbed the residents' attention and time, and the generally unfavorable results of occasional farming experiments did nothing to distract them toward husbandry. Only with the arrival of Acadian refugees from Baie Verte and Tatamagouche, and the attempts to establish discharged soldiers and a few Germans along the Mira, was a major effort made at agricultural settlement. If it be argued that there was not enough time before 1758 to test these

73. AC, C11B-*10*, 23.
74. Don Antonio d'Ulloa, *A Voyage to South America* (1772), 2, 376.

attempts, it is also true that many of the "acclimatized" Acadians gave up after two or three years and the "veterans'" settlement was apparently a failure, although we know little about the others. Residents of Louisburg with capital established some moderately successful farms along the Mira River and between Louisburg, Catalogne Lake, and Mira Bay, but such provided no useful economic test of agricultural capabilities for ordinary settlers, and these farms could supply no significant fraction of the colony's needs. The attempt of one Draguon, the owner of the largest farm along the river, to sell his property to Drucourt, the last French governor, elicited the following comment from him: "Il est constant que la dépense indispensable pour cultiver la terre, au point d'en avoir du bled, excèdera, de beaucoup, la recette . . . ."[75]

Livestock fared better than crops and clearly contributed more to the economy, although there never were large numbers of animals and the single large importation (by Acadian refugees to Grand Narrows in 1751) largely disappeared after one winter. The marshy areas provided a good deal of summer forage. "Hitherto they have been able to reap no sort of grain; but they have a vast deal of meadow-lands in some parts of the woods, on mossy grounds, and on the banks of rivers, which produce excellent pasture."[76] Yet the possibilities of making hay to carry the livestock over the winter were so limited as to keep a sharp curb on cattle numbers. In fact, the De la Roque count of 1752 gave a total of only about 573 cattle, 232 swine, 230 sheep, 54 horses, and 10 goats for the entire island (see Table 7.2).

The livestock were very unevenly distributed. More than two-fifths of the cattle (243) were found in the Lennox Passage-St. Peters area. More than three-fifths of the horses (34) and sheep (154) were in Louisburg and its environs. Relative to population, Acadians at Sydney Harbour and Grand Narrows had the most swine (63). Some areas had surprisingly few animals: Gabarouse had only six swine, St. Ann but two cows, Little Bras d'Or a cow, a bull, and three goats, Main-à-Dieu an ox, a cow, and a calf, Baleine one cow and seven sheep, and the Lorraines but four sheep. Southwest of Louisburg there were no sheep; in Louisburg and locations north to Sydney Harbour sheep outnumbered swine. In the Acadian settlements the ratio of sheep to swine was about 1 : 3 (although the sheep clearly had suffered severely

75. Surlaville, *Les Derniers Jours*, p. 125.
76. Pichon, *Genuine Letters*, p. 15.

TABLE 7.2 *Livestock recorded in the De la Roque census of 1752*

Place	Undifferentiated cattle	Oxen	Heifers and cows	Calves	Bulls	Goats	Horses	Swine	Sheep
Gabarouse	–	–	–	–	–	–	–	6	–
St. Esprit	–	–	10	3	–	–	2	–	–
L'Ardoise	18	4	17	5	1	–	4	14	–
St. Peters	25	39	63	8	2	–	3	22	–
Isle Madame (north coast)	–	8	28	16	–	–	1	7	–
Petit-de-Grat	–	3	12	–	1	–	–	1	–
R. Inhabitants	–	12	23	1	2	–	1	9	–
Chapel Island*	–	1	2	–	–	–	1	2	6
Grand Narrows	–	15	13	2	–	–	–	29	10
St. Ann	–	–	2	–	–	–	–	–	–
Little Bras d'Or	–	–	1	–	1	3	–	–	–
Spanish Bay	–	17	26	7	–	4	–	34	11
Lingan	–	8	14	–	–	–	–	–	–
Port Morien	–	13	23	2	–	–	7	13	17
Mira	–	2	24	10	2	3	2	8	15
Scatarie I.	–	–	3	1	–	–	–	–	6
Main-à-Dieu	–	1	1	1	–	–	–	–	–
Baleine	–	–	1	–	–	–	–	–	7
Lorraine	–	–	–	–	–	–	–	–	4
Louisburg and environs	79	–	–	–	–	–	34	87	154
Total	122	123	263	56	9	10	54	232	230

* On Bras d'Or Lake near St. Peters.

Source: Joseph, Sieur de la Roque, "Tour of Inspection made by the Sieur de la Roque," AC *Report for 1905* (1906), pp. 3–172.

during the previous winter). It would be interesting to know if the
livestock numbers had been substantially greater before 1745 and if
these figures for 1752 represent only the rather haphazard beginnings
of a recovery which would have started with the repatriation of 1749.

At any rate, even though conditions for stock raising seemed greatly
superior to those for grain farming in Cape Breton, at least for the
summer season, the wintering problem and the need to use the animals
for food if the people were to survive may have kept the numbers
small. The experience of the Acadians who wintered at Grand Narrows
in 1751/52 is instructive. Assuming that the 1752 data for both Grand
Narrows and for the several localities around Spanish Bay all apply to
this group, then, from August until the next March the numbers of
livestock were diminished as shown on Table 7.3. The horses and sheep
seem to have suffered most severely; perhaps the Acadians were holding on to the cows and sows as "capital" with which to reestablish
themselves in Acadia. Moreover we know that there was a good demand in Louisburg for horses for the West Indies. Also cattle and swine
could survive the winter with poor shelter better than could sheep and
they were less likely victims of wolves and bears. However it is also
possible that we are making too much of the winter's perils. Most of
the Acadians gave up and returned to their Fundy homelands very
soon thereafter and perhaps they had decided to do so before De la
Roque visited them and simply had sold their livestock in a good
market knowing that they could replace them at much lower prices
back home in Minas or Chignecto.

Our fullest source of comments on agriculture is perhaps biased; it
consists of Surlaville's notes attached to copies of official correspondence of the early fifties, especially of Governor le Comte de Raymond.[77] Raymond was an irrepressible enthusiast for agricultural
settlement who sincerely believed that the island could develop a self-
sufficient agriculture, and Surlaville was dubious. In discussing Raymond's agricultural efforts and optimism, Drucourt (his successor as
governor, 1754–58) observed: "Comme il l'a fait dans ses mémoires,
que le terrain de l'Isle Royalle est susceptible de production de touts
grains, et que mesme, elle se peut fournir elle-mesme assés pour se
passer de l'étranger, voilà ce qui est reconnu faux depuis trente-cinq
ans que l'on en a fait des essais et toujours inutilement."[78]

77. Surlaville, *Les Derniers Jours.*   78. *Ibid.*, p. 125.

TABLE 7.3 *Decline in numbers of livestock owned by Acadian immigrants to Cape Breton over the winter 1751/52*

Livestock	August 1751	March 1752	
		Grand Narrows and Spanish Bay	All Acadians*
Cattle	230	80	173
Sheep	173	21	82
Swine	181	63	83
Horses	17	0	2
Goats	0	4	4

* The last column includes all livestock owned by all who might be interpreted as being Acadians.
Source: See Table 7.2.

The Fishery[79]

Of the three major bases of the island's economy—trade, government expenditure, and the fishery—the last was the most important. It had been the principal reason why the French retained Cape Breton in 1713 and subsequently bargained so hard (and successfully) for its return in 1748.

The fishery was for cod and was similar to that described for the nearby Canso area, for the same period, in Chapter 6. At first it was almost entirely a boat (shallop) fishery prosecuted by residents or visiting ships relatively close inshore, but a schooner fishery which

79. The basic sources are those used throughout this chapter: the C11B series of the Archives des Colonies held by the Archives Nationales in Paris, largely copied in the Public Archives of Canada, series C11B. The originals have been used extensively by La Morandière in *Histoire de la pêche*. There are occasional materials in the C11A series and in the various municipal archives of the ports from which the fishing ships came. Also, there are useful references in the Public Record Office (London) holdings, especially the CO 217 series, which are largely copied in the AC, NSA series. Harold A. Innis has used the AC holdings extensively both in appropriate sections of *The Cod Fisheries: The History of an International Economy* (1954), and in "Cape Breton and the French Regime" (1935). McLennan, *Louisbourg*, has many observations on the fishery. I have been able to check most of the documentary sources used and have found some additional interesting material not used by any of the above.

exploited the more distant banks grew up in the 1720's and became increasingly more important. For the purposes of this chapter the sloop-rigged vessels (*batteaux*) and those with schooner-rigs (*goélettes*), roughly in the same size range and functionally indistinguishable, are both included as "schooners."[80]

Whether caught by schooner or shallop, the fish were dried ("made" or "cured") on beaches or "flakes," usually a matter of some weeks. The labor was divided between the fishermen and a shore crew. In the case of the shallop fishery the fish were brought in daily, as a rule, and headed, cleaned, and salted on shore. On schooners the heading, cleaning, and initial salting took place on board. The drying or curing procedure was similar in either case although the schooner fish usually had to be washed first to remove excess salt. The longer the fish remained in salt before air curing began the less attractive they tended to become for the premium markets for dry fish in the Mediterranean. The Paris market had developed a taste for the "green" fish in the sixteenth and seventeenth centuries as these were made by vessels from France fishing on the banks and returning to cure the fish in France, but this kind of fish—larger, darker in color, and necessarily much more heavily impregnated with salt—brought a significantly lower price as the eighteenth century progressed than the small, white, lightly salted product of the inshore dry fishery. That of the schooners, as in Canso and New England at the same period, was a product somewhat less attractive but making up in quantity for the lower price per quintal.

Ordinarily a schooner produced about two and a half times as much fish in a season as did a shallop. A schooner had a crew of five men;

---

80. The *chaloupe* was a vessel of normally five to six tons burden, a rugged if undecked vessel, and manned by a crew of three. It rarely went far from shore but had to be able to survive quite severe storms with high waves. The origin of the *goélette*, or schooner—a two-masted, lateen-rigged vessel of twenty to fifty tons (perhaps most usually of twenty-five or thirty tons)—is uncertain; it may have been developed in Bermuda. But it was from New England that the schooner fishery spread to Newfoundland, Cape Breton, Canso, and other parts of Nova Scotia's southern coast, and perhaps most of the vessels used even in Cape Breton were built in New England. There is some confusion at first as to what a schooner was. Sometimes "sloop" (which is how I have translated *batteau*), technically a one-masted vessel, may have meant the same thing. In the earliest years both *charroys* (heavy, lumbering vessels of thirty feet in length, so that the word might be translated as "barge") and brigantines of forty to fifty tons were used in fishing, but must have been replaced rapidly by the more maneuverable schooners or sloops.

initially there were more but the procedure of managing with five was soon learned from New England. A shallop operation ordinarily involved two shallops fishing (with a boatmaster and crew of two each) and a shore team of four (a header and cleaner, a salter, a boy-of-all-work, and a beachmaster who tended the drying fish). The shore crew was necessary for the constant care of the curing fish, which had to be turned frequently to avoid wetting by rain or dew or "burning" from too much sun. The schooners needed shore crews too; even if the fish were already cleaned and salted they had to be washed and then tended as did the shallop catches. Two shallops (the catch of one would not support a shore crew) required more men than a schooner, and produced less fish, but the fish was often of better quality and the investment in equipment was less.

The fishery was markedly seasonal. The main season ran from April to the end of September when the residents and visiting French ships competed for cod both inshore and on the banks. This was followed by a very chancy winter fishery which was pursued by the residents from mid-November through January.[81] It was conducted from coves and harbors all along the east and south coasts from Cape North to the Strait of Canso although usually there was not much between Ingonish and Little Bras d'Or.

The fishing enterprise quickly became a competition between local residents and entrepreneurs who sent out ships from France. Unlike the situation in the sixteenth and seventeenth centuries, these vessels rarely engaged in the fishery directly (i.e., by handlines over the side). They could hardly risk anchoring out over the banks and they were too inefficient inshore. They used exactly the same equipment as the residents: either shallops or schooners. The competition thus was technically, if not in ultimate resources, on equal terms. The ships ordinarily anchored in or near the cove or harbor from which their small vessels were operating but sometimes they stayed at Louisburg (no doubt for such amenities of metropolitan life as the capital provided).

In terms of the geography of settlement and economic enterprise on Cape Breton Island during the French regime the position of the residents in competition with the fishing ships from France is of major importance. Since they used the same small vessels and other equip-

81. This was *la pêche d'automne*. It is described at length in AC, C11B-*21*, 208–29: "Mémoire sur les habitants de L'Isle Royale," by Le Normant de Mézy, March 1739.

ment, and often competed for the same labor, it would have been very hard to distinguish the two by observation in any given cove during any given summer. But the residents were Cape Bretoners. They could not move easily as seasonally, or from year to year, the fish concentrated over different offshore banks or along different sections of the shoreline. Moreover, they stayed on the island; what they earned also remained for the local economy; and, at least after the end of the winter fishery in mid-January, they were the only inhabitants of most of the outports.

The ships from France were usually classified by the record-keepers at Louisburg as "for trade only," "for trade and fishery," or "for fishery only." The classifications were loose. Some of the ships supposed to have been for trade only are believed to have hired shallops and schooners to fish for them; some of the ships ostensibly in the area to fish apparently did not do so. Ships of any of these categories could, and did, take cargoes of fish back to Europe. The ships had an initial advantage over the residents in terms of resources and lines of credit, and few residents had the means to engage in the schooner fishery to the banks when schooners were introduced in the 1720's. Initially the ships depended on the inshore fishery with shallops too, but they shifted more rapidly to an emphasis on schooners. As time went on the residents engrossed an ever larger proportion of the shallop fishery and the ships coming from France turned more and more to the use of schooners, but throughout the period some ships continued to engage in the inshore shallop fishery and the residents, especially in Louisburg, acquired some schooners.

The fishery developed very rapidly after the move from Placentia in 1713 and 1714. In 1716 there were some two thousand fishermen, about half employed by residents and about half from crews of visiting ships, each group employing some two hundred shallops.[82] Without

82. It would be tedious to cite the documents or other sources for each figure mentioned in what follows: the chief sources for all are the C11B series and the censuses in G1-467, and at key points the specific document will be noted. As in the cases of Newfoundland and Canso there are many statistical summaries for individual years, although rarely is exactly the same kind and variety of information given for any two years in a row. The French did not use a standard "Heads of Inquiry" form as did the British Board of Trade. Among the categories included one place or another were: numbers of fishing ships, of trading or sack ships, of combined trading and fishing ships, of hands on the ships, the region or country (often individual ports) from which the ships came, and the harbors or coves where the

regard to the changing value of money, the fishery produced from roughly 1,500,000 to 3,500,000 livres worth a year, or approximately 100,000 to 175,000 quintals of dried fish. The best years were from the mid-1720's through the mid-1730's. The dislocations of open or undeclared war seriously reduced the amount in the 1740's and 1750's and of course there was a complete hiatus in 1746, 1747, and 1748. Nevertheless nearly 2,000,000 livres worth was produced in 1743 and just over that amount in 1753. The number of ships coming from France for the fishery each year was usually between forty and sixty; a peak of seventy-three (by the records) was reached in 1739, although the largest figure for total money return was of 3,500,185 livres in 1733.

From as early as 1718 through the second and third decades of the century, the residents operated, on the average, a total of about three hundred shallops each year. The peak year in numbers was 1731, with 366, and the size of their shallop fleet did not start to tail off rapidly until the early 1740's. The number of shallops operated by the fishing ships, on the other hand, fluctuated much more widely and generally was much smaller. After 1720 they employed as many as one hundred shallops in only one year, and in four different years they used fewer than thirty.

Most years the total catch from shallops (generally more than two hundred quintals per boat) averaged more than 100,000 quintals. The best year of record was 1731 when 366 shallops of the residents and seventy-eight operated by ships produced 138,000 quintals (98,000 in the regular season and 40,000 in the winter season). The ship-sponsored fishery continued to be important, however, as the ships moved more rapidly than the residents to the use of schooners which averaged about five hundred quintals of fish each season. But with the general decline of the fishery in the early 1740's, the overall use of schooners declined more rapidly than did that of shallops. The chief schooner users, the ships, could withdraw from the fishery quite easily simply by not setting out from France, or by moving to some other fishing area, but the residents had little alternative but to keep on fishing even when prices were low.

----

ships made their headquarters; also, the numbers of shallops, sloops, or schooners employed by the ships, of shallops and schooners used by the residents, and of hands employed by the residents; also, the locations of the residents, and the amounts of fish produced, variously broken down, for particular years.

Commonly, the total shallop fishery produced two to five times the amount of fish brought in and cured by the schooners. The highest catches from schooners and shallops combined were recorded in the early 1730's: 165,000 to 170,000 quintals a year. By 1740 the figure had dropped to 124,000 and, by 1744, to 69,000.[83]

The ships came from many French ports and there were interesting shifts during the period, but Norman, Breton, and Basque ports predominated. Most years there were many vessels from Canada and the French West Indies but the degree to which colonial vessels, often schooners, other than those definitely belonging to Cape Breton, participated in the fishery is not always clear.[84]

There was an initial reluctance, by those who had been using Plaisance as a base, to shift to Cape Breton; the latter was seen chiefly as a dry shore-fishery area and many of the French vessels were oriented toward the Paris market which, by long habit, had developed a preference for the larger darker and saltier green fish produced by fishing on the banks. But the higher world prices for the dry fish prevailed and the shift was made; good seasons in 1714 and 1717 helped to quiet the misgivings. In 1716 there were eleven Basque vessels (chiefly from St. Jean-de-Luz and Bayonne), five from Granville, one from Nantes, and seven or eight from St. Malo. In 1717, forty-four ships came from France, three from Canada, and four from the West Indies. The last seven vessels and twenty-four of the French ships made their headquarters at Louisburg, six summered in the Isle Madame area, two at Ingonish, and the rest in coves more or less "suburban" to Louisburg;

83. For a general review of the data see Innis, "Cape Breton," pp. 59–61. These figures were checked in detail for 1737, 1738, and 1739 in AC, C11B-*20*, 134, 243; C11B-*21*, 151; and C11B-*26*, 100–101, and some discrepancies were noted so the figures should be used with caution.

84. In the peak year of 1733 there were sixty French ships from the following ports: St. Jean-de-Luz, 16; St. Malo, 16; Bayonne, 8; Nantes, 6; Morlaix, 3; La Rochelle, 3; Marennes, 2; Granville, 2; Les Sables d'Olonne, 2; Bordeaux, 1; and Marseilles, 1. AdC, C11B-*14*, fol. 232. Quoted in La Morandière, *Histoire de la pêche*, 2, 678. Also in 1733 there were 22 ships from the French West Indies, 10 from Quebec, and 32 from New England recorded. In 1753, of 273 ships (of actual record) arriving in the island, 43 were from France: St. Malo, 10; Bayonne and St. Jean-de-Luz, 9; Bordeaux, 8; La Rochelle, 6; Les Sables d'Olonne, 4; Nantes, 2; Dunkirk, 2; Lorient, 1; and Cherbourg, 1. In addition 17 came from Canada, 57 from the French West Indies, and 156 from New England. AdC, C11B-*33*, fol. 495, quoted in La Morandière, *Histoire de la pêche*, 2, 687.

TABLE 7.4   *The fishery in Cape Breton in 1727*

Location	Location of ships from France		Fishing undertaken by French ships		Fishing undertaken by residents	
	In trade only	In trade and fishery	Shallops employed	Schooners employed	Shallops employed	Schooners employed
North coast						
Ingonish*	9	4	10	3	59	7
St. Ann	–	1	–	1	–	–
Louisburg hinterland						
Lingan	–	–	2	–	13	–
Scatarie I.	–	2	7	–	18	–
Baleine	–	1	6	–	19	–
Lorraine	–	–	–	–	23	–
Louisburg*	18	23	20	39	30	10
South coast						
Fourchu	–	–	–	–	19	–
St. Esprit	–	–	10	–	33	–
Michaud	–	–	–	–	6	–
Petit-de-Grat	–	3	14	–	19	1
St. Peters*	–	–	–	–	–	2
Total	27	34	69	43	239	20

* In addition to the French ships there were 29 from Canada (5 to Ingonish, 23 to Louisburg, and 1 to St. Peters), 12 from the West Indies (11 to Louisburg and 1 to Ingonish) and 21 from New England (20 to Louisburg and 1 to Ingonish). There is no hard information as to which were trading only and which also engaged in the fishery. It is believed that the North American ships were small and largely traders. Whatever fish they caught may not have been included in the Cape Breton totals.

Source: AC, C11B-*9*, 67.

three in Gabarouse Bay, three at Baleine, two at Main-à-Dieu, and four on Scatarie Island.⁵⁵ Although the inhabitants were much more widely scattered, the ships from France continued to concentrate in the three areas of Ingonish, the Louisburg region from Gabarouse to Mira bays, and the coves of Isle Madame to the south.

There is no such thing as a "typical" year, but detailed information for 1727, 1733, and 1744, although not complete or comparable in all categories, may serve to give a view of the locational pattern of the

85. AC,C11B-*1*(2), 276–81.

TABLE 7.5   *The fishery in Cape Breton in 1733*

| | Fishing undertaken by French ships | | Fishing undertaken by residents | | |
| | | | Summer | | Winter |
	Shallops employed	Schooners employed	Shallops employed	Schooners employed	Shallops* employed
North coast					
Aspy	14	–	–	–	–
Nagasson(?)	–	–	–	–	4
Ingonish	2	–	54	5	72
Isle d'Orléans (also Ingonish?)	–	–	14	3	12
Louisburg hinterland					
Little Bras d'Or	–	–	–	–	24
Lingan	–	–	8	–	2
Scatarie I.	–	1	23	10	4
Baleine	14	1	30	–	24
Lorraine	4	–	41	–	11
Louisburg	10	55	26	13	18
South coast					
Fourchu	–	–	31	–	32
St. Esprit	–	–	46	–	14
Michaud	–	–	6	–	4
Petit-de-Grat	9	4	17	–	8
Total	53	61	296	31	229†

* There were no schooners in the winter fishery.
† The document shows a total of 233 but the individual entries give this total.
Source: AC, C11B-*14*, 162.

fishery (see Tables 7.4, 7.5, 7.6). We may divide the coves and harbors into three sections: (1) those north of St. Ann; (2) those from Little Bras d'Or to Gabarouse Bay (the Louisburg hinterland); and (3) those along the south coast. On the basis of converting one schooner to two and one-half shallops in terms of fishing efficiency (500 to 750 quintals per year as against 200 to 300), the fishing enterprise was divided between the French ships and the residents of Cape Breton in the three years as shown on Table 7.7.

Ingonish was the principal fishing port outside of Louisburg, reaching a peak of ninety-one shore-based shallops in 1731. Peak numbers

TABLE 7.6   *The fishery in Cape Breton in 1744*

Location	Ships from France		Fishing under-taken by French ships		Fishing under-taken by residents	
	In trade and fishery	Fishing only	Shal-lops em-ployed	Schoon-ers em-ployed	Shal-lops em-ployed	Schoon-ers em-ployed
North						
Ingonish	4	–	–	–	29	–
St. Ann	–	–	–	–	–	–
Louisburg hinterland						
Little Bras d'Or	–	–	–	–	–	–
Lingan	–	–	–	–	8	–
Scatarie I.	–	–	–	–	10	–
Baleine	–	–	8	–	27	–
Little Lorraine	–	–	–	–	34	–
Louisburg*	15	14	2	28	20	6
South coast						
Fourchu	–	–	2†	–	13	–
St. Esprit	–	–	–	–	15	–
Michaud	–	–	–	–	3	–
Petit-de-Grat	–	–	–	–	20	–
St. Peters	–	–	–	–	–	–
Total	19	14	12	28	179	6

* In addition 36 ships had come to Louisburg to trade, 12 each from Canada, the West Indies, and Acadia, and 28 prizes, captured from the English, had been brought to Louisburg.

† No doubt employed by a ship stationed at Louisburg.

Source: AC, C11B-*26*, 100–101.

of shallops operated in the fishery were reached in other places in the years indicated in Table 7.8. Louisburg itself stood out far beyond even Ingonish. It usually had more than a third of the total fishery and the overwhelming majority of all schooners employed by residents and ships (forty-seven of sixty-seven, sixty-one of ninety-two, and twenty-eight of thirty-four) in the three years cited.

As in Newfoundland, the master of the first ship to arrive in a cove became "admiral" for the season, assigning portions of the beach to later comers. But unlike Newfoundland of the same period, in Cape Breton, residents had legally defensible rights to specified portions of

TABLE 7.7   *The regional distribution of the fishing enterprise on Cape Breton in terms of shallop units employed (one schooner equated to two and one-half shallop units)*

Region	1727 French ships	1727 Residents	1733 French ships	1733 Residents	1744 French ships	1744 Residents
	SHALLOP UNITS EMPLOYED					
North coast	20	76.5	16	88	0	29
Louisburg hinterland	142.5	128	170.5	185.5	80	114
South coast	24	84.5	19	100	2	51
Total	186.5	289	205.5	373.5	82	194
	PERCENTAGE OF SHALLOP UNITS EMPLOYED					
North coast	10.7	26.5	7.8	23.5	0	15.0
South coast	12.8	29.2	9.2	26.7	2.4	26.3
North and South	23.5	55.7	17.0	50.2	2.4	41.3
Louisburg hinterland	76.5	44.3	83.0	49.8	97.6	58.7
	100.0	100.0	100.0	100.0	100.0	100.0
Ratio of resident to French ships, in shallop units	1.5 : 1		1.8 : 1		2.4 : 1	

Source: Calculated by the author from scattered data in the AC, series C11B series, especially: C11B-*9*, 67; C11B-*14*, 162; and C11B-*26*, 100-101.

TABLE 7.8   *Peak years for number of shallops operating in Cape Breton ports other than Louisburg*

Location	Number of Shallops	Year
Ingonish	91	1731
Lingan	17	1726
Scatarie I.	27	1730
Baleine	45	1729
Lorraine	39	1729
Fourchu	34	1731
St. Esprit	46	1733
Petit-de-Grat	19	1729

Source: Harold A. Innis, "Cape Breton and the French Regime" (1935), p. 58.

the beaches. A series of *ordonnances* and *arrêts* makes clear, however, that the residents had such priorities only if they used them themselves for fishing, and that certain areas were reserved for French ships.[86]

The requirement of two shallops to make a shore-fishing operation feasible meant a need for ten men as a minimum for any resident fishery entrepreneur and even if he headed the shore crew as beach-master and had the help of some grown sons, he had to employ a good deal of seasonal labor. Most of this came from France and the individuals became engagés of a habitant or of a ship's master for a season or for a period of up to three years. Those who wintered in the island provided the needed labor for the *pêche d'automne.* Labor shortages led to severe competition for engagés among the habitants themselves and between them and the ships. The use of alcohol to get them to sign on (some signed as many as three contracts for the same season) and their jumping contracts to get higher wages, led to a good deal of litigation, and a number of official arrêts designed to stop abuses, which are reported in the documents. Indeed spiraling wages (including hidden "fringe benefits" like the payment of passages to and from France) threatened the stability of the fishery and led to severe regulations, although the periodic reissue of essentially the same rules, and even specified wages for individual duties, suggests that the problem was never fully controlled.[87]

With all the difficulties, the persistence of the resident shallop fishery indicates that it provided a living at least. If many habitants fell

---

86. La Morandière, *Histoire de la pêche, 2,* 669–71, has a detailed discussion of the problem.

87. See La Morandière, *Histoire de la pêche, 2,* 672–76. A memoir of March 1739 in AdC, C11B-*21,* fol. 297, shows how narrow the margin could be for a two-shallop operation (q = quintals of dry cod):

Wages for 2 maîtres de chaloupe	@ 38 q. =	76 q.
" " 4 fishermen	@ 36	= 144
" " 1 beachmaster	@ 45	= 45
" " 1 salter	@ 24	= 24
" " 1 header (and cleaner?)	@ 20	= 20
" " 1 garçon ou mousse	@ 18	= 18
Passage from France of 8 men	@ 4	= 32
Provisions for 10 men		72
Equipment and salt for 2 shallops		157
Total costs		588 q.

If the normal catch was no more than 300 quintals per shallop, the profit at best was only 12 quintals (which, at 10 or 12 livres per quintal, yields only 120 to 150 livres) and it was often reckoned at only 200 quintals. However the resident usually

inextricably in debt to merchants and suppliers of food, salt, and gear, others prospered to the extent of acquiring schooners which allowed a greater profit in season and could be used for coasting trade (cabotage) and voyages to the West Indies or even France in the off season. And there is no doubt that the residents engrossed ever more of the total catch. The vessels from France became increasingly only trading or sack ships. In 1739, of fifty-four ships from France, twenty-one engaged in trade only and of the thirty-three others perhaps only twenty were heavily involved in the fishery. Cod was their preferred return cargo, however, and at an average of two thousand quintals per vessel it required anywhere from fifty to eighty ships to take the annual cod harvest back to Europe.

The great year-to-year fluctuations in success in the fishery remind one of the vicissitudes of the fur trade of Canada. A few examples from official correspondence may serve to illustrate the problems that contributed to those ups and downs. In 1716 the merchants were alarmed by taxes imposed to support the garrison and many fewer ships came from France. In 1724 an excellent summer fishery at Louisburg and Scatarie faded out in the autumn whereas Ingonish had one of its best winter fisheries, suggesting an aberrant migration of the cod.[88] In 1726 Le Normant and St-Ovide complained of losses from November storms.[89] A good fishery faced a poor market in 1733 and much of the cod remained unsold.[90] In the same year both St-Ovide and Levasseur reported many fewer ships coming from France and lower prices for cod as a result of poorer markets in Europe.[91] Two years later an unusually difficult season of rain and fog seriously interfered with both fishing and curing.[92] In 1742, Du Quesnel wrote of poor fishing and the high cost of supplies.[93]

Moreover, the fishing industry itself provided a wide variety of complaints. It was alleged that: schooners fishing twelve to fifteen miles offshore threw offal overboard and kept the cod from coming in; there were too many small boats competing in some areas; wages were

was his own beachmaster and if he obeyed the law he did not pay passage money, so perhaps a fair living was possible. It is interesting that a quintal of cod was, in fact, the chief practical monetary standard of the colony.

88. AC, C11B-7, 96.   89. AC, C11B-8, 20.   90. AC, C11B-14, 273.
91. AC, C11B-14, 108–9.
92. AC, C11B-17, 38: St-Ovide to the Minister, Louisburg, August 1735.
93. AC, C11B-24, 65.

excessively high; prices of provisions and supplies were out of balance with prices received; fishermen staked by one merchant sold their cod to others for cash; the governor or commandant bought up supplies on his own account and sold them at monopoly prices; liquor was used to suborn fishermen from their contracts or was so freely available it served to demoralize them; and so on—the list of such laments, preserved in the records, is a long one.[94]

In conclusion, a geographical view of the fishery of Cape Breton Island in the first half of the eighteenth century should emphasize that its location, in scattered harbors and coves along the Atlantic coast, generally with immediate hinterlands in which the soil was relatively poor, the vegetation often scrubby, and the climate at its dampest and foggiest, certainly inhibited the fishermen, who formed the chief civilian population outside of Louisburg, from branching out into plant and animal husbandry. It further suggests that if each possible beach in each possible cove, each year, had been used to its fullest, Cape Breton well might have supported several times the number of resident fishermen that it did and have yielded an income to France that might have overcome the chronic neglect with which the island was treated in most years of peace.

Commerce and Supplies[95]

Perhaps the major handicap of Cape Breton's economy throughout most of the French regime was the chronic shortage of supplies, particularly of food. A report of 1738 illustrates the complaints that were reiterated monotonously: ". . . la dizette de vivres dont la colonie a été affligé depuis deux ans et celles auxquelles elle a été sujette cy devant, ont aporté une préjudice nottable au commerce et à l'établissement de l'isle . . . ."[96] Earlier complaints had found the garrison on short rations, fishermen unable to work in the winter (or even the summer

94. See esp. AC, C11B-*20*, 207–11: 1738, and C11B-*21*, 90–96, 208–29: 1738.
95. There is a rather full discussion of this problem in Innis, "Cape Breton," and many of the relevant sections of pertinent documents are printed in Harold A. Innis, ed. *Select Documents in Canadian Economic History, 1497–1783* (1929). A summary discussion of the significance of the problem in relation to New England can be found in Clark, "New England's Role."
96. AC, C11B-*20*, 45. Bourville and Le Normant, Louisburg, October 1748.

fishery), and even of engagés returning to France.[97] In 1742 du Quesnel addressed the same problem in terms of the resulting high prices:
"Les vivres sont icy au dessus de dix à douze louis le quintal, il n'est pas
possible que la colonie subsiste et l'habitant est sans crédit, sans
resources, et dès qu'il est un pais en debet, il ne peut pas s'en relever."[98]
The year 1742 was one of the worst: in May, June, and July sailors on
ships at Louisburg and other harbors were limited to one pound of
bread a day.[99]

Since agriculture had failed, the supplies could come only from
France, Canada, Acadia, or (usually illegally) from New England.[100]
There were a number of difficulties associated with direct supplies from
France. The French ships complained that they faced ruinous competition from New England which had the support of the colonial
officials.[101] On the other hand the colonial officials consistently complained that the supplies from France were inadequate,[102] and, moreover, despite the needs for foodstuffs and basic supplies (bread and
biscuits in particular), French vessels tended to bring cargoes more
profitable to their owners.[103] At one point it was averred that the ships
had not even brought enough for their own needs and bought from the
colony's inadequate stores for the return trip to France.[104] The inhabitants complained in 1738 that colonial officials were buying up supplies
from the French ships and withholding them until prices rose[105] and the
Canadians complained that the French ships sometimes held up sup-

97. See AC, C11B-3, 34: 1718; C11B-14, 61: 1733; and C11B-19, 50: 1737, for
example.
98.   AC, C11B-24, 65.
99. AdC, C11B-38, fol. 39, quoted in La Morandière, Histoire de la pêche, 2, 664.
100. McLennan has assembled records of shipping at Louisburg for fourteen
years of the period from 1726 to 1743. In those selected years there was a total of
901 vessels arriving from France, with a high of 84 in 1731 and a low of 43 in 1737.
Of 275 from Canada the range was from 31 in 1730 and 1734 to 6 in 1737; a total
of 271 from the French West Indies ranged from 9 in 1727 to 32 in 1743. New
England's reported inbound ships numbered 623, rising from 22 in 1727 to 78 in
1743. The secular trend was for shipping from France and Canada to decrease and
for that from Acadia and New England to increase. McLennan, Louisbourg,
appendix 5, p. 382.
101. AC, C11B-20, 25–27: Louisburg, September 1727. For the period 1750 to
1753 see AC, C11C-9, 236–43.
102. AC, C11B-19, 50: Louisburg, 1737, provides an example.
103. AC, C11B-19, 109, 112: Louisburg, 1737.
104. AC, C11B-10, 56: 1728.
105. AC, C11B-20, 207–17: a long petition, of twenty-one resident fishermen,
sent from Louisburg in 1738. Duvivier was singled out as a major culprit.

plies for a better price and later were forced to throw them on the market forcing prices down so that the Canadians lost money.[106]

Apparently there was a variety of reasons why Canada was an unreliable source of supply. There were few local merchants able to buy the cargoes on the arrival of the Canadian ships, no adequate warehouses where cargoes might be stored, and ship's captains were discouraged by the slow process of disposing of cargoes to the perennially indigent inhabitants.[107] Further, they objected to competition from New England which sometimes made prices in Louisburg lower than in Quebec itself.[108] The late opening of the St. Lawrence River contributed to late arrival of vessels from Quebec and a poorer competitive position with respect to France and New England. The quality of supplies from Quebec, notably flour, was criticized.[109] On at least one occasion Du Quesnel and Bigot had sent to New England for flour on a request from Hocquart, the flour to be forwarded to Canada to relieve an expected shortage there.[110]

Nevertheless substantial supplies did come from Canada. Between 1726 and 1743 there were two years when more than thirty vessels arrived therefrom at Louisburg, and five years in which from twenty to thirty came (although the trend was for decreasing numbers as time went on).[111]

In 1726, of forty-one vessels clearing from Quebec, twenty-six were destined for Cape Breton (indeed, ten were owned there). Their cargoes were chiefly food (biscuits, flour, peas, beans, and a little meat), quite a lot of tobacco, and some lumber. In 1728, of the same number of vessels clearing Quebec (forty-one), thirty-two sailed for Cape Breton; in 1729 the proportion was twenty-three out of thirty-seven. We have a much more detailed breakdown of cargoes for the nineteen vessels that arrived in 1732 from Quebec. All brought wheat flour and dried white peas and all but one brought biscuits. In total, they supplied 3,028 quintals (hundred-weight) of flour (some eight tons per vessel), 6,450 quintals of biscuits, and 2,698 quintals of dried peas. Three vessels brought seventeen quintals of salt beef and pork, eleven vessels some 2,330 livres of tobacco, six vessels some 1,850 pine

---

106. AC, C11B-*14*, 141–48: 1733, and C11B-*19*, 50: 1737.
107. AC, C11B-*21*, 156: 1739.
108. AC, C11B-*7*, 140: 1725. See also C11B-*20* and *26*.
109. AC, C11A-*54*, 44–45: 1731.
110. AC, C11B-*25*, 3–5: Louisburg, August 1743.
111. McLennan, *Louisbourg*, p. 382.

planks ten feet long, and five vessels 58,000 shingles.[112] There are similar records for 1733 and 1735–37.

Isle St-Jean proved an unreliable source of supply because of slowness of agricultural development and various local problems, notably the recurrent plagues of mice.[113] Such exports as it was able to provide consisted chiefly of fish and in the fifties it was often a food deficit area itself as it received a flood of refugees from Baie Verte and Tatamagouche.[114] Probably it had a net import of foodstuffs throughout the period from 1720 to 1755 as it acquired increasing numbers of people from Acadia.

The activity of the Acadians in clandestine trade with Cape Breton has been discussed in some depth in Chapter 6, and there is a detailed inventory of the Acadian imports to Louisburg and their value in 1740 (see Table 6.12). One more example of the nature of the traffic may suffice. An observer at Louisburg in 1726 saw four vessels loaded in Acadia which brought "eighty odd Oxen and Cows, great Store of Sheep, and other fresh Provisions, and a great quantity of Furrs; being thus furnished with Vessels and with the Timber of Nova Scotia to build others . . . they are enabled to vie with us in the Foreign Fish Trade and reap as much benefit from Nova Scotia as if they were still Proprietors thereof."[115] Writing in 1741 from Annapolis, Governor Mascarene observed that he ". . . could not prevent those of Cape Breton who were in great want of these Commodities [foodstuffs] to resort to the many uninhabited harbours on our Eastern Coast and Bay Verte where by means of a communication by land with the Settlements of Manis and Chignecto they drew from those places whole droves of cattle and other Provisions in which they were assisted [by] the french Inhabitants and it is strongly presumed were supported by our English traders . . . ."[116] In addition to the main categories of livestock, wheat, flour, and furs, the Nova Scotia mainland supplied oak timber for the fortifications and ship building at Louisburg;[117] it also supplied the best large masts.

Yet, with all the Acadian contributions added to those of France, Canada, and Isle St-Jean, supplies were still inadequate. The often

112. AC, F2B p. 3: "Commerce des Colonies," 1732.
113. AC, C11B-10, 90: 1728, and C11B-20, 156–59: 1738.
114. See esp., D. C. Harvey, *The French Regime in Prince Edward Island* (1926) and my *Three Centuries and the Island.*
115. AC, NSA-17, 33–34, 125–26: Bradstreet to Lords of Trade, March 1725/26.
116. AC, NSA-25, 135–36.   117. AC, NSA-26, 35–36: 1743.

rather large deficit remaining was made up from New England despite the fact that most of such trade contravened the mercantilist regulations of both Britain and France and was technically a smuggling operation as, in the eyes of the British, was Louisburg's trade with the Acadians. Not only did the Louisburg officials wink at it, but at times they encouraged it, both because of the real need of the colony and because its extra-legal nature made it possible for the officials to profit from it through kickbacks, bribes, and shares in profits.

The New England supplies were varied and filled a wide variety of local needs: cattle, sheep, beef, pork, eggs, poultry, wheat, flour, corn, potatoes, turnips, onions, apples, cider, and building materials of all kinds (shingles, planks, bricks, etc.), in addition to the schooners and sloops often sold with their cargoes. Such supplies competed especially with those from Canada and France and as early as 1725 the merchants and ships' captains of Louisburg protested to Brouillan de St-Ovide.[118] In 1731 he admitted allowing "trois ou quatre petits bâtiments Anglais . . . de vendre ses petits cargaisons" consisting of articles of which the colony had desperate need: planks, brick, livestock, maize, apples, turnips, and onions.[119] On occasion he sent directly to New York to buy flour[120] and he strongly defended the trade as absolutely necessary for survival, claiming, however, that he allowed vessels from there to bring only bricks, timber, live animals, and other specified articles and insisted upon them taking in exchange coal, brandy, wine, and so forth, to the benefit of the colony and French merchants.[121] When official eyebrows were raised his answer was always to point to the inadequacies of supplies from France, about which protests were constant.[122]

One suspects that although the trade with New England probably was always greater than the French documents imply, it may not have been as important as might be suggested by the official and unofficial reports from British observers at Canso, who had every reason to exaggerate it in order to get firmer action for its suppression. In 1726, one such observer, Bradstreet, noted that the market at Louisburg for New Englanders ". . . . occasioned such plenty of fresh Provisions

118. AC, C11B-*7*, 138–40: October 1725.   119. AC, C11B-*12*, 35.
120. AC, C11B-*14*, 40: October 1733 (one of a great many instances).
121. AC, C11B-*10*, 57: November 1728.
122. See, for example, AC, C11B-*14*, 61–63: November 1733; C11B-*19*, 50: November 1737; C11B-*19*, 112: December 1737; and C11B-*20*, 207: October 1738.

there that the Price of one Sheep at Canso was Equivalent to that of two at Cape Britton . . . ."[123] A memorial from several masters of ships trading to Canso, written around 1731, claimed:

That there is at present a great trade carried on by the French in the Harbour of Cansoe who come from the Island Gaspye & Cape Breton, and sell great Quantities of Martinico Rum, Molassus & sundry Commodities from old France as Brandy, Wine, Linnens, & ca. to the Fishermen at Cansoe & who come there yearly from other places and barter those Commoditys for Fish caught by the English which enhances the price of Fish & also proves a very considerable Detriment to the Ships which yearly come from England in order to purchase their Cargoes of Fish there not only by the French getting part of ye fish for those contraband Commoditys but also is a manifest Loss to those Brittish Ships who cannot sell the Lawful Commoditys they bring with them in order to purchase fish ye People at Cansoe being continually stock't by the French so [that] the advantage which might accrue from our own & Plantation Commodities is lost thereby as well as Ye French being enabled to purchase the greatest Quantities of Fish and supplying the Marketts in the Mediterranean therewith and more especially Italy which is yearly overstock'd with fish brought thither in French ships tho great part of it is caught by our own people as above . . . .[124]

The chief transgressors from the English side at Canso clearly were New Englanders. The "Canso" area was conceived to include Chedabucto Bay, Isle Madame, and the south coastal havens of Cape Breton. Petit-de-Grat was one of the principal sites of the illegal trade.[125] In this archipelagic area it was very easy to make a rendezvous if official disapproval at Canso proper or Louisburg began to show its teeth.[126] There was a tendency for both New England and Cape Breton fishermen to sell their fish either at Louisburg or Canso, depending on the price. Thus Bigot, *commissaire-ordonnateur* (in effect, intendant) at Louisburg, claimed that fish brought there from the southern coastal havens of the island was often "English."[127]

Harold Innis long ago pointed out that one of the greatest weaknesses of France in the seventeenth and eighteenth centuries, as compared with Britain at the same time, was her failure to develop a

123. AC, NSA-*17*, 34.
124. AC, NSA-*20*, 134–35, quoted in Innis, *Select Documents*, p. 129.
125. AC, C11B-*22*, 207: 1740.
126. The British maintained a rather inadequate fort and garrison at Canso for most of the period. See Chapter 6.
127. AC, C11B-*21*, 123: October 1739.

coordinated system of exploiting the geographical diversity of the western hemisphere. The key elements in such an integrated commercial network, as developed by the British, were a productive mid-latitude agricultural area, a maritime cod-fishery realm, and extensive tropical sugar plantations, with a concomitant "triangle" of trade involving the mother country.[128] The failure lay not only in the slow agricultural development of Canada but perhaps rather more in the problem of maintaining sailing ship connections which had to cope with the closed season in the St. Lawrence River from November to May, the hurricane season in the West Indies in the late summer and early autumn when sailing conditions were best to the north, and the calendars of the fishery on the one hand and the canefields on the other. Cape Breton at the heart of the triangle was magnificently situated to provide rest, refreshment, refitting, warehousing, and exchange facilities—in brief, to be the central cog in a machine that was never able to function properly. To the degree that it did play its destined commercial role it was, ironically, as a trading entrepôt that tied the British and French systems together in the creation of a technically illegal triangular trade between New England, the French West Indies, and old France itself.

In the period from 1720–1745, thus, Cape Breton became a major trading entrepôt in the northwestern Atlantic, a position it resumed again between 1749 and 1758. Much of the trade was French—with the homeland, Canada, or the French West Indies—but an increasing volume of it was with New England. The Yankee vessels brought much-needed supplies to Cape Breton and either sold the vessels there for specie, or returned to New England with goods from France and, especially, the French West Indies. Two reports on the New England trade in the 1740's emphasize the importance of West Indian products which New England could not obtain in adequate quantity in its legal trade with the British Antilles. In 1743 Hibbert Newton, the collector of customs, writing from Canso on September 1, said there were at that time eighteen colonial ships in Louisburg and that eighty to ninety a year called there, often resulting in the sale of the vessels as well as the

---

128. Innis, "Cape Breton," pp. 51, 84–86. Note also AC, C11A-*3*, 151–61: "Mémoire touchant le commerce de Canada aux Isles Antilles françaises de l'Amérique," 1670, for an early appreciation of the possibilities by the Canadian officials.

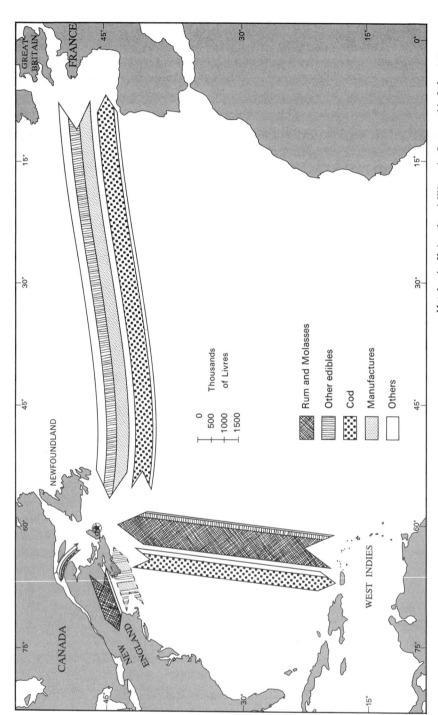

Fig. 7.7 Louisburg: Trade Flow Pattern, 1752/53.

Map by the University of Wisconsin Cartographic Laboratory

cargoes and, in turn, taking back to New England chiefly rum and molasses.[129] Another source, from 1746, made a round estimate of one hundred New England vessels a year going to Louisburg in the early forties, ranging from five to four hundred tons (but being chiefly small ones). His list of goods moving from New England at that time included tar, pitch, turpentine, resin, beef and pork, butter and cheese, bread and flour, horses and cattle of all kinds, cider, apples, onions and corn, and cabinet-maker's goods. In the return cargoes to New England, besides rum, molasses, and sugar he noted coffee and indigo (also probably from the West Indies), as well as East Indian goods; drugs, brandy, wine, oil, sail cloth, cordage, iron, and various manufactures.[130]

The documentary record emphasizes a trend of increasing dependence of Louisburg on supplies from New England, in the face of the inadequacy of supplies from France, Canada, or even Acadia. The recorded values and quantities of Louisburg's trade with Acadia, New England, Canada, the West Indies, and France in 1740 and 1752 give a rather clear picture of some of the classical triangles of trade operating in fine disregard of the mercantilist restrictions of Britain and France (see Tables 7.9 and 7.10).

In the interval between the French reoccupation of Louisburg and the resumption of regional hostilities in 1755, the New England trade may have reached its peak. Cornwallis, writing from Halifax in November 1751, estimated that there were one hundred and fifty English vessels at Cape Breton in that year,[131] and Governor Lawrence made the same complaint in 1754: "We sometimes see six or seven sloops in a day pass by this Harbour Loaded for that place; and we have certain intelligence of Thirty Vessels now in that Harbour who sail'd very lately from Boston loaded with Provisions."[132]

Subsidiary Economic Enterprise

Minor industrial activity in Cape Breton was largely a matter of lumbering, some ship-building, stone-quarrying, and brick-making, and a little coal-mining. Lumbering was conducted at St. Peters, River

129. AC, NSA-*26*, 30–33. He estimated that the trade involved 6,000 hogsheads of rum and molasses a year to New England.

130. [William Bollan] actually by Captain Samuel Holland, *The Importance and Advantage of Cape Breton, Truly Stated and Impartially Considered, with Proper Maps* (1746), pp. 118–19.

131. AC, NSA-*43*, 135–44.   132. AC, NSA-*55*, 119–20.

TABLE 7.9   *Trade of Louisburg: Selected exports (value in livres)*

	to New England		to Canada		to West Indies		to France
Exports	1740	1752	1740	1753	1740	1753	1753
Dried cod	—	—	—	—	—	488,256	605,680
Bank cod (in casks)	—	—	—	—	—	28,890	38,700
Cod, unspecified	—	—	—	—	198,264	—	—
Fish oil	—	—	—	—	2,535	—	47,600
Salmon	—	—	—	—	1,040	—	4,590
Furs and hides	—	—	—	2,800	—	—	15,586
Horses	—	—	—	—	—	17,800	—
Tobacco	—	—	732	15,334	—	—	—
Cloth	—	—	—	6,336	—	—	—
Shoes	—	—	—	2,940	—	—	—
Coal	2,010	—	—	—	1,425	—	4,832
Tar	—	—	3,200	—	—	—	—
Oak planks	—	—	—	—	975	—	2,570
English planks	—	—	—	—	—	24,343	—
Planks of the country	—	—	—	—	2,472	17,513	—
Casks, knocked down	—	—	—	—	—	21,235	—
Stavewood	—	—	—	—	—	24,113	—
Other wood products	—	—	—	—	5,313	—	—
Flour	—	—	—	—	28,039	—	—
Tafia (rum)	46,475	233,550	56,880	59,760	—	—	—
Molasses	18,400	333,080	15,720	—	—	—	—
Sugar	—	40,350	11,100	—	—	—	—
Coffee	—	27,000	16,380	7,162	—	—	—
Rice	—	—	4,000	—	—	—	—
Wine	—	—	3,800	—	—	—	—
Wine and brandy	1,000	20,400	—	—	—	—	—
Miscellaneous	2,793	300	2,964	16,826	2,925	51,714	16,247
Total	70,678	654,680	114,776	111,158	242,988	673,864	735,805

Sources: AC, F2B and J. S. McLennan, *Louisbourg from its Foundation to its Fall, 1713–1758* (1918).

TABLE 7.10   *Trade of Louisburg: Selected imports (value in livres)*

Imports	from Acadia	from New England	from Canada		from West Indies		from France
	1740	1740	1740	1752	1740	1752	1752
Skins and furs	5,423	—	—	—	—	—	—
Livestock	13,796	8,679	—	800	—	—	—
Tobacco	—	—	—	1,457	4,825	22,104	—
Cloth and cloth-ing	—	—	—	1,020	—	1,350	229,259
Sailcloth	—	—	—	—	—	—	23,834
Fishing gear	—	—	—	—	—	—	138,879
Other iron and copper products	—	834	—	—	—	—	64,774
Wood and wood products	167	17,778	607	1,941	—	—	—
Furniture	—	5,916	—	—	—	—	—
Axes and hatchets	30	4,488	—	—	—	—	—
Flour	1,146	—	106,528	—	—	—	30,173
Biscuits	50	—	75,000	—	—	—	—
Other food	5,516	9,634	7,260	—	—	5,997	176,364
Tafia (rum)	—	—	—	—	150,040	445,770	—
Molasses	—	—	—	—	78,780	543,263	—
Sugar	—	—	—	—	11,591	75,967	—
Coffee	—	—	—	—	5,652	52,377	—
Wine	—	—	—	3,700	5,750	8,000	167,540
Soap	—	—	—	—	6,978	—	—
Salt	—	—	—	—	—	—	97,418
Olive oil	—	—	—	—	5,460	5,670	9,672
Miscellaneous	812	1,118	7,108	4,359	239	19,749	186,226
Total	26,940	48,447	196,503	13,277	269,315	1,180,247	1,124,139

Sources: See Table 7.9.

Inhabitants, Little Bras d'Or,[133] St. Ann, at Spanish Bay, and along the Mira River. Most of the lumber was used for local building needs or shipped to Louisburg. In 1743 a report from Canso had it that French from Cape Breton went to "Picton" (possibly "Pictou" on the Nova Scotia mainland and, therefore, legally British) to winter for the purposes of building small vessels and cutting oak and masts for transport back to the ship-building activities of the island proper.

Quite early the demands of Louisburg for fuel led to major wood-cutting activity in many places. Thus St. Peters sent some ten batteaux loaded with firewood to the capital in 1736, and there are constant references to the problem of firewood—a major one for Halifax, too, in its first decades.[134]

The building of vessels for the fishery (shallops, schooners, and sloops) and even of larger vessels was established early and continued into the 1750's. The first firm record appears to be that of 1733 when fourteen vessels were built in ports outside of Louisburg. Table 7.11 contains some scattered evidence of an activity that persisted through the early 1750's at least. It is interesting that shallop building is never recorded and that although a distinction is always carefully made between slooped-rigged (batteaux) and schooner-rigged (goélettes) vessels for the bank fishery and the coastal trade, each type varied widely in size.

The localization of vessel construction outside of Louisburg itself had some relationship to the availability of satisfactory timber, at Ingonish, St. Ann, Boularderie's place on Little Bras d'Or, Spanish Bay (only after 1750), Mira Bay, and St. Peters. Except for Scatarie Island (and that only once) none of the many other central and south coast fishing coves are mentioned. Interestingly Holland's references to evidence of small-craft construction at Justeaucorps and Chéticamp on the Gulf coast are nowhere confirmed in the French sources.

It is doubtful that Cape Breton Island during the French regime ever reached its full potential in the building of vessels larger than the undecked shallops for the inshore fishery because it was so easy to buy sloops and schooners, and even larger vessels, from the New England-

133. For Verderonne (Boularderie) Island, Holland reported that several saw-mills had been operated by Boularderie, but whether he based this information on evidence or report is uncertain. Holland also reported sawmills at Sydney Harbour. Harvey, *Holland's Description,* p. 65.

134. See Chapter 8.

TABLE 7.11   *Construction of vessels on Cape Breton (scattered records, by tonnage)*

Year and Location	Undifferentiated vessels	Goélettes (Schooners)	Batteaux (Sloops)	Brigantines
1733 (14 vessels)				
Little Bras d'Or	90, 45, 30, 20	–	–	–
St. Ann	160, 50, 30	–	–	–
Ingonish	90, 35, 35	–	–	–
Scatarie I.	15, 12	–	–	–
St. Peters	40, 35	–	–	–
1736 (5 vessels)				
Louisburg	–	–	–	70
Mira Bay	–	25	45	–
St. Ann	–	–	35	–
Little Bras d'Or	–	–	38	–
1737 (9 vessels)				
Louisburg	120,80	–	–	–
Little Bras d'Or	100,25	–	–	–
Ingonish	120, 70, 50	–	–	–
St. Peters	50, 30	–	–	–
1738 (10 vessels) (no breakdown)				
1750 (12 vessels)				
Mira Bay	–	40, 40, 40, 18	15	–
Little Bras d'Or	–	40	–	–
Sydney Harbour	–	–	15	–
St. Peters	–	40	37, 35, 30, 30	–

Sources: 1733—J. S. McLennan, *Louisbourg from its Foundation to its Fall, 1713–1758* (1918), p. 388; *1736*—AC, C11B-*18*, 133. Three batteaux of 35, 30, and 25 tons were also built on Isle St-Jean; *1737*—McLennan, *Louisbourg*, p. 388. However, Charles de La Morandière (*Histoire de la pêche française de la morue dans l'Amérique septentrionale*, 1962, 2, 677) has uncovered evidence of fourteen vessels of 50 to 121 tons, quoting AN, AdC, C11B, fol. 14. *1738*–AC, C11B-*20*, 115-20; *1750*—AC, C11B-*29*, 205. There were also seven built in Isle St-Jean and three recorded in "Acadie."

ers. In the mid 1720's John Bradstreet had reported from Canso that he ". . . saw ten New England sloops and schooners, and one Ship in the Harbour of Louisburg, all to be sold to the French both Vessels and Cargoes."[135] In 1736, when only five vessels were built on the island, seven schooners were bought from New England (three of fifteen tons, and one each of twenty, twenty-three, twenty-five, and sixty tons).[136] In 1738 six purchases were recorded by October[137] and we assume that this buying was a steady procedure through the 1730's and early

135. AC, NSA-*17*, 33–34: 1725/26.   136. AC, C11B-*18*, 133.
137. AC, C11B-*20*, 115–20.

1750's. During the somewhat freer relations with New England in the inter-war period from 1749 to 1755 the purchases were on a larger scale: twenty-four vessels in 1749, thirty in 1750, and twenty-four again in 1754.[138]

The average size of the ships built locally in the three years cited was fifty-five, fifty-six, and seventy-four tons. Indeed the twenty-four ships bought in 1754 had a larger total tonnage (1,773 as compared with 1,668) than the thirty bought in 1750.[139] It seems probable that the larger vessels were being acquired as much or more for trade as for fishing. As with other New England trade, that for vessels, technically illegal, was at least tacitly approved by the Louisburg authorities and, at times, even openly defended.[140] Without such purchases it seems doubtful that the schooner-fishing industry on the nearby banks could have been maintained.

Coal mining, rather surprisingly, was badly neglected. Coal was used chiefly by passing ships or for fuel at Louisburg, though some attempts were made to ship it to France. A probably unjustified fear of spontaneous combustion made shipowners wary even when it could have served as useful cargo, in place of ballast, for return journeys to France.[141] The awareness of the existence of a valuable, largely unused resource is, however, evident in many documentary references to it. The Baron d'Huart, writing from Louisburg in September 1752, expatiated on the amount and quality of the coal and of its possible value to France in reducing the need for imports. In his wise essay, *Pensées diverses sur L'Isle Royale,* written in 1752, Surlaville observed:

Cape Breton has many coal mines which we ought to exploit fully. Each year we send substantial sums of money to England for coal. Why not load all the government ships, which come here and would otherwise return empty, with coal and why not oblige the [returning] merchant vessels to take some coal in place of ballast which could be unloaded at any French port and thence

138. McLennan, *Louisbourg,* p. 385. Those bought in 1750 included eight sloops (of 15, 30, 45, 50[2], 60[2], and 100 tons), seventeen schooners (of 6, 12, 20, 25, 30, 40[3], 50[2], 60[2], 80[2], 85, 90, and 100 tons), and five brigantines (of 60, 80[3], and 90 tons). AC, C11B-*29*, 75–83, 202–5. In that year the largest vessels built on Cape Breton were three schooners of 40 tons each.

139. McLennan, *Louisbourg,* p. 385.

140. AC, C11B-*25*, 15: Louisburg, October 1743.

141. Bigot discussed the problems of the deterioration of coal during storage and shipment to France. AC, C11B-*24*, 118–19: Louisburg, October 1742.

transported wherever needed? It might be advantageous for His Majesty to employ one or two chains of convicts in mining it for their maintenance would not cost more here than elsewhere. If it is feared that the coal might set the ships on fire it is well known that it cannot ignite spontaneously and needs only a little care to prevent accident.[142]

142. *Les Derniers Jours,* pp. 266–67. My translation.

8

Mid-Century Transition

𝄢

THE DECADE of the 1750's was a climactic one in the historical geography of Maritime Canada. The present Canadian section of the expanded Acadia of the seventeenth century, territorially almost identical with Sir William Alexander's dream of a New Scotland, was reunited as one British colony of Nova Scotia. France was eliminated as a political and military power in the region. The bulk of the Acadian population was forcibly removed and, for the first time, significant numbers of non-French, Protestant settlers were introduced from the British Isles and the European continent. But neither of the two population groups which were to dominate Nova Scotia's next century, Highland Scottish crofters and New England farmers, were yet present in anything but token numbers.

The old Acadia had largely died but the new Nova Scotia was still in gestation as the decade came to a close; it was an end and a beginning superimposed, a period of rapid and traumatic transition. Much of the countryside became a *tabula rasa;* the legacy of French occupation of Cape Breton Island and of most of the mainland areas was extremely scanty. Yet the hard-won dyked lands of Chignecto, Minas, and Annapolis and the axe-cleared fields of Isle St-Jean bore testimony to the past and, with characteristic stubbornness and tenacity, a remnant of the Acadian people remained, or returned, to form the nucleus of an ultimately important segment of the regional population. Men from New England's harbors, still largely based at home, continued to harvest the cod from its coastal waters, to cure their catches on its beaches

330

and rocky strands, and to dominate what little regional commerce there was. These two groups carried the human threads that tied the old Acadia and the new Nova Scotia into one continuous entity.

THE COURSE OF EVENTS

The military and political events of these years, which gave a solid meaning for the first time to the concept of a British Nova Scotia, legally established in 1713 but given the fabric of reality only with the founding of Halifax, are well known and well reported in many historical studies.[1] The war of 1744–48, with the capture and return of Louisburg and the comings and goings of armed bands of Canadians and Indians through their settlements, was far less significant to the Acadians than the events it set in train. To start with, the restoration of Louisburg to the French, in 1749, made necessary the foundation of its counterpart British base in the magnificent harbor of Chebucto, site of the rendezvous of the remnants of the ill-fated fleet of Admiral the Duc d'Anville, in 1746. There, in the course of three years, several thousand immigrant settlers were introduced including a large body of Continental Protestants, principally German in culture but with a minority of French speakers.

French Activity in the early 1750's

The previously rather vague French claims to the territory of present eastern Maine and New Brunswick became specific and were supported by garrisons near the mouth of the Saint John River and a fort, Beauséjour, on a ridge in the Chignecto marshes just northwest of the lower Missaguash River and across from the old settlement of Beaubassin[2] (see Figure 8.3). When the British countered with Fort Lawrence on a similar, parallel, ridge on the Beaubassin bank of the Missaguash and the French added Fort Gaspereau near Baie Verte, the first clear, *de facto* boundary of peninsular Nova Scotia was drawn and the seventy-five year old Cumberland Basin settlement was split in

1. See, for example, W. S. MacNutt, *The Atlantic Provinces: The Emergence of a Colonial Society, 1712–1857* (1965), ch. 2.
2. The British formally claimed the present New Brunswick area but largely neglected it except for the Acadian settlements west of the Missaguash in the Chignecto isthmus and those along the Memramcook, Petitcodiac, and Shepody rivers.

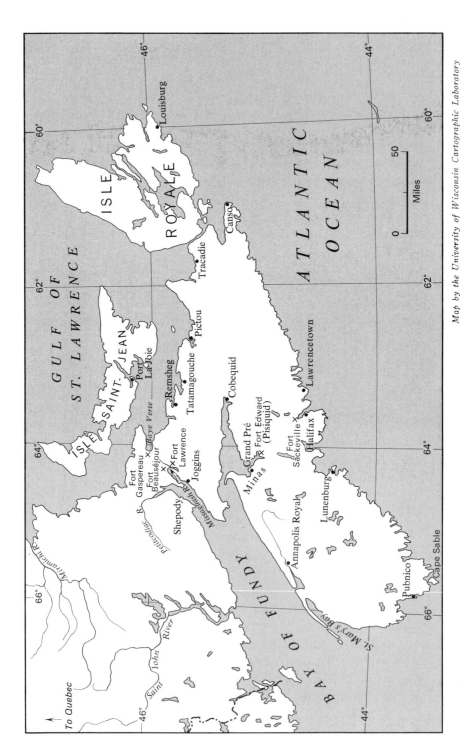

Fig. 8.1 Nova Scotia in 1755.

Map by the University of Wisconsin Cartographic Laboratory

two. French aggressiveness in boundary claims was associated with their desire for bargaining power in their deeper concern to control the upper Ohio River Valley and its connections with Louisiana, the upper Great Lakes, and the great western fur resources beyond the lakes. But they also wished to maintain pressure on New England, Halifax, and Annapolis and to protect Louisburg, their valuable fishery there, and the Canadian lifeline to Europe through Cabot Strait and the Gulf.

By the end of 1750 an armed truce existed locally but it was much nearer formal warfare than that preceding 1744. The governors at Louisburg and Halifax might exchange polite notes, and New England vessels by the score might trade at the French harbor, but the tension between the two forces confronting each other across the Missaguash River rarely relaxed, and the Acadians in Minas and Cobequid were sharply reminded of the precarious state of affairs by the building and garrisoning of a blockhouse at Grand Pré in Minas in 1749 and, in the spring of 1750, the establishment of Fort Edward (near present Windsor) at Pisiquid and the opening of a road from Halifax.

By both open and clandestine means, and perhaps largely through the ecclesiastical apparatus by which the Acadians long had had formal and persistent ties with Quebec and Louisburg, the French authorities tried to induce the Acadians to remove themselves, their goods, and their animals to the French side of the Missaguash or, initially or subsequently, to French territory on Cape Breton and Isle St-Jean.

In the Cumberland Basin (at Beaubassin itself, and the settlements along the La Planche, Nappan, Maccan, and Hébert rivers, especially) and in the Cobequid settlements, where the old route of livestock droving for Cape Breton began on its way across the height of land to Tatamagouche (see Figure 6.4), they enjoyed some success before 1755. Most of the emigrés moved to St-Jean where, in preceding years, a substantial French-speaking population, largely Acadian in origin, had become established.

There were, too, some defections from the Pisiquid settlement, where English disapproval of some rather open collaboration with Canadian forces in the 1740's created an air of uneasiness and distrust In the largest settlement of Minas and in Annapolis, where the avoid ance of British surveillance was more difficult, the influence of th⸍ clergy less strong (or the missionaries less inclined to encourage disaffection), and the dangers from the Indians less imminent, there appears to have been little emigration.

The threats both of withdrawal of religious ministrations and of harassment by the Indians were employed by the French, chiefly by the Abbé Le Loutre and the missionaries most closely associated with him, although even as vicar-general of Acadia he was not able to persuade some of the priests at Minas and Annapolis to cooperate. When Colonel Charles Lawrence (later governor) first came with troops to challenge La Corne's occupation of the site of Fort Beau-séjour, the houses and church of the old Beaubassin village were destroyed by fire, the weight of the evidence strongly suggesting that it was done by Indians under Le Loutre's orders.[3] The people then had no option but to retire to the other side of the Missaguash and find cramped and makeshift quarters there as refugees. The same tactics were used against a number of settlers at Cobequid. On the whole the refugees were understandably unhappy during the next five years and some at least returned to their old homes. Word of their plight no doubt influenced the majority of the inhabitants, even of the most disturbed areas of Pisiquid and Cobequid, to stay put,[4] although at the end, shortly before the formal deportation of 1755, most of the residents of Cobequid did leave.

The Establishment of Halifax

Meanwhile, as the Acadians were leaving or being dispersed the full apparatus of British government, the shadow of which had existed at

3. The Abbé Jean-Louis Le Loutre was a controversial figure whose zealotry was alternately condoned and condemned by the officialdom of Quebec and Louisburg, but he was generally supported because he was the acknowledged center of French influence among the Micmac of the peninsula, whom he had served since 1737 when he took up his first missionary post with them on the Shubenacadie River. Abbé Henri-Raymond Casgrain, in his notably dispassionate comments on Le Loutre in "Coup d'oeil sur l'Acadie" (1888), admitted the likelihood that the militant priest had ordered the destruction of the village but Casgrain remained confident that his vows as a priest would not have allowed him to connive at the destruction of the church. Yet one can well conceive a rationalization that its destruction by fire was preferable to its desecration by heretical British soldiers.

4. See especially *Les Derniers Jours de l'Acadie (1748–1758). Correspondances et mémoires. Extraits du portefeuille de M. le Courteois de Surlaville, Lieutenant-Général des Armées du Roi* [et] *Ancien Major des troupes de l'Île Royale,* ed. and ann. Gaston du Boscq de Beaumont (1899), pp. 99, 122, 126, 135, and a summary in J. B. Brebner, *New England's Outpost: Acadia before the Conquest of Canada* (1927), pp. 177–78.

Annapolis for four decades, was being established in Nova Scotia. Interest centers on Halifax, the hurriedly organized naval base and staging area for the armies which destroyed French power east of Quebec. Inevitably the government set up by the new governor, Lord Cornwallis (who took over immediately from Mascarene), was quasi-military, although British civil and representative forms were steadily introduced by pressure from influential New England residents. Cornwallis resigned the governorship in 1752 and was replaced by Colonel Peregrine Thomas Hopson who had commanded at Louisburg in the British occupation of 1745–49. Hopson's fourteen-month tenure of office was a smooth one. His successor, Colonel Charles Lawrence, was made lieutenant-governor in 1754 and governor in 1756, a post he retained until his death in 1760. An able military officer, he was rather arbitrary and authoritarian as governor and in constant embroilment with the New Englanders who attacked him and posed as good democrats, often chiefly to cover their own smuggling and peculations. Undoubtedly the New Englanders on his council (he postponed organizing an assembly until 1758) did influence the harshness of his attitude toward the Acadians.

If there was little accomplished in the way of agricultural development by new immigrants in the 1750's there were, nevertheless, some important beginnings made between the La Have River and Chezzetcook Inlet on the central south coast, particularly in the magnificent harbor of Chebucto. The foundation and early years of Halifax have been well described in many places.[5] Roughly two thousand settlers arrived in the "first fleet" with Cornwallis in late June of 1749.[6] The immigrants, assembled rapidly and, despite inducements to get retired or discharged soldiers and sailors[7] (or because of them), probably not very well screened, were a mixed bag; Cornwallis estimated that fewer than one hundred of the soldiers and perhaps twice that number of

5. See especially T. B. Akins, "History of Halifax City" (1895). There are very clear accounts by Cornwallis and Hugh Davidson in their dispatches found in AC, NSA-*34* through NSA-*39*. A summary of Davidson's oral account of Halifax as given to the Board of Trade in 1750 is in AC, NSA-*39*, 77–83, and is printed in Adam Shortt, V. K. Johnston, and Gustave Lanctot, *Documents Relating to Currency, Exchange and Finance in Nova Scotia, with Prefatory Documents, 1675–1758* (1933), pp. 318–20.

6. Some 2,576 people were on the thirteen vessels, probably more than 500 being officers and crew. See Akins, "History of Halifax," p. 5.

7. "Acquisition and Trade of Halifax" (1755).

sailors and civilians were both able and willing for the kind of work that
had to be done.[8]

The settlement was located, after a false start or two, on the eastern
side of the present Halifax peninsula, across from present Dartmouth
Cove, about three miles south of the Narrows leading into Bedford
Basin and just at the foot of the steep hill on which the citadel now
stands (see Figure 8.1). The decision not to build on the shores of
Bedford Basin, one of the most commodious and best protected natural
harbors in North America, if not in the whole world, was based chiefly
on the assumption that fishermen would not be willing to push the
extra five miles coming and going.[9] However, the outer harbor between
the Narrows and McNab Island was quite well protected from the
open sea by the latter. Moreover, location on a narrow-necked peninsula proved to be a boon in defending the settlement from Indian
attacks in its first decade, and both naval and merchant vessels saved
much time in the reduced distance from the open sea. The chief
deficiency of the site in 1749 was the lack of an adequate fresh water
stream.

Enough land was cleared in the first summer to get the settlers on
shore.[10] By September, when 1,574 settlers were victualed, a palisade
had been erected about the area cleared for the settlement and a square
completed "at the top of the town."[11] In September the number on
government rations rose to 1,675 and by October three hundred houses
were "covered" and a road had been cut from the town to the head of
the bay (presumably Fort Sackville).[12] The houses or huts would
appear to have been made largely from logs, poles, and bark acquired
in clearing the site and from its immediate neighborhood. Some frames
and other building materials came from Boston but there were delays
in getting sawmills working (necessarily away from the nearly stream-
less peninsula) because of threat of Indian attack and low water from
an unusually dry season. A gridiron pattern of streets was laid out.[13]
Clearly many of the lots had the rudest of wooden shelters or even
tents: "Many unfortunate People died of Cold the first Winter after
their Settlement. This indeed, may be imputed to the Want of Houses,

8. AC, NSA-*34*, 202–5: Cornwallis to Lords of Trade, Halifax, July 1749.
9. *Ibid.*, pp. 189–98: Cornwallis to Bedford, Chebucto, July 1749.   10. *Ibid.*
11. AC, NSA-*35*, 44–51.   12. *Ibid.*, pp. 55–58, 101–6.
13. Streets were 55 feet wide in fact, although projected for 60 feet, with blocks
320 by 120 feet, each containing 16 lots of 40 by 60 feet. Akins, "History of
Halifax," pp. 10–11.

which only such as could build were able to obtain; and to see the vast Flakes of Snow lying about the Tents of those who had been accustomed to warm fires about Newcastle and London, was enough to move the Heart of Stone."[14]

Meanwhile the settlers poured in; more shiploads came from Europe and, by Cornwallis' estimate, over one thousand from Louisburg and the colonies to the southwest, to share in the greatest public porkbarrel yet opened in British North America. By June of 1750 Cornwallis thought the population had doubled since the arrival of the first fleet of transports, and many hundreds more came in the latter half of that year. At the beginning of 1751 it was estimated that 750 houses had been built and 200,000 bricks (for chimneys and foundations) made.[15] By the end of the same year another report estimated six hundred houses inside the ten-foot-high palisade and five hundred outside it in the "suburbs" where lots had been laid out before the end of 1749.[16]

A major accretion to the population, and an acute problem for the government, was provided by the arrival of several thousand "Foreign Protestants" from France, Switzerland, and German states in the Rhineland.[17] The Lords of Trade, with the concurrence of the Privy Council, had decided to undertake a systematic colonization with Swiss and other Continental Protestants, "found by experience" to be "a sober and industrious sort of People."[18] The first proposals for directing people of this sort to Nova Scotia date back to 1717,[19] but such immigrants had been pouring into New York and Pennsylvania, in particular, for decades and this effort can be seen as an attempt to divert part of that stream.

The first vessel-load of some three hundred arrived in 1750 (seventeen died in passage and subsequent mortality suggested too large a

14. John Wilson, *A Genuine Narrative of the Transactions in Nova Scotia since the settlement, June, 1749, till August the 5th, 1751* . . . (n.d.), pp. 10–11. Written about 1751. Quoted in Harold A. Innis, ed., *Select Documents in Canadian Economic History, 1497–1783* (1929), pp. 172–73.

15. *Journal of the Commissioners for Trade and Plantations, January 1749/50 to December 1753* (1932), p. 116.

16. Anon., *The Importance of the Settling and Fortifying of Nova Scotia* . . . (1751), in AC, *Catalogue of Pamphlets, 1,* No. 152, p. 23.

17. W. P. Bell, *The "Foreign Protestants" and the Settlement of Nova Scotia* (1961), has assembled their record in massive detail.

18. Quoted in Bell, *Foreign Protestants,* p. 107, from a report by the Board of Trade to the Privy Council. The experience presumably was that of Pennsylvania.

19. *Ibid.,* p. 33.

proportion of elderly and infirm), although there had been six or seven dozen in Cornwallis' ships' lists of 1749 who had names suggesting similar origins. Bell estimates the total landed in Halifax from 1749 through 1752 to have been 2,724 (something fewer than one thousand heads of families or single men), and makes a valiant effort to sort out areas of origin and occupations.[20] The Palatinate, Württemberg, Hesse-Darmstadt, Montbeliard, and Switzerland accounted for the bulk of them but at least a score of other states from the Netherlands and Alsace to Danzig are believed to have been represented. About three dozen families had French names (chiefly the Montbeliards) and were presumably French-speaking, and almost all the rest, the overwhelming majority, spoke German.[21] In occupations they were diverse. Some half (a bit fewer) of the heads of family were farmers or husbandmen and another quarter were included under the rubrics: carpenters or joiners, bakers, masons or stone-cutters, shoemakers, tailors, smiths, weavers, millers, surgeons, and coopers. A further forty-three categories suggested the wide variety of skills available to the new settlement. In Halifax itself the major concentration of the "foreigners" was near the neck of the peninsula, establishing the district name of "Dutch Settlement" which it was to retain.

In the summer of 1753 Halifax spread over thirty-five of its rectangular blocks, although extant "views" of the city drawn as late as 1757 suggest that most of the dwellings were still small, rough, and unattractive in appearance.[22] A good many apparently were horizontal log cabins of the kind the Acadians had been building for a century, perhaps boarded over.[23] The population did not grow nearly as rapidly as one might have supposed from the large number of recorded immigrants, and the steady flow of merchants, fishermen, and the like from New England. Ever since the first year the movement away of the disaffected and disenchanted had been large and active. Those involved

20. *Ibid.*, pp. 284–85.
21. The name by which their descendants became known (Lunenburgers, after their settlement west of Halifax) came from one of the titles of the Hanoverian monarchs (Dukes of Braunschweig-Lüneberg) and should not be linked in any other way with Lüneburg Heath or Town. Perhaps fewer than fifteen families came from northwestern Germany. Bell, *Foreign Protestants*, pp. 287–91.
22. See reproductions, especially by one Short, in Sir John G. Bourinot's "Builders of Nova Scotia: An Historical Review" (1899). They are discussed in Harry Piers, "Artists in Nova Scotia" (1914).
23. See Chapter 4, note 70.

were chiefly individuals physically and temperamentally unsuited to the rough regime of life, and chiefly English, although some of the foreign Protestants, as we have noted in the discussion of the Mira River settlements in Cape Breton, made their way there with the help of Acadians at Pisiquid and Cobequid. There was a balancing infusion of thoroughly acclimatized New Englanders. This is not to imply moral superiority in the latter group, which included many of the rumsellers, smugglers, and feeders at the public trough who had debauched Louisburg.[24] But it also included many fishermen and responsible, if hardheaded, traders and they may have done as much as the governmental, military, and naval apparatus to get Halifax solidly established.

The Establishment of Lunenburg

An historiographic idée fixe about Acadia has been that the foreign Protestants were destined to be "salted in" among the Acadians to water down the strength of their enthusiasm for the French faith and culture, and thus make the latter more amenable to British sovereignty. Certainly Governor Shirley of Massachusetts had advocated this in respect to potential New England immigration. However, Bell shows quite convincingly[25] that the official plans for the Continentals involved their settlement in discrete townships (perhaps with English settlers intermixed), that only two of the first five were planned for the Fundy borderlands, and that, as in Morris' plans,[26] the latter were to border the Acadian settlements but not to overlap significantly with them. Whatever the interpretation of the evidence, it was obviously impractical in 1751, 1752, or 1753 to plan to settle these people in the Fundy area and to expose them thus to Indian attacks. The whole military establishment at Halifax could not have protected them, if deployed for that purpose alone. Equally they were an enormous burden on the public treasury in Halifax, producing no food for themselves, and when, at length, the idea of any location on the Bay of

24. The Parliamentary votes for Halifax in the first seven years gave some measure of the opportunities: 1749, £40,000; 1750, £57,583; 1751, £53,928; 1752, £61,493; 1753, £94,616; 1754, £58,447; 1755, £49,418. "Acquisition and Trade of Halifax."

25. Bell, *Foreign Protestants,* pp. 317–27.

26. PRO, A & WI-*63*, 106: "Report by Captain [Charles] Morris to Governor Shirley upon his Survey of Lands in Nova Scotia available for Protestant Settlers, 1749." Printed in AC *Report for 1912* (1913).

Fundy was abandoned, an eligible spot on the Atlantic coast was sought for them.[27]

The experience in attempting to farm the ungenerous soil of the Halifax area had made it clear, by 1752, that whatever other virtues the Chebucto area may have had, it shared with the Atlantic coast generally, from Cape Sable to Cape Canso, a very low agricultural potential. There was one notable exception—the surface of the drumlins in the central and western areas of present Lunenburg County and the eastern area of present Queens (see Figure 2.1 and End papers). Since the first Razilly settlement of 1632, more than 120 years before, the agricultural potential of the La Have-Mirligueche area had been demonstrated abundantly. As we have seen, there had been settlement there off and on throughout this period and several families still resided there when Cornwallis visited it on his way to Chebucto in 1749 and wrote of "very comfortable wooden houses, covered with bark, a good many Cattle and Sheep, and clear Ground for more than serves themselves."[28] Hopson had ascertained that there were at least four hundred acres of "cleared land" (actually largely grown up in brush and not necessarily easier to clear than a mature forest and that the peninsula (on the neck of which the town of Lunenburg grew up) could be defended with a picket palisade as that of Halifax had been[29] (see Figure 8.2).

The decision on the site having been made, transports were hired from New England[30] and for several weeks after the first vessels made the trip in June of 1753 several of them were employed in ferrying people, effects, and supplies from Halifax to "Merligash" (actually renamed Lunenburg in an action of the council of May 10).

27. So far from even wanting the Foreign Protestants near the French, at this point there was a rather strong feeling, especially because of many desertions associated with their unhappiness at being cooped up in Halifax, that they should be moved even farther away. AC, NSA-*48*, 69: 1752. Moreover, it was still hoped to keep the Acadians on their lands and Governor Hopson was sure, in October of that year, that if he sent Foreign Protestants among them, the Acadians would leave. AC, NSA-*49*, 62–80: Hopson to Lords of Trade, October 1752.

28. AC, NSA-*34*, 103–9.

29. Hopson's reasons for choosing Mirligueche are scattered through his dispatches. See those for May 26 and July 23, 1753, in AC, NSA-*54*. In the latter, pp. 67–83, he emphasized the fine harbor.

30. Wasting no opportunity the masters of these sloops and schooners brought lumber, livestock, bricks, hay, and other typical local commodities from home, to sell in Halifax. PRO, CO-*221*, 110–19.

As in downtown Halifax today, one faces, in the town of Lunenburg, streets of very steep slope, because of the decision made by Morris to impose on unsuitable terrain a strict gridiron pattern: eight streets lengthwise of the hill and five crossing "uphill" streets.[31] The protective palisade across the neck of the peninsula was just at the western edge of the town site. There were block houses there and on the eastern edge of the town and, beyond the latter, some garden lots before the bulk of the rocky, infertile area of the peninsula was reached. Rapidly houses were built, often of horizontal square-hewn logs, sometimes of vertical poles or pickets for the walls with boards nailed on.[32] Just as the settlers were of varied means, despite the "poor mouth" that most of them had displayed during their stay at Halifax, so their houses varied in quality.

The number of settlers estimated for 1754 is indicated in the victualing allowance asked for that year—nearly £10,000 for some 1,955 settlers for twelve months. This request also indicates little confidence on the part of the authorities that they could supply their own food.[33] There was some rebelliousness by the settlers over real or imagined deprivations in the summer of 1753 and an "insurrection" in December of that year which has received at least as much attention as it deserves,[34] but that was the end of any mutinous activity.

Little farming activity was undertaken during the first year of the Lunenburg settlement although some thirty-acre farm lots (fifty chains deep by seven and one-half chains wide, the length at right-angles to a road or base line) were marked out just beyond the townsite (see Figure 8.2). From late 1753 through 1754 more such lots were laid out over a large area. In about half the cases a base line more or less parallel to the coast and about forty chains from it was run giving each

31. The central of these was 80 feet wide, those parallel to it 48 feet, and the more or less horizontal streets only 40 feet. In all there were 42 blocks, 280 by 120 feet, or somewhat smaller than in Halifax, with lots of 40 by 60 feet—the same size as those in the capital. Bell, *Foreign Protestants*, pp. 426–27.

32. M. B. DesBrisay, *History of the County of Lunenburg* (1895), p. 38, has a description of one built in 1757 with slotted corner posts into which rough-hewn planks for the walls were fitted, one above another, shingled on the outside and boarded within. This house was 26 by 14 feet in plan and the rooms on the ground floor were only six feet high.

33. "Dry stores"—i.e., flour, dried peas, and the like—were obtained from the British colonies to the south; "wet stores," especially beef and pork in casks of brine, usually came from Ireland.

34. Bell, *Foreign Protestants*, pp. 450–68.

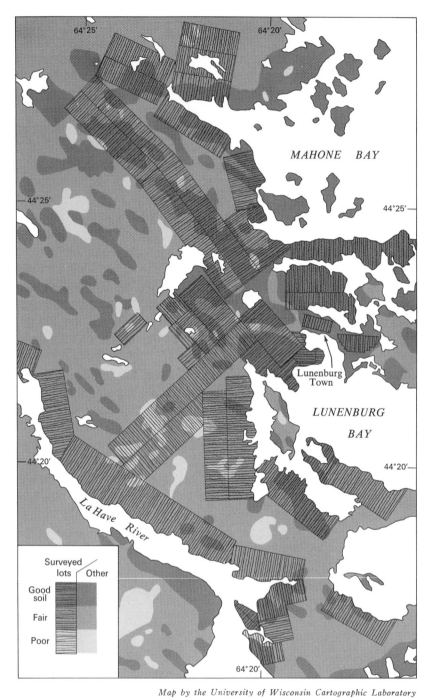

64°25'   64°20'

MAHONE BAY

44°25'   44°25'

Lunenburg
Town

LUNENBURG

BAY

44°20'   44°20'

La Have River

Surveyed lots	Other
Good soil	
Fair	
Poor	

64°20'

Map by the University of Wisconsin Cartographic Laboratory

Fig. 8.2 Lunenburg Settlement: Surveyed Lots in Relation to the Quality of
the Soil.

lot just short of 500 feet of tidewater frontage.[35] As Bell points out, many present-day roads are orientated according to these survey lines. Interestingly, this first formal prior survey for rural settlement under British auspices in present maritime Canada followed a pattern of very elongated rectangles or trapezoids which, although only of a little more than five to one in proportion, was reminiscent of the *rangs* of *rotures* in Canada and anticipatory of the layout of individual holdings in the framework of Holland's survey of Isle St-Jean in the next decade.[36] The size was less than a perhaps expectable fifty acres, possibly because otherwise there would have been too little land available near enough to Lunenburg to make its working from a village base practicable.

In the period from 1756 through 1758 the forested wilderness of interior Nova Scotia was controlled by mixed groups of Acadians or Canadians and Micmac. The King's writ, in fact, extended little beyond the settlements at Halifax, Lunenburg, Lawrencetown (see below), and the forts at Annapolis, Pisiquid (Edward), and Chignecto (Cumberland). As the most exposed and least protected settlement, Lunenburg suffered especially from this guerilla activity.[37]

Until 1758 the Cape Sable Acadian settlements had been little disturbed and had received some accretions from Annapolis. Some seventy-two people had been rounded up in 1756 but the final "clean-up" was deferred until 1759. Rightly or wrongly the successive attacks on Lunenburg have been attributed to groups based in that area. At any rate a number of such attacks, with killing, scalping, or kidnapping of settlers occurred and the work of clearing and settling was greatly impeded as families retreated to the town or men were called for militia duty. There was also some interruption of sea connections with Halifax by French privateers. The number killed or wounded at Lunenburg was never large but the attacks continued until 1759 when, of necessity, supplies of ammunition and other encouragement from the French at Louisburg and Quebec ceased. There is no doubt about the attacks, but there is little proof that the Acadians *per se* were involved.

35. Seven and one-half chains is 495 feet; if the coastline was irregular the shoreline often measured much more, and the actual area of the lots varied considerably.

36. See especially R. C. Harris, *The Seigneurial System in Early Canada* (1966), and A. H. Clark, *Three Centuries and the Island* (1959).

37. As we should doubtless call it today; in the language of the 1940's it might have been dignified by the term "Resistance."

The Abortive Lawrencetown Settlement

Only one formal settlement other than those at Halifax and Lunenburg was undertaken in the transition period of the 1750's. In 1752 the
indefatigable Charles Morris, whose investigations and surveys never
seemed to cease and who, after Mascarene's retirement, knew the
peninsula of Nova Scotia far more intimately than any other of the
official group,[38] reported on old French settlements in the Chezzetcook
area east of Halifax and opened the question of a "plantation" in that
region. Indeed the Lords of Trade envisaged that location for the
Foreign Protestants but Hopson chose Lunenburg instead, chiefly because of the former's poor harbor facilities (see Figure 8.1). There was
little official enthusiasm for any extension to the east; the tentative
settlements on the Dartmouth side of Halifax harbor, established because of adequate water for saw-milling, had been severely mauled by
the Indians. By the time Lawrence took over as acting-governor, in
1754, there cannot have been as many as five families there. Nevertheless, in that year twenty settlers were given what must have seemed
most generous grants of 1,000 acres each in a settlement named Lawrencetown to be made between Cole Harbour and present Chezzetcook.
Some two hundred regulars and a few rangers were detailed to cut a
road to the new town which, like Lunenburg, was on a peninsula which
could be "picketed in," and to protect the settlers as they built homes
and set about clearing land. The project faced many difficulties and the
protection needed was so obviously beyond the possible or probable
advantages that in 1757 the troops were withdrawn and the project
abandoned, little having been accomplished.

POPULATION   NUMBERS
AND   DISTRIBUTION

The Acadians

An estimate of the numbers and distribution of Acadians at mid-century was made in Chapter 6. In the succeeding five or six years before

38. He was, unquestionably, Nova Scotia's first practical field geographer. For an
earlier attribution of this honor to a later figure, see A. H. Clark, "Titus Smith,
Junior, and the Geography of Nova Scotia in 1801 and 1802" (1954).

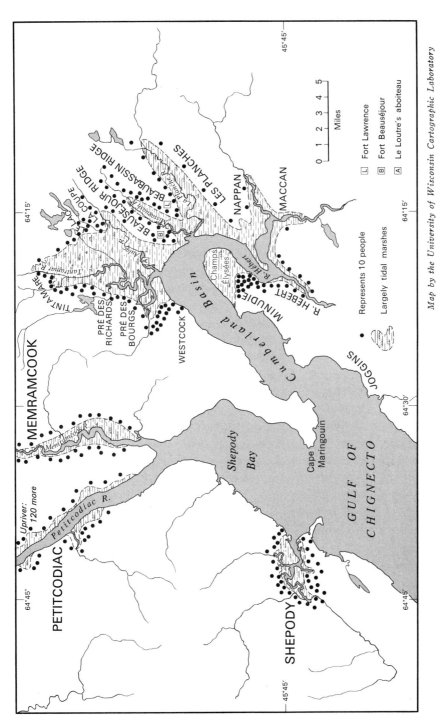

Fig. 8.3 Chignecto Settlements: Population as of 1750.

Map by the *University of Wisconsin Cartographic Laboratory*

the round-ups and deportations, the hypothesized 1,750 of Annapolis
may have reached 2,000 and the assumed 2,500 of Minas proper may
have increased as much or more. Probably at least as many of the
Pisiquid settlers left as the natural rate of increase would have added
to the settlement up to 1754, so our best estimates for early 1755 would
be for somewhere between 1,000 and 1,500 persons along the Avon, St.
Croix, and Kennetcook rivers.[39] Actual deportation figures are somewhat imprecise but from various sources Bernard has assembled the
totals shown in Table 8.1. These are clearly substantially fewer than
the numbers of residents before the round-up began, but are somewhat
closer to such totals in Annapolis and Minas than elsewhere.

TABLE 8.1 *Numbers of
Acadians deported from the
Bay area, 1755–60*

Grand Pré	2,182
Annapolis	1,664
Pisiquid	1,100*
Beaubassin	1,100*
Total	6,050*

* Approximately.
Source: Antoine Bernard,
Histoire de l'Acadie (1939), pp.
61–62.

The large movements to Tatamagouche and Remsheg from Cobequid Bay, from the Cumberland Basin settlements east of the Missaguash to the west of that river, and from the shores of the Strait of
Northumberland to Isle St-Jean and even to Quebec and Cape Breton,
make estimates of numbers and locations dubious when we look north
of Pisiquid. In 1752 a rough census of settlements in the Chignecto
area west of the Missaguash (Cumberland Basin), disclosed nearly
twice as many "refugees" as old settlers (see Table 8.2). A more
complete breakdown of the population for this area, but in 1754, is
shown in Table 8.3.

39. "Upwards of 1,000 people" were rounded up and deported from Pisiquid in
October of 1755. "Journal of Colonel John Winslow, of the Provincial Troops,
while Engaged in Removing the Acadian French Inhabitants from Grand Pré, and
the Neighbouring Settlements, in the Autumn of the Year 1755," Nova Scotia Historical Society *Collections, 3* (1883), *4* (1885). Quotation is from *4,* 178.

TABLE 8.2   *Acadian population in the Chignecto area, 1752*

Location	Old residents	Refugees	Total
Cumberland Basin			
Fort Gaspereau	0	83	83
Baie Verte	5	127	132
Portage	0	19	19
Pont à Buot	5	90	95
La Coupe	34	15	49
Le Lac	78	421	499
Beauséjour	114	93	207
Westcock	61	28	89
Pré des Bourgs	24	37	61
Pré des Richards	40	24	64
Tintamare	152	120	272
TOTAL	513	1,057	1,570
Shepody Basin			
Memramcook	245	46	291
Petitcodiac	351	1	352
Shepody	359	8	367
TOTAL	955	55	1,010
Fort Beauséjour garrison			
and employees	–	–	280
GRAND TOTAL	1,468	1,112	2,860

Source: AC, G1-*466*, 267–98. There are a number of lists which give rather different totals for what purports to be the same population.

The locational origin of the refugee groups in the Chignecto area is not easy to determine. For 1752 we have some scattered, incomplete, and contradictory information from the manuscript census compendium.[40] One list gives districts of origin of 56 of 280 families thus: (1) from beyond Chignecto Bay, thirteen (three single men from Annapolis, three families from Cobequid, two from Pisiquid, and five from Minas); (2) from east of the Missaguash, thirty-five (four from Minudie, three from Maccan, five from Nappan, eight from Rivière Hébert, three from Les Planches (near Amherst), six from La Butte, and six from Old Beaubassin; (3) from west of the Missaguash, eight (all from Westcock). It is interesting that eight families should have left Westcock and seven families of some thirty people entered it (see Tables 8.2 and 8.3). Another nominal list (and thus more convincing) identified the origin of 958 people (see Table 8.4). A similar and later, or more complete, listing made some slight changes. The Minas Basin

40. AC, Gl-*466*, 279, 288, 291–98.

TABLE 8.3 Distribution of the 2,897 Acadians west of the Missaguash River, 1754

Location	Old inhabitants					Refugees settled					Refugees not settled				
	Men	Women	Boys	Girls	Total	Men	Women	Boys	Girls	Total	Men	Women	Boys	Girls	Total
Cumberland Basin															
Westcock	11	11	17	25	64	7	7	8	11	33	–	–	–	–	–
Pré des Bourgs	10	10	18	12	50	6	7	15	11	39	–	–	–	–	–
Pré des Richards	6	5	11	9	31	4	3	7	8	22	–	–	–	–	–
Tintamare	32	31	70	51	184	11	10	19	14	54	–	–	–	–	–
La Coupe	5	6	16	13	40	–	–	–	–	–	–	–	–	–	–
Le Lac	18	19	52	27	116	21	21	35	37	114	26	25	57	36	144
Beauséjour	16	17	31	22	86	20	20	21	28	89	8	10	14	15	47
La Butte Roger	4	4	5	5	18	–	–	–	–	–	–	–	–	–	–
Jolicoeur	–	–	–	–	–	13	13	34	30	90	–	–	–	–	–
Pont à Buot	–	–	–	–	–	12	11	16	20	59	7	8	14	13	42
Portage	–	–	–	–	–	9	9	24	17	59	–	–	–	–	–
Baie Verte	–	–	–	–	–	26	26	40	40	132	–	–	–	–	–
Fort Gaspereau	–	–	–	–	–	4	4	9	11	28	–	–	–	–	–
Total (1,541)	102	103	220	164	589	133	131	228	227	719	41	43	85	64	233
Western Chignecto															
Shepody, Petit-codiac, and Memramcook	170	172	396	362	1,100	28	27	57	40	152	–	–	–	–	–
Cape Tormentine	–	–	–	–	–	10	10	16	16	52	–	–	–	–	–
Chimougouick*	–	–	–	–	–	8	8	12	9	37	–	–	–	–	–
Cap St-Laurent*	–	–	–	–	–	3	3	4	6	16	–	–	–	–	–
Total (1,357)	170	172	396	362	1,100	49	48	89	71	257	–	–	–	–	–

* Location uncertain.
Source: J. C. Webster, The Forts of Chignecto (1930), p. 37.

TABLE 8.4 *District of origin of 958 people in the Chignecto area, 1752*

District	Number of heads of family	Number of people
Cobequid	5	30
Minas	11	41
Minudie	29	164
Rivière Hébert	20	112
Maccan	13	80
Nappan	23	149
La Butte	15	84
Les Planches	7	41
Beaubassin	33	156
Westcock	18	101
	174	958

Source: AC, G1-*466*, 288–98.

as a whole increased from 71 to 155 people, Minudie to 169, Maccan and La Butte to 86, Les Planches to 59, Beaubassin to 190, and Westcock to 115. Nappan was down seven to 142 and the total had grown to 1,114. This is so close to the total of refugees by place of temporary residence (as given in Table 8.2) that one may assume that it represents a more careful and complete identification of origin.[41]

The locations of the various places of origin east of the Missaguash, and of reception west of that river, are shown on Figure 8.3. The total for Cumberland Basin east of the Missaguash in the most complete list is 854. Thus, roughly, we may assume that, in the mid-1750's, the Cumberland branch of Chignecto Bay held some 1,500 people and the Shepody Bay estuaries roughly 1,000, or 2,500 in all.

These lists give us the only rough notion we have of relative distribution of population in eastern Cumberland Basin at mid-century before Forts Lawrence and Beauséjour divided the area; after 1750 these southeastern settlements were mostly deserted but clearly many Acadians stayed as close to their old homes as possible with the hopes of returning. We cannot estimate very accurately the numbers leaving the Gulf ports for the period after 1750. Almost certainly they exceeded

41. W. R. Bird, *A Century at Chignecto* (1938), p. 80, attributes these last two lists to 1753 and 1754, by what evidence is not stated. He also identifies the engineer, Franquet, as the source, which seems reasonable. Apparently some of the higher estimates (e.g., Rameau's) have involved counting these refugees twice.

2,500 and may have reached 4,000 to 5,000, but 3,000 is suggested here as a more likely maximum. To sum up all of these suggestions and inferences, the total population of Acadians in the Chignecto Bay area and in the peninsula proper might have reached 11,000 to 12,500 by 1755 without emigration; it is concluded that, in all, 8,000 to 9,500 remained in the summer of "le grand dérangement."

There have been many attempts to make an accounting of the numbers and locations of the Acadians between 1755 and 1763, and they have led to widely varying figures. The number deported in 1755 probably represents only two-thirds to three-fourths of those actually resident at the beginning of the year. Some hundreds left for the other nearby French territories; the substantial Cape Sable-Pubnico settlement was not touched in 1755 and it absorbed escapees from Annapolis in particular. A few may have lived with the Indians in the peninsula's interior wilderness, but we conclude that most of those who avoided the round-up of 1755 found temporary homes or shelter in the territory of present New Brunswick, on the Saint John River, near Chaleur Bay, or along the Miramichi River. Between 1758 and 1762 some two thousand were rounded up, one place or another, perhaps half of those who had escaped original deportation from the areas of present New Brunswick and peninsular Nova Scotia.

In 1756 Lawrence estimated "about five hundred of the Inhabitants still lurking about in the Woods."[42] Depending on the extent of "the Woods" this was probably a gross underestimate. There was a steady trickling in of individuals to give themselves up at one or another of the forts at Chignecto, Pisiquid, or Annapolis; these were generally quartered at Halifax. In 1758 a refugee group on the Saint John River was partly rounded up and partly dispersed and its houses and outbuildings burned.[43] Most of the settlers may have escaped to Quebec or the Miramichi and the mortality must have been heavy, for food supply was marginal. The same year part of the Cape Sable group was seized. The next year some two hundred more surrendered or were captured on the Saint John and transferred to Halifax and a similar number coasted down from Miramichi and surrendered at Fort Cum-

---

42. Lawrence at Halifax to Governor Shirley in Boston, February 18, 1756. Printed in *Nova Scotia Archives. I* (1869), p. 297.

43. The Canadian officer, Boishebert, was hoping to use the settlement as a base for attacks on either New England or Nova Scotia in that "year of decision" for New France.

berland. Also in 1759, 152 more persons surrendered at Cape Sable, and were shipped to England via Halifax.[44] In 1760 another sweep up the Saint John netted three hundred prisoners who were brought to Halifax.[45] In April of 1761, the current governor, Belcher, estimated about 1,540 Acadians still in the province apart from some 440 at Halifax from earlier surrenders and captures, 240 at Chignecto, and some 1,300 at Restigouche and Miramichi.[46] In the same year 787 of the latter group were captured at Nipisiguit and 335 of them were sent to Halifax charged with piracy, the rest making submission and promising to come in as they had an opportunity to.[47] Belcher thought there were many more in the province.

Non-Acadians

Something of population growth in Halifax and Lunenburg, the only significant nuclei of non-Acadian civilian population before 1760, has been indicated above. The peak of such population in Halifax may have been reached at five to six thousand just before the establishment of Lunenburg. By 1760, when Halifax, after its first decade of excitement and glory, was sinking into the role of a standby military and naval outpost of empire, to be held in readiness for war but as cheaply as possible, the population probably decreased to fewer than three thousand.[48] We are confident that the New England contingent grew steadily in its proportion of the whole. As the public and military expenditures dwindled the opportunities for laborers diminished and the members of this group, predominantly from England, found it easy to ship out as deck hands for Massachusetts or the other colonies. From 1753 to 1760 the Lunenburg population fluctuated between one and two thousand, perhaps averaging something like fifteen hundred.

In 1758 some fifty-nine souls from the Louisburg area, including some of the few Protestant Germans who had deserted from Halifax,

44. Lawrence to Pitt, November 3, 1759, Nova Scotia Archives, *1*, 308.
45. Lawrence to Lords of Trade, from Halifax, May 11, 1760. Summarized in AC *Report for 1894* (1895), p. 221.
46. Belcher to Lords of Trade, at Halifax, April 14, 1761. Summarized in AC *Report for 1894* (1895), p. 226. This group may have been partly composed of refugees from Isle St-Jean.
47. Belcher to Egremont, from Halifax, January 9, 1762. Summarized in AC *Report for 1894* (1895), p. 229.
48. Akins, "History of Halifax," p. 69, estimated 2,500 for 1763.

made their way to Cape Breton, and been settled along the Mira River, were moved to Lunenburg and given help in getting established (remarkably generous treatment), although Bell's researches have discovered that only two of the family names of the seventeen families in this group survived until modern times. He thinks the others may have moved out soon thereafter to Halifax. Certainly there was a good deal of movement to and from Halifax in the later 1750's including single men and heads of families who could find work to get cash for the many things they needed (clothes, tools, and the like) which they could not raise themselves nor obtain from the government bounty. In 1769 there appear to have been some 350 men and 1,114 women and children, and roughly 600 milking cows in the settlement.[49] There had been a "weeding out" of the weaker, as well perhaps as some of the more enterprising, through death, accident, Indian attacks, and the like, but especially we may suppose through emigration to Halifax. In 1767 some 264 "Germans and other foreigners" were resident at Halifax, a number consonant with other estimates of the late fifties and early sixties cited by Bell,[50] who turned up thirty-five to forty names in Halifax at later periods who were listed at Lunenburg in the 1750's. Before the New England invasion the total civilian population of present Nova Scotia cannot have been far from a total of some 6,000 souls, with the Lunenburgers and Acadians forming slightly less than half of the total.

ECONOMIC ACTIVITY

The Acadians

Until 1755 the Acadians carried on their normal agricultural and pastoral activities as described in Chapter 6 with little change in Annapolis, Minas, and the Shepody estuaries, but faced greater or lesser degrees of disturbance elsewhere. Apparently they continued their illegal trade in livestock, meat, hides, and grain with the French

49. DesBrisay, *History of Lunenburg*, p. 54. A count for 1767 lists for Lunenburg a total of 1,417 people of "German and other Foreign" derivation out of a total of 1,468 in the township, suggesting further emigration to balance natural increase. See also "A General Return of the Several Townships in the Province of Nova Scotia for the first day of January, 1767," Nova Scotia Historical Society *Collections*, 7 (1891), opp. p. 56.
50. *Foreign Protestants*, pp. 615–23.

in the areas of present New Brunswick, Prince Edward Island, and Cape Breton Island, either on their own or through New England traders, if we may judge from the number of proclamations and acts to suppress such activity which originated in Halifax.[51] Interestingly the specific mention of rye, barley, and oats, along with wheat and peas, suggests an increasing variety in their cereal and pulse production.

Of settlements other than Annapolis and Minas, Pisiquid may have been least disturbed but the exodus from Cobequid was large and the Cumberland Basin settlements east of the Missaguash River were nearly deserted. Those in the basin lands west of that river not only lived under the shadow of imminent conflict but had large numbers of refugees quartered among them, and the effort of the Abbé Le Loutre to develop his pet aboiteau project on the upper Aulac River, under conditions of virtually forced labor, must have further disrupted their normal routine.[52] Much more nearly normal activities were maintained in the Shepody estuaries, where the refugees were fewer and the surveillance of the fort commander less imminent.

After the dispersion, the nearly complete destruction of the settlers' buildings, and the slaughter or driving away of the livestock, the Acadians who escaped deportation were driven to a virtually Indian mode of existence. In the Cape Sable-Pubnico area life proceeded more normally until they, too, were removed in 1758 and 1759, but hunting and fishing inevitably had played a larger role in an area where there was little opportunity to dyke tidal lands and the farming of the "upland" (i.e., non-marsh) areas was unrewarding. In the Shepody estuaries a group of thirty Acadians were rounded up (near the head of tide on the Petitcodiac) in 1758, but generally the fields and dykes lay deserted and untended there, as in the other dyked land areas, after 1755. The concentrations on the Saint John River and at the various estuaries on the Gulf coast engaged in some little agriculture and, where possible, fished but must have depended heavily on hunting for their food.

The Lunenburgers

By what can only be described as rare good luck, the initial settlement at Lunenburg encompassed the largest single block of potential

51. Some of the many examples will be found in AC, NSB-*7*, 75–78, 79–83, 110–16: 1754, and NSB-*8*, 54–62: 1755.

52. J. C. Webster, *The Forts of Chignecto* (1930), p. 33

good crop soils on the whole Atlantic Coast of Nova Scotia (see Figure 8.2 and Chapter 2) composed of Wolfville and Bridgewater loams on the low, rolling drumlins which formed much of the terrain. There has been a lot of misunderstanding implicit in the interpretation of the famous Lunenburg schooner fishery of the nineteenth century as a case of environmental determinism. In that view, a people of largely inland agricultural tradition was dumped unceremoniously on a stern and rockbound coast and, facing an inhospitable environment for farming, found their faces turned to the sea as the only way to make a living. Without in anyway denigrating the fishery achievement of the nineteenth century, it certainly must be remembered that most of the Lunenburgers, for most of their history, were farmers, that their farming success was solid and continuing, and that their achievements as husbandmen, if less romantic and spectacular, supplied a firmer, deeper, and wider economic base over the years than did their accomplishments as builders and operators of fishing schooners. If there is a shred of argument left in this history for the environmental determinists it lies rather in the fact that, by a stroke of good fortune, they did in fact settle on a small area of remarkably good farming land in marked contrast to the none-too-fertile soils of the peninsula as a whole. Perhaps this, along with the character of the people and the relative degree of exposure to Indian attack, ought to be seen as a major reason for the success of Lunenburg in contrast with the failure of Lawrencetown.

Initially Colonel Lawrence, in charge of the settlement, encouraged the sowing of oats, barley, turnips, and potatoes but discouraged the bread grains (wheat, rye, and Indian corn) as taking too much out of the land until the settlers had manure. They still lacked livestock at the beginning of the second summer (1754), yet by December of that year some hundred or more had gone to settle on their "country lots" and a first distribution of livestock had been obtained from New England. Each "unit" of livestock was distributed by lot to two families, the units consisting of one cow and one sheep, or five or six sheep, or one sow and one goat, or four sheep and two goats. There were units also for single men of various classes. There was some uncounted distribution of poultry. Bulls, rams, billygoats, and boars were kept collectively in one of the commons reserved at either edge of town and appropriate charges made for their services. Unhappily, in the winter of 1754/55 a large part of the livestock died from exposure and malnutrition.

In 1755 some Acadian livestock (probably mostly cattle, and fewer than one thousand head), available after the deportation, appear to have been driven to Halifax and taken by sea to Lunenburg. How many were involved we do not know.[53] A number of indications, not very well documented, lead us to conclude that a group of Lunenburgers may have ventured through the woods to Minas in 1756, rounded up some cattle and horses which had survived the winter unattended, and managed to drive a few score back across the peninsula. If indeed they did, it was a spectacular feat for there was no good track except Indian trails, which inevitably used water connections. One must assume that most of the ultimate livestock population of the Lunenburg settlement came from New England.

It had been intended that victualing of Lunenburg should be cut off as early as 1755 and it is clear that each year more and more of the settlers were becoming relatively self-sufficient in amount (if not in kind) of food,[54] but large numbers were still on government rations during most of the period. Not only the Indian raids but the weather posed severe problems. A prolonged drought in the summer of 1757 seriously depleted whatever crops the settlers may have had and the harsh winter of 1758/59 destroyed quantities of stored roots and some of their animals. They approached adequate numbers of livestock only slowly and whatever agricultural surpluses they may have had to sell in Halifax (potatoes, turnips, and possibly cabbages) did not go far toward helping them meet their shortages of bread grains and meat. Firewood and cooperage materials (staves, hoops, and butts) found a good market in the capital too and firewood was sent even to Boston.[55] By October of 1754 there were five sawmills built, three by the Lunenburgers themselves and two by outsiders in Mahone Bay to the northeast, but such saw-milling as was undertaken before 1760 barely sufficed to supply their own great needs and the beginnings of the great and justly famous Lunenburg fishery of later times had not yet been made.[56] In the period, major roads had been opened to present Mahone Bay and the La Have River opposite present Bridgewater. However the

53. Bell, *Foreign Protestants*, pp. 488–89.

54. See Bell, *Foreign Protestants*, ch. 12, for citation of relevant documents for the period.

55. AC, NSA-*56*, 76–104: 1754.

56. A 1762 report declared that "they have no inclination for the Fishery tho' well situated for that purpose." AC, NSA-*67*, 18–63, quoted in Innis, *Select Documents*, p. 243.

"roads," eight feet wide, must have been the roughest sort of cart-tracks through the stumps, rocks, and swamps. There were many proposals for a road to Halifax but all were abortive.

Lawrencetown and the South Coast generally

Of these settlements there is not very much to be said. As along the whole Atlantic coast, except where, between Mahone Bay and Petite Rivière, the slate-derived drumlin field of present Lunenburg and Queens counties reaches the sea, the soils of the coastal areas are most unrewarding and, despite repeated trials, have never afforded a reasonable return for a concentration on plant or animal husbandry. Living between the sea and the forest its inhabitants, to the degree that they have been successful primary producers, have had to derive most of their living from one or the other. The exploitation of the land in an agricultural sense, as more than two centuries of subsequent history has demonstrated abundantly, was doomed to be limited to patchy fields of wild or tame hay, oats, potatoes, or vegetables. These amounted to little more than garden plots, and along with a cow or two, a few swine, and some poultry, had to be tended by the women while the men were fishing or lumbering.

Halifax

By the same token, agriculture could not, and of course did not, provide any kind of a reasonable economic base for the settlers around Halifax harbor. The thin soils were soon exhausted of their modicum of fertility by a few seasons of sparse crops. Every effort was made, indeed, to encourage the production of hay, grain, and roots in the Chebucto Bay lands by bounties granted from time to time, but the production was negligible. The references in official documents, and by unofficial observers, are somewhat contradictory. One report (which by internal evidence sounds like special pleading) asserted, in 1758: "Fifteen hundred Acres of Land, upon the Peninsula, have been clear'd and fenced in, by the Inhabitants, sowed with Grass, and planted with Potatoes, and other Roots and garden stuff, and some Grain and above Twenty Houses built, on the Farm Lotts; of all this land the soldiers have pillaged the Produce and entirely destroy'd the Fences and buildings, except two or three, very remote. At least forty Houses, in the suburbs, have been pull'd down and burnt, by the soldiers . . . ."[57] The apparently most disinterested and dispassionate account of Halifax extant, of 1762, reviewed the agricultural activity of the previous thirteen years.[58] At that time the town, including both suburbs, had some seven hundred houses and about 2,500 people, most of them living directly or indirectly from public expenditures. There was not, in the judgment of the writer, "one Family in the town nor in the parts Circumjacent that subsist by Husbandry." By the aid of an excise tax on liquor, Cornwallis had provided a bounty of one pound sterling per acre fenced and cleared of woods. This led to the fencing and clearing of about one-third of the 3,000-acre Halifax peninsula, which had been divided into five-acre lots for farming purposes, ". . . but all the land being covered with fall'n Trees and the moss becoming dry by removing the Trees, was fired and with extreme violence (as dry moss burns like wild fire) . . . and discovered that the Soil in general was covered with a bed of stones, and no attempts have been made since of improving them . . . ."[59] Precisely the same experience was had with the 220-acre lots surrounding the harbor and Bedford Basin. Lawrence, alarmed at the cost of hay imported from Massachusetts, had given substantial bounties for hay production and stone fencing of fields to keep out the animals, but even with liberal applications of dung the production failed to come anywhere close to justifying the bounties. Despite all the efforts to establish Dartmouth as a self-supporting suburb there were, in 1762, only two families there cutting wood.

Except for fish, which must always have been plentiful and cheap and a mainstay of the diet of the mass of the people,[60] virtually all the food was brought in to Halifax from elsewhere; under pressure, and in inadequate amounts, it came from the Acadians until 1755 (including live animals and salted meat derived from the confiscations of that year) and, both before and after, from New England, New York, and Pennsylvania. Trading and fishing vessels bound therefrom to Halifax, used whatever open hold capacity they had available to bring supplies

57. AC, NSA-*62*, 11–23: "State of facts relating to the complaints of the Freeholders of Nova Scotia." Excerpts have been printed in Innis, *Select Documents*, pp. 228–30.

58. AC, NSA-*67*, 18–63: "Description of the Several Towns in the Province of Nova Scotia."

59. *Ibid.* Printed in Innis, *Select Documents*, p. 241.

60. True, it is rarely referred to, but one is reminded of the adage that "what everyone knows is never in the newspapers."

(including, as we have seen, hay) to a good cash market. This trade, together with that in rum, was the major device by which so much of the heavy government spending in Halifax found its ultimate way south. Fortunately for Halifax the settling there of increasing numbers of traders and fishermen from New England kept some of this bounty from leaking away.

A substantial effort went into the local exploitation of forest products although, at best, that production could reduce only slightly the heavy demands for firewood, squared timber, masts, planks, boards, and cooperage needs. The wood about Halifax in the fifties was chiefly maple, birch, beech, ash, and a little oak, but up the basin were fine stands of pines fit for masts of thirty-inch diameter.[61] The difficulties of maintaining sawmills, necessarily away from the peninsula because of the need for water power, in the face of Indian attacks, were extreme, and the needs for fuel in the bitter, damp weather led to much wood that had gone into buildings or fences being used for firewood each winter. The lack of stoves, which did not become widespread in Nova Scotia for another century (although the Lunenburgers must have known of them and wished for them), meant the same excessive use of wood in inefficient fireplaces which plagued New England's first two centuries. Some firewood did come from Pisiquid in the early years, but the hostile attitude of the Indians led to the refusal of the Acadians to try to bring it in. Some came from Lunenburg—and even from New England.

These problems suggested further efforts to work the coal mines at Joggins, at the entrance to Cumberland Basin. Since the seventeenth century every vessel standing in to that basin on the tide in clear weather had seen the seams of coal exposed on the cliffs and various attempts to exploit it, despite the completely exposed roadstead and the extreme tidal range, had been made with very little productive result. Moreover the mercantilist bias of the Lords of Trade made them rigorously opposed to the development of any coal mines in the area lest it encourage manufacturing industry and so compete with the home industry.[62] One of nature's blessings, in their view of things in the mid-eighteenth century, was that New England had not been so endowed.

61. *Journal of the Commissioners for Trade and Plantations, January 1749/50 to December 1753* (1932), p. 3.
62. AC, NSA-*46*, 135: Whitehall, March 6, 1752.

As early as 1750 construction of two vessels for the fishery was under way[63] and the building of shallops and schooners apparently continued throughout the decade. But shortages and heavy imports suggest that wood exports, except perhaps of barrels for and with fish, were negligible from Halifax.[64] A bounty act of 1757 for encouraging the building of stone walls made clear in its preamble that ". . . there are no other Materials at hand to fence the same [i.e., the "Lotts"] but Stones."[65] As we have seen there was some use of brick and stone in building, but the lack of locally available sandstone or limestone meant that it had to come from a distance, sometimes as ships' ballast.

If agriculture, lumbering, mining, or quarrying all were negligible in the Halifax area, nevertheless the fishery, closely associated with the very active commercial enterprise, seems to have made substantial strides in the decade. Halifax shared with Canso (and later largely replaced it) and with Louisburg after 1758, the roles of both a fishery base and an entrepôt for the collection and shipping of fish to the continental colonies, the West Indies, and Europe. We are, however, short of precise figures for Halifax. A report of 30,000 quintals cured in Nova Scotia in 1750[66] may have applied chiefly to Canso, but the frequent mention of bounties, and of regulations about the export of fish from Halifax suggests that local activity was substantial.[67] The fishing schooners left for the banks as early as March,[68] and whereas the drying of fish apparently was not a major occupation in Halifax itself in the first decade, its harbor apparently was an important base for the schooner fishery.

The documents have frequent indirect references to trade although it is hard to find specific figures for total imports and exports of individual years. The expenditure of hundreds of thousands of pounds and the

63. AC, NSA-*36*, 5–11: Mauger reporting in London to the Lords of Trade on the first phase of the Halifax settlement.

64. There is one suggestion of export of wood and wood products in an Act of Council of October 1754, in Halifax, which carefully regulated the measurements and quality of a wide variety of wood exports, and of the barreling in which fish and other commodities were to be shipped. AC, NSB-7, 129–51.

65. AC, NSB-*9*, 32–37.

66. AC, NSA-*39*, 77–83: Hugh Davidson's personal report to the Lords of Trade in London, November 8, 1750.

67. Writing of 1750, Akins avers (without citation of evidence, however) that "Halifax Harbor was the resort of a large number of fishing vessels." Akins "History of Halifax," p. 19.

68. *Ibid.*, p. 25.

entry of scores of ships each year with supplies for the garrison attest the degree to which Halifax must have become a major, and profitable shipping center.

THE REMOVAL OF THE ACADIANS

The outstanding event of the transition period was the deportation and dispersion of most of the Acadians. Its impact has drawn a strong thread through much of the discussion of this chapter. The details have been described in so many publications[69] that it would be a work of supererogation to repeat them here; such as are relevant to our present purposes have been included above.

By any objective reading of the evidence the overwhelming majority of Acadians in Annapolis and Minas remained truly neutral in sentiment through the troubled years of the early forties and fifties, and a substantial proportion of those in Cobequid, Pisiquid, and the Chignecto settlements may have done so too although, for those west of the Missaguash, and in the Memramcook, Petitcodiac, and Shepody settlements, such neutrality under French military control would have been hard to maintain. However unreasonable it may have seemed to British officialdom that people, living on soil recognized in open treaties for nearly four decades by the French as British (as the lands on the peninsula clearly were), should have refused consistently to accept one of the most widely recognized responsibilities of a subject (loyalty to the sovereign authority and willingness to bear arms in its defense), in retrospect their lack of open support for people of their own language, faith, and traditions from Canada and Cape Breton (which the missionaries had kept very much alive since 1710) seems even more remarkable. The explanation must lie in their primary concern with a love for their ancestral lands, however clouded their legal title, and for their distinctive way of life. Their folk memories reached back over a century of repeated attack and counterattack, with alternating success and control by the two competing powers, and they seemed to have had an almost intuitive wariness of deep involvement on either side that might give an excuse to the eventual victor to deprive them of their rich but hard-won grainfields and pastures behind the dykes.

69. Largely based upon "The Journal of Colonel John Winslow," pp. 71–196, and Placide Gaudet, "Acadian Genealogy and Notes" (1906).

The most equivocal aspect of the situation was the relationship of the Acadians with the Indians; more than anything else this may have led to the eventual tragedy of wholesale deportation. The successful maintenance of their settlements for more than a century gives evidence, more persuasive than any documentary record, of a harmonious *modus vivendi* with the Micmac. This was greatly aided by two factors: a good deal of intermarriage in the seventeenth century (although apparently much less in the eighteenth) which had created blood ties, and the fact that active proselytization by the missionaries for more than a century had firmly attached the Indians to the same faith. In peace and war the Micmac passed by and through the Acadian settlements, traded fur, feathers, game, and canoes for goods obtained by the Acadians from Boston or Louisburg, and maintained their traditional ways of life in the vast interior that the Acadians traversed but never settled. An almost symbiotic relationship of mutual tolerance and support grew up between the two cultures.

When the French authorities incited, on the peninsula and particularly against Halifax after 1749, the same sort of savage Indian guerrilla warfare that had been prosecuted so successfully and for so long on the New England borders, the Indians of necessity came and went near, or through, the Acadian settlements, particularly those of Chignecto, Cobequid, and Pisiquid. There is little evidence of direct Acadian collaboration but they rarely reported Indian movements. They probably were not as fearful of retaliatory Indian attacks as they pretended to be, in avoiding the role of informers, but they did look on the Indians as a more permanent element of the environment than either British or French authority.

The degree of sympathy for, or identification with, the interests of Quebec, Louisburg, or metropolitan France among the Acadians was understandable, indeed almost inevitable, and requires no explanation or excuse. It seems to have been moderate, rather detached, and to have changed little over the years. On the other hand the New England attitude toward the Canadians and their Indian allies, after more than a century of bloody frontier warfare, steadily hardened and came to dominate the thinking of the British authorities in Annapolis and Halifax. The French use of Indians on the peninsula in the 1740's and 1750's turned much of this bitterness toward the Acadians. It was very easy for the soldiers and settlers at Halifax, in this atmosphere, to hold the Acadians in some degree responsible for the wounding, killing, and

scalping that took place even within hailing distance of the new fortress. The embers of the chronic suspicion of French and "papists"
took little to be fanned into a flame that was to ravage the great
innocent mass of the Acadians along with the few guilty. "Religious
freedom" (a somewhat ambiguous term in view of the civil disabilities
for Roman Catholics under British law of the time) might have been
guaranteed to the Acadians by treaty but they were of a hated faith,
they shared this faith with the Indians, and, as a result, they could be
expected to aid and abet them. And while the Indians were rarely
caught, the Acadians were there, in their homes and fields, to bear the
full force of the reaction.

There is no simple explanation of the ultimate decision to uproot the
Acadians, destroy their homes, confiscate their lands and livestock, and
deport them. Proposals to remove them, if they refused to take unqualified oaths of allegiance, had been discussed openly in official correspondence since the capture of Port Royal in 1710. As a corollary there
had been repeated promotions of schemes for settling either New
Englanders or Old World Protestants, either among them or on their
vacated lands. Yet the arguments for allowing the Acadians to remain[70]
were persuasive and, indeed until the late 1750's, there was no strong
and unfulfilled demand for land in Nova Scotia by the ordinary New
England settlers who would in fact occupy it. In the event, the movement into the vacated lands was slow and reluctant. Moreover, as we
have seen, for a variety of reasons the Foreign Protestants who were
brought to Halifax in the early fifties were ultimately settled elsewhere.

The suggested motives for the deportation of implacable, cold-
blooded vengeance for Indian attacks, or of calculated chicanery designed to profit from the disposal of Acadian lands and stock on the
part of Governor Lawrence and his advisers, are not supported by
adequate evidence. The unhappy event has to be seen, rather, as the
result of a number of converging developments: the increasing bitterness of the undeclared war after 1750; the emigration of several
thousand Acadians, largely on their own initiative, to areas under
French sovereignty or control; the intransigence of the remaining
Acadians in their refusal to take the oath of allegiance; the undermin-
ing of British confidence by dismaying military reverses in the interior
of the continent despite the capture of the Chignecto forts in 1755; the

70. Notable among these was the need to have a local farming population to
supply the garrison with food.

local freedom of action which their fall made possible; the rise of temperature of New England attitudes toward both French and Indians which was fed by the cumulative frustrations that began with the return of Louisburg to the French in 1749; and the impatient and injudicial temperament of Governor Lawrence.

In the moral and political climate of the time, and in consciousness of the ease with which the people of any nation in our own time can rationalize similar operations,[71] it may be surprising that deportation was so long delayed. Had the British had the means to effect it and to support their garrisons without the Acadian crops, flocks, and herds, it would very likely have occurred many years earlier. Upon calm review, and despite the horror with which (even lacking Longfellow's effective propaganda) we should inevitably view it today, the conclusion is almost inescapable that if the area were to remain safely in British hands in the midst of a bitter struggle for survival between the British and French empires in North America (the ultimate outcome of which seemed very much in doubt in 1755), the Acadians would have had to take, and to have proved their sincerity in so doing, an unqualified oath of allegiance or be forced to leave. All the evidence affirms that they never would have taken such an oath except under a degree of duress that would have nullified its meaning, and that they never would have left Annapolis or Minas, at least, except by force.

In extenuation of the highly emotional attitude of Acadian historians to the "grand dérangement," however, one can advance more than a natural reaction to the uprooting of their forefathers from their ancestral lands. Lawrence went ahead with the deportation program without authority from Britain, acted callously, if not indeed brutally and dishonestly, in the process and, largely on his own, decided upon the unhappy policy of distributing them through the British American colonies rather than allowing them to go to French colonies to the solace of traditions and culture of their own faith and tongue. If the removal is considered to have been inevitable, the manner of effecting it can have little rational apologia. J. B. Brebner well summed up the story of the Acadians in the years after 1755:

. . . of how over six thousand peaceful farming people were by force and strategem rounded up and hurriedly [perhaps an imprecision] placed on transports and distributed from Massachusetts to South Carolina; of how

71. Consider, for example, the removal of Americans and Canadians of Japanese origin from the Pacific coast in World War II.

others took refuge in the forests of what are now New Brunswick, Prince Edward Island, and Quebec, or made their way to Quebec City, the Ohio valley, and Louisiana; of how some of them who escaped the first seizure only to be made captives in the terrible guerilla campaign of the succeeding years were sent to France and England or allowed to join the French in St. Pierre and Miquelon or the West Indies; or of how many lost their lives from starvation, exposure, ship-wreck, and the hazards of war. . . . For eight years the destruction and dispersal went on. . . . Only the coming of peace in 1763 put an end to it. Then individuals and groups of Acadians began to find their ways back to their homeland and, although they were not allowed to take up their old properties, they found abiding places here and there in what are now the three Maritime Provinces of Canada.[72]

THE RETURN OF THE ACADIANS

One of the great difficulties in estimating numbers and location of Acadians after 1760 comes from the extraordinary mobility of different groups and the yearning for their homes that kept them as close as possible to the Fundy dyked-land areas, or drew them back thereto by the hundreds from their ports of disembarkation southward along the Atlantic coast. Many of those picked up on the Saint John or along the Gulf from 1758 to 1762 may have had such a history. Moreover scores filtered back into the peninsula itself, as near to their original homes as possible. Concern as to how many there were, where they were, and what to do with them occupies a prominent place in the official correspondence of the early 1760's. In the spring of 1764 Governor Wilmot estimated some 1,056 in or near Halifax, 227 near Fort Edward (Pisiquid), 91 at Annapolis, and 388 near Fort Cumberland, a total of 1,762,[73] to which might have been added a few score on the Island of St. John and some hundreds along the Saint John River, the Gulf coast north of Chignecto, and in the southern Cape Breton-Canso area. In late 1764 a group of roughly six hundred of those at Halifax hired vessels at their own expense and sailed for the French West Indies.[74]

With the collapse of French resistance in North America much of the ostensible purpose in removing the Acadians had disappeared and

72. Brebner, *New England's Outpost*, pp. 224–26. See also A. G. Doughty, *The Acadian Exiles* (1916), esp. ch. 10.

73. Enclosure in Wilmot to Halifax, March 22, 1764, at Halifax. Summarized in AC *Report for 1894* (1895), p. 252.

74. Wilmot to Halifax, at Halifax, December 18, 1764. *Nova Scotia Archives. I,* 350.

the original ambivalence of the British authorities about the removal
was reflected in many of the dispatches of the later 1750's and early
1760's. With the entry of the New Englanders, ignorant of the management of the dyked lands, there are repeated requests for Acadian aid
(the tail-end of a hurricane in 1759 had severely damaged dykes and
aboiteaux over a wide area) and the government in Halifax found the
maintenance of the Acadians interned there a heavy financial burden.[75]
The refusal of the southern colonies to accept them, their unwillingness
to go to Quebec, and the costs of shipping them to France or the West
Indies also played their parts. At the end of 1762 the Lords of Trade
concluded that further removal was neither necessary nor politic.[76] In
October of 1764 Lieutenant-Governor Francklin had persuaded the
council in Halifax to offer land to some 165 families of Acadians, if
they were prepared to take the oath (as a large number were), on the
basis of fifty acres for each head of a family and ten acres more for
each member of their households. They were to be settled in rather
widespread locations, well away from the sea; thirty families at Halifax, fifteen at Lunenburg, and ten families apiece in each of a dozen
other places.[77] Other plans for different distributions and larger allotments were also considered. In 1767 and 1768 the "Acadian shore"
settlement of present Digby County along St. Mary's Bay was laid out
for the Acadians and others were allowed to return to the old settlements at Pubnico.

Despite these grudgingly encouraging moves many of the Acadians
became downhearted when it became clear that the marshland areas of
Annapolis, Minas, and Cumberland basins were to be closed to them
and they went off voluntarily to Quebec, St. Pierre and Miquelon
(despite strong efforts to prevent this), or to France. Thus the estimates of population for 1771 were still low (see Table 8.5).

Probably the additions to the population on the peninsula were few
thereafter, although some may have moved from St. Pierre and Miquelon to Cape Breton Island and others have left Quebec for the Shepody
Bay region. Thus, in the 1780's, Chéticamp on Cape Breton's west
coast drew some from the French islands off Newfoundland's southern

75. Belcher to Colonel Forster, at Halifax, June 18, 1761. *Nova Scotia Archives
I*, 317–18.
76. Minutes of the Proceedings of the Lords Commissioners of Trade and
Plantations, December 3, 1762. *Nova Scotia Archives. I*, 337–38.
77. Beamish Murdoch, *A History of Nova-Scotia or Acadie* (1865–67), 2, 443.

TABLE 8.5 *Distribution of Acadians, 1771*

Location	Number of families	Number of people
Cape Breton		
Neirichak (Arichat)	33	174
Petit Degras (Petit-de-Grat)	9	37
Des Kousses (D'Escousse)	15	73
St-Pierre-Lardoise (St. Peters and L'Ardoise)	11	63
Labrador (Lake Bras d'Or)	7	32
Louisbourg	4	22
Baye de Gabarus	6	38
		439
The Peninsula		
Windsor	17	82
Halifax et environs	24	118
Chezzetcook	17	96
Cap de Sable	12	50
Baye Ste-Marie	24	98
		444
Present New Brunswick area		
Rivière St-Jean	37	158
Ft. Cumberland	16	70
Memramcook	23	87
Petkoodiak	14	51
		366
Total		1,249

Source: British Museum, Add. MS 19071, fol. 125. Printed in *Collection de documents inédits . . . sur le Canada et l'Amérique,* comp. Henri-Raymond Casgrain, 2 (1889), 83–84.

coast, but most, probably, from a variety of locations in southern Cape Breton and both sides of the Strait of Northumberland.[78] The spread of the Acadians from the 1770's onward was rather like that after 1670; sons or more adventurous oldsters moved out of existing settlements to start new ones. Two distributions recorded for 1790 and 1803 (Tables 8.6 and 8.7) may serve to indicate something of the geography of the Acadian reestablishment.

The presence of many new names, unknown in any of the old Acadian records, indicates that there had been an infusion of non-Acadian families from various places but the overwhelming majority of

78. Père Anselme Chiasson, *Chéticamp, Histoire et Traditions acadiennes* (1961), pp. 29–31.

TABLE 8.6 *Distribution of Acadian families in the Maritime Provinces in 1790*

Cape Sable and St. Mary's Bay	110
Cape Breton and Tracadie (Antigonish County)	130
Cumberland (chiefly west of the Missaguash and probably largely in the Shepody estuaries)	140
Chezzetcook	30–35
Isle St-Jean	66
Miramichi and Chaleur Bay	200–300

Source: British Museum, Add. MS 19071 fol. 127. Printed in *Collection de documents inédits . . . sur le Canada et l'Amérique,* comp. Henri-Raymond Casgrain, *2* (1889), 85.

TABLE 8.7 *Acadians in the Nova Scotian peninsula (excluding Minudie) in 1803*

St. Mary's Bay (Clare Township, Digby County)	1,080
Tousquet (probably present Yarmouth to present Shelburne, especially Pubnico)	400
Chezzetcook and Prospect (present Halifax County)	520
Canso (present Antigonish, Guysborough, and Richmond counties)	1,584
Chéticamp (Inverness County)	353
Total	3,937

Source: From the report of an episcopal visit (the first to Acadian lands since 1685) by Mgr. Denaut, summarized in François-Edmé Rameau de Saint-Père, *Une Colonie Féodale en Amérique; l'Acadie (1604–1881)* (1889), *2,* 255–56. In addition he estimated 742 for Prince Edward Island, 351 for the Magdalen Islands, 1,162 for Minudie and the Shepody estuaries, 2,121 on the Gulf coast of present New Brunswick, and 446 in present Madawaska County, N. B. This total of 8,759 included some in present Cumberland County, so that Nova Scotia thus had a total in excess of 4,000, and more than in either present Prince Edward Island or New Brunswick. Rameau infers from similar ecclesiastical evidence that the total had increased to 11,630 by 1812, thus approaching or exceeding the totals of sixty years earlier.

families clearly stemmed from pre-dispersion stock. Indeed the multiplication of individual families led to whole villages or groups of villages becoming dominated by one or two names and the necessary resort to patronymics, or toponymics (locality descriptions) such as "la forêt" or "la rivière," to sort out the individuals.

PREPARATION FOR THE NEW ENGLAND IMMIGRATION

After the capture of Louisburg in 1758 and the slow attrition of Acadian and Indian resistance, the rather faltering promotion of settlements by New Englanders on the old Acadian lands and on the harbors of the south coast gathered steam. A very inaccurately optimistic description of the evacuated Acadian lands was circulated in Halifax and New England in the autumn of 1758. Claims of 100,000 acres of plowlands and the same quantity of pasture, orchard, and garden in the old Acadian lands were made therein by Lawrence.[79] In 1759 more details or claims were released. The home government had some doubt about plans that clearly favored New Englanders over discharged British soldiers but Lawrence answered them that ". . . every soldier that has come into the Province, since the establishment of Halifax, has either quitted it or become a dram-seller."[80]

The groundwork for the actual New England settlements, which did not properly get under way until the year of Lawrence's death (1760), and signaled the end of the transition, was laid in a number of ways. An assembly that Lawrence, despite repeated clear directives from the Lords of Trade, had avoided calling for five years, from a mixture of sound reasons and sheer casuistry (in rationalization of his doubts about democracy and New Englanders), came into being and the assurance of a popular voice in government was given. The province was divided into five counties of Annapolis, Kings, Cumberland, Lunenburg, and Halifax (see End papers).[81] A typically New England township system of land grants was used: units of twelve miles square

79. AC, NSA-*62*, 193–96.

80. AC, NSA-*64*, 11: 1760. This widely-quoted exaggeration matches an earlier one that all the disbanded soldiers had become privateers. Both hyperboles made their points, however; the soldiers did not take to fishing or farming and did not make good pioneers. See Thomas C. Haliburton, *An Historical and Statistical Account of Nova Scotia* (1829), *1*, 235.

81. In terms of present boundaries (with some minor adjustments; see End papers), Cumberland was about as it is now, except that it did not include the Parrsboro-Cape Chignecto area. This latter was part of a far larger Kings County, which surrounded Minas Basin, taking in present Kings, Hants, and Colchester counties.

or just under 100,000 acres.[82] Each head of family was to receive 100 acres of wild woodland, and each member of the family 50 acres in addition, with a limit of 5,000 acres per family. Each ten years was to see one-third of the area cultivated or enclosed and further grants were not to be made until the earlier conditions were fulfilled. Then the settlements at Grand Pré (Horton), Canard (Cornwallis), Pisiquid (Falmouth), and Annapolis (north side, Granville, south side, Annapolis) were put in train. Associations were formed in New England, deputations inspected the lands and formal grants were given. At the same time similar plans were made for Atlantic harbors, led off by Liverpool. Then, in 1760, the settlers started to come, perhaps nearly two thousand in that year,[83] and the transition was at an end. The new province, British in the majority of its population, its government, and its traditions, as well as in formal sovereignty, had taken shape. In eleven years Acadia truly had become Nova Scotia.

82. This was about four times the area of a survey township of the township-section-range system used for western lands in both the United States and Canada.
83. AC, NSA-*64*, 127.

9

Conclusion

❧

In the Introduction it was noted that the establishment and evolution of the region, Acadia, from the early seventeenth to the mid-eighteenth centuries, with which this study has been concerned, was one of innumerable individual developments in the process of the expansion of peoples and cultures from western Europe to mid-latitude lands overseas which followed the great explorations of the fifteenth and sixteenth centuries. For more than three hundred years the process continued, to North America, southern South America, South Africa, Australia, and New Zealand. Initially the principal hearths were the British Islands, France, and the Low Countries although the German-speaking states made massive contributions in the eighteenth century and, before the process had run its course, many millions had been drawn, as well, from Iberia, Scandinavia, and from Europe eastward and southward to the Balkans, the Black Sea, and the Urals. Here and there important contingents came from Africa and Asia. But the process really began on the eastern coasts of North America in what are now the United States and Canada, and was dominated in the sixteenth and seventeenth centuries by French and English, the latter accompanied by large groups from other parts of the British Isles.

It was also emphasized that there are a number of ingredients that contribute to the basic human geography of any of these areas at any time. Of fundamental importance are the natural characteristics, the antecedent cultural occupation and its effects, the nature of the invad-

370

ing culture, and the regional and world-wide contexts of the political, commercial, and strategic relationships of the region. In these last, relative location is of the utmost importance and not just in regard to bordering areas, vital as these usually are, but in connection with broader avenues and patterns of trade and of international military rivalries. Into the mixture that was Acadia went elements from all of these categories and it has been the concern of this study to describe the manner in which they blended to form the changing geography of a century and a half. No human geography is ever static, for populations fluctuate in size and people relocate themselves as cultures change with innovation and diffusion, as nature undergoes faster or slower mutations (often, as in biotic and pedological changes, markedly assisted by cultural process), and as, under the technology that any group commands and the goals of cultural development it sets for itself in any period, the balance of population and resources may be progressively altered. In microcosm, Acadia in evolution illustrates all of these intertwined processes which result in changing geographical character, but its record challenges some of the widely accepted generalizations that have been made about such processes.

Historical investigations of changing institutions, ideas, geographies, or whatever, may have many purposes. The most basic concern probably always is, and should be, to set down as carefully as resources of time, facilities, and skill allow, the accurate record of relevant phenomena and events. In the historical geography of the overseas expansion of Europe there are scores or hundreds of such studies to be made and very few yet completed. Thus the next stage, or purpose, of historical investigation, to attempt some broad generalizations, may be premature—to say the least—for historical geographers. Nevertheless, after a brief review of some of the aspects of the evolving Acadian geography described in detail in the foregoing chapters, that record will be used as the basis for a critical examination of one of the more widely accepted theories about the history of North American settlement.

In Chapter 2 the ingredients of nature in Acadia were discussed. They were affected somewhat, but perhaps not very much, as they changed slowly over ten thousand years or more, by a thin and spasmodic occupation by hunting, gathering, and fishing peoples. Their significance to the Acadians may be seen especially in comparisons and contrasts with the latters' homeland. In terms of relative location

Acadia was part of the peninsular and archipelagic easternmost extension of the North American continent which forms the eastern margin
of the Gulf of St. Lawrence. Nearest to Europe of the continental areas
settled therefrom, this region (now known so appropriately as Atlantic,
or Maritime, Canada) was simply the unsubmerged portion of a great
eastward projection of the continental shelf which culminated in the
Grand Bank. Parts of the area were nearer to the British Isles than to
the Mississippi River and nearer to Paris than to New Orleans. The
influence of the sea was always pervasive, notably in the cold Labrador
currents offshore, the vast resources of demersal fish in the shallow
waters over much of the shelf, the persistent fogs, the gales, and the
easy access of ocean shipping (particularly for the small shallow-draft
vessels common in the seventeenth and early eighteenth centuries).
Acadia itself, the southeastern margin of this great area, had the
additional dividend from its location that the course of the global tidal
surges, combined with the shelving and narrowing of the Gulf of Maine
to a focus in the Bay of Fundy, led to one of the largest tidal ranges
known anywhere in the world. Newfoundland and Cape Breton Island
were superbly situated in relation to Great Circle sailing routes across
the North Atlantic to serve as entrepôts in the triangular, quadrangu-
lar, pentagonal, and other geometrical trading patterns that developed,
especially in the eighteenth century.

In latitude the new lands, settled by the ancestral Acadians, were
roughly the same as Hokkaido, Mongolia, the Crimea, Patagonia,
New Zealand's South Island or, more to the point here, those of south
central France itself. Port Royal had the latitude of Bordeaux, Beaubassin and Louisburg that of La Rochelle or Lyons, and Grand Pré that
of St-Etienne and Grenoble. Thus they shared the same seasonal length
of day and night and angle of the sun. But any resultant expectations
of closely similar climates were unfulfilled. The summers were somewhat chillier in Acadia chiefly because of cooling offshore currents; the
winters, in the lee of a super-cooled high-latitude continent, were
markedly colder with a persistent and often quite deep snow cover
unknown in most of France. The precipitation was much heavier than
that in the homeland at all seasons, the winds stronger and, in the
Acadian's waterside location, the fogs more persistent. The influence of
the sea also was felt in a marked delay of the seasons. April temperatures in France correspond with those of October; in the Acadian lands
they were, on the average, some ten degrees Fahrenheit cooler in the

spring than in the autumn month; both summer and winter came on with laggard step.

In surface form and geological structure and composition Acadia was a somewhat subdued northern fringe of the Appalachian rough-lands which extend in a broad belt from Alabama to Gaspé and New-foundland. Large areas of ancient crystalline rocks were exposed at the surface but there also were many areas of softer sedimentaries, gener-ally of much less roughness and elevation; none of the hill lands was high enough really to deserve the name of mountain. In relief and elevation the Acadian area corresponded roughly with that of Northern France from Brittany and Normandy through the Paris basin to the western slopes of the Vosges; in these terms most of the Acadians were in a familiar sort of environment.

By the seventeenth century of our era the forests of France, what-ever their character may have been five millennia before, had become a reflection of those thousands of years of clearing, fire, selective cutting, and more or less indiscriminate rooting, grazing, and browsing by swine, cattle, sheep, and goats. Wood for fuel and construction was often a scarce and precious commodity to be grown and husbanded with great care. Buildings and bridges characteristically were of stone, roofs of slate or tile. In Acadia, in contrast, although in the English colonies to the south (and even more in New Spain and Peru) short-ages of wood were to appear after a century and a half of occupation and rapidly expanding forest exploitation and although, in isolated instances, this was paralleled in the maritime areas of New France in the problems of supply of timbers and firewood for the fortress town of Louisburg, wood of adequately wide variety, broadleaf or conifer, was essentially a free and unlimited resource. Wild animals had long been rare in France, to be hunted or snared on private estates or parks only at the risk of a poacher's cruel fate. In Acadia, game, hunted directly or bartered from the Indians, was plentiful, free to all to hunt and relatively easily available. Even by the middle of the eighteenth cen-tury the forest wilderness appears to have been little altered except, perhaps, for more frequent forest fires; the animals, the fowl, the fish of lake, stream, or estuary were, like the trees, still available to the Acadians in almost unlimited supply. The abundance of animal protein and fat in their diet (they were producing surpluses of livestock and barnyard fowl very early as well) must have been one of the greatest contrasts with the experience of their French forefathers.

One of the greatest differences between the European heartland and the Acadians' New World home was that of soil fertility. It is difficult even to guess what the level of such fertility, west of the Rhine and the Alps, and north of the Mediterranean and the Pyrenees, may have been when farming peoples started penetrating the area five thousand years ago. By the seventeenth century of our era the level of fertility of most of the lowland soils of France, maintained by manuring and fallowing, was much greater than that of the heavily podzolized forest soils of Maritime Canada. In a sense the Acadians by-passed this problem by relying on the soils of the sediment-rich tidal flats, dyked away from the sea, but perhaps the neglect of the "dry land" soils, reflecting their generally low fertility, played a major role in the peripheral concentration of settlement and so affected the nature of their settlement patterns and fundamental economy in a very direct way.

The Acadians themselves were the second major ingredient of this new geographical entity. Transplanted Frenchmen, in part military officers, land owners, government bureaucrats, merchants, and ecclesiastics, but chiefly peasants, sailors, disbanded military of low rank, fishermen, servants, and *engagés* of wide variety, they made homes for themselves and found ways of making a living in a strange, wild land across one of the world's stormiest oceans from their homeland. With them they brought all the inherited residue of their long history in the lands that had become, or were becoming, France and, however altered (sometimes rather rapidly), they retained much of their impedimenta of tradition, preference, and prejudice. Of especial importance was a common language and, after the very first years, a common religious adherence. Medieval forms of allegiance and methods of land holding had been much altered in France by 1600 and were largely irrelevant to their ways of life in Acadia by 1750. Nevertheless, following the *coûtume de Paris* or one of the similar "customs" which traditionally established the relationship of people in medieval societies to each other and to the land (allowing, of course, for the many changes of the late medieval and early modern periods) most Acadians must have assumed that everyone must indeed "hold" land as a concession from some lord (*seigneur*) who held in turn from some superior lord or, ultimately, the crown. In New France's Canada, along the St. Lawrence, there was some recognizable relationship in land-holding structure to the traditions of these ancient customs, in its seigneurial system, although a recent study by R. C. Harris argues that the system had far less effect on the settlement geography of the St. Lawrence valley than has hitherto been supposed.[1] In Acadia the seigneurial structure was often so shadowy that the very word "system" is a contradiction in terms. Yet, although the Acadians were as obstinate in their claims to the use of particular pieces of land as any New Englander or Virginian, and strongly resisted all attempts to reorganize or even resurvey the cadastral chaos that had resulted from rather haphazard squatting by the first pioneers in any of their areas of settlement, it is doubtful that any Acadian had a conception of anything like the Anglo-Saxon institution of freehold. Probably their willingness to pay the pittances involved in the nominal *cens et rentes,* and fines of alienation, to some person or persons who claimed them, was rather more a matter of establishing their rights to hold what lands they did, and to pass them on to their heirs, than a slavish following of Old World medieval traditions in the New. It is true that, unlike the very full records of concession, inheritance, and transfer of individual rotures and the often deeply involved relationships between seigneur and censitaire, which are recorded for Canadian seigneuries, we have almost nothing of the kind for Acadia. Indeed we have to piece together what we know largely from inference and from official British records for the period after 1710. Yet it seems a reasonable conclusion that, however loose and inchoate their land-holding "system" was, it retained many of the traditional French ancestral forms until long after the British conquest of that year.

France has long coastlines, from Flanders to Britanny and the Basque country on the Atlantic, and along the Mediterranean, and many of the first Acadians had lived in coastal Britanny, Normandy, or on the Biscayan littoral, but the vast majority of Frenchmen, and probably most of the Acadians (notably the immigrants before 1654 who contributed so largely to the ultimate Acadian population), were inland people, living in areas devoted to a mixed farming economy in which grains (chiefly wheat), pulses (chiefly peas), *Brassicas* (chiefly cabbages and turnips), apples, a wide variety of traditional French garden plants, and the standard western European barnyard animals and poultry, played major roles. Even on the ocean margins and in areas like the channel coasts and the Biscayan shores, where a great

1. R. C. Harris, *The Seigneurial System in Early Canada* (1966).

tidal range offered the opportunity to extend farming almost into the
sea, the French predilection for agriculture as opposed to maritime
occupations was notable. The Acadians, almost to a man, lived, thrived
and expanded their settlements within the sight and smell of salt water.
They did fish and they made good use of the sea for transportation,
just as they exploited effectively the endless forests so alien to their
tradition. But their primary, if necessarily divided, attention was always given to their crops and animals, and in that emphasis they
reflected the strength of their ancestral legacy.

Such traditions showed their force in many ways. Nova Scotia is not,
and never has been, a very suitable area for the growing of wheat, the
preferred grain crop of most of France, yet the Acadians persisted in
making it the chief object of their husbandry. They introduced their
traditional *pommes, poires, prunes,* and *cerises* (and probably also
pêches and *abricots*) although only the apples did well. Fortunately
the turnips, cabbages, and a wide range of *legumes, salades,* and *herbes*
so important to their traditional cuisine, thrived as did the livestock,
large and small. It is evident that visitors from France found the diet,
however rich in protein and fat, rough and heavy, but also that it was
the product of traditional French cookery and peasant taste.

Least changed of all the inheritances from France probably was the
religious faith, and with it a fondness for the ritual and forms of
organization of the Roman Catholic church. Very early in its history
New France was for all practical purposes barred to Protestants. Often
the Acadians were without pastors or saw them rarely on the missionaries' itinerant rounds. But, usually, there were resident priests in most
of the settlements and often they appear to have been the temporal as
well as spiritual advisers and leaders of the communities. The loyalty
of the Acadians to France, or New France, as entities in themselves,
may never have been strong but their sense of cultural continuity, of
unshakeable devotion to ancestral ways, was expressed as clearly as it
was possible to do in their love and respect for their faith, its dogma,
and its rites. It is said that sometimes they were a bit slow in paying
tithes or in having their infants baptised, when either was inconvenient, but it is also evident that the threat of even temporary denial of
the sacraments or, *in extremis,* the hint of excommunication, sufficed to
give effect to a pastor's judgment on many a dispute concerning the
affairs of this world rather than the next.

Unquestionably the presence of Micmac Indians throughout the period that Acadia was a recognized and recognizable territory on the map of the world contributed a special quality to the human geography of the Acadians that was not quite duplicated in any other North American area. Except in rare and isolated instances the Micmac lived with them in full harmony, the Acadians tending their crops and herds for the most part while the Indians fished and hunted. The occasional suggestions of Indian agriculture (notably at Mirligueche, i.e. Lunenburg, and possibly at Musquodoboit or one of the other south coast harbors) seems to have been chiefly the activity of halfbreeds. Just how much intermarrying or interbreeding there was is uncertain and the bulk of it may have taken place before the Razilly group arrived in 1632. It is likely that liaisons, on both sides of the blanket, continued throughout the Acadian period, chiefly between young Acadian men and Indian girls during the winter hunting period, and that some of the offspring may have been accepted in time into the Acadian communities, but most métis children of the first generation were brought up in their mother's homes as Indians. However, the existence of a large métis group at Mirligueche for many years does suggest some identification of the halfbreeds as different from either group and a *de facto* segregation. At any rate, the associations that produced the métis do not appear to have disturbed the even tenor of interracial relationships. Perhaps because the Acadians did not live in or destroy the forest, and the Micmac had little use for the tidally flooded lands, neither group coveted the other's territory. They were able to carry on their separate modes of life without economic conflict and, indeed, to assist each other a good deal by barter. There was no good reason for disputes and a great deal of advantage to both sides in continued peace. European artifacts, if not European technology, became very important to the Indians, and in dozens of ways the Acadians learned from the Micmac —in hunting, fishing, and fowling, in the making and use of canoes, the fabrication of clothing, especially footgear, from fur and skin, and the use of native plants for food, herbal remedies, and dyes. Perhaps nothing was of more use to the Acadians in all of this than birch bark, universally available and with dozens of uses beyond that for canoes, notably for insulating houses and for making containers of all kinds. The general picture for a century and a half was that of a harmonious and almost symbiotic mutual interdependence of the two groups.

The Acadians had every reason to know that their land, unattractive as it might seem to others in terms of its own resources of soil, timber, minerals or, after the seventeenth century, of fur, was a key location on the borderlands between English and French strategic interests in North America. In the seventeenth century Port Royal and Chignecto suffered repeated raids from New England and after its sovereignty (at least that of present peninsular Nova Scotia) was recognized as British in the treaty of Utrecht, it was subject to much harassment directed from Quebec or Louisburg. Sometimes this was by Canadian troops; more often it was by Indians, armed, subsidized, and supervised by the officials of the two fortress towns of New France. The Acadians themselves were not the object of these attacks, and only incidentally its victims, and they were always suspected by the British of aiding them at least covertly; moreover the French military authorities, sometimes supported by their priests who usually were appointed by the Bishop of Quebec, made it clear that they expected the Acadians' cooperation. Somehow the Acadians almost always avoided direct participation even when armed forces numbering in the hundreds moved through their settlements, or troops from Canada or Massachusetts were quartered upon them. Yet, for at least half a century they played the unenviable role of the Belgians of North America.

Any picture of an isolated, bucolic existence, sheltered from the effects of great power military conflict and commerce has to be further redrawn in terms of the Acadian trading activity with the outside world, at times quite vigorous and in some volume. The New England connection, vital to their needs for a wide variety of goods, was maintained at least intermittently during the French regime and, undoubtedly, was their main source of supply in the eighteenth century. Nor did French commercial connections cease with the British capture of Port Royal in 1710. Direct exchange between the dyked-land Acadian settlements and Canada was always minimal; the two sectors of New France produced much the same kind of product of which neither experienced dire shortages. But Cape Breton, renamed Isle Royale, and its fortress of Louisburg were in constant, urgent need of surplus Acadian food and, despite every effort by the British garrison at Port Royal to stop it, the trade continued briskly as the military establishment of Cape Breton built up. Moreover, Louisburg developed into a significant entrepôt of Atlantic trade, with vessels from Canada, France, the French West Indies, and (again, despite all British efforts at its interdiction) from New England, crowding its docks, and this gave the Acadians relatively easy access to a wide variety of European,

Mediterranean, West Indian, and colonial British American goods. The Fundy settlements enjoyed a markedly favorable balance of trade with Cape Breton Island; it provided a metal currency which gave them an advantageous bargaining posture vis-à-vis the shrewd Yankee peddlers with whom they continued to do the trading that provided them with their most critically needed imported goods. There is every reason to suppose that the proclivity in driving hard bargains, in which the French peasant always has been celebrated as a good match for the Yankee, Scottish, Syrian, or Jewish merchant, was one of the many cultural inheritances that the Acadians retained and nurtured.

The theme of this book has been that of changes in a people and in the area they occupied. It has been emphasized that it is only one among innumerable instances in the history of mankind in which an area has been invaded by an alien people with a well developed and complex culture and their retinue of exotic plants and animals. The problem is to interpret the record so as to place the Acadians and Acadia properly in the extremely varied continuum of experience that the full catalog of such invasions represents. At one extreme we can see, as in the case of New Zealand in the two centuries since the first visit of James Cook, a vast alteration in the face of the earth. In contrast, it is arguable that, except for a few hundred square miles which the Acadians farmed (and most of that, reclaimed tidal marshland) the landscape, flora, fauna, and pre-European culture and economy of Acadia had altered very little indeed by 1760. If any significant change had occurred it was a change in the people themselves, a transformation of Frenchmen into Acadians. This was similar to the process through which their distant ancestors had gone when Franks and other German tribes had settled in different parts of Roman Gaul as part of the great folk movements of early medieval times. However, it differed in many ways from those distant relocations of population in Europe.

There was, to begin with, little of the racial or cultural intermixture which had been so important in the Old World. More significant here, the Acadians, as all people who move into new and largely unoccupied lands of hunting and gathering folk must, had to do without the age-old accumulation of capital in terms of cleared fields, hedges, fences or walls, permanent buildings of all kinds, roads and bridges, improved harbors, and most of the laboriously created social machinery of politics, law, and commercial exchange. In an institutional sense, with the exception of the stout cloak of religion, a thin veil of seigneurial trappings, and the spasmodic, absentminded attention paid to them by the French and British governments, they were stripped to rags. Pragmatic to a fault, they were effective empiricists, working out much of their own ways of living together, freely adapting remembered modes, or the often feebly attempted institution of new ones by their governors, to their own needs and convenience. Most of these adaptations were quite firmly established by 1710 and thereafter they clung to them with the same peasant stubbornness and conservatism for which their forbears had been notorious in Europe. The degree of transmutation they underwent was a seventeenth-century phenomenon paralleling that of New England; the eighteenth century witnessed its crystallization and its settling into new rigidities. One might perhaps venture the generalization that change is rapid on a new frontier only until changes satisfactory to new circumstances are effected; thereafter it may be resisted as much or more than in long established settlements.

A detailed analysis and exposition of the changing geography of Acadia might be expected to fit into one or another of the historiographic theses which historical geographers have found useful as frames of reference in attempting to see the broader relevance of their empirical studies. Scholarly prudence does not allow broad generalizations from the few such studies yet undertaken in North America but it seems to be legitimate, and perhaps imperative, that each of them should be viewed from such an historiographic perspective. For an eastern Canadian region the two interpretative formulas that would seem most likely to be appropriate are "Laurentianism" (or its offshoot, "metropolitanism") which has been most widely accepted by Canadian historians, and the "frontier thesis" which has been in the forefront of the attention of their colleagues in the United States for more than half a century.[2] Both theories are very strongly geographical in their implications.

The Laurentian school, led by Harold Innis, stressed the importance of the role of regional concentration on the production of export staples and on the problems of technology and investment in moving them from their source areas to world markets. "Metropolitanism" picked up one of its predecessor's ancillary themes, that of commercial organi-

2. See J. M. S. Careless, "Frontierism, Metropolitanism and Canadian History" (1954), Morris Zaslow, "The Frontier Hypothesis in Recent Canadian Historiography" (1948), and Marvin Mikesell, "Comparative Studies in Frontier History" (1960).

zation, underlined the significance of transportation, and added the recognition of the dominating influence of "home" areas or of major urban centers. Yet, although two of the major staple trades, for fur and fish, were of prime importance immediately east and west of the Acadian farmlands, and although the Acadians participated to some degree in both, neither was central to the Acadian economy nor did the Acadians develop any other comparable staple products. Their transportation technology was simple and undemanding. Their trading, of great importance to themselves and to the Island of Cape Breton in the eighteenth century, nevertheless cannot be considered to have been a dominant element of their economy. Nor does the added dimension of "metropolitanism" really apply. Neither Paris, Quebec, or, later, Louisburg or Boston, played any dominant role in influencing Acadian economic activity. The impact of France before 1710, and of Britain after, was largely the negative one of neglect.

It might be thought possible to interpret the Acadian experience in a derivative way from its marginal association with the great staple trades or its probably even more marginal significance to the New England economy. Just how important it was to the latter is a question still to be researched, but a quick judgment, based on the small size of the Acadian population and the small amount of Acadian production that went into commerce, is that the Acadian supply and market roles were very minor in their effect on the course of economic development in the nearest British colonies. Although it is clear that Acadia, as a region, was very important indeed to the strategic interests of New England vis-à-vis New France as a whole, the Acadians *per se* played a very small strategic role. To sum up, neither the Laurentian theoretical framework nor its derivatives are closely relevant in the Acadian context.

On the other hand, Acadia can be argued to have been in a "forest frontier" situation throughout its history. There, a group of European immigrants was long exposed to whatever shaping or molding effects such an experience might be seen to have had. The "frontier model" of Frederick Jackson Turner and his followers thus would seem to be a much more appropriate one in which to apply the parameters of the Acadian experience. As the best known of all the theories applied to North American history, which has been persistently attacked, defended, and restated (if not, as many would have it, slain and resurrected) during the three-fourths of a century since its pronouncement, such an attempt to match it against the Acadian record should, at least,

bring the more significant aspects of that record into bolder relief.[3]
There is even the modest hope that it may help with the further
refinement and reinterpretation of the theory itself. One of the most
perceptive Turnerian critics, George W. Pierson, has commented:

. . . Turner's frontier essays should be "controlled" by comparisons of a
somewhat different sort: for instance by the study of other populations and
other frontiers. Were the *habitants* of Lower Canada affected as were the
Virginians or Vermonters by the American wilderness? Evidence is being
marshalled to indicate that the Pennsylvania Germans, at least, were not.[4]

From the opposite camp a leading neo-Turnerian apologist has added:

While the over-all Turner thesis has been applied to physical expansions of
other nations and to the spread of Europeans in general, the conclusions of
these applications have never been sorted out and tied together. Secondly, the
comparative work and techniques of other disciplines have been largely
ignored.[5]

Finally, it was one of the most formidable Turnerians, Avery O.
Craven, who has repeatedly emphasized that "local history was human

3. The best single source in the history of conflicting fashions, arguments, and
trends in frontier historiography is *The Frontier Thesis*, ed. R. A. Billington
(1966). Billington, the most cogent and influential of latter-day Turnerians, nevertheless presents a balanced picture and a splendid, highly selective, annotated
bibliography. The heart of his own apologia, a much better balanced evaluation
than those of earlier, less critical disciples, appears in his *America's Frontier
Heritage* (1966), but it permeates all of his writings, notably the extremely popular
and influential text, *Westward Expansion,* now in its third edition (1967). No
serious student of North American history can be unaware of some of the greatest
pieces of writing supportive of Turner's ideas such as Walter Prescott Webb's *The
Great Plains* (1931) and Merle Curti's *The Making of an American Community: A
Case Study of Democracy in a Frontier County* (1959), or, indeed of the more
formidable attacks led directly by such doughty antagonists as Richard Hofstadter,
"Turner and the Frontier Myth" (1949), Fred A. Shannon, *An Appraisal of Walter
Prescott Webb's The Great Plains* (1940), Henry Nash Smith, *Virgin Land: The
American West as Symbol and Myth* (1950), and David M. Potter, *People of
Plenty: Economic Abundance and the American Character* (1954). The thesis has
been tested and applied in every country in which a similar frontier has existed,
notably in Australia, New Zealand, Canada, and South Africa (see esp., *The
Frontier in Perspective,* ed. W. D. Wyman and C. B. Kroeber, 1957), and even in
Russian and Chinese contexts. The pervasive influence of the thesis is discussed in
J. L. M. Gulley, "The Turnerian Frontier, A Study in the Migration of Ideas"
(1959).
4. George W. Pierson, "The Frontier and Frontiersmen of Turner's Essays"
(1940), p. 478.
5. Ellen von Nardroff, "The American Frontier as a Safety Valve: The Life,
Death, Reincarnation and Justification of A Theory" (1962). Quotation is from
p. 61 of Billington, ed., *The Frontier Thesis.*

history."[6] The experience of the Acadians should serve as a reasonable control, it has been observed in this instance by a geographer, and it is local history in Craven's sense—one of the segments of reality which any historiographic theory must accommodate.

The frontier thesis, as refined and elaborated between 1893 and Turner's death in 1932 in more than a dozen of his papers, and since by scores of sympathetic scholars, has many aspects. Most pertinent geographically were the matters of location at any time and of changes in location through time. The critical locale, the frontier, was most simply conceived as the outer edge of settlement. It also came to be seen plurally as several lines or zones which might pass through a given geographical location as the leading edges of successive waves of different classes of entrepreneurial interest (fur trading, mining, cattle raising, and farming). But at any time a frontier had a definable location and extent, and that location, in respect of the people and resources behind it, of the local resources, exploitative techniques, and cultural groups within it, and of the nature and distribution of resources, economies, and people (if any) beyond it, was a vital element in terms of the political or socio-economic significance it may have had. The obvious implications of strong degrees of environmental influence, if not control, led the thesis to be embraced warmly by the geographers contemporary with its early twentieth-century heyday and then, often almost as uncritically, rejected by latter-day geographers in a methodological revulsion against the naiveté of single-factor causation. Equally intriguing, geographically, was the concept of progressive movement through space until, in the last decade of the nineteenth century, the frontier ran out of space in the United States, although the thesis has continued to be applied to twentieth-century developments on the fringes of the northern lands and in various parts of Asia, Africa, South America, and Australasia.

It was the impact of the combined natural and cultural characteristics of this very special, if transitory, environment which, according to Turner, transformed the sons and grandsons of European immigrants into that celebrated transatlantic entity, Crèvecoeur's "new man."[7] In the closing paragraph of his seminal paper of 1893 Turner observed:

6. Avery O. Craven has written two appraisals of Turner and his ideas: "Frederick Jackson Turner" (1937), and "Frederick Jackson Turner, Historian" (1942).

7. J. Hector St. John (Michel Guillaume St-Jean de) Crèvecoeur, *Letters from an American Farmer* . . . (1782), and *idem, Qu'est-ce qu'un Américain* (reprinted, 1943).

For a moment, at the frontier, the bonds of custom are broken and unrestraint is triumphant. There is not *tabula rasa*. The stubborn American environment is there with its imperious summons to accept its conditions; the inherited ways of doing things are also there; and yet, in spite of environment, and in spite of custom, each frontier did furnish a new field of opportunity, a gate of escape from the bondage of the past, and freshness, and confidence, and scorn of older society, impatience of its restraints and its ideas, and indifference to its lessons have accompanied the frontier.[8]

Twenty-one years later, as the thesis was still being refined and elaborated he added: "American democracy was born of no theorists dream; it was not carried by the *Sarah Constant* to Virginia nor in the *Mayflower* to Plymouth. It came stark and strong and full of life out of the American forest, and it gained new strength each time it touched a new frontier."[9] Turner saw men shedding their old cultural impedimenta under the impact of the new life, developing newer, simplified, pragmatic solutions to answer the problems of the environment. They became more primitive, yet more inventive, more democratic and yet, paradoxically in part, more individualistic, more self-sufficient and more self-reliant, more controlled by expansive dreams and yet, withal, more materialistic.

In Acadia, as elsewhere on the continent, upon initial occupance, the bonds of custom *were* noticeably strained, but certainly not broken, and it cannot be said either that unrestraint was triumphant or that any sort of anarchic individualism arose or was, by necessary accommodation, transformed into a democracy at all like that which Turner described. From the middle 1630's, for a period of two decades, the Acadians in La Have and Port Royal learned, individually and collectively, under the firm paternal eye of d'Aulnay de Charnisay, how to make a satisfactory living in that new world, so different from the old in so many ways. As in the case of the first major invasions of New England, these immigrant Frenchmen had excellent relations with the Indians and, unlike later generations of colonial Englishmen, they maintained them throughout their history. Thus one of the basic catalysts of transformation, in the Turnerian view of the American frontier, was lacking: fear of, and constant or repeated conflict with, the Indians. Nor did their pattern of economic activity change significantly throughout their history. It is true that the primary motives of the

8. Frederick Jackson Turner, "The Significance of the Frontier in American History" (1894), p. 227.

9. Frederick Jackson Turner, "The West and American Ideals" (1914), p. 245.

Razilly settlement, and certainly those of its subsequent history under d'Aulnay, were centered around the making of profits from trading with the Indians. Moreover, up to the time of the Acadian dispersion in 1755, such trading went on, by merchants and officials before 1710 but also, continuously after 1654, by the individual Acadians themselves. A second motive for the establishment of the original settlement had been to provide a base for the cod fishery. This soon faded into the background as a concern of the original leaders of the colony but the Acadians continued to fish in their own rivers and estuaries and out in the Bay of Fundy itself and to supply manpower to the Atlantic cod fishery, spasmodically at least, throughout their history. Finally it is abundantly attested that the Acadians traded what surpluses they had, or what goods they could acquire from the Indians, for things they could not themselves produce, to New England, France, Canada, and, in the eighteenth century, to Cape Breton Island. But, from the beginning, the Acadians were, primarily and fundamentally, peasant-like farmers, living chiefly from their crops and animals, and their varied ancillary activities, including hunting and wood cutting, were carried on not in any structured chronological succession, but concurrently. Assuming that dyked-land farming was employed generally by the mid-1650's it is probable that the basic patterns and practices of rural life had not changed very substantially a century later.

Yet the Acadians did adopt a way of farming life markedly different from that of most of their French ancestors or from that of their contemporaries in Canada, New England, or the most southern English colonies. We attribute this chiefly to experiments made in the period before the English interregnum at Port Royal from 1654 to 1670, when the use of tidally flooded lands became the principal focus of agricultural activity. This was, clearly, a peculiar and unique environmental opportunity that inherited experience and the imagination of some individual or small group invited them to exploit, and the success of which, given ample areas of tidal flats to develop and an absolute population growth (with very limited immigration) which did not overtax the supply, kept them close to such lands through the whole period with which we are concerned. Perhaps the development of a Turnerian succession was made difficult if not impossible both by the generally much lower level of fertility of the other kinds of lands into which they could have expanded, and by the lack of immigration which held down the rate and amount of population increase.

The period from 1654 to 1670 may have been the most critical one for the course of their development. They were quite cut off from France and largely ignored by the Crown-Temple group in control at Port Royal whose interest was only in the fur trade. Acclimatized and acculturated in one generation to a viable economy in this new land they were left almost entirely to their own devices for nearly another generation, a period of time long enough to demand of them a very high degree of self-reliance. Lacking governmental control in almost all of the operations and activities of their daily lives, and with claimants of seigneurial rights (which were, in any event, very light burdens) having no official force behind them, the Acadians achieved a *modus operandi* of occupying new land, settling disputes, trading individual skills and surpluses, and developing the rest of the aspects of team-work necessary to build dykes, aboiteaux, and drainage channels and, no doubt, houses and other structures and the small sailing vessels which became increasingly more important to them. It may have been the attempts by French governors after 1670 to re-establish a firm, paternal, central control which encouraged migration from Port Royal to Chignecto and Minas and the fact, or threat, of such movement was enough to lighten the official hand in the mother settlement lest the local supplies of food on which the officials depended so heavily should be seriously threatened by depopulation. Governors were constantly complaining of *"demi-republicaine"* attitudes in the outer settlements.

In terms of the slogans of the French Revolution, more than a century after this judgment of the Acadians, there certainly was, among them, a marked degree of personal freedom of action, although just how much of the full content of "liberté" they had may be questionable. "Egalité" seems to have been a general quality of social life, perhaps less from a breaking down of social stratification than from its failure to develop; here the frontier model may have a good deal of relevance. Although we are poorly informed as to matters of social precedence, it is likely that a somewhat elite social circle existed around the governor during the French regime, including the officials, the officers of the garrison, and members of the leading families—that is, those with seigneurial rights and pretensions, in particular, like the Le Borgnes, d'Entremonts, La Tours, and La Vallières. We can gauge this in part from the marriage alliances recorded in the parish registers. But the same registers affirm that these families also contracted marriages with a great many other "ordinary" families and there is much other evidence to suggest a relatively free "vertical mobility" economically, through above average success in farming, milling, or trading. On the whole there is little to indicate that social distinctions mattered very much, especially in the outlying settlements, and whatever their force they probably declined in influence in the eighteenth century. If there was a minority group discriminated against socially, it may have consisted of métis, for most of these lived with the Indians or far away from the major settlements.

"Fraternité" is another word with broad and varied connotations, but both the increasingly intertwined blood connections of the people, evident from the very large number of dispensations for consanguinity in marriages in the eighteenth century, and the day to day needs for agricultural cooperation in the dyked-land areas, made the stereotype individualism of the Kentucky frontiersman relatively rare among the people. Their constant and essential interdependence was of a far stronger kind than the occasional gathering of frontiersmen for a barn-raising or corn-shucking bee.

But perhaps the key question, in trying to fit the frontier model, is whether one can speak of "democratie" with any degree of assurance either under the 1654–1670 interregnum or under either of the succeeding French and British regimes. During the former, with no superior authority to which to turn, the Acadians did manage to solve everyday problems of *meum* and *tuum* and anti-social behavior in one or another pragmatic fashion; with the return of authority they, as readily, showed a willingness to bring their questions to a French governor or *commissionaire-ordonnateur* or to an English governor or council. Throughout, the ecclesiastical apparatus provided a workable mechanism for solving many interpersonal problems. There must have been a large measure of informal, practical democracy but there is no indication of a theoretical view of any degree of sovereignty residing in the majority of the people, rather than in the divinely guided head of state, or that the arithmetic of head counting supplied the best basis for permanent or temporary policy decisions. Of course the neo-Turnerians have argued that the democracy theme in the frontier thesis is valid specifically in the American (presumably U. S.) context. Billington insists that "Turner was speaking of *American* democracy, not democracy in general, when he generalized upon the frontier experience"[10] But then, one asks, what is, indeed, "American" in the seventeenth and eighteenth century contexts with which we are concerned?

10. Billington, ed., *The Frontier Thesis*, p. 69.

It might be argued that the Acadian experience differed so markedly from that of the American frontier as it moved up to and across the Appalachian roughlands in part because of the Acadians' relative isolation from the world at large. Not only had the continental frontiersmen to face constant battles with the Indians but they were ever a part of the interplay of tactics and grand strategy in the continuing conflict of English, later American, French, and Spanish interests in the continental interior. Yet the Acadians, as we have seen, often were even more deeply involved in the international power struggle although, like most of their rural contemporaries in Europe or among European derived groups in North America, most Acadians were illiterate and doubtless poorly informed of the nature and course of the international political and commercial forces for which they acted as pawns.

If degree of self-sufficiency is one of the diagnostic characteristics of the frontier experience the Acadians may qualify quite as well as most of the groups from whose history Turner derived his generalizations. Their economy was subsistent to an important degree and they could "make do" very well on their own for food, clothing, and shelter. But just as the interior frontiersman—even of the first waves—could not do without guns, powder, shot, axes, and knives and demanded many other things when they were available, so the Acadians made constant use of a wide variety of goods from the markets of the world. From the English colonies came most of their necessary iron, hardware, tools and implements, the metal fittings for their boats, mill machinery, cordage and canvas, and a wide variety of oddments from the usual stock-in-trade of the Yankee sea-peddlers. Through Cape Breton came cloth, wine, and brandy from France and transshipped tropical products from the French Antilles. To emphasize their isolation, or to stress their self-sufficiency, is, in comparative terms, a rather gross distortion of the actual record. Yet one wonders if they were so very different from the normal (or Turnerian) frontiersman in that: perhaps their access by sea to New England and Cape Breton, despite all the obstacles put in the way of such intercourse, gave them commercial advantages superior to those who had to make long trips on foot or horseback for needed exotic supplies and whose transport problems inhibited the growing of crops of large bulk, but relatively low value, for sale.

It is glaringly obvious that the American frontier moved far more rapidly than did that of the Acadians which, in a century and a half, had pushed only as far as the estuarine marshland areas of the northern and eastern extremities of the Bay of Fundy, except for very small outliers on the Atlantic coast and the Strait of Northumberland, and to Isle St-Jean or (rather minor) to the southern fringes of Cape Breton. However, the Acadian settlement was not static in location, it did spread out and, especially in Isle St-Jean (the later Prince Edward Island), it occasionally did climb out of the dyked tidal lands on to the "upland" or "dry land" soils where the process of clearing, stumping, making farms, and planting orchards, differed little from that in western Massachusetts, New York, Virginia, or Kentucky. Again it might be pointed out that the Acadians rarely moved as individuals living in isolated farmsteads at great distances from their old homes. The nature of dyked-land agriculture required the continuously cooperative efforts of at least several men. Yet there often were individual Acadian families, or groups of fewer than half a dozen, settled by themselves for long periods and even the first "invasions" of Minas, Cobequid, Beaubassin, Shepody, or Memramcook initially involved very small groups. Moreover, most of the experience on the moving American frontier must have involved groups as large; indeed, the occasional truly isolated pioneer in the wilderness must have been so small a part of the total experience as to have contributed comparatively little to the resulting characteristics of society and economy.

Perhaps the aspects of the frontier thesis which are least useful in measuring the Acadian experience are those associated with the "safety-valve" theory—whether that is a cadaver, as Shannon claimed, or very much alive in a somewhat different incarnation, as Von Nardroff argues.[11] It was not population pressure or land shortages that led to migration. It is true that the abundance of land elsewhere did allow free movement out of the Port Royal (Annapolis) settlement to the Minas and Chignecto "colonies" and this does seem to have affected the age distribution and perhaps the initiative of the people left at home as the more adventuresome younger folk moved out. But this is hardly a safety-valve: Acadia has little to contribute to this aspect of the frontier model.

There can be no doubt that the experience of the Acadians took place in a "frontier" situation, and that, partly as a result, they did become a people distinctly different from the immigrant group from which they derived in many ways. Yet the changes which occurred and

11. Von Nardroff, "The American Frontier as a Safety Valve."

the ways in which they developed, often differed widely from that expectable from the Turnerian model, despite the fact that much of their situation seems to have been comparable to that of the interior American pioneers. This may mean simply that the model is not as broadly comprehensive in its utility for the interpretation of North American settlement history as has been supposed. It may be useful, therefore, to recapitulate some of the characteristics of the Acadians or of their experience which did differ significantly from those of the people and history of the British American colonies to the south. The most important of these may have lain in the relative harmony of their relationships with the Indians, the lack of immigration to combine with natural population growth to provide distinct population pressure on the land, and the lack of fertile soil, except for the tidal flats, near enough or otherwise accessible enough to them to invite farther or more rapid movement. Perhaps the nearest possible attractive areas, of the Connecticut, Hudson-Mohawk, or St. Lawrence valleys, had they not been pre-empted by others, as they were, still would have lain rather too far away. But, had such areas of soil existed in upland New Brunswick, Maine, or Appalachian Quebec a distinct conflict with Montagnais, Naskapi, Malecite (or other Abenaki tribes), or the Iroquois might have resulted.

At an early stage in the development of the frontier thesis, Benjamin Wright attempted to assess it against the experience of the Canadians in the St. Lawrence Valley:

> In both theory and fact, France was a despotism; there was almost no self-government, local or national. The essentials of this system were transferred to Canada and remained during the entire period of French control. . . . It is clear that the conditions which inevitably exist in frontier communities do set a temporary limit to the possibilities of such areas, but it would seem equally certain that they do not primarily determine the character of the institutions which are to be planted there. The customs and ideas brought by the settlers from an older civilization are of vastly more importance in shaping the history of the new lands. None of the American frontiers was ever "free from the influence of European ideas and institutions." The colonists who settled the first American frontiers altered remarkably little the principles which they inherited from their European ancestors.[12]

The dean of American historical geographers, Carl O. Sauer, has added:

12. Benjamin F. Wright, "American Democracy and the Frontier" (1930), p. 352.

. . . civilized man retains many attributes and activities of his particular situation when he transfers himself to a frontier community. No groups coming from different civilizations and animated by different social ideals have reacted to frontier life in identical fashion. The kind of frontier that develops is determined by the kind of group that is found in it. The eternal pluralism of history asserts itself on the American frontier: there was no single type of frontier nor was there a uniform series of stages. The nature of the cultural succession that was initiated on any frontier was determined by the physical character of the country, by the civilization that was brought in and by the moment of history involved.[13]

Using the Acadian experience as a case study, it may be reasonable to conclude that frontier historians, following the Turnerian model, and in understandable reaction against the underemphasis of environmental contexts by cultural determinists, have let the pendulum swing too far and allowed themselves to undervalue the role of cultural inheritance. It may be futile, or worse, to speculate on what the region we have called Acadia might have become, or what its inhabitants might have developed into, had the Alexander colony of Nova Scotia in the 1620's not been dispossessed by Razilly's immigrants and, instead, expanded under English or Scottish control to become the northernmost colony of the eastern seaboard, under the control of, and with a population derived from, the British Isles. Dyked-land farming might, or might not have been developed; there would have been quite as much reason for it to have done so as in the case of the Acadians. The people might have drifted west to New England or to New York, as the Acadians did not do to Canada, or, like the Acadians, they might have created a viable and lasting geographical entity with minimum immigration or emigration. But, had the New England occupation of Nova Scotia in the 1760's, the influx of Loyalists in the 1780's, or the Highland Scottish invasions of the early nineteenth century, been thus anticipated, we surely should have expected results quite different from those which did follow. The writer's guess would be that such developments would have fitted the Turnerian model very much better than those which did occur. Much more marked individualism, democratic ideas of responsible and representative government, and the full train of Turner's "frontier" characteristics might well have developed just as it is argued that they did in the more southern European colonies.

13. Carl O. Sauer, "Historical Geography and the Western Frontier" (1929). Quotation is from p. 49 of a reprinting in *Land and Life: A Selection from the Writings of Carl Ortwin Sauer,* ed. John Leighly (Berkeley, 1963), pp. 45–52.

The conclusion is that we must recognize the importance of the fact that the Acadians were transplanted Frenchmen, not English, Scots, or Ulstermen and, however altered in their new homes, that they retained a good measure of that cultural inheritance. So, of course, did those from the British Isles, but it was a different inheritance, and it led them in a different direction—specifically into more rapid and progressive change and, it is argued here, to some of the characteristics which have been attributed to the frontier milieu. If Acadia was no more truly a New France than Canada, and perhaps rather less, it was, still, a colony of only partly transformed Frenchmen; the British American colonies to the south were those of British Islanders or Rhineland Germans, in large measure, with the latter rapidly acculturating themselves to the framework established by a century of prior English occupation. The seeds of what were to emerge and be identified as frontier characteristics in the Ohio Valley, the Bluegrass or Nashville basins were, in this view, always there to be nourished into full bloom if the institutional and environmental contexts were favorable. In large part such seeds were simply not present in the Acadian ancestral culture and, even when parallel experiences suggest the calling forth of parallel responses, if the model is valid and useful, we find that they evolved in their own, and often quite different ways.

There is no desire here, and particularly not by a geographer, to swing the pendulum back to historical theories which attempted to explain American colonial life in terms of the institutions of medieval Germanic tribes. Environmental context, institutional as well as physical and biotic, is always of vital importance. But it is argued that we must never forget the degree to which the Atlantic colonies of English or French in North America in the seventeenth and eighteenth centuries were, in fact, still cultural suburbs of Europe. For historiographic treatment of North America's changing geographies during more than three centuries of European occupation and control we need an explanatory model which, while embodying all useful or relevant socio-economic theory, and the fullest possible appreciation of the significance of the inherent (or culturally altered) attributes of nature, as the frontier model essayed to do, nevertheless does include in its formulation a fully adequate representation of the parameters of cultural inheritance. Such a model must be as useful in the interpretation of Acadia and the Acadians as of Kentucky, Arkansas, Ontario, Wisconsin, or Alberta.

Nor will such a model be comprehensively useful until it is so constructed as to take fully into account what the writer would call the locational co-ordinates of the phenomena it considers. To most historians, it would seem, interests of geographers are confined closely to matters of the natural environment of culture. Geographers are very glad to accept this responsibility but it is by no means their central concern. The latter is, rather, where things are in relation to each other, and it is the significance of both absolute and relative location which interests them most deeply. That is to say, again drawing on the example of Acadia and the Acadians as detailed in this volume, the geographer would insist on a full appreciation of the location of Acadia with respect to the rest of the world, the location and direction of the lines of interregional communication which affected it, the size and shape of the region itself, its internal areal differentiation of nature and culture, and the intraregional lines of connection or barriers to communication within it. Much of this is comprehended in the rubric "patterns of settlement and economic activity" but that is susceptible to an interpretation that is too static and which ignores the changing functional interconnections through space which, very often, show most clearly the significance to culture of the relative location of its elements. It is not either explicit or implicit in the usual formulation of Turnerian theory.

The usefulness of any model which may be conceived to accommodate the empirical findings of geographically biased historical research thus depends in great part upon its ability to illuminate these matters of relative and absolute location. Such a model, if it is to help in interpreting the Acadian experience, should be able to embrace both the antecedent natural and cultural properties of the locale of that experience and the extent and character of the relationships developed with adjacent areas.[14] Thus, for any area, large or small, however analytically or arbitrarily delimited, we must interpret its changing character always in terms of what it was like at the beginning of our period of interest (the basic ingredients, so to speak) and, throughout that period, constantly keep in mind the changing characteristics of its adjacent areas

14. This type of conceptualization has been explored within the context of the location of immigrants within a nineteenth century American city by David Ward. See his "Antecedence and Adjacence; Locational Attributes of Central Residential Districts" (1964), and "The Emergence of Immigrant Ghettoes in American Cities: 1840–1920" (1968).

by which it always must be affected to a degree and to, or through, which its lines of communication with the rest of the world must extend.

No amount of argument, in itself, is as likely to convince a thoughtful and informed reader as the clearest possible record of what actually happened in the process of change in any regional human geography. As well as it was possible for the writer to do, this has been set down above for Acadia and the Acadians. By what has been written there, and represented in its maps and charts, the author has illustrated as clearly as he can his conception of what a regional exposition of historical human geography should involve. Giving full value to the importance of antecedence and adjacence and the locational co-ordinates of its phenomena, it is an attempt to give an account of geographical change as an occupying culture or cultures with persistent vitality acted upon, reacted to, and blended with both nature and neighboring cultures through time.

REFERENCE MATTER

Studies of Acadian Origins in France

MOST OF the research on French Canadian origins in France has been concentrated on Quebec, the "Canadian" section of New France.[1] Louis Hamilton[2] made a valiant effort for the Acadians but his distribution of 221 living Acadian names, the most probable provincial origin of which, in France, can be determined with some accuracy, suffers from the fact that he has not made separate determinations for the earliest group which contributed most to the cultural and biological inheritance,[3] nor has he been able to take into account

1. J.-B.-A. Ferland *Cours d'histoire du Canada* (1861 and 1865), and F.-X. Garneau, *Histoire du Canada depuis sa découverte jusqu'à nos jours* (1845–48), were among the earliest historians to give attention to the problem, but their interest was confined to Quebec. Cyprien Tanguay's exhaustive *Dictionnaire Généalogique des familles canadiennes depuis la fondation de la colonie jusqu'à nos jours* (1871–90), has no counterpart in Acadia. N. E. Dionne, *Les Canadiens-Français; Origine des familles emigrées de France, d'Espagne, de Suisse, etc., pour venir se fixer au Canada, depuis la fondation de Québec jusqu'à ces derniers temps, et signification de leurs noms* (1914), made no division between Canada and Acadia, nor has the work of most of the linguists other than Geneviève Massignon (*Les Parlers Français d'Acadie*, 1962), e.g. S. A. Lortie ("De l'origine des Canadiens-français," 1903) been directed to Acadian origins.
2. Louis Hamilton, *Ursprung der französischen Bevölkerung Canadas* (1920).
3. Of the group at Port Royal after 1635, known surnames that have survived, compiled from parish registers and other records, are, according to Antoine Bernard, Aucoin, Gaudet, Martin, Dugas, Trahan, Landry, Pitre, Melanson, Caissy, Colleson, and Pesely. *Histoire de l'Acadie* (1939), p. 20. These would be drawn from the fifteen or twenty married engagés among Razilly's original three hundred and from the Scots. Others have posited that the first Melanson, if a Scot, arrived during the interregnum after 1654. Bernard suggests that the following names were

the vast disparity of numbers bearing the different names now. His suggestion that, whereas three out of ten Acadian heads of family may have come from Normandy or Britanny, only 58 per cent in all came from the coastal provinces, and that thirty-four of the forty-seven provinces of the country were represented, challenges conventional views. The difficulties of his research were very great; he depended on Rameau, Haliburton, and others, who had made lists from a wide variety of censuses and other documentary records. He checked all the parish records, petitions, etc., that he could find but many, of course, have been lost. The dispersion of 1755 was particularly hard on Acadian records. He faced the fantastically variable orthography of the names, inevitable among an illiterate people and in an age which placed little value on consistency in spelling. Thus it is very difficult to tell whether one is dealing with different spellings of the same name or with two different names. Providing the writing has been read correctly the identity between Robecheaux, Robichaux, Raubichou, and Robichaud, for example, is evident; but when faced with Peauxtie and Pothier, it is only probable that they are the same family name.

Hamilton came up with 479 Acadian names of which 190 have completely disappeared and 68 could not be reasonably assigned to a particular provincial origin. He was left with 221 living Acadian names the provincial origins of which he felt confident.

Table A.1 shows the number of names originating from each province among the first ten contributors. The distribution of Canadian names among the same provinces is given for comparison.

The small proportion from Poitou conflicts with Massignon's hypothesis discussed in Chapter 5.[4] Many of the names borne by those in Razilly's first contingent of settlers and by subsequent families introduced by d'Aulnay are those common in areas which were parts of the estates of Charles de Menou d'Aulnay or of his mother, Nicole de Jousserand. At least twenty of the names in the 1671 census of Acadia[5] were the same as those of censitaires of one or the other of the two, although no further identification could be made.

---

established somewhat later, although before 1671, whether by marriage of single men to daughters or widows of the above or by new immigration, and whether entirely at Port Royal or not, is not made clear: Bourgeois, Doucet, Cyr, Boudrot, Savoie, Béliveau, Blanchard, Brault, Hébert, Dupuis, Daigle, Petitpas, Robichaud, Leblanc, Bourg(Bourq), Poirier, Richard, Thibaudeau, Girouard, Saulnier, Terriau, and Cormier. *Ibid.*, p. 20.

It is interesting that Émile Lauvrière also gives a list of names of those coming after the immigrants of 1632, similar to the preceding but with some changes in orthography and some clearly different names: Doucet, Bourgeois, Petipas, Boudrot, Terriault, Daigre, Sire, Poirier, Richard, Leblanc, Thibaudeau, Girouard, Granger, Comeau, Cormier, Robichaud, Hébert, Blanchard, Brault, Morin, and Béliveau. *La Tragédie d'un peuple* (1922), p. 81.

4. Massignon, *Les Parlers Français.*

5. The 1671 nominal census can be found in AC G1-466, 2–13 and has been printed many times.

TABLE A.1 *Inferred provincial origins in France of living Acadian family names, for the ten leading provinces*

French province	Acadia		Canada
	Number of names	Per cent* of total	Per cent* of total
Bretagne	32	14½	9
Normandie	28	13	14
Guienne	18	8	5½
Île-de-France	11	5	5
Picardie	11	5	5
Gascogne	11	5	4½
Bourgogne	9	4	5
Champagne	9	4	5
Poitou	9	4	3
Franche-Comté	7	3	3
37 other provinces	76	34½	41
Total	221	100	100

* Percentages recalculated from Hamilton's basic data.
Source: Louis Hamilton, *Ursprung der französischen Bevölkerung Canadas* (1920).

Massignon concluded that the coincidence allowed the strong inference that a substantial number of the earliest Acadians, and of those who contributed disproportionately to the later population because of this precedence in time, had come from inland, northeastern Poitou.[6]

Of course many other names were introduced between 1632 and 1671 and it is possible to resolve the conclusions of both Hamilton and Massignon if we remember how complete was the list of names considered by the former and how limited the number associated with the d'Aulnay lands. Many of Hamilton's names were those of fishermen, soldiers, sailors, trappers, *coureurs*

6. The seigneurie of d'Aulnay was roughly coincident with the modern commune of Martaizé in the Departement de Vienne. It lies south of Loudon and north west of Chatellerault. Vienne was roughly the inland one-third of the old province of Poitou. D'Aulnay's estates, together with those of his mother, may have included the villages of d'Angliers, d'Aulnay, and la Chaussée.

After examining the registers of the parish of la Chaussée, situated in the general area, she reported that more than half of the entries, from 1626 to 1650, involved names of families recorded in the 1671 census in Acadia. These included: Babin, Belliveau, Bertrand, Bour, Brault (or its feminine equivalent, Braude), Brun, Dugast, Dupuy, Gaudet (or feminine, Gaudette), Giroire, Joffriau, Landry, Le-Blanc, Morin, Poirier, Raimbaut, Savoie, Thibodeau. The following names, borne by the wives of 1671 Acadians, also appear: Chevrat, Gautier, Guion (Dion?), Lambert, and Mercier. The names of Blanchard, Bourg, Brault, Giroire, Godet, Guerin, Poirier, and Terriot were found among those of the censitaires of d'Aulnay's mother. See Massignon, *Les Parlers Français, 1,* 35–36.

du bois, and adventurers who attached themselves to the settlement at various times later in the century and who might be expected to have come from almost anywhere in France; the seaports must have been mixing-pots for the poor and unfortunate who drifted there or had been uprooted from inland homes for military or naval service.

Some of the names were derived from men of the La Tour group by marriage into the Port Royal population. A notable example are the d'Entremonts. Their ancestor, Philippe Mius d'Entremont, was conceded the land around Pubnico Bay by La Tour. The family returned to their old lands after the dispersion and expanded rapidly; the surname is overwhelmingly dominant in that district today.

Bibliography

‌

THE BIBLIOGRAPHY is organized into three general sections. The first of these includes the references for Chapter 2 ("The Endowment of Nature") and Chapter 3 ("The Micmac Indians: First Residents of Acadia") of the text. The second discusses unpublished documents and manuscripts. In the third section published materials consulted, other than those relating directly to Chapters 2 and 3, and including collections of manuscripts in print, are listed in alphabetical order.

WORKS CONSULTED FOR CHAPTERS 2 AND 3

The following abbreviations are used in this section: NSSS, Nova Scotia Soil Survey; *P(T)NSIS, Proceedings (and Transactions) of the Nova Scotian Institute of Sciences;* and *PTRSC, Proceedings and Transactions of the Royal Society of Canada.*

Geology and Physiography

Daly, R. A. "Physiography of Acadia," *Bulletin of the Museum of Comparative Zoology, Harvard University,* Geological Ser. 5, *38* (1901), 71–106.
Dawson, (Sir) J. W. *Acadian Geology.* Edinburgh, 1855; London, 1868. Also supplements: Edinburgh, 1860; London, 1878. Many other editions.
———. *The Geology of Nova Scotia, New Brunswick and Prince Edward Island.* London, 1891. A revised edition of *Acadian Geology.*
Goldthwait, J. W. *Physiography of Nova Scotia.* (Geological Survey of Canada, No. 140.) Ottawa, 1924.
Hickox, C. F., Jr. *Pleistocene Geology of the Central Annapolis Valley, Nova Scotia.* (Nova Scotia Mines Department, Memoir No. 5.) Halifax, 1962.
Hogg, W. A. *Pleistocene Geology of Pictou County.* (Nova Scotia Research Foundation.) Halifax, 1953.

Johnson, D. W. *The New England–Acadian Shoreline.* New York, 1925. This includes material from many of his briefer papers.

Prest, W. H. "On the Nature and Origin of the Eskers of Nova Scotia," *PTNSIS for 1917–18, 14* (1919), 371–93.

Stockwell, C. H., ed. *Geology and Economic Minerals of Canada.* (Geological Survey of Canada.) 4th ed., Ottawa, 1957.

Wilson, J. Tuzo. "Drumlins of Southwest Nova Scotia," *PTRSC*, ser. 3, *32* (1938), sec. 4, 41–47.

The Shoreline

Churchill, F. K. "Recent Changes in the Coastline in the County of Kings, Nova Scotia," *PTNSIS for 1923–24, 16* (1927), 84–87. \

Ferguson, S. A. *Strait of Canso Map Area, Nova Scotia.* (Geological Survey of Canada, Paper 46–12.) Ottawa, 1946.

Ganong, W. F. "The Vegetation of the Bay of Fundy Salt and Diked Marshes: An Ecological Study," *Botanical Gazette, 36* (1903), 161–86, 280–302, 349–67, 429–55.

Goldthwait, J. W. *Physiography of Nova Scotia.* (Geological Survey of Canada, No. 140.) Ottawa, 1924.

Johnson, D. W. *The New England–Acadian Shoreline.* New York, 1925.

Lyon, Charles J., and Goldthwait, J. W. "An Attempt to Cross-Date Trees in Drowned Forests," *Geographical Review, 24* (1934), 605–14.

Schott, Carl. *Die Kanadischen Marschen.* (Schriften des Geographischen Instituts der Universität Kiel, Band 15, Heft 2.) Kiel, 1955.

Oceanography

Fisheries Research Board of Canada. *Index and List of Titles, Publications of the Fisheries Research Board of Canada, 1901–1954.* (Bulletin No. 10.) Ottawa, 1957.

Hachey, H. B. *The General Hydrography of the Waters of the Bay of Fundy.* (Canada, Joint Committee on Oceanography, Atlantic Oceanographic Group.) St. Andrews, N.B., 1952.

———. *Oceanography and Canadian Atlantic Waters.* (Fisheries Research Board of Canada, Bulletin No. 134.) Ottawa, 1961. This provides an introduction, incorporates ideas from his many detailed studies, and has an extensive bibliography.

McLellan, H. B., Lanzier, L., and Bailey, W. B. "The Slope Water off the Scotian Shelf," *Journal of the Fisheries Research Board of Canada, 10* (1953), 155–76.

Marmar, H. A. "Tides in the Bay of Fundy," *Geographical Review, 12* (1922), 195–205.

Officer, C. B., and Ewing, M. "Geophysical Investigations in the Emerged and Submerged Atlantic Coastal Plain," *Bulletin of the Geological Society of America, 65* (1954), 653–70.

Climate

Bilham, E. G. *The Climate of the British Isles*. London, 1938.

Boughner, C. C. "The Climate of the Atlantic Provinces," *Public Affairs, 3* (1940), 114–18.

Boughner, C. C., and Potter, J. D. "Snow Cover in Canada," *Weatherwise, 6* (December 1953), 155–59, 170–71.

Boughner, C. C., and Thomas, M. K. *Climatic Summaries for Selected Meteorological Stations in Canada, Newfoundland and Labrador.* 2 vols. (Canada, Dept. of Transport, Meteorological Division.) Toronto, 1948.

Canada, Bureau of Statistics. "Climatic Tables," *Canada Year Book*. Ottawa, various years.

Canada, Meteorological Branch. *Climatic Summaries for Selected Meteorological Stations in . . . Canada*. Various volumes and addenda. Toronto, 1947, 1954, etc.

———. "Breakup and Freeze Data of Rivers and Lakes in Canada," Circular 3156, ICE-2. Toronto, 1959.

Great Britain, Meteorological Office. *Climatological Atlas of the British Isles*. London, 1952.

Jacobs, L. *The Meteorology of the Gulf of St. Lawrence . . . .* Ottawa, 1945.

Longley, R. W. "Mean Annual Temperatures and Running Mean Temperatures for Selected Canadian Stations," Canada, Meteorological Branch, Circular 2481, TEC-186. Toronto, 1954.

Putnam, D. F. "The Climate of the Maritime Provinces," *Canadian Geographical Journal, 21* (1940), 134–47.

Shinfield, L., and Slater, D. F. "The Climate of Toronto," Canada, Meteorological Branch, Circular 3352, TEC-327. Toronto, 1960.

Thomas, M. K. *A Bibliography of Canadian Climate, 1763–1957*. Ottawa, 1961.

———. "Climatic Trends Along the Atlantic Coast of Canada," *PTRSC*, ser. 3, *49* (1955), Oceanographic session, 15–21.

———. *Climatological Atlas of Canada*. Ottawa, 1953.

———. "Monthly Fog Data." Canada, Meteorological Branch, Circular 2944, CLI-15. Toronto, 1957.

U.S. Navy Hydrographic Office. *Naval Air Pilot Weather Summary—Nova Scotia, New Brunswick, Southeastern Quebec*. Washington, 1943.

U.S. Weather Bureau. *Preliminary Report on Climate and Weather of Northwestern Europe*. (Weather Research Center, Ser. 3.) Washington, 1942.

Vegetation

Bentley, P. A., and Smith, E. C. "The Forests of Cape Breton in the Seventeenth and Eighteenth Centuries," *PNSIS, 24* (1956), pt. 1, 1–15.

Chapman, V. J. "A Note on the Salt Marshes of Nova Scotia," *Rhodora, 39* (1937), 53–57.

Clark, A. H. "Titus Smith, Junior, and the Geography of Nova Scotia in 1801 and 1802," *Annals of the Association of American Geographers, 44* (1954), 291–314.

Cunningham, G. C. *Forest Flora of Canada.* (Canada, Dept. of Northern Affairs and National Resources, Forestry Branch, Bulletin No. 121.) Ottawa, 1958.

Dore, W. G., and Roland, A. E. "The Grasses of Nova Scotia," *PNSIS, 20* (1942), 177–298.

Drinkwater, M. H. *The Tolerant Hardwood Forests of Northern Nova Scotia.* (Canada, Dept. of Northern Affairs and National Resources, Forestry Branch, Forest Research Division, Technical Note No. 57.) Ottawa, 1957.

Drummond, A. J. "How Plant Life is Distributed in Canada and Why," *Canadian Institute Transactions* (now Royal Canadian Institute), *8* (1910), 23–39.

Fassett, Norman C. "The Vegetation of the Estuaries of North-Eastern North America," *Proceedings of the Boston Society of Natural History, 39* (1928), 73–130.

Fernald, M. L. "Flora of Nova Scotia," *American Journal of Botany, 51* (1918), 237–47.

Fernow, B. E., Howe, C. D., and White, J. H. *Forest Conditions of Nova Scotia.* Ottawa, 1912.

Ganong, W. F. "The Vegetation of the Bay of Fundy Salt and Diked Marshes: An Ecological Study," *Botanical Gazette, 36* (1903), 161–86, 280–302, 349–67, 429–55.

Gorham, Eville. "Titus Smith, a Pioneer of Plant Ecology in North America," *Ecology, 36* (1955), 116–23.

Hawboldt, L. S. "Aspects of Yellow Birch Dieback in Nova Scotia," *Journal of Forestry, 45* (1947), 414–22.

Hawboldt, L. S., and Bulmer, R. M. *The Forest Resources of Nova Scotia.* (Nova Scotia Dept. of Lands and Forests.) Halifax, 1958.

Loucks, O. L. "A Forest Classification for the Maritime Provinces," *PNSIS, 25* (1962), pt. 2, 86–167.

Nichols, G. E. "The Hemlock–White Pine–Northern Hardwood Region of Eastern North America," *Ecology, 16* (1935), 403–22.

———. "The Vegetation of Northern Cape Breton Island, Nova Scotia," *Transactions of the Connecticut Academy of Arts and Sciences, 22* (1918), 249–467.

Roland, A. E. "Flora of Nova Scotia," *PTNSIS, 21* (1945), pt. 3, 95–642.

Rowe, J. S. *Forest Regions of Canada.* (Canada, Dept. of Northern Affairs and Natural Resources, Forestry Branch, Bulletin No. 123.) Ottawa, 1959.

Schott, Carl. *Die Kanadischen Marschen.* (Schriften des Geographischen Instituts der Universität Kiel, Band 15, Heft 2.) Kiel, 1955.

Soils

Cann, D. B., and Hilchey, J. D. *Soil Survey of Antigonish County, Nova Scotia.* (NSSS Report, No. 6.) Truro, 1954.

————. *Soil Survey of Lunenburg County, Nova Scotia*. (NSSS Report, No. 7.) Truro, 1958.

————. *Soil Survey of Queens County, Nova Scotia*. (NSSS Report, No. 8.) Truro, 1959.

Cann, D. B., Hilchey, J. D., and MacDougall, J. I. *Soil Survey of Digby County, Nova Scotia*. (NSSS Report, No. 11.) Truro, 1962.

————. *Soil Survey of Guysborough County, Nova Scotia*. (NSSS Report, No. 14.) Truro, 1964.

————. *Soil Survey of Halifax County, Nova Scotia*. (NSSS Report, No. 13.) Ottawa, 1963.

————. *Soil Survey of Shelburne County, Nova Scotia*. (NSSS Report, No. 9.) Truro, 1960.

Cann, D. B., Hilchey, J. D., and Smith, G. R. *Soil Survey of Hants County, Nova Scotia*. (NSSS Report, No. 5.) Truro, 1954.

Cann, D. B., and Wicklund, R. E. *Soil Survey of Pictou County, Nova Scotia*. (NSSS Report, No. 4.) Truro, 1950.

Harlow, L. C., and Whiteside, G. B. *Soil Survey of the Annapolis Valley Fruit Growing Area*. (Dominion of Canada, Department of Agriculture, Technical Bulletin No. 47.) Ottawa, November 1943. First of the NSSS reports but not so numbered.

McDonald, J. H. *Annual Report of the Department of Agriculture for 1934*. Section on soils. Halifax, 1935.

Whiteside, G. B., Wicklund, R. E., and Smith, G. R. *Soil Survey of Cumberland County, Nova Scotia*. (NSSS Report, No. 2.) Truro, 1945.

Wicklund, R. E., and Smith, G. R. *Soil Survey of Colchester County, Nova Scotia*. (NSSS Report, No. 3.) Truro, 1948.

The Micmac and Related Themes

Adney, E. Tappan. "The Malecite Indians' Names for Native Berries and Fruits and Their Meanings," *Acadian Naturalist, 1* (1944), 103.

Bailey, Alfred G. *The Conflict of European and Eastern Algonkian Cultures, 1504–1700: A Study in Canadian Civilization* (New Brunswick Museum, Monograph Ser. No. 2), Saint John, N. B., 1937.

Dixon, R. B. "The Early Migrations of the Indians of New England and the Maritime Provinces," *Proceedings of the American Antiquarian Society*, new ser., *24* (1914), 65–76.

Hutton, J. A. "The Micmac Indians of Nova Scotia to 1834." Unpublished M.A. thesis, Dalhousie University, Halifax, 1961.

Jenness, Diamond. *The Indians of Canada*. 5th ed. Ottawa, 1960.

Johnson, Frederick, ed. *Man in Northeastern North America*. (Papers of the R. S. Peabody Foundation for Archeology.) Boston, 1946. See especially papers by J. M. Cooper and Regina Flannery on the Northeastern Indian hunters.

Leighton, Alex H. "The Twilight of the Indian Porpoise Hunters," *Natural History, 40* (1937), 410–16, 458. A description of porpoise hunting as practiced years ago by the Micmac Indians of Nova Scotia.

McIlwraith, T. F. "Micmac," *Encyclopedia Canadiana, 7,* 60. Ottawa, 1966.

Piers, Harry. "Brief Account of the Micmac Indians of Nova Scotia and Their Remains," *PTNSIS, 13* (1911–12), 99–125.

Rogers, Norman McLeod. "Apostle to the Micmacs," *Dalhousie Review, 6* (1926–27), 166–76. Re Abbé Pierre Maillard.

Smith, H. I., and Wintemberg, W. S. *Some Shell-Heaps in Nova Scotia.* (National Museum of Canada, Anthropological Ser. No. 9.) Ottawa, 1929.

Speck, Frank G. *Beothuk and Micmac.* New York, 1922.

———. "Culture Problems in Northeastern North America," *Proceedings of the American Philosophical Society, 65* (1926), 272–311.

Speck, Frank G., and Hadlock, W. S. "A Report on Tribal Boundaries and Hunting Areas of the Malecite Indians of New Brunswick," *American Anthropologist,* new ser., *48* (1946), 355–74.

Stuckenrath, R., Jr. "The Debert Site: Early Man in the Northeast," *Expedition, 7* (1964), 20–29.

VanWart, Arthur F. "The Indians of the Maritime Provinces, Their Diseases and Native Cures," *Canadian Medical Association Journal, 59* (1948), 573–77.

Wallis, W. D. "Historical Background of the Micmac Indians of Canada." In *Contributions to Anthropology, 1959.* (National Museum of Canada, Bulletin No. 173.) Ottawa, 1961, pp. 42–63.

Wallis, W. D., and Wallis, R. S. *The Micmac Indians of Eastern Canada.* Minneapolis, 1955.

———. *The Malecite Indians of New Brunswick.* (National Museum of Canada, Anthropological Ser. No. 40.) Ottawa, 1957.

UNPUBLISHED DOCUMENTS AND MANUSCRIPTS

The heart of this study is based largely on manuscript material only a few parts of which have been printed intact or in various excerpts. Most of the manuscript material available for the study of the Acadians, in terms of their settlement, economy, and society, consists of official French and English correspondence and records. The great bulk of these have been copied, by hand or photographically, and the copies deposited in the Public Archives of Canada (AC), which also hold some original material for this period. Other major collections may be found in the Archives de la province de Québec and in the Public Archives of Nova Scotia. The most important originals are in the Archives Nationales in Paris (AN), especially the Archives des Colonies (AdC), and in the Colonial Office series of the British Public Record Office in London. Nevertheless, bits and pieces were located in a wide variety of depositories in France, the United Kingdom, Canada, and the United States.

The best guides to the AC holdings are a series of *Preliminary Inventories* of their different Manuscript Groups. These also specify where various widely scattered guides and indexes to their holdings may be found, chiefly in various AC annual *Reports* and in D. W. Parker, *A Guide to the Documents in the Public Archives of Canada, 7* (1914), and its supplements. No attempt will be made here to list all the depositories where information can be found. But attention is called to the "Bibliographical Notes" in J. B. Brebner, *New England's Outpost: Acadia Before the Conquest of Canada,* Columbia University Studies in History, Economics, and Public Law, No. 293 (New York, 1927). The location of specific documents is indicated where they are cited.

The series of the Archives Nationales, Archives des Colonies, copied for AC (in Manuscript Group 7) which have proved most useful include:

AC designation		AN, AdC designation
Ser. 2	B	Lettres envoyées, 1663–1789
Ser. 3	C11A	Correspondance générale, Canada, 1540–1784
Ser. 4	C11B	Correspondance générale, Île Royale, 1712–1762
Ser. 5	C11C	Amérique du Nord, 1661–1670
Ser. 6	C11D	Correspondance générale, Acadie, 1603–1714
Ser. 18	F2B	Commerce des Colonies, 1714–1790
Ser. 20	F3	Collection Moreau St-Méry, 1492–1798
Ser. 21	F5A	Missions et cultes religieux, 1658–1782
Ser. 22	G1	Registres de l'État civil, recensements et divers documents, 1721–1784
Ser. 23	G2	Registres des Greffes du Conseil Supérieur de Louisbourg, 1711–1758

Unquestionably, the vast amount of material for the period before 1710 on Acadia is in C11D, and for the period after 1713 on Cape Breton Island in C11B. Of absolutely central value are the censuses, often nominal, frequent, and in painstaking detail, which have been collected in G1. To facilitate reference, the AN, AdC designations are used for the series but the AC copies were those used in the great majority of cases and the volume numbers and pagination refer to them. There was some use made also of AC copies from the AN, Archives de la Marine (AC, MG5), Archives de la Guerre (AC, MG4), and the Archives de la Ministère des Affaires Étrangères (esp. Correspondance Politique, Angleterre, and Mémoires et Documents, Amérique [also AC, MG5]). AC, MG9, Provincial, Local and Territorial Records, Section B8 (Nova Scotia Church Records) contains several parish registers in copies. AC, MG18 (Pre-Conquest Documents) has a section F (Acadie et Nouvelle-Écosse), a section L (British Officers), and a section N (Military Documents) in which one or more useful bits were found.

The relevant materials in the Manuscript Room of the British Museum and in the Public Record Office were seen there in large part but, again AC has transcribed or photocopied the most useful materials in AC, MG11 (Transcripts of Papers in the British Museum and Colonial Office papers from the Public Record Office). A somewhat incomplete attempt has been made to locate material seen in London in the AC copies; where successful the AC citation is given as likely to prove more useful to North American scholars. The principal Colonial Office papers used included NSA, CO 217 (including later Nova Scotia and Cape Breton material) and NSB (Executive Council Minutes).

Unhappily, we are without a large part of the kind of material upon which similar studies of the Canadian section of New France can be based. While Acadia was under French control the governmental and legal apparatus can be described as, at best, skeletal. After 1710 we have more information recorded in the actions of the council at Annapolis Royal, but we are without the enormously useful censuses of the French regime. We have nothing equivalent to the Ordonannces des Intendants, the Registres de la prévôté de Québec, or the records of the seigneurial courts.

Fragmentary parish records have survived for what little one can tell from them (see Placide Gaudet, "Acadian Genealogy and Notes," 1906). Those of the parish of St. Jean Baptiste of Annapolis Royal for 1702–50 are in Halifax. Those of St. Charles of Grand Pré for 1709–48 repose in somewhat damaged form in the archives of the Archdiocese of New Orleans. The greater part of the registers of Beaubassin for 1712–48 were discovered more than half a century ago at Rochelle in France (Archives départmentales de la Charente-Maritime). Finally, the Archives de l'archevêché de Québec has some fragments of the registers at Beaubassin dating from the end of the seventeenth century. Copies of all these are now in AC in Manuscript Groups 1 (G1 and G2) and 9 (38), and, to anticipate, some fragments for Beaubassin and Minas (Rivière des Mines) for 1679–86 and Shepody (Chypody) and Petitcodiac (Pedkodiac) have been published as Acadian Church Records.

Understandably, the Public Archives of Nova Scotia has a substantial holding of relevant documentary material, which is catalogued in consecutively numbered groups. Material of interest to this work is chiefly in the first 28 groups. Much of it consists of copies of PRO, BM (British Museum), AN, or AC material, but there are many originals, some not duplicated elsewhere. Of special interest were groups 4a and 4b (documents regarding the Acadians, 1720–51 and 1749–69); 5 to 11 (dealing with the administration at Annapolis Royal, 1711–49); 12–13½ (relations with New England); 16–18 (correspondence between London and Annapolis Royal); 19 (Louisburg-London correspondence, 1745–49); and 26 (parish records at Port Royal-Annapolis Royal). Many of the PANS holdings have been published.

A few other manuscript items of unusual importance should be mentioned. "A Breif Survey of Nova Scotia," which J. B. Brebner and others conclude was written by Captain Charles Morris about 1749, is in the Library of the Royal Artillery Regiment at Woolwich, and a photocopy is in AC, catalogued as MG18, F10. I depended on my own transcription of the original; the photocopy is difficult to read. It is incomparably the best extant description of Acadia and the Acadians at mid-eighteenth-century (although with all the inherent bias of a New Englander). PANS holds an unusually interesting undated manuscript by Isaac Deschamps, a major Halifax figure of the

1760's and the 1770's, on Acadian agriculture and dyke-building, and the original diaries of Titus Smith, Jr., the naturalist. The correspondence of Colonel Charles Lawrence with his subordinate, Monckton, gives some useful views of the region in the critical early months of 1755. The originals are in the Vernon-Wager papers in the Library of Congress but AC has copies. The Chalmers Collection of Letters and Documents relating to Nova Scotia in the New York Public Library proved useful.

Finally, BM, PRO, PANS, and Archives de la province de Quebec, in particular, have excellent collections of originals or photocopies of maps of the area made throughout the period of interest; the writer holds photocopies of many of those which are not available for study in published form, as in Marcel Trudel, *Atlas historique du Canada Français,* Quebec, 1961. Individual maps were turned up in many places, e.g., the Newberry Library in Chicago holds a magnificent *Carte Marine* of Port Royal as of 1708 or 1709 (see Fig. 5.8).

Other Published Works and Documentary compendia

A substantial number of documents and related contemporary materials have been published. No attempt has been made to include in the following list all of those consulted, but it is meant to include all that have been cited. Major media for such publication include the annual reports (under various titles) and special publications of AC, PANS, Archives de la province de Québec, and the New Brunswick Museum; the *Collections* and special publications of the New Brunswick Historical Society, Nova Scotia Historical Society, and Royal Society of Canada; and the Champlain Society series. Special attention should be directed to certain collections: H.-R. Casgrain, 1888; Placide Gaudet, 1906; H. A. Innis, 1929; A. Shortt, V. K. Johnston, and G. Lanctot, 1933; W. I. Morse, 1935; *Nova Scotia Archives, I,* 1869, *II,* 1900, *III,* 1908, and *IV,* 1967; P.-G. Roy, 1927–29; Surlaville, 1899; R. G. Thwaites, 1896–1901; and J. C. Webster, 1934. For those published by *Le Canada-Français,* see P.-G. Roy, 1924. In addition, many such materials for the period have been reproduced in whole or in part, abridged, paraphrased, and sometimes translated, in such later publications as F.-E. Rameau de Saint-Père, 1859; Rameau, 1877 and 1889, and Beamish Murdoch, 1865–67. Occasionally, the *Preliminary Inventories* of the different Manuscript Groups in AC have an indication of where their materials have appeared in print.

The most comprehensive single bibliographical listing of published works dealing with Acadia and the Acadians may be that appended to Geneviève Massignon, 1962. In addition, one should note: N. E. Dionne, 1906; J. P. Edwards, 1921; Gustave Lanctot, 1951; Philip Garigue, 1956; W. F. E. Morley, 1967; and Norah Story, 1967.

The following abbreviations have been used in this section: AC, Public

Archives of Canada; CHA, Canadian Historical Association; *CHR, Canadian Historical Review;* NBHS, New Brunswick Historical Society; NSHS, Nova Scotia Historical Society; PANS, Public Archives of Nova Scotia; *PTRSC, Proceedings and Transactions of the Royal Society of Canada.*

Acadian Church Records, 1679–1757. Mobile, Ala., 1964. Has fragments from Beaubassin and Rivière aux Mines for 1679–1686, and "Pedko-diac" and "Chypody" for 1755–1766. A series of pamphlets.

Acadiensia Nova, 1578–1779: New and Unpublished Documents and other Data Relating to Acadia, ed. W. I. Morse. 2 vols. London, 1935.

"An Account of Nova Scotia in 1745," NSHS *Collections, 1* (1879), 105–9.

An Account of the Present State of Nova Scotia in two Letters to a Noble Lord. London, 1756. AC, Catalogue of Pamphlets, *1,* No. 189.

"Acquisition and Trade of Halifax," *The Gentleman's Magazine, 25* (1755), 261–64.

Akins, Thomas B. "History of Halifax City," NSHS *Collections, 8* (1895), 3–272.

Alexander, Sir William (later Earl of Stirling). *An Encouragement to Colonies.* London, 1624.

Anderson, William Patrick. *Micmac Place-Names.* (Geographic Board of Canada.) Ottawa, 1919.

Archibald, Sir A. G. "The Expulsion of the Acadians," NSHS *Collections, 5* (1887), 11–95.

Arsenault, Bona. *L'Acadie des ancêtres: avec la généalogie des premières familles acadiennes.* Quebec, 1955.

———. *Histoire et généalogie des Acadiens.* 2 vols. Quebec, 1965.

Bailey, Alfred G. *The Conflict of European and Eastern Algonkian Cultures, 1504–1700: A Study in Canadian Civilization.* (New Brunswick Museum, Monograph Ser. No. 2.) Saint John, N. B., 1937.

Barbeau, Marius. "Types des maisons acadiennes," *Le Canada Français,* ser. 2, *29* (1941–42), 35–43.

Baudry, René. "Aux Sources de l'Histoire de l'Acadie et des Provinces Maritimes," CHA *Report* (1955), pp. 62–68.

Bell, Winthrop P. *The "Foreign Protestants" and the Settlement of Nova Scotia: The History of a Piece of Arrested British Colonial Policy in the Eighteenth Century.* Toronto, 1961.

Bernard, Antoine. *L'Acadie vivante: histoire du peuple acadien de ses origines à nos jours.* Montreal, 1945.

———. *Histoire de l'Acadie.* 2nd ed., Moncton, 1939.

———. *Histoire de la Louisiane de ses origines à nos jours.* Quebec, [1953?].

———. *Histoire de la Survivance Acadienne: 1755–1935 . . . .* Montreal, 1935.

Biard, Pierre. *Missio Canadensis.* Albany, 1870. *See also* Thwaites, R. G., ed., *Jesuit Relations, 2,* 58–118.

———. *Relation de la Nouvelle France, de ses terres naturel de païs, & de ses habitans, item, du voyage des Peres Iesuits aus dictes contrées, & de ce qu'ils y ont faict jusques à leur prinse par les Anglois.* Lyons, 1616. *See also* Thwaites, R. G., ed., *Jesuit Relations, 3,* 21–284; *4,* 9–165.

————. Various letters to the General and his Provincial of the Society of Jesus. In Thwaites, R. G., ed., *Jesuit Relations, 1,* 125–83, 188–92; *2,* 3–56.

Biggar, H. P. *The Early Trading Companies of New France: A Contribution to the History of Commerce and Discovery in North America.* Toronto, 1901.

————. *The Precursors of Jacques Cartier, 1497–1534: A Collection of Documents Relating to the Early History of the Dominion of Canada.* (AC publications, No. 5.) Ottawa, 1911.

————. *The Voyages of Jacques Cartier.* (AC publications, No. 11.) Ottawa, 1924.

————, ed. *The Works of Samuel de Champlain.* 6 vols. (Champlain Society publications, new ser.) Toronto, 1922–36.

Billington, R. A. *America's Frontier Heritage.* New York, 1966.

————, ed. *The Frontier Thesis.* New York, 1966.

————. *Westward Expansion.* 3rd ed., New York, 1967.

Bird, J. Brian. "Settlement Patterns in Maritime Canada, 1687–1786," *Geographical Review, 45* (1955), 385–404.

Bird, Will R. *A Century at Chignecto: The Key to Old Acadia.* Toronto, 1928.

————. *Done at Grand Pré.* Toronto, 1955.

Bishop, Morris. *Champlain.* New York, 1948.

[Bollan, William]. *See* Holland, Samuel, *The Importance and Advantage . . . .*

A Boston Merchant of 1745: or, Incidents in the Life of James Gibson, A Gentleman Volunteer at the Expedition to Louisburg. Boston, 1847.

Bourinot, Sir John G. "Builders of Nova Scotia, An Historical Review," *PTRSC,* ser. 2, *5* (1899), sec. 2, iii–197. Separately published, same title, Toronto, 1900.

————. "Cape Breton and Its Memorials of the French Regime," *PTRSC, 9* (1891), sec. 2, 173–343. Contains much original material.

————. *Historical and Descriptive Account of the Island of Cape Breton and of Its Memorials of the French Régime.* Montreal, 1892.

Brebner, J. B., ed. "Canadian Policy toward the Acadians in 1751," *CHR, 12* (1931), 284–86.

————. *New England's Outpost: Acadia before the Conquest of Canada.* (Columbia University Studies in History, Economics, and Public Law, No. 293.) New York, 1927.

————, ed. "Subsidized Intermarriage with the Indians," *CHR, 6* (1925), 33–34.

Brown, Richard. *A History of the Island of Cape Breton . . . with Some Account of the Discovery and Settlement of Canada, Nova Scotia, and Newfoundland.* London, 1869.

Burt, A. L. "The Frontier in the History of New France," CHA *Report* (1940), pp. 93–99.

Butel-Dumont, G. M. *Conduite des français par rapport à la Nouvelle Écosse.* London, Paris, 1756.

"The Cadillac Memoir." *See* Laumet de Lamothe de Cadillac.

A Calendar of Two Letter-Books and one Commission-Book in the Possession of the Government of Nova Scotia, 1713–1741, ed. Archibald M. Mac-Mechan. Halifax, 1900. Widely catalogued and referred to as *Nova Scotia Archives. II.*

Calnek, W. A. *History of the County of Annapolis . . . .* Toronto, 1897. *See also* supplement by A. W. Savary, Toronto, 1913.

Campbell, George G. *The History of Nova Scotia.* Toronto, 1948.

Carayon, Auguste, ed. *Première Mission des Jésuites au Canada.* Paris, 1864.

Careless, J. M. S. "Frontierism, Metropolitanism and Canadian History," *CHR, 35* (1954) 1–21.

Casgrain, Abbé Henri-Raymond. "Les Acadiens après leur dispersion, 1755–1775," *PTRSC, 5* (1887), sec. 1, 15–91.

———, comp. *Collection de documents inédits: Documents sur le Canada et l'Amérique. 1* and *2, Documents sur l'Acadie.* Quebec, 1888–89.

———. "Coup d'oeil sur l'Acadie," *Le Canada Français, 1* (1888), 115–34.

———. "Éclaircissements sur la question acadienne," *PTRSC, 6* (1888), sec. 1, 23–75.

———. *Une Seconde Acadie: l'Île Saint-Jean, Île du Prince-Édouard sous le régime français.* Quebec, 1894.

———. *Les Sulpiciens et les prêtres des missions étrangères en Acadie 1676–1762.* Quebec, 1897.

Census of Canada, 1870–71. Ottawa, 1876.

Chabert de Cagolin, Joseph B. *Voyage fait par ordre du Roi en 1750 et 1751 . . . pour rectifier des cartes des côtes de l'Acadie . . . .* Paris, 1753.

Champlain, Samuel de. *Oeuvres. See* Laverdière, C. H., ed.

———. *Des Sauvages . . . .* Paris, 1603.

———. *Les Voyages . . . .* Paris, 1613.

———. *Voyages et descouvertes faites en la Nouvelle France, depuis l'année 1615, jusques à la fin 1618 . . . .* Paris, 1619.

———. *Les Voyages . . . . Canada . . . .* Paris, 1632.

———. *Works. See* Biggar, H. P., ed.

Charlevoix, P.-F.-X. de. *Histoire et description générale de la Nouvelle France, avec le journal historique d'un voyage fait par ordre du Roi dans l'Amérique septentrionale.* 3 vols. Paris, 1744. The journal appeared in English translation in 1761 and was retranslated and edited by Louise P. Kellogg, Chicago, 1923. Two English translations of the *History* are readily available: J. G. Shea, trans. and ed., 6 vols. New York, 1866–72, and N. F. Morrison, ed., with memoir and bibliography, New York, 1900.

Chiasson, Père Anselme. *Chéticamp, Histoire et Traditions acadiennes.* Moncton, 1961.

Chipman, W. "The Life and Times of Major Samuel Holland, Surveyor-General, 1764–1801," *Papers and Records of the Ontario Historical Society, 21* (1924), 11–90.

Church, [Benjamin]. *The History of the Great Indian War of 1675 and 1676, commonly called Philip's War. Also, the old French and Indian wars, from 1689 to 1704. By Thomas Church, esq., with numerous notes and an appendix by Samuel G. Drake*. Rev. ed. Hartford, n.d. Many earlier editions dating from 1716.

Clark, A. H. "Acadia and the Acadians: The Creation of a Geographical Entity." In *Frontiers and Men,* ed. John Andrews. Melbourne, 1966, pp. 90–119.

———. *The Invasion of New Zealand by People, Plants and Animals*. New Brunswick, N. J., 1949.

———. "New England's Role in the Underdevelopment of Cape Breton Island during the French Regime, 1713–1758," *Canadian Geographer, 9* (1965), 1–12.

———. *Three Centuries and the Island: A Historical Geography of Settlement and Agriculture in Prince Edward Island, Canada*. Toronto, 1959.

———. "Titus Smith, Junior, and the Geography of Nova Scotia in 1801 and 1802," *Annals of the Association of American Geographers, 44* (1954), 291–314.

Clark, A. H., and Innis, D. Q. "The Roots of Canada's Geography." In *Canada: a Geographical Interpretation,* ed. John Warkentin. Toronto, 1968, pp. 13–53.

Clark, Jeremiah S. "Micmac Place Names in the Maritime Provinces of Canada." In S. T. Rand. *Micmac Dictionary*. Charlottetown, P.E.I., 1902, pp. 179–92.

Collection des manuscrits contenant lettres, mémoires et autres documents historiques relatifs à la Nouvelle-France recueillis aux Archives de la Province de Québec ou copiés à l' étranger. 4 vols. Quebec, 1883–85.

Comeau, F. G. J. "The Origin and History of the Apple Industry in Nova Scotia," NSHS *Collections, 23* (1936), 15–30.

Commissioners for Trade and Plantations. *See Journal of the Commissioners* [etc.].

Conquest of Cape Breton. London [1745?].

Considerations sur les Differends . . . Touchant l'Acadie. The Hague, 1761.

Cormier, P. C. *L'Origine et l'histoire du nom Acadie, avec un discours sur d'autres noms de lieu Acadiens*. Winnipeg and Moncton, 1966.

Couillard-Després, Azarie. *Charles de Saint-Étienne de La Tour, gouverneur, lieutenant-général en Acadie, et son temps, 1593–1666*. Arthabaska, P.Q., 1930. A slightly revised version in 1932.

———. "Les Gouverneurs de l'Acadie sous le régime français, 1600–1710," *PTRSC,* ser. 3, *33* (1939), sec. 1, 219–88.

———. *Histoire des Seigneurs de la Rivière du Sud et de leurs alliés Canadiens et Acadiens*. St-Hyacinthe, P.Q., 1921.

Couillard-Després, Azarie. *En Marge de La Tragédie d'un Peuple de M. Emile Lauvrière.* Bruges, 1925.

———. *Observations sur l'histoire de l'Acadie française de M. Moreau.* Montreal, 1919.

———. "Aux Sources de l'histoire de l'Acadie," *PTRSC,* ser. 3, 27 (1933), sec. 1, 63–81.

Courville, Louis-Léonard Aumasson, Sieur de. "Journal of Louis de Courville." In *Journals of Beauséjour . . . ,* ed. J. C. Webster, Sackville, N. B., 1937.

———. "Mémoire du Canada," *Rapport de l'Archiviste de la Province de Québec, 1924–25* (1925), pp. 94–96.

———. *Mémoires sur le Canada depuis 1749 jusqu'à 1760.* Quebec, 1838 and 1873.

Craven, Avery O. "Frederick Jackson Turner." In *Marcus W. Jernegan Essays in American Historiography,* ed. William T. Hutchinson. Chicago, 1937, pp. 408–24.

———. "Frederick Jackson Turner, Historian," *Wisconsin Magazine of History, 25* (1942), 408–24.

Crèvecoeur, J. Hector St. John (Michel Guillaume St-Jean de). *Letters from an American Farmer . . . .* London, 1782.

———. *Qu'est-ce qu'un Américain?* Princeton, 1943.

Crowell, Edwin. *A History of Barrington Township, and Vicinity, Shelburne County, Nova Scotia, 1604–1870 . . . .* Yarmouth, 1923. (Material gathered by Alfred Doane.)

Curti, Merle E., *et al. The Making of an American Community: A Case Study of Democracy in a Frontier County.* Stanford, 1959.

Daligaut, Marguerite. "Les Acadiens de Belle-Île-en-Mer," *La Société Historique Acadienne,* Cahier *11* (1966), 5–11.

Daviault, Pierre. "Les noms du lieux au Canada," *PTRSC,* ser. 3, 42 (1948), sec., 1, 43–52.

———. *Le Baron de Saint-Castin, Chef abénaquis.* Montreal, 1939.

David, Albert. "Messire Pierre Maillard, Apôtre des Micmacs," *Bulletin des Recherches Historiques, 35* (1929), 365–75.

Davis, Harold A. *An International Community on the St. Croix (1604–1630).* (University of Maine *Studies,* ser. 2, No. 64.) Orono, Me., 1950.

Dawson, R. MacGregor. "Place Names in Nova Scotia." Paper read before the Linguistic Circle of Manitoba, Winnipeg, 1960.

DeCazes, Paul. "L'Episode de l'Ile de Sable," *PTRSC,* 10 (1892), sec. 2, 7–15.

D'Entremont, Henri Leander. *The Baronnie de Pombcoup and the Acadiens: a History of the Ancient "Department of Cape Sable". . . .* Yarmouth, N. S., 1931.

———. *The Forts of Cape Sable in the Seventeenth Century.* Centre East Pubnico, N. S., 1938.

De Forest, Louis Effingham. *Louisbourg Journals, 1745.* New York, 1932.

Demeulle, Jacques. "Mémoire touchant le Canada et l'Acadie, 1687." In *Les Nouvelles Annales des voyages et des sciences géographiques*. Paris, 1884.
———. "Un Recensement de l'Acadie en 1686," *Bulletin des Recherches Historiques, 38* (1932), 677–96.
Denys, Nicolas. *Description Géographique et historique des costes de l'Amérique septentrionale, avec l'histoire naturelle du païs*. 2 vols. Paris, 1672.
———. *The Description and Natural History of the Coasts of North America (Acadia)*, trans. and ed. W. F. Ganong. (Champlain Society publications, 2.) Toronto, 1908.
DesBrisay, M. B. *History of the County of Lunenburg*. Toronto, 1870. 2nd. ed., 1895.
Deschamps, Isaac. Undated MS on Acadian agriculture and dyke-building. PANS (uncatalogued).
Deschamps, Leon. *Isaac de Razilly*. Paris, 1887.
"Description of Nova Scotia," *Daily Gazetteer* (London), June 14, 1746.
Dièreville, [N.?], Sieur de. *Relation du voyage du Port Royal de l'Acadie . . . .* Paris, 1708. Many subsequent editions in French, English, and German.
———. *Relation of the Voyage to Port Royal in Acadia or New France*, trans. Alice Webster, ed. with notes, J. C. Webster. (Champlain Society publications, 20.) Toronto, 1933.
Dionne, N.-E. *Les Canadiens-Français; Origine des familles emigrées de France, d'Espagne, de Suisse, etc., pour venir se fixer au Canada, depuis la fondation de Québec jusqu'à ces derniers temps, et signification de leurs noms*. Quebec and Montreal, 1914.
———. *Champlain*. New York, 1926.
———. *Inventaire chronologique des ouvrages publiées a l'étranger en diverses langues sur Québec et la Nouvelle-France (1534–1906)*. Quebec, 1906.
Doughty, Arthur G. *The Acadian Exiles, a Chronicle of the Land of Evangeline*. Toronto, 1916. 2nd ed., 1920.
Douglass, William (M.D.). *A Summary, Historical and Political, of the First Planting, Progressive Improvements, and Present State of the British Settlements in North America*. 2 vols. Boston, 1755.
Douville, Raymond and Jacques-Donat Casanova. *La Vie Quotidienne en Nouvelle-France: le Canada de Champlain à Montcalm*. Paris, 1964.
Downey, Fairfax. *Louisburg, Key to a Continent*. Englewood Cliffs, N.J., 1965.
D'Ulloa, Don Antonio. *A Voyage to South America*. London, 1772. Spent some time at Louisburg and reports on it.
Eaton, A. W. H. *Chapters in the History of Halifax, and the Rhode Island Settlers in Hants County, Nova Scotia*. New York, [1920?]. Reprints of fifteen articles appearing in *Americana* from 1915 to 1918; the relevant articlé was the first, "The Founding of Halifax," *Americana, 10* (1915), pt. 1, 269–88.

Eaton, A. W. H. *The History of Kings County, Nova Scotia; Heart of the Acadian Land, 1604–1910.* Salem, Mass., 1910.

Edwards, Joseph P. *The Public Records of Nova Scotia.* Halifax, 1920.

———. "Sources of Canadian History, with Special Reference to Nova Scotia," NSHS *Collections, 20* (1921), 155–66.

Faribault, G. B., ed. *Catalogue d'ouvrages sur l'histoire de l'Amérique, et en particulier sur celle du Canada, de la Louisiane, de l'Acadie, et autres lieux.* Quebec, 1837.

Fauteux, Noël. *Essai sur l'industrie au Canada sous le régime français.* 2 vols. Quebec, 1927.

Fergusson, C. Bruce. *The Boundaries of Nova Scotia and its Counties.* (PANS *Bulletin,* No. 22.) Halifax, 1966.

———. "Cabot's Landfall," *Dalhousie Review, 33* (1953), 257–76.

———. "Eighteenth-Century Halifax," CHA *Report* (1949), pp. 32–39.

———. *The Public Archives of Nova Scotia.* (PANS *Bulletin,* No. 19.) Halifax, 1963.

———, ed. *Uniacke's Sketches of Cape Breton and Other Papers Relating to Cape Breton.* Halifax, 1958.

Ferland, J.-B.-Antoine. *Cours d'histoire du Canada.* 2 vols. Quebec, 1861 and 1865.

Fiedmont, Louis Thomas Jacau, Sieur de. *The Siege of Beauséjour in 1755, a Journal of the Attack on Beauséjour written by Jacau de Fiedmont, Artillery Officer and Acting Engineer at the Fort,* trans. Alice Webster, ed. J. C. Webster. Saint John, N.B., 1936.

Firestone, O. J. "Farming in Nova Scotia in the Seventeenth Century," *Public Affairs, 6* (1943), 152–58.

Floyer, Captain Matthew. "Journal of the March by the River Shebenaccadia, August, 1754," PANS *Report* (1957), pp. 17–20.

Folsom, George, ed. "Expedition of Capt. Samuel Argall . . . to the French Settlements in Acadia . . . 1613," New York Historical Society *Collections,* ser. 2, *1* (1841), 335–42.

Forbin, Victor. "Les Français d'Acadie et leur langue," *La Nature* (1929), 222–24. A review of Pascal Poirier's, *Le Parler Franco-Acadien et son origine.*

Franquet, Louis, Le Sieur. "Le Voyage de Franquet aux Iles Royale et Saint-Jean (1751)," *Rapport de l'archiviste de la province de Québec, 1923–24* (1924), pp. 111–140.

Fraser, Colonel Alexander. "Nova Scotia: The Royal Charter of 1621," *Transactions of the Royal Canadian Institute, 14* (1922), pt. 1, 69–122.

Frégault, Guy. *La Civilisation de la Nouvelle-France (1713–1744).* Montreal, 1944.

Froidevaux, Henri. "Origine du mot 'Acadie'," *Journal de la Société des Américanistes de Paris,* nouv. ser., *12* (1920) 267–68.

Frye, "Col." "Extract of a letter from Col. Frye to his excellency the governour of Nova Scotia, dated, Fort Cumberland, Chignecto, March 7,

1760," Massachusetts Historical Society *Collections,* ser. 1, *10* (1809), 115–16.

Ganong, W. F. "Additions and Corrections to Monographs on the Place Nomenclature, Cartography, Historic Sites, Boundaries, and Settlement Origins of the Province of New Brunswick," *PTRSC,* ser. 2, *12* (1906), sec. 2, 3–157.

———. *Crucial Maps in the Early Cartography of the Atlantic Coast of Canada,* ed. with introduction and notes by T. E. Layng. Toronto, 1964. Based on a series of studies in *PTRSC,* 1929 to 1937.

———. *The History of Miscou and Shippegan.* Rev. and enlarged from the notes of W. F. Ganong by Susan B. Ganong. Saint John, N.B., 1946.

———. "A Monograph of the Cartography of the Province of New Brunswick," *PTRSC,* ser. 2, *3* (1897), sec. 2, 313–427.

———. *A Monograph of the Evolution of the Boundaries of the Province of New Brunswick.* Ottawa, 1901.

———. "A Monograph of Historic Sites in the Province of New Brunswick," *PTRSC,* ser. 2, *5* (1899), sec. 2, 213–357.

———. "A Monograph of the Origins of Settlements in the Province of New Brunswick," *PTRSC,* ser. 2, *10* (1904), sec. 2, 3–185.

———. "A Monograph of the Place-Nomenclature of the Province of New Brunswick," *PTRSC,* ser. 2, *2* (1896), sec. 2, 175–289.

———. "The Origin of the Place-Names, Acadia and Norumbega," *PTRSC,* ser. 3, *11* (1917), sec. 2, 105–11.

———. "Richard Denys, Sieur de Fronsac, and his Settlements in Northern New Brunswick," *NBHS Collections,* No. 7 (also listed as vol. 3, No. 1) (1907), pp. 7–54. This is also listed as item No. 4 in a series entitled "Historical-Geographical Documents Relating to New Brunswick."

———. *Sainte Croix (Dochet) Island: A Monograph.* Saint John, N.B., 1945.

Garigue, Philip. *A Bibliographical Introduction to the Study of French Canada.* Montreal, 1956.

Garneau, F.-X. *Histoire du Canada depuis sa découverte jusqu'à nos jours.* 3 vols. Quebec, 1845–48. The 3rd edition, 1859, was expurgated under ecclesiastical pressure. The 4th edition, 1882, was somewhat edited. The Paris editions, 1913–20, used the original text. The eighth and final edition was Paris, 1944.

———. *History of Canada . . . to 1840–41.* Montreal, 1860; 3rd ed., 1866. This translation by Andrew Bell of the expurgated 3rd edition (Quebec, 1859), of Garneau's classic is unsatisfactory.

Gaudet, Placide. "Acadian Genealogy and Notes," AC *Report for 1905* (Ottawa, 1906), *2,* app. A, pt. 3, i–xxxiv, 1–55, 1–372.

———. *Le Grand Dérangement.* Ottawa, 1922.

———. "Notes to accompany the Plan of the River of Annapolis Royal." *See* Knox, Captain John.

———, ed. "Les Seigneuries de l'ancienne Acadie," *Bulletin des Recherches Historiques, 33* (1927), 343–47.

"A General Return of the Several Townships in the Province of Nova Scotia for the first day of January, 1767," NSHS *Collections, 7* (1891), opp. 56.

A Genuine Account of Nova Scotia . . . . London and (repr.) Dublin, 1750. This has been attributed to either John Wilson or Otis Little.

A Geographical History of Nova Scotia. London, 1749 and 1755. Also published in translation as *Histoire Géographique de la Nouvelle-Écosse, contenant le detail de la situation de son étendue et de ses limites.* London, 1749. The original has been attributed to both Otis Little and John Wilson.

Gerin, Leon. *Aux Sources de notre histoire: les conditions économiques et sociales de la colonisation en Nouvelle France.* Montreal, 1946.

———. "La Première Tentative de colonisation française en Amérique," CHA *Report* (1931), pp. 49–60.

Gibson, James. *A Journal of the Late Siege . . . against the French at Cape Breton* . . . . London, 1745. Reprinted in *A Boston Merchant of 1745: or, Incidents in the Life of James Gibson, a Gentleman Volunteer at the Expedition to Louisburg.* Boston, 1847.

Gilroy, Marion. *A Catalogue of Maps, Plans and Charts in the Public Archives of Nova Scotia.* (PANS *Bulletin 1,* No. 3.) Halifax, 1938.

Gipson, Lawrence H. "Acadia and the beginnings of modern British Imperialism." In *Essays in Modern English History in Honor of Wilbur Cortez Abbot.* Cambridge, Mass., 1941, pp. 177–202.

Gorham, Eville. "Titus Smith, a Pioneer of Plant Ecology in North America," *Ecology, 36* (1955), 116–23.

Gorham, R. P. "Landmarks in Early Maritime Agriculture," *Scientific Agriculture* (now *Canadian Journal of Agricultural Science*), *6* (1926), 249–55.

Gould, Harley H. "The Acadian French in Canada and in Louisiana," *American Journal of Physical Anthropology, 28* (1941), 289–312. Physical studies of Acadian descendants in Louisiana, New Brunswick, and Prince Edward Island.

Graham, Gerald S. *Empire of the North Atlantic: the Maritime Struggle for North America.* Toronto, 1950.

Groulx, Lionel Adolphe. *Histoire du Canada française depuis la découverte.* 4 vols. Montreal, 1950–52. 2nd ed., 2 vols. Montreal, 1962.

Gulley, J. L. M. "The Turnerian Frontier, a Study in the Migration of Ideas," *Tijdschrift voor Economische en Sociale Geografie, 50* (1959), 65–72 and 81–91.

Hakluyt, Richard. *The Principall Navigations Voiages and Discoveries of the English Nation.* London, 1589. See photo-lithographic facsimile, Cambridge, 1965. One of the best known versions of scores, abridged, supplemented, etc., in many languages, is *The Principal Navigations, Voyages, Traffiques & Discoveries of the English nation.* (Hakluyt Society publications, extra ser., *1–12.*) Glasgow, 1903–5.

Hale, Robert. "Journal of a Voyage to Nova Scotia made in 1731 by Robert Hale of Beverly," Essex Institute *Historical Collections, 42* (1906), 217–44.

Haliburton, Thomas C. *An Historical and Statistical Account of Nova Scotia* . . . . 2 vols. Halifax, 1829. A considerable expansion and revision of his *A general description* . . . . Halifax, 1823.

Hamilton, Louis. *Ursprung der französischen Bevölkerung Canadas.* Berlin, 1920.

Hannay, James H. *History of Acadia, From its First Discovery to the Surrender to England, by the Treaty of Paris.* Saint John, N.B., 1879; London, 1880.

––––––. *History of New Brunswick.* 2 vols. Saint John, N.B., 1909.

Hanotaux, Gabriel, and Martineau, Alfred A. *Histoire des colonies françaises.* 6 vols. Paris, 1929–33.

Hardy, Georges. *Histoire sociale de la colonisation française.* Paris, 1953.

Harris, R. C. *The Seigneurial System in Early Canada: A Geographical Study.* Madison, 1966.

Hart, C. E. "Notes on the Fate of the Acadians," *CHR, 5* (1924), 108–17.

Harvey, Daniel Cobb. *The French Regime in Prince Edward Island.* New Haven, 1926.

––––––, comp. and ed. *Holland's Description of Cape Breton Island and Other Documents.* (PANS publications, No. 2.) Halifax, 1935.

––––––. ed. *See* Lawrence, (Colonel) Charles.

––––––. "Sir William Alexander and Nova Scotia," NSHS *Collections, 30* (1954), 1–26.

Hawkins, C. G. "The Origins of the Nova Scotia Lumber Trade," *Public Affairs, 9* (1946), 108–11.

Herbin, John F. *Grand Pré* . . . . 2nd ed., Toronto, 1900.

Hofstadter, Richard. "Turner and the Frontier Myth," *The American Scholar, 18* (1948–49), 433–43.

Holland, Captain Samuel. *Description of Cape Breton Island. See* Harvey, D. C., ed.

––––––. *The Importance and Advantage of Cape Breton, Truly Stated and Impartially Considered (With Proper Maps).* London, 1746. AC, Catalogue of Pamphlets, *1*, No. 121. Attributed to William Bolan.

Huguet, Adrien. *Jean de Poutrincourt, fondateur de Port-Royal en Acadie, vice-roi du Canada, 1557–1615* . . . . (Société des Antiquaires de Picardie, *Mémoires,* No. 44). Paris, 1932.

The Importance of Cape Breton Consider'd in a Letter to a Member of Parliament from an Inhabitant of New England. London, 1746. AC, Catalogue of Pamphlets, *1*, No. 120. The author uses the pseudonym "Massachusettenois."

The Importance of the Settling and Fortifying of Nova Scotia . . . . London, 1751. AC, Catalogue of Pamphlets, *1*, No. 152.

Innis, Harold Adams. "Cape Breton and the French Régime." *PTRSC,* ser. 3, *29* (1935), sec. 2, 51–87.

––––––. *The Cod Fisheries: The History of an International Economy.* Toronto, 1940. Rev. ed., Toronto, 1954.

Innis, Harold Adams. *The Fur Trade in Canada: An Introduction to Canadian Economic History*. Toronto, 1930. Rev. ed., Toronto, 1956.

————, ed. *Select Documents in Canadian Economic History, 1497–1783*. Toronto, 1929.

Insh, G. P. "Sir William Alexander's Colony at Port Royal," *Dalhousie Review, 10* (1929–30), 439–47.

Jefferys, Thomas. *The Conduct of the French in relation to Nova Scotia from its First Settlement to the Present Time . . . . In a Letter to a Member of Parliament*. London, 1754.

————. *The Natural and Civil History of the French Dominions in North and South America*. London, 1760.

Johnstone, James Chevalier de. *Memoirs of the Chevalier de Johnstone*. 3 vols. Aberdeen, 1870–71. He was in Louisburg from 1752 to 1758, through all of the last siege.

Journal of the Commissioners for Trade and Plantations, January 1749/50 to December 1753, London, 1932; *January 1759 to December 1763*, London, 1935; *January 1764 to December 1767*, London, 1936.

A Journal of the proceedings of the Late Expedition to Port Royal, on Board Their Majesties' Ship, The Six-Friends. Boston, 1928.

Knox, Captain John. *An Historical Journal of the Campaigns in North America for the Years 1757, 1758, 1759, and 1760 by Captain John Knox . . .* , ed. Arthur G. Doughty. 3 vols. Toronto, 1914–16. This includes Placide Gaudet's "Notes to accompany the Plan of the Rivers of Annapolis Royal."

La Boische de Beauharnois, Charles de, and Hocquart, Gilles. "Letter . . . to Le Comte de Maurepas." In *Documents Relative to the Colonial History of the State of New York, 10* (1858), 3–19. *See* under O'Callaghan, E. B., ed.

Lagrange, Louis Chancels de. "Voyage fait à l'Isle Royale ou de Cap Breton en Canada, 1716 . . . ," *Revue d'histoire de l'Amérique-française, 13* (1959), 424–34.

Laing, David, ed. *Royal Letters, Charters, and Tracts Relating to the Colonization of New Scotland and the Institution of the order of Knights Baronets of Nova Scotia, 1621–1638*. (Bannatyne Club publications, No. 14.) Edinburgh, 1867.

La Morandière, Charles de. *Histoire de la pêche française de la morue dans l'Amérique septentrionale*. 2 vols. Paris, 1962.

Lanctot, Gustave. "L'Acadie et la Nouvelle-Angleterre, 1603–1763," *Revue de l'Université d'Ottawa, 11* (1941), 182–205, 349–70.

————. "L'Établissement du Marquis de La Roche à l'île de Sable," CHA *Report* (1933), pp. 33–42.

————. *Histoire du Canada*. 3 vols. Montreal, 1960–63.

————. *A History of Canada*. 3 vols. Cambridge, Mass., 1963, 1964, and 1965. *1* (to 1663) trans. Josephine Hambleton; *2* (1663–1713) and *3* (1713–63) trans. Margaret Cameron.

————. *L'Oeuvre de la France en Amérique du Nord. Bibliographie selective et critique.* Paris and Montreal, 1951.

La Roque, Joseph, Sieur de. "Tour of Inspection made by the Sieur de la Roque." AC *Report for 1905* (Ottawa, 1906), *2,* app. A, pt. 1, 3–172. Includes complete nominal census of Cape Breton and Isle Saint-Jean.

Laumet de Lamothe de Cadillac, Antoine. "The Cadillac Memoir of 1692," ed. W. F. Ganong. NBHS *Collections, 13* (1930), 77–97.

Lauvrière, Émile. *La Tragédie d'un peuple: histoire du peuple acadien de ses origines à nos jours.* 2 vols. 4th ed., Paris, 1922. (Cover gives 1923.)

Laverdière, C. H., ed. *Oeuvres de Champlain.* 6 vols. Quebec, 1870.

Lawrence, (Colonel) Charles. *The Journals and Letters of Colonel Charles Lawrence.* Introduction by D. C. Harvey. (PANS *Bulletin* No. 10.) Halifax, 1953. A day-by-day account of the founding of Lunenburg from the Brown MSS in the British Museum.

Lawson, Mrs. William. *History of the Townships of Dartmouth, Preston and Lawrencetown.* Halifax, 1893.

Le Blanc, Dudley, J. *The True Story of the Acadians.* Lafayette, La., 1937.

Le Blanc, Emery. *Les Acadiens.* Montreal, 1963.

Le Blant, Robert. *Un Colonial sous Louis XIV. Philippe de Pastour de Costebelle, Gouverneur de Terreneuve puis de l'Île Royale, 1661–1717.* Dax, 1935.

————. "Une Corsaire de Saint-Domingue en Acadie, Pierre Morpain, 1707–1711," *Nova Francia, 6* (1931), 195–208.

————. "Les Études Historiques sur la colonie française d'Acadie, 1603–1713," *Revue d'histoire des colonies, 35* (1948), 84–113.

Le Clercq, Chrestien. *New Relation of Gaspesia, with the Customs and Religion of the Gaspesian Indians.* . . . trans. and ed., with a reprint of the original, by W. F. Ganong. (Champlain Society publications, *5.*) Toronto, 1910.

————. *Nouvelle relation de la Gaspesie.* . . . Paris, 1691.

Le Jeune, Louis M. *Tableaux synoptiques de l'histoire de l'Acadie: fascicule special (1500–1700).* Quebec, 1918.

Le Loutre, Jean-Louis, Abbé. "Une autobiographie de l'abbé Le Loutre (1709–1772)," ed. Albert David, from a MS in the Archives des Missions Étrangères à Paris. *Nova Francia, 6* (1931), 1–34.

————. "Description de l'Acadie." *See* under Casgrain, H.-R., comp., *Collection de documents inédits* . . . , *1,* 41–43.

Lemieux, O. A. "The Development of Agriculture in Canada During the 16th and 17th Centuries." Unpublished Ph.D. dissertation, University of Ottawa, 1940.

Lescarbot, Marc. *Histoire de la Nouvelle France* . . . . Paris, 1609. Rev. and enlarged, 1617. Many editions and translations. *See esp. History of New France by Marc Lescarbot,* trans. and ed. W. L. Grant. (Champlain Society publications, *1, 7, 9.*) Toronto, 1907–14. *See also, Nova Francia: Description of Acadia, 1606,* Pierre Erondelle's translation of 1609, reprinted, with introduction by H. P. Biggar, New York, 1928, and two items in Thwaites, R. G., ed., *Jesuit Relations, 1,* 49–113, and *2,* 119–92.

Letourneau, Firmin. *Histoire de l'agriculture (Canada français).* Montreal, 1950.

"Lettre de Talon au ministre Colbert," November 1671, *Rapport de l'archiviste de la province de Québec pour 1930–31* (1931), pp. 163–67.

Lincoln, Charles Henry, ed. *Correspondence of William Shirley.* New York, 1912.

Little, Otis. *The State of Trade in the Northern Colonies Considered with an Account of their Produce and a Particular Description of Nova Scotia.* London, 1748. Little was a New Englander who lived some time at Annapolis Royal, 1736ff. He may have written some of the anonymous items for this period.

Lom d'Arce, Louis-Armand de, Baron de Lahontan. *Mémoires de l'Amérique septentrionale on la Suite des voyages de Mr le Baron de Lahontan.* The Hague, 1703.

———. *Nouveaux Voyages . . . dans l'Amérique septentrionale . . . .* The Hague, 1703. *See also,* Thwaites, R. G., ed. *New Voyages . . . .*

Longfellow, Henry Wadsworth. *Evangeline: A Tale of Acadia.* Boston, 1847.

Lortie, Stanislaus Alfred. "De l'origine des Canadiens-français." In *L'Origine et le parler des Canadiens-français,* ed. Adjutor Rivard. Paris, 1903, pp. 5–12.

Lounsbury, R. G. "Yankee Trade at Newfoundland," *The New England Quarterly, 3* (1930), 607–26.

Lower, A. R. M. "The Maritimes as a Strategic Point in North America," *Public Affairs, 4* (1940), 57–60.

McGrail, T. H. *Sir William Alexander, First Earl of Stirling: A Biography.* Edinburgh, 1940.

McLennan, J. S. *Louisbourg from its Foundation to its Fall, 1713–1758.* London, 1918.

Macleod, J. E. A. "Lord Ochiltree's Colony," *Dalhousie Review, 4* (1924), 308–16.

McLeod, R. R. *Markland or Nova Scotia.* Berwick, N.S., 1903.

MacNutt, W. Stewart. *The Atlantic Provinces: The Emergence of a Colonial Society, 1712–1857.* Toronto, 1965.

———. *New Brunswick, a History: 1784–1867.* Toronto, 1963.

MacVicar, W. M. *A Short history of Annapolis Royal . . . .* Toronto, 1897.

Maillard, Pierre. *An Account of the Customs and Manners of the Mickmackis and Maricheets savage nations . . . .* London, 1758. Maillard was a missionary to the Micmac in the 1730's, 1740's, and 1750's, and was based on Cape Breton.

Mairobert, Mathieu François Pidanzat de. *Discussion Sommaire sur les anciennes limites de l'Acadie, et sur les stipulations du Traité d'Utrecht . . . .* Basle, 1755.

Marsh, Henry. *A proposal for raising a Stock of Two millions of pounds for forming a settlement on each side of a large river in Acadia* . . . . London, 1720.

Martell, J. S. "Pre-Loyalist Settlements around Minas Basin." Unpublished M.A. thesis, Dalhousie University, Halifax, 1933.

———. "The Second Expulsion of the Acadians," *Dalhousie Review, 13* (1933–34), 359–71.

Martin, Ernest. *Les Exilés Acadiens en France, aux XVIII° siècle et leur établissement en Poitou.* Paris, 1936.

Mascarene, Paul. "Letter from Paul Mascarene to Governor Shirley, Annapolis-Royal, April 6, 1748," Massachusetts Historical Society *Collections*, ser. 1, *6* (1799), 120–26.

Massignon, Geneviève. *Les Parlers Français d'Acadie (enquête linguistique).* 2 vols. Paris, 1962.

Mémoires des Comissaires du roi et de ceux de Sa Majesté britannique sur les possessions et les droits respectifs des deux couronnes en Amérique. 4 vols. Paris, 1755–57.

Mémoires sur le Canada, 1749–1760. 2nd printing, Quebec, 1873. Tentatively attributed by Brebner to Franquet.

The Memorials of the English and French Commissaries Concerning the Limits of Nova Scotia or Acadia. 2 vols. London, 1755. Simultaneously published as *Mémoires des Commissaires du roi et de ceux de Sa Majesté britannique* . . . . 4 vols. Paris, 1755–57.

Mikesell, Marvin. "Comparative Studies in Frontier History," *Annals of the Association of American Geographers, 50* (1960), 62–74.

Minutes of His Majesty's Council at Annapolis Royal, 1736–1749, ed. C. Bruce Fergusson. Halifax, 1967. Widely catalogued and referred to as *Nova Scotia Archives. IV.*

Monro, Alexander. *New Brunswick: with a brief outline of Nova Scotia and Prince Edward Island.* Halifax, 1855.

Moreau, Celestin. *Histoire de l'Acadie française (Amérique septentrionale) de 1598 à 1755.* Paris, 1873.

Morley, W. F. E. *The Atlantic Provinces.* Vol. 1 of *Canadian Local Histories, a Bibliography.* Toronto, 1967.

[Morris, (Captain) Charles]. "A Breif Survey of Nova Scotia." Unpublished MS in the Library of the Royal Artillery Regiment, Woolwich. Photocopy in AC, MG18, F10.

Morris, Charles. "Report by Captain Morris to Governor Shirley upon his Survey of Lands in Nova Scotia available for Protestant Settlers, 1749." Enclosure in Shirley to Bedford, Boston, February 18, 1749. PRO, "America & West Indies," *63,* 106. AC *Report for 1912* (Ottawa, 1913), pp. 79–83.

———. "Judge Morris' Remarks Concerning the Removal of the Acadians," NSHS *Collections, 2* (1881), 158–60.

Morse, W. I., ed. *Pierre Du Gua, sieur de Monts; records: colonial and "Saintongeois."* London, 1939.

Morse, W. I., ed. *See Acadiensia Nova.*

Murchie, Guy. *Saint Croix, the Sentinel River.* New York, 1947.

Murdoch, Beamish. *A History of Nova-Scotia, or Acadie.* 3 vols. Halifax, 1865–67.

Nicholson, Colonel Francis. "The Journal of Col. Nicholson at the Capture of Annapolis, 1710," NSHS *Collections, 1* (1879), 59–104.

Nova Scotia Archives. I. See: Selections from the Public Documents . . . .

Nova Scotia Archives. II. See: A Calendar of Two Letter-Books . . . .

Nova Scotia Archives. III. See: Original Minutes of His Majesty's Council . . . .

Nova Scotia Archives. IV. See: Minutes of His Majesty's Council . . . .

O'Callaghan, E. B., ed. *Documents relative to the Colonial History of the State of New York, procured in Holland, England and France by John Romeyn Brodhead, esq., agent* . . . . 15 vols. Albany, 1853–87.

Oleson, T. J. *Early Voyages and Northern Approaches, 1000–1632.* (Canadian Centenary Series, *1.*) Toronto, 1963.

Original Minutes of His Majesty's Council at Annapolis Royal, 1720–1739, ed. Archibald M. MacMechan. Halifax, 1908. Widely catalogued and referred to as *Nova Scotia Archives. III.* Note that the continuation of this series is *Minutes of His Majesty's Council at Annapolis Royal, 1736–1749,* ed. C. B. Fergusson. Halifax, 1967.

Parker, D. W., *A Guide to the Documents in the Manuscript Room of the Public Archives of Canada.* Ottawa, 1914. There are many supplements.

Parkman, Francis. *The Jesuits in North America in the Seventeenth Century.* Boston, 1894.

———. *Pioneers of France in the New World.* (Frontenac Edition.) Boston, 1910.

Patterson, F. H. *Acadian Tatamagouche and Fort Franklin.* Tatamagouche, N.S., 1947.

———. *History of Tatamagouche.* Halifax, 1917.

———. "Old Cobequid and its Destruction," NSHS *Collections, 23* (1936), 49–88.

Patterson, George. *A History of the County of Pictou, Nova Scotia.* Montreal, 1877.

———. "Sable Island, Its History and Phenomena," *PTRSC, 12* (1894), sec. 1, 3–44.

———. "Sir William Alexander and the Scottish Attempt to Colonize Acadia," *PTRSC, 10* (1892), sec. 2, 79–107.

[Pichon, Thomas]. *Genuine Letters and Memoirs, Relating to the Natural, Civil, and Commercial History of the Islands of Cape Breton and Saint John from the First Settlement . . . to 1758. By an impartial Frenchman.* The Hague and London, 1760. See also the French edition of the same year, *Lettres et mémoires pour servir à l'histoire naturelle, civil et politique du Cap Breton depuis son établissement jusqu'à la réprise de cette isle par les Anglois en 1758.* Pichon, also known as Thomas Tyrrell, was a spy for the British and, after the capture of Beauséjour, where he served after leaving Cape Breton, he lived in England.

Piers, Harry. "Artists in Nova Scotia," NSHS *Collections, 18* (1914), 103–6.

Pierson, George W. "The Frontier and Frontiersmen of Turner's Essays," *Pennsylvania Magazine of History and Biography, 64* (1940), 454–78.

Pietraszek, Bernadine. "Anglo-French Trade Conflicts in North America, 1702–1713," *Mid-America, 35* (1953), 144–74.

Poirier, Pascal. *Origine des Acadiens.* Montreal, 1874.

———. *Le parler franco-acadien et son origine.* Quebec, 1928.

Pote, Captain William, Jr. *The Journal of Captain William Pote, junior, during his captivity in the French and Indian War, 1745–47.* 2 vols. New York, 1896.

Potter, David M. *People of Plenty: Economic Abundance and the American Character.* Chicago, 1954.

Rameau de Saint-Père, François-Edmé. *Une Colonie Féodale en Amérique (L'Acadie, 1604–1710).* Paris, 1877. Essentially, this is the first volume of the 1889 work.

———. *Une Colonie Féodale en Amérique: l'Acadie (1604–1881).* 2 vols. Paris, 1889.

———. *La France aux colonies: études sur le développement de la race française hors de l'Europe, par E. Rameau. Les Français en Amérique: Acadiens et Canadiens . . . .* Paris, 1859.

Raymond, William O. "Earliest route of travel between Canada and Acadia . . . ," *PTRSC,* ser. 3, *15* (1921), sec. 2, 33–46.

———. "Nova Scotia under English Rule: From the Capture of Port Royal to the Conquest of Canada, 1710–1760," *PTRSC,* ser. 3, *4* (1911), sec. 2, 55–84.

———. *The River St. John: Its Physical Features, Legends and History from 1604 to 1784.* Sackville, N.B., 1943. See the earlier edition, *History of the River St. John.* Saint John, N.B., 1905.

Remarks on the French Memorials Concerning the Limits of Acadia; Printed at the Royal Printing House at Paris and distributed by the French Ministers to all the Foreign Courts of Europe . . . . London, 1756. The maps are useful.

Richard, Édouard. *Acadie: reconstitution d'un chapitre perdu de l'histoire d'Amérique.* 2 vols. Paris, 1895. Published in New York in the same year as *Acadia: Missing Links of a Lost Chapter of American History.* 2 vols. New York, 1895.

Robinson, B. E. "Grand Pré of the Acadians," *Canadian Geographical Journal, 11* (1935), 76–84.

Robitaille, J. Édouard. "L'Agriculture en Acadie," *Le Canada Français, 5* (1920), 23–27.

Roy, J.-Edmond. *Rapport sur les archives de France relatives à l'histoire du Canada.* (AC publications, No. 6.) Ottawa, 1911.

Roy, Pierre-Georges. *Inventaire des concessions en fief et seigneurie, fois et*

*hommages, et aveux et dénombrements, conservés aux archives de la
Province de Québec.* 6 vols. Beauceville, P.Q., 1927–29.

Roy, Pierre-Georges. "Les sources imprimées de l'histoire du Canada-français; Collection de documents inédits sur l'Acadie publiés par le Canada-
Français," *Bulletin des recherches historiques, 30* (1924), 186–90.

Rumilly, Robert. *Histoire des Acadiens.* 2 vols. Montreal, 1955.

Sauer, Carl O. "Historical Geography and the Western Frontier." In *The
Trans-Mississippi West,* ed. James F. Willard and Colin B. Goodykoontz.
Papers Read at a Conference Held at the University of Colorado, June
18–June 21, 1929. Boulder, Col., 1930.

Saunders, R. M. "The First Introduction of European Plants and Animals into
Canada," *CHR, 16* (1935), 388–406.

Savoie, Francis. *L'Île de Shippegan.* Moncton, 1967.

Seguin, R. L. *Équipement de la ferme Canadienne aux xviie et xviiie siècles.*
Montreal, 1959.

Selections from the Public Documents of the Province of Nova Scotia, "Papers
Relating to the Acadian French, 1714–1755," ed. Thomas B. Akins,
Halifax, 1869. Widely catalogued and referred to as *Nova Scotia Archives. I.*

Shannon, Fred A. *An Appraisal of Walter Prescott Webb's The Great Plains.*
(Vol. 3 of *Critiques of Research in the Social Sciences.*) New York, 1940.

Shortt, Adam, Johnston, V. K., and Lanctot, Gustave, eds. *Documents Relating to Currency, Exchange and Finance in Nova Scotia, with Prefatory
Documents, 1675–1758.* Ottawa, 1933.

Shurtleff, H. R. *The Log Cabin Myth.* Cambridge, Mass., 1939.

Slafter, E. F. *Sir William Alexander and American Colonization. . . .* (The
Prince Society.) Boston, 1873.

Smethurst, Gamaliel. *A Narrative of an Extraordinary Escape . . .* London,
1774. Reprinted and ed. W. F. Ganong. *NBHS Collections,* No. 2
(1905), 33 pp.

Smith, Henry Nash. *Virgin Land: The American West in Symbol and Myth.*
Cambridge, Mass., 1950.

Story, Norah. *The Oxford Companion to Canadian History and Literature.*
Toronto, 1967.

Sulte, Benjamin. *L'Acadie Française. Mélanges historiques, 16.* 2nd ed.,
Montreal, 1930. This is material from Sulte, *Histoire des canadiens-français,* annotated and edited by Gérard Malchelosse.

―――. *Histoire des Canadiens français, 1608–1880.* 8 vols. Montreal,
1882–84.

―――. "Origin of the French Canadians" (with map), *PTRSC,* ser. 2, *11*
(1905), sec. 2, 99–119.

―――. "Poutrincourt en Acadie, 1604–1623," *PTRSC,* ser. 1, *2* (1884), sec.
1, 31–50.

Surlaville, Michel le Courteois, Sieur de. *Les Derniers Jours de l'Acadie
(1748–1758). Correspondances et mémoires. Extraits du portefeuille
de M. Le Courteois de Surlaville, Lieutenant-Général des Armées du Roi*

[*et*] *Ancien Major des troupes de l'Ile Royale,* ed. and ann. Gaston du Boscq de Beaumont. Paris, 1899.

Tanguay, Cyprien. *Dictionnaire Généalogique des familles canadiennes depuis la fondation de la colonie jusqu'à nos jours.* 7 vols. Montreal, 1871–90.

Thomas, John. "The Diary of John Thomas," NSHS *Collections, 1* (1879), 119–40. Thomas was a surgeon in Winslow's expedition of 1755 and worked with the deportation forces.

Thwaites, R. G., ed. *The Jesuit Relations and Allied Documents: Travels and Explorations of the Jesuit Missionaries in New France, 1610–1791.* 73 vols. Cleveland, 1896–1901.

———, ed. *New Voyages to North America by the Baron Lahontan.* 2 vols. Chicago, 1905.

Trudel, Marcel. *Atlas Historique du Canada Français des origines à 1867.* Quebec, 1961.

———. *The Seigneurial Regime.* (CHA Historical Booklet, No. 6.) Ottawa, 1956.

Trueman, G. J. *Marsh and Lake Area of Chignecto Bay (with map).* (Natural History Society of New Brunswick.) Saint John, 1899.

Turner, Frederick Jackson. "The Significance of the Frontier in American History." *Annual Report of the American Historical Association for the Year 1893.* Washington, D. C., 1894, pp. 199–277.

———. "The West and American Ideals," *Washington Historical Quarterly, 5* (1914), 243–57.

Vetch, Samuel. "Papers Connected with the Administration of Governor Vetch," NSHS *Collections, 4* (1885), 64–112.

Vigneras, Louis-André. "Letters of an Acadian Fur Trader, 1674–1676," *New England Quarterly, 13* (1940), 98–110.

Von Nardroff, Ellen. "The American Frontier as a Safety Valve: The Life, Death, Reincarnation and Justification of a Theory," *Agricultural History, 36* (1962), 123–42.

"W., J." *A Letter from a gentleman in Nova Scotia to a person of distinction on the continent describing the present state of government in that colony . . .* (signed "W. J."). London, 1756.

Ward, David. "Antecedence and Adjacence: Locational Attributes of Central Residential Districts." *Abstracts of Papers, Twentieth International Geographical Congress.* London, 1964, pp. 277–78.

———. "The Emergence of Immigrant Ghettoes in American Cities: 1840–1920," *Annals of the Association of American Geographers, 58* (1968), 343–59.

Webb, Walter Prescott. *The Great Plains.* Boston, 1931.

Webster, J. C., trans. and ed. *Acadia at the End of the Seventeenth Century: Letters, Journals and Memoirs of Joseph Robineau de Villebon, Commandant in Acadia, 1690–1700, and other contemporary documents.* (New Brunswick Museum, Monograph No. 1.) Saint John, N.B., 1934.

———. *The Career of Abbé Le Loutre in Nova Scotia.* Shediac, N.B., 1933.

Webster, J. C. *The Forts of Chignecto: A Study of the Eighteenth Century Conflict Between France and Great Britain in Acadia.* Shediac, N.B., 1930.

———. *A History of Shediac, New Brunswick.* Sackville, 1928.

———, ed. *Journals of Beauséjour; Diary of John Thomas; Journal of Louis de Courville.* (PANS, Special Publication.) Sackville, N.B., 1937.

———. *Thomas Pichon "The Spy of Beauséjour."* Sackville, N. B., 1937. His life in Europe and North America. French documents translated by Alice Webster.

Wheeler, G. A. "Fort Pentagoët and the French Occupation of Castine," *Collections and Proceedings of the Maine Historical Society,* ser. 2, *4* (1893), 113–23.

———. *History of Castine, Penobscot, and Brooksville, Maine.* Bangor, 1875.

Wilkins, E. H. "Arcadia in America," *Proceedings of the American Philosophical Society, 101* (1957), 4–30.

Williamson, James A. *The Cabot Voyages and Bristol Discovery under Henry VII.* (Hakluyt Society publications, ser. 2, No. 120.) Cambridge, England, 1962.

Wilson, John. *A Genuine Narrative of the Transactions in Nova Scotia since the settlement, June, 1749, till August the 5th, 1751 . . .* London, n.d. [1751 or 1752]. Very good on Halifax in 1751. Wilson was an inspector of stores with the first fleet.

Wilson, Isaiah W. *A Geography and History of the County of Digby, Nova Scotia, from 1604–1895.* Halifax, 1900.

Winslow, John. "Journal of Colonel John Winslow, of the Provincial Troops, while Engaged in Removing the Acadian French Inhabitants from Grand Pré, and the Neighbouring Settlements, in the Autumn of the Year 1755," *NSHS Collections, 3* (1883), 71–96, and *4* (1885), 113–246.

Winthrop, John. *The History of New England from 1630 to 1649 . . . with notes . . . by James Savage.* New ed., 2 vols. Boston, 1883.

Winzerling, Oscar. *Acadian Odyssey.* Baton Rouge, 1966. Exiles to France, then to Louisiana, 1784–85.

Wood, W. C. H. *The Great Fortress.* Toronto, 1915.

Wright, Benjamin F. "American Democracy and the Frontier," *The Yale Review, 20* (1930), 349–65.

Wright, Esther Clark. "Cumberland Township: A Focal Point of Settlement on the Bay of Fundy," *CHR, 27* (1946), 27–32.

———. *The Miramichi: A Study of the New Brunswick River and of the People who Settled Along It.* Sackville, N.B., 1945.

———. *The Petitcodiac: A Study of the New Brunswick River and the People who Settled Along It.* Sackville, N. B., 1945.

———. *The Saint John River.* Toronto, 1945.

Wyman, Walker D., and Kroeber, Clifton B., eds. *The Frontier in Perspective.* Madison, 1957.

Zaslow, Morris. "The Frontier Hypothesis in Recent Canadian Historiography," *CHR, 29* (1948), 153–67.

Index

Abenaki, 57

Aboiteaux (clapper valves): at Shepody, 147; Dièreville's account of, 161; described, 162, 238–40; Le Loutre's, at Chignecto, 240, 240*n;* communal labor on, 252; mentioned, 30, 48, 231, 365

Acadia: strategic importance of, 9, 77, 372, 378; pre-Columbian occupation of, 56; origin of name, 71–72; extent of, 71–74; comparison with Nova Scotia, 72–73; earliest lodgements in, 77–78; outports, early 18th c., 223–30; latitude, 372; Turner's frontier thesis and, 384–93

Acadian economy: importance of agriculture in, 158, 375; self-sufficiency of, 176, 388; commercial nature of, 231; degree to which subsistence, 231. *See also* Agriculture; Fishery; Trade

Acadians: relations with Micmac of, 68–70, 88–89, 128, 129*n*, 361, 377; blamed for Indian attacks, 69, 195, 361–62; identification of, with Nova Scotia, 74; arts and skills among, 100, 176, 177; Scots among, 101; origins of, 101, 131, 374, 375–76, 397–400; prior knowledge of, of dyking, 101–3; role of priests among, 113*n*, 189–91; characteristics of, 115, 150, 260–61, 375, 380, 385–88; complaints of laziness of, 151, 158–60, 231–32, 260; agriculture as chief occupation of, 158; problems of British

government with, 186, 333, 363; and oath of allegiance, 188, 191, 196–97, 362–63, 365; use of, in government by British, 188–89; political neutrality of, 193–95, 200, 360, 361, 378; marriages among, 203–5; New England immigrants wish aid of, in dyking, 356; effects of French origin on, 374–76, 379; importance of religious faith to, 376; commercial interests of, 378–79; compared to English colonists, 384–85, 388–90; Turnerian thesis not applicable to, 385; social structure of, 386–87; governmental and legal institutions of, 387. *See also* Agriculture; Deportation; Fishery, cod; Land tenure; Population; Seigneurial system; Trade

Acadian surnames: French origin of, 101, 101*n*, 397–400; Scotch origin of, 101, 101*n*, 397*n;* number of, 131–32; similarities among, 366–67

Agricultural produce: markets for Acadian, 230

Agricultural settlement: role of women in, 89

Agricultural surpluses, 173, 231–32

Agriculture, Acadian: on the uplands, 54–55, 219; at trading-posts, 85–86; before 1630's, 87, 88; importance of, in economy, 158, 375; described, 158–76, 230–44; suitability of marsh-lands for, 161, 162; statistics on, 163–75 *passim,* 233–38 *passim;* commer-

Cape Breton fishery, 304–14 *passim*
Schott, Carl, 30, 46
Scots: settlement at Port Royal of, 83–84, 87, 91, 99, 101; date of settlement, 83*n;* hypothesized among early Acadian settlers, 101; exact location of settlement, 103*n;* Highland, 330
Scurvy, 78, 166
Sealing, 61, 153, 268
Seal oil: try-works at Chedabucto, 156
Sedgwick, Robert, 94, 111*n*
Seguin, R. L., 232, 233
Seigneurial system, Acadian: and organization of land at La Have, 95; institutions of, in Acadia, 106; seigneurial dues, 114–15; J.-E. Roy's map of Acadian grants, 115; list of grants in Acadia, 115–18; as framework of land tenure, 120, 121, 195; operation of, under British, 195, 197–98; significance of, in Acadia, 374–75; compared with Canadian, 375; scanty information on, 375
Seigneuries: in Acadia, 113–21; lack of information about, 114; J. B. Brebner on, 114–15; Minas, 118–19; Port Royal district, 132; Beaubassin, 141–42; Cobequid, 219; Cape Breton, 283
Settlement: early deterrents to, 7; antecedents of, 75–77; of Chignecto, 109; of Minas, 109; pattern of, at Port Royal, 132–34, 135; expansion of, from Port Royal, 139–40; and upland-marshland controversy, 158–60; pattern of, at Minas, 216–17; in Cape Breton, 280–93 *passim*
Shad, 60, 150, 151, 179, 246
Shadberries, 17, 62, 62*n;* at Canso, 157
Shallops: Micmac use of, 63*n;* in Minas, 247; in Cape Breton fishery, 305–14 *passim;* building of, 326, 359
Sheep: at Port Royal, 86, 167; at Chignecto, 143; pasturing of, 159; uses for wool of, 165, 243; kinds of, in Acadia, 167–68; at Lunenburg, 354; mentioned, 113*n*, 231. *See also* Agriculture; Livestock
Shelburne Harbour area: population, 130, 153, 224; description of, 153,

224; mentioned, 123*n. See also* Port Razoir
Shepody Bay area: squatters in, 144; description of, 145–48; livestock in, 147; population, 147, 210, 211, 220, 222; land tenure in, 198; marshland in, 221; refugees in, 353; mentioned, 111, 203*n. See also* Chignecto
Shepody estuary, 352–53
Shepody River, 111
Sherbrooke, 96, 108
Shickshock Mountains, 11
Shipbuilding: Acadian materials for, 177, 249; in Acadia, 256; in Cape Breton, 326–28; at Halifax, 359–60.
Shirley, William, 271, 339
Shoreline: Nova Scotia, 21–22; Strait of Northumberland, 22
Shubenacadie district, 219
Shubenacadie River, 59, 150, 156, 220
Shubenacadie (seigneurial grant), 118, 219
Sloops, fishing, 304, 304*n. See also* Fishery, cod
Smith, Titus, Jr., 39–44 *passim*
Snowfall: in Nova Scotia, 34–35
Snowshoes, 64, 135
Soil: Acadian use of, 53–55; fertility of, in dyked marshland, 237; Acadian and French, compared, 374
Soils, Nova Scotia: nature of regolith of, 49–50; acidity of, 50; effect of vegetation on, 50; areas of best, 50–51; in Annapolis-Cornwallis Valley, 51–52; in Cumberland County, 52; poor characteristics of, 52; in Lunenburg County, 52, 354; in Yarmouth County, 53; at Lawrencetown, 356
Souriquois. *See* Micmac
South Carolina, 363
Spain: fishing from, 75; war with, 193, 229; mentioned, 7, 78, 267
Spanish Bay: as possible capital of Cape Breton, 270; description of, 284–85; Acadians at, 285; population, 285; vessel-building at, 326; mentioned, 264
Specie, 183. *See also* Currency
Speck, Frank, 57
Spinning, 165

Spruce, 44, 51
Squatters, Acadian, 198
Stewart, (Sir) James, fourth Lord Ochiltree, 84, 267
Stirling, Earl of. *See* Alexander, Sir William
Subercase. *See* Auger
Sulte, Benjamin, 100
Surlaville, Michel Le Courteois, Sieur de, 273, 302, 328–29
Swine, 86, 87, 113*n*, 143, 167–68, 173, 244, 354. *See also* Agriculture; Livestock
Switzerland, 337
Sydney Harbour. *See* Spanish Bay

Tadoussac, 9, 78
Taiga. *See* Forests
Talon, Jean, 28, 126, 180
Tamarack, 46
Tantramar district: new settlement at, 111; population, 221–22, 347–48
Tantramar marsh, 220–21, 238, 240
Tantramar River, 111, 221
Tatamagouche: settlements at, 117, 203*n*, 218, 228; trade routes via, 219, 252–58 *passim;* trade at, 220; refugees go to, 346
Taverns: at Canso, 229
Taxes, 198, 357
Temple, Sir Thomas, 107, 107*n*, 111, 111*n*
Tennycape, 219
Terriau, Pierre, 148
Test and Corporation Acts, 188
Thebok, 223
Thibaudeau, Pierre, 145–47, 178
Thierry, Father, 69*n*
Thwaites, R. B., 57*n*
Tibierge, M., 182
Tibogue, 200, 223
Tidal flats: Cornwallis Valley, 51–52; in Yarmouth County, 53. *See also* Dyked marshland; Marshland, tidal
Tidal marshland. *See* Dyked marshland; Marshland, tidal
Tidal range: in Bay of Fundy, 24; effects of hurricanes on, 24; deposition of silts due to, 25, 27; problems with, at Pisiquid, 218; cause of difficulties

in loading coal, 358; importance of, 372
Tierce, 246
Timber: cut at Pictou, 249; reserved for crown at Annapolis, 249; cut at Spanish Bay, 285
Tintamare, 221–22, 347–48
Tobacco: Indian use of, 57*n*, 62*n;* growing of, 230
Toboggans, 64
Tonge's Island, 142
Tools, 91, 95, 176, 232–33
Trade. *See* Canso; Fur trade; Halifax; Indians; Lunenburg; New England; Trade, Acadian; Trade, Cape Breton
Trade, Acadian: with New England, 111, 139, 143, 149, 153, 175–76, 180–84, 192, 231–32, 243, 254, 255, 378; for implements and tools from New England, 176; with Canso, 180; exports, 180–83; imports, 180–83, 255; with French West Indies through New Englanders, 181; barter and use of currency, 183–84; goods needed by Acadians, 183–84; with West Indies, 229, 247, 260; attempts to control, at Annapolis, 230; clandestine, with Cape Breton, 230; with Indians, 75, 254, 361; vessels used in, 254–55, 256; with Louisburg, 254–57 *passim;* commercial surpluses for, 255; for British goods via New England, 256; favorable balance in, with Cape Breton, 260; with New York, 319; illegal, with France, 352–53; with Halifax, 357. *See also* Fur trade; Trade, Cape Breton
—, Cape Breton: with Acadia, 256, 257–61, 318–19, 323, 353; in cattle, 260; with West Indies, 267, 321, 323, 356, 364; and supplies needed at Louisburg, 315–25; with Canada, 317–18, 321, 323; with France, 317–18, 321, 323; participation of officials in, 319–20; with New England, 319–20, 321, 323, 328; clandestine, 319–20, 328; effects of seasons on, 321; number of ships involved in, 321, 323
Tradesmen, Acadian, 176–77
Trahan, Guillaume, 113